Stahleisen-Wörterbuch
Iron and Steel Dictionary

Stahleisen-Wörterbuch

Deutsch – Englisch
Englisch – Deutsch

Iron and Steel Dictionary

German – English
English – German

4., erweiterte Auflage
4th, enlarged edition

Herausgegeben vom / Edited by
Verein Deutscher Eisenhüttenleute
German Iron and Steel Institute

Verlag Stahleisen mbH

Vorwort zur vierten Auflage

Seit der ersten Veröffentlichung im Jahre 1958 hat sich das Stahleisen-Wörterbuch Deutsch – Englisch/Englisch – Deutsch der raschen technischen Weiterentwicklung in der Eisen- und Stahlindustrie laufend angepaßt. Enthielt die 1. Auflage jeweils rund 7 500 deutsche und englische Stichwörter, so ist das Volumen in der vorliegenden 4. Auflage bereits auf mehr als 12 500 Begriffe in jeder der beiden Sprachen gewachsen. Das Wörterbuch wird damit auch in der Neuauflage ein unentbehrliches Hilfsmittel für den internationalen fachlichen Erfahrungsaustausch.

Wiederum haben zahlreiche Fachleute aus Industrie, Forschung, Verbänden und Behörden an der Überarbeitung und Erweiterung des aufgenommenen Wortschatzes mitgewirkt. Ihnen allen gilt unser herzlicher Dank.

Verein Deutscher Eisenhüttenleute

Dr.-Ing. D. Springorum
Geschäftsführendes Vorstandsmitglied

Das Werk ist urheberrechtlich geschützt. Die dadurch begründeten Rechte, insbesondere die der Übersetzung, des Nachdrucks, der Wiedergabe auf photomechanischem oder ähnlichem Weg und der Speicherung in Datenverarbeitungsanlagen, bleiben, auch bei nur auszugsweiser Verwertung, vorbehalten.

© 1987 Verlag Stahleisen mbH, Düsseldorf
Bearbeitung der 4. Auflage / Revision of the 4th edition:
Dipl.-Ing. Kerstin Garbracht, Redaktions- und Industrie-Presse-Service

Printed in Germany

ISBN 3-514-00355-6

Foreword to the fourth Edition

Since its first publication in 1958, the Iron and Steel Dictionary German – English/English – German has been continually adapted to the rapid advances in the iron and steel industry. Whereas the first edition included some 7,500 German and English entries each, this fourth edition has grown to more than 12,500 terms in each language. The new edition of the dictionary has thus become an indispensable aid in sharing technical experience at an international level.

A large number of specialists from the industry, R & D, professional associations and administrative bodies have again contributed to the revision and extension of the terms covered by the dictionary. To all of them our heartfelt thanks.

German Iron and Steel Institute

Dr.-Ing. D. Springorum
Executive Director

This work is subject to copyright. All rights are reserved, whether the whole or part of the material is concerned, specifically those of translation, reprinting, reproduction by photocopying machine or similar means, and storage in data banks.

© 1987 Verlag Stahleisen mbH, Düsseldorf
Bearbeitung der 4. Auflage / Revision of the 4th edition:
Dipl.-Ing. Kerstin Garbracht, Redaktions- und Industrie-Presse-Service

Printed in Germany

ISBN 3-514-00355-6

Benutzerhinweise

Die vorliegende 4. Auflage des Stahleisen-Wörterbuches wurde Computer-unterstützt erstellt. Dadurch ergeben sich einige Besonderheiten in der Sortierung, die vor allem im I. Teil (deutsch – englisch) zum Tragen kommen:

– Alle Begriffe wurden alphabetisch bis zum letzten Buchstaben jedes Wortes durchsortiert.
– Erläuterungen in runden Klammern kennzeichnen oft eine bestimmte Verwendung der Vokabel und wurden deshalb ebenfalls mit bei der Sortierung berücksichtigt.

Die deutschen Umlaute *ä, ö, ü* sind wie *a, o, u* alphabetisch eingeordnet, das deutsche ß wie ss.

Wörter oder Buchstaben in eckigen Klammern [ ] können weggelassen werden, ohne daß sich die Bedeutung in der anderen Sprache ändert.

Wörter in runden Klammern ( ) dienen zur Erläuterung z. B. des Fachgebietes oder stellen ein Synonym dar.

Sind bei einem Stichwort in beiden Sprachen Wörter in runden Klammern eingefügt, so entspricht das erweiterte Stichwort einer erweiterten Übersetzung. Es müssen also entweder in beiden Sprachen die Klammerwörter weggelassen oder in beiden Sprachen hinzugefügt werden.

In Teil I (deutsch – englisch) gilt der Gedankenstrich – in den deutschen Bedeutungen als Wiederholungszeichen für das erste Wort der Zeile. Zur besseren Übersicht ist z. B. der Ausdruck „in eine Liste eintragen" unter dem Buchstaben „L" (wie Liste) zu finden als: „Liste, in eine – eintragen".

Abkürzungen

m	= Maskulinum	*pl*	= Plural
f	= Femininum	*(am.)*	= amerikanisch
n	= Neutrum	*s. a.*	= siehe auch

Notes for the user

The present 4th edition of Iron and Steel Dictionary as a product of computer aided publishing shows some characteristics concerning assortment, especially in the I. part (German – English):

- All keywords have been sorted alphabetically letter by letter.
- To distinguish keywords with a very special technical meaning from commonly used expressions words in round brackets have also been criterion for assortment.

The German umlauts *ä, ö, ü* are arranged alphabetically as *a, o, u*, the German ß as ss.

Words or letters in square brackets [ ] can be omitted without changing the meaning in the other language.

Words in round brackets ( ) give further information referring to a special field or a synonym.

When words are added in both languages in round brackets against the keyword the extended alphabetic keyword corresponds to the extended translation. If, therefore, the word in brackets is included in one language, the corresponding word must also be included in the other language.

Abbreviations

m	= Masculine		*pl*	= Plural
f	= Feminine		*(am.)*	= American
n	= Neuter		*s. a.*	= see also

Inhalt

	Seite
I. Teil: Deutsch – Englisch	2
II. Teil: Englisch – Deutsch	203

Contents

	page
Part I: German – English	2
Part II: English – German	203

I. Teil:
Deutsch/Englisch

Part I:
German/English

A

Abbau *m* decomposition; exploration
abbauen (gewinnen) work
abbauwürdig workable
abbeizen pickle
abbiegen (Strangguß) bend
abbinden combine; fix; react with
Abbinden *n* **(des Stickstoffs)** fixation
abbinden (Ti) chloridise; fix
abbinden (Zement) set (cement)
Abblasen *n* grit-blasting
abblasen (mit Sand) sandblasting
Abblasen (mit Schrot oder mit Sand) blast cleaning
Abblaseschieber *m* blow-off valve (cowper)
abblättern chip off; flake; scale; spall
Abblättern *n* exfoliation; flaking; peeling; scaling
Abblättern *n* **(Schienen)** spalling
Abbrand *m* loss; loss by burning; melting loss (in a liquid medium); oxidizing loss (in a gaseous medium); scaling loss
Abbrandelektrode *f* consumable electrode
Abbrand *m* **(Elektroden)** burn off
Abbrandverhältnis *n* melting loss condition; scaling loss condition
Abbrausen *n* **(Draht)** sull coating
abbrechen break up; dismantle
abbremsen slow down
abbrennen burn off; dewax (powder met.); scale
Abbrennschweißung *f* resistance flash welding
Abbrennstumpfschweißen *n* flash butt welding
Abbrenn[stumpf]schweißung *f* flash [butt] welding
abbröckeln scale
Abbrucharbeiten *fpl* dismantling
Abbruchschrott *m* demolition scrap
Abdecken *n* capping
Abdeckmasse *f* covering agent for melts
abdichten caulk; pack; tighten
abdrehen turn off
Abdrücken *n* **(Rohre)** run a hydraulic pressure test
Abdruckverfahren *n* replica technique
Abdruck *m* **(Walzdrahtfehler)** roll [guide] mark
abfackeln bleed
Abfall *m* decline; decrease; discard; scrap; waste
Abfallbeizen-Aufarbeitung *f* regeneration of spent pickle liquor
Abfallbeseitigung *f* waste disposal
Abfallende *n* short end
Abfallerzeugnis *n* by-product; residuary product; waste product
Abfallkohle *f* waste coal
Abfallkoks *m* scrap coke
Abfallstoffe *mpl* waste materials
Abfallverbrennungsanlage *f* incinerator; waste incineration plant
abfangen (Schmelze) block; catch; scotch
Abfangschmelze *f* catch carbon heat
Abflachung *f* bevel
Abfluß *m* outlet
Abflußrohr *n* discharge pipe; drain [pipe]; exit pipe; exit tube; outlet pipe
Abfuhrrollgang *m* delivery roller table; exit roller table; run-out roller table
Abgabe *f* tax
Abgänge *mpl* abatement (of furnace); discharge; effluent (of furnace); emission (of furnace)
Abgarung *f* **(Koks)** carbonisation
Abgas *n* exhaust gas; flue gas; spent gas; stack gas; waste gas
Abgasabführung *f* waste gas main
Abgas-Entnahmesonde *f* waste gas probe
Abgasfackel *f* excess burner; surplus gas burner
Abgaskanal *m* waste heat flue
Abgaskanal-Schlacke *f* **(Wärmeofen)** flue cinder
Abgasprüfer *m* flue gas tester

Abgasschieber m flue gas valve
Abgasthermometer n flue gas thermometer
Abgasüberwachung f waste gas control
Abgas-Umwälzbeheizung f waste gas recirculation heating
Abgasumwälzung f waste gas recirculation
abgefedert spring-supported; sprung
abgeflacht flattened
abgekürztes Verfahren n short-cut method
abgeleitet derivative
abgeleiteter Wert m derivative
abgeschnittenes Ende n crop end
abgeschrägt bevelled; chamfered; skewed
abgesetzte Verformung f stepped extrusion
abgesetzt (Stempel) stepped
abgesetzt (Welle) eccentric
abgestimmt (EDV) tuned
abgestumpft blunted; dulled; truncated
abgestütztes Gewölbe n sprung roof
abgießen cast; pour; teem; teem off
abgleichen equalize; reset
abgraten burr; clip; fettle; trim
Abgraten n clipping; deburring; trimming
Abgratmaschine f burr removing machine; deburring machine; flash trimmer
abgrenzen limit
Abgriff m tap
Abgriff m **(EDV)** pickup
Abguß m cast; casting; pouring; teeming
Abhandlung f paper; treatise
abhängige Veränderliche f dependent variable
Abhängigkeit f dependence
abhängig von dependent on
Abhaspelvorrichtung f pay-off reel
abheben draw; shrink away; take off
Abhebepunkt m **(Stranggießen)** shrink point

Abheber m off-loader
Abhitzedampfgewinnung f waste heat steam recovery
Abhitzekessel m waste heat boiler
Abhitzeverwertung f waste heat utilization
abkanten bevel; chamfer
Abkantpresse f bending-off press
Abkantprofil n flanged profile
abkippen dump; pour; tip
abklatschen dab
abklingen decay; diminish
Abklingkonstante f **(innere Reibung)** decay constant
Abkohlung f **(Kokerei)** incomplete decarbonizing; partial decarbonizing
Abkohlung f **(Stahl)** partial decarburization
abkühlen chill; cool; refrigerate
Abkühlkurve f cooling curve
Abkühlung f coolant
Abkühlungsbottich m cooling vat
Abkühlungsgeschwindigkeit f cooling rate
Abkühlungsmittel n coolant
abkuppeln disconnect
Abladeanlage f dumper
Abladeplatz m dump
Ablage f **(für Kaltstrang)** cradle
Ablageplatz m tip
Ablagerung f **(von Schadstoffen)** deposit (of contaminants); settling (of contaminants)
ablängen shear to length
Ablaß m discharge; drain
ablassen discharge; tap
ablaufen lassen drain
Ablaufhaspel f pay-off reel; pouring reel; uncoiler
Ablaufkasten m unwinding box
Ablaufprogramm n sequential programm
Ablaufprogrammsteuerung f sequential control
Ablauf- und Planungsforschung f operations research
ablegen lay down

Ablehnungsbereich *m* region of rejection
ableiten deduct; derive; draw off
Ableitung *f* derivation
Ablesefehler *m* dial error; reading error
Ablesung *f* reading
Ablichtung *f* light print
abliefern deliver
Ablieferung *f* delivery
ablöschen (Kalk) slake
Ablöschtemperatur *f* temperature of quench
Ablöseenergie *f* activation energy
ablösen detach
Abluft *f* exhaust air; waste air
Abmaß *n* allowable variation; off-size; permissible variation; variation in dimension
Abmessung *f* dimension; ga[u]ge; size
Abnahme *f* acceptance; decline; decrease; decrement; drop; inspection; reduction
Abnahmebeamter *m* inspector
Abnahmebescheinigung *f* approval note
Abnahme *f* drop
Abnahme *f* **je Stich** draft; reduction per pass
Abnahme *f* **(je Stich)** draft
Abnahmeprotokoll *n* acceptance report
Abnahmeprüfprotokoll *n* inspection report
Abnahmeprüfung *f* acceptance test; reception test
Abnahmeprüfzeugnis *n* inspection certificate
Abnahmestichprobe *f* acceptance-sampling
Abnahmestichproben-Verfahren *n* acceptance-sampling
Abnahmeverweigerung *f* rejection
Abnahme *f* **(von Maschinen)** inspection
abnehmbar detachable; removable
abnehmen detach; take off
Abnehmer *m* receiver

abnutzen scuff; wear off
Abnutzung *f* abrasion; wear; wear and tear
Abnutzungsbeständigkeit *f* wear-resistance; wearability
abplatzen chip off; flake; peel; shell; spall; split away
Abplatzung *f* bursting; flaking
Abprallverlust *m* rebound loss
abpressen (von Rohren) run a hydraulic pressure test
Abpreßversuch *m* hydrostatic test
Abquetschrolle *f* consolidation roll
Abquetschrolle *f* **(Beizen)** wringer roll
Abquetschrolle *f* **(Bramme)** squeeze roll
abrauchen vaporize
Abraum *m* overburden; rubble
abreiben abrade; rub off; wear by rubbing
Abreißkraft *f* **(Tiefziehen)** fracture load
abrichten dress
Abrieb *m* abrasion
Abriebfestigkeit *f* abrasion resistance
Abriebkorrosion *f* fretting corrosion
Abrollhaspel *f* uncoiler; uncoiling reel
abrösten (Erze) roast
abrunden chamfer; round off
Abrundung *f* chamfer; fillet; rounding off; tailoring
Absatz *m* disposal; sale; offset; recess; double teem (surface defect); step; teeming arrest (surface defect)
Absaugeanlage *f* exhausting plant; sucking-off plant; suction plant
Absaugegerät *n* suction apparatus
Absaugehaube *f* suction hood
absaugen draw off; exhaust; suck off
abschälen peel off
abschalten break; detach
Abschaltleistung *f* rupturing capacity
Abschaltmoment *n* cut out torque
abschäumen blow
abscheiden deposit; settle out
Abscheider *m* separator
abscheren cut off; shear; shear off
Abscherung *f* shear

Abscherwirkung f shearing action
Abschiebevorrichtung f pusher; pushing device
Abschirmung f shielding
abschlacken deslag; slag off; tap slag
Abschlagen n **des verlorenen Kopfes** topping
Abschläger m **(Gießerei)** fettler
abschleifen abrade; grind off
abschließen trap
Abschluß m bargain
Abschlußkonten npl final accounts
Abschlußring m sealing ring
Abschlußventil n shut-off valve
abschmelzen flash off; fuse; melt off
Abschmelzofen m consumable-arc furnace
Abschmelzschweißverfahren n fusion welding
Abschmieren n greasing; lubricating
abschmirgeln grind with emery
abschmoren scale
Abschneidegesenk n cut off [die]
abschneiden crop; cut off; shear
Abschneidstempel m **(Umformen)** cropping tool
abschopfen crop
abschrägen bevel; chamfer; scarf
Abschrägung f bevel; chamfer
abschrauben unscrew
Abschreckalterung f quench ag[e]ing
Abschreckaustenit m retained austenite
Abschreckbiegeprobe f quench bending test [specimen]
Abschreckdauer f quenching time
abschrecken chill; quench
Abschrecken n quenching
Abschrecken n **gestuftes** step quenching
Abschrecken n **schnelles** rapid quenching
Abschreckgeschwindigkeit f rate of cooling
Abschreckhärten n quench hardening
Abschreckmittel n quenching medium
Abschrecktemperatur f quenching temperature

Abschrecktiefe f depth of chill
Abschreckung f chill
Abschreckwerkzeug n fuller
Abschreibung f depreciation
Abschreibung f **kalkulatorische** depreciation allocation
abschuppen scale
abschütten discharge
Abschweißofen m wash heating furnace
absenken withdraw
Absenken n **der Gicht (Hochofen)** descent of charge
Absenkformmaschine f drop platetype moulding machine
Absenkgeschwindigkeit f **(Stranggießen)** withdrawal speed
Absenkwalze f withdrawal roll
Absetzbecken n sedimentation basin; settling tank (gas cleaning)
absetzen deposit; offset; settle out; step
absetzen (= **Absatz bilden**) step
Absetzkammer f **(Staub)** settling chamber
absieben screen [out]; sieve; sift
Absorption f absorption
Absorptionsquerschnitt m neutron absorption cross section
abspalten spall; split off
abspänen chip
absperren check; cut-off; lock
absperren (Leitung) cut off; shut off
Absperrhahn m stop cock
Absperrschieber m gate valve; slide valve
Absperrteile npl cut-off devices (e. g.: valves)
Absperrventil n retaining valve
absplittern spall; splinter; split off
Absplittern n spalling
Abspritzen n sull coating
abspülen rinse; swill
Abspulgerät n pay-off reel
Abstechdrehbank f slicing lathe; trimming lathe
abstechen cut off; tap; teem; trim
Abstechen n tapping
Abstechstahl m parting-off tool

abstehen lassen kill
abstehen lassen (Schmelze) dead melt
absteifen stiffen; thicken
Absteifen *n* stiffening
Absteifung *f* staying
abstellen shut off
Abstich *m* run-off; tap; tapping
Abstichfolge *f* casting cycle
Abstichladung *f* jet tapper (am.)
Abstichloch *n* tap hole
Abstichrinne *f* launder; runner; tapping spout
Abstichschlacke *f* flush slag; flushing cinder
Abstich-zu-Abstich-Zeit *f* tap-to-tap time
abstrahlen sand-blast
Abstrahlungsverlust *m* radiation loss
Abstreckbarkeit *f* stretchability
Abstreckdrücken *n* flow turning; shear spinning; spin forming (tubes)
Abstrecken *n* ironing
abstreichen skim
Abstreifen *n* stripping
abstreifen (Kokillen oder Dorn) strip
Abstreifer *m* stripper [guide]; wiper
Abstreifhalle *f* stripping bay
Abstreifkran *m* stripping crane
Abstreifmeißel *m* guard; stripping plate
Abstreifplatte *f* stripper plate
Abstrich *m* dross; scum
abstufen grade; step
Abstufung *f* gradation
Abstufung *f* **der Einflußgrößen** level of factors
abstützen prop; reinforce; spring; strut; support
Abstützung *f* bracing
Abszisse *f* abscissa axis
abtasten scan
Abtaster *m* **(EDV)** scanner
Abtastglied *n* scanning element
Abteilungsleiter *m* departmental manager; superintendent
abteufen sink
abtrennen cut

Abtrieb *m* **(Stranggießen)** output shaft
abtropfen drain
abtropfen (Draht) drain
Abwärmekessel *m* waste heat boiler
Abwärmeverwertung *f* waste heat recuperation; waste heat utilization
Abwärme-Verwertungsanlage *f* waste heat utilization plant
Abwasser *n* sewage; waste water
Abwasser-Kläranlage *f* waste water clarifying plant
Abwasserpumpe *f* waste water pump
Abwasserreinigung *f* waste water cleaning
Abwasser-Rückgewinnungsanlage *f* waste water recovering plant
abweichen deviate
abweichen (= unterscheiden) diverge
Abweichung *f* departure; deviation; difference; error
Abweichungssumme *f* deviance
Abweichung *f* **zulässige** allowable variation
Abwesenheit *f* absence
Abwesenheit *f* **(von Arbeitern)** absenteeism
Abwickelgerüst *n* **(z. B. für Drahtringe)** swift
abwickeln uncoil; unwind
Abwischer *m* wiper
abwracken break up; wreck
Abwurftisch *m* **(Sinter)** deflector table
abziehen draw down; draw off; pull slag; unwind; withdraw (die/powder met.)
abziehen (Schlacke) tap
Abziehrolle *f* pinch roll; withdrawal roll
Abzug *m* draft; hood; off-take
Abzugshaube *f* hood
Abzugskanal *m* flue; off-take
Abzugsmantelmatrize *f* **(Pulvermet.)** retracting die
Abzugsrohr *n* discharge duct
Abzugsrohrleitung *f* downtake
Abzugsschlacke *f* boilings
Acetylen-Erzeugungsanlage *f* acety-

lene production plant
Acetylen-Schneidverfahren n acetylene cutting
Achsbüchse f axle box
Achse f arbor; axis; axle; shaft
Achsenverhältnis n axial ratio
Achskasten m axle box
Achslager n axle box; journal bearing; journal box
Achslager n mit seitlichen Federstützungen laterally sprung axle bearing
Achsschenkelschleifmaschine f axle journal grinding machine
Achtkantstahl m octagons
Achtstrang-Gießmaschine f eight-strand continuous casting machine
Ac-Punkt m Ac-point
Ader f strand; vein
Adhäsionskraft f adhesive power; bonding force
Adjustage f finishing department; finishing shop
Adjustagemaschine f dressing and straightening machine; ending machine
Adsorptionseigenschaften fpl adsorptive properties
Adsorptionsvermögen n adsorptive capacity
Affinität f affinity
Agglomerat n agglomerate
Aggregatzustand m aggregate state
Akkordarbeit f job work; piece work
Akkordarbeiter m incentive operator; piece worker
Akkordleistung f task-work performance
Akkordlohn m contract rate; piece rate wages
Akkordvorgabe f rate fixing standard
Akkumulator m accumulator; electric storage battery
Aktie f share
Aktionär m shareholder; stockholder
Aktiva npl **(Bilanz)** assets
aktives Glied n **(EDV)** active element
Aktivierbarkeit f **(Reaktorstähle)** activatibility
Aktivierungsenergie f activation energy
Aktivierungsmittel n activating agent
Aktivkohle f activated carbon
akustographisches Bildwandler-Verfahren n acoustographic imaging system
Akzeptanz f acceptance
alitierter Stahl m calorized steel
alkalimetrisch alkali measuring
alkalisch alkaline
alkoholische Salpetersäure f **(Ätzen)** alcoholic nitric acid
Allotropie f allotropy
Alpacca n nickel silver
Alpha-Eisen n alpha iron
Alpha-Mischkristall m alpha solid solution
Alteisen n scrap iron
altern age
Altern n **nach Deformation** strain ag[e]ing
Alterung f ag[e]ing
Alterungsbehandlung f ageing treatment
Alterungsbeständigkeit f resistance to ag[e]ing
Alterungsempfindlichkeit f sensitivity to ag[e]ing; susceptibility to ag[e]ing
Alterungsriß m ageing crack
Alterungssprödigkeit f ag[e]ing brittleness
Altschrott m capital scrap
Alumetieren n aluminium plating
Aluminierungsofen m aluminizing furnace
Aluminiumfolien-Anlage f leaf aluminium rolling mill
Aluminiumoxid n **(Tonerde)** alumina
Aluminiumplattieren n aluminium plating
Aluminiumsilicat n aluminium silicate
aluminothermisches Schweißen n thermite welding
Amboß m anvil
Ammoniak n ammonia

Ammoniakgewinnungsanlage f ammonia recovery plant
Ammoniaklösung f ammonium solution
Ammoniakspaltgas n cracked ammonia
Ammoniakwäscherei f ammonia recovery plant
Ammoniakwasser n ammonia water; liquid ammonia
Ammoniak n wäßriges aqueous ammonia
Ammoniumsulfat n di-ammonium sulphate
Analog-Digital-Umformer m analogue-digital-converter
Analogiemodell n simulator
Analogrechner m analogue computer
Analyse f analysis
Analysengerät n analytic equipment
Analysenkontrollprobe f reference material
Analysenwaage f analytical balance
analytische Chemie f analytical chemistry
Anätzung f **(Fehler beim Kaltwalzen)** etching
Anbau m extension
anbieten offer; tender
anblasen blow
Andruckrollen-Biegeverfahren n back-up roll bending
Andruckrollen fpl back-up rolls
Anfahrdiagramm n start-up graph
anfahren start
Anfahrkopf m **(Stranguß)** dummy bar head
Anfahrstrang m dummy bar; starting bar
Anfahrstück n dummy bar
anfallen form; result
Anfälligkeit f **(für)** liability to; sensitiveness (to); susceptibility (to)
Anfangskorrosionsgeschwindigkeit f initial corrosion rate
Anfangsquerschnitt m initial [pass] section; starting section
Anfasmaschine f chamfering machine

Anfertigung f manufacture
anfeuchten (Steine) temper
Anforderung f requirement; strain
Anfrage f inquiry; request
anfressen corrode; erode; gall; pit; seize
Angaben fpl data
angeben advance
Angebot n offer; tender
Angebot n unverbindliches offer without obligation
Angebot n verbindliches binding offer
angegossen cast in one with; cast integral with; cast-on
angeheftet (zum Schweißen) set-up
angelernter Arbeiter m semi-skilled worker
angeln (= mit Schwanzende versehen) tag
Angestellter m employee; salaried worker
angetriebener Rollgang m live roller table
angewandte Chemie f applied chemistry
angewandte Statistik f applied statistics
Angießen n start of casting
angleichen adapt
Angleichung f adapt[at]ion
angreifen bite; corrode
Angriffsfreudigkeit f aggressivity; rate of attack
Angriffsmittel n aggressive medium
anhalten stop
anhaltend persistent
Anhaltszahlen fpl auxiliary data; reference data
Anhängerverfahren n system used in calculating price extras on basic price list
Anhänger m **(Wagen)** trailer
Anhängeschild n tag
Anhäufung f **von Mattschweißen** recurrent lap; surging lap
anheizen fire; light up
Anisotropie f anisotropy
Anker m tie element

Ankerbelastung f (einer elektr. Maschine) armature load
Ankerbolzen m anchor bolt; tie bolt
Anker m (eines Hochofens) belt
Ankerreihenschaltung f (elektr. Antrieb) series armature circuit
Ankerrohr n axial conduit
Ankersäule f buck-stay
Ankerschiene f tie bar
Ankerschraube f anchor bolt; foundation screw
ankörnen centre; mark
Anlage f equipment; installation; layout; plant
Anlage f eines Stichprobenverfahrens sample design
Anlage f eines Versuches design of an experiment
Anlagekosten pl capital costs; costs of installation; establishment charges; initial costs
Anlagentechnik f plant engineering; plant techniques
Anlagevermögen n fixed assets
Anlaßätzung f temper etch
Anlaßbeständigkeit f retention of hardness
Anlaßdauer f tempering time
anlassen anneal; draw; start; temper
Anlaßfarbe f temper colour
Anlaßfestigkeit f as tempered tensile strength
Anlaßgefüge n structure as tempered
Anlaßhärte f as tempered hardness; retention of hardness; tempered hardness
Anlaßofen m tempering furnace
Anlaßsprödigkeit f temper brittleness
Anlaßtemperatur f tempering temperature
anlaufen tarnish
anlaufen lassen sull coat
Anlauffarbe f annealing colour
Anlaufkohlenstoff m melt-down carbon
Anlaufmoment n starting moment
Anlaufzeit f rise time (automatic control); settling time (automatic control)
Anlaufzeit f (Gamma-alpha-Umwandlung) incubation time
Anlernling m learner; trainee
anliegend adjacent
Anmeldetag m (Patent) filing date
Anmeldung f (Patent) application
annähern approach
Annahme f receipt
annehmbare Qualitätsgrenzlage f acceptable quality level (AQL)
Annippelvorrichtung f für Elektroden electrode joining and lifting nipple equipment
Anode f anode
anodische Amalgamvoltametrie f anodic voltametry
anodischer Schutz m (Korrosion) anodic protection
anordnen arrange
Anordnung f arrangement; lay-out
Anordnung f nach der Größe series arranged according to magnitude
anpassen adapt; adjust; fit; match
Anpassen n von Kurven curve fitting
Anpaßstein m (Lichtbogenofengewölbe) broken ring segment
Anpassungsfähigkeit f flexibility
anprallen impinge
Anpreßdruck m contact pressure
Anpreßkraft f contact force
anregen excite
anreichern concentrate; enrich
anreichern mit Kohlenstoff caburize
Anreicherung f concentration; enrichment
anreißen trace
anreißen (= **Risse bekommen**) crack superficially
Anriß m flaw; incipient crack; incipient tear
Ansammlung f (Drahtziehen) accumulation
Ansatz m lug; shoulder
Ansatz m (auf Ofenwänden) scar
Ansätze mpl accretions
Ansatz m (Hochofen) scab
Ansatzmatrize f shouldered die

Ansatz m **(Oberflächenfehler)** scab
Ansatz m **(Schachtofen)** scaffold
Ansaugeleistung f suction output; suction power
Ansaugleitung f suction line
Anschaffungskosten pl initial costs
Anschlag m dog
Anschlag m **(Drahtziehen)** first draw
Anschläger m **(Kran)** hanger-on; striker
Anschlagvorrichtung f arresting device
anschließen join[t]
Anschluß m connection
Anschlußklemme f connecting terminal
Anschlußstück n gooseneck; nipple
Anschlußwert m **(elektr.)** connected load
anschmieden forge-on
anschneiden gate
Anschneiden n **(von Formen)** gating (of moulds)
Anschnitt m ingate
Anschnitt-Technik f gating (of moulds)
anschrauben screw on
anschweißen weld on
Anschweißende n **(Rohre)** safe end
Anschweißschraube f welding stud
ansetzen (Bad) strain
Ansintern n **des bei Herdreparaturen aufgeworfenen Dolomits** sticking of dolomite during bottom fettling
Anspannung f strain
anspitzen sharpen; swage
Anspitzen n **(Stauchen)** nosing
Ansprechempfindlichkeit f sensitiveness (to)
Ansprechwert m input resolution (automatic control)
anstauchen head; upset
Anstellkraft f **(Stranggießen)** contact force
Anstellschraube f screw down
Anstellsteuerung f adjusting control; screw down control
Anstellvorrichtung f adjusting equipment

Anstich m coat
Anstichquerschnitt m initial [pass] section; leading pass section
Anstichwelle f **(Bandrichten)** bite mark
Anstoß m impact; impetus
anstreichen coat; swab
Anstrichmittel n coat[ing] material; paint[ing] medium
Anteil m amount; share
Anthrazit m anthracite [glance coal]; glance coal
antiferromagnetische Fernbereichsordnung f (in Einkristall) long range antiferromagnetic order
Antimon n antimony
Antrieb m impetus; input; input shaft
Antriebselemente npl driving elements
Antriebskraft f driving power
Antriebsmotor m driving motor
Antriebsritzel n driving pinion
Antriebsspindel f **(Walzen)** spindle
Antriebswelle f driving shaft
Antrophometrie f anthropometry
anwärmen warm up
Anwendung f application
Anwendungsbereich m field of application; scope
Anwendungsmöglichkeit f applicability
anzapfen bleed
Anzapfung f **(EDV)** tap
Anzapfventil n **(Hochofen)** bleeder valve
Anzeichnen n **(von Blechen)** marking
Anzeige f display (computer); indication
Anzeigegerät n indicating instrument
anzeigen indicate
Anzeigetafel f indicator board
anziehen tighten
Anziehungskraft f attractive force
Anzug m draught
Anzug m **(Kaliber)** draft; taper
anzünden ignite
AOD-Verfahren n argon oxygen decarburization process
Apparatebau m construction of appa-

ratus (plant manufacture)
Äquivalentleitfähigkeit f equivalent conductivity
Arbeit f energy; job; work
Arbeiter m operative; operator; worker; workman
Arbeitersiedlung f workmen's quarter
Arbeiter m **zeitweilig entlassener** lay off workman
Arbeitsablauf m work proceeding
Arbeitsamt n employment bureau; labo[u]r office; state employment bureau
Arbeitsanalyse f job analysis
Arbeitsanforderung f job requirement
Arbeitsaufgabe f work task
Arbeitsaufwand m energy expended; work expended
Arbeitsbedingungen fpl working conditions
Arbeitsbelastung f load
Arbeitsbeschreibung f job description
Arbeitsbühne f working platform; working stage
Arbeitseinsatz m man-power
arbeitsfähig able to work
Arbeitsfläche f working face
Arbeitsgemeinschaft f study group; working party
Arbeitsgruppe f crew; team; working group
Arbeitshub m working stroke
Arbeitshygiene f industrial hygiene
Arbeitskraft f man-power
Arbeitsleistung f labour efficiency; work output
Arbeitslosenunterstützung f dole; unemployment benefit
Arbeitsloser m unemployed [man]
Arbeitsmedizin f industrial medicine
Arbeitsmethode f method of working
Arbeitsmittel n operational facility; operational means
Arbeitsphysiologie f work physiology
Arbeitsplan m working program
Arbeits[platz]bewertung f job evaluation
Arbeitspsychologie f work psychology
Arbeitssoziologie f work sociology
Arbeitsspannung f operating voltage
Arbeitsstudie f time and motion study
Arbeitsstudium n work study
Arbeitsstunde f man hour; working hour
Arbeitsvorbereitung f works scheduling
Arbeitsvorgang m operation
Arbeitswalze f work[ing] roll
Arbeitsweise f works practice
Arbeitswirkungsgrad m energy efficiency
Arbeitswissenschaft f ergonomics
Arbeitszeit f machining time; operating time; working time
Argonpfannenspülung f argon ladle purging
arithmetisches Mittel n arithmetic mean
arm an low in
Armaturen fpl accessories
Armco-Eisen n Armco iron; ingot iron
Armierung f casing
Ar-Punkt m Ar-point
arsenige Säure f arsenious acid
Arsenik n white arsenic
Arsenkies m arsenic pyrites
arteigen inherent
Art und Weise f mode
Asbest m asbestos
Asche f ashes
Aschenrückstand m ash residue
Asphaltüberzug m **(warm aufgetragen)** asphalt sheeting
Asselwalzwerk n Assel mill
Atemschutzgerät n breathing apparatus
athermische Umwandlung f athermal transformation
atmosphärische Korrosion f atmospheric corrosion
Atomabsorptions-Spektrometer n atomic absorption spectrometer
Atomenergie f nuclear energy
Atomfluoreszenzspektrometrie f atomic-fluorescence spectroscopy
Atomgewicht n atomic weight

Atomkern *m* atomic nucleus
Atomkraftwerk *n* atomic power plant; nuclear power plant
Atomreaktor *m* nuclear reactor
Atramentverfahren *n* atrament process (see phosphate coating)
Ätzbild *n* etching figure
ätzen corrode; etch
ätzend corrosive
Ätzgrübchen *n* etch pit
Ätzmittel *n* etchant; etching [re]agent; etching medium; mordant
Aufbau *m* composition; construction; erection; structure
Aufbauchung *f* **(Ziehstein)** fattening
aufbauen build up; construct; erect
Aufbauschmelze *f* build-up heat
Aufbauschneide *f* built-up edge
aufbereiten concentrate; condition; dress
aufbereitetes Wasser *n* treated water
Aufbereitung *f* **durch Absieben (Erz)** dressing by screening
Aufbereitung *f* **durch Auswaschen** dressing by washing
Aufbereitung *f* **durch magnetische Trennung** dressing by magnetic separation
Aufbereitungs-Heberad *n* ferris wheel
Aufbereitungsstammbaum *m* system of ore dressing
aufblähen bulge; expand
aufblähen (Steine) bloat
aufblasen blow up
Aufblasstahl *m* BOF steel
Aufblasverfahren *n* top blowing process
Aufbrausen *n* effervescence
Aufbrennen *n* **des Stichloches mit der Sauerstofflanze** burning out the tap hole with the oxygen lance
Aufdampfen *n* **(Metallüberzug)** vapor deposition
Aufdornbarkeit *f* **(Rohre)** expandability
aufdornen broach (e.g. finish plate bolt holes)
aufeinanderlegen (Bleche) match

Aufenthalt *m* stay[ing time]
auffangen (ein Gas) collect (a gas)
auffangen (Gas) trap
Auffangschmelze *f* catch carbon heat
Auffederung *f* roll spring
Auffederung *f* **(Draht)** swelling
auffrischen top up
Aufgabeapparat *m* donkey arms
Aufgabeteller *m* feeder table
aufgehen swell
aufgehen (Pulvermet.) expand
Aufgehmaß *n* spring factor (powder met.)
aufgespaltene Versetzung *f* dissociated dislocation; extended dislocation
aufhalten trap
Aufhängevorrichtung *f* **für Steine** attachment of bricks; suspension of bricks
Aufhängung *f* suspension
Aufhärtbarkeit *f* maximum hardness obtainable
Aufhärtung *f* excessive hardening; hardness increase
Aufhaspeln *n* **in Ringen (Bandstahl)** coiling
Aufklärung *f* elucidation
aufkohlen carbonize; carburize
Aufkohlen *n* carburization
Aufkohlen *n* **mit Roheisen** carburization by pig iron
Aufkohlung *f* carbonization
Aufkohlungsbeschleuniger *m* energizer in carburizing
Aufkohlungsmittel *n* carburizing agent
Aufkohlungspulver *n* carburizing powder
aufladen load
Aufladen *n* loading
Auflage *f* bearing surface
Auflagefläche *f* bearing area; seating
Auflagerentfernung *f* distance between supports
Auflagetränkung *f* infiltration (powder met.)
Auflaufhaspel *f* coiler; winding drum
auflegieren alloy up
Auflichtmikroskopie *f* incidental light

microscopy
auflösen decompose; dissolve
Auflösung f dissolution
Auflösungsfähigkeit f solvent power
Auflösung f **von Versetzungen** anihilation of dislocations
Auflöten n **(von Stahlplättchen)** steel facing
aufmauern wall up
Aufnahme f absorption
aufnehmen (z. B. Kohlenstoff) absorb
aufnippeln (Elektrode) screw on
aufpumpen blow up
aufreißen burst
Aufriß m elevation; sectional view
Aufrollvorrichtung f coiling device
Aufsatz m treatise
aufsaugefähig absorbent
Aufsaugevermögen n absorption capacity
aufschichten stack
aufschlagen impinge
Aufschlämmung f slurry
Aufschließbarkeit f capacity for decomposition
aufschlußreich significant
Aufschmelzen n fusing; melting on; sintering
Aufschmelzgeschwindigkeit f meltdown rate
Aufschmelzriß m **(Schweißen)** liquation cracking
Aufschreibung f **(Blatt)** log sheet
aufschrumpfen shrink on
Aufschweißbiegeprobe f bead bend test
Aufschweißbiegeversuch m weld bead bend test
aufschweißen build up; weld on
Aufschweißen n steel facing
Aufschweißen n **(oder Auflöten) von Hartmetallplättchen** hard-facing
Aufschweißlegierung f filler metal; hard-facing alloy
Aufseher m boss
Aufsetzkübel m set-down bucket
Aufsichtsbeamter m supervisor
Aufsichtsrat m board [of directors]

aufspalten burst
Aufspaltung f cleavage (X-rays)
Aufspannvorrichtung f chuck; clamping device; fixture; jig; work holding attachment
aufspulen coil; spool; wind up
aufstampfen stamp on; tamp down
Aufsteckkopf m **(Thermoelement)** disposable head
Aufsteigen n elevation
Aufstellung f assembly; erection; establishment; installation; mounting
Aufsticken n nitriding; nitrogen pick-up
auftragen build up; deposit
Auftragen n application
auftragen (Schutzüberzug) apply (a protective coat)
Auftrag m order
Auftrag m **(Schicht)** coat
Auftragschweißung f build-up welding; deposit welding; overlaying welding; surface-layer welding; surfacing
Auftragsmetall n build-up metal; deposit metal
auftreffen impinge
Auftrefffläche f impinging face
Auftrennung f discontinuity
Auftrieb m **(Gas)** buoyancy
Auftriebsfreistrahl m buoyancy plume
Auftrittspotential n appearance potential
auftropfen apply by dropping
Auf- und Abbewegung f lufting
Aufwallen n ebullition; effervescence
Aufwalzung f **(Stranggießen)** opening up of crack by rolling
Aufwand m expenditure
Aufwärtsströmung f rising flow
aufweiten beck; bulge; enlarge; flare
Aufweitung f **im Rißgrund** expansion of the base of the crack
Aufweitung f **(Ziehstein)** enlargement
Aufweitversuch m bulging test; drift test; expansion test
Aufweitversuch m **(Rohr)** expanding test

Aufweitwalzwerk n expanding mill
Aufweitwalzwerk n **(Rohre)** becking mill
aufwickeln coil; wind
Aufwickeln n **in Rollen** winding in coils
Aufwickler m **mit spiralenförmiger Bandspeicherung** spiral looper accumulator
Aufzug m chain; elevator (am.); lift
Aufzugführungsschiene f elevator tee [guide]
Augenschutz m eye protection
Auger Elektronenspektroskopie f Auger electron spectroscopy
ausbauchen belly; bulge
Ausbauchen n bulging
Ausbauchung f camber
Ausbauchung f **(eines Ofenschachtes)** batter; stack batter
ausbauen dismantle
ausbauen (Walzen) take off
ausbessern revamp
Ausbeulen n buckling
Ausbeute f output
Ausbildung f form
ausblasen blow down; blow out; exhaust
ausbohren bore out
Ausbrechen n **von Teilchen (aus der Walzoberfläche)** shelling
ausbreiten spread
ausbringen put out; yield
Ausbringen n output
Ausbruch m **(Schienen)** shelly spot
ausbuchsen bush
Ausbuchtung f bulge
ausdehnen expand; extend
Ausdehnung f dilatation; expansion; extension; increase
Ausdehnungskoeffizient m expansion coefficient
Ausdrückmaschine f scraper
ausfahrbarer Herd m car-bottom hearth; mobile hearth
Ausfällen (Drahtziehen) soaping out
Ausfall m **(Generator)** outage
Ausfallmuster n type sample
Ausfallrutsche f billet chute

Ausfallzeit f downtime
ausflammen flame out
ausfließen discharge; flow out
Ausflockung f flocculation
Ausfluß m discharge
Ausflußöffnung f orifice
Ausfugmasse f jointing mixture
Ausführhund m stripper guide
Ausführmeißel m delivery guide
Ausführung f achievement
ausfüttern fettle; line
Ausgang m exit; issue; outlet
Ausgangsdicke f initial thickness
Ausgangsgröße f initial size; output variable
Ausgangswerkstoff m initial material; starting material
ausgaren lassen carbonize; let well carbonize
ausgelaufener Block m bled ingot
ausgelegt sein be laid out
ausgerundetes Kaliber n curved groove
ausgeschlissener Ziehstein m worn die
ausgestanztes Stück n blank
Ausgießen n **(Lager)** lining
Ausgitterung f checker work
ausgleichen balance; compensate; equalize; soak
Ausgleichen n blending (of powder grain size)
Ausgleichgetriebe n differential gear
Ausgleichsgerade f best fit line
Ausgleichsgerade f **(durch Korrelationsrechnung)** partial regression line
Ausgleichsgrube f soaking pit
Ausgleichsherd m soaking chamber; soaking hearth
Ausgleichsleitung f compensation leads
Ausgleichstrichter m surge hopper
Ausgleichszone f soaking zone
Ausglühen n full annealing
Ausguß m discharge; drain; lip; nozzle; outlet
Ausgußrinne f spout

aushalten endure; last; stand
ausheben eject
Auskehlung f groove
Auskleidung f lining
Ausklinkmaschine f coping machine
Ausklinkpunkt m disengagement point
Auskohlung f total decarburization
Auskolkung f cratering
auskuppeln uncouple
ausladend angeordnet overhung
Ausladung f gab; overhang; swing
Ausladung f **(Drehkran)** working radius
Ausladung f **(Hochofen)** throat
auslagern age
Auslagerungsbehandlung f ageing treatment
ausländische Arbeitskraft f foreign labour
ausländische Arbeitskräfte fpl imported workers
Auslaß m delivery; discharge; outlet pipe
Auslaßführung f exit guide
Auslaßschütz n outlet gate
Auslaßventil n escape valve
Auslastung f load factor
Auslauf m down-spout; outlet
Auslauf m **ausgekleideter** dabbed spout
auslaufen bleed; leak
Ausläufer m leaker; tail
Auslaufrohr n delivery pipe
Auslaufrollgang m delivery roller table
Auslaufseite f **(der Walzen)** catcher's side (of rolls); delivery side (of rolls); outgoing side (of rolls)
Auslaufteil n exit section
auslegen lay out
Ausleger m cantilever
Auslegerkran m boom type jib crane; jib crane
auslesen assort; sort
auslösen disengage; trip
Auslöser m **(EDV)** trigger
Ausmauerung f bricking up; lining; masonry; walling up

Ausnutzung f utilization
auspacken (Formen) shake out
Auspuff m exhaust
Auspuffgas n exhaust gas
Ausreißer m freak value (data); maverick; outlier
ausrichten adjust; set; straighten
Ausrichtmaschine f balancing machine
Ausrichtungsgrad m **(Kristall)** orientation index
ausrücken disconnect; disengage; throw out
Ausrüstung f equipment
Ausschachtung f excavation
ausschalten break [a circuit]; cut out; disconnect
Ausschalter m breaker; circuit breaker
ausscheiden precipitate
Ausschlag m amplitude; swing
Ausschlag m **(Ultraschall)** deflection
Ausschlagvorrichtung f arresting device
Ausschleppverlust m **(beim Beizen)** entrainment loss
Ausschnitt m clip
Ausschuß m discard; scrap; waste
Ausschußblech n waste sheet; waster
Ausschuß m **für Betriebswirtschaft** Industrial Engineering Committee
Ausschwingversuch m test by free oscillations
Außenachslager n axle-bearing outside the wheels
Außendruck m external pressure
Außendurchmesser m major diameter; outside diameter
Außenhandel m foreign trade
Außenluft f ambient air; ambient atmosphere
Außenschicht f case
Außenwand f **des aufsteigenden Gas- oder Luftkanals (SM-Ofen)** bulkhead
Außenzone f rim
außer Betrieb m **setzen** shut down
außermittig off centre

außermittige Lage f eccentricity
außermittige Lagerlast f eccentric bearing load
aussondern sort
Aussonderung f segregation; sorting out
aussortieren (Schrott) segregate
Aussparung f clearance
ausspritzen squirt
Ausstechen n trepanning
ausstehende Verpflichtungen fpl liabilities
ausstoßen eject
ausstoßen (von Gasen) knock out
Ausstoß m **(Gas)** discharge; emission
Ausstoßpresse f extruding press
Ausstoß m **(von Gasen)** evolution
Austauschstahl m substitute steel
Austauschstromdichte f exchange current density
Austauschwerkstoff m substitute material
Austenit m austenite
Austenitformhärten n ausforming
Austenitformpatentieren n ausform-patenting
austenitischer Stahl m austenitic steel
austenitisieren austen[it]ize
Austenitisierung f austen[it]izing
austiefen sink
Austrag m discharge
austragen discharge
Austrag m **(Erz)** yield
Austragschieber m discharge plough
Austritt m exit
Austrittsbalken m delivery beam
Austrittsgeschwindigkeit f delivery speed; velocity of exit
Austrittsseite f **(an der Walze)** catcher's side
Auswahl f sampling
auswählen assort; sample; select
Auswahlverfahren n sampling
Auswaschen des Stranges n **(Stranggluß)** decanting of the strand; draining of the strand
Auswaschung f cavitation; washing attack

Auswechselteil n **an Generatorgasbrennern** scotch block
Ausweichplatz m siding
auswerfen eject
Auswerfer m ejector
Auswertung f analysis; evaluation
Auswuchtmaschine f balancing machine
Auswurf m discharge; effluent; emission; slopping; spatter and slopping; spittings
Ausziehvorrichtung f drawing device
Auszubildender m apprentice
Auszugmaschine f **(Ofen)** withdrawing machine (furnace)
Autogenes Schweißen n gas [fusion] welding; oxyacetylene welding
Autokorrelation f autocorrelation
Autokran m automotive crane
Automatenschweißung f automatic welding
Automatenstahl m easy-machining steel; free-cutting steel; free-machining steel
Automatenweichstahl m soft free-cutting steel; soft free-machining steel
automatische Badspiegelregelung f **(Strangguß)** automatic steel level control
automatische Kupplung f **(Eisenbahn)** automatic coupling
automatisieren automate
automatisiertes Verfahren n automated process
Automatisierung f automation
Autoradiographie f autoradiography
Axialbeanspruchung f axial load

B

backen bake; burn; cake
Backenbrecher m jaw crusher
Backenbremse f cheek brake
backende Kohle f bituminous coal; caking coal
Backenfutter n jaw chuck

Backfähigkeit f caking capacity; coking capacity
Bad n bath
Badaufkohlen n bath carburizing
Badbewegung f bath agitation
Badbewegung f **induktive** electromagnetic stirring of the bath
Badcarbonitrieren n cyaniding
Badnitrieren n salt bath nitriding
Badofen m bath furnace
Badpatentieren n bath patenting
Badspiegelregelung f **automatische (Stranguß)** automatic steel level control
Bagger m dredger
Baggerschlacke f dredging slag
Bahn f face; track
Bahn f **(Kaliber)** body
Bainit m bainite
Bainithärten n bainitic hardening
Bainitstufe f bainite
Balkenherd-Glühofen m walking-beam annealing furnace
Balkenherdofen m rocker-bar type furnace; walking beam [type] heating furnace
Ballast m **(Hochofen)** inert materials
Ballen m bale; ball; barrel; bunch
Ballenlänge f barrel length; body length; face length
Ballenpresse f baling press
Ballen m **(Walze)** body
Balligkeit f camber; crown
Balligkeit f **der Walze** roll camber; roll crown
Balligkeitssteuerung f crown control
Band n belt; strip; tape
Bandabschneidmaschine f strip cutting-off machine
Bandage f tyre
Bandagendraht m tie-wire
Bandbegichtung f **(Hochofen)** conveyor belt charging
Bandbremse f strip brake
Banddicken-Meßgerät n ga[u]ge measuring device; strip thickness measuring device
Banddickenregelung f **automatische** automatic ga[u]ge control
Banddurchlauf-Glühanlage f continuous strip annealing line
Banddurchziehofen m continuous strand furnace
Bandende n tail end of strip
Bandförderer m belt conveyor
Bandgießen n thin strip casting
Bandhaspel f reel for strip
Bandkantensteuerung f edge positioner
Bandlaufebene f **angestrebte** pass-line
Bandmaß n tape
Bandmöllerungsanlage f conveyer belt burdening installations
Bandoberseite f top side of the strip
Bandpellet n straight grate pellet
Bandrichtmaschine f strip straigthening machine
Bandring m coil
Bandrolle f belt idler
Bandsäge f band saw
Bandschaufellader m conveyor-type bucket loader
Bandschleifmaschine f flexible belt sander
Bandschreiber m strip chart recorder
Bandsinteranlage f strand sintering plant
Bandsintern n strand sintering
Bandspan m ribbon chip
Bandspeicher m magnetic tape memory
Bandstahl m iron hoop; steel hoop; strip steel
Bandstahlbund n coil of strip
Bandstahl-Glühofen m strip annealing furnace
Bandstahlwalzwerk n hoop mill; strip [steel] mill
Bandsteifigkeit f strip stiffness
Bandunterseite f bottom side of the strip
Bandverbinder m belt fastener
Bandverzinnen n strip tinning
Bandwaage f conveyor type weigher

Bandwalzwerk n strip [rolling] mill; strip [steel] mill; strip mill; wide strip mill
Bandwickler m strip winder; taping machine
Bandwölbung f strip crown
Bandzugsteuerung f strip tension control
Bär m button; skull; tup
Barren m billet
Bart m burr; flash
Bart m **(Nägel)** whiskers
Base f base
Basenaustauscher m base-exchanger
Basengrad m basicity
basischer Siemens-Martin-Ofen m basic open hearth furnace
basische Schlacke f basic slag
basische Schlackenführung f basic slag practice; working with a basic slag
basisches feuerfestes Erzeugnis n basic refractory [product]
basisches Futter n basic lining
basisches Roheisen n basic pig iron
basische Zustellung f basic lining
Basizität f basicity
Basizitätsgrad m slag ratio
Basizitätsverhältnis n slag ratio
Bauart f design; type
bauartgenehmigungspflichtig subject to design certification
Baublech n structural steel plate
Bauch m **(Konverter)** belly; body
bauen build
Baukastenprinzip n building block principle; mechanical assembly technique (MAT); modular building brick principle; unit construction principle
Baukosten pl building costs; costs of construction
Baumann-Abdruck m sulphur print
Baumaschine f machine for structural engineering
Baustahl m structural shapes; structural steel
Baustahlmatte f reinforcing wire mesh; welded wire fabric; welded wire mesh
Baustellenschweißung f field welding; site welding
Baustoff m building material
Bauteil n structural member
Bautentrocknung f drying of building
Bauwesen n construction; engineering
Bauxit m bauxite
Beanspruchbarkeit f capacity to withstand stresses
beanspruchen strain; stress
Beanspruchung f load; stress; strain
beanstanden reject
Beanstandung f complaint; objection; rejection
bearbeiten machine; treat; work
Bearbeitung f treating; working
Bearbeitungsdauer f machining time; time-consuming lag
Bearbeitungsstufe f machining step
Bearbeitungswerkstatt f mechanical workshop
Bearbeitungszeit f machining time
Bearbeitungszugabe f allowance
Becher m shell
Becherbruch m cup-and-cone fracture; cupping
Becherwerk n bucket conveyor; bucket elevator
Bedampfung f sputtering (electron microscope)
bedecken cover
Bedeutung f significance
bedeutungsvoll significant
Bedienung f attendance; operation; service
Bedienungsbühne f operator's platform
Bedienungshebel m operating lever
Bedienungsmann m attendant; operative; operator
beeinflußbare Zuschlagskosten pl burden; controllable [extras]
Befehlsfolge f control sequence
Befehlsgerät n order transmitting device

befestigen fasten; fix
befördern convey
Beförderung f delivery
Befund m analysis
begichten burden
Begichtung f burdening
Begichtung f **mit Hängebahn** charging by aerial ropeway; charging by trolley conveyor
Begichtungsaufzug m top-charging hoist
Begichtungsvorrichtung f charging gear
Begleitelement n accompanying element; tramp element
Begrenzungsgrad m **der Breitung (Walzen)** limiting spread factor
Begrenzungsschalter m limit switch
behalten retain
Behälter m bin; bunker; case; container; hopper; tank; trough
behandeln treat
Behandlung f treatment
Behandlungszustand m condition of treatment
Beharrungszustand m steady-state condition (automatic control)
beheizen fire; heat
Beheizung f firing; heating
Beheizungseinrichtung f heating installation
beidrehen (Kristall vor der Erstarrungsfront) turn into line with
beidseitiges Pressen n double action pressing
Beimengung f admixture; impurity
beißend castic; caustic
Beiwert m coefficient; factor
Beizablauge f pickling acid waste; spent pickle liquor; spent pickling solution; waste pickle liquor
Beizabwasser n waste pickle liquor
Beizanlage f pickling plant
Beizausrüstung f pickling equipment
Beizbad n pickling bath
Beizbarkeit f capacity for pickling
Beizbast m pickling deposit
Beizbedarf m pickling agents

Beizbehälter m pickling vat
Beizblasen fpl pickling blistering; pickling blow holes
Beizbottich m pickling tank; pickling vat
Beize f mordant
beizen pickle
Beize f pickle; pickling bath
beizend caustic
Belzerei f pickling department
Beizflüssigkeit f pickling fluid
Beizinhibitor m pickling inhibitor
Beizkasten m pickling vat
Beizkorb m pickling basket; pickling crade
Beizlösung f pickling solution
Beizmaschine f pickling machine
Beizmittel n pickling agent
Beizprobe f pickle test
Beizrückstand m pickling residue
Beizrückstände mpl carbon smut
Beizsprödigkeit f pickle brittleness
Beizstrecke f pickling line; pickling section
Beizzusatz m inhibitor; pickling compound
bekämpfen abate; combat
Bekämpfung f abatement; combat
Bekleidungsblech n coating sheet; curtain wall plate; curtain wall sheet; lining sheet
beladen charge; fill; load [up]
Beladevorrichtung f loader; loading device
Belag m coat; cover; facing; lining
Belagblech n floor plate
Belagskorrosion f deposit attack
Belastbarkeit f loadability; working stress
Belastbarkeit f **(Elektroden)** loading capability
belasten charge
Belastung f burdening; charge; load
Belastung f **(= Überhang)** bias
Belastung f **dynamische** dynamic load
Belastungsdauer f time under load
Belastungsfähigkeit f load (carrying) capacity

Belastungskurve f loading curve; loading diagram; stress curve; stress diagram
Belastungsschwankung f **(Lichtbogenofen)** load swing
Belastung f **stoßweise** pulsating load
belegen coat; face
Belegexemplar n voucher copy
Belegstück n reference sample
beleuchten illuminate; light
belichten expose (phot.)
Belichtung f exposure
Belichtungszeit f exposure time
Belohnung f award
Belüfter m ventilating device
Belüftung f ventilation
Belüftungselement n aeration cell (corrosion)
Belüftungsklappe f ventilating flap
Bemessung f dimensioning; sizing
Bemessungsgrundlage f dimensioning basis
Benetzbarkeit f wettability
Benetzungsfähigkeit f wetting power
Benetzungsmittel n wetting agent
Benetzungswinkel m wetting angle of contact
Bentonitbinder m bentonite binder
benutzen use
Benutzung f use
Benzin n distillate fuel; light petroleum distillate
Benzol n benzene; benzol
beratender Ingenieur m consulting engineer
Beratungsstelle f **für Stahlverwendung** advice centre for steel use
berechnen calculate; compute
Berechnung f calculation; computation
Bereich m range; reach
Bereichsanpassung f **(EDV)** scaling
Bereichstruktur f **(Kristall)** domain structure
Bergbahn f mountain railway
Bergbau m mining
Bergbauausrüstung f mining equipment

Berge mpl tailings
Bergeversatz m debris; pack; stope filling; stowage
Bergwirtschaft f mining activity
Berieselungsturm m scrubber; spray tower; wash tower
Berieselungswäscher m spray scrubber
Berstdruck m bursting pressure
bersten burst
Berufsgenossenschaft f employers' liability insurance association
Berufsgruppe f occupational group
Berufskrankheit f occupational disease
beruhigen abate; deoxidize; kill
beruhigter Stahl m fully killed steel; killed steel; solid steel
Beruhigung f deoxidizing
Berührungsfläche f area of contact
Berührungskorrosion f crevice corrosion at contact
Beryllium n beryllium
Besatzgewicht n loading capacity
Besatzstein m filler brick
Besatzung f crew
besäumen trim
Besäumen n trimming
Besäumschere f side cut shear; trimming shear
beschädigte Kante f damaged edge
Beschädigung f damage
Beschädigung f **durch Bandagieren** band dent
Beschädigung f **durch Krantransport** crane dent
Beschädigung f **durch metallischen Überzug** metal dent
Beschädigung f **durch Richtmaschine** roller straightening dent
Beschaffenheit f condition; nature; state
Beschäftigungsgrad m employment factor
Beschallung f acoustic irradiation
Beschichtung f coating
Beschichtungswalze f applicator roll
beschicken burden; charge; feed; load

Beschicken *n* loading
Beschickung *f* burden; charge; feed; load
Beschickung *f* **absatzweise** batch charging
Beschickungsbühne *f* charging platform
Beschickungsgeschwindigkeit *f* feeding rate
Beschickungsgeschwindigkeit *f* **(Ofen)** charging rate
Beschickungskran *m* charging by batches; charging crane
Beschickungsmulde *f* charging box
Beschickungssäule *f* **(Hochofen)** stock column
Beschickungsseite *f* charging side; feeding side
Beschickungstrichter *m* feed hopper
Beschickungsvorrichtung *f* feeding device
Beschickvorrichtung *f* charging device; feeding device
beschlagen tarnish
beschleunigen accelerate
Beschleunigung *f* acceleration
Beschleunigungsmittel *n* accelerator; activating agent; catalyst
beschmieren daub
Beschneiden *n* **von Kanten** edge trimming
Beschneiden *n* **von Kanten (Band)** edging; side shearing
beschnittene Kante *f* sheared edge
beschränken limit
beschränkend restrictive
Beschwerde *f* complaint; trouble
Besetzung *f* **einer Gittergeraden** packing of a lattice direction (X-rays)
Bessemerstahl *m* Bessemer steel; acid Bessemer steel
Bessemerverfahren *n* Bessemer process; acid Bessemer process; acid converter process
beständig constant; stable
Beständigkeit *f* stability
Bestandsführung *f* **(EDV)** stock registration

Bestandteil *m* component (part)
Bestandteil *m* **(Gefüge)** constituent
Bestellgewicht *n* ordered weight
bestimmen determine; evaluate; limit
Bestimmung *f* determination; evaluation
bestrahlen irradiate
bestreichen smear; sweep
bestücken tip
Beta-Rückstrahlung *f* back scatter of beta rays
Betatron *n* betatron
Beton *m* concrete
Betondichtungsmittel *n* concrete sealing agent
Betonprüfmaschine *f* concrete testing machine
Betonrippenstahl *m* ribbed reinforcing bars
Betonstahl *m* concrete reinforcing steel bars; reinforcing bar
Betonstahlmatte *f* concrete reinforcing [steel] mat; welded wire reinforcing fabric; wire fabric
Betonware *f* concrete product; concrete ware
Betrag *m* amount
Betrag *m* magnitude
betreiben exploit; operate
Betrieb *m* operation; plant; practice; service
Betrieb *m* **in** operating
Betrieb *m* **in - setzen** launch; put into operation
betriebliches Rechnungswesen *n* cost [factory] accounting; works cost accounting
Betriebsablaufsteuerung *f* operating sequence control
Betriebsabrechnungsbogen *m* overhead expense distribution sheet
Betriebsanlage *f* mill; operational plant
Betriebsanlagen *fpl* facilities
Betriebsaufschreibung *f* operational record[ing]
Betriebsbericht *m* operating report

Betriebsbericht *m* (Zahlenaufstellung) log
Betriebsblatt *n* (z.B. SEB) works engineering specifications
Betriebsbuchhaltung *f* cost accounting department; factory accounting
Betriebschef *m* superintendent; works manager
Betriebsdaten *npl* operational data
Betriebsdauer *f* time of operation
Betriebsdruck *m* working pressure
Betriebseinrichtung *f* operating equipment; processing line
Betriebserfahrung *f* operational experience
Betriebsergebnis *n* operating result; practical result
Betriebsergebnisse *npl* operating results
betriebsfertig ready for operation
Betriebsfestigkeitsversuch *m* fatigue test under operational stresses
Betriebsführung *f* management; plant management
Betriebsgesellschaft *f* subsidiary manufacturing company
Betriebsingenieur *m* engineer in charge
Betriebskennzahlen *fpl* operating characteristics
Betriebsklima *n* shop morale
Betriebskosten *pl* operating costs
Betriebslagereinrichtung *f* stores equipment; warehouse equipment
Betriebslehre *f* go-no-go gauge
Betriebsleiter *m* boss; departmental manager; plant superintendent; shop manager; works manager
Betriebspsychologie *f* industrial psychology
Betriebsrat *m* shop committee
Betriebsrechner *m* operational computer
Betriebsregelsatz *m* servo-mechanism
betriebsreif ready for industrial application
Betriebsreife *f* service stage

Betriebsschmelze *f* production cast; production heat
Betriebsschwingversuch *m* fatigue test under actual service conditions
Betriebsselbstkosten *pl* operation first costs; operation prime costs
Betriebssicherheit *f* operating safety
Betriebsspannung *f* working voltage
Betriebsstoff *m* operating material
Betriebsstörung *f* break-down; operating trouble
Betriebsunfall *m* mill accident; works accident
Betriebsunterbrechung *f* break-down; stoppage
Betriebsversuch *m* production trial; service test
Betriebsweise *f* mode of operation
Betriebswirtschaft *f* industrial engineering; industrial management; plant economics
Betriebszahlen *fpl* operating figures; operating numbers
Betriebszeit *f* manned time; time of operation
betupfen dab
Beugung *f* diffraction
Beugung langsamer Elektronen low energy electron diffraction
Beule *f* bulge; dent; ding
Beulenbahn *f* buckling line
Beurteilung *f* assessment; valuation
Beurteilungsmaßstab *m* method of evalution
Beurteilungsverfahren *n* method of evalution
Beutelfilter *m* bag filter
bewegen agitate; handle; move
beweglich mobile; movable
bewegliche Herstellungskosten *pl* mobile prime costs; variable prime costs
bewegliche Kupplung *f* (Rohr) flexible joint
bewegte Konten *npl* active accounts
bewegte Last *f* moving load
Bewegung *f* agitation; handling (material); motion; movement

Bewehrungsmatte f rod mats for concrete reinforcement
bewerten assess; estimate; evaluate
Bewertung f appreciation; assessment; valuation
Bewertungskurve f weighting curve
Bewirtschaftung f control
Bewitterungsversuch m weathering test
bezeichnen mark
bezeichnend significant
Beziehungsschaubild n correlogram
bezogen specific
bezogen auf converted to
bezogener Arbeitswirkungsgrad m specific energy efficiency
Bezugsprobe f reference test piece
Bezugsstrecke f sampling length
Bezugswert m reference value; relative value
biegbare Röhren fpl flexible tubing
Biegeapparat m bending apparatus
Biegebeanspruchung f bending stress
Biegebruchfestigkeit f ultimate bending strength
Biegedauerfestigkeit f fatigue strength under bending stress
Biegedauerfestigkeit f im Schwellbereich fatigue strength under repeated bending stresses; pulsating bending fatigue limit
Biegedehnung f bending strain
Biegedrillknicken n torsional-flexural buckling
Biegeentzundern n scale removal by bending
Biegefähigkeit f bend test ductility
Biegefestigkeit f bending strength; flexural strength
Biegegesenk n snaker
Biegekraft f bending force
Biegemaschine f bending machine
Biegemoment n bending moment
biegen camber
biegen (Strangguß) bend
Biegepresse f bending press
Biegepunkt m **(Stranggießen)** straightening point; tangential point

Biegerichten n bending and straightening
Biegeriß m bending crack
Biegerollen fpl bending rolls
Biegeschlagversuch m bending impact test
Biegeschwellfestigkeit f pulsating fatigue strength under bending stresses
Biegespannung f bending stress
Biegesteifigkeit f flexural rigidity
Biegeumformen n forming by bending
Biegeversuch m bending test; flexure test
Biegeversuch m **(Hin-und-Her-Biegeversuch)** alternating bend test; to-and fro-bend test
Biegewalze f bending roll
Biegewechselfestigkeit f fatigue strength under reversed bending stresses
Biegewechselfestigkeitsversuch m fatigue test under reversed bending stresses
Biegewechselzahl f bending cycles
biegsam flexible; pliable
biegsamer Kaltstrang m articulated dummy bar; flexible dummy bar
Biegsamkeit f flexibility
Biegung f bend; flexure; offset
biegungsfrei gezogener Draht m dead-drawn wire
Bienenkorb-(Koks)ofen m beehive (coke) oven
Bilanz f consolidated statement; statement [of accounts]
Bilanz f **(kaufm.)** balance (sheet)
Bilanz f **technische** balance
bildsam ductile; plastic
bildsame Formgebung f plastic deformation; plastic shaping
Bildsamkeit f ductility
Bildsamkeit f forgeability; malleability; plasticity
Bildungsenergie f free energy of reaction
Bildungswärme f enthalpy; heat of formation

binärdekadisches System *n* binary-coded decimal system
binäre Legierung *f* binary alloy
binäres System *n* binary system
Binärziffer *f* binary digit; bit
Bindedraht *m* baling wire; binding wire; tying wire
Bindefähigkeit *f* binding power
Bindemetall *n* auxiliary metal (powder met.); binder (powder met.)
Bindemittel *n* binding; binding agent; bonding agent; bond; binding wax; jointing; linkage; linking primer
binden tie
Bindeton *m* bonding clay
Bindung *f* binding; compound; linkage
Birne *f* converter
Birnenform *f* converter shape
Biß *m* bite
Bißverhältnis *n* bite ratio
Bißweite *f* width of a bite
Bitumen-Asbest-Überzug *m* **(Korrosionsschutz)** bitumen-asbestos-mastic
Bitumenkorrosionsschutz *m* **(Rohrinnenseite)** bitumen lining
Bituminierung *f* bituminization
blähen swell
Blähgrad *m* **(Koks)** swelling index; swelling property
blank beizen bright pickle
Blankdraht *m* bare wire
Blankdrehen *n* bright turning
blankgedreht bright turned
blankgezogen (Draht) bright drawn; cold drawn
Blankglühen *n* bright annealing
Blankglühofen *m* bright-annealing furnace
Blankhärten *n* bright hardening
blank machen blank
Blankstahl *m* bright steel; cold drawn steel
Blankwalzöl *n* straight mineral oil
Blankziehen *n* bright-drawing
Blankzieherei *f* bright-drawing shop
Blasarbeit *f* blowing operation
Blase *f* blister

blasen blow
Blase *f* blow hole; bubble
Blaseigenschaft *f* blowability
Blaseignung *f* blowability
Blasemeister *m* blower
Blasen *n* blowing
Blasenbildung *f* **(Block)** blistering
Blasenbildung *f* **(Flüssigkeit)** bubbling
blasenfrei not blistered (steel)
Blasenkette *f* bubble chain
Blasenloch *n* pit hole
Blasenverdampfung *f* nucleate-boiling
Blasezeit *f* blowing period
Blasform *f* tuyre
Blasformebene *f* tuyre level
Blasfrischen *n* oxygen refining; pneumatic refining
Blasrohr *n* blast pipe; blow pipe
Blasschlacke *f* chromium-bearing slag
Blasstahlkonverter *m* basic oxygen furnace (BOF)
Blasstahlwerk *n* BOF shop; basic oxygen steelmaking plant
Blatt *n* blade; leaf; sheet
blättchenförmig flaky
Blattfeder *f* laminated spring; leaf spring
Blaubiegeprobe *f* blue brittle bend specimen
Blaubruch *m* blue brittleness; blue shortness
Blaubrüchigkeit *f* blue brittleness; blue shortness
Bläuen *n* blu[e]ing (e.g. sheet)
Blauglühen *n* blue annealing; open annealing
Bläuofen *m* blu[e]ing furnace
Blaupause *f* blue print
Blausprödigkeit *f* blue brittleness; blue shortness
Blech *n* plate
Blechabfälle *mpl* plate clippings; sheet clippings; sheet scrap
Blecharbeiten *fpl* plate structures
Blechbearbeitungsmaschine *f* plate working machine

Blechbehälter *m* sheet metal container
Blechbiegemaschine *f* plate bending machine
Blech *n* **breites** wide plate; wide sheet
Blechbürstmaschine *f* plate brushing machine
Blechdoppler *m* plate doubler
Blecheinfettmaschine *f* sheet greasing machine
Blech *n* **erster Wahl** prime sheet
Blechhalter *m* blank holder
Blechkantenanbiegepresse *f* plate-edge bending press
Blechkonstruktionen *fpl* fabricated steel sheet products and structures
Blechlehre *f* plate ga[u]ge; sheet ga[u]ge
Blechmantel *m* metal jacket; steel casing; steel jacket
Blech *n* **(mittel)** jobbing sheet; light plate; medium plate; medium sheet
Blech *n* **(Oberbegriff)** sheets and plates
Blechpaket *n* sheet pack; stack of sheets; sticker
Blechpanzer *m* steel casing; steel sheet casing; steel shell
Blechprüfmaschine *f* plate testing machine
Blechrichtmaschine *f* sheet straightening machine
Blechschere *f* plate shears
Blechschraube *f* tapping screw
Blechschrott *m* plate scrap; sheet scrap
Blechstapler *m* sheet-metal stacking machine
Blechtafel *f* sheet panel
Blechträger *m* plate girder
Blechtrockentisch *m* plate drying table
blechummantelter Stein *m* ferroclad brick; metal cased brick
blechverarbeitende Industrie *f* sheet fabricating industry
Blechwalze *f* plate roll
Blechwalzwerk *n* **(fein)** sheet [rolling] mill
Blechwalzwerk *n* **(grob)** plate [rolling] mill
Blechzange *f* plate gripping tongs
Blech *n* **zweiter Wahl** mender
Blei *n* lead
Bleibadhärten *n* lead hardening
Bleibadkessel *m* lead bath vat
bleibende Durchbiegung *f* set
bleibende Gesamtverformung *f* total plastic strain
bleibende Regelabweichung *f* sustained deviation (am.)
bleibende Verformung *f* permanent set
bleichen bleach
Bleipatentieren *n* lead patenting
Bleischaum *m* **(Feuerverzinken)** lead froth
Blende *f* diaphragm; orifice; screen
Blindaufkohlen *n* pseudocarburising
Blindaufkohlen *n* **(ohne Aufkohlungsmittel)** blank carburizing
blindes Kaliber *n* blind pass; dummy pass
Blindhärten *n* blank hardening
Blindhärtungsversuch *m* blank hardness test
Blindlaststoß *m* blind load impulse (arc furnace); wattless power (arc furnace)
Blindleistung *f* relative wattless power
Blindnitrieren *n* pseudonitriding
Blindnitrieren *n* **(ohne Nitriermittel)** blank nitriding
Blindstich *m* blind pass
Blindstrom *m* reactive current; wattless current
Blindversuch *m* blank test
Blindwalze *f* dummy roll; idle roll
Blindwert *m* blank [value]
Blindwiderstand *m* reactance
Blitztrockner *m* flash baker
Block *m* ingot
Blockabstechmaschine *f* ingot parting machine
Blockabstreifer *m* ingot stripper; stripper [guide]
Blockabstreifkran *m* ingot stripping crane

Blockaufsatz *m* dozzle; feeder head; hot top; shrink head casing
Block *m* **ausgelaufener** bled ingot
Blockausziehkran *m* ingot drawing crane
Block-Brammen-Walzwerk *n* ingot slab mill
Blockbrecher *m* ingot breaker; ingot crusher
Blockdrehbank *f* ingot lathe
Blockdrücker *m* ingot pusher
Block *m* **durch Nachgießen in den Lunker ausgefüllter** slop ingot
Blockeinsetzkran *m* ingot charging crane
Blockende *n* crop
Blockende *n* **oberes** top
Blöcke *mpl* **zufällig ausgewählte** randomised blocks
Blockfähre *f* ingot [transfer] car; ingot buggy
Blockform *f* ingot mould; mould
Blockgerüst *n* blooming [mill] stand; cogging [mill] stand; roughing [mill] stand
Block *m* **in der Kokille steckengebliebener** mould sticker; sticker
Blockkaliber *n* blooming pass; cogging pass; roughing pass
Blockkipper *m* ingot tilter; ingot tipping device
Blockkokille *f* ingot mould
Blockkopfbeheizung *f* hot topping feeder head heating
Blockkran *m* ingot [handling] crane
Blocklänge *f* solid length
Block *m* **mit ausgeprägten Gasblasen** blown ingot; blowy ingot
Blockputzen *n* chipping
Blockputzerei *f* chipping [shop]
Blockrest *m* ingot butt
Blockschale *f* bottom splash (surface defect); curtaining (surface defect); double skin (surface defect)
Blockschaum *m* ingot scum
Blockschere *f* bar-cutting machine; bloom shears
Blockschrott *m* bloom scrap; heavy scrap; scrap of blooms
Blockseigerung *f* ingot segregation; ingotism; major segregation
Blockstraße *f* blooming train; cogging train
Block *m* **vorgewalzter** bloom
Blockwagen *m* ingot [transfer] car; ingot buggy; ingot chariot
Blockwalze *f* blooming roll; cogging roll
Blockwalzwerk *n* blooming mill; cogging mill
Blockzange *f* ingot dog; ingot tongs
Bock *m* frame; trestle
Bockkran *m* gantry [crane]
Bodenbart *m* bottom fin (ingot); bottom flash (ingot)
Bodenbart *m* **(Block)** bottom fin; bottom flash
Bodenbelag-Winkelstahl *m* floor cover angle sections
bodenblasender Konverter *m* bottom blown converter
Bodenblech *n* bottom plate
Bodendicke *f* **(Fließpressen)** base thickness
Bodenecho *n* **(Ultraschall)** bottom echo
Bodenerschütterung *f* ground vibration
Bodenkörper *m* insoluble phase; sludge
Bodenkorrosionsversuch *m* soil corrosion test
Bodenkühlung *f* **(Hochofen)** underhearth cooling; underhearth cooling
Bodenplatte *f* bottom plate; groundplate
Bodenreißer *m* cup base fracture
Bodensau *f* furnace sow; salamander
Bodenstampfmaschine *f* bottom ramming machine; plug ramming machine
Bodenstein *m* bottom block; hearth block
Bogen *m* arc; arch; bend; sheet; sweep
Bogenentladung *f* arc discharge

bogenförmig curved
Bogengießanlage f bow type continuous casting machine; curved mould casting machine; curved mould continuous casting machine
Bogenstranggießanlage f curved mould continuous casting machine
Bogen m sweep
Bogenstranggießmaschine f bow-type continuous casting machine
Bogenzahnkupplung f curved teeth coupling
Bohnerz n bean ore
Bohrbank f boring machine
bohren bore; drill
Bohren n boring
Bohren n (mit Spiralbohrer) drilling
Bohrer m (Facharbeiter) driller
Bohrerherstellung f drill manufacture
Bohrgestänge n boring tools
Bohrloch n bore hole; well; drill hole
Bohrmaschine f boring machine; drilling machine
Bohröl n boring oil; soluble oil
Bohrölwasser n cutting fluid emulsion; soluble oil emulsion
Bohrprobenehmer m drillings sampler
Bohrrohr n drill tube
Bohrspäne mpl borings
Bohrspindel f boring bar
Bohrstahl m boring tool; drill steel
Bohrstange f boring bar
Bohr- und Fräsmaschine f boring and milling machine
Bohrung f bore; bore hole; diameter of bore
Bohrwelle f drilling shaft
Bolzen m arbor; bolt
Bolzenkopfschmiedemaschine f bolt-head forging machine
Bolzenschweißung f stud welding
Bombierung f camber; crown bow
Bombierung f (Blech) bow; crown
Bombierung f (Walzen) camber
bondern (siehe Phosphatieren) bonderize (see phosphate coating)
Bor n boron

Bordeisen n cask hoop
Bördelmaschine f flanging machine
bördeln bead; border
Bördelnaht f double-flanged joint
Bördelrohr n flanged pipe
Bördelversuch m flanging test
Borieren n boriding
Boroxid n boric oxide
Borsäure f boric acid
Borstahl m boron steel
Böschungswinkel m (einer Schüttung) angle of repose
Bote m carrier
Bottich m tank; vat; vessel
Bowdenzug m Bowden wire
Bramme f slab
Brammenblock m slab ingot
Brammendrehvorrichtung f slab turning device
Brammenkaliber n slabbing pass
Brammenschere f slab shears
Brammenwalzwerk n slab cogging mill; slabbing mill
Brammenwendevorrichtung f slab turn-over device
Brandmauer f fire-proof wall
Brandriß m fire check; fire crack
Brandrißabdruck m (Walzdrahtfehler) fire crack transfer mark
Brandriß m (in Kokillen) crazing
Brandschutz m fire protection
brauchbar efficient; serviceable
Brauchbarkeit f efficiency
Brauchwasser n water fit for industrial use
Brauneisenerz n bog iron ore; limonite
Brauneisenoolith m oolitic limonite
Brauneisenstein m brown hematite; brown iron ore
bräunen burnish
brauner Rauch m brown fume
Braunkohle f lignite
Braunkohlenbrikett n brown-coal briquette; lignite briquette
Braunkohlen-Großabbauanlage f equipment for large open cast brown coal mining

Braunstein *m* manganese ore
Brechanlage *f* (Erzaufbereitung) crushing plant
brechen crush
brechen (von Emulsionen) split
Brecher *m* breaker; crusher
Brechkoks *m* crushed coke
Brechstange *f* breaker bar
Brechtopf *m* breaker block
Brechwalze *f* cracker; crusher roll
Breitband-Walzwerk *n* wide strip mill
Breite *f* breadth
breiten spread; widen
Breite *f* width
Breiteisen *n* broad tool
Breitenänderung *f* spread
Breitflachstahl *m* universal [mill] plate; wide flat steel
Breitflanschträger *m* broad flanged beam; wide-flanged beam; wide-flanged joist
breitfüßig broad flanged
Breitfußschiene *f* flange rail; flat bottom rail
Breitstrahlbrenner *m* broad jet burner
Breitung *f* spread
Breitungsstich *m* broadsiding pass; spreading pass
Breitung *f* **vollkommen verhinderte** spread fully contained
Bremsautomatik *f* automatic slow down
Bremsberg *m* braking incline
bremsen brake
Bremse *f* brake
bremsen drag
Bremshaspel *f* drag reel
Bremskeil *m* chock
Bremskraft *f* braking power
Bremstrommel *f* brake drum
Bremszug *m* back tension
brennbar combustible
Brenndauer *f* burning period; duration of burning
brennen bake; burn; calcine
Brennen *n* burning; calcination; roasting
brennen (Pellets) fire

Brenner *m* blow pipe; burner; torch
Brennerkopf *m* burner tip; gas port block; gas port end
Brennermaul *n* burner mouth
Brennerstein *m* burner port
Brennfleck *m* arcing zone; fire spot; impingement
Brenngas *n* fuel gas
Brennhärtemaschine *f* flame-hardening machine
Brennhärten *n* flame hardening
Brennkammer *f* combustion chamber
Brennkammer *f* **(Glühofen)** fire box
Brennofen *m* baking oven; burning kiln; calcining kiln; kiln
Brennöl *n* fuel oil
brennputzen deseam
Brennputzen *n* flame chipping; flame descaling; flame deseaming; flame scarfing; torch deseaming
Brennschacht *m* combustion chamber
Brennschneiden *n* flame cutting; gas cutting; oxyacetylene cutting; torch cutting
Brennschneidmaschine *f* flame-cutting machine
Brennschwinden *n* **(ff. Steine)** firing shrinkage
Brennstoff *m* combustible; fuel
Brennstoffteilchen *n* fuel particle
Brennstoffverbrauch *m* fuel consumption
Brennwachsen *n* **(ff. Steine)** firing expansion
Brikett *n* briquette
Brikettieranlage *f* briquetting plant
brikettieren briquette
Brikettierfähigkeit *f* briquetting property
Brillenschieber *m* goggle valve
Brinellhärte *f* Brinell hardness
Brinell-Kugeldruckprobe *f* Brinell hardness test
bröckelig brittle; crumbly
brodeln bubble
Bronzelager *n* bronze bearing
Bruch *m* break; break-down; breakage; burst; failure; fracture

Bruchaussehen n fracture appearance
Bruchdehnung f elongation after fracture
Brucheinleitung f fracture initation
Bruchfestigkeit f ultimate tensile strength
Bruchfläche f cleavage plane; surface of fracture
Bruchgefüge n fracture
brüchig brittle
brüchige Fläche f (Blockfehler) spongy surface
Brüchigkeit f brittleness; shortness
Bruchlastspielzahl f number of alternations to fracture; number of cycles to fracture
Bruchmechanik f fracture mechanics
Bruchprobe f break-down test; fracture test
Bruchschrott m broken scrap; lump scrap
Bruchsicherheit f security against failure
Bruchspannung f breaking stress; ultimate stress
Bruchstelle f fracture face
Brückenbildung f (Bunker) arching
Brückenbildung f (Ultraschall) arcing
Brückengleis n bridge rail
Brückenwaage f weighbridge
brünieren burnish
Brünieren n burnishing
Brunnen m well
Buchse f box
Büchse f bush; bushing; lining
Buchsenkette f bush chain
Büchsenwinkel m (Fließpressen) die angle
Buckelblech n buckled plate; buckled sheet
Budgetrechnung f budgetary control; industrial budgetary control
Bügelsäge f hack saw
Bund n bunch; bundle; coil; shoulder
Bundbildlinie f coil build-up
Bündel n bunch
Bündelanlage f bundling plant
bündeln bundle
Bündel n (Rohrbündel) bank (of tubes)
Bündeltasche f cradle
Bundgewicht n coil weight
Bundhubwagen m coil lift truck
Bundpatentieren n coil patenting
Bund n (Schraube) collar
Bundverpackungslinie f coil packing line
Bundvorbereitung f coil preparation
Bundwickelmaschine f coil winder
Bunker m bin; bunker; silo
Bunkerfüllstand m level of filling in a hopper; material level in a bin
Bunkerfüllstandanzeiger m level indicator for bunker
Buntmetall n non-ferrous metal
Büro n office
bürsten brush
Bürste f brush
Bürstmaschine f brushing machine
Butzen n (beim Walzen von Stahlringen) centre punching

C

calcinieren calcine
Calcinierofen m calcining kiln
calcinierte Soda f anhydrous sodium carbonate
Calcinierung f calcination
Calciowüstit m calcio-wustite
Calciumcarbid n calcium carbide
Calciumferrit n calcium ferrite
Calorisieren n calorising
Carbid n carbide
Carbidanordnung f carbide spacing
Carbidausscheidung f carbide precipitation
Carbidvergröberung f coarsening of carbides
Carbidverstärkung f carbide strengthening
Carbidzeiligkeit f carbide bending
Carbonitrieren n carbonitriding
Carbonyleisen n carbonyl iron

Carburierung f carburation; carburisation

Carburierung f (im SM-Ofen) carburetting

Cer n cerium

Cermet n cermet

Chamotte s. Schamotte

Charge s. Schmelze

Chargier...s.a. Beschick[ungs]...

chargieren charge

chargierfähig in furnace sizes; in handy sizes

chargierfähige Stücke npl pieces in handy sizes

Charlier-Probe f Charlier check

Chemie f chemistry

chemisch beständiger Stahl m stainless steel

chemisches Potential n chemical potential

chemische Technologie f chemical technology

chemische Waage f analytical balance

chemische Zusammensetzung f chemical composition

chemisch gebundener Stein m chemically bonded brick

chemisch-technologische Prüfung f chemico-technological test

Chi-Quadrat-Probe f chi-square test

chlorieren chloridise; chlorinate

chlorieren (z. B. Kalk) chlorinate

chromatieren chromating

chromatisieren chromating

chromatographische Prüfung f chromatographic analysis

Chromausbringen n chromium recovery

Chromeisenerz n chrome iron ore; chromite

Chromeisenstein m chrome iron ore

chromieren chromising

Chromitstein m chrome brick

Chrom-Magnesit-Stein m chrome-magnesite brick

Chrom-Nickel Stahl m chrome nickel steel; chromium nickel steel

Chromstahl m chrome steel

Chromstahlguß m cast chromium steel [material]; chromium steel casting [product]

Chromstein m chrome brick

Chromüberzug m chrome coating; chromium coating

Chromverarmungstheorie f (interkristalline Korrosion) chromium depleted-zone theory

Cobaltstahl m cobalt steel

COD = crack opening displacement COD = crack opening displacement

Compound... siehe Verbund ...

Container m flowbien

Coulometer n coulometer

Cowper m cowper; hot blast stove

Cowperstein m cowper brick; hot blast stove brick

cracken crack

Cyanbadhärten n bath cyaniding; cyanide hardening; cyaniding

D

Dach n roof

Dachblech n roofing sheet

Dachpfannenblech n roofing sheet

Dachrutsche f elevated inclined chute

Dachschwelle f (Eisenbahnoberbau) sole plate (permanent way)

Dachziegel m roof tile; tile

dämmen bank; damp down

Dämmstoff m insulating material

Dämmstoff m (Isolierstoff) insulating material

Dampf m fume; steam; vapour

Dampfanlassen n steam bluing

Dampfarmaturen fpl steam fittings

Dampfdruck m vapour pressure

dämpfen bank; bank (furnace); damp

Dampferzeuger m flash steam boiler

Dampferzeugungsanlage f steam generation plant

Dampffaß n steam drum

Dampfgutschrift f steam credit

Dampfhammer *m* steam hammer
Dampfkessel *m* steam boiler; stocker
Dampfkesselfeuerung *f* steam boiler firing
Dampfkolbengebläse *n* steam blowing engine; steam piston blowing engine
Dampf-Kraftwerk *n* steam power station
Dampfkran *m* steam crane
Dampfmantel-Gaserzeuger *m* steam-jacket gas producer
Dampfmaschine *f* steam engine
Dampfrohr *n* steam pipe
Dampfstrahlgebläse *n* steam jet blower
Dampfturbine *f* steam turbine
Dämpfung *f* attenuation; damping
Dämpfung *f* **(Schwingungskreis)** damping
Dämpfungsfähigkeit *f* damping capacity
Dampfversuch *m* **(Korrosion)** steam test
Dampfzerstäubung *f* steam atomising
Datei *f* data file; file
Datenabruf *m* data recall
Datenaufschreibung *f* data recording
Datenbank *f* data bank; data base
Datenerfassung *f* data acquisition; data logging; data recovery
Datenfluß *m* data flow
Datensammlung *f* data collection
Datenstellenzahl *f* number of data places
Datenstrukturierung *f* data structure concept
Datenübertragung *f* data transfer
Datenübertragungseinrichtung *f* data circuit-terminating equipment
Datenverarbeitung *f* electronic data processing
Datenverarbeitungsaufgabe *f* data processing task
Datenzugriffsmethode *f* data access method
Datenzugriffsmodul *n* data file access module

Dauerbeanspruchung *f* fatigue stress
Dauerbetrieb *m* continuous operation; continuous running; continuous service
Dauerbiegeversuch *m* fatigue bend test; flexure fatigue test
Dauerbruch *m* fatigue failure; fatigue fracture
Dauerelektrode *f* continuous electrode
Dauerfestigkeit *f* endurance limit; fatigue strength; fatigue stress; endurance strength; fatigue resistance
Dauerfestigkeitsverhältnis *n* fatigue ratio
Dauerfestigkeitsversuch *m* fatigue strength test
Dauerflußversuch *m* continuous flow test
Dauerformguß *m* die casting; gravity die casting; permanent mould casting
Dauerform-Gußstück *n* die casting; gravity die casting; permanent mould casting
Dauerfutter *n* back lining; outer lining; safety lining
Dauerhaftigkeit *f* durability
Dauerhaltbarkeit *f* service life
Dauerkerbschlagversuch *m* notched bar impact fatigue test
Dauermagnet *m* permanent magnet
Dauermagnetwerkstoff *m* permanent magnet material
dauern endure; last
Dauerprüfmaschine *f* fatigue testing machine
Dauerschallverfahren *n* continuous wave transmission method
Dauerschlagbiegefestigkeit *f* repeated impact bending strength
Dauerschlagbiegeversuch *m* repeated impact bending test
Dauerschlagfestigkeit *f* resistance to repeated impact
Dauerschlagfestigkeitsversuch *m* impact endurance test; repeated impact test

Dauerschlagversuch *m* repeated impact test
Dauerschlagzugversuch *m* repeated impact tension test
Dauerschwingbeanspruchung *f* cyclic stress; fatigue loading alternating stress
Dauerschwingbruch *m* fatigue fracture
Dauerschwingfestigkeit *f* fatigue endurance limit; fatigue strength
Dauerschwingversuch *m* fatigue test; full scale fatigue test
Dauerstandfestigkeit *f* creep rupture strength
Dauerstandverhalten *n* creep behaviour
Dauerstandversuch *m* creep rupture test; creep test
Dauertauchversuch *m* total immersion test
Dauerverdrehversuch *m* repeated torsion test; torsion fatigue test
Dauerversuch *m* endurance test; fatigue test
Dauerversuch *m* **mit Wechselbeanspruchung** alternating stress test
Dauerwechseldrehversuch *m* alternating torsion fatigue test
Dauerwechselfestigkeit *f* fatigue strength under completely reversed stress
Daumenschlepper *m* dog-bar type conveyor
Decke *f* coat; cover; roof
Deckel *m* cover; cover lid; lid; roof (arc furnace); top crust (in tundish or mould)
Deckelabhebewagen *m* **für Tieföfen** cover lifting bogie for pit furnaces
Deckelauflage *f* roof skewback
Deckelbildung *f* **(Block)** capping (ingot); ingot top crust; top freezing (ingot)
Deckel *m* **(in Gießwanne oder Form)** top crust (in tundish or mould)
Deckelwagen *m* cover carriage; soaking-pit cover carriage

Deckemail *n* cover coat enamel
Deckenbalken *m* overhead beam
Deckengewölbe *n* arched roof
Deckenstein *m* roof brick
Deckfähigkeit *f* covering ability
Deckglas *n* slide (microscope)
Decklage *f* **(Schweißen)** final pass; final run
Deckring *m* top plate on mould
Deckschicht *f* protective layer; surface layer; top coat
Deckvermögen *n* covering ability
Defektelektron *n* defect electron
Dehnbarkeit *f* ductility; flexibility
dehnen strain
Dehnen *n* elongating; extending; stretching
Dehnen *n* **(Längen)** lengthening
Dehnfuge *f* expansion joint
Dehngrenze *f* permanent limit of elongation
Dehngrenze *f* **technische** 0.2% proof stress
Dehnschraube *f* necked-down bolt
Dehnung *f* dilatation; elongation; extension; stretch
Dehnung *f* **(s. a. Bruchdehnung)** expansion; strain; stretch
Dehnungsausgleicher *m* bellows; expansion pipe bellows
Dehnungsmesser *m* extensometer; strain ga[u]ge
Dehnungsmeßstreifen *m* strain ga[u]ge
Dehnungsstufe *f* elongation step
Dehnungszone *f* stretched zone
Dekaleszenz *f* decalescence
dekapieren descale (in acid); pickle
Delta-Eisen *n* delta iron
Delta-Gamma-Umwandlung *f* delta-gamma transformation
Delta-Mischkristall *m* delta solid solution
Demontage *f* dismantling
demontieren dismantle
Dendrit *m* dendrite
Dendritenarmabstand *m* dendrite arm spacing

Dendritenstrukturzone f dendritic zone
dendritisch dendritic
Dengeln n thinning; wheting
Denitrieren n denitriding; nitrogen removal
Deponie f dumping [refuse]
Deputatkohle f allowance coal
Desintegrator m disintegrator
Desorption f desorption
Desoxidationslegierung f deoxidation alloy
Desoxidationsmittel n deoxidant; deoxidiser; deoxidising agent
Desoxidationsschlacke f deoxidising slag
desoxidieren deoxidise
Destillation f distillation
destillieren distill
Diagramm n chart; graph
Diagrammrolle f drum for recorder
Diagrammscheibe f disc for recorder
Dialogauskunft f on-line enquiry
Dialogmonitor m TP monitor
Dialogprogrammgenerator m dialogue program generator
Dialogverarbeitung f on-line processing
Diamantkegel m diamond cone
Diamantmetallegierung f diamond bearing alloy
Diamantziehstein m diamond drawing die
Dicalciumferrit m dicalcium ferrite
Dicalciumsilicat n dicalcium silicate
dicht close; dense; leak-proof; tight
dichtbrennen (ff. Steine) vitrify
dichten caulk
Dichte f consistence; density
dichten joint; lute
Dichten n jointing
Dichtenfehler m density defect
dichtester Wert m mode
Dichtgas n seal gas
Dichtheitsschweiße f tightness weld
Dichtigkeit f (Ofen) degree of sealing
Dichtschweißung f caulk welding; seal welding

Dichtung f join[t]; join[t]ing; packing; seal; stuffing
Dichtungsmasse f (für Mauerwerk) filler; jointing compound; tightening material
Dichtungsring m gasket; packing ring; seal ring; stuffing
Dichtungsschweißung f caulk welding; seal welding
Dicke f diameter; ga[u]ge; thickness
Dickenmeßgerät n thickness ga[u]ge
Dickenregelung f automatic ga[u]ge control
Dickenverhältnis n (beim Walzen) exit thickness to roll diameter ratio in %
dicke Stelle f high spot
dickflüssig semifluid; viscous
Dickstoffpumpe f sludge pump; slurry pump; slush pump
Dickteerabscheidung f coal tar extraction
Dielektrizitätskonstante f dielectric coefficient; permittivity; specific inductive capacity
Dieselmotor m diesel engine
Differential-Flammenphotometrie f differential flame photometry
Differentialthermoanalyse f (DTA) differential thermal analysis
Differenz f
Differenzdruck m differential pressure; orifice measurement
differenzverzinntes Weißblech n differentially coated tinplate
Diffraktometer n diffractometer
diffundieren diffuse
Diffusion f diffusion
Diffusion f **bei turbulenter Strömung** eddy diffusion
Diffusionschromieren n chromium diffusion coating
Diffusionsglühen n homogenising
Diffusionskoeffizient m diffusion coefficient
Diffusionsschweißen n diffusion welding
Diffusionsverfahren n **für Metallüberzüge** diffusion coating

Digitalanzeige f digital display
digital arbeitende Anlage f digitally operating installation
Digitalausgabe-Einheit f digital output unit
digitale Datenspeicherung f digital data storage
digitale Informationsverarbeitung f digital data processing
Digitaleingabe-Einheit f digital input unit
digitaler Zustand m digital state
digitales Verknüpfungsglied n logic element
Digitalrechner m digital computer
dimensionslose Kennzahl f dimensionless parameter
Dinasstein m dinas brick; ganister brick; silica brick
DIN (Deutsches Institut für Normung) German Industrial Standards Institute
Dipolmoment n dipole moment
Direkthärten n direct hardening
direkt prozessgekoppelt on-line
Direktreduktion f direct reduction; solid state reduction
Diskussion f consideration; discussion
Dispersionshärten n dispersion hardening
Dispersionskneter m dispersion kneader
Dispersionsmittel n dispersing agent
Dissoziationsgrad m degree of dissociation
Distanzblech n spacer sheet
Divergenz f divergence
Dolomit m dolomite; magnesia-limestone
Dolomitanlage f dolomite plant
Dolomitbrennofen m dolomite calcining kiln
dolomitischer Kalk m dolomitic lime[stone]
Dolomitklinker m clinkered dolomite
Dolomit-Schleudermaschine f dolomite centrifuging machine
Dolomitstein m dolomite brick

Dolomitsteinpresse f dolomite brick press
Domflansch-Winkelstahl m angle sections with webs of unequal thickness
Doppelanlassen n double tempering
Doppelbohrung f twin-bore
doppelbrechend birefringent
Doppelbrechung f birefringence
Doppelduowalzwerk n double two-high mill; double-duo
Doppelhärten n double hardening
Doppelherdofen m dual-hearth furnace
Doppelkopf-Ablaufhaspel f double head pay-off reel
Doppelkopfschiene f bull head rail
Doppelkurbel f drag-link mechanism
doppeln double; fold
Doppelplattenkeilschieber m **(Winderhitzer)** double disc wedge valve
Doppelpreßtechnik f double press[ing] technique
Doppelreduzierstraße f double cold reducing mill
Doppelscheiben-Ziehmaschine f double-block drawing machine
Doppel-T-Eisen n H-beam; H-girder
Doppel-T-Träger m I-beam; girder; joist; standard beam
Doppelverzinken n double galvanising
Döpperstahl m punch steel
Doppler m doubler
Dopplung f double draw; lamination; lap
Dopplung f **(im Stahlblock)** lamination
Dorn m arbor; core rod; drift; mandrel; piercer
Dorn[bolzen] m bolt
Dornen n off-hand piercing
Dornhubwagen m boom truck; ram truck
Dornstapler m mandrel piler
Dornwiderlager n mandrel thrust block
Dornziehen n drawing over mandrel; plug drawing

Dosierbandwaage f controlled feed belt weigher; metering-type belt scales
dosieren meter
Dosierpumpe f controlled volume pumpe; metering pump
dotieren dope
Drachenzähne mpl **(im Konus einer Torpedopfanne)** pointed cobblestoning
Draht m wire
Drahtader f wire strand
Drahtbearbeitungsmaschine f wire-working machine
Drahtbund n bundle of wire
Drahtbürste f wire brush
Drahtdicke f wire ga[u]ge
Draht m **dunkelgeglühter** black annealed wire
Drahtdurchmesser m diameter of wire
Drahtelektrode f welding rod; wire electrode
Drahterzeugnis n wire product
Drahtgaze f wire gauze
Drahtgeflecht n wire netting
Draht m **(gezogener)** wire
Drahtglas n armoured glass; wire glass
Drahtglühen n wire annealing
Drahthaspel f rod reel; wire [rod] reel
Drahtkorn n cut wire; wire shot
Drahtlehre f wire ga[u]ge
Drahtlitze f wire strand
Draht m **mit galvanischem Überzug** fully galvanised wire
Draht m **mit geringer Querschnittsabnahme gezogen** mild drawn wire; soft drawn wire
Draht m **nach Verzinken wärmebehandelt** galvanneal wire
Drahtpatentierofen m wire patenting furnace
Drahtreduktion f **mit Hammermaschinen** rotary hammer swaging
Drahtring m wire coil
Drahtring m **ohne Spannungen aufgewickelt** dead cast wire coil
Drahtschälmaschine f wire peeling machine

Drahtschere f wire cutter
Drahtschrott-Wickler m cobble-baller
Drahtschweißmaschine f wire welding machine
Drahtseil n cable; wire cable; wire rope
Drahtseilbahn f aerial railway; funicular railway; aerial ropeway; cable railway
Drahtseilbahn f **(elektr.)** telpher-line
Drahtseilbetrieb m cable drive; cable transmission
Drahtseilkübel m mine kibble
Drahtseilschloß n cable joint
Drahtseiltrieb m cable drive
Drahtstift m pin; wire-nail; tack; wire nail
Drahtverwindeanlage f wire twisting machine
Drahtvorwalzgerüst n rod mill rougher
Draht m **(Walzdraht)** wire rod
Drahtwalzwerk n rod [rolling] mill; wire [rolling] mill; wire rod mill
Drahtzange f pliers; wire cutter
Drahtzaun m wire-fence
Drahtziehen n wire drawing
Drahtziehen n **mit Gegenzug** back pull wire drawing; reactive wire drawing
Drahtzieher m wire drawer
Drahtzieherei f wire drawing plant
Drahtziehfett n wire drawing grease
Drahtziehmaschine f wire drawing machine
Drahtzug m wire drawing block
Drall m twist
Drallabscheider m cyclone dust collector; cyclone separator; high centrifugal force cyclone
Drallarbeit f work done in twisting
Drallbrenner m swirl burner
Drallbüchse f twist[ing] guide
Drallführung f twist[ing] guide
Drallrohr n swirl promoter
Drallrollen fpl roller twister units
Dreharbeit f turning
Drehautomatenteil n automatic lathe component

Drehbank f lathe; turning lathe
Drehbankherz n carrier
drehbar revolvable; rotary; swivelling; turning
Drehbedampfung f **(Elektronenmikroskop)** rotary sputtering
Drehbewegung f rotational motion; turning motion
Drehbohrschneide f drill-bit; rotary bit
Drehbrechen n breaking by twisting
drehen revolve; rotate; turn
drehend revolving
Dreher m turner
Drehfestigkeit f twisting strength
Drehflammofen m rotary reverberatory furnace
Drehführung f twist guide
Drehgelenk n swivel-joint
Drehgestell n bogie frame
Drehgestell n **(beim Drehofen zum Wiedererhitzen)** revolving hearth
Drehherdofen m rotary hearth furnace
Drehkolbengebläse n rotary piston blowing engine
Drehkonverter m rotary converter
Drehkorbhaspel f laying reel
Drehkran m rotary crane; slewing crane
Drehkreuz n capstan
Drehkristallaufnahme f rotating crystal photograph
Drehling m tool [holder] bit
Drehmeißel m turning tool
Drehmesser n turning tool
Drehmoment n starting moment; torque
Drehofen m rotary furnace
Drehpol m center of rotation
Drehpunkt m fulcrum; pivot
Drehpunkt m **des Wechselwagens** turning place
Drehrohrofen m revolving cylindrical furnace; revolving tubular kiln; rotary kiln
Drehrohr-Sinterofen m rotary sintering kiln
Drehrost-Gaserzeuger m revolving grate gas producer; rotary grate gas producer

Drehscheibe f turntable
Drehschieber m rotary [slide] valve
Drehschurre f rotary chute
Drehschwingprüfstand m torsional vibration test[ing] stand
Drehspäne mpl swarf; turnings
Drehspulmeßwerk n moving-coil measuring system
Drehstabdauerfestigkeit f rotating beam fatigue test
Drehstahl m cutting tool; turning tool
Drehstrahltaster m offset tool depth ga[u]ge
Drehstrom m alternating current; three phase alternating current; three phase current
Drehstrom-Gleichstrom-Umformer m three phase to direct current motor generator set
Drehstrommotor m three phase [current] motor
Drehteller m rotary feed table; swift
Drehtisch m revolving table; rotary table; turntable
Drehtischpresse f rotating table press
Drehtrommelofen m drum type kiln
Drehung f revolution; rotation; torsion; turn; wrench
Drehung f **(Schraubenschlüssel)** wrench
Drehverfahren n turning techniques
Drehverlappen n lock forming by twisting
Drehwinkel-Meßumformer m angle of rotation transducer
Drehzahl f number of revolutions; speed
Drehzahlabfall m rpm drop; speed drop
Drehzahlverlauf m speed characteristic
Drehzapfen m pivot
dreieckig three-cornered; triangular
Dreieckschaltpunkt m delta connection
dreifach threefold
Drei-Glocken-Gichtverschluß m three bell hopper arrangement

Dreikantschraube f triangle head cap screw
Dreikantstahl m triangular section steel
Dreilagenblech n three-ply plate; triangular section
Dreilagenstahl m three-layer steel; two sided clad steel
Dreilagenstahlblech n soft center steel sheet
Dreilochdüse f three-hole nozzle
Dreiphasen-Sterngegenparallelschaltung f three-phase star inverse parallel connection
Dreischichtbetrieb m three shift operation
Dreistoffsystem n ternary system
Dreistrangmaschine f three strand machine
Dreistufenfilter m **(Spektralanalyse)** three-stage transmission filter
dreistufig three-stage; three-step
Dreiwalzengerüst n three-high rolling stand
Dreiwellenkompensator m concertina-type expansion joint
Dressierblumen fpl feathering
dressieren skin pass; level
Dressieren n skin pass rolling; temper [pass] rolling
Dressiergerüst (siehe Nachwalzgerüst)
Dressierwalze f skin pass roll
Dressierwalzwerk n skin pass mill; temper [pass] mill; temper [pass] rolling mill
Drillingsguß m triple casting
Drillknicken n torsional buckling
Drillmoment n twisting moment
Drillwulststahl m twisted [reinforcement] bulb steel
Drop-Weight-Probe f drop-weight trial
Drossel f **(elektr.)** choking coil; reactance coil; throttle
Drosselklappe f butterfly valve; throttle valve
Drosselleistung f **(Lichtbogenofen)** supplementary reactor rating

drosseln choke; throttle
Drosselspule f **(Lichtbogenofen)** line reactor (am.); supplementary reactor
Drosselventil n butterfly valve; choker valve; throttle valve
Druck m compression; pressure; thrust
Druckabfall m pressure drop
Druckausgleichbehälter m surge tank
Druckbeanspruchung f compression load; compression stress; compressive stress
Druckbehälter m pressure vessel
Druckbogen m sheet [printing]
drücken push; spin
Drücken n spinning
Drücken n **(Blechumformen)** metal spinning
Drücken n **von Außenborden** spinning of external flanges
Drücken n **von Hohlkörpern** spinning of hollow items
Drücken n **von Innenborden** spinning of inside beads
Drücker m pusher
Druckerausgabe f **(EDV)** print-out
Druckerei f printing office
Druckereimaschine f printing machine
Druckerweichung f **(ff. Steine)** softening under load (refractory bricks)
Druckfeder f pressure spring
Druckfestigkeit f compression strength; crushing strength; resistance to crushing
Druckfeuerbeständigkeit f refractoriness-under-load
Druckflüssigkeit f hydraulic fluid
Druckförderer m dispenser
Druckgasentschwefelung f desulphurisation of pressure gas
Druckgebläse n forced draft fan
Druckgefäßversuch m pressure vessel test
Druckguß m die casting; high pressure die casting; pressure die casting; pressure pouring
Druckgußstück n pressure die casting

Druckhöhe f head
Druckkessel m high pressure boiler; high pressure container; high pressure tank
Druckkraft f **(Pressen)** compressive force
Drucklager n thrust bearing
Druckluft f compressed air
Druckluftanlage f compressed-air system
Druckluft-Gesenkhammer m compressed air drop hammer
Drucklufthammer m compressed air hammer
Drucklufthärten n air blast quenching
Druckluftheber m air lift pump
Druckluftkessel m compressed air container; compressed air tank
Druckluftleitung f compressed air line
Druckluftmeßgerät n pressure ga[u]ge
Druckluftwerkzeug n compressed air tool; pneumatic tool
Druckmantel m pressure shell
Druckmarkierung f pressure marking
Druckmeßdose f pressure cell
Druckmesser m manometer; pressure ga[u]ge
Druckminderventil n pressure reducing valve
Druckmutter f screw-down nut
Druckpumpe f forcing pump
Druckregler m pressure governor
Druckschmierung f forced lubrication
Druckschraube f adjusting screw; main screw; screw down
Druckschweißung f pressure welding
Druckschwellbereich m range for pulsating compressive stresses
Druckschwellfestigkeit f compression pulsating fatigue strength
Drucksintern n sintering under pressure
Druckspannung f compression stress
Druckspritzverfahren n pressure spray process
Druckstab m compression member
Drucktopf m **(Walzen)** pressure pad; pressure piece
Druckumformen n compressive reforming; pressure forming
Druckverdüsungspulver n atomized powder
Druckverformung f compression strain
Druckverlust m loss of pressure
Druckversuch m compression test; crushing test
Drückwalzen n roller spinning
Drückwalzen n **über kegeligen Dorn** roller spinning over conical mandrel
Drückwalzen n **über zylindrischen Dorn** roller spinning over cylindrical mandrel
Druckwasser n hydraulic water; pressure water
druckwasserstoffbeständiger Stahl m steel for high-pressure hydrogenation vessels
Druckwiderlager n **(Rohrwalzwerk)** thrust block bearing
Dualphasenstahl m dual phase steel
Dualsystem n binary system
Dübel m dowel; peg
Dunkelfeldaufnahme f dark field image
dünn thin
Dünnflüssigkeit f fluidity
Dünnschichtverfahren n **(für Stahldrähte)** thin foil technique
Dünnschliff m thin section; transparent cut
Dunstglocke f haze dome
Duo-Kaltwalzwerk n two-high cold reduction mill
Duostraße f two-high [rolling] mill
Duowalzwerk n two-high [rolling] stand
Duplex-Mikro-Struktur f micro-duplex structure
Duplexstahl m compound steel; duplex steel
Duplexverfahren n duplex[ing] process
Duraluminium n duralumin

durcharbeiten knead; squeeze; thoroughly work
Durchbiegen n **der Arbeitswalzen** whipping of the work rolls
Durchbiegung f out of straightness
Durchbiegung f **bleibende** permanent set; set
Durchbiegung f **(elastisch)** deflection
Durchbiegung f **gesamte** overall deflexion
Durchbiegung f **(quer)** flexure
Durchbiegungsmesser m deflection indicator
durchbrechen blow; break through; pierce
durchbrennen mit Sauerstoff clear with oxygen
Durchbruch m break-out
Durchdringung f penetration
durchdrücken pushing through
Durchdrücken n extruding
Durchfluß m flow; passage
Durchflußmesser m flow meter
Durchfluß-Thermoelement n suction pyrometer
Durchflutungsprüfung f magnetic flow detection
Durchgang m travel
Durchgangsloch n throughhole
durchgehend continuous; full-length; through
Durchhang m slack
Durchlaufentgasung f continuous degassing
Durchmesser m radius
Durchstoßofen m continuous pusher type furnace; pusher type furnace
Düse f die; jet; nozzle; tuyre
Düsenabstreifverfahren n jet process
Düsenarbeitsfläche f die reduction zone; die working zone
Düsenausgang m die exit
Düsenauslauf m die exit
Düsenboden m plug bottom; tuyre bottom; wind box
Düseneinlauf m die entrance; die mouth
Düseneintritt m die mouth

Düseneintrittswinkel m angle of die taper; die approach angle; die entrance angle
Düsenform f contour of hole; die shape
Düsenhalter m die holder; tuyre holder
Düsenkanal m die channel
Düsenleistung f die tonnage
Düsenöffnung f die aperture
Düsenquerschnitt m nozzle cross sectional area; tuyre area
Düsenrohr n blast pipe
Düsenstock m blast connection; boot leg; pen stock; tuyre stock
Düsenwand f die chanel surface; die wall
Düsenwand-Neigungswinkel m die wall taper
Düsenwinkel m die approach angle

E

eben dead-flat
Ebene f plane
ebener Dehnungszustand m uniaxial elongation
ebener Spannungszustand m uniaxial stress
ebener Winkel m plane angle
Ebenheit f **des Bandes** strip flatness
ebenmäßiger Angriff m uniform attack (corrosion)
ebnen level
Eckbeschlag m corner casting (on freight container)
Eckenwinkel m **(Spanen)** effective cutting angle
Eckigkeit f angularity
Eckleistung f peak power
Edelgas n inert gas; rare gas
Edelguß m high-strength cast iron; special cast iron
Edelstahl m high-grade steel; special steel
Edelstahlguß m special steel casting

Edenbornhaspel f laying reel
EDV-System n data processing system
EDV-technische Anpassung f data system adjusted application
Effektivwert m effective value
eichen calibrate
Eichkurve f calibration curve
Eichlösung f calibration solution
Eichprobe f calibration test piece
Eichstrich m gradation; measuring line
Eigengewicht n dead weight
Eigenkorrelation f autocorrelation
Eigenschaft f attribute; property
Eigenschrott m home scrap; plant scrap
Eigenschwingung f natural oscillation
Eigenspannung f internal stress; residual stress
Eigenverbrauch m internal consumption; own use
Eigenwärme f sensible heat
Eignungsprüfung f qualification test
Eimer m bucket
Einarbeitung f practice; training
Einbau m assembly; insertion; mounting
einbauen build in; fit in; insert; install; mount; set
Einbaustück n chock; insert
einbetten embed
Einbettmaterial n packing material
einbeulen dish
Einbindung f integration
einblasen blow into; inject
Einblasen n **(von Gichtstaub)** injection (of blast furnace flue dust)
Einbrandkerbe f groove; notch; weld toe
Einbrandtiefe f depth of penetration
Einbrandzone f penetration zone
einbrennen burn in
Einbrennen n baking; curing; burning [in]; firing in
einbuchten dish
eindeutig clear
Eindicken n thickening

Eindringen n penetration
Eindringkörper m **(bei der Härteprüfung)** penetrating body
Eindringtiefe f depth of penetration
Eindruck m identation; impression
Eindruckbeständigkeit f sag resistance
Eindrücken n impressing; indenting
einfach simple
Einfachabschneiden n single cropping
Einfachbiegen n single bending
einfache Handelsgüte f commercial grade; commercial quality; ordinary quality
Einfachhärten n single hardening
Einfachpreßtechnik f single press technique
einfädeln (in Kaliber) thread
Einfädelvorrichtung f threading device
Einfahrgeschwindigkeit f entry speed
Einfallswinkel m **(Ultraschall)** angle of incidence
einfassen border
Einfassungseisen n casement section; frame section; sash section
einfetten grease; lubricate
Einflußrohr n central gate
Einflußuntersuchung f factorial analysis
Einflußversuch m factorial experiment
einfrieren chill; freeze
Einfügung f insertion
einführen enter; introduce
einführen (in Kaliber) thread
Einführung f entry guide; inlet; introduction
Einfüllöffnung f charging hole; filling hole
Eingabe-Primärstatus m input primary status (IPS)
Eingabe-Sekundärstatus m input secondary status (ISS)
Eingabezeit f input time interval
Eingang m **(Empfang)** receipt
Eingangsgröße f input (signal); input variable
Eingangsinformation f input information

Eingangsschlüssel *m* bell mouth; mouth of die
Eingangsschlüssel *m* **(des Ziehsteins)** bell mouth
Eingangsverbindung *f* input connection
Eingangswert *m* input value
eingearbeitet incorporated
eingeblasen injected
eingekeilt keyed in
eingeölt oiled finish; slushed
eingeschmolzener Fremdstoff *m* fused-in extraneous matter
eingespanntes Gewölbe *n* sprung arch
eingewalzter Splitter *m* rolled-in scrap
Eingießende *n* pouring end
eingießen (füllen) charge into; pour
eingipflig unimodal
Eingriffsbereich *m* zone of contact
Einguß *m* ingate; runner gate
Eingußrinne *f* feed runner
Eingußrohr *n* central gate; trumpet
Eingußrohr *n* **(steigender Guß)** tunnel
Eingußtrichter *m* down gate; gate; sprue
einhaken hook in; hook on
Einhalsen *n* botting
Einhalsen *n* **durch Drücken** contracting by spinning
Einhandbrenner *m* one hand burner
Einhärtbarkeit *f* potential hardness increase
Einhärtetiefe *f* hardness penetration [depth]
einhauen (Walzen) rag; roughen
Einheit *f* item; unit
einheitlich standard; uniform; unitary
Einheitsformat *n* unit form; unit shape
einheizen heat
Einkaliber-Stopfenwalzwerk *n* single groove plug mill
einkapseln encase
Einkauf *m* purchasing department
Einkaufsabteilung *f* purchasing department
einkerben nick; notch; rag; roughen; score; scotch
Einknicken *n* **(Kaltwalzen)** buckling (of coil)
Einkreislanze *f* one circuit lance
Einkristall *m* monocrystal; single crystal
Einlage *f* insert
Einlagedraht *f* **(für Gummibereifung)** bead
Einlagenschweißung *f* single pass welding
Einlagerung *f* dispersion; inclusion
Einlagerungsmischkristall *m* interstitial solid solution
Einlaß *m* admission; inlet
Einlaßführung *f* entering guide; entry guide
Einlaßöffnung *f* intake
Einlaufkohlenstoff *m* melt-down carbon
Einlaufperiode *f* running-in period
Einlaufrollgang *m* run-in roller table
Einlaufschlacke *f* melt down slag
Einlaufteil *m* entry section
Einlegedraht *m* bead
Einlochdüse *f* single hole nozzle
Einölmaschine *f* lubrication machine
einordnen arrange in order
Einprägen *n* stamping (characters into the surface of a workpiece)
Einregelungsbrenner *m* self inspiration burner
Einreißen *n* tearing in
Einreißen *n* **der Kante** edge tearing
einrichten adjust; equip; install; set
Einrichtung *f* apparatus; device; appliance; arrangement; equipment; establishment; facility; installation
Einrichtung *f* **(z. B. einer Versuchsstation)** installing; setting up
Einriß *m* flaw
Einrollen *n* curling
Einrollmaschine *f* **(für Rohrstreifen)** cold roll forming machine
Einsatz *m* burden; charge
Einsatzfähigkeit *f* availability for use; readiness
einsatzhärten case harden

Einsatzhärten n case hardening
Einsatzhärtetiefe f specified depth of case hardening; thickness of case hardening
Einsatzhärtung f carburisation
Einsatzmittel n **(für Einsatzhärten)** carburiser
Einsatzmittel n **(für Einsatzhärtung)** case hardening carburiser; case hardening compound
Einsatz m charge
Einsatzofen m batch operated furnace
Einsatzschicht f case
Einsatzstahl m case hardening steel
Einschallwinkel m **(Ultraschallprüfung)** angle of sonic radiation
Einschaltdauer f power-on period; switching period (motor)
einschalten connect a circuit; connect into circuit
Einschalter m switch
Einschalt-Verzögerung f raising delay
Einschichtemaillieren n single-layer enameling
Einschienenbahn f monorail
Einschlackenverfahren n single slag process
Einschleifen n seat grinding
einschließen trap
Einschluß m inclusion
Einschlüsse mpl **von Feuerfeststoffen** brick inclusions
einschmelzen melt down; smelt down
Einschmelzen n smelting down
Einschmelzen n **(Umschmelzen)** melting down
Einschmelzkohlenstoff[gehalt] m melt-down carbon
Einschmelzschlacke f melt-down slag
Einschneiden n lancing
Einschnitt m indentation
Einschnürdehnung f elongation with necking
einschnüren neck
Einschnürung f constriction; necking [down]; reduction of area
Einschnürung f **an beiden Enden des Hauptgewölbes (SM-Ofen)** knuckle (open hearth furnace)
einschränkend restrictive
Einschränkung f restriction
Einschroten n partial parting by chiseling
Einschwingen n **eines Ermüdungsanrisses** initiation of a fatigue crack
einseitige Neigung f bias
einseitiges Pressen n single action pressing
Einseitigkeit f bias
Einseitigkeit f **der Probenahme** bias of sampling
Einsenken n die hobbing
Einsenken n **(kalt)** hobbing
Einsetzbühne f charging floor
einsetzen caburise; case harden; charge; insert
Einsetzen n **mit Rutschen** chute charging
Einsetzmaschine f ground level charging machine
Einsetzmulde f charging box
Einsetzofen m batch operated furnace
Einspannbacke f chuck jaw
einspannen chuck; clamp; grip; mount
Einspannkopf m clamping head; gripping head
Einspannlänge f ingoing wire
Einspannung f insertion; mounting
Einspannvorrichtung f clamp; jig
Einsparung f saving
Einspeisen n feeding
Einspeisetrafo m supply transformer
Einspritzen n partial spreading
Einspritzpumpe f injection pump
Einspritzventilator m injection fan
Einspruch m complaint; protest
Einspruch m **einlegen gegen ein Patent** oppose a patent
Ein-Stapel-Ofen m single stack furnace
Einstechschleifen n plunge cut grinding
einstecken enter; insert; introduce
Einsteckseite f **(vor der Walze)** entry side of rolls; roller's side
Einsteigtür f access door

einstellen adjust; center; set; time
Einstellung f adjustment
Einstellwinkel m **(Spanen)** angle of incidence; tool cutting edge angle
Einstellzeit f **(EDV)** response time
Einstich m insertion; introduction; pass
Einstoßen n reducing
Einstoßvorrichtung f pusher; pushing device
Einstrangbetrieb m single strand
Einstrang-Durchlaufofen m single strand continuous furnace
Einstrang-Gießmaschine f single strand casting machine
Einstrangverfahren n single strand process
Einströmungsrohr n intake
Einstufen-Dauerschwingversuch m fatigue test in one load stage
einstufig single-stage
Einstufung f grading; grouping
einstürzen collapse
Eintauchelektrode f immersion electrode
eintauchen dip; immerse; sink in
einteilen grade
einteiliger Walzständer m monolithic roll housing
eintreten enter
Eintrittswinkel m **(Walzen)** entering angle
Eintröpfelung f dropping in
Einwaage f weighed sample
einwalzen roll in
Einwalzung f rolled-in extraneous matter; scrap mark
Einwegaufblas-Tiefofen m one-way top-fired soaking pit
Einwegofen m single way furnace; uniflow furnace
Einwirkung f effect; operation
Einwirkungsbereich m **(Gas)** sphere of action
einzapfen mortise
Einzelachsbüchse f individual journal box
Einzelantrieb m individual drive; single drive

Einzelbestand m **(im Lager)** single on-hand quantity
Einzelblock m bull block; single block
Einzelheit f detail; item
Einzellos n batch
einzelner Posten m item
Einzel- oder Doppelüberlappverbindung f single or double shear lap joint
Einzel- oder Mehrpunktschweißprobe f single or multiple spot welding specimen
Einzelplattenkassette f **(für Datenspeicherung)** single disc cartridge
Einzelton m pure tone
Einzelton-Analysator m sound analyser
Einzelversuch m single test
Einzelwalzenantrieb m **bei Duo-Umkehrstraßen (Zwillingsantrieb)** twin drive
einziehen infiltrate; neck; reduce; retract
Einziehzange f pulling-in dog
Einzweckmaschine f single-purpose machine-tool
Einzylinder-Dampfmaschine f single cylinder steam engine
Eisberg m **(Eisenschwammberg im Ofen)** iceberg
Eisen n iron
Eisenabstichloch n iron notch
Eisenausscheidung f iron precipitation
Eisenbad n iron bath
Eisenbahnbedarf m railway material
Eisenbahnoberbaustoffe mpl rail accessories
Eisenbahnradreifen m railway tyre
Eisenbahnschiene f rail
Eisenbahn-Transportkessel m railway transport vessel
Eisenbahn-Verladeanlage f railway loading installation
Eisenbahnwagenbau m railway wagon construction
Eisenbahn-Werkstätte f structural engineering workshop

Eisenbahnzeug *n* railway material; track material
Eisenbau-Werkstätte *f* shop for steel structures; shop for structural engineering
Eisenbegleitelement *n* companion element; incidental element; minor constituent
Eisenbergwerk *n* iron mine
Eisenbestimmung *f* determination of iron
Eisenbeton s. **Stahlbeton**
Eisencarbid *n* iron carbide
Eisendraht *m* iron wire
Eisenerz *n* iron ore
Eisenerzbrikett *n* ferric oxide briquette; iron ore briquette
Eisenerz-Koks-Pellet *n* ore coke pellet
Eisenerz-Lagerstätte *f* iron ore deposit
Eisenerzstücke *npl* half roasted lumps of iron ore
Eisenerzvorbereitung *f* ore beneficiation
Eisengehalt *m* iron content
eisengesättigt iron saturated
Eisengießerei *f* iron foundry
Eisengießerei-Erzeugnisse *npl* cast-iron products
Eisenglanz *m* iron glance; kidney ore; oligiste iron ore; specular iron ore
Eisenglimmer *m* micaceous iron ore
Eisenguß *m* cast iron; iron casting
eisenhaltig ferriferous
Eisenhütte *f* ironworks
Eisenhüttenchemie *f* iron works chemistry
Eisenhüttenkunde *f* ferrous metallurgy
Eisenhüttenmann *m* steel man
Eisenhüttenwerk *n* iron and steel plant; iron and steel works
Eisenhüttenwesen *n* ferrous metallurgy; iron and steel manufacture; metallurgy of iron
Eisen *n* **im Abstichloch erstarrt** chestnut
Eisenkies *m* **(FeS$_2$)** iron pyrites

Eisen-Kohlenstoff-Schaubild *n* iron carbon diagram
Eisennickelkies *m* iron nickel pyrites; nicopyrite; pentlandite
Eisenoxid *n* ferric oxide
Eisenoxidrauch *m* iron oxide fume
Eisenoxidul *n* ferrous oxide
Eisenpecherz *n* pitticite
Eisen-Phosphor *n* iron phosphide
Eisenportlandzement *m* iron Portland cement; slag Portland cement
Eisenpulver *n* iron powder
Eisenrinne *f* metal runner
Eisenrückgewinnungsanlage *f* iron recovery plant
eisenschaffende Industrie *f* iron and steel producing industry
eisenschüssiger Kalk *m* ferruginous lime
Eisenschwamm *m* DRI (= direct reduced iron); metallised iron ore; sponge iron
Eisenschwamm *m* **aus Stückerz** sponge iron made from lump ore
Eisenschwammpellet *n* sponge iron pellet
Eisenseife *f* iron soap
Eisenspat *m* spathic iron
Eisensulfat *n* ferrous sulfate
Eisenträger *m* **(Baustahlträger)** steel girder
Eisen- und Stahlerzeugnisse *npl* iron and steel products
Eisen- und Stahlhandel *m* iron and steel trade
eisenverarbeitende Industrie *f* steel processing industry
Eisenvitriol *n* copperas; green vitriol; iron sulphate
Eisenwerk *n* iron works
Eisenwerkstoff *m* ferrous material
elastische Formänderung *f* elastic deformation
elastische Formänderungsarbeit *f* elastic energy of deformation
Elastizitätsgrenze *f* elastic limit
Elastizitätsmodul *m* Young's modulus; elastic modulus; modulus of elasticity

Elektriker m electrician
elektrische Batterie f electric storage battery
elektrische Beheizung f electric heating; electric heating plant
elektrische Drahtseilbahn f telpher line
elektrische Elementarladung f elementary charge
elektrische Feldstärke f electric field strength
elektrische Leitfähigkeit f electrical conductivity
elektrische Maschinen fpl electrical machinery
elektrisches Feld n electrical field
elektrische Steuerung f electric control
elektrische Verschiebung f electric displacement
elektrische Verteileranlage f distribution plant for electric current
elektrische Zentrale f electric power house; power station
Elektroanstauchen n electro thermal upsetting; upending by the electric heating method
Elektroblech n electric[al] quality sheet; magnetic sheet; silicon steel sheet
Elektrochemie f electrochemistry
elektrochemische Beweglichkeit f electrochemical mobility
elektrochemisches Ablösen n (Zinküberzug) electro-chemical stripping
elektrochemische Spannungsreihe f electro-chemical series
elektrochemisches Potential n electrochemical potential
Elektrode f electrode
Elektrode f **kalkbasisch umhüllte** electrode with basic sheath
Elektrode f **mit Flußmittel** fluxed electrode
Elektrodenabstand m (**Spektralanalyse**) spark gap
Elektrode f **nackte** bare wire electrode
Elektrodenarm m electrode arm

Elektrodenaufbau m electrode joining
Elektrodenaufbau m **auf dem Ofen** electrodes on-furnace assembling
Elektrodenaufbau m **neben dem Ofen** electrodes off-furnace assembling
Elektrodenbruch m electrode scrap; electrode waste
Elektrodeneintauchtiefe f depth of electrode immersion
Elektrodenhalter m electrode holder
Elektrodenköcher m electrode case
Elektrodenkraftzylinder m electrode-pressure cylinder
Elektroden fpl **kreisförmig angeordnet** electrodes arranged in a circle
Elektrodenregelung f electrode control system
Elektrodenteilkreis m pitch circle
Elektrodenverbrauch m electrode consumption
Elektroerosion f spark erosion; spark machining
Elektrofahrzeug n electric vehicle
Elektrofilter m electro [gas] filter; electrostatic precipitator
Elektroflaschenzug m electric pulley block
Elektrogasschweißen n electro gas welding
Elektrohängebahn f electric overhead trolley; telpher line
Elektrohochofen m electric shaft furnace
Elektrokarren m electric truck
Elektrolyse f electrolysis
elektrolytische Durchlaufverzinkung f bethanising
elektrolytische Nickelunterschicht f (**bei Weißblech**) electrodeposited nickel undercoat
elektrolytisches Polieren n electrolytic polishing
elektrolytisches Veredeln n electroplating
elektrolytisches Verzinnen n electrolytic tinning
elektrolytisch verzinkt electrogalvanised

elektrolytisch verzinntes Weißblech *n* electrolytic tinplate
Elektrolytpulver *n* electrolytic powder
Elektromagnet *m* electromagnet
elektromagnetisch electromagnetic
elektromagnetischer Gegenstrom *m* electromagnetic counter current; electromagnetic inverse current
Elektromechaniker *m* electrician
elektromotorische Kraft *f* **(EMK)** electromotive force (EMF)
Elektronenbeugung *f* electron diffraction
Elektronendämpfungsverfahren *n* electron attenuation process
Elektronen-Flachstrahlkanone *f* broad beam electron gun
Elektronenkanone *f* **mit Fremdbeschleunigung** electron gun with external acceleration
Elektronenkanone *f* **mit Selbstbeschleunigung** electron gun with built-in self-acceleration
Elektronenmikroskop *n* electron microscope
elektronenmikroskopische Aufnahme *f* electron-micrograph
Elektronenmikrosonde *f* microprobe analyser
Elektronenrechner *m* electronic computer
Elektronen-Ringstrahlkanone *f* annular jet discharge electron gun
Elektronenröhre *f* electronic valve
Elektronenschale *f* electron shell
Elektronenstrahler *m* electron gun
Elektronenstrahl-Mikroanalyse *f* electron probe microanalysis
Elektronenstrahl-Schmelzverfahren *n* electron beam melting process
Elektronenstrahlschneiden *n* electron beam cutting
Elektronenstrahlschweißen *n* electron beam welding
Elektronenniederschachtofen *m* electric low shaft furnace
elektronische Datenverarbeitung *f* electronic data processing

Elektroofen *m* electric furnace
Elektrophorese *f* electrophoresis
elektroplattieren electroplate
Elektroreduktionsofen *m* electric arc reduction furnace; electric ore reduction furnace
Elektroroheisen *n* electric furnace iron
Elektroschlacke-Schweißen *n* electro slag welding
Elektroschlackeumschmelzen *n* **(ESU)** electroslag refining (ESR); electroslag remelting (ESR)
Elektroschlackeumschmelzverfahren *n* **(ESU)** electro slag remelting (ESR)
Elektroschmelzschweißen *n* electric fusion welding
Elektroschweißer *m* arc welder
Elektrostahl *m* electric [furnace] steel
Elektrostauchverfahren *n* upsetting with electric resistance heating
Elektrotechnik *f* electrical engineering; electrotechnics
elektrothermisch electrothermal
Elektro-Trockenfilter *m* electro dry filter
Elektroturbogebläse *n* electric turbo blower
Elektrowerkzeug *n* electric driven tool
Elektrozug *m* electric hoist
Elementarwürfel *m* unit cell
Elementarzelle *f* unit cell
Elin-Hafergut-Verfahren *n* firecracker welding
Elysieren *n* electro forming
Emaillierblech *n* enameling sheet
emaillieren enamel
Emaillierofen *m* enamel[ing] oven
Emission *f* emission
Emissions-Elektronenmikroskop *n* electron emission microscope
Emissions-Flammenphotometrie *f* emission flame photometry
EMK-Sonde *f* EMF cell; solid electrolyte cell
EMK *f* **(Zellspannung)** emf (cell voltage)

E-Modul *m* modulus of elasticity
Empfang *m* receipt
Empfindlichkeit *f* **(gegen)** sensitiveness (to); susceptibility (to)
Empfindlichkeitsregler *m* sensitivity regulator
Emulsion *f* emulsion
Ende *n* **abgeschnittenes** crop end
Endenschere *f* crop shears
Endergebnis *n* upshot
endotherm endothermic
Endprobe *f* final sample
Endschalter *m* limit switch
Endstein *m* **(Ziehen)** finishing die (drawing)
Endstellung *f* final position
Energie *f* energy
Energiebedarf *m* power required
Energiebedarfsdeckung *f* satisfaction of energy requirement
Energiefluß *m* energy flow
Energiequelle *f* energy source
Energieumwandlung *f* power conversion
Energie- und Stoffwirtschaft *f* economy; organisation of power and material supply; power and material
Energieverbrauch *m* energy consumption; power consumption
Energieverbundwirtschaft *f* integrated power system
Energieverlust *m* loss of energy; loss of power
Energieversorgung *f* power supply
energiewirtschaftliches Verbundsystem *n* power supply interlinked system
Energiewirtschaftsingenieur *m* energy manager
Energiewirtschafts-Schwerpunkt *m* focal point of power economy
eng narrow
Engen *n* **durch Drücken** contracting by spinning
Engpaß *m* bottle-neck
engster Querschnitt *m* bottle-neck
entarteter Perlit *m* degenerate pearlite

Entaschungsanlage *f* ash removal [device]; ash removal plant
Entbenzolung *f* **mit Kühler und Wärmetauscher** debenzoling by cooler and heat exchanger
Entchromen *n* dechroming
Entfall *m* discard
entfernen remove
Entfernen *n* **der Gangart** removal of gangue
Entfestigung *f* removal of workhardening
entfetten degrease; dewax
Entfettung *f* degreasing
Entfettungsmittel *n* degreasing agent
entflammen set alight
entgasen degas; degasify; evaporate
entgaster Stahl *m* killed steel
Entgasung *f* **(von Schmelzen)** degassing
Entgiftung *f* decontamination; detoxication
entgraten debur; flash trim
Enthalpie *f* enthalpy
enthalten contain
enthaltend containing
enthärtetes Wasser *n* softened water
Enthärtungsanlage *f* softener
entkohlen decarburise
Entkohlungswirkung *f* carbon drop; decarburising effect
entkuppeln discharge; disengage; uncouple
Entladeanlage *f* unloading facilities
entladen discharge; empty; unload
entlassen discharge
Entlassung *f* discharge
Entlastung *f* removal of load; stress removal
Entlastungsventil *n* bleeder valve
entleeren empty
Entleerungsanlage *f* detarring plant
Entlüften *n* ventilation
Entlüftung *f* breather; venting
Entlüftungsanlage *f* ventilating system
Entmagnetisieren *n* demagnetising
Entmischung *f* phase separation; segregation; separation

Entnitrieren s. Denitrieren
entölen de-oil
Entöler *m* oil separator
Entphenolung *f* des Gaswassers phenol extraction from the gas water
Entphosphorung *f* dephosphorisation
Entropie *f* entropy
entrosten derust
Entrostung *f* rust removal
Entrostungsmittel *n* derusting agent
Entsalzen *n* desalting
Entsalzen *n* **(Meerwasser)** desalination
entsalztes Wasser *n* desalinated water
entschlacken deslag; remove slag
Entschlackungsmittel *n* deslagging agent
entschlämmen deslime; free from mud
Entschlüßler *m* decoder
Entschwefelung *f* desulphurisation
Entschwefelungsanlage *f* desulphurisation plant
Entschwefelungsmittel *n* desulphurisation agent
entsilicieren desiliconize
entspanntes Wasser *n* low-surface tension water
Entspannung *f* removal of stress; stress relieving
Entspannungsglühen *n* stress relieving annealing
entstauben dust off; remove dust
Entstauber *m* dust catcher
Entstaubung *f* dust extraction; dust removal
Entstaubungsanlage *f* dust catcher; dust removing plant; dust-collecting machine
Entstaubungsgrad *m* degree of dust extraction; degree of dust removal
Entstickung *f* removal of nitrogen
Entteerungsanlage *f* detarring plant
entwässern dewater; drain
Entwässerung *f* dewatering
Entwässerungsanlage *f* draining plant

Entwässerungsrohr *n* drainage pipe
entwickeln (Rauch) evolve; produce
Entwicklung *f* trend
Entwicklungsrichtung *f* trend
Entwurf *m* design; device; plan
Entzinkung *f* dezincification
entzünden ignite
entzundern (bei Blöcken) descale
Entzunderung *f* descaling
Entzunderungsanlage *f* descaling plant
Entzündung *f* ignition
Epilamenreibung *f* near contact friction
epitaxiales Oxid *n* epitaxial oxide
Epoxid *n* epoxy
erbauen build
erblasen blow
Erdgas *n* natural gas
erdiges Erz *n* earthy ore
Erdnaphtha *n* rack oil
Erdöl *n* petroleum
Erdschluß *m* earth connection; earth fault; earth leakage
Erdung *f* earth connection; earthing
Erdungskabel *n* earth lead; work lead (am.)
Erfahrungswahrscheinlichkeit *f* empirical probability
Erforschung *f* investigation; research
ergänzen amplify; complete
ergeben result
Ergebnis *n* issue; result; yield
Ergonomie *f* ergonomics
ergreifen grasp
Erhaltungsbetrieb *m* maintenance department
Erhaltung *f* **(z. B. durch Ausbesserung)** salvage
Erhebung *f* elevation
erhitzen heat
Erhitzungsmikroskop *n* hot stage microscope
erhöhen bring up; increase
Erholung *f* elastic recovery
Erholungsglühen *n* recovery annealing
Erichsen-Tiefung *f* cupping index

erkalten cool
Erkaltung f cooling
Erkennung f identification
Erklärung f elucidation
Erläuterung f elucidation
Ermüdung f fatigue
Ermüdung f bei niedriger Lastspielzahl low cycle fatigue
Ermüdungsbruch m fatigue failure; fatigue fracture
Ermüdungskorrosion f fatigue corrosion
Ermüdungsriß m fatigue crack
Ermüdungsversuch m endurance test; fatigue test
erneuern renew; restore
erodieren erode
Erörterung f consideration; discussion
Erosion f erosion
Erosionskorrosion f corrosion erosion
Erosionsverhalten n erosion characteristics
erproben test
erregen excite
errichten construct; erect
Errichtung f (eines Werkes) erection (of a mill)
Ersatz m replacement; substitution
Ersatzbad n replenishing solution
Ersatzfehlergröße f (zerstörungsfreies Prüfen) calibrated standard defect size
Ersatzgerüst n replace stand; spare stand
Ersatzgetriebe n substitute gear; substitute mechanism
Ersatzteil n spare part
Erscheinung f phenomenon
Erscheinungsbild n hypothetical postulate
Erschmelzung f im Lichtbogen electric arc melting
Erschmelzungsart f melting process
erschöpfend exhaustive; sufficient
Erschöpfung f exhaustion
Erschütterung f concussion; shock
erschütterungssicher shock proof
ersetzen replace

Ersparnis f saving
erstarren coagulate; freeze; set; solidify
Erstarren n freezing
erstarrender Metallblock m solidifying pig
erstarrtes Eisen n im Abstichloch chestnut
Erstarrung f solidification
Erstarrungsbereich m solidification range
Erstarrungspunkt m freezing point
erster Zug m (beim Kaltziehen) ripping; rumpling
Ertrag m increase; output; output yield; profit; yield
Erwachsenenschulung f adult training
Erwärmdauer f heating time
Erwärmen n blu[e]ing
Erwartung f expectation
Erwartungswert m expectation value
erweichen resolve; soften
Erweichungsprobe f squatting test
Erweichungspunkt m fusion point; sagging point; sintering point; softening point
erweitern enlarge; expand; extend; flare; widen
Erweiterung f boss; enlargement; extension
Erweiterungsfunktion f extender function
Erweiterungsglied n extender element
Erz n ore
Erzabfälle mpl tailings
Erzader f ore vein
Erzaufbereitung f ore concentration; ore dressing
Erzaufbereitungsanlage f ore dressing facility; ore dressing plant; ore preparation plant
Erzausschuß m ore committee
Erzbrecher m ore crusher
Erzbunker m ore bin; ore storage bunker
erzen (Erz zusetzen) ore up

erzeugen (Dampf) produce; raise
Erzeuger *m* producer
Erzeugnisse *npl* **in der Fertigung** work in progress
Erzeugung *f* fabrication; manufacturing; output; production
Erzeugungsangaben *fpl* output data; production data
Erzeugungsleistung *f* production rate
Erzeugungsmenge *f* output
Erzeugung *f* **(Strom)** generation
Erzfrachter *m* ore freighter
Erzfrischverfahren *n* direct process for the production of wrought iron
erzführend ore bearing
Erzgicht *f* ore burden
erzhaltig ore bearing
Erzkonzentrat *n* ore concentrate
Erzlager *n* source of ore
Erz *n* **leicht reduzierbares** easily reducible ore
Erz *n* **mulmiges** earthy ore; friable iron ore
Europäische Gemeinschaft für Kohle und Stahl (EGKS) *f* European Community for Steel and Coal (ECSC)
exotherm exothermic

F

Fabrikgebäude *n* factory building
Facharbeiter *m* expert workman; skilled worker; skilled workman
Fachliteratur *f* technical literature
Fachmann *m* expert; specialist
Fachwerk *n* framework; truss
Fachwerkknoten *m* framework knote
Fachwerkträger *m* lattice girder
Fackel *f* **(Abgas)** excess gas burner; surplus gas burner
Faden *m* **(Faser)** filament
Fadenkristall *m* whisker
Fadenlunker *m* axial [fine] porosity; central porosity; coky centre
Fadenzeiger *m* hair line pointer
fahrbar mobile; movable; travelling

fahrbarer Roheisenmischer *m* mixer type hot metal car
fahrbarer Rollgang *m* travelling roller table
fahrbare Trommelpfanne *f* mobile drum type ladle
Fahrdrahtaufhängung *f* contact wire suspension (electric traction)
fahren travel
Fahrschiene *f* overhead beam
Fahrzeug *n* car; vehicle
Fahrzeugfeder *f* vehicle spring
faktorielle Versuchsplanung *f* factorial design
Fakturiermaschine *f* invoice typewriter
Fallbär *m* drop; tup
Fallbeschleunigung *f* acceleration due to gravity; acceleration of free fall
Fallbirne *f* drop weight; tup
Fallbügel *m* chopper bar
Fallbügelregler *m* chopper bar controller
Fallbügelüberwachung *f* chopper type monitoring
fällen precipitate
Falle *f* trap
fallend direct teem; top pour; top-cast
fallender Guß *m* top pouring
Fallengießen *n* direct casting; top pouring
fallend [ver]gießen direct teem; downhill teem; teem direct; teem downhill; top-cast; top-pour
Fallgewichtsversuch *m* falling weight test
Fallhammer *m* drop hammer; drop press; drop stamper; monkey
Fallhärteprüfer *m* hardness drop tester
Fallhärteprüfung *f* drop hardness test; impact ball hardness test
Fallprobe *f* falling weight test; shatter test
Fallrohr *n* down-comer; downpipe
Fällung *f* precipitation
Fällungsdesoxidation *f* precipitation deoxidation

Fällungspulver *n* precipitated powder
Fallversuch *m* **(DWT)** drop weight test
Fallwerk *n* **(Schrottzerkleinerung)** skull cracker
falsche Einstellung *f* maladjustment
Falschluft *f* entrained air; false air; infiltrated air; inleaked air
Faltbund *n* folded bundle
Falte *f* fold; pincher
Falte *f* **(beim Schmieden)** cold shut
falten crinkle; double; fold
Faltenbildung *f* formation of wrinkles
Faltenhalter *m* annular holder; annular ring; clamping ring
Falte *f* **(überwalzte)** cold lap
Faltungsriß *m* fold crack; fold crevice; seam
Faltversuch *m* bending test; flattening test; folding test
Falzblech *n* sheet with good bending properties
falzen bead; fold; notch
Falzen *n* **(Anlegen eines Bordes)** seaming
Falzen *n* **durch Drücken** seaming by spinning
Fangstoff *m* getter (powder met.)
Faraday-Konstante *f* Faraday constant
farbdurchdringend dye-penetrant
Farbpyrometer *n* colorimetric pyrometer
Farbschicht *f* film of paint
Farbspritzverfahren *n* paint spraying process
Faser *f* chamfer; fiber; filament
faseriger Bruch *m* fibrous fracture
faseriges Pulver *n* fibrous powder
Faserstruktur *f* fibering; fibrous structure
Faserverbundwerkstoff *m* fibre reinforced material
faserverstärktes Metall *n* fibre reinforced metal
Faserverstärkung *f* fibre reinforcement
Faß *n* barrel
fassen contain; grasp; grip; seize
Fassondrehteil *n* special shape turned part

Faßreifen-Bandstahl *m* supporting hoop for barrels
Fassung *f* border; casing; mount
Fassung *f* **(bei Ziehsteinen)** die holder
Fassungsvermögen *n* capacity; holding capacity
Fassung *f* **(Ziehstein)** mount
faul brittle
faulbrüchig short-brittle
Faustregel *f* rule of thumb
Fazit *n* break-down; net result; upshot
Fazit *n* **(Schlüsselergebnis)** sum total
Feder *f* spring; tongue
Federblatt *n* spring blade; spring leaf; spring plate
Federblech-Biegeversuch *m* spring plate bend test
Federdraht *m* spring wire
Federdruckmesser *m* spring pressure gauge
Federführungshülse *f* spring housing
Federkeil *m* feather key; fitting key
Federkennlinie *f* load deflection curve for spring
Feder *f* **kleiner Abmessung** light-gage spring
Federmatrize *f* spring supported die
federnde Aufhängung *f* spring suspension
Federn-Schwingprüfmaschine *f* scragging machine for testing springs
Federprüfmaschine *f* spring testing machine
Federring *m* spring washer
Federscheibe *f* **(screw)** spring washer
Feder-Sicherheitsventil *n* spring-operated safety valve
Federstahl *m* spring steel
Federstahldraht *m* spring steel wire
Feder und Nut *f* slot and groove; tongue and groove
Fehlabmessung *f* **(beim Kaltwalzen)** off-ga[u]ge
Fehlen *n* absence; absenteeism; lack
Fehler *m* defect; error; fault
Fehlerbereich *m* confidence interval
Fehler *m* **durch nicht genau übereinander sitzende Gesenkhälften** mismatch; offset

Fehlerecho n defect echo; flaw echo
Fehlererscheinung f fault
fehlerfreie Probe f sound test piece
Fehlergrenze f limit of error
fehlerhaft defective; faulty
Fehlerortungsstab m **(Ultraschall)** flaw location scale
Fehlerprüfgerät n defects detecting device
Fehlerquelle f bias; source of defect; source of error
fehlgeordnete Legierung f disordered alloy
Fehlguß m faulty cast; mis-run [casting]; off-cast; waste casting; waster
Fehlordnung f disorder (structure)
Fehlordnungsgrad m degree of disorder
Fehlschicht f absenteeism
Fehlschlag m failure
Fehlschmelze f misfit cast; off-heat
Fehlstelle f defect; void
Fehlwalzung f cobble
feilen file
Feile f file
Feilenstahl m file steel
Feilspäne mpl filings
fein bearbeitet finish-machined
Feinblech n metal sheet; sheet; sheet metal; works annealed sheet
Feinblech-Vorwalzgerüst n **mit ungehärteten Gußwalzen** soft mill
Feinblech-Walzwerk n sheet [rolling] mill
Feindehnungsmessung f micro-train measurement
Feineisen n small sections
feinen deoxidize; purify; refine
Feinentstaubung f secondary dust removal
Feinerz n fine ore; ore fines
Feingefüge n fine structure; microstructure
feingeschliffen precision ground
Feinguß m precision casting
Feinkoks m coke fines; rubbly culm coke
Feinkorn-Desoxidation f grain size control by deoxidizing practice
feinkörnig fine-grained; small grained
feinkörniger Bruch m fine-grained fracture; sappy fracture
feinkörniges Gefüge n fine-grained structure; sappy structure
feinkörniges Roheisen n close-grained pig
Feinkornstahl m close grained steel; fine grained steel
Feinmessung f precision measurement
feinnadelig acicular
Feinpore f micropore
Feinpulver n fine powder
Feinreinigung f fine cleaning; fine purification; secondary cleaning
Feinschneiden n fine-edge blanking
Feinsilicium n fine silicon
Feinstahl-Walzwerk n light section rolling mill; small-section rolling mill
Feinstanteil m superfines
Feinstbearbeitung f microfinishing
Feinstblech n black plate
feinste Abmessung f finest ga[u]ge
Feinstpulver n sub-sieve powder
Feinstraße f small section mill
feinstufiger Vorschub m sensitive feed
Feinstziehschleifen n superfinishing
Feinungsschlacke f final slag; refining slag
Feinvakuum-Elektronenstrahlschweißen n medium high vacuum electron beam welding
Feinzerkleinerung f fine grinding (powder met.)
Feinzerkleinerung f **fester Metalle** comminution of solid metals
Feinzink-Destillationsanlage f zinc destillation plant
Feinzug m finishing pass
Feld n country
Feldanweisung f field definition
Feldelektronenmikroskop n field electron microscope
Feld n **(Gewölbe)** roof panel
Feldionenmikroskopie f field ion mi-

croscopy
Feldstärke *f* field intensity
Feldvariable *f* field variable
Felge *f* rim
Fenster *n* **(EDV)** gate
Fensterstahl *m* sash and casement sections; window framing steel
Ferien *pl* holidays; vacation
Ferngas *n* grid gas; long-distance gas
Ferngasnetz *n* gas grid; grid
Ferngasverdichter *m* compressor for grid gas transmission; compressor for long distance gas transmission
Ferngasversorgung *f* grid gas supply; long-distance gas supply
Ferngeber *m* teletransmitter
Ferngreifer *m* remote control[led] grab
Fernheizung *f* long distance heating
Fernheizungsanlage *f* district heating plant
Fernleitung *f* long-distance pipeline
Fernmeldeanlage *f* telecommunication system
Fernmeßgerät *n* telemeter
Fernmessung *f* telemetering
Fernordnung *f* long range order
Fernschreiber *m* teleprinter; telewriter
Fernsehmikroskop *n* quantitative television microscope
Fernsehsignal *n* video-signal
Fernsehübertragung *f* television transmission
Fernsender *m* remote transmitter
Fernsteuerung *f* remote control
Fernübertragung *f* **von Meßgrößen** tele-transmission of measured values
Ferrit *m* ferrite
ferritischer Stahl *m* ferritic steel
Ferritkorn *n* ferrite grain
Ferritspieß *m* ferrite lath
Ferrocarbidstein *m* ferrocarbide brick
Ferroclipstein *m* ferroclip brick
Ferrokoks *m* ferro-coke
Ferrolegierung *f* ferro alloy
ferromagnetisch ferromagnetic
Ferromangan *n* ferro-manganese
Ferromolybdän *n* ferro-molybdenum
Ferrosilicium *n* ferro-silicon
ferrostatischer Druck *m* ferrostatic pressure
Ferrotitan *n* ferro-titanium
Ferrowolfram *n* ferro-tungsten
fertig ready (for operation)
Fertigbauteil *n* prefabricated member
Fertigbearbeitung *f* finish machining
fertigblasen blow full
Fertigdichte *f* **(Pulvermet.)** final density
Fertigdrehbank *f* finishing lathe
Fertigerzeugnis *n* finished goods; finished product
Fertiggerüst *n* finisher; finishing stand
Fertiggesenk *n* finisher
Fertigglühung *f* final annealing
Fertigkaliber *n* finishing groove; finishing pass
Fertigkeit *f* art
Fertiglänge *f* effective length; finished length
fertigmachen finish
Fertigmaß *n* finished size
Fertigschlacke *f* final slag; finishing slag; refining slag
Fertigsinterung *f* final sintering operation
Fertigstapel *m* stack of finished steel sheets
Fertigstich *m* shaping pass
Fertigstraße *f* finishing train
Fertigteil *n* finished part
Fertigung *f* production
Fertigungsablauf *m* production flow
Fertigungssteuerung *f* production control
Fertigungszeit *f* manufacturing time; production time
fertigwalzen finish [roll]
Fertigwalzwerk *n* finishing [rolling] mill
fest constant; solid
Festbett *n* static bed
Festbrennen *n* **auf den Führungen** sticking in the guides (lamination)

Festbundtisch *m* tight coil table
feste Kosten *pl* fixed costs
feste Länge *f* exact length
feste Lösung *f* solid solution
feste Phase *f* solid stage
fester Zustand *m* solid state
festes Roheisen *n* pig iron
festfressen gall; jam; scour; seize
festhaftend firmly adhering; firmly bonded to
festhaftender Überzug *m* fast coating
Festigkeit *f* consistence; resistance; strength; tenacity; tensile strength
Festigkeitseigenschaften *fpl* mechanical properties; strength characteristics; strength properties; tensile properties
festigkeitsgerecht properly proportioned for stress and strain
Festigkeitsschweiße *f* strength weld; tightness weld
festklemmen jam
Festkörper *m* solid; solid-state body
Festpreis *m* fixed price
feststehend fixed; stationary
feststellen determine; observe; state
Feststellung *f* identification
Feststellvorrichtung *f* arresting device
Feststoff *m* solid; solid matter
Feststoffreduktion *f* reduction of solids
fest werden congeal
Festwertregelung *f* control with fixed set-point; fixed set point control; set value control; set-point
Fett *n* **in - arbeitend (Lager)** grease packed
Fettkalk *m* fat lime
Fettkohle *f* caking coal; cannel coal; coking coal; gas coal
Fett- oder Schmutzgrübchen *npl* grease or dirt marks (surface defect); grease or dirt pits
Fettöl *n* fatty oil
Fettschmierpresse *f* grease gun
Fettschmierpumpe *f* grease pump
feucht damp
Feuchtigkeit *f* humidity; moisture
Feuchtigkeitsgeber *m* humidity cell

Feuchtigkeitsgradmesser *m* **(bei festen Stoffen)** moisture meter
Feuchtigkeitskorrosion *f* aqueous corrosion
Feuchtigkeitslagerversuch *m* high humidity and condensation test
Feuchtigkeitsmeßgerät *n* dewpoint recorder
Feueraluminieren *n* hot dip aluminising
feuerbeständig fire resisting; non-scaling; scale-resisting
feuerbeständiger Guß *m* fire-resisting casting; heat-resisting casting
Feuerbeständigkeit *f* **(eines Steines)** refractibility; refractory quality
Feuerbeton *m* refractory concrete
Feuerbrücke *f* fire-bridge
feuerfest fire proof; fire resisting; refractory
Feuerfestausbruch *m* **(Entfallstoff)** refractory breaks
feuerfeste Anstrichmasse *f* refractory coating
feuerfeste Auskleidung *f* refractory lining
feuerfeste Ausmauerung *f* fireproof lining
feuerfeste Flickmasse *f* refractory patching mass
feuerfeste Masse *f* refractory mixture
feuerfester Baustoff *m* refractory building material
feuerfester Leichtstoff *m* light weight refractory; low density refractory
feuerfester Mörtel *m* refractory cement; refractory mortar (am.)
feuerfester Stein *m* firebrick; refractory brick
feuerfester Ton *m* fire-clay; refractory clay
feuerfestes Graphit-Ton-Erzeugnis *n* plumbago [refractory]
feuerfeste Stampfmasse *f* refractory ramming mixture
Feuerfestigkeit *f* refractability; refractoriness
Feuerfest-Industrie *f* refractories industry

feuergefährlich inflammable
Feuerkratze f rake
Feuerleichtstein m light-weight refractory brick
Feuerlöscher m fire extinguisher
Feuermelder m fire detector
Feuerraum m **(Ofen)** combustion chamber
Feuerschweißen n forge welding
Feuerspritzenwagen m fire-engine
Feuerung f fire place; firing; heating
Feuerungsanlage f firing plant
Feuerverzinken n hot [dip] galvanising; hot dip galvanising
feuerverzinkt hot [dip] galvanised
feuerverzinntes Weißblech n hot-dipped tinplate
Feuerverzinnung f hot tinning
Feuerzement m refractory mortar
Filmverdampfung f film-boiling
Filter m filter
Filteranlage f filter plant
Filter n **(EDV)** strainer
filtern filter
Filterschlauch m filter bag
filtrieren filter; percolate
Finanzbuchhaltung f financial accounts department
Finanzkonten npl finance accounts
Finite-Elemente-Verfahren n finite element method (FEM)
Firmenschild n name plate
Firnissen n varnishing
Firstblech n ridging plate
Fischauge n fish eye
Fischschuppe f fish scale
Fischschwänze mpl fish tails
Fittings pl fittings
fixe Länge f specified length
Fixierbad n fixing bath
Flachbahnkaliber n **(Walzwerk)** bull-head pass
Flachbahnwalze f flat roll; plain suface roll (am.)
Flachbiegeversuch m flat-bending test
Flachblech n plain sheet
Flachbramme f flat slab
Flachdraht m flat wire

Fläche f area; face; plane; sheet; surface
Flacheisen n flat bar
Flacheisen n **mit abgerundeten Kanten** chain section
Flächenberieselungskühler m spray cooling tank
Flächenbeziehungsgesetz n area relation law
Flächendiagonale f **des Elementarwürfels** cube face diagonal
Flächendruck m pressure per unit of area; pressure per unit of surface
Flächeneinheitslast f unit load
Flächenfräsen n surface milling
Flächeninhalt m area
Flächenlängsriß m longitudinal facial crack
Flächenpressung f surface pressing
Flächenquerriß m transverse facial crack
Flächenraum m area
Flächenverschleiß m wear of top face
flachgewalzte Erzeugnisse npl flat rolled products
Flachgewinde n square thread
Flachhalbrundstahl m flat half rounds
Flachherdmischer m flat-hearth type mixer
Flachkaliber n box groove; box hole; box pass
Flachknüppel m slab billet
Flach-Längswalzen n flat longitudinal rolling
Flach-Längswalzen n **von Hohlkörpern** flat longitudinal rolling of hollow items
Flach-Längswalzen n **von Vollkörpern** flat longitudinal rolling of solid bodies
Flachlasche f flat joint
Flachnaht f flat face fillet weld
Flachprägen n flat; surfacing
Flach-Querwalzen n flat transverse rolling
Flachrecken n **mit Breitung** upsetting
Flachschleifen n surface grinding
Flach-Schrägwalzen n flat skew rolling

Flachstab m flat bar
Flachstahl m flat rolled steel; flat steel bar; flats
Flachstahl-Warmwalzen n hot rolling of flats
Flachstauchen n hammer forging
Flachstich m flat pass
Flachverformung f plain strain
flachwalzen flat rolling; slab
Flachwalzen n **von Runddraht** flat rolling of round wire
flachwandig (Kokillen) plane sided
Flachwulststahl m bulb plate
Flachzerreißstab m flat tensile test bar
Flachzeug n flat product
Flachziehen n flat drawing
flackern flare; flare flicker; flicker
Flamme f flame; luminous flame
flammen burn
Flämmen n flame descaling; flame deseaming; flame scarfing
flammenbeheizt reverberatory
Flammenfeldlöten n multiple gas jet brazing
Flammenhärten n flame hardening
Flammenionisationsdetektor m flame ionization detector
Flämmhobeln n flame gouging
Flammofen m air furnace; reverberatory furnace
Flammpunkt m flash point; kindling point
Flämmputzen n deseam
Flammrohrkessel m fire-tube boiler; flue boiler
Flammstrahlen n flame deseaming; scarfing
Flansch m fixed flange; flange
flanschen border
Flanschenrohr n flange tube
Flanschstärke f restraint stress
Flanschträger m flanged beam
Flanschverbindung f flange joint
Flanschverschraubung f flanged head bolt
Flaschenbatterie f gas cylinder manifold

Flaschenbündel n battery of cylinders
Flaschengas n **(zum Schweißen)** gas in bottles (for welding)
Flaschenhalskokille f bottle top mould
Flaschenwagen m cylinder trolley
Flaschenzug m pulley block; tackle
flechten strand
Fleck m flaw
Flecken m stain
fleckig mottled
fleckiges Blech n stained sheet
flicken fettle; patch; reline; repair; revamp
Flickmasse f **(für Ofenherde)** patch
fliegend angeordnet overhung
fliegender Wechsel m flying change
fliegende Schere f flying shears
Fliehkraft f centrifugal force
Fliehkraftabscheider m centrifugal separator
Fliehkraftregler m flyball governor
Fliehkraft-Staubabscheider m centrifugal dust separator; cyclone dust collector
Fließarbeit f line assembly work
Fließband n assembly line
Fließband n belt conveyor
Fließbedingung f yield criterion
Fließbett n fluidized bed
Fließdauer f flow rate
Fließdruck m yield pressure
Fließdrücken n flow turning
Fließdruckpresse f impact extrusion press
fließen creep; flow; run; yield
Fließen n creeping
Fließfiguren fpl Lüders' lines; stretcher lines
Fließfiguren fpl **(Bleche)** flow lines; lines of stress; surface bands
Fließgeschwindigkeit f flow rate
Fließgrenze f flow limit
Fließkurve f stress strain curve
Fließofen m continuous furnace
Fließpressen n impact extrusion
Fließpressen n **(kalt)** cold extrusion
Fließpressen n **mit starrem Werkzeug** impact extrusion with rigid tool

Fließpressen *n* **mit Wirkmedien** impact extrusion with action media
Fließpressen *n* **(warm)** hot extrusion
Fließpreßgeschwindigkeit *f* extrusion rate
Fließscheide *f* no[n]slip point
Fließscheide *f* **(beim Walzen)** neutral point
Fließspan *m* flow chip
Fließspannung *f* yield stress
Fließverhalten *n* flow characteristics
Fließvermögen *n* flowability
Fließvorgang *m* continuous process; yielding; yielding phenomenon
Fließwiderstand *m* flow stress
Fließzeit *f* flow rate
Fließzeit-Meßgerät *n* flow meter
Flimmern *n* flickering
flittriges Pulver *n* flaky powder
Flocke *f* flake
Flockenausbildung *f* flocculation
Flockenbildung *f* flake formation
Flockenriß *m* flake
Floppy disk-Laufwerk *n* floppy disc drive
Flossenrohr *n* finned tube
Flotation *f* flotation
Flöz *n* bed; deposit; layer; seam; vein
Flöz *n* **nichtabbauwürdiges** unworkable bed
flüchtig volatile
flüchtige Bestandteile *mpl* volatile components; volatile matter
Fluchtlinie *f* alignment
Flugasche *f* flue ash; fly ash
Flügel *m* blade; vane
Flügelschraube *f* wing screw
Flugrost *m* initial easily removable rust
Flugstaub *m* flue dust
Fluidität *f* fluidity
Fluoreszenz-Magnetpulver-Verfahren *n* magnetic particle method
fluormetallische Verstärkungsfolie *f* fluorometallic intensifying screen
Flurfördereinrichtung *f* ground level transportation gear
Fluß *m* flow

Flußbild *n* flow diagram
flüssig fluid; liquid
flüssige Phase *f* liquid stage
flüssiger Sumpf *m* liquid crater; liquid initial bath
flüssiges Eisen *n* molten iron
flüssiges Roheisen *n* hot metal
Flüssiggas *n* liquid gas
Flüssigkeit *f* fluid; liquid
Flüssigkeitsgetriebe *n* fluid gear
Flüssigkeitsreibung *f* fluid film friction
Flußmittel *n* flux; fluxing agent
Flußmittel *npl* **für das Beizen** fluxes for pickling; galvanising
Flußsäure *f* hydrofluoric acid
Flußspat *m* fluorspar
Flußstahl *m* ingot steel
Fluxen *n* fluxing; magnetic particle testing
Fokalisierungsstrom *m* focusing current
Folgeprüfung *f* sequential analysis of variance; sequential test
Folgeregelung *f* follow-up control; program control; servo-mechanism
Folgeregler *m* cascade control [system]
folgerichtig consistent
Folgerichtigkeit *f* consistency
Folgeschneiden *n* follow-die cutting
Folgesteuerung *f* sequential control
Folgestichprobe *f* sequential sampling
Folgestichprobenverfahren *n* sequential method of sampling
Folge *f* **von Querrissen auf gezogenem Draht** broken back; cracked back
Folie *f* film; foil; leaf
Foliennahtschweißen *n* foil butt seam welding
Folienwalzwerk *n* foil rolling mill
Förderanlage *f* conveying plant; hauling installation; hauling plant
Förderband *n* belt conveyor; conveying belt; conveyor belt
Förderbandöfen *mpl* conveyor belt furnaces
Förderbrücke *f* bridge conveyor; conveying bridge

Förderer

Förderer *m* conveyor
Fördererz *n* crude ore; run-of-mine
Fördergefäß *n* carrier
Fördergerüst *n* headgear; pithead gear
Fördergestell *n* cage; hoisting cage; pallet
Fördergut *n* goods in conveying plant
Förderkasten *m* skid
Förderkette *f* conveyor chain
Förderkohle *f* green coal
Förderkorb *m* cage; skip
Förderkübel *m* skip
Fördermaschine *f* drawing engine; hoist; winding gear
Fördermenge *f* output
Fördermenge *f* **(Pumpe)** delivery
Fördermittel *n* conveying appliance
Fördermittel *npl* conveying appliance
Fördermittel *n* conveying device
Fördermittel *npl* conveying device; means of transportation
fördern convey; hoist; promote; wind
Förderschacht *m* crawing shaft; drawing shaft; hoist shaft
Förderseil *n* winding rope
Förderturm *m* head frame; pit hoist; pithead frame; winding tower
Forderung *f* debt
Forderungen *fpl* accounts receivable
Förderwagen *m* mine car; mine tram; transfer car
Form *f* mo[u]ld; shape; tuyre
Formänderung *f* deformation
Formänderungsarbeit *f* deformation work
Formänderungsfestigkeit *f* yield stress
Formänderungsverlauf *m* process of deformation
Formänderungsvermögen *n* deformability
Formänderungswiderstand *m* deformation resistance
Formänderungswirkungsgrad *m* **(beim Drahtziehen)** theoretical to actual die pull ratio
formbar ductile; plastic

Formbarkeit *f* compactibility
Formbeständigkeit *f* retention of shape; stability of shape
Formbiegen *n* form bending
Formblatt *n* form; schedule
Form *f* **(der Modellabdruck)** pattern
Formdrehen *n* form turning
formen form; mo[u]ld; shape
Formen *n* **durch Stoßwellen** explosion forming; hydrosparking
Formenrüssel *m* tuyre nozzle; tuyre snout
Formfaktor *m* **(Sphärizität)** formfactor (sphericity)
Formgebung *f* forming operation; shaping
formgerecht true to shape
Formiergas *n* forming gas
Formkoks *m* formed coke
Formling *m* blank
Formmaschine *f* moulding machine
Formmaske *f* shell mould
Form *f* **neue** new shape
Form *f* **nichtausgefüllte** short poured mould
Formpressen *n* **mit Grat** closed-die press forming with flash
Formpressen *n* **ohne Grat** closed-die press forming without flash
Formrecken *n* stretch forming
Formrundkneten *n* rotary swaging
Formrundkneten *n* **von Außenformen** rotary swaging of external shapes
Formrundkneten *n* **von Innenformen** rotary swaging of internal shapes
Formsand *m* loamy sand; moulding sand
Formschleifen *n* profile grinding
Formschlichte *f* mould wash
Formschwärze *f* black mould dressing; black wash; blacking; moulding blackening; slip blackening
Formstahl *m* section; section[al] steel; steel shape; structural shape; structural steel
Formstahl-Walzwerk *n* section [rolling] mill; shape [rolling] mill; structural [steel rolling] mill

Formstanzen *n* die forming by drawing; press die forming
Formstauchen *n* closed-die upsetting
Formstein *m* shaped brick
Formstich *m* shaping pass
Formstoff *m* moulding material
Formzahl *f* stress concentration factor
Formziehen *n* **im Gesenk** die forming by drawing
forschen search
Forschung *f* research
fortschreitendes Bördeln *n* progressive flanging
fortschreitendes Stichprobenverfahren *n* sequential analysis of variance
Fragebogen *m* questionnaire; schedule
fräsen cut; mill
Fräser *m* cutter; milling cutter
Fräsermesser *n* cutter blade
Fräsmaschine *f* milling machine
Frässpäne *mpl* millings
Fräs- und Bohrmaschine *f* milling and boring machine
Fräs- und Bohrwerk *n* milling and boring machine
freie Energie *f* **(Helmholtz)** Helmholtz free energy
freie Energie *f* **im Normalzustand** free energy in standard state
freie Enthalpie *f* **(Gibbs)** Gibbs free energy
freier Druchgang *m* clearance
freier Druchlaß *m* clearance
freies Biegen *n* free bending
freies Elektron *n* **(Leitungselektron)** free electron (conduction electron)
freies Runden *n* off-hand rounding
freie Standardreaktionsenthalpie *f* standard free energy of reaction
freie Überschußenthalpie *f* excess free energy
Freiflächenverschleiß *m* wear of top face
Freiformen *n* off-hand forming under compression conditions; open die forming

freiformgeschmiedetes (vorgeschmiedetes) Werkstück *n* pre-shaped (blocked) workpiece
Freiformschmieden *n* hammer forging; open die forging
Freiform-Schmiedestück *n* smith hammer forging
Freihandschleifen *n* offhand grinding
Freilufttransformator *m* outdoor transformer
Freistrahlbrenner *m* free jet burner
frei von systematischen Fehlern unbiased
Freiwinkel *m* clearance angle; setting angle
Fremdatom *n* foreign atom
fremdbeheizter Rekuperator *m* externally fired hot blast heater
Fremdkapital *n* borrowed capital
Fremddrechner *m* host computer
Fremdrost *n* extraneous rust; rust from external sources
Fremdschallpegel *m* external sound level
Fremdschrott *m* bought scrap; external scrap
Fremdstoff *m* **(Luftverunreinigung)** foreign substance; pollutant
Fremdstrom *m* current from external source (corrosion)
Fremdstrombezug *m* external power supply
Frequenz *f* frequency
Frequenzeinbruch *m* frequency break
Frequenzgang *m* frequency response; harmonic reponse
fressen cut; erode; gall; pit; scour; seize
Fressen *n* seizing
fressend corrosive
fressender Verschleiß *m* galling; plucking; seizing
Fressen *n* **des Ventilsitzes** scouring of the valve seat
friemeln cross roll
Friemelwalzwerk *n* reeler; reeling mill (for tubes)
frischen blow; oxidise; refine

Frischen n carbon drop; carbon elimination; oxidation
Frischerz n feed ore
Frischgas n unburnt gas
Frischgefäß n refining vessel
Frischgeschwindigkeit f rate of carbon drop; rate of carbon elimination
Frischluft f infiltrated air; primary air
Frischperiode f oxidising period; refining period
Frischschlacke f oxidising slag
Frischverlauf m progress of refining
Frischwirkung f oxidising reaction; refining action
fritten s. sintern
Frühinvalidität f early disability
Frühschicht f early shift
Fuchs m flue uptake; skimmer; stack flue; syphon; uptake
Fugazität f fugacity
Fugazitätskoeffizient m fugacity coefficient
Fügen n joining
Fügen n **durch Bördeln** joining by flanging
fühlbare Wärme f sensible heat
fühlen feel; probe
Fühler m feeler ga[u]ge; indicator; probe; sensor
fühlergesteuert tracer-controlled
Fühlhebel m feeling lever; touching lever
führen conduct; lead
Führerstand m driver's compartment
Führung f guidance; guide; management; operation; practice; working
Führung f **der Schmelze** working of the melt; working the heat
Führung f **(Maschinenteil)** guide
Führung f **(Ofen)** operation
Führungsbogen m ramp roof
Führungsbüchse f guide bush
Führung f **(Schmelze)** working
Führungsgröße f command variable; reference input
Führungskasten m guide box
Führungskratzer m guide mark; guide scar; guide scratch

Führungslänge f bearing length
Führungslänge f **(Ziehstein)** length of parallel
Führungsregler m master controller
Führungsring m driving band
Fülldichte f apparent density
Füllgewicht n fill
Füllgewicht n **(Pulvermet.)** fill
Füllhöhe f die fill
Füllkoks m bed coke
Füllmasse f filler
Füllmittel n **(Schmierung)** extreme pressure additive
Füllraum m filling space
Füllrumpf m bin; hopper
Füllstandsregelung f control of level in a bin
Füllstein m filling brick
Füllstellung f **für flüssiges Roheisen** charging position for molten pig iron
Füllstellung f **für Kalk** charging position for lime
Füllstoff m filler
Fülltrichter m feed hopper
Füllvolumen n filling volume
Füllwagen m charging car; charging larry; larry [car]
füttern bush

G

Gabel f fork; shank
Gabelpfanne f bull ladle; shank ladle
Gabelprobe f fork-test bar
Gabelstapler m fork lift truck; fork piler
Gallkette f plate link chain
Gallsche Gelenkkette f Gall's chain
Galmei m calamine
galvanische Kette f galvanic cell
galvanische Korrosion f galvanic corrosion
galvanisches Element n galvanic cell
galvanisches Überziehen n electrocoating
galvanisieren galvanise

galvanostatische Impulsmethode f galvanostatic pulse method
Gamma-Eisen n gamma iron
Gamma-Mischkristall m gamma solid solution
Gang m course; seam; vein
Gangart f gangue; tailings
Gangartentfernung f removal of gangue
Gang m **(des Hochofens)** course; passage; path running; working; run; vein; working
gangförmiges Vorkommen n occurence in veins
Ganghöhe f **(Steigung)** lead
Gangspalte f fault; fissure; vein; vein fissure
ganzbasisch all basic
ganze Zahl f integer
Ganzwölber m **(ff. Stein)** end arch; wedge brick
garen refine
Garnitur f lining
Garschaum m kish
Garschaumgraphit m kish graphite
Garungsdauer f carbonising period; carbonising time
Garungszeit f coking time
Gas n gas
Gasabfang m down-comer
Gasabscheider m gas separator
Gasabzug m down-comer; gas flue; gas off-take
Gasanalyse f gas analysis
Gasanreicherung f enrichment of gas
Gasarmaturen fpl gas pipeline accessories and fittings
Gas n **(auf einen Ofen) geben** (= anheizen)
Gasaufkohlungsofen m gas carburising furnace
Gasaufnahme f gas pick-up
Gasauslaßventil n bleeder valve
Gasausnutzung f degree of chemical utilisation of gas
Gasaustritt m **aus den Koksöfen** discharge (or: release) of gas from the coke ovens

Gasbehälter m gas holder; gasometer
gasbeheizter Schmiedeofen m gas [fired] furnace
Gasbeheizung f gas firing
Gasbeizen n gas pickling
Gasblase f blow hole; gas bubble; pin hole
Gasbrenner m blower; gas burner; gas jet; gas port
Gascarbonitrieren n gas carbonitriding
gasdicht gas-tight
Gasdichtemesser m effusiometer; gas density ga[u]ge
Gasdurchlässigkeit f gas permeability; permeability to gas; porosity
Gasdüse f gas jet; gas tuyre
Gase npl **im Stahl** occluded gases
Gaseinsatzhärtung f gas carburising
Gaseinschluß m blow hole; gaseous inclusion; occlusion
Gasentwicklung f development of gas
Gaserzeuger m gas producer
Gasfang m down-comer; gas offtake
Gasfanghaube f gas collecting hood
Gasgenerator m gas producer
Gasglocke f gas bell; gas holder
Gasheizkammer f gas regenerator chamber
Gaskammer f gas chamber
Gaskanal m gas duct; gas flue
Gaskohle f bituminous coal; gas coal
Gaskoks m gas coke
Gaskompressor m gas compressor
Gaskühlanlage f gas cooling plant
Gaskühler m gas cooler
Gaskühlung f gas cooling
Gasleitung f gas conduit; gas line; gas pipe; gas pipeline
Gasmangel m deficiency of gas; lack of gas
Gasmaschinenzentrale f gas engine power house
Gasmaske f breather (am.); gas mask
Gasnitrieren n dry nitriding; gas nitriding
Gasofen m gas furnace
Gasometer m gasometer

Gasphase f gas phase
Gasprobe-Entnahmevorrichtung f gas sampling device
Gasprüfer m gas detector
Gasreduktion f gas-type reduction
Gasreinigung f gas cleaning; gas purification
Gasreinigungsanlage f gas cleaning plant; gas purifying plant
Gasrohr n gas pipe
Gasröstofen m **(Erze)** gas-fired calcining kiln
Gassammelbehälter m gas holder
Gassammelleitung f **(Vorlage)** gas collecting main
Gassauger m gas aspirator; gas extractor
Gasschlauch m gas hose
Gasschleuse f gas seal
Gasschmelzschweißung f gas [fusion] welding; oxacetylene welding
Gasschneiden n gas cutting
Gasschweißen n torch welding
Gasspaltung f gas cracking; gas reforming
Gasspürer m gas detector
Gas n **starkes** rich gas
Gasstocher m gas poker
Gastrennanlage f gas separating plant
Gastrocknung f gas drying
Gasumsetzer m gas reformer
Gasventil n gas valve
Gasverarbeitungsanlage f gas processing plant
Gasverbundnetz n interlinked gas grid system
gasvolumetrisch gasometric
Gaswäscher m gas scrubber
Gaswasserbeseitigung f gas water removal
Gaszähler m gas meter
Gaszementieren n gas carburising
Gaszufuhr f gas pipe
gattieren burden; calculate the burden
Gattieren n making the mixture
Gattierung f burden calculation

gebeizt (zu stark) over-pickled
Geber m transmitter
Gebläse n blast; blower; blowing engine; fan; ventilator
Gebläsedruck m blast pressure
Gebläsehaus n blast engine house; blower house; blowing engine house
Gebläseluft f blast
Gebläselufthärten n air-blast quenching
Gebläsemaschine f blast engine; blower; blowing engine
gebläutes Blech n blued plate
gebogene Kokille f curved mould
gebogener Stahlring m bent steel ring
gebogener Träger m cambered girder
gebogenes Blech n buckled sheet
gebrannt burnt
gebrannter Kalk m burnt lime; quicklime
gebrannter Ton m grog
Gebrauch m appliance
Gebrauchsmuster n registered design; registered pattern; utility patent
Gebrauchsspannung f working stress
gebundener Kohlenstoff m combined carbon; fixed carbon
gebundener Rang m tied rank
gedämpfter Hochofen m banked blast furnace; damped-down blast furnace
gedämpfter Luftraum m attenuated air space
Gedinge n bargain; contract
Gedingearbeit f piece work
gedreht (Oberflächenzustand) finish as turned; turned finish
gedrungenes Oval n flat sided oval
geeignet machen render suitable
Gefälle n drop; gradient; inclination; slope
gefälltes Pulver n precipitated powder
Gefäß n bucket; receiver; receptacle; vessel
gefederte Matrize f floating die
gefrieren freeze; refrigerate

Gefrierpunkt *m* freezing point
Gefüge *n* microstructure; structure; texture
Gefügebild *n* micrograph
Gefügegrundmasse *f* matrix
Gefügerichtreihe *f* series of reference diagrams; structure rating chart
Gefügeumwandlung *f* structural transformation
Gefügeunterschied *m* structural difference
gegen den Uhrzeigersinn *m* counterclockwise
Gegendrall *m* back twist
Gegendruckturbine *f* back-pressure turbine
Gegenelektrode *f* counter electrode
Gegenführung *f* steady
Gegengewicht *n* balance weight; counterweight
Gegenhalter *m* overarm
Gegenhalter *m* **(beim Nieten)** dolly bar
Gegenhalter *m* **(Fräsmaschine)** overarm
Gegenkopplung *f* inverse feedback; negative feedback
Gegenkraft *f* reacting force
Gegenlauffräsen *n* conventional milling; upcut milling; upmilling
gegenläufig moving in opposite directions
Gegenläufigkeit *f* contra effect
Gegenpol *m* opposite pole
Gegenprobe *f* check test
Gegenschlaghammer *m* counterblow hammer
gegenseitiges Ausweichen *n* mutual repulsion
gegensinniger Kurvenverlauf *m* negative correlation
Gegensprechanlage *f* intercom [system]
Gegenstand *m* item; object; subject
Gegenstrom *m* counterflow
Gegenstrom-Wärmeaustauscher *m* counter-current heat exchanger; counterflow heat exchanger

Gegentakt *m* push pull
Gegenwirkung *f* contra effect
Gegenzug *m* back pull
Gegenzugziehen *n* draw with back pull; draw with back tension
gegliederte Unterlagen *fpl* ranked data
geglüht annealed
geglühtes Pulver *n* annealed powder
geglüht und gehärtet oberhalb des Umwandlungsbereiches *m* supercritically annealed and quenched
geglüht vom Lieferanten mill annealed
gegossener Glühtopf *m* cast annealing pot
gegossener Rohling *m* cast blank; casting
Gehalt *m* concentration; content
Gehalt *n* salary
Gehalt *m* yield
Gehaltsempfänger *m* salary earner
gehäufter Wert *m* cumulant; cumulative value
Gehäuse *n* box; cage; case; casing; housing; shell
geheizter Tiefofen *m* live [soaking] pit
Gehörschädigung *f* hearing impairment
Gehörschutz *m* ear protection
Gehörüberwachung *f* audio monitoring
geknicktes Blech *n* buckled sheet
gekörnte Schlacke *f* granulated slag
Gekrätz *n* dross; refuse
gekreuzte Nicols *pl* crossed nicols
gekröpfte Kurbelwelle *f* crankshaft
gekrümmt curvilinear
gekümpelter Kesselboden *m* dished head
Gelenk *n* articulation; hinge; joint; knuckle; link
Gelenkbandprofil *n* hinge profile
Gelenk-Scharnier *n* hinge
Gelenkspindel *f* articulated spindle
Gelenkspindel-Bohrmaschine *f* multiple drill pass
gelenkte Erstarrung *f* controlled directional solidification

gelenkte Oxidation *f* controlled oxidation
gelochtes Blech *n* perforated plate
gelockerte Stelle *f* **(Gefüge)** discontinuity
gelöschter Kalk *m* slaked lime
gemahlene Schamotte *f* grog
gemahlenes Pulver *n* ground powder; milled powder
gemauerte Pfanne *f* brick lined ladle
Gemeinkosten *pl* burden overhead cost; expense; general expense; overhead cost
gemeinsam common
gemeinsamer Markt *m* Common Market
gemeinsames Ziehen *n* combined drawing
Gemeinschaftsforschung *f* cooperative research
Gemenge *n* batch
Gemisch *n* mixture
gemischte Logik *f* mixed logic
gemischtes Hüttenwerk *n* integrated iron and steel plant
gemustertes Blech *n* pattern sheet
genau close; exact; precise
genaues Aufeinanderlegen *n* **von Blechen (vor dem Glühen)** sheet sweep
Genauguß *m* investment casting
Genauigkeit *f* accuracy; precision
genau prüfen scan
Genauschmieden *n* precision forging
Genehmigungsdatum *n* **(Patent)** date granted
geneigt inclined; oblique
geneigter Flansch *m* sloping flange
geneigter Hochofen *m* down-comer
Generaldirektion *f* head office
Generatorblech s. Elektroblech
Generatorgas *n* producer gas
Generator *m* **(Gas)** producer
Generatorkohle *f* producer coal
genormt standardised
geöffneter Formkasten *m* open moulding box
Geologie *f* geology

geologisches Untersuchungsverfahren *n* geological research procedure
geometrisches Mittel *n* geometric mean
Geophysik *f* geophysics
geprägtes Blech *n* embossed sheet
gepunktete Kurve *f* dotted line
gerade straight
Geradeausziehmaschine *f* straight line drawing machine
gerade Länge *f* **(Draht)** length
geraderichten straighten
gerade vom Ring *m* **ablaufend** straight cast
Geradheit *f* straightness
geradkettig **(Moleküle)** straight chained
Geradverzahnung *f* straight tooth bevels
gerändelte Kante *f* milled edge
Gerät *n* apparatus; device; appliance; device
Gerätekonfiguration *f* **(EDV)** hardware configuration
Geräuschdämpfung *f* soundproofing
Geräuschgrundpegel *m* background noise
Geräuschpegel *m* noise level
Geräuschspektrum *n* frequency analysis
geregelte Atmosphäre *f* controlled atmosphere
gerichtete Erstarrung *f* directional solidification
gerichtetes Blech *n* flat sheet
gerinnen coagulate; congeal
Gerinnen *n* congealing
gerippt ribbed; ripped
Geröll *n* boulder; bowlder
geronnene Masse *f* congelation
geröstetes Eisenerz *n* roasted iron ore
Geruchsbelästigung *f* nuisance from odours; obnoxious odour
Gerüst *n* frame; scaffold; stand; trestle
Gerüst *n* **(Baugerüst)** staging
Gesamteisenbestimmung *f* determi-

gesetzlich geschützter Name

nation of total iron
Gesamtentkohlung f complete decarburisation
Gesamtgewicht n total weight
Gesamtkohlenstoff m total carbon
Gesamtkonzeption n integrated system
Gesamtlebensdauer f fatigue limit
Gesamtpräzision f **(Probenahme)** overall precision
Gesamtprobe f total specimen
Gesamtquerschnittsabnahme f overall reduction
Gesamtschallpegel m overall noise
Gesamtschneiden n combination blanking and piercing
Gesamtstrahlungspyrometer n ardometer; rayotube pyrometer; total radiation pyrometer
Gesamtverfügbarkeit f **(EDV)** total reliability
Geschäftsbericht m annual report
Geschäftsleitung f company management
geschliffen ground
geschliffener Stab m ground bar
geschliffener Zustand m ground finish
geschlossener Formkasten m closed moulding box
geschlossener Walzenständer m closed top type housing; housing of the close top type
geschlossenes Gleitlager n sleeve bearing; slide bearing
geschlossenes Kaliber n box groove; box hole; closed pass
geschlossenes Spiralseil n locked coil rope
geschlossenes Stauchkaliber n tongue and groove pass
Geschmeidigkeit f ductility
geschnittene Kante f cut edge; sheared edge
geschnittene Länge f cut length
geschränkt offset
geschützter Schwinger m **(Ultraschallprüfung)** protected crystal
geschweißter Behälter m welded container

geschweißter Stoß m welded joint
geschweißtes Rohr n welded pipe
geschweißte Stumpfnaht f welded butt joint
Geschwindigkeit f rate; speed; velocity
Geschwindigkeitskonstante f rate constant
Geschwindigkeitspotential n velocity potential
Gesenk n boss; die [block]; steel die; swage
Gesenkbiegen n die bending
Gesenkbördeln n die flanging
Gesenkdrücken n die squeezing
Gesenkformen n die forming
Gesenkformen n **mit ganz umschlossenem Werkstück** closed-die forming
Gesenkformen n **mit teilweise geschlossenem Werkstück** die forming with partly enclosed work
Gesenkhammer m swaging hammer
Gesenkmatrize f hob
Gesenk n **mit gebrochener Teilfuge** lock die
Gesenkrichten n die straightening
Gesenkrinne f **zur Aufnahme des Grates** gutter
Gesenkrunden n radial die forming
Gesenkschmieden n die forging; drop forging; swaging
Gesenkschmiedepresse f drop forging press
Gesenkschmiederohling m dummy
Gesenkschmiedestahl m drop forging die steel
Gesenkschmiedestück n die formed part; drop forging; swaged forging
Gesenkschmiede- und Kalibrierpresse f forging and sizing press
Gesenksicken n die beading
Gesenkstauchen n die upsetting
Gesenkziehen n die forming by drawing
Gesetzgebung f **zur Reinhaltung der Luft** clean air regulations
gesetzlich geschützter Name m registered name; trade mark

gesichert significant
gesicherte Dezimalstelle f significant digit
gespaltene Enden npl split ends
Gespann n bottom plate
Gespannguß m group casting
Gespann-Mauermasse f bottom pouring masonry mixture
Gespannplatte f bottom casting; bottom pouring plate; group teeming bottom plate; group teeming stool (am.); stool for bottom casting
gesprenkelt mottled
gestaffelt arranged in steps; staggered
gestaffelte Walzstraße f staggered roll[ing] train
Gestalt f profile; shape
gestalten form; shape
Gestaltfestigkeit f strength depending on design; strength depending on shape
Gestaltung f design; forming; shaping
Gestaltungskurve f design curve
gestampfter Boden m rammed bottom; tamped bottom
Gestänge n linkage of bars
Gestängerohr n drill pipe
gestanztes Loch n punched hole
Gestehungskosten pl original cost; prime cost
Gesteinsbohrer m rock drill
Gesteinsbohrstahl m mining drill steel
Gestein n **taubes** barren gangue
Gestell n chassis; cradle; well; frame; hearth; rack; trestle; well
Gestellbelastung f hearth load
Gestelldurchbruch m break out
Gestellpanzer m hearth casing; hearth jacket
gesteuerte Kühlung f controlled cooling
gestopftes Windloch n blind tuyre
gestörtes Gefüge n disturbed structure
gestrichelte Kurve f dashed line
gestrichelte Linie f **(Kurve)** broken line (curve)

gestuftes Abschrecken n step quenching
gestuftes Warmauslagern n progressive ageing
gestutzt (Statistik) truncated
gesund sound
geteilte Matrize f split die
geteiltes Kaliber n knife pass
Getriebe n drive; driving gear; gear[ing]
Getriebemotor m geared motor
Getriebestufe f gear speed
Getter m getter
Gewährleistungsumfang m guarantee range
Gewaltbruch m spontaneous fracture
gewalzter Durchmesser m **des Walzgutes** rolled diameter of stock
Gewebedraht m fabric wire
gewellte Kokille f corrugated mould
Gewerbeaufsichtsamt n industry control office
Gewerbehygiene f industrial hygiene
Gewerbemüll m industrial garbage
gewerblicher Rechtsschutz m industrial legal protection
Gewerkschaft f trade union; union
Gewicht n weight
Gewichtsabweichung f discrepancy in weight; weight deviation
gewichtsanalytisch gravimetric
Gewichtung f weighting
Gewinde n screw-thread; thread
Gewindebohren n tapping
Gewindebohrer m screw tap; tap
Gewindebolzen m threaded pin
Gewindedrücken n thread rolling; thread spinning
Gewindeflansch m screwed flange
Gewindefurchen n thread grooving
Gewindegrund m root
Gewindekupplung f threaded coupling
Gewinderohr n threaded pipe
Gewinderollen n flat-die thread rolling
Gewindeschneiden n thread cutting
Gewindeschneiden n **(außen)** threading
Gewindeschneiden n **(innen)** tapping

Gewindeschneider m chaser; tap
Gewindeschneidmaschine f screwing machine
Gewindeschneidwerkzeug n screw cutting tool
Gewindespitze f crest
Gewindestahl m chaser
Gewindestange f threaded rod
Gewindesteigung f screw pitch
Gewindestift m grub screw; headless screw
Gewindewalzen n round die thread rolling
Gewindewalzen n im Durchlaufverfahren thread rolling by the throughfeed method
Gewindewalzen n im Einstechverfahren thread rolling by the plungecut method
Gewindewalzmaschine f thread rolling machine
Gewinn m profit
Gewinnanteil m bonus
Gewinnbeteiligung f profit sharing
gewinnen exploit; win
Gewinnspanne f margin
Gewinn- und Verlustkonten npl profit and loss accounts
Gewinnung f im Tagebau mining by open-cast method; open-cut mining
Gewinnung f im Tiefbau mining by deep level workings
Gewinnung f unter Tage underground winning
gewogenes Mittel n weighted average; weighted mean
gewöhnlich ordinary; straight
Gewölbe n arch; arched roof; roof
Gewölbeausschnitt m roof portion
Gewölbebogen m arch; sprung arch
Gewölbehaltbarkeit f life of arched roof; roof life
Gewölbelängsschub m longitudinal thrust of the roof
Gewölbe n mit beweglichem Widerlager sprung type roof
Gewölbe n mit festem Widerlager roof with fixed skewback

Gewölbenase f wall arch nose
Gewölbeniederhalter m holding down member (open hearth furnace)
Gewölbescharen fpl arch rings
Gewölbeschub m thrust of roof
Gewölbestein m roof brick
Gewölbestich m rise of crown; rise of the crown; roof rise
Gewölbeteil f portion of the roof
Gewölbezwickel m wall arch nose
gewölbter Kesselboden m dished head
gewölbter Tiefofendeckel m arched soaking pit lid
gewölbtes Band n full strip
gezogener Stabstahl m drawn steel bar
Gicht f batch; burden charge; furnace throat; furnace top; throat; top
Gichtbrücke f **(Hochofen)** skip bridge
Gichtbühne f charging platform; top platform
Gichtdurchmesser m stack diameter; throat diameter
Gichtenfolge f charging sequence; cycle of charges
Gichtgas n blast-furnace gas; top gas
Gichtgasabzug m downtake
Gichtgasabzugsrohr n downcomer
Gichtgasfackel f excess blast-furnace gas burner; furnace bleeder; surplus blast-furnace gas burner
Gichtgasgebläse n blast furnace gas-driven blowing engine
Gichtgasleitung f blast furnace gas main; top gas main
Gichtgasrückführung f recycling of top gas
Gichtgegendruck m hight top ressure
Gichtglocke f furnace top bell; stopper bell
Gichtkübel m charging basket (am.); charging bucket (am.); receiving hopper; skip
Gicht f **(Möller)** charge
Gichtöffnung f furnace throat; furnace top; throat opening
Gichtschlamm m washing tower sludge

Gichtsonde f charge level [indicator]; indicator; stock level [indicator]; stock line ga[u]ge; stock line recorder

Gichtstaub m blast furnace flue dust; flue dust; throat dust

Gichtstaubbrikettierungsanlage f flue dust briquetting plant

Gichttrichter m furnace top hopper; receiving hopper

Gichtverschluß m bell and hopper [arrangement]; blast furnace top closing device; closing device; cup and cone arrangement; throat stopper

Gichtverschluß m durch Tellerventile valve seal-type top-charging

Gießader f strand

Gießaufsatz m dozzle; feeder; hot top; sinkhead

Gießbühne f pouring platform; teeming platform

gießen bottom pour; cast; cast up-hill; teem; teem direct; top pour; top-cast

Gießen n casting

Gießen n mit verlorener Gießform investment casting

Gießer m caster; casting pit operative; founder; foundryman

Gießerei f foundry

Gießereianlagen und -einrichtungen fpl foundry plants and equipments

Gießereibedarf m foundry materials

Gießereierzeugnis n foundry product

Gießereihilfsstoff m foundry auxiliary material

Gießereikoks m foundry coke

Gießereikran m foundry crane

Gießereiroheisen n foundry pig iron

Gießfehler m casting defect

Gießform f mo[u]ld

Gießgeschwindigkeit f casting speed; teeming rate

Gießgrube f casting pit; open pit

Gießhalle f casting bay; pouring bay

Gießkelle f casting ladle

Gießkolonne f casting team

Gießkopf m feeder head; hot top; runner head; shrink head; sinkhead

Gießkran m casting crane; pouring crane

Gießloch n jet

Gießlöffel m casting ladle; shank

Gießmaschine f casting machine

Gießpfanne f casting ladle; pouring ladle; shank; teeming ladle

Gießpfannenschnabel m pouring ladle lip

Gießplatte f casting plate

Gießplatz m casting pit

Gießpreßschweißen n molten metal pressure welding; pressure thermit welding

Gießpulver n casting flux

Gießrinne f jet; launder; pouring spout; runner

Gießschmelzschweißen n non-pressure thermit welding

Gießschnauze f pouring lip

Gießschweißen n cast welding

Gießspiegel m liquid metal level [in mould]; meniscus; surface of metal (in a mould)

Gießspiegelmeßsystem n molten level measurement system

Gießspiegelregelung f mould level control

Gießspirale f spiral [mould]

Gießstelle f casting pit

Gießstopfen m ladle stopper

Gießstrahlbehandlung f pouring stream treatment

Gießsturz m mold

Gießtrichter m bell; centre riser; centre runner; down-gate; git; pouring gate; sprue; trumpet

Gießtrommel f casting drum

Gießwagen m casting bogie; casting car; pouring car

Gießwalzen n direct strand reduction

Gießwanne f tundish

Gießwellen fpl reciprocation marks

Gift n poison

giftig poisonous

Gips m gypsum; plaster

Gipsabgußverfahren n plaster casting method

Gitter *n* grating; grid
Gitter *npl* interpenetrating lattices
Gitter *n* lattice; trellis
Gitterbaufehler *m* lattice defect
Gitterdraht *m* fence wire
Gitterfachwerk *n* framed structure
Gitterfehlstelle *f* vacant site in lattice
Gitterheizfläche *f* checker heating surface
Gitterhohlstein *m* hollow checker brick
Gitterkammer *f* checker chamber
Gitterleerstelle *f* lattice vacant site
Gittermast *m* girder pole; lattice mast; latticed girder pole
Gitterpackung *f* checkerwork
Gitterpunkt *m* grid point
Gitterrost *m* lattice grate
Gitterschweißmaschine *f* grid welding machine
Gitterspektrometer *n* grating spectrograph
Gitterstein *m* checker brick
Gitterstörung *f* lattice defect; lattice distortion
Gitterstruktur *f* lattice structure
Gitterumwandlung *f* lattice transformation
Gitterwerk *n* checker work; checkers
Glanz *m* gloss
Glanzblech *n* bright [polished] sheet
Glanzeisenstein *m* oligiste iron ore
Glanzkohle *f* anthracite; coal
Glanzverchromen *n* burnished chroming
Glaseinschmelzdraht *m* sealing wire
Glasfaserfilter *m* glass fiber filter
glashart glass hard
glasieren glaze
glasige Schlacke *f* vitreous slag
glasig werden vitrify
Glaskopf *m* **(Roteisenstein)** kidney ore
Glasschmierung *f* glass lubrication
Glasur *f* glaze; glazing
Glattdrücken *n* planishing
glätten burnish; planish; polish; reel; smooth
Glätten *n* flattening (of sheets); passing; patent flattening; skin
Glattendrohr *n* plain end tube
Glätten *n* **(von Feinblech)** skin passing
glattes Gewölbe *n* plain roof
glatte Walze *f* plain roll
Glattprägen *n* compression surface finishing; smooth
Glattschachtgitter *n* chimney type checkers
Glättungstiefe *f* peak to mean line height
Glattwalze *f* plain roll; smooth roll
Glattwalzen *n* **im Einstechverfahren** finish rolling by the infeed method
Glattwalzen *n* **von Rohren im Durchlaufverfahren** reeling of tubes by the through-feed method
Glattwalzen *n* **von Stäben im Durchlaufverfahren** finish rolling of bar stock by the through-feed method
Glättwalzwerk *n* reeler; reeling mill; smoothing rolls
gleichartig homogeneous
Gleichartigkeit *f* homogeneity
gleichbleibend constant
gleichgerichtet unidirected
gleichgerichtete Kristalle *mpl* equiaxed crystals
Gleichgewicht *n* balance; equilibrium
Gleichgewichtseinstellung *f* obtaining of equilibrium
Gleichgewichtskennzahl *f* equilibrium index
Gleichgewichtskonstante *f* equilibrium constant
Gleichgewichtsschaubild *n* equilibrium diagram
Gleichgewichtstemperatur *f* equilibrium temperature
Gleichgewichtswert *m* equilibrium value
Gleichgewichtszustand *m* equilibrium
Gleichheitsprüfung *f* parity check
Gleichlauf *m* synchronism
Gleichlauffräsen *n* downcut milling
Gleichmaßdehnung *f* elongation without necking; uniform elongation
gleichmäßig homogeneous

gleichmäßiger Angriff *m* uniform attack
Gleichmäßigkeit *f* uniformity
Gleichrichter *m* electric rectifier
gleichschenkliger rundkantiger Winkelstahl *m* round edge equal angles
gleichschenkliger scharftkantiger Winkelstahl *m* square edge equal angles
gleichschenkliger Winkel *m* equal-leg angle
gleichschenkliges Dreieck *n* isosceles triangle
Gleichschlagseil *n* Lang's lay rope
Gleichschrittöfen *mpl* double walking beam furnaces
Gleichstrom *m* direct current (D.C.)
Gleichstrommotor *m* D. C. motor; direct current motor
Gleichstrom-Plasmabogen-Generator *m* direct-current arc plasma jet excitation source
Gleichstromschweißmaschine *f* DC-welding machine
Gleichstromschweißverfahren *n* DC-welding techniques
Gleichung *f* equation
Gleichversuch *m* comparative test
Gleichwertigkeitskoeffizient *m* equivalence coefficient
gleichzeitig simultaneous
Gleis *n* trace; track
Gleisanlage *f* railway track
Gleisbau *m* plate-laying
Gleisbaumaschine *f* track laying machine
Gleisbremsanlage *f* rail brake
gleisgebunden railmounted; trackbound
Gleisrad *n* runner
Gleiswaage *f* wagon weighbridge
Gleitachslager *n* plain axle bearing
Gleitbahn *f* pallet; slide
Gleitbonderflüssigkeit *f* anti-friction bonderising bath
Gleitebene *f* sliding plane
gleiten glide; slide; slip
gleitender Durchschnitt *m* moving average
Gleitfeder *f* sliding feather key
gleitfester Typ *m* friction-grip type
Gleitfläche *f* pallet; slide
Gleitkufe *f* landing skid
Gleitlager *n* plain bearing; sleeve bearing
Gleitlinie *f* slip line
Gleitlinienstreifen *m* slip band
Gleitlinientheorie *f* slip line theory
gleitloses Ziehen *n* non slip drawing
Gleitmittel *n* lubricant; sliding agent
Gleitmodul *m* modulus of elasticity; shear modulus
Gleitreibung *f* sliding friction
Gleitrohr *n* skid pipe
Gleitschiene *f* pellet slide bar; skid [rail]
Gleitschuh *m* sliding shoe
Gleitsystem *n* slip system
Gleitverlust *m* frictional loss
Gleitwiderstand *m* resistance to slip
Gleitziehbiegen *n* form bending by a sliding-action draw
Gleitziehen *n* drawing (by a sliding action); slip-type drawing
Glied *n* element; link; term
Gliederkaltstrang *m* articulated dummy bar; chain type dummy bar
glimmen glow
Glimmentladung *f* glow discharge
Glimmnitrieren *n* glow nitriding
Globularkristall *m* equiaxed crystal
globulitische Kernzone *f* equiaxed crystal core zone
globulitische Randzone *f* chill crystal zone
Glocke *f* bell
Glockenkurve *f* **(Gaußsche)** bell-shaped curve
Glühanlage *f* annealing plant
Glühbehälter *m* annealing box
Glühdauer *f* annealing time
glühen anneal; calcine; glow; normalise
Glühen *n* annealing; flash annealing
Glühen *n* **auf kugeligen Zementit (GKZ)** spheroidising

Glühen *n* **zwischen zwei Zügen (Kaltziehen)** inter-pass annealing
Glühfaden-Pyrometer *n* disappearing filament optical pyrometer (D.F.)
Glühfarbe *f* temper colour
Glühfehler *m* defect arising in annealing (ingots)
Glühfestigkeit *f* annealed tensile strength; as annealed tensile strength
glühfrischen malleablize by graphitisation
Glühhaube *f* annealing bell; annealing hood
Glühkiste *f* annealing box
Glühlampe *f* bulb
Glühmuffel *f* annealing muffle
Glühofen *m* annealing furnace
Glührand *m* **(Bandfehler)** annealed stained edge; black edge; snaky edge
Glührohr *n* annealing tube
Glührückstand *m* ignition residue
Glühtopf *m* annealing pot
Glühverlust *m* ignition loss
Glühzunder *m* mill scale
Glühzyklus *m* heat cycle
Glut *f* glow
Göpel *m* drawing engine; winch
Graben *m* ditch; trench
Grad *m* degree
Gradeinteilung *f* graduation; scale
Granatenstahl *m* shell steel
Granulat *n* granulated material
Granulationsanlage *f* granulating plant
Granulierrinne *f* granulating spout
granulierte Schlacke *f* granulated slag
Graph *m* graph
graphische Darstellung *f* graphical representation; plot
Graphit *m* graphite; plumbago
Graphitelektrode *f* graphite electrode
graphitisch graphitic
Graphitisierung *f* graphitisation
Graphitknötchen *n* graphite nodule
Graphitkohle *f* graphitic carbon
Graphitkohlenstoff *m* graphitic carbon

Graphitlager *n* graphite bearing
Graphitstabofen *m* graphite rod furnace
Grat *m* burr; fin; flash
Gratrippe *f* fin
Gratriß *m* fin crack
Grat *m* **(überwalzt oder überschmiedet)** cold lap
graues Roheisen *n* grey pig
Grauguß *m* grey [cast] iron
Grauguß s. **Gußeisen mit Lamellengraphit**
gravieren engrave
Gravieren *n* die sinking
Gravur *f* cut; cut [in a die]; impression [of finished drop forging]
Greifbagger *m* drag-line excavator
greifen bite; grip; seize
Greifer *m* grab [bucket]; grapple bucket
Greiferbrücke *f* chain gripper bar
Greiferkran *m* grab crane
Greifkanter *m* **(Walzen)** grip type tilter
Greifvorrichtung *f* catcher
Greifwinkel *m* **(Walze)** angle of bite; angle of contact
Greifzange *f* gripping tongs
Grenze *f* limit
Grenzfall *m* extreme case
Grenzfläche *f* interface
Grenzflächenreibung *f* boundary friction
Grenzflächenspannung *f* interfacial tension
Grenzformänderungskurve *f* forming limit curve
Grenzmaß *n* limiting size
Grenzmerkmal *n* limiting characteristic value
Grenzpackdichte *f* limiting density
Grenzreibung *f* boundary friction
Grenzschicht *f* boundary layer
Grenzschichtdicke *f* thickness of boundary layer
Grenzschmierung *f* boundary lubrication; thin film lubrication
Grenzwert *m* threshold value
Grenzwertsatz *m* **(Statistik)** central limiting value theorem

Grenzziehverhältnis n limiting drawing ratio
Grieß m gravel; grit
Griff m **(am Gesenkschmiedestück)** sprue
Griffstelle f point of contact
grob coarse
Grobätzung f macro-etching
Grobblech n heavy plate; plate
Grobblech-Walzwerk n plate [rolling] mill
Grobbrecher m boulder crusher
Grobeinstellung f rough adjustment
Grobentstaubung f preliminary dust extraction
Grobgut n oversized material
Grobkorn n coarse grain; open grain
Grobkornanfälligkeit f susceptibility to grain coarsening
Grobkornglühen n coarse grain annealing
grobkörniger Stahl m coarse-grained steel
Grobkornstahl m coarse grain steel
Grobpore f macropore
Grobpulver n coarse powder
Grobreinigung f primary cleaning
Grobstraße f rolling train for heavy products
Grob- und Feinkokssieberei f screening of lump coal and culm
Grobvakuum-Elektronenstrahlschweißen n vacuum electron beam welding
Grobwalzwerk n blooming mill
Grobzerkleinerung f coarse breaking; coarse crushing; coarse grinding
Grobzug m coarse draft; coarse drafting
Größe f quantity; size; variable
Größe f **(EDV)** datum (pl.: data)
Größenfaktor m size factor
Größenklassierung f classification by dimensions
Größenordnung f order of magnitude
Größenprobe f size sample
Größenverteilung f size distribution
Großkesselanlage f large boiler plant

Großprobe f gross sample
Großraumheizung f central heating of large rooms
Großraum-Tiefofen m large compartment soaking pit
großtechnisch commercial; industrial
Großversuch m large-scale production trial
Großwinkelkorngrenzen fpl high angle tilt boundaries
Großzahlauswertung f statistical interpretation
Großzahlforschung f frequency research
Großzugversuch m wide-plate test
Grübchen n pit
Grübchenbildung f pitting
Grübchenbruch m dimpled fracture
Grübchen n **(Oberflächenfehler)** steel pit
Grube f coal mine; colliery; pit trench; trench; underground level
Grubenausbaustahl m colliery arches
Grubenbahn f pit railway
Grubenbau m underground winning
Grubenglühen n pit annealing
Grube f **(Untertagebau)** underground level
Grube f **unter Wasser setzen** flood a mine with water
Grundanstrich m priming coat
Grundbeschichtung f priming coat
Grundbesitz m real estate
Grunddrehzahl f **(Walzwerk)** base speed of mill
Grundfläche f base
Grundgesamtheit f parent population; population
Grundierung f primer
Grundlage f base; basic principle
Grundlinie f base
Grundlohn m basic wage rate
Grundmasse f matrix
Grundmetall n base metal; parent metal
Grundnahtfehler m root-bead defect
Grundplatte f base-plate; bed-plate; ground-plate

Grundrichtung f trend
Grundriß m plan view
Grundschaltzeichen n general symbol
Grundsorte f basic type
Grundstahl m base steel
Grundstoff m base material; elementary substance
Grundstoffindustrie f primary industry
Gründung f foundation
Grundverknüpfung f logical connective
Grundwasser n subterranean water
Grundwerkstoff m base material; parent material
Grünfestigkeit f green strength
Grünling m green compact
Grünpellet n green ball; green pellet
Grünsand m green sand
Grünsandkern m green sand core
Gruppenarbeit f team work
Gruppenbildung f grouping
Gruppierung f grouping
Grusofen m breeze oven
gültig valid
Gummi n rubber
Gummidichtung f rubber gasket
gummigefederte Räder npl rubber spring wheels; wheels with spring action by rubber
Gummischlauch m rubber hose
Gummitreibriemen m rubber drive belt
Gurt m belt
Gurtförderer m belt conveyor
Guß m cast; casting; pouring; tap
Gußblase f blow hole
Gußblock m **mit flüssigem Kern** bled ingot
Gußbruch m broken castings; cast-iron scrap
Gußeisen n cast iron
Gußeisen n **mit Kugelgraphit** ductile cast iron; nodular [graphite] cast iron; spheroidal graphite cast iron
Gußeisen n **mit Lamellengraphit** grey cast iron
Gußeisen n **mit Stahlschrottzusatz** semi-steel

Gußeisen n **mit Zwischenstufengefüge** acicular cast iron
gußeiserne Formstücke npl iron castings
Guß m **gehärteter** hardened casting
Güte f closeness (estimation); grade; quality
Güte f **der Anpassung** goodness of [best] fit; quality of fit
Gütegruppe f **(von Stählen)** quality group
Güterumschlag m turn-round (of goods)
Güterwagen m freight car; goods wagon
Gütestufe f grade; quality
Güteüberwachung f quality control
Gütevorschrift f quality specification
Gütezahl f quality index

H

Haarhygrometer n hair hygrometer
Haarkristall m whisker
Haarriß m check; hair [line] crack; pull crack; shatter crack; tiny crack
Habitusebene f habit plane
haften adhere
Haftfähigkeit f adherence; adhesive strength
Haftfestigkeit f adhesive strength; firmness
Haftmittel n adhesive
Haftreibung f static friction
Haftung f adhesion
Haftvermögen n bonding strength; contact power
Haken m hook
Hakenbahn f **(für Drahtringe)** hook conveyer
Hakenkanter m tilting fingers
Hakenkette f chain sling with hook
Hakenplatte f hooked tie plate
Hakenschraube f screw hook
halbautomatische Schweißung f semi-automatic welding

halbberuhigt semi killed
halbberuhigter Stahl *m* balanced steel; semi killed steel; semi rimming steel
halbflaches Halbzeug *n* half flat semifinished product
Halbgasfeuerung *f* half gas firing
halbgeröstete Eisenerzstücke *npl* half roasted lumps of iron ore
halbhart half hard
halbiert mottled
halbkontinuierliches Walzwerk *n* semicontinuous rolling mill
Halbkreisfräser *m* concave milling cutter; convex milling cutter
Halbkugelpunkt *m* **(Schmelzbarkeit von Kohle)** hemisphere temperature
Halbleiter *m* semi conducter
Halbreibung *f* static friction
halbrunder Walzdraht *m* half round wire rod
Halbrundstahl *m* half rounds
Halbschalenkorb *m* clamshell type charging bucket
halbtechnisch pilot; semi commercial
Halbwarmverformung *f* warm working
Halbwertsbreite *f* defect depth; half line width; half time width
Halbwertzeit *f* half life
Halbwölber *m* **(ff. Stein)** half wedge brick
Halbzeug *n* semi finished products; tube rounds
Halbzeug *n* **für Röhren** tube rounds
Halbzeugputzerei *f* semi product conditioning department
Halbzeug-Walzwerk *n* rolling mill for semi finished products
Halbzeugzurichtung *f* processing of semi finished product
Halde *f* dump; heap; tip
Halle *f* bay; shop
Haltbarkeit *f* durability; life; life durability; stability; strength
Haltedauer *f* dwell period; holding period; soaking time
Halten *n* holding; maintaining; stopping
Haltepunkt *m* Ac-point; arrest point; change point; charge point; critical point; recalescence point; transformation point
Haltestift *m* fixing pin
Haltevorrichtung *f* jigging
Haltezeit *f* holding time; retardation time
haltig bearing; containing
Hämatit *m* hematite; iron glance; kidney ore
Hämatitroheisen *n* hematite pig iron
Hammer *m* hammer
Hammerbär *m* ram (tup)
Hämmerbarkeit *f* malleability
Hammerbrecher *m* hammer crusher (hammer mill)
Hammerkopf *m* hammer head
hämmern hammer; peen
Hammerschlag *m* scale
Hammerschraube *f* tee head bolt
Hammerschweißung *f* forge welding
Hammerständer *m* frame
Hämmerverdichten *n* compacting by swaging
Hammerwerk *n* forge; hammer mill
Handarbeit *f* manual operation; manual work
Handelsbilanz *f* trade balance
Handelsblech *n* merchant sheet; sheet metal of commercial quality
Handelsfeinblech *n* commercial grade sheet; commercial quality sheet
Handelsguß *m* jobbing casting
Handelsgüte *f* commercial grade; commercial quality
Handelspolitik *f* foreign trade policy
Handelssorte *f* commercial quality
Handelsstabstahl *m* merchant bars
handelsüblich commercial
handfest geschraubt hand tight
handhaben handle
Handhebel *m* hand lever
Handmeißel *m* hand chisel
Handpfanne *f* bull ladle; shank ladle
Handregelung *f* manual control
Handschweißen *n* manual welding
Handstampfer *m* hand rammer

Hanfseil n hemp rope
Hängebahn f aerial railway; aerial ropeway; overhead trolley; telpher line
Hängebahnofen m overhead conveyor furnace
Hängedecke f suspended arch; suspended roof
Hängemeißel m hanging guard
Hängen n (der Gicht) hanging; scaffolding
Hängestützgewölbe n semi suspended roof
Hängewand f suspended wall
harmonisches Mittel n harmonic mean
Hartauftragsschweißung f hard facing; surfacing (am.)
härtbar hardenable
Härtbarkeit f hardenability
Hartbrennen n heat hardening; induration
härten harden
Härte f hardness
Härteader f (Bandfehler) shadow line
Härtearbeit f hardening
Härtebeständigkeit f capacity for retaining hardness
Härteempfindlichkeit f sensitivity to hardening; susceptibility to hardening
Härtegut n hardening stock
Härte f im abgeschreckten Zustand as quenched hardness
Härtemaschine f hardening machine
Härten n curing; hardening; interrupted hardening; stepped hardening
Härten n aus der Warmumformhitze hardening from hot forming temperature
Härten n örtliches local hardening
Härteofen m hardening furnace
Härteprüfmaschine f hardness testing machine
Härteprüfung f hardening test
Härtequerschnitt m sectional area of hardening
Härterei f hardening shop

Härteriß m hardening flaw; heat treatment crack
Härteschicht f case
Härtestreuband n hardness scatter band; scatter band of Jominy hardenability
Härtetiefe f case depth; depth of case; depth of chill; hardness penetration
Härtetiegel m hardening crucible
Härte- und Vergüteanlage f hardening and heat treating plant
Härteverlauf m variation in hardness
Härteverzug m deformation due to hardening; distortion due to hardening
hartgezogener Draht m hard drawn wire
hartgießen case harden; chill cast
Hartgummi m hard rubber
Hartguß m chill casting; chilled cast iron
Hartgußwalze f chilled roll
Hartherd m rammed and sintered bottom
Hartlegierung f cemented carbide; cutting alloy; hard metal
Hartlot n brazing solder; hard solder
hartlöten braze
Hartlötofen m brazing furnace
hartmagnetischer metallischer Sinterwerkstoff m hard magnetic sintered material
Hartmanganerz n black hematite; psilomelane
Hartmetall n cemented carbide alloy; hard metal alloy; sintered carbide alloy; tungsten carbide alloy
hartmetallbestücktes Werkzeug n carbide tipped tool
Hartmetall-Legierung f carbide alloy; cemented carbide alloy; hard metal alloy; sintered carbide alloy; tungsten carbide alloy
Hartmetallplättchen n cemented carbide [alloy] tip
Hartmetallschneide f cutting edge of hard metal
Hartmetallwerkzeug n carbide cutting tool

Hartmetall-Ziehstein *m* hard metal draw die

Hartstahlguß *m* high carbon steel casting

Hartstahl *m* **(unlegiert)** high carbon steel

Hartstoffpulver *n* hard material powder

Härtung *f* hardening

Härtungsgefüge *n* **(Drahtfehler)** hard spots

Härtungsrißempfindlichkeit *f* hardening crack sensitivity; hardening fracture sensitivity

Hartverchromen *n* hard chromium plating

Hartzinn *n* pewter

Harz *n* resin

Haspel *f* coiler; gear; haulage gear; recoiler; reel; tackle; whim; winch; windlass

Haspelanlage *f* reeling plant

haspeln coil; reel; wind

Haspelofen *m* hot box; reel furnace

Haspelzug *m* reel tension

Haubenblock *m* hot top ingot

Haubenglühofen *m* bell type annealing furnace; hood type annealing furnace

Haubenglühofen *m* **mit Strahlheizrohren** radiant tube bell type annealing furnace

Haubenkühlung *f* hood cooling

Haubenmasse *f* exothermic feeder head mixture

Haubenofen *m* bell type furnace; portable cover furnace; top hat furnace

Haubenriß *m* hanger crack

Hauen *n* ragging

häufen accumulate; bunch; heap; pile; stack

Haufen *m* batch; bunch; heap

Haufensand *m* spillage sand

häufig frequent

Häufigkeit *f* frequency

Häufigkeitskurve *f* frequency curve

Häufigkeitsschaubild *n* frequency diagram

Häufigkeitsverteilung *f* frequency distribution

Hauptabmessungen *fpl* leading dimensions

Hauptast *m* **(Dendriten)** primary arm

Hauptbetrieb *m* main production department

Hauptblasrohr *n* blast main

Hauptgaeleitung *f* gas main

Hauptgewölbe *n* main roof

Hauptmasse *f* bulk

Hauptschalter *m* master switch

Hauptspannung *f* principal stress

Hauptverwaltungsbüro *n* head office

Hauptwindleitung *f* blast main

Hebebock *m* jack

Hebebühne *f* elevating platform; lifting device

Hebel *m* jack; lever

Hebelarmbeiwert *m* **(Walzen)** lever factor

Hebelbeziehung *f* lever relationship rule

Hebelgesetz *n* level rule; lever principle

heben hoist; lift; raise

Hebetisch *m* lifting table

Hebe- und Zufuhrvorrichtung *f* magazine elevator feeder

Hebevorrichtung *f* elevator (am.); feeder

Hebezeug *n* hoist; hoisting apparatus; lifting apparatus

heb- und senkbar vertically adjustable

Heftdraht *m* stitching wire

heften tack

Heftschweiße *f* stitch welding; tack weld

Heimathafen *m* home port

heißblasen blow up; use hot blast

Heißbruch *m* hot shortness

heißbrüchig burnt

Heißdruckfestigkeit *f* **(ff. Steine)** hot compression strength

Heißextraktion *f* vacuum hot extraction

Heißflämmen *n* flame scarfing

Heißgutförderer *m* hot material conveyor

Heißkühlung f hot cooling
Heißluftleitung f hot air duct
Heißnachpressen n hot repressing
heißpressen hot press
Heißriß m clink
Heißspülbehälter m hot immersion tank
Heißwasserteil n hot water part
Heißwind m hot blast
Heißwind-Kupolofen m hot blast cupola
Heißwindleitung f hot blast pipe
Heißwindofen m Cowper; hot blast furnace; hot blast stove
Heißwindschieber m hot blast [slide] valve
Heizdüse f **(Gasschweißen)** preheat bore; preheat gas way; preheat orifice
Heizer m fireman; heater; stoker
Heizfläche f heating surface
Heizgas n fuel gas
Heizgasleitung f fuel gas conduit
Heizgas-Sammelkanal m heating flue
Heizkoks m combustion coke; fuel coke
Heizkraft f calorific power; calorific value
Heizleiterlegierung f metallic resistance material
Heizleiter-Werkstoff m heating conductor material
Heizöl n bunker C-standard oil; fuel oil
Heizschacht m combustion chamber
Heiztischmikroskop n hot stage microscope
Heizung f firing; heating; heating flue
Heizwert m calorific power; gross caloric power (am.)
Heizwert m **oberer** upper caloric value
Heizwert m **unterer** lower caloric value; net caloric power (am.)
Hellfeldaufnahme f bright field image
hemmen check; drag; inhibit; lag; stop
Herausschmelzen n melting out
herausziehen draw out
Herd m fire place; hearth; mobile hearth

Herdbelastung f metallurgical load on a furnace
Herdbreite f width of the hearth
Herdfläche f hearth area
Herdflächenleistung f output of hearth surface
Herdfrischen n hearth refining
Herdfrischverfahren n charcoal hearth process; open hearth process
Herdgewölbe n arched roof of hearth; knuckle; ramp
Herdlänge f length of the hearth
Herdofen m hearth type furnace
Herdpflege f bottom [hearth] maintenance; care of the hearth
Herdquerschnitt m section of the hearth
Herdschmelzverfahren n hearth type melting process
Herdsohle f hearth bottom
Herdstahlwerk n hearth type steelmaking plant
Herdtiefe f depth of the hearth
Herdwagenofen m bogie hearth furnace; car bottom furnace
herkömmliche Erschmelzung f traditional melting
Herstellänge f standard length produced
herstellen fabricate; produce
Herstellen n **eines Ziehendes (Rohr)** nozzling
Herstellung f manufacture; production
Herstellungskosten pl manufacturing costs
Herstellungsverfahren n production process
Herstellung f **von Gehäusen** caseing
herunterfrischen blow down
herunterschmelzen bring down; melt down
herunterwalzen break down; cog down; roll down; rough down
Herunterzieh-Eigenschaften fpl drawing down properties
Hespenstahl m fence bar; fencing iron
heterogen heterogeneous

heterogene Zone f mushy zone
hierarchisches Prozeßrechnersystem n hierarchical process computing system
Hilfsarbeiter m labourer; unskilled workman
Hilfsbetrieb m auxiliary department; service department
Hilfsgröße f auxiliary variable
Hilfskranzug m auxiliary crane hoist
Hilfsmetallegierung f auxiliary metal alloy
Hilfs- und Nebenbetrieb m service and secondary process department
hindern check; inhibit
hinreichend sufficient
Hinterachse f rear axle
hintereinander angeordnete Walzgerüste npl stands in tandem
hintereinander (geschaltet) in series; series
hinteres Ende n tail end; trailing end
Hinterkipper m end dumping truck
Hintermauerung f brick backing
Hinterschneidung f undercut
Hinterstampfung f backing
Hinterwalzer m catcher
Hin- und Herbiegeversuch m alternating bending test; reverse bend test
Hin- und Herverdrehversuch m reverse torsion test
hinzufügen add
Hitze f heat
Hitzebelastung f thermal load
hitzebeständig heat resistant; refractory; resistant to heat
hitzebeständiger Stahl m heat resisting steel
Hitzebeständigkeit f heat resistance; refractoriness
Hobelmaschine f planing machine
Hobelmesser n planing tool
hobeln plane
Hochbau m building trade
Hochbaustahl m steel for building construction; steel for structural steelwork
Hochbehälter m elevated tank; high level tank; surge tank
Hochbunker m high level storage bunker; overhead hopper
Hochdruckarmaturen fpl high pressure accessories and fittings
Hochdruckgasleitung f high pressure gas main
Hochdruckmanometer n high pressure manometer
Hochdruckschmiermittel n high pressure lubricant
Hochdruckteil n high pressure part
Hochdruckverfahren n (Hochofen) high top pressure operation
Hochdruckzusatz m (Schmieren) extreme pressure additive
Hochenergieumformung f high energy rate forming
hochfester Baustahl m high strength structural steel
hochfester Stahl m high strength steel; high tensile steel
hochfestes Gußeisen n high duty cast iron
hochfeuerfester Stein m highly refractory brick
Hochfrequenz-Induktionsofen m coreless induction furnace; high frequency induction furnace
Hochfrequenzofen m coreless induction furnace
hochgekohlter Stahl m high carbon steel
Hochgeschwindigkeitsbrenner m high velocity burner
Hochgeschwindigkeitsumformen n high speed forming
Hochglanzblech n bright-luster sheet; high-mirror-finished sheet
hochheben lift; raise
hochkantig on edge
hochkant stellen edge; place on edge; upend
hochklappbares Schutzglas n flip-up window
Hochlage f upper shelf
Hochlauf m elevated inclined chute
hochlegierter Stahl m high alloy steel

Hochleistungsbrenner *m* high output burner
Hochleistungsfeder *f* heavy duty spring
Hochleistungslichtbogen *m* high current arc
Hochleistungslichtbogenofen *m* UHP furnace
Hochleistungs-[Lichtbogen]ofen *m* ultrahigh power [arc] furnace
Hochleistungswäscher *m* high energy scrubber
Hochofen *m* blast furnace
Hochofenanlage *f* blast furnace plant
Hochofenbetrieb *m* blast furnace operation; blast furnace practice
Hochofenbetrieb *m* **mit Gegendruck an der Gicht** high top pressure operation of blast furnace
Hochofenbunker *m* blast-furnace hopper
Hochofenerzeugnis *n* blast-furnace product
Hochofenerzeugung *f* blast-furnace output
Hochofengas *n* blast-furnace gas
Hochofengebläse *n* blast-furnace blower
Hochofen *m* **gedämpfter** banked blast furnace; damped-down blast furnace
Hochofengerüst *n* blast-furnace framework; blast-furnace steel structure
Hochofengestell *n* hearth
Hochofenkoks *m* blast-furnace coke
Hochofenmantel *m* blast-furnace shell
Hochofenmauerwerk *n* blast-furnace brickwork; blast-furnace masonry
Hochofenpanzer *m* blast-furnace steel jacket
Hochofenprofil *n* blast-furnace lines
Hochofenreise *f* blast-furnace campaign
Hochofenschacht *m* blast-furnace shaft; blast-furnace stack; shaft; stack
Hochofenschaumschlacke *f* blast-furnace foamed slag
Hochofenschlacke *f* blast-furnace slag
Hochofenschlackenzement *m* blast-furnace slag cement
Hochofenwind *m* blast-furnace blast
Hochöfner *m* blast furnace man; blast furnace operator
Hochregallager *n* high-bay warehouse
Hochspannungsanlagen *fpl* high-voltage lines and equipment
Hochspannungsfunkenerzeuger *m* high voltage spark generator
Höchstdrehmoment *n* maximum torque
Höchstdruck *m* E.P. (= extreme pressure)
hochstegig deep webbed
höchstes Betriebsmoment *n* working peak torque
höchstfester Stahl *m* super high strength steel
Hochstraße *f* elevated road; flyover
Hochstrombahn *f* heavy current conductors
höchstzulässiger Konzentrationswert *m* maximum allowable concentration
Hochtemperatureigenschaften *fpl* high temperature properties
Hochtemperaturfestigkeit *f* strength at elevated temperature; strength at high temperatures
Hochtemperaturversprödung *f* high temperature brittleness
Hochvakuum-Elektronenstrahlschweißen *n* high-vacuum electron beam welding
Hochvakuumlichtbogenofen *m* high-vacuum arc furnace
Hochvakuumofen *m* high-vacuum melting furnace
hochwarmfeste Legierung *f* high temperature alloy
hochwertig high quality
hochwinden hoist
Höcker *m* knuckle (reheat furnace)
Höckerplatte *f* hump plate

Höhe f height; level; level height
Hohe Behörde f The High Authority
Höhenschwund m shrinkage in height
höhenverstellbar retractable
höhere Temperatur f elevated temperature
Hohlachse f hollow axle
Hohlbeitel m gouge
Hohlblockstein m hollow brick; hollow shape
Hohlbohrer m hollow drill
Hohlbohrstahl m hollow drill steel
Hohldornen n hollow-punch piercing
Hohlelektrode f hollow electrode
Hohlgeschoß n shell
Hohl-Gleitziehen n drawing of tubular bodies; sinking
Hohlguß m hollow casting; slush casting
Hohlkehle f fillet
Hohlkehlnaht f (Schweißen) concave fillet weld
Hohlkörper m hollow [body]
Hohlmeißel m gouge
Hohlprägen n embossing
Hohlprofil n hollow section
Hohl-Quer-Fließpressen n transverse tubular impact extrusion
Hohl-Quer-Strangpressen n transverse tubular extrusion
Hohlraum m cavity
Hohl-Rückwärts-Fließpressen n indirect tubular impact extrusion
Hohl-Rückwärts-Strangpressen n indirect tubular rod extrusion
Hohlschmieden n hollow forging
Hohlstein m hollow brick; hollow shape; tile
Hohlstein m (Rekuperator) tile
Hohlstrangpressen n hollow extrusion
Höhlung f cavity
Höhlung f concavity
Höhlung f cupping; hollow
Höhlung f sweep
Höhlung f void
Hohlung f (Walze) sweep
Hohl-Vorwärts-Fließpressen n direct tubular impact extrusion

Hohl-Vorwärts-Strangpressen n straight tubular rod extrusion
Hohlwalze f hollow roll
Hohlwalzwerk n rotary piercing mill
Hohl-Walzziehen n roll drawing of hollow items without central tool
Hohlziegel m hollow brick; hollow shape
hohlziehen cup
Hohlzug m (Rohr) sinking
Holeintritt m die mouth
Holzkohle f charcoal
Holzkohlenfrischverfahren n charcoal hearth process
Holzkohlengrieß m charcoal breeze
Holzkohlen-Roheisen n charcoal pig iron
homogen homogeneous
homogenisieren homogenize
Homogenität f homogeneousness
Homogenitätsbereich m region of homogeneity
Honen n honing
Honmaschine f honing machine
Hooke'sches Gesetz n Hooke's law
Hordentrockner m drying hurdle
Hordenwäscher m hurdle type scrubber; hurdle washer; hurdle washing tower; wet scrubber
horizontales Schweißen n horizontal position welding
Horizontalkammerofen m vertical flue oven
Hosenrinne f bifurcated launder; forked runner; forked tapping spout
Hosenrollgang m Y-roller table
Hub m lift; stroke
Hubbalkenförderer m walking beam conveyer
Hubbalkenofen m rocker bar type furnace; walking beam furnace
Hubbegrenzer m stroke arresting device
Hubbewegung f (Kran) lifting movement
Hubbrücke f bascule bridge
Hubgeschwindigkeit f hoisting speed
Hubhöhe f stroke length

Hubmagnet *m* lifting magnet
Hubmarken *fpl* **(Stranggießen)** oscillation marks; reciprocation marks; ripple marks
Hubstange *f* **für Glocke** bell lifting rod
Hubstapler *m* fork lift truck
Hubsystem *n* walking beam system
Hubuntersatz *m* stillage
Hubwagen *m* lift[ing] truck; tiering truck; truck
Huckepackmotoren *mpl* piggyback motors
Hüllinie *f* crest line
Hüllprofil *n* **(Rauheitsmessung)** rolling circle envelope
Hülse *f* shell
Hund *m* **(Abstreifmeißel)** stripper guide
Hürde *f* cradle
Hutkühlung *f* cone cooling system
Hut *m* **(LD-Verfahren)** taphole
Hütte *f* metallurgical plant; metallurgical works; mill; plant; works
Hüttenbedarf *m* auxiliary material for iron and steel works
Hüttenbims *m* foamed slag; pumice slag
Hüttenflur *m* mill floor level; shop floor level
Hüttenkalk *m* powdered blast-furnace slag; slag lime
Hüttenkoks *m* metallurgical coke
Hüttenkunde *f* metallurgy
Hüttenmann *m* ironworker; metallurgist
Hüttenmauerstein s. **Hüttenstein**
Hüttenrohzink *n* crude zinc
Hüttensand *m* granulated blast-furnace slag
Hüttenschwemmstein *m* foamed slag brick; pumice slag brick
Hüttenstein *m* granulated slag brick
Hüttenwerk *n* ironworks; metallurgical plant
Hüttenwerkskran *m* iron and steel works crane
Hüttenwolle *f* slag wool
Hüttenzement *m* blast-furnace slag cement

Hybridrechner *m* hybrid computer
Hybridstation *f* balanced station; combined station
Hydraulikguß *m* castings for hydraulic structures
Hydraulikkolben *m* hydraulic piston
hydraulische Entzunderung *f* hydraulic descaling
hydraulische Maschine *f* hydraulic machine
hydraulische Presse *f* hydraulic press
hydraulischer Akkumulator *m* hydraulic accumulator
hydraulischer Antrieb *m* hydraulic drive
hydraulischer Haubenofen *m* hydraulically operated bell type furnace
hydraulische Schmiedepresse *f* hydraulic forging press
hydraulische Steuerung *f* hydraulic control
hydraulische Winde *f* hydraulic jack
Hydridpulver *n* hydride powder
hydrieren hydrogenate
Hydrierwerk *n* hydr[ogen]ation works
Hydrodynamik *f* hydrodynamics
hydrodynamische Reibung *f* hydrodynamic friction
hydrodynamisches Ziehen *n* hydrodynamic drawing
hydrodynamische Walztheorie *f* hydrodynamic theory of rolling
hydromatisches Ziehwerkzeug *n* hydromatic drawing tool
Hydrometallurgie *f* hydrometallurgy
hydrostatisches Hohl-Vorwärts-Fließpressen *n* hydrostatic direct tubular impact extrusion
hydrostatisches Pressen *n* hydrostatic compacting
hydrostatisches Voll-Vorwärts-Fließpressen *n* hydrostatic direct impact extrusion of rods
hydrostatisches Vorwärts-Fließpressen *n* hydrostatic direct impact extrusion
hydrostatisches Vorwärts-Strangpressen *n* hydrostatic direct rod extrusion

hypereutektoidischer Stahl *m* hypereutectoid steel
Hystereseisschleife *f* hysteresis loop
Hysteresisverlust *m* hysteresis loss

I

ideal ideal
ideale Lösung *f* ideal solution
ideal plastisch perfectly plastic
Identifizierung *f* identification
Ilgnersatz *m* Ilgner [type motorgenerator]
im Anschluß *m* **an (Walzwerk)** in tandem with
im gegossenen Zustand *m* as cast
im Gesenk geschmiedetes und gewalztes Reinsteisen *n* swaged and rolled high-purity steel
im Gesenk *n* **hohlschmieden** deep pierce
im gezogenen Zustand *m* as drawn
im Kreuzstoß *m* **geschweißte Rohre** one tube welded across on top of another
Immission *f* pollution of in-house atmosphere
Immobilien *fpl* dead stock; real estate
Impedanz *f* impedance
impfen inoculate (cast iron); seed
Impfen *n* seeding
Impfstoff *m* inoculating agent
Impfstoff *m* **(Gußeisen)** inoculant
Impfung *f* **(Gußeisen)** inoculation
Implantmethode *f* implant method
Implantversuch *m* implant test
imprägnieren impregnate
Imprägnierungsmittel *n* impregnating agent
Impuls *m* impulse
Impuls-Echo-Verfahren *n* impulse reflection method; pulse echo technique
Impuls-Fernsteuerung *f* impulse type remote control
Impulsformer *m* pulse shaper

Impulsform *f* **(Ultraschall)** pulse envelope
Impulsgeber *m* impulse sender; pulse generator
Impulslärm *m* impact noise
Impulszähler *m* impulse counter
im Uhrzeigersinn *m* clockwise
im Vergleich *m* **mit (oder: zu)** in comparison with
im warmgewalzten Zustand *m* in the hot rolled condition
in Bau *m* under construction
in Betrieb *m* operating
in Betrieb *m* **setzen** launch; put into operation
inchromieren chromise
Indikatorgas *n* tracer gas
Induktionserhitzen *n* induction heating
Induktionshärten *n* induction hardening
Induktionsofen *m* induction furnace
Induktionsrinnenofen *m* core type induction furnace
induktive Badbewegung *f* electromagnetic stirring of the bath; induction stirring
induktives Rühren *n* induction stirring
induktives Rühren der Schmelze *f* electromagnetic stirring of the bath
induktives Schweißen *n* induction welding
Induktivität *f* inductance
Industrieabfall *m* industrial waste
Industrieabwasser *n* industrial waste water
Industriebauten *mpl* industrial structures
Industriebetrieb *m* industrial operation; industrial undertaking
Industrielärm *m* industrial noise
Industriemüll-Sinteranlage *f* industrial waste sintering plant
Industrieofen *m* industrial furnace
Industriewasser *n* processing water
ineinandergeschachtelte Gitter *npl* interpenetrating lattices (X-rays)
ineinandergreifende Sondersteine *mpl* **mit Aufhängung** interlocking [suspended] bricks

in eine Gleichung *f* **einführen** introduce into an equation
in eine Liste *f* **eintragen** include in a list; list; schedule
Inertgas *n* inert gas
Informationsbedarf *m* information demand
Informationsfluß *m* information flow
Informationsübernahme *f* read in of information
informationsverarbeitendes Gerät *n* information processing device
Informationsweg *m* information path
Infrarotsteueranlage *f* infrared control system
Infrarotstrahlungsofen *m* infrared radiation furnace
Ingangsetzen *n* starting
Ingenieur *m* chief engineer
Ingenieurberatung *f* engineering consultancy
Ingenieurbüro *n* consulting engineer's
Ingenieurschule *f* technical school for engineers
in geringer Entfernung *f* **voneinander** frequent
in geschlossenem Gesenk in der Presse hergestellt press forging
Inhibitor *m* inhibitor
Inhomogenität *f* inhomogeneity
Injektorbrenner *m* gas welding blow pipe; low pressure torch
in Kalibern gewalzter Rohrstreifen *m* grooved skelp
Inkrement-Probenahme *f* increment sampling
Inkrement-Teilungsverfahren *n* increment division method
innen interior
Innenabsaugung *f* internal evacuation; internal exhaust
Innenachslager *n* axle bearing inside the wheels
Innenblech *n* metal plate insert
Innenblech *n* **(ff. Steine)** metal plate insert
Innenblech *n* **(Gewölbe)** metal plate insert (arch)

Innenborden *n* **durch Drücken** spinning of inside beads
Innendruckversuch *m* **mit Luft** air pressure test
Innendruckversuch *m* **mit Wasser** hydraulic test
Innengewindeschneiden *n* tapping
Innengewinde-Schneidmaschine *f* tapping machine
Innenlunker *m* cavity
Innenriß *m* internal crack; internal fissure; shatter crack
Innenschweißen *n* internal welding
Innensechskantschraube *f* hexagonal socket head cap screw
innere Energie *f* internal energy
innere Oxidation *f* internal oxidation
innige Vermischung *f* intimate mixing
in Palettenverpackung *f* palletised
Instandhaltung *f* maintenance; upkeep
instandsetzen condition; repair
Instandsetzungskosten *pl* reconditioning costs; repairing costs
integrierte Pegelmessung *f* integrated level measurement
in Teilmengen *fpl* **von** in increments of
interatomare Verbindung *f* interatomic bond
interdendritisch interdendritic
interdendritischer Graphit *m* interdendritic graphite
Interdiffusion *f* interdiffusion
Interferenzschichten-Mikroskopie *f* interference coating microscopy
interkristalline Brüchigkeit *f* cleavage brittleness
interkristalline Korrosion *f* intercrystalline corrosion; intergranular corrosion
interkristalliner Bruch *m* intercrystalline fracture
interkritische [Wärme]behandlung *f* intercritical [heat]treatment
intermediäre Phase *f* intermediate phase
intermetallische Verbindung *f* intermetallic compound

intermittierende Betriebsweise f intermittent operation
Invarstahl m Invar steel
Inventurbestand m inventory on-hand quantity; inventory stock
Investitionsgüter npl capital goods
Ionenaustausch m ion exchange
Ionenbindung f ionic bonding
Ionenstärke f ionic strength
Ionenstörstelle f ionic defect
Ionisierungszustand m **(Spektralanalyse)** ionisation state
ionitrieren ionitriding
Ionitrieren n ionitriding
IPE-Träger m **(IPE-Reihe)** IPE-beam (European section)
Irrstrom m stray current
Irrtumswahrscheinlichkeit f level of significance
Isochrone f isochronous curve
ISO-Entwurf m ISO draft
Isolator m insulator
Isolierrohr n insulating tube
Isolierstein m insulating brick
Isolierstoff m insulating material
isolierter Draht m insulated wire
Isolierung f insulation; isolation
isotherme Umwandlung f isothermal transformation
Isotop n isotope
Isotopen-Dickenmeßanlage f thickness measuring device using isotopes
Isotopenhäufigkeit f abundance of isotopes
ISO-Vorentwurf m ISO rough draft
Ist-Kosten pl actual costs
Ist-Leistung f actual production
Ist-Messen n determination of actual size
Ist-Profil n actual section; measured profile
Ist-Wert m actual value

J

Jenkin-Biegeversuch m Jenkin's bend test

J-Integral n integral J
Joch n magnet yoke
Jodzahl f **(Schmieren)** iodine number
Jominy-Kurve f Jominy curve
Jominy-Versuch m Jominy test
justieren adjust; fit; set

K

Kabelband n cable tape
Kabelbandstahl m cable tape steel
Kabeldraht m cable wire
Kabelkanal m cable duct
Kabelschutz m cable protection
Kabelschutzrohr n cable protection pipe
Kabelverseilmaschine f cable-stranding machine
Käfigläufer m cage rotor
Kaliber n box groove; box hole; box pass; closed pass; groove; hole; open groove; open pass; pass
Kaliberanzug m taper of a groove
Kaliberbauart f pass design
Kaliberbearbeitungsmaschine f roll pass dressing machine
Kaliberdruck m bite; draft
Kaliberöffnung f clearance between collars
Kaliberrand m collar
Kaliberreibungsbeiwert m effective coefficient of friction in the groove
Kaliberwalze f grooved roll
kalibrieren calibrate; design roll passes; size
Kalibrieren n coining; coining (press); pass design; roll drafting; roll pass design; sizing
kalibrierte Walze f grooved roll
Kalibrierung f roll drafting; roll pass design
Kalibrierwalzwerk n sizing mill
Kaliseife f potassium soap
Kalium n potassium
Kalkabscheidung f calcium precipitation

kalkbasische Umhüllung f (Schweißdraht) lime-basic covering
kalkbasisch umhüllte Elektrode f electrode with basic sheath
Kalkblasanlage f lime injection equipment
Kalkbrennofen m lime-burning kiln
Kalkbunker m lime bunker
Kalkdinasstein m ganister brick (am.); lime dinas brick
Kalkelend n lime set; troubles due to an excess of lime
Kälken n **(Draht)** liming
kalkgebundener Silicastein m lime-bonded silica brick
kalkhaltig calcareous; calciferous
kalkiges Erz n calcareous ore; limey ore
Kalk m lime
Kalk m **gebrannter** burnt lime
Kalk m **gelöschter** slaked lime
Kalkmilch f milk of lime
Kalksplitt m limestone chips
Kalkstein m limestone
Kalk-Tonerde-Gemisch n lime-alumina mixture
kalkulatorische Abschreibung f depreciation allocation
Kalk m **ungelöschter** quicklime
Kalorie f unit of heat
Kalorimeter n calorimeter
Kalorisieren n calorising
kalottenförmig dome-shaped
Kaltabkanten n cold edge trimming
Kaltarbeitsstahl m cold work steel
Kaltaushärtung f room temperature precipitation hardening
Kaltauslagern n natural ag[e]ing
Kaltband n cold [rolled] strip
Kaltband-Profilwalzwerk n cold roll forming machine
Kaltbeanspruchung f cold straining; cold working
Kaltbiegen n cold bending
Kaltblechschere f cold shear
Kaltbonderverfahren n cold bonderising
Kaltbruch m cold shortness

kaltbrüchig cold short
Kaltbrüchigkeit f coldshortness
Kaltdruckfestigkeit f **(ff. Steine)** cold compression strength
Kältebeständigkeit f antifreezing quality; cryogenic strength; resistance to cold
Kalteinsenkpresse f die typing press; hobbing press
Kältemaschine f refrigerating machine
kalt erblasen cold-blast
Kaltfließpressen n cold extrusion
Kaltformgebung f cold forming
kaltgepilgertes Rohr n cold pilgered tube; rocked tube
kaltgestauchter Draht m cold headed wire; cold heading wire
kaltgewalzter und kaltgereckter Draht m cold-worked steel
kaltgewalztes Band n cold-rolled strip
kaltgezogener Stahl m cold drawn steel
kalthämmern peen
Kalthärtbarkeit f strain hardenability
Kalthärtung f strain hardening; wear hardening; work hardening
Kaltläufer mpl cold shuts
Kaltlaufversuch m cold run trial
Kaltlötstelle f cold junction
Kaltnachpressen n cold repressing
Kaltnachwalzen n cold rerolling; skin pass rolling
Kaltnachwalzwerk n pinch pass rolling mill; temper mill; temper pass rolling mill
Kaltphosphatieren n cold phosphating
Kaltpilgern n cold pilger rolling
Kaltpressen n cold compacting; cold pressing
Kaltpreßmuttern-Eisen n cold-press nut-iron
Kaltpreßschweißen n cold welding
Kaltprofil n cold rolled section
Kaltrecken n cold straining; cold working
Kaltrißbildung f **unter der Naht** cold cracking under the weld

Kaltsäge f cold saw; hack saw
Kaltscherbarkeit f capacity for cold shearing
Kaltschlagdraht m cold heading wire
Kaltschlagmatrize f piercing die
Kaltschlagschmieden n cold impact forging; impacting
Kaltschlagstahl m cold heading steel; cold upsetting steel
Kaltschweiße f cold shut
Kaltspritzbehälter m cold rinse tank
Kaltsprödigkeit f cold brittleness
Kaltstauchen n cold heading; cold upsetting
Kaltstauch- und Kaltfließpreßstähle mpl steels for cold upsetting and cold extrusion
Kaltstrang m dummy bar; starting bar
Kaltstrangeinfahren n introduction of dummy bar
Kaltstrangpressen n cold extruding
Kaltstrang m **(Stranggießen)** dummy bar
Kaltumformbarkeit f cold workability
Kaltumformen n cold forming; cold reforming; cold shaping; cold working
Kaltverarbeitung f cold working
kaltverfestigen flow-harden; strain harden
kaltverfestigter Stahl m strain hardened steel
Kaltverfestigung f strain hardening; strengthening by cold working; wear hardening; work hardening
Kaltverformung f cold forming; cold reduction; cold straining; cold working; deformation at low temperatures
Kaltverwinden n cold twisting
kaltverwundener Bewehrungsstahl m cold twisted reinforcing steel
Kaltwalze f cold roll
kaltwalzen cold roll
Kaltwalzen n cold rolling
Kaltwalzgerüst n cold rolling mill
Kaltwalzwerk n cold reduction mill; cold rolling mill
Kaltwand-Vakuumofen m cold wall vacuum furnace

Kaltwasser-Prüfdruck m cold water test pressure
Kaltwindofen m cold blast furnace
Kaltwindschieber m cold blast sliding valve
Kaltwindzusatzleitung f temper air line
kaltzäh tough at subzero temperature
kaltzäher Stahl m cryogenic steel; low-temperature steel; steel having a high impact strength at low temperature
kaltzäher Stahlguß m steel castings having high impact strength at low temperature; cryogenic steel casting
kaltziehen cold draw
Kaltziehmatrize f cold drawing tool
Kaltzug m cold draw
Kameraabtastung f camera scanning
Kamin m chimney; stack
Kaminschieber m chimney damper; chimney slide valve; stack valve
Kaminwirkung f chimney effect
Kamm m cam; cog
Kammergewölbe n arch of a chamber
Kammerofen m batch [type] furnace; chamber furnace; retort oven
Kammerschweißen n enclosed resistance welding
Kammrad n cog[ged] wheel
Kammrad m mit versetzten Zähnen staggered tooth pinion
Kammwalze f pinion
Kanal m conduit; duct; uptake
Kanalguß m sewer castings
Kanalofen m tunnel type furnace
Kanalradpumpe f channel wheel pump
Kanalstein m runner brick
Kante f border; edge
kanten edge; turn; turn over
Kantenabrundung f rounding off of the edges
Kantenbeschädigung f handling break
Kantenbeschädigung f **(durch eine Haspel)** reel break
Kantenbeständigkeit f **(Pulvermet.)** green strength

Kantenfestigkeit f edge strength
Kantenlängsriß m longitudinal corner crack
Kantenquerriß m transverse corner crack
Kantenriß m corner crack; edge break
Kantenrissigkeit f tendency to edge corner
Kantenwelle f (Kaltband) edge wave
Kanter m manipulator for turnover
Kant- und Verschiebevorrichtung f manipulator for turning-over and shifting; side guards manipulator
Kantvorrichtung f manipulator; tilting device; turning over device
Kaolinsand m kaolin sand
Kapazitätsabgleich m capacity adjustment
Kapazitätsauslastung f capacity utilisation
Kapillarrohr n capillary tube
Kapillartränkung f infiltration by capillary force
Kappe f hood; top
Kappenstahl m pit arch steel
Kappenständer m housing of the open top type
Kapsel f casing
Karbonitrieren n carbonitriding
Karburierung f carburation; carburetting; carburisation
Kardangelenk n Cardan joint; Hooke's universal joint
Karosserie f autobody
Karosserieblech n autobody sheet; automobile-body sheet; car body sheet; motorcar body sheet
Karre f car; cart; truck
Karte f card; chart
Karteischrank m index card cabinet [library]
kartengesteuerter Streifenlocher m card-controlled tape punch
Kartenlocher m card punch
Kartusche f cartridge
Karusselldrehbank f boring machine with revolving table; vertical boring and turning mill; vertical turret boring machine

Karussellofen m revolving furnace
Kaschierung f lamination
Kasten m box; case; tray
Kastenaufkohlen n pack carburising
Kastenförderer m flask conveyer
Kastenglühen n box annealing; close annealing; flask annealing
Kastenglühofen m box annealing furnace
Kastenkaliber n box groove; box hole; box pass
Katalysator m catalyst
Kathodenschutz m cathodic protection
Kathodenstrahlröhre f cathode ray tube
Kathodenzerstäubung f cathode sputtering
kathodischer Schutz m cathodic protection
kathodischer Schutzüberzug m cathodic oxide coating
Kausche f thimble
Kavitation f cavitation
kavitationsbeständig resistant to cavitation
Kavitationskorrosion f cavitation corrosion
Kegelbrecher m cone crusher
Kegeldruckprobe f cone thrust test
Kegeldruckversuch m cone thrust test
Kegeleindruck m cone impression
Kegelfallpunkt m pyrometric cone equivalent
Kegelfeder f elliptic spring
Kegelhärteprüfung f cone hardness test
Kegelrad n bevel gear; mitre gear
Kegelrad-Geradverzahnung f straight tooth bevel gear
Kegelrad-Spiralverzahnung f spiral tooth bevel gear
Kegelrollenlager n conical roller bearing; tapered roller bearing
Kegelstauchversuch m cone upset test; conical compression [upsetting] test
Kegelstift m taper pin

Kegeltrieb *m* bevel gear drive
Kehlnaht *f* double fillet weld; hollow weld; rounded weld; single fillet weld
Kehlnahtmeßlehre *f* fillet ga[u]ge
Kehlnahtschweiße *f* fillet welded connection
Kehlnahtschweißen *n* fillet weld
Kehrwert *m* reciprocal value
Keil *m* cotter; key; peg; stopper; wedge
Keilanstellung *f* wedge adjusting equipment
Keilbiegen *n* V-form bending
keilförmiger Querschnitt *m* **(Band)** wedge section; wedge shape
Keilnut *f* keyway
Keilprüfung *f* fillet weld break test
Keilprüfung *f* **(schmelzgeschweißter Stumpfnähte)** fillet weld break test
Keilriemen *m* V-belt
Keilschneiden *n* wege-action cutting
Keilstahl *m* key bar
Keilstein *m* key; wedge
Keilwelle *f* **(aus dem Vollen herausgearbeitet)** spline[d] shaft
Keilwellennut *f* groove
Keilwinkel *m* **(Spanen)** lip angle
Keilzugprobe *f* wedge-draw specimen
Keilzug-Tiefungsverfahren *n* wedge draw cupping test
Keim *m* embryo; nucleus
Keimbildung *f* nucleation
Kenngröße *f* index; parameter
Kennkurve *f* operation characteristic (OC)
Kennzahl *f* characteristic value; statistic
Kennzahlen *fpl* characteristic data; data
Kennzeichen *n* attribute
kennzeichnen mark
Kennzeichnung *f* characterisation
Kennzeichnung *f* **(von Erzeugnissen)** identification marking
keramisch ceramic
Kerb *m* channel; charpy; groove; nick; notch

Kerbbiegeprobe *f* nick bend test; nicked fracture test; notch bend test
Kerbbiegeversuch *m* nick bend test; nicked fracture test; notch bend test
Kerbdauerstandversuch *m* notched creep test
Kerbdurchmesser *m* notch diameter
Kerbempfindlichkeit *f* notch sensitivity
Kerben *n* grooving
Kerbfallprüfung *f* notch bending test
Kerbprobe *f* notched sample
Kerbschlagarbeit *f* notch impact energy
Kerbschlagarbeit *f* **an Spitzkerbproben nach ISO-V** Charpy-V-notch (CVN)
Kerbschlagbiegeversuch *m* impact test; notched bar impact bend test
Kerbschlagprüfung *f* notched bar impact test
Kerbschlagversuch *m* impact test
Kerbschlagzähigkeit *f* absorbed energy per cross sectional area
Kerbschlagzähigkeit *f* **(ISO-V)** CVN-toughness
Kerbsprödigkeit *f* notch brittleness
Kerbverdrehversuch *m* notched torsion test
Kerbwirkung *f* notch effect
Kerbwirkungszahl *f* fatigue notch factor; fatigue strength reduction factor
Kerbzugversuch *m* notched tension test
Kern *m* center; core; nucleus
Kernblasmaschine *f* core blower
Kernbock *m* chaplet
Kerndurchmesser *m* **(Gewinde)** minor diameter
Kernenergie *f* nuclear energy; nuclear power
Kerngefüge *n* core structure
Kernhaltestift *m* dabber
Kernhärtbarkeit *f* core hardenability
Kernhärten *n* core hardening
Kernkraftwerk *n* nuclear power station
kernloser Induktionsofen *m* coreless induction furnace; high-frequency induction furnace

Kernmarke f core print
Kernmasse f core mixture
Kernnagel m chaplet
Kernöl n core oil
Kernphysik f nuclear physics
Kernprogramm n task
Kernreaktor m nuclear reactor
kernrissig exhibiting internal cracks
Kernrückfeinen n core refining
Kernrückfeinung f core refining
Kernseigerung f core segregation
Kernspaltung f nuclear fission
Kernspeicher m **(EDV)** core memory; core store
Kernstütze f chaplet
Kerntrockenkammer f core baking oven
Kernzerschmiedung f forging burst
Kessel m boiler; hood; shell
Kesselanlage f boiler plant
Kesselanschlüsse mpl boiler connections; boiler mountings
Kesselblech n boiler plate
Kesselboden m boiler bottom; boiler end; dished head
Kesseleinmauern n boiler setting
Kesselfeuerung f boiler firing; boiler furnace
Kesselhaus n boiler house
Kesselhaus-Überwachungsanlage f boiler house control plant
Kesselrohr n boiler tube
Kesselschuß m drum; drum of a boiler
Kesselspeisewasser n boiler feed water
Kesselspeisewasseraufbereitungsanlage f boiler feed water preparation; boiler feed water softening plant
Kesselstein m boiler scale
Kesselsteinablagerung f scale deposit
Kesselsteinentfernung f boiler scale removal
Kesselstein-Lösungsmittel n boiler scale solvent
Kesseltrommel f boiler accessories; boiler drum
Kessel m **und Kesselarmatur** f boiler and fittings

Kesselzubehör n boiler accessories
Kette f chain
Kettenachse f chain shaft
Kettenflaschenzug m chain block; chain hoist
Kettenförderer m bucket conveyor; bucket elevator
Kettenglied n chain link
Kettenkaltstrang m articulated dummy bar
Kettenkaltstrang m **(Stranggießen)** chain type dummy bar
Kettenrad n chain wheel
Kettenrost-Beschickvorrichtung f chain grate stoker
Kettenschleier m chain curtain
Kettenstahl m chain steel
Kettenzahnrad n sprocket
Kettenziehbank f draw bench with chains
Kies m gravel; pyrites; shot
Kiesabbrand m calcined pyrites
Kieselgur f kieselguhr
kieseliges Erz n siliceous ore
Kieselsäure f silica; silicic acid
kinematische Viskosität f kinematic viscosity
Kinetik f kinetics
kinetische Energie f kinetic energy
kippbarer Vorherd m tilting type [hot metal] receiver
kippen dump
Kippen n tipping
kippen (Pfanne) tip
Kipper m tipp[l]er
Kippherd m tilting hearth
Kippkübel m skip car; tipping bucket; tilting skip
Kippkübel-Begichtung f skip filling
Kipplager n rocker bearing
Kippmoment n tilting moment
Kippofen m rocking type furnace; tilting furnace
Kippfanne f tilting ladle
Kippschalter m reversible switch
Kippstuhl m tilting device; tipping device; up-ender
Kipptisch m tilting table

Kippvorrichtung f dumping device (am.); tilting device; tipping device
Kippwagen m dump cart
Kippwiege f rocker
Kiste f box
kistengeglühtes Feinblech n box annealed sheet
Kistenglühofen m box annealing furnace; close annealing furnace
Kitt m putty
kitten lute
klaffender Querriß m pull
Klammer f cramp
klammern brace; clip; cramp
Klappdorn m collapsible mandrel
Klappe f clack valve; door; flap valve; gate; top; trap
Kläranlage f clarifying plant
Klärbecken n settler; settling basin; settling tank
klären clarify
Klarlack m clear coat
Klärschlamm m settling slime; settling sludge
Klarschriftcodierer m character encoder
Klärsumpf m hopper
Klärwerk n cleaning plant
Klasse f class
Klassenbreite f class range
Klassengrenze f class limit
Klassenhäufigkeit f class frequency
Klassenmitte f class centre
klassieren class; grade; size
Klassieren n **der Erze** grading of ores; sizing of ores
Klassierrüttelsieb n classifying jigging screen; grading jigging screen; sizing jigging screen
Klassiersieb n classifying screen; grading screen; sizing screen
Klassierung f **der Erze** classification of ores
Klaubanlage f picking plant
Klaubband n sorting belt
Klauenfett n neat's foot oil
Klauenkupplung f crab
Klavier[saiten]draht m piano wire

Klebekraft f adhesive strength
kleben adhere; stick
Kleben n **(des Walzgutes an der Walze)** cobbling
Kleben n **(dünner Bleche)** sticking
Kleber m cobble; sticker
Klebestelle f **(Oberflächenfehler)** contact spot; contract spot; sticker mark
Klebeverbindung f adhesive bonding
Klebmittel n adhesive
klebriger Gichtstaub m sticky blast-furnace flue dust
klebrige Schlacke f tacky slag
Klebsand m loamy sand; sticky sand
Kleeblattmuffe f clover leaf sleeve
Kleeblattzapfen m clover leaf neck; wobbler
Kleie-Putzmaschine f **(Weißblech)** branning machine
Kleinbessemerbirne f baby Bessemer converter
Kleineisenzeug n small iron ware
Kleinschrott m light-weight scrap
kleinstes Quadrat n least square
Kleinwinkelkorngrenze f small angle grain boundary
klemmen gall; jam; seize
klemmen (sich) gall
Klemmplatte f clamping plate; clip
Klemmrolle f pinch roll
Klettern n **von Versetzungen** climb of dislocations
Klima n **(am Arbeitsplatz)** state of the atmosphere (at the workplace)
Klimaanlage f air conditioning plant
Klimatisierung f air conditioning
Klinge f blade
Klinke f latch
Klinkenbett n cam-type bed; dog-type bed; pawl-type bed
Klinkenschlepper m pawl type skid
Klirrfaktor m harmonic distortion factor
Klopfdichte f tap density
klopfen (rütteln) rap
Klopfvolumen n tap volume
Klotzschlacke f block slag
Klumpen m cluster

Klumpenauswahlverfahren n cluster sampling
Klumpenbildung f (Schlacke) lumping
Klumpenstichprobenverfahren f cluster sampling
Knabberschneiden n (Blech) nibbling
Knagge f cam; dog
Knaggenschlepper m dog-bar type conveyor
Knappheit f shortage
Kneifen n sucking
Kneifstich m knife pass
knetbar kneadable
kneten knead; squeeze
Knetlegierung f forgeable alloy
Knick m break; coil break; kink
Knickbauchen n acute-angle bulging
Knickbeanspruchung f buckling stress
Knickbiegen n V-die bending; bulging
Knick-Dauerstandversuch m creep buckling test
knicken break; buckle; crinkle
Knickfestigkeit f buckling resistance; buckling strength; column strength
Knicklänge f effective length
Knickspannung f buckling stress
Knickstelle f **im Band** coil wrench mark
Knickstelle f **im Blech** sheet wrench mark
Knickung f local buckling
Knickversuch m buckling test
Knickvorgang m process of buckling
Knie n knuckle
Kniehebel m toggle
Kniestück n elbow; gooseneck; pen stock
Kniestück n **(des Düsenstocks)** boot leg
Knochen m **(Gießen)** knuckle; sprue
Knopf m button
Knotenblech n gusset [plate]
Knotengraphit m chunky graphite
Knüppel m billet
Knüppelfolge f billet sequence
Knüppelordner m billet unscrambler
Knüppelputzerei f billet bank
Knüppelschere f billet shears

Knüppelstoßofen m pusher type billet heating furnace
Knüppelwalzwerk n billet mill
Koaleszenz f coalescence
Kobalt n cobalt
kochen boil
Kochen n boiling; ebullition
kochender Stahl m wild steel
Kochsalz n common salt
Kochsalzgitter n rocksalt lattice
Kochversuch m boiling test; test in boiling liquids
Koeffizient m coefficient
Koerzitivkraft f coercive force
kohäsive Zone f cohesive Zone
Kohle f carbon; coal
Kohleaufdampfverfahren n carbon replica technique
Kohlebürste f carbon brush
Kohleelektrode f carbon electrode
kohlehaltig carbonaceous
Kohlelager n carbon bearing
Kohle-Lichtbogenschweißen n carbon arc welding
Kohle f **minderwertige** crop coal; low grade coal
Kohlenaufbereitungsanlage f coal washing and grading plant
Kohlenaufgabeeinrichtung f coal charging device
Kohlenbergwerk n coal mine; colliery
Kohlenbeschickvorrichtung f stoker
Kohlenbrechanlage f coal crushing plant
Kohleneisenstein m black band; carbonaceous ironstone
Kohlengewinnung f exploitation of coal; output of coal; raising of coal; winning of coal
Kohlengrus m beans; breeze; peas
Kohlenmischanlage f coal mixing plant
Kohlenmonoxid n carbon monoxide
Kohlenmonoxidvergiftung f carbon monoxide poisoning
Kohlensack m belly; bosh parallels
Kohlensäure f carbon dioxide
Kohlenstaub m coal dust; pulverised coal

Kohlenstaubfeuerung f coal dust firing plant
Kohlenstaub-Feuerungsanlage f pulverised coal firing plant
Kohlenstaubgasbrenner m pulverised coal/gas combined burner
Kohlenstoff m carbon
Kohlenstoffabfall m carbon drop
kohlenstoffarmer Schnellautomatenstahl m low carbon free-cutting steel
kohlenstoffarmer Stahl m low carbon steel
kohlenstoffarmer Thomasstahl m Thomas low carbon steel
kohlenstoffarmer weicher Stahl m low carbon steel; mild steel
Kohlenstoffaufnahme f carbon pickup
Kohlenstoffbestimmungsgerät n carbon analyser
Kohlenstoff m **enthaltend** carbonaceous
Kohlenstoffgerüst n carbon network
kohlenstoffgesättigtes Eisen n carbon saturated iron
kohlenstoffreicher Stahl m high carbon steel
Kohlenstoffstahl m **(unlegierter Stahl)** plain carbon steel
Kohlenstoffstein m carbon block; carbon brick
Kohlenstoff m **zugeben** carburise
Kohlenstoffzustellung f carbon lining
Kohlenturm m coal storage tower; coal tower
Kohlenturmgurtförderer m coal tower conveyor
Kohlenwäsche f coal washing plant
Kohlenwassergasanlage f carburetted water gas installation
Kohlenwasserstoff m hydrocarbon
Kohlenwertstoff m coal by-product
Kohlenwertstoffgewinnungsanlage f coal by-products recovery plant
Kohleschleifbügel m carbon slip stirrup
Kohleschleifkontakt m carbon sliding contact

Kohleschleifstück n carbon slip piece; carbon trolley shoe
Kohlestabofen m carbon rod furnace
Kohletiegel m carbon crucible
Kohlevergasung f coal gasification
Kohlevergasungsanlage f coal-to-gas plant
Kokerei f coke oven plant; coking plant
Kokereigasbehandlung f coke-oven gas processing
Kokereinebenerzeugnis n coke by-product; coke derivative
Kokille f chill; ingot mould; mould
Kokille f **mit dem dünnen Ende oben** small end up (S.E.U.) mould
Kokille f **mit dem weiten Ende oben** big end up mould; wide end up (W.E.U.) mould
Kokillenanstrichmittel n ingot mould coating material; ingot mould dressing material; mould wash
Kokillenband n series of moulds
Kokillenbruch m ingot mould scrap; mould scrap; scrap of ingot moulds
Kokillenglasur f ingot mould glasing
Kokillenguß m chill casting; die casting; gravity die casting
Kokillenhartguß m chilled casting
Kokillenhaube f hot top
Kokillenhubtisch m mould frame
Kokillenlack m ingot mould coating; ingot mould varnish
Kokillenschlichte f ingot mould blackening
Kokillenschluckvermögen n swallowing capacity of moulds
Kokillenspritzeinrichtung f ingot mould washing plant
Kokillenuntersatz m ingot mold stool (am.); ingot mould bottom plate
Kokillenwand f mould wall
Koks m coke
Koksaufbereitungsanlage f coke preparation plant
Koksausdrückmaschine f coke pusher machine; pusher ram
Koksbrechanlage f coke crushing plant

Koksbunker *m* coke bunker; coke storage bin
Koksfeinkohle *f* coking fines
Koksfestigkeit *f* coke strength
Koksgas-Sauerstoff-Brenner *m* mixed coke oven gas-oxygen burner
Koksgerüst *n* coke network
Koksgrus *m* breeze; coke breeze
Kokskammer *f* carbonisation chamber; coking chamber
Koks *m* **kleinstückiger** breeze; small coke
Kokskohle *f* bituminous coal; coking coal
Kokskohlenentladung *f* dumping of coking coal
Kokskohlenkomponentenbunker *m* service bunker
Kokskohlenturm *m* coking coal tower
Kokskuchenführungswagen *m* coke guide
Kokslösche *f* coke dust
Kokslöschturm *m* coke quench tower
Kokslöschwagen *m* coke quenching car
Koksofen *m* coke oven; stove
Koksofenbatterie *f* battery of coke ovens
Koksofengas *n* coke oven gas
Koksofengas *n* **ungemischtes** straight coke oven gas
Koksofentür *f* coke oven door
Koks-Ölverbrauch *m* coke-oil rate
Koksrampe *f* coke loading bay; coke wharf
Koksrampenband *n* coke side bench
Koksrückstand *m* residual coke
Kokssatz *m* coke rate
Kokssiebanlage *f* coke screening plant
Koksverbrauch *m* coke consumption
Koksverladung *f* coke loading
Kolben *m* piston
Kolbengebläse *n* gas piston blower; reciprocating blowing engine
Kolbenhub *m* piston stroke
Kolbenpumpe *f* piston pump
Kolbenring *m* piston ring

Kolkbreite *f* width of cratering
Kolklippe *f* cratering lip
Kolkung *f* cratering
Kollapsring *m* ring inside a filter bag
Kollektiv *n* **(Großzahlforschung)** lot; universe
Kollergang *m* edge mill; edge runner; muller; pan grinder; roller pug mill
kollern pan grind
Kolloidlösung *f* colloidal solution
Kolorimetrie *f* colorimetry
kombinierter Brenner *m* combined burner
Kommandoprogramm *n* user program procedure
Kommission *f* **der Europäischen Gemeinschaften (KEG)** European Communities Commission (ECC)
Kommissionierung *f* dispatch
Kommissionierungslager *n* dispatch warehouse
Kommunikationsprozess *m* communication process
Kompaktdichte *f* particle true density
Kompakt-Durchlaufglühverfahren *n* compact continuous annealing process
Kompaktzugproben *fpl* compact tensile specimens
Kompensator *m* bellows expansion joint; expansion pipe
Kompensator *m* **(Dehnungsausgleicher)** bellows expansion joint; expansion pipe
Compound.....siehe Verbund ....
Kompressionsmodul *m* **(K-Modul)** modulus of compression
Kondensationsanlage *f* condenser plant
Kondensator *m* capacitor
Kondensieren *n* condensation
Kondenstopf *m* steam trap
Kondenswasserkorrosion *f* corrosion by condensed water
Konditionierer *m* **(LD-Gasreinigung)** conditioner
Konfektionierung *f* packaging
Konfektionierungsplanung *f* packaging planning

Konfektionierungssteuerung f packaging control
Konfluenzanalyse f confluence analysis
Königstein m cluster bottom mould; king brick; runner core; spider
Königswasser n aqua regia
konisches Getriebe n bevel gear
Konizität f conicity; taper
Konode f tie line
Konsistenz f consistence; consistency
Konstante f constant
konstitutionelle Unterkühlung f constitutional supercooling
konstruieren build
Konstrukteur m designer
Konstruktion f design
Konstruktionsmerkmal n constructional feature
Konstruktionsrohr n structural pipe
Kontaktelektrode f touch rod
Kontaktschweißen n contact welding
Kontaktwerkstoff m contact material (powder met.)
Konten npl **der innerbetrieblichen Vorgänge** accounts of movements within the business
Kontenrahmen m frame of accounts; model chart of accounts
Kontingent n quota
kontinuierliches Kühlungs-Umwandlungsschaubild n continuous cooling transformation curve
kontinuierliches Sauerstofffrischverfahren n continuous oxygen refining process
kontinuierliches Walzwerk n continuous [rolling] mill
kontinuierliches ZTU-Diagramm n continous cooling transformation curve (CCT)
kontinuierliche Wärmebehandlung f continuous heat treatment
Konto n account
Kontraktionszahl f Poisson's ratio
Kontrollanalyse f check analysis
Kontrolle f control; inspection
kontrollierte ausgeglichene Stichprobe f balanced sample

Kontrollschaubild n control chart
Kontrollversuch m checking test
Konus m cone; taper
Konuswinkel m approach angle; entrance angle
Konvektion f convection
Konvektionskühlung f convection cooling
Konvektor m convector; heat-conducting plate
Konverter m converter; vessel
Konverterantrieb m converter drive
Konverterauswurf m converter slopping and spatter
Konverterbetrieb m converter shop
Konverterboden m converter bottom; plug; solid converter bottom
Konverterboden-Einsetzwagen m converter bottom mounting car
Konverterboden-Stampfmaschine f converter bottom tamping machine
Konvertereinhausung f converter casing; enclosure protective walls
Konverterfutter n converter lining
Konvertergefäß n converter vessel
Konverterhut m conical converter top; converter hood
Konverterkamin m converter chimney
Konverterlager n converter bearing
Konvertermantel m converter shell
Konvertermittelstück n belly
Konvertermündung f converter mouth
Konverterstahl m basic oxygen furnace steel; converter steel
Konverter-Trocknungsanlage f converter drying plant
Konzentrat n concentrate
Konzentration f concentration
Konzentrationsstein m enriched matte
konzentriert concentrated
Konzernbilanz f consolidated statement
Koordinate f co-ordinate
Koordinatenpapier n graph paper
Kopf m head; port[end]; top
Kopfanstauchen n **im Gesenk** die heading
Kopfbart m top fin; top flash

Kopfhöhe f headroom
Kopfkühlungselement n **(an Kippöfen)** chill
Kopfschere f squaring shears
Kopfschrott m top discard scrap
Kopfteil m top
Kopfwand f end wall
Kopplung f interface
Korb n basket; bucket; cage
Korbbeschickung f basket charging; bucket charging
Korbverseilmaschine f cage stranding machine
Kordeln n diamond knurling
Korn n grain; particle
Kornaufbau m grain structure
Kornband n size distribution
Kornbildung n granulation
körnen center; granulate
Körnen n center punching; punch marking
Körnereinschläge mpl gauge marks; pop marks
Kornfeinen n grain refining
Kornfeinung f **(Wärmebehandlung)** grain refinement
Kornform f particle shape
Korngefüge n grain structure
Korngrenze f grain boundary
Korngrenzenangriff m grain boundary attack; intergranular attack
Korngrenzenbruch m intergranular fracture
Korngrenzendiffusion f boundary diffusion; interfacial diffusion
Korngrenzenhärtung f grain boundary hardening
Korngrenzenkorrosion f intergranular corrosion
Korngrenzennetzwerk n grain boundary network
Korngrenzenwanderung f grain boundary migration
Korngröße f grain size [number]; particle size
Korngrößenbereich m grain size range; particle size range
Korngrößeneinteilung f grain classification

Korngrößenfraktion f grain size fraction
Korngrößenklasse f particle size fraction
Korngrößenverteilung f grain size distribution; particle size distribution
körniges Gefüge n granular structure
Kornklassierung f grain sizing; particle sizing
kornorientiertes Blech n grain oriented sheet
Körnung f degree of grain coarsening; grain coarsening; granulation
Körnungskennlinie f granulation characteristica [curve]
Körnungsnetz n particle-size network
kornverfeinerter unlegierter Manganstahl m grain refined C-Mn steel
Kornvergröberung f grain coarsening
Kornverteilungskurve f granulation characteristica [curve]
Kornwachstum n grain growth; increase of grain size
Kornzertrümmerung f shattering of grains
Kornzusammensetzung f size grading
Körperschallmessung f measurement of sound conducted through solids
korpuskuläre Verunreinigung f corpuscular pollution
Korpuskularstrahlung f corpuscular radiation
Korrelationskoeffizient m correlation coefficient
korrodieren corrode
Korrosion f corrosion
Korrosion f **durch Wasserstoff** hydrogen induced corrosion (HIC)
Korrosionsart f type of corrosion
korrosionsbeständig resistant to corrosion
Korrosionsbeständigkeit f corrosion resistance; rust resisting property; stainless property
Korrosionselement n corrosion cell
Korrosionsermüdung f corrosion fatigue
Korrosionsform f appearance of corrosion

Korrosionsgeschwindigkeit f rate of corrosion
Korrosionshemmung f corrosion inhibition
Korrosionsnarbe f corrosion pit
Korrosionsriß m corrosion crack
Korrosionsschutz m corrosion protection; protection against corrosion
Korrosionsschutzmasse f anti corrosion mixture
Korrosionsschutzmittel n anti corrosive compound
Korrosionsunterwanderung f corrosion creep
Korrosionswiderstand m corrosion resistance
Korrosion f **unter Ablagerungen** corrosion under deposits
Korrosion f **unter mechanischer Beanspruchung** corrosion under mechanical stress
Korrosion f **unter Sauerstoffverbrauch** oxygen consumption type of corrosion
korrosiv corrosive
Korundstein m corundum brick
Kosten pl cost[s]
Kostenabteilung f cost department
Kostenanalyse f cost analysis
Kostenanteil m **des Arbeitslohnes** labour element of cost
Kostenart f cost type
Kostenermittlung f cost finding
Kostenersparnis f cost saving
Kostenkonto n cost account
Kostenpreis m cost price
Kostenrechnung f cost accounting; costing
Kostenrechnungs-Richtlinien fpl cost calculation guidelines
Kostenstelle f cost center
Kostenträger m cost bearer
Kostenumlage f **nach Gebrauchsdauer** cost allocation on the basis of equipment life
Kostenumlage f **nach Raumgröße** cost allocation on the basis of floor space
Kostenumlage f **nach Stoffverbrauch** cost allocation on the basis of material cost
Kostenumlage f **nach Umsatz** cost allocation on the basis of sales volume
Kostenvergleich m cost comparison
Kostenvoranschlag m estimate
kracken crack
Kraft f force; power
Kraftangriff m application of load
Kraftantrieb m power drive
Kraftausbeute f **beim Drahtziehen** length of wire drawn per unit of power consumed
Kraft-Durchbiegungs-Messung f load deflection measurement
Kräftebestimmung f stress analysis
Kräfterzeugungsanlage f power plant
Kräftezusammensetzung f composition of forces
Kraftfahrzeug n motor car
Kraftmeßdose f load cell
Kraftmeßglied n dynamometer
Kraftschalter m actuator; pilot relay
Kraftstoff m engine fuel
Kraftübertragung f power transmission
Kraft-Verlängerungskurve f load extension curve
Kraftwagenblech n autobody sheet; motor-car body sheet
Kraftwagenmotor m motor-car engine
Kraftwerk n power house; power station
Kraftwirkungsfiguren-Ätzverfahren n strain line etching
Kraftwirkungsfiguren fpl stretcher lines; stretcher strains
Kragarm m cantilever
Kragenkristallisator m **(ESU)** collar mould (ESR)
Kragenziehen n collar forming; collaring holes by drawing
Krammstock m skimmer rod
Kran m crane
Kranfahrsicherung f crane travel safety device

Kranführer *m* crane driver; crane operator
Krangetriebe *n* crane gear
Kranhaken *m* crane hook
Krankatze *f* crane trolley
Krankette *f* burden chain
Kranpfanne *f* crane-operated ladle
Kranschiene *f* crane rail
Kranzgewölbe *n* ringed roof
Kranz *m* **(Rad)** rim
Kratzbeständigkeit *f* resistance to scratching
kratzen score; scrape; scratch
Kratzendraht *m* card wire
Krätzer *m* rabble
Kratzer *m* scratch
kräuseln curl
Kreditanspannung *f* overextended current liabilities
Kredithöhe *f* **(bei Verrechnungsabkommen)** swing
Kreidung *f* chalking
Kreisblattschreiber *m* circular-chart recorder
Kreisblende *f* circular aperture
Kreisbogen *m* arc
Kreisbogen-Stranggießmaschine *f* bow type continuous casting machine
Kreiselbrecher *m* gyratory crusher; rotary crusher
Kreiselgebläse *n* turboblower
Kreiselverdichter *m* centrifugal compressor
Kreisfrequenz *f* angular velocity; gyro-frequency; pulsatance
Kreisführung *f* circular template
Kreislauf *m* circuit
Kreislaufkohle *f* recycled coal
Kreislaufschrott *m* own scrap arisings
Kreissäge *f* circular saw
Kreisschere *f* circular shears; rotary shears
krempen flange
Kreuzgelenk *n* Hooke's universal joint
Kreuzrollgang *m* transverse roller table
Kreuzschlag *m* reverse twist

Kreuzschlagseil *n* ordinary lay rope; regular lay rope
Kreuzschlitzschraube *f* cross recessed screw
Kreuzstoß geschweißte Rohre *npl* **(im ...)** one tube welded across on top of another
Kreuzstrom-Wärmeaustauscher *m* cross flow heat exchanger
Kreuzung *f* crossing
Kreuzungsstoß *m* cross joint
kreuzverzahnter Fräser *m* staggered teeth milling cutter
kriechen creep
Kriechgeschwindigkeit *f* creep rate; creep speed
Kriechgrenze *f* limiting creep stress
Kriechverhalten *n* creep behaviour
Kriechwiderstand *m* creep resistance
Krippmaschine *f* **(für das Drahtweben)** crimping machine
Kristallbildung *f* acicular structure; crystallisation
Kristallerholung *f* crystal recovery
Kristallgitter *n* crystal lattice
kristallin crystalline
kristalliner Bruch *m* crystalline fracture
Kristallisation *f* crystallisation
Kristallisator *m* mould
Kristallkorn *n* crystal grain
Kristallorientierung *f* crystal orientation
Kristallseigerung *f* crystal segregation; microsegregation; minor segregation
Kristallstruktur *f* crystal structure
Kristallwachstum *n* crystal growth
kristallwachstumshemmender Zusatz *m* doping material
kritischer Abkühlungsverlauf *m* critical cooling rate
kritische Schubspannung *f* critical shear stress
kritisches Feld *n* critical range
kritisches Kornwachstum *n* critical grain growth
Kronengestell *n* uncoiling device

Kronenmutter f castellated nut
kröpfen bend at right angles; crank; offset
Kröpfen n cranking; offsetting
Krümeln n granulating of sinter mix
Krümmer m bend; elbow
Krümmung f camber; curvature; knuckle
Kübel m bucket; tray; tub; vat
Kübelaufzug m bucket conveyor; bucket elevator
Kübelbegichtung f basket charging; bucket charging (am.); tub filling
Kübelwagen m bucket car; skip car
kubisch-flächenzentriertes Gitter n cubic face centered lattice; face centered cube space lattice
kubisch-raumzentriertes Gitter n body centred cubic lattice; cubic body centered lattice
Kuchen m cake
Kugel f ball; bullet; sphere
kugeläquivalenter Durchmesser m equivalent spherical drop diameter
Kugeldruck-Härteprüfung f ball hardness test; ball indentation test
Kugeldruckversuch m ball hardness test; ball indentation test
Kugelfallhärte f scleroscope hardness
kugelförmiger Zementit m spheroidised carbide
Kugelgelenk n ball joint
Kugelglühen n spheroidising
Kugelgraphit-Gußeisen n nodular [graphite] cast iron; nodular cast iron; spheroidal graphite cast iron
kugelig globular; spheroidal
kugeliger Kristall m equiaxed crystal
kugeliges Pulver n globular powder; spherical powder
Kugeligglühen n spheroidising
Kugelkette f bead chain
Kugellager n ball bearing
Kugellagerstahl m ball bearing steel
Kugelmühle f ball mill
Kugelpackung f packing of spheres
Kugelsintern n nodulising
Kugelstrahlen n shot peening

Kugelventil n globe valve
Kühlband n controlled cooling conveyor
Kühlbett n cooling bank; cooling bed
Kühler m condenser
Kühlhaube f cooling cover; cooling hood
Kühlkasten m coolers; cooling box; monkey
Kühlluft f cooling air
Kühlmittel n coolant
Kühlmittelzuführung f coolant supply pipe
Kühlöl n soluble oil
Kühlplatte f cooling plate
Kühlring m cooling ring
Kühlrohr-Walzenlager n **(Bronze)** cooling tube roll bearing (bronze)
Kühlschale f cooling jacket; mould; mould cooling jacket
Kühlschatten m skid mark
Kühlschrott m scrap for cooling
Kühlspannungsriß m cooling crack
Kühlstraße f water mill
Kühlturm m chimney cooler; cooling tower
Kühlung f cooling
Kühlung f **in ruhender Flüssigkeit** cooling in a static fluid; cooling in a static liquid
Kühlung f **in strömender Flüssigkeit** flow boiling cooling
Kühlwasserbecken n cooling basin
Kühlwasserleitung f cooling water pipe
Kümpelerzeugnisse npl dished products; flanged products
kümpeln dish; flange
Kümpeln n coning; dishing
Kümpelpresse f circular flanging press; dishing press; flanging press
Kundendienst m service
Kundenguß m jobbing casting
Kunstharzlager n synthetic resin bearing
Kunstharzüberzug m plastic coating
künstlich artificial
künstliche Bewitterung f artificial weathering

künstliches Altern *n* artifical ag[e]ing
kunststoffbeschichtetes Stahlblech und -band *n* plastic coated sheet and strip
Kunststoff *m* plastic
Kunststoffolien *fpl* **aufwalzen** laminate
kupferhaltig copper bearing
Kupferstahl *m* copper steel
Kupfersulfatprüfung *f* copper sulphate test
Kupferüberzug *m* coppering
Kupolofen *m* cupola [furnace]
Kuppel *f* dome
Kuppelgewölbe *n* dome
Kuppelmuffe *f* coupling box
Kuppelspindel *f* coupling spindle
Kuppeltemperatur *f* dome temperature
Kuppelzapfen *m* wobbler
Kupplung *f* clutch; coupling; crab
Kupplung *f* **automatische (Eisenbahn)** automatic coupling
Kupplungsbüchse *f* coupling bush
Kupplungswelle *f* coupling shaft
Kurbel *f* crank
Kurbelpresse *f* crank press
Kurbelwelle *f* crankshaft
Kurbelwellenfertigung *f* manufacturing of crank shaft
Kurbelzapfen *m* crank pin; wrist pin
Kurve *f* curve; path
Kurvenanpassung *f* curve fitting
Kurvenlänge *f* path length
Kurvenlineal *n* French curves; curve template
Kurvenrollgang *m* curved roller table
Kurvenschar *f* family of curves; group of curves
Kurvenscheibe *f* cam
Kurvenverlauf *m* course of curve; trace of curve
kurze Anwärmhitze *f* flash heat
kurzer Flußstahlblock *m* butt ingot
kurzes Nachrichten *n* restriking; tapping
kurze Stützen *fpl* stub column
kurzfristige Verbindlichkeiten *fpl* current liabilities

kurzgeschlossen (Stromkreis) earthed; grounded (am.)
Kurzhubgesenkhammer *m* short-stroke drop hammer
Kurzprüfverfahren *n* accelerated test
Kurzzeitlösung *f* fast acting solution

L

labil labile
Laborant *m* laboratory assistant
Laboratorium *n* assay office; laboratory
Laboratoriumsforschung *f* laboratory research
Laboratoriumsgerät *n* laboratory apparatus; laboratory appliance
Labyrinthfaktor *m* tortuosity factor
Lack *m* lacquer; varnish
Lackabdruck *m* lacquer print
lackieren varnish
lackieren (Band) lacquer
lackiert lacquered; varnished
Lacksysteme *npl* paint systems
Ladebehälter *m* loading bunker
Ladebrücke *f* loading bridge
Ladebühne *f* charging platform
Ladefähigkeit *f* loading capacity
Ladegestell *n* skid
Laderampe *f* loading ramp
Laderaum *m* freight space
Ladung *f* loading
Ladungszahl *f* charge number
Lage *f* bed; condition; course; layer; location; pack; position; situation; state; tier
Lagekugel *f* **(Röntgen)** projection sphere
Lager *n* deposit; seam; stock [house]; store; support; warehouse
Lagerausgießung *f* bearing lining
Lagerbestand *m* warehouse on-hand quantity
Lagerblech *n* bracket
Lagerbock *m* box; porter bar; supporting bracket

Lagerbüchse f bearing box
Lagerdruck m bearing pressure
Lagerfuge f joint of the bed
Lagerfutter n babbitt; brass
Lagergehäuse n bearing box
Lagergröße f stock size
Lagerhalle f warehouse
Lagerhaltung f store-keeping
Lagerkragen m bearing collar
Lagerlänge f (Walzstäbe) mill length
Lager n **(Maschinenelement)** bearing
Lagermetall n babbitt [metal]; bushing metal
lagern locate; rest; stock; store; support
Lagerortstamm m warehouse master file
Lagerplatz m stock pile; stock yard; storage yard; stocking ground; yard
Lagerplatzstamm m warehouse locations master file
Lagerreibung f bearing friction
Lagerschale f axle box; bearing bush[ing]; bearing lining; brass; bush[ing]
Lagerspiel n bearing play
Lagerständer m bearing pedestal
Lagerstätte f deposit
Lagertragfähigkeit f bearing capacity
Lagerung f storage
Lagerwesen n warehouse control
Lage f **verlegen (von Steinen)** lay a course of (bricks)
Lamellenbremse f muliple disk brake
Lamellengraphit m flake graphite; lamellar graphite
Lamellenpumpe f lamella pump
Lamellenreibungskupplung f disc clutch
laminieren laminate
Länge f length
längen lengthen
Längen n extending by stretching
Längen[aus]dehnung f linear expansion
Längenausdehnungskoeffizient m linear expansion coefficient
langgestreckte Moleküle npl long chain molecules
langkettige Moleküle npl long chain molecules
länglich oblong
Langloch n oblong hole
Langsamkühlung f slow cooling
Längsdehnung f linear expansion
Längskraft f longitudinal force
Längsnahtschweißen n straight bead welding
Längsprobenahme f longitudinal sampling
Längsriß m longitudinal crack; split
Längsschneiden n slitting
Längsschnitt m longitudinal section
Längsschwund m shrinkage in length
Längsspannung f membranar residual stress
Längsstich m longitudinal pass
Längsstrecken n elongation
Längsstreckung f elongation
Langstab m long test bar
Längsteilen n slitting
Längsteilschere f slitting shears
Längsträger m stiftener
Längsüberwalzungsfehler m pinch
Längswalzen n longitudinal rolling
Längswelle f line shaft
Langtischfräsen n plano-milling
Langzeitbad n slow acting bath
Langzeitversuch m long-time test
Lanze f lance
Lanzenfangvorrichtung f lance safety gear
Lanzenfrischen n refining steel by top-blowing
Lanzenkosten pl lance cost
Lanzenschlitten m lance carriage
Lanzenwagen m lance carrier
läppen (Oberfläche) lap
Lärmbekämpfung f noise abatement
Lärmminderung f noise reduction
Lärmschutz m protection against noise
Lasche f fish-plate; splice bar
Laschenbolzen m bolt
Laschennietung f butt-joint riveting
Laschenstoß m strap joint assembly

Laschen und Platten *fpl* **(Eisenbahn-Oberbau)** joint bars and fishplates
Laser-Mikrosonde *f* laser microprobe
Laserstrahl *m* laser beam
Last *f* burden; load
Lastangriffspunkt *m* point of [application of] load
Lastbolzen *m* load lug
Lastenaufzug *m* freight elevator
Lasthaken *m* load hook
Lasthebemagnet *m* lifting magnet
Lästigkeit *f* **(Lärm)** annoyance (noise)
Lastkraftwagen *m* truck
Lastschalter *m* **(Lichtbogenofen)** tap changer
Lastspielzahl *f* number of cycles
Lasttraverse *f* loading beam
Last *f* **(Ventil)** lift
Lastverteilung *f* **(Strom)** dispatching
Lastwechsel *m* reversal of stress
Lastwechselfrequenz *f* frequency of load alternations; frequency of load cycles
latente Wärme *f* latent heat
Lauf *m* course; run; travel; way
Laufbahn *f* raceway
Laufbüchse *f* bush[ing]; liner
laufen run
laufend continuous
Läufer *m* leaker; rotor; runner
Läuferstein *m* **(Kokerei)** stretcher brick
Lauffläche *f* bearing face; bearing surface; running surface; tread
Laufflächenwalze *f* tread roll
Laufgewicht *n* sliding weight
Laufkarte *f* route card
Laufkatze *f* crab; skip hoist; trolley
Laufkran *m* overhead travelling crane (OTC); travelling crane
Laufrad *n* rotor wheel; traversing wheel
Laufring *m* race
Laufschlacke *f* running slag
Laufsteg *m* catwalk
Lauf- und Führungsbüchsen *fpl* run and guide bushes
Laufweg *m* path length

Laufzapfen *m* journal; neck
Laufzeit *f* transit time; travel time
Lauge *f* alkaline solution; base; leach; lye
laugen lye
laugenbeständig lye-resisting; resistant to caustic embrittlement
laugenrißbeständig resistant to caustic cracking
Laugensprödigkeit *f* caustic cracking; caustic embrittlement
Lautstärke *f* loudness level (dB)
LD-AC-Verfahren *n* LD-AC process
LD-Verfahren *n* LD process; top blowing process
Lebensdauer *f* life; life-time
Leck *n* leak
lecken leak
leckende Form *f* leaking tuyre
ledeburitischer Stahl *m* ledeburitic steel
Ledeburit *m* ledeburite
Ledermanschette *f* U-leather; crimped leather; cup leather
leer empty
Leere *f* emptiness; vacuum
Leergicht *f* **(Hochofen)** non-coke charge; non-ore charge
Leerlauf *m* idle operation
Leerlaufzeit *f* idle-running period; idle-running time; non-load time
Leerstelle *f* vacancy
legieren alloy
legierter Stahl *m* alloy[ed] steel
legiertes Band *n* alloy strip
Legierung *f* alloy
Legierungsbunker *m* alloyant hopper
Legierungserz *n* alloy ore
Legierungszusatz *m* alloying addition
Legierungszwischenschicht *f* **bei Weißblech** tinplate alloy layer
Lehm *m* clay; loam
Lehre *f* ga[u]ge; template
Lehrling *m* apprentice
Lehrwerkstatt *f* industrial workshop; instructional workshop; teaching workshop
Leichtbau *m* light ga[u]ge design

Leichtbauweise f weight saving construction
leichte Kehlnaht f hollow weld
leichter Formstahl m light sections
Leichtmetall n light metal
Leichtprofil n light section
Leichtstein m light-weight brick
Leistung f capacity; efficiency; operation rate; output; performance; power; production; working capacity
Leistungseinstufung f merit rating
leistungsfähig efficient
Leistungsfähigkeit f capacity; efficiency; power
Leistungsfaktor m power factor
Leistungsgewicht n power-to-weight ratio
Leistungsgrad m efficiency; efficiency factor; performance index
Leistungskabel n power cable
Leistungslohn m accelerating incentive; steepening incentive
Leistungsmerkmal n user facility
Leistungsspitzen-Begrenzungs-Automatik (LBA) f automatic power peak limitation
leistungsstark high power
Leistungssteigerung f increase of ouput
Leistungssummenkurve f cumulative load curve
Leitblech n baffle plate; deflector plate
leiten carry; conduct; convey; lead
leitender Ingenieur m Chief Engineer
leitendes Gleitstück n brush
Leiter m director
Leiter f ladder; scale
Leiter m **(eines Unternehmens)** manager
Leiter m **(elektr.)** conductor
Leitfähigkeit f conductivity
Leitfähigkeit f **(magnet.)** conductibility
Leitschiene f guide rail
Leitspindel f lead screw; leading spindle
Leitspindel-Drehbank f sliding cutting lathe

Leitstrahl m focal radius
Leitsystem n control system
Leitung f cable; direction; lead; line
Leitung f **(Betriebsleitung)** management
Leitung f **(elektr.)** conduction; wire
Leitungsdraht m line wire
Leitungsdruck m pipe-line pressure
Leitungsrohr n line pipe
Leitungsverlegen n wire laying
Leitungswasser n mains water; top water; town water
Leseband n sorting belt
Leseeinheit f **für Disketten** floppy disc reader
Leuchtbildwaage f illuminated dial balance
Leuchtgas n city gas; coal gas; town gas
Leuchtmelder m signal light
Leuchtschaltbild n illuminated mimic panel
Leuchtstofflampe f vacuum tube lamp
Leuchtstoffröhre f fluorescent strip lamp; vacuum tube lamp
Lichtbogen m arc; electric arc
Lichtbogenbeheizung f heating by arc
Lichtbogenbereich m arc flare region
Lichtbogenofen m arc furnace
Lichtbogenofen m **elektrischer** electric arc furnace
Lichtbogenofen m **mit Schwenkdeckel** swing roof arc furnace
Lichtbogen-Preßschweißen n arc pressure welding
Lichtbogen-Schaukelofen m swing type arc furnace
Lichtbogenschneiden n arc cutting
Lichtbogenschweißen n arc welding
Lichtbogen-Widerstandsofen m resistance-arc furnace
Lichtbogenzünden n striking the arc
lichtelektrischer Verstärker m photoelectric amplifier
lichte Weite f clearance; inside diameter
Lichtgitter n lattice grate (for lighting)
Lichtgriffel m light pen

Lichtmikroskopie f optical microscopy
Lichtpause f light print
Lichtquelle f light source; luminous source
Lichtrufanlage f light signal plant
Lichtschnitt m light-section
Lichtschranke f light barrier
Lichtstärke f intensity of light
Lichtstrahlschweißen n laser welding
Lieferbedingungen fpl terms of delivery; terms of supply
Lieferfrist f date of delivery; term of delivery
liefern supply
Liefertermin m delivery promise
Lieferung f delivery; supply
Lieferwerk n supplier
Lieferzustand m condition of delivery
Liegegeld n demurrage
Liegezeit f exposure time; holding time; stay[ing time]
Limonit m brown hematite; limonite
lineares Programmieren n linear programming
Linie f curve; line
Liniennetz n system of coordinates
Linienschnittverfahren n (Korngröße) intercept method; interrupted segment method
Linksgewinde n left-handed thread
Linksschweißung f left hand welding
Liquidität f current financial strength
Liquidusfläche f liquidus [area]
Liquiduslinie f liquidus [line]
Liste f list; schedule; table
Liste f **aufstellen** draw [up] a list; schedule
Liste f **eintragen (in eine...)** include in a list; list; schedule
Lithium n lithium
Litze f strand; stranded wire
Litzendraht m strand wire
Lizenz f license
Lizenzgeber m licenser
Lizenzgebühr f royalty
Lizenznehmer m licensee
Lizenzvertrag m license agreement
Loch n hole; pin hole

Lochband n perforated tape; punched tape
Lochblech n perforated plate
Lochdorn m mandrel; piercer; piercing mandrel; plug
Lochdurchmesser m diameter of bore
lochen pierce; punch
Lochen n hollow forging; piercing; piercing holes
Locher m punch
löcherartige Ausfressung f honeycomb type erosion
Löcher npl **(Bandfehler)** holes
Löcher npl **bilden** pit
Lochfeile f riffler
Lochfräser m slotting cutter
Lochfraß m pitting
Lochfraßkorrosion f selective corrosion
Lochfraßpotential n pitting corrosion potential
Lochkarte f perforated card; punch[ed] card
Lochkartenleser und -stanzer m punched card reader and punch
Lochkartensteuerung f punched-card control
Lochkorrosion f pitting
Lochplatte f **(Schmieden)** swage block
Lochprobe f punching test
Lochschweiße f plug weld
Lochstanze f punching press
Lochstein m perforated brick
Lochstempel m die; piercing die; piercing mandrel; punch
Lochstreifen m perforated tape; punched tape
Lochstreifenleser m tape reader
Lochsuchgerät n pinhole detector
Loch- und Ziehpresse f punching and drawing press
Lochung f perforation
Lochversuch m punching test
Lochwalzwerk n piercer; piercing mill
Lochwerkzeug n punching tool
lockeres Gefüge n porous structure
lockern loosen
Lockerstelle f discontinuity

Lockfeuer n pilot fire
Löffel m bucket; spoon
Löffeldampfbagger m steam shovel
Löffelprobe f spoon test specimen
logische Grundverknüpfung f logical connective
logische Programmanpassung f adapting program logic
Lohn m wage
Lohnanreiz m wage incentive
Lohnempfänger m wage earner
Lohnkosten pl labour costs; wage costs
Lohnliste f payroll
Lohnwalzen n hire rolling; job rolling
Lokalelement n **(Korrosion)** local cell; local element
Lokomotive f engine; locomotive
Lore f buggy (am.); tram
lösbar detachable; resoluble
löschen discharge; unload
löschen (Feuer) extinguish
löschen (Kalk) slake
löschen (Koks) quench
Löschen n quenching
Löschen n **(Kalk)** slaking
Löschrampe f quenching wharf
Löschtrog m water trough
Löschturm m quenching tower
Löschwagen m quenching car
Lösemittel n solvent
lösen dissolve; loosen; release
Lösewalzwerk n detaching mill
Losgröße f lot size
Löslichkeit f solubility
Löslichkeit f **im festen Zustand** solid solubility
Löslichkeit f **im flüssigen Zustand** liquid solubility
losmachen loosen
Los n lot; unit
Lösung f dissolution; loosening; solution
Lösung f **(dissoziierte)** dilute solution
Lösung f **(einer Schraube)** release
Lösung f **(feste)** solid solution
Lösung f **(ideale)** ideal solution
Lösung f **(rasch wirkende)** fast acting solution

Lösungsbehandlung f solution [heat] treatment
Lösungsentropie f solution entropy
Lösungsfähigkeit f solvent capacity; solvent power
Lösungsglühen n solution annealing; solution heat treatment (precipitation hardening)
Lösungsmittel n solvent
Lösungswärme f heat of solution
Lötbarkeit f brazeability; capacity for soldering
Lötbrenner m brazing torch; soldering burner
Lötbruch m **(Feuerverzinken)** stress corrosion by molten zinc
Lötbrüchigkeit f solder brittleness
löten braze
Löten n brazing; soldering
Lötkolben m copper bit; soldering iron
Lötmetall n brazing solder; pewter; solder; spelter
Lötnaht f soldered seam
Lötrohr n blow pipe
Lötrohrflamme f blow-pipe flame
Lötstelle f brazed joint; soldered joint
Lötwasser n soldering fluid
Lötzinn n soldering tin
Lücke f gap
Lückengrad m voidage; voids fraction
Lückengradverteilung f distribution of voids
Luftabkühlung f air cooling; uncontrolled cooling
Luftabschluß m exclusion of air; hermetically sealed
Luftabschrecken n air quenching
Luftaustausch m air interchange
Luftblase f blow hole
Luftdämpfung f air damping
Lufteinblasrohr n air inlet pipe
lüften vent
Lüfter m fan; ventilator
Lufterhitzer m air heater
Luftfahrtwerkstoff m aviation material; material for aircraft industry
Luftfeuchtigkeitsmesser m hygrometer

Luftfilter *m* air filter
Luftfrachtverkehr *m* air freight traffic; air transport
Luftführung *f* air pipeline
luftgekühlt air-cooled
Lufthammer *m* air hammer; air lift gravity hammer
Lufthärten *n* air hardening
Lufthärtestahl *m* air hardening steel
Luftheizkammer *f* air regenerator chamber
Luftkammer *f* air chamber
Luftkanal *m* air duct; air flue; air uptake; uptake
Luftkissen *n* air cushion
Luftklappe *f* air flap valve
Luftkühler *m* air cooler
Luftpatentieren *n* air patenting
Luftreinhaltung *f* air pollution control
Luftreiniger *m* air cleaner
Luftschacht *m* air duct
Luftschicht *f* layer of air; stratum of air
Luftschieber *m* damper
Luftschleier *m* air blast
Luftschmierung *f* air lubrication
Luftschütz *n* air break contact; air gap relay
Luftschutz *m* air raid precautions; air raid protection
Luftstrahl *m* air jet
lufttrocken air dry
Luftüberschuß *m* excess air
Lüftungsanlage *f* ventilation plant
Lüftungsaufsatz *m* ventilator cowl
Luftverunreiniger *m* air pollutant; source of air pollution
Luftverunreinigung *f* air pollution
Luftverunreinigungs-Bekämpfung *f* air pollution abatement
Luftvorwärmer *m* air heater; air preheater; economiser; recuperator
Luftwäscher *m* air washer
Luftweg *m* air duct
Luftzerlegungsanlage *f* air disintegration plant
Luftzug *m* air draft; air duct; air flue; air uptake; vent
Luftzuggewölbe *n* air uptake

Luftzuleitung *f* blast main
Lunker *m* blow hole; pipe; shrink hole; shrinkage cavity; sink hole
Lunkerabdeckmasse *f* anti-pipe compound; pipe eliminator; pipe eradicator
Lunkerbildung *f* piping; shrinking

M

Maerz-Boelens-Ofen *m* Maerz-Boelens furnace; pork pie furnace
Maerz-Gitter *n* Maerz checkers
Magazineinrichtung *f* stores equipment; warehouse equipment
magere Steinkohle *f* uninflammable coal
Magerkohle *f* dry burning coal; feebly caking coal; glance coal; lean coal; non-caking coal; semi-bituminous coal; weakly caking coal
Magnesia *f* magnesia
Magnesidon-Spezialstein *m* magnesidon special brick
Magnesiowüstit *m* magnesio-wüstite
Magnesit-Chromerz-Stein *m* magnesite chrome brick
Magnesitmehl *n* fine-grained mag
Magnesit-Stampfmasse *f* magnesite ramming mass
Magnesitstein *m* magnesite brick
Magnesium *n* magnesium
Magnesiumoxid *n* burnt magnesite
Magnet[ab]scheider *m* magnetic grader; magnetic separator
Magnetband *n* magnetic tape
Magnetbandeinheit *f* magnetic tape reel
Magnetbandspeicher *m* tape recorder
Magnetbandspule *f* magnetic tape reel
Magnetbandsteuerung *f* magnetic tape control
Magnetblasenspeicher *m* bubble memory
Magneteisenstein *m* magnetic iron ore

Magnetfeldglühen *n* magnetic annealing
Magnethammer *m* magnetic hammer
magnetische Anisotropie *f* magnetic anisotropy
magnetische Bandumlenkwalze *f* magnetic roll for strip
magnetische Feldstärke *f* magnetic field strength
magnetischer Fluß *m* magnetic flux
magnetische Rißprüfung *f* magnetic flaw detection
magnetisches Altern *n* magnetic ag[e]ing
magnetisches Drehfeld *n* magnetic rotating field
magnetisches Joch *n* magnet yoke
magnetische Störung *f* magnetic change
magnetische Vorzugsrichtung *f* prefered direction of magnetisation
Magnetisierbarkeit *f* magnetizability
magnetisierende Röstung *f* magnetic roasting
Magnetisierungsachse *f* magnetisation axis
Magnetisierungskraftline *f* line of magnetic force
Magnetit *m* magnetic iron ore; magnetite
Magnetkernspeicher *m* magnetic core memory
Magnetkies *m* magnetic pyrites
Magnetkran *m* magnet crane
Magnetmesser *m* magnetic flow meter
Magnetostriktion *f* magnetostriction
magnetostriktive Ultraschallprüfung *f* magnetostrictive ultrasonic test
Magneto-Strukturprüfgerät *n* magnetic structure examination apparatus
Magnetplattenspeicher *m* disc store; magnetic disc memory
Magnetpulver-Prüfverfahren *n* magnaflux testing method; magnetic powder testing method
Magnetstahl *m* magnetic steel
Magnettrommel *f* magnetic drum

Magnetventil *n* solenoid valve
Mahlanlage *f* crushing plant
Mahlbarkeit *f* grindability
mahlen crush; grind; mill; pulverize
Mahlkörper *m* crusher ball
Mahlläufer *m* muller
Mahlwerk *n* breaker
Makrogefüge *n* macrostructure
Makrohärteprüfung *f* macro hardness test
makroskopischer Reinheitsgrad *m* degree of freedom from coarse non-metallic inclusions
Manganerz *n* manganese ore
manganhaltig manganiferous
Manganhartstahl *m* austenitic manganese steel; manganese steel; straight manganese steel
Mangan-Silicium *n* silico-manganese
Mangan-Silicium-Stahl *m* silico-manganese steel
Manganstahl *m* manganese steel
Mangan-Stahlguß *m* manganese steel casting
Mangel *m* defect; deficiency; lack; shortage
Manipulator *m* manipulator
Mann hinter der Walze *m* catcher
Mannloch *n* man hole
Mannschaft *f* crew; team
Mantel *m* case; casing; jacket; shell
Mantelbrenner *m* multi-fuel annular burner system; shell burner
Mantelstahlrohr *n* jacketted jet pipe
Mantelstützwalze *f* sleeve back-up roll
Mantelwalze *f* chill cast roll
Marke *f* mark
Markiervorrichtung *f* marker
Martensit *m* martensite
Martensitanlassen *n* martensite tempering
Martensitaushärten *n* marag[e]ing
martensitaushärtender Stahl *m* marag[e]ing steel
martensitisch martensitic
martensitische Härtung *f* martensite hardening
martensitischer Stahl *m* martensitic

Martensitpunkt *m* Ms point; martensite transformation point
Martensitzerfall *m* martensite breakdown
Maschendraht *m* netting wire
Maschensieb *n* mesh screen; mesh sieve
Maschenweite *f* aperture
Maschenweite *f* **(Sieb)** mesh; size
maschinell festgeschraubt machine tight
Maschinenausschuß *m* Committee of Mechanical Engineers
Maschinenbau *m* mechanical engineering
Maschinenbaustahl *m* engineering steel; machine construction steel; machinery steel; steel for mechanical engineering
Maschinenbetrieb *m* engineering department; mechanical engineering department
Maschinenguß *m* casting for machine construction; castings for general engineering; engineering castings; machine casting
Maschinenhaus *n* engine house; machine house; power station; winding engine house
Maschinenschlosser *m* fitter
Maschinenstamm *m* machine master file
Maschinenständer *m* standard
Maschinenwesen *n* mechanical engineering
Maschine *f* **zum Verkröpfen und Ab- oder Durchsetzen** joggling machine
Maschine *f* **zur spanlosen Herstellung von Schrauben** machine for forming screws
Maschinist *m* machinist
Maß *n* degree; dimension; extent; ga[u]ge; measure; rate; size
Maßabweichung *f* dimensional variation; permitted dimensional tolerance; size variation; variation in dimension

Maßänderung *f* change in dimension
Masse *f* bulk; mass
Masseformerei *f* dry-sand moulding
Massekopfkokille *f* hot top mould; sinkhead mould
Massekopfkokille *f* **(mit dem weiten Ende oben)** big end up mould
Massel *f* pig
Masselbett *n* pig bed
Masselbrecher *m* pig breaker
Masselform *f* bed pig; pig mould
Masselformmaschine *f* pig moulding machine
Masselgießmaschine *f* pig-casting machine
Masselschläger *m* pig breaker
Massel-Schlagwerkskran *m* pig-breaking travelling crane
Massenbruch *m* mass fraction
Massenerzeugung *f* bulk production
Massengehalt *m* mass fraction
Massengutumschlag *m* bulk handling
Massenherstellung *f* mass production; quantity production; tonnage production
Massenkonzentration *f* mass concentration
Massenschwächungskoeffizient *m* mass absorption coefficient; mass attenuation coefficient
Massenspeicher *m* mass storage device
Massenspektrometrie *f* mass spectrometry
Massenstrom *m* mass [bulk] flux
Massenstromdichte *f* mass flux density
Massenwirkungsgesetz *n* mass action law
maßgeblicher Querschnitt *m* ruling section
maßgenau true to dimension; true to size
Maßgenauigkeit *f* dimensional accuracy
Maßgrenze *f* **(Spielraum)** tolerance
Maßhaltigkeit *f* accuracy to ga[u]ge; accuracy to size; dimensional accuracy; trueness to ga[u]ge

mäßig moderate
massiver Ferrit *m* bulk ferrite
Massiv-Lochen *n* indirect impact extrusion of hollow items
Massivprägen *n* closed-die coining; coining
Massivpressen *n* coining
maßprägen size
Maßprägen *n* sizing
Maßstab *m* rule; scale
Maßtoleranz *f* tolerance on size
Maßvorstoß *m* measuring stop
Maßwalzwerk *n* sizing [rolling] mill; sizing rolls
Mast *m* mast; pole
Material *n* material; stock
Materialbedarf *m* stock requirement
Materialbegleitkarte *f* process card
Materialbestand *m* stock on-hand quantity
Materialbewegung *f* stock transfer
Materialentnahme *f* material withdrawal
materialflußorientiert stock-control oriented
Materialfreigabe *f* stock release
Materiallagerplatz *m* depot
Materialplan *m* stock plan
Materialprüfung *f* materials testing
Materialstamm *m* material master file
Materialverfolgung *f* material tracking
Materialwirtschaft *f* material management
Mathematik *f* mathematics
mathematisches Modell *n* mathematical model
Matratzendraht *m* mattress wire
Matrize *f* die
Matrizenarmierung *f* **(Fließpreßen)** die ring
Matrizenblock *m* die block
Matrizenmantel *m* die bolster
Matrizenstahl *m* die steel
Matrizenwalze *f* bottom roll
Matrize (Untergesenk) lower die
Mattblech *n* dull-finish sheet; terne plate
matte Oberfläche *f* dull finish

matte Schmelze *f* cool melt
mattieren tarnish
Mattschweiße *f* lap
Mattschweiße *f* **(Blockfehler)** cold shut; teeming lap
Mauer *f* wall
mauern brick
Mauerwerk *n* brickwork
Maul *n* throat
Maurer *m* bricklayer; mason
maximale Arbeitsplatzkonzentration *f* **MAK (an Schadstoffen)** maximum concentration at the work place
McQuaid-Ehn-Korngröße *f* McQuaid grain size
Mechaniker *m* mechanic
mechanisch beschädigte Oberfläche *f* bruised surface
mechanische Bearbeitung *f* machining
mechanische Oberflächenbeschädigung *f* dog leg; manipulator mark
mechanisches Einstellglied *n* mechanical focussing mechanism
mechanische Technologie *f* mechanical technology
mechanische Werkstätte *f* machine shop; mechanical workshop; repair shop
mehrachsiger Spannungszustand *m* multi-axial stress condition
Mehrbandanlage *f* multi strand line
mehrdimensionale Verteilung *f* multi variate distribution
Mehrdüsenlanze *f* multiple nozzle lance
Mehreinflußversuch *m* multiple factor experiment
mehrfach manifold; multiple
Mehrfachabbiegen *n* multiple folding
Mehrfachabschneiden *n* multiple cropping
Mehrfachaufteilung *f* cross classification
mehrfach gegliederte Tabelle *f* cross tabulation
Mehrfachkeilbiegen *n* multiple V-form bending

Mehrfachpreßtechnik f multiple pressing
Mehrfachschlagversuch m multiple blow [impact] test
Mehrfachschreiber m multiple recorder
Mehrfachteilung f joint distribution
Mehrfachziehmaschine f multiple drawing bench; multiple drawing machine
Mehrfachziehstein m compound drawing die
Mehrfachzug m multiple drafting; multiple drawing
Mehrfarbenschreiber m multicolour plotter; multicolour recorder
mehrgerüstiges Walzwerk n multiple stand rolling mill
mehrkantiger Block m **(mit eingezogener Seitenfläche)** corrugated ingot; fluted ingot
Mehrkosten pl excess costs
mehrphasige Legierung f polyphase alloy
Mehrrollen-Kaltwalzwerk n cold rolling cluster mill
Mehrscheibenkupplung f multiple disc clutch
Mehrstoffsystem n multicomponent system
mehrsträngige Gießmaschine f multi[ple] strand casting machine
Mehrstufen-Dauerschwingversuch m multi stage fatigue test
Mehrstufenkühlung f multi stage cooling
mehrstufige Gasreinigung f multiple stage gas cleaning
Mehrzonenofen m multiple zone furnace
Mehrzweckofen m all purpose furnace
Meißel m chisel; ga[u]ge
meißeln chip; chisel
Meißelstahl m chisel steel
Meister m boss; foreman
meliert mottled
Membranventil n membrane valve
Menge f amount; output; quantity

Mengenmesser m fluid flow meter; volumeter
Mengenregler m volume regulator
Mengenwert m quantile
Menschenführung f personnel management
Mergel m marl
Merkmal n attribute; feature
Merkmalsklasse f category
Meßbereich m measuring range
Meßblende f measuring orifice
Meßdose f dynamometer
Meßeinrichtung f measuring device
messen measure
Messen n callipering; ga[u]ging; measuring; metering
Messer n blade; cutter
Messer m meter
Messerhalter m blade holder
Messerkopf-Schleifmaschine f cutter head grinding machine
Messerschnittkorrosion f interfacial corrosion; knife-edge corrosion
Messerstahl m cutlery steel
Meßfehler m measuring error
Meßfühler m detecting element; primary element (am.); sensing device
Meßgenauigkeit f precision of measurement
Meßgerät n measuring instrument
Meßgeräteschrank m measuring instrument cupboard
Meßglied n measuring means; measuring unit
Meßgröße f measured variable
Messing n brass; yellow brass
Messinglager n brass bearing
Meßkolben m graduated flask
Meßlänge f ga[u]ge length
Meßleitung f measuring leads; measuring pipe
Meßnadel f feeler ga[u]ge; measuring probe
Meßort m measuring point
Meßschenkel m measuring arm
Meßschiene f measuring rail
Meßschwert n test rod
Meßstelle f measuring junction; measuring point

Meßstellenumschalter m measuring point change-over switch
Meßumformer m measuring transmitter; transducer; transmitter
Messung f measurement
Messung f mit Staurand diaphragm measurement; orifice measurement
Meßwarte f measuring station
Meßwerkzeug n measuring tool
Meßwert m measured value
Meßwerte mpl data
Meßwerterfassung f data collection
Meßwertgeber m pick-up; primary element
Meßwertschreiber m data logger
Meßwertspeicherung f data storage
Meßwertverarbeitung f data processing
Meßzahl f index number
Metallbad n metal bath
Metallbearbeitungsöl n machining oil; metal working oil
Metallblecheinlage f metal insertion
Metalleinsatz m metallic charge
Metallhüttenkunde f metallurgy
Metall-Inertgasschweißen n MIG welding; inert gas metal arc welding
metallische Einlage f metallic insert
Metallkeramik siehe Pulvermetallurgie
Metall-Keramik-Werkstoff m cermet
Metallkleben n bonding of metals; metal bonding
Metallklumpen m slug
Metallkunde f metallography; physical metallurgy
metallkundliche Prüfung f metallurgical test
Metall-Lichtbogenschweißen n metallic-arc welding
Metall-Metalloid-Sinterwerkstoff m sintered metal-metaloid-material
Metallographie f metallography
metallographischer Schliff m microsection
Metallphysik f metal physics
Metallplatte f sheet

Metallrückstände mpl metal residues
Metallsäule f head of metal
Metallschicht f layer
Metall-Schutzgasschweißen n inert gas metal arc welding
Metallseife f metal soap
Metall n seltenes rare metal
Metallspritzen n metal spraying
Metallüberzug m metallic coating
Metallurgie f chemical metallurgy; metallurgy; process metallurgy
metallurgischer Vorgang m metallurgical process
metallverarbeitende Industrie f metalworking industry
Metallwaren fpl metal goods; metal ware
Metallzuführung f unter dem Gießspiegel immersion pouring; submerged pouring
metastabil metastable
Meteoreisenstein m aerosiderite; meteoric iron
Metergewicht n weight per meter
Methan n methane
Mikroätzen n micro etching
Mikrobewegungsanalyse f micromotion analysis
Mikrogefüge n microstructure
Mikrohärte f microhardness
mikrolegierter Baustahl m micro alloyed structural steel
Mikrometerschraube f micrometer ga[u]ge
Mikropelletieren n micro pelletising
Mikropore f micropore; microvoid
Mikroschliff m microsection
mikroskopischer Reinheitsgrad m microscopic degree of purity
Mikrosonde f microprobe
Mindermaß n undersize
minderwertig low grade
Mindestzugfestigkeit f minimum tensile strength
Mineralbestandteil m (Kohle) mineral component; mineral matter
Mineralien npl accessory minerals
Mineralogie f mineralogy

Mineralöl n mineral oil
Miner-Summierung f miner summation
Minette f minette; oolitic [iron] ore
mischbar miscible; mixable
Mischbrenner m proportioning mixer
mischen blend; mix
Mischer m hot metal mixer; mixer
Mischerroheisen n mixer metal
Mischerzpellet n mixed ore pellet
Mischgas n mixed gas
Mischkristall m mixed crystal; solid solution
Mischkristallhärtung f solid solution hardening
Mischkristallseigerung f solid solution segregation
Mischkristallverfestigung f solid solution hardening; solid solution strengthening
Mischpfanne f bull ladle
Mischphase f mixed phase
Mischreibung f mixed friction
Mischung f blend; compound; mixture
Mischungsbett n fines bed
Mischungsentropie f entropy of mixing
Mischungslücke f two-phase region
Mischungsverhältnis n mixing ratio
Mischungswärme f heat of mixture
Mischung f vom Mischbett reclaimed material
Mitarbeiter m **(Mitverfasser)** contributor
mitnehmen pick up
Mitnehmer m cam; carrier; catch; cog
Mittel n agent; appliance; compound; device
Mittelband n medium wide strip
mittelbar indirect
Mittelblech n jobbing [sheet]; light plate; medium sheet
Mittelblech-Walzwerk n jobbing plate mill; jobbing sheet mill
Mitteldraht m medium ga[u]ge wire
Mittelfrequenz-Umformer m medium frequency converter; medium frequency transformer
Mittelgerüst n intermediate roll stand

Mittel n **(mathem.)** mean
Mittelpunkt m center [point]
Mittelstahl-Walzwerk n rolling mill for medium-sized products
Mittelstein m **(eines Blockgespannes)** centre brick
Mittelstraße f intermediate mill
Mittelwalze f central roll; centre roll; middle roll
Mittelwalzwerk n intermediate rolling mill
Mittelwert m average; mean value; median
Mittelwertschreiber m average data recorder
Mittelwertsgerade f line of best fit
Mittelzug m medium drawing
Mittenfrequenz f centre frequency
Mittenrauhwert m centre line average height (CLA); root mean square height (RMS)
Mittenwelle f **(Kaltband)** full center
Mittenwelligkeit f **(Band)** medium waviness
mittige Beanspruchung f axial stress
mittlere Abweichung f standard deviation
mittlere chemische Zusammensetzung f average chemical composition
mittlere freie Weglänge f mean free path
mittlere quadratische Abweichung f mean square deviation
mittlerer Fehler m mean error; standard error
mittlerer Formkasten m cheek
Mitveränderlichkeit f co-variation
Modell n model; pattern
Modell n **mathematisches** mathematical model
Modellsand m facing sand
Modellschreinerei f pattern shop
Modellversuch m simulation test
Modifikation f modification
Modul m modulus
möglicher Fehler m accidental error
Möglichkeit f chance; possibility

Mohrscher Spannungskreis *m* Mohr circle [of stresses]
Molalität *f* molality
molare Masse *f* molar mass
molare Wärmekapazität *f* molar heat capacity
Molarität *f* amount of substance concentration; molarity
Molekularsieb *n* molecular sieve
Molenbruch *m* mole fraction
Möller *m* burden; homogenised ore burden; prepared ore burden; stock
Möllerausbringen *n* burden yield
Möllerberechnung *f* burden calculation; burdening
Möllergewicht *n* burden ratio
möllern blend; burden
Möllersonde *f* charge level indicator; stock line indicator; stock line gauge; stock line recorder
Möllerung *f* burdening
Möller *m* **vorbereiteter** homogenised ore burden; prepared ore burden
Möllervorbereitungsanlage *f* burden preparation plant
Möllerwagen *m* larry car
Molwärme *f* **bei konstantem Volumen (Druck)** heat at constant volume (pressure); molecular heat at constant volume (pressure)
Molybdän *n* molybdenum
Momentumlagerung *f* redistribution of moments
Moniereisen *n* concrete reinforcing steel bars
Monotonie *f* monotonic state
Montage *f* assembling; assembly
Montageingenieur *m* assembly engineer
Montageunternehmer *m* erector of industrial plant
Montanindustrie *f* mining industry
Monteur *m* fitter
montieren assemble; erect; mount
morsch brittle
Mörtel *m* mortar
Mörtelfuge *f* cement joint
Motor *m* motor
Motorenbau *m* engine manufacture; motor construction
Motorschürfwagen *m* motor scraper
Muffe *f* coupling box; socket
Muffel-Durchziehofen *m* continuous muffle type furnace
Muffelofen *m* muffle furnace
Muffelofen *m* **(Härteofen)** gas fired furnace
Muffenkupplung *f* sleeve coupling
Muffenrohr *n* bell and spigot pipe; faucet pipe (am.); socket pipe
Mühle *f* mill
Muldenofen *m* crucible furnace
Müllbeseitigung *f* waste disposal
Müllmischanlage *f* refuse mixing plant
Müllverbrennungsanlage *f* refuse incineration plant
Mündung *f* nose
Mündung *f* **(Konverter)** mouth
Mundungsbär *m* bug; mouth skull
Mündungsring *m* LD lip ring; lip ring
mürbe brittle

N

Nabe *f* boss; hub
nacharbeiten finish
Nacharbeiten *n* dressing
Nachbearbeitung *f* **nach dem Sintern** post sintering operations
nachbehandelte Oberfläche *f* treated surface
Nachbehandlung *f* aftertreatment
Nachbildung *f* simulation
nachblasen after-blow
nach dem Verzinken wärmebehandelter Draht *m* galvannealed wire
nach der 1. Probe *f* **(beim SM-Ofen)** before going on
nach der ersten Überschmiedung *f* after first pass
nachdrehen dress
Nachdrücken *n* resqueezing
Nacheilung *f* **(Walzen)** backward slip (rolling); lagging; peripheral recession

nachgearbeitete Kanten fpl dressed edges
nachgeben yield
nachgiebige Verbindung f flexible connection
nachgießen after-pour; feed; repour
nachglühen reanneal
Nachhall m reverberation
Nachkalkulation f historical costing
Nachlaufregler m follower control device; remote control device
nachmessen check
Nachmessen n checking dimensions; controlling sizes
Nachprägen n resizing
Nachpressen n repressing
nachpressen (Pulvermet.) repress
nachprüfen check; control; verify
nachprüfen (messen) recheck
Nachprüfung f recheck; verification
Nachreinigung f secondary cleaning
Nachrichtenanlage f signaling equipment
Nachrichtenspeicher m message storage unit
Nachsaugen n (Blöcke) feeding
nachschärfen (Beizbad) regenerate; top up
Nachschlacke f (Hochofen) roughing slag
Nachschlagen n restriking
Nachschleifen n regrinding
Nachschneiden n final trimming; finish shaving
nachschweißen re-weld
Nachschwindung f after-contraction
Nachsetzen n subsequent charging
Nachsetzstein m (für SM-Ofengewölbe) filler brick
Nachsintern n high sintering; resintering
nachspüren trace
nachstellbar adjustable
nachstellen adjust
Nachstellzeit f integral action time; reset time
Nachtarbeit f night shift; night turn
Nachtschicht f night turn; night-gang; night-shift
Nachwachsen n (ff. Steine) after-expansion
nachwalzen reroll
Nachwalzen n skin pass rolling; temper rolling
Nachwalzgerüst n sizing stand; skin pass mill stand
nachwärmen sadden
Nachwärmofen m reheating furnace
Nachwuchs m recruits (for training)
Nachzerkleinern n secondary crushing
Nachziehen n stretch reducing by roll drawing
Nachzug m follow up draft
Nadel f needle; pin; pricker
Nadelboden m needle bottom; pinhole plug
Nadeldraht m needle wire
nadelförmig acicular
nadelförmige Kristallbildung f (Stahlblock) scorching
nadelförmige Struktur f (Stahlblock) acicular structure
Nadelfräsen n (zur Beseitigung von entkohlten Schichten) microscalping
nadeliges Pulver n acicular powder
Nadelkristall m acicular crystal
Nadellager n needle bearing
Nadelstichpore f pinhole
Nagel m nail; tack
nageln nail
Näherung f approximation
Nahförderanlage f short distance conveying plant
Nahordnung f short range order
Naht f blister; fin; fine; seam; weld
nahtlos seamless
nahtlos gewalztes Rohr n seamless tube
nahtlos gezogenes Rohr n solid drawn tube
Nahtschweißung f seam welding
Naht f (überwalzte) lap
Namensaktie f registered share
Namensschild n name plate

Näpfchen *n* **(Tiefzug)** cup
Napfziehversuch *m* cupping test
Narbe *f* mark; pit; scar
Nase *f* cam; nose
Nasenprofil *n* bulge profil; ribbed flats
Nase *f* **(Vorsprung)** lug
Naßabscheider *m* water spray collector; wet separator
naßblank gezogener Draht *m* bright wet drawn wire
Nässegehalt *m* **(Probenahme)** moisture content
Naßelektrofilter *m* wet electro filter
Naßentstaubung *f* wet dust removing
Näßeprobe *f* moisture sample
Naß[gas]reinigung *f* wet [gas] cleaning
naß gezogener Draht *m* **(mit heller Oberfläche)** lacquer drawn wire; wet drawn wire
Naßklassieren *n* wet sizing
Naßkühlturm *m* wet cooling tower
Naßlöschen *n* wet quenching
naßmagnetische Aufbereitung *f* wet magnetic dressing
Naßmahlung *f* wet grinding
Naßreiniger *m* scrubber; tower washer; wet scrubber
Naßverzinkung *f* wet galvanising
Naßzug *m* wet drawing
Natriumsulfat *n* sodium sulphate
Natronlauge *f* caustic soda
Naturgas *n* natural gas
naturhart naturally hard
Naturkante *f* mill edge
natürlich natural
natürliches Altern *n* natural ag[e]ing
Naturumlauf *m* natural circulation
Naturversuch *m* **(Korrosion)** field test
Nebelhärten *n* fog quenching
Nebelschmierung *f* mist lubrication
Nebenast *m* **(Dendriten)** secondary arm (dendrites)
Nebenbetriebe *mpl* auxiliaries; auxiliary plants and shops
Nebenecho *n* mode echo
nebeneinander angeordnete Walzgerüste *npl* train of stands

Nebenerzeugnis *n* by-product; derivative
Nebengestein *n* country rock
Nebengleise *npl* siding
Nebenschluß *m* shunt
Nebenschlußmotor *m* shunt wound motor
Nebenschneide *f* end cutting edge; front cutting edge; trail edge
Nebenspannung *f* secondary stress
Nebenzeit *f* downtime; idle period
Neigung *f* batter; slope; susceptibility
Neigung *f* **(Steigung)** inclination
Neigung *f* **(Tendenz)** tendency
Neigungswaage *f* inclination balance
Neigungswinkel *m* **(Spanen)** rake angle; slope angle; tool cutting edge inclination; top rake
Neigung *f* **zu Weichfleckigkeit** liability to the formation of soft spots
NE-Metall *n* non-ferrous metal
Nenndrehzahl *f* nominal speed
Nenner *m* denominator
Nennkraft *f* **einer Presse** press rating
Nennkurzschlußspannung *f* impedance voltage
Nennleistung *f* nominal capacity; rated capacity; rated power
Nennleistung *f* **(Ofentransformator)** name plate rating
Nennmaß *n* nominal size
Nennscheinleistung *f* apparent power; apparent rating; nominal rating
Nennwert *m* nominal value
Nennzahl *f* rating
Nest *n* cluster
Neststichprobe *f* cluster sampling
Neststichprobenverfahren *n* cluster sampling
Nettolohn *m* net wage
Netto-Wärmeverbrauch *m* net heat consumption
Netzanschluß *m* mains circuit connection
netzartige Rißbildung *f* alligator cracking
Netzbelastung *f* supply system loading

Netzebene f grate plane
netzförmig reticular
Netzfrequenz f line frequency (am.); mains frequency
Netzfrequenz-Induktions-Tiegelschmelzofen m line frequency induction crucible melting furnace
netzgeführt system-controlled
Netzplan m graph; network plan
Netzplantechnik f production and evaluation review technique
Netzspannungsschwankung f fluctuation in the mains voltage
Netzwerk n crazing; crocodile skin; lattice
Netzzerfall m disappearance of network pattern
neuer Erfindungsgedanke m **(Patent)** novel object of invention; novelty
Neusilber n nickel silver
neutrale Aufwands- und Ertragskonten npl non-operating income and expenditure accounts
neutrale Linie f **(eines Walzkalibers)** pitch line
neutraler Aufwand m non-operating expenditure
neutralisieren neutralise
Neutronenaktivierung f neutron activation
Neutronenbestrahlung f neutron radiation
neu zustellen reline
Neuzustellung f new lining; relining
Nibbeln n **(Blech)** nibbling
nichtangetriebener Rollgang m idle roller table
Nichteisenmetall n non-ferrous metal
nicht entschwefelt undesulphurised
nicht entzundertes Band n black strip
nicht formhaltig off-size
nicht fortschreitender Dauerbruch m non-propagating fatigue crack
nicht leitend non-conducting
nichtlineare Korrelation f curvilinear correlation
nichtlineares Glied n non-linear member

nichtmagnetisierbarer Stahl m non-magnetizable steel
nicht maßhaltig non-sizing; offga[u]ge; running out
nicht maßhaltig geschnitten not cut to pattern
nichtmetallischer Einschluß m non metallic inclusion
nicht nachgewiesen (in Tabellen: n. n.) not determined
nichtrostend non corroding; rustless; stainless
nichtrostender Stahl m stainless steel
nichtselbsttätige Regelung f non automatic control
nichtspanabhebend chipless; swarfless
nichtwirbelnde Düse f **(Stranggießen)** non swirl nozzle
Nickel n nickel
Nickelstahl m nickel steel
niederblasen blow down; blow out
niederbringen sink
Niederdruckgasleitung f low pressure gas main
Niederdruckmanometer n low pressure manometer
Niederdruckzylinder m low pressure cylinder
Niederfrequenzofen m low frequency induction furnace
Niederfrequenzschweißen n low frequency welding
Niederhaltedruck m stripper pressure
Niederhalter m blank holder
Niederschachtofen m low shaft [blast] furnace
Niederschlag m deposit; precipitate
niederschlagen abate; deposit; precipitate
niederschmelzen melt down
niederschmelzen (umschmelzen) melt down
Niederschrift f **(EDV)** printout
Niederspannungsanlage f low tension plant
Niederspannungsautomat m low tension automatic circuit breaker

Niederspannungsgenerator *m* low voltage generator
niedrig gekohlter Stahl *m* low carbon steel
niedriglegierter Stahl *m* low alloy steel
niedrigster Leerlauf *m* low idle [run]
Niedrigtemperaturzerfall *m* **NTZ** low temperature break LTB; reduction degradation index RDI
Nierenbruch *m* **(Schiene)** shatter crack
Niet *m* rivet
nieten rivet
Nietloch *n* rivet hole
Nietmaschiene *f* riveting machine
Nietprüfung *f* rivet test
Nietschweiße *f* plug weld
Nietstahl *f* rivet steel
Nietstempel *m* snap riveting set
Nietverbindung *f* riveted joint
Niob *n* columbium; niobium
Nippel *m* nipple
Nitrid *n* nitride
Nitridbildner *m* nitride former; nitriding agent
Nitrieren *n* nitriding
Nitrierhärten *n* nitriding; nitrogen hardening
Nitrierhärtetiefe *f* depth of nitration
Nitrierstahl *m* nitriding steel
nitrierte Schicht *f* nitrided case
Niveau *n* level
Nocken *m* cam; lug
Nockenherdofen *m* notched hearth furnace
Nockenwelle *f* camshaft
Nomogramm *n* nomogram; straight-line chart
Norm *f* standard
normalglühen normalise
Normalglühen *n* normalising
normalisierendes Umformen *n* normalising forming
Normalkiste *f* base box (sheets)
Normalkraft *f* normal force
Normalleistungsofen *m* regular power furnace

Normalprofil *n* standard [structural] section; standard [structural] shape
Normalspannung *f* normal stress
Normalstein *m* standard square [brick]
Normalverteilung *f* normal distribution
Normblende *f* standard orifice
Normdüse *f* standard nozzle
Normenvorentwurf *m* rough draft of a standard
Normfallbeschleunigung *f* standard acceleration of free fall
Normgröße *f* standard size
Normprobe *f* standard specimen
Normstahl *m* standard steel
Normteil *n* standard part
Normung *f* standardisation
Normvorschrift *f* standard specification
Notabstich *m* **(Hochofen)** cast through the cinder notch
Notbremse *f* emergency brake
Notfall *m* emergency
Notform *f* auxiliary tuyre
Notstromaggregat *n* emergency power unit
Nullanschlag *m* zero dead stop
Nulleinstellung *f* zero setting
nuten groove; slot

O

Oberbär *m* upper ram
Oberbaumaterial *n* permanent way material; track material
Oberdruck *m* top roll pressure
oberer Heizwert *m* gross caloric power (am.); upper caloric value
oberer Schmiedesattel *m* **(das Obergesenk)** upper die block
oberes Teil *n* top
obere Streckgrenze *f* upper yield point
obere Zwischenstufe *f* upper bainite structures
Oberfläche *f* area; surface; surface area

Oberflächenabdruck *m* **(Mikroskopie)** surface replica
oberflächenaktiver Stoff *m* surface active agent
Oberflächen-Aufreißung *f* **(durch Zusammenkleben beim Walzen)** sticker break
Oberflächenbehandlung *f* surface treatment
Oberflächenbeschaffenheit *f* surface condition; surface finish; surface quality
Oberflächeneindruck *m* **(Kaltwalzen)** mark
Oberflächenfehler *m* surface defect; surface imperfection
oberflächenhärten case harden
Oberflächenhärte *f* skin hardness
Oberflächenhärten *n* surface hardening
Oberflächenkonzentration *f* surface concentration
Oberflächenporen *fpl* pepperbox; pinholes; pitted surface; skin holes
oberflächenrein flawless surface finish
Oberflächenriß *m* seam; surface crack; surface tear
Oberflächenschutzmittel *n* surface protective agent
Oberflächenspannung *f* surface tension
Oberflächenveredelung *f* finishing; surface treatment
Oberflächenvorbehandlung *f* **für das Kaltfließpressen** cold extrusion finish
Oberflächenzustand *m* finish quality; surface quality
oberflächliches Walzen *n* **mit geringem Druck** pinch rolling; skin pass rolling; temper [pass] rolling
Obergesenk *n* hob
Oberkasten *m* upper frame [cope]
Oberkolben *m* upper ram
Obersatteltraverse *f* top tool carrier
Oberschwingung *f* harmonic oscillation

Oberspannung *f* primary voltage
Oberstempel *m* upper punch
Oberwalze *f* top roll; upper roll
Objekttisch *m* **(Mikroskop)** stage
Objektträger *m* **(Elektronenmikroskop)** specimen holder
Obligation *f* bond
OBM-Verfahren *n* Q-BOP process
Ofen *m* furnace; stove
Ofenalter *n* age of the furnace
Ofenatmosphäre *f* furnace atmosphere
Ofenauskleidung *f* furnace lining
Ofenbär *m* salamander
Ofenbegichtung *f* charging
Ofenbetrieb *m* furnace operation; furnace practice
Ofen *m* **(Brennofen)** kiln
Ofen *m* **für satzweisen Einsatz** batch furnace
Ofenfutter *n* furnace lining
Ofengang *m* furnace working
Ofengefäß *n* furnace casing; furnace shell; furnace vessel
Ofen *m* **(Kokerei)** oven
Ofenkopf *m* port block; port end
Ofenmantel *m* furnace casing
Ofenmauer-Dichtungsmasse *f* jointing compounds for furnace masonry
Ofenmauerung *f* furnace lining
Ofenraum *m* furnace chamber; hearth
Ofenraum-Druckregelung *f* furnace pressure control
Ofenreise *f* campaign; furnace campaign
Ofensau *f* salamander; sow
Ofenstock *m* mantle
Ofentür *f* furnace door
Ofenwarte *f* furnace control station
Ofenzunder *m* furnace scale
Offenbundglühofen *m* open-coil annealing furnace
offene Kokille *f* open top mould
offenes Gesenk *n* open die; plain die
offenes Gleitlager *n* plain bearing
offenes Kaliber *n* open groove; open pass

offene Steuerung f open loop control
offen prozeßgekoppelt on-line open loop
Öffnung f aperture; opening; orifice
Öffnungswinkel m **(Ultraschall)** angle of beam spread
Öffnungswinkel m **(Ziehdüse)** approach angle
ohmscher Widerstand m ohmic resistance
Oktavspektrum n octave analysis
Okularmikrometer n ocular micrometer
Öl n oil
Ölabdichtung f oil seal
Ölabscheider m oil separator
Ölanlassen n oil tempering
Ölbrenner m oil burner
Öldruckkabel n oil filled cable
ölen oil
Ölfeuerung f oil firing
Ölfilm m oil film
Ölflutlager n oil film bearing
ölhaltende Schicht f foil-retaining layer
ölhaltig oil emulsive; oily
Ölhärten n oil hardening; oil quenching
Ölhärter m oil hardening steel
Ölhydraulik f oil hydraulics
Ölkarburierungsanlage f oil carburising plant
Ölkeil m oil wedge
Ölkühler m oil cooler
Ölnebelschmierung f oil mist lubrication; oil mist spray; oil spray lubrication
OLP-Konverter m oxygen lance powder converter
Ölschiefer m oil shale
Ölspargerät n apparatus to economise oil
Öltränkung f oil impregnation
ölvergüteter Draht m oil quenched and tempered wire
ölverseuchtes Erdreich n oil contaminated soil
Ölwechsel m oil change
Operations- und Fehleranzeigen f operation and error indicators
Optimierung f optimisation
optisches Pyrometer n optical pyrometer
Orangenhaut f **(Bandfehler)** orange peel
Ordnung f array; order
Ordnungs-Umwandlung f order transformation
Ordnungszahl f atomic number
organischer Stoff m organic matter
Organosol n organosol
Orientierungsabhängigkeit f orientation dependence
Orthosilicat n orthosilicate
ortsfest stationary
Ortskoordinaten fpl coordinates
Öse f eye; lug; staple
osmotischer Druck m osmotic pressure
Oszillation f oscillation
Oszillograph m oscillograph
Ovalkaliber n oval groove; oval pass
Oxidation f calcination
Oxidationsmittel n oxidant
Oxidbelag m oxide film
Oxideinschluß m oxide inclusion
Oxideinsprenkelung f **(Kaltwalzen)** broken oxide
Oxidhaut f oxide skin
oxidieren oxidise

P

paarweise gewalzte Bleche npl doubles
Pack m pack
Päckchen n parcel
packen pack
Packlage f bottoming material
Packmaschine f packing machine
Packung f packing; stuffing
Packungsdichte f packing density
Paddelmischer m paddle mixer
Paket n box; pack

Paketieren *n* briquetting; bushelling; fag[g]oting
Paketierschrott *m* fag[g]ot iron; fag[g]oting scrap
paketierter Eisenschrott *m* baled scrap; fagotted iron [scrap]
Paketschneiden *n* **(Blech)** mill shearing
Paketwalzen *n* pack rolling
Paketwärmofen *m* fag[g]oting furnace; pack heating furnace; sheet heating furnace
Palette *f* pallet
Panzer *m* casing
Panzer *m* **(Hochofen)** jacket; steel jacket; steel plate lining
Panzerplatte *f* armour plate
Panzerplatten-Walzwerk *n* armour plate rolling mill
Papiersack *m* paper bag
parallele Längsfehler *mpl* **durch Überwalzen** tramlines
Parallelflanschträger *m* parallel flanged beam; parallel flanged joist
Parallelversuch *m* replication
Paramagnetismus *m* paramagnetism
Parameter *m* parameter; statistic
Parkerverfahren *n* Parkerising
Parry-Kegel *m* Parry type cup and cone arrangement
Parry-Verschluß *m* Parry type cup and cone arrangement
Partialdichte *f* mass concentration
Partialdruck *m* partial pressure
partielle Ableitung *f* partial derivative
partielles Stauchen *n* incremental forging
Passiva *npl* liabilities
Passivierbarkeit *f* capacity for passivation
passivieren deaden (flotation)
Passivierung *f* passivation
Passivität *f* passivity
Passivschicht *f* passive layer
Paßmaß *n* nominal size
Paßschraube *f* shoulder screw
Paßstück *n* fitting piece
Passung *f* fit

Passungsrost *m* galling rust
Passwortsicherung *f* password protection
Pastenaufkohlen *n* paste carburising
Pastenverfahren *n* paste process
Patentamt *n* patent office
Patent *n* **angemeldet** patent applied for
Patent *n* **anmelden** apply for a patent
Patentanmeldung *f* patent application
Patentanspruch *m* **berichtigen** revise a claim
Patentanspruch *m* **vorwegnehmen** anticipate a claim
Patentanwalt *m* patent agent
Patentbeschreibung *f* patent specification
Patenteinspruch *m* opposition to a patent
Patent *n* **erteilen** grant a patent
patentieren patent; patent (wire)
patentierter Seildraht *m* **mit besonders hoher Zugfestigkeit** high strength patented wire rope
patentierter Stahldraht *m* patented steel wire
Patentinhaber *m* patentee
Patentschrift *f* letters patent
patentschutzfähige Neuheit *f* patentable novelty
Patentverletzung *f* infringement of a patent
Patentvorbenutzung *f* prior use
Pause *f* blue print
pausen trace
PD-Regler *m* proportional plus rate [derivative] action controller
Pech *n* pitch
Pechkohle *f* caking coal; pitch coal
Pegel *m* **(air pollution)** ga[u]ge
Pegelwert *m* ga[u]ge reading (air pollution)
Pellet *n* pellet
pelletieren pelletise
Pelletierteller *m* balling disc; pelletising disc
Pelletiertrommel *f* pelletising drum
Pelletierung *f* pelletising

Pendelglühen n cycle annealing
Pendelhammerschlagwerk n pendulum impact test machine
Pendelklappe f shuttle valve
Pendellager n self aligning bearings
pendeln cycle
pendelnd hunting
pendeln mit Schweißelektrode weave with electrode (welding)
Pendelrollenlager n self aligning roller bearing
Pendelsäge f oscillating saw
Pendelschleifmaschine f swing grinding machine
Pendelung f oscillation
Perforiermaschine f perforating machine
Periode f (elektr.) cycle
Perioden fpl **je Sekunde** cycles per second
Periodensystem n **der chemischen Elemente** periodic system
periodisches Walzen n **(im Gesenk)** die rolling
Peritektikum n peritectic
peritektische Umwandlung f peritectic transformation
perlenschnurartige Carbidausscheidung f discontinuous chain type of carbide precipitation
Perlit m pearlite
perlitarmer Sonderbaustahl m **(PAS)** fine grained low pearlite structural steel
Perlitguß m pearlite cast iron
perlitisch pearlitic
perlitischer Stahl m pearlitic steel
perlitische Struktur f perlitic structure
Perlitisieren n isothermal annealing
Perlitkorn n pearlite grain
Perlkoks m pea coke; rubbly culm coke
Permeabilität f permeability
Personalbestand m number of operatives
Personalbüro n staff department
Personalkosten pl payroll
Personenaufzug m passenger lift

Petrochemie f petrochemistry
petrographischer Dünnschliff m petrographic thin section
Petroleum n petroleum
Petrolkoks m petroleum coke
Pfahlramme f pile driver
Pfanne f ladle
Pfanne f **abstehen lassen** hold a ladle
Pfannenabdeckmasse f ladle covering compound
Pfannenaufheizanlage f ladle heating plant
Pfannenausgießzeit f ladle emptying time
Pfannenausguß m ladle lip; nozzle of a ladle
Pfannenausmauerung f ladle lining
Pfannenbär m button; salamander; skull
Pfannenbedienungsmann m ladle operator
Pfannenbehandlung f ladle treatment
Pfannenblech n roofing sheet
Pfannenbock m ladle stand
Pfannenentgasung f ladle degassing
Pfannengabel f ladle shank
Pfannengehäuse n ladle casing; ladle shell
Pfannengießzeit f ladle pouring time
pfannenmetallurgische Nachbehandlung f ladle metallurgy aftertreatment
Pfannennachbehandlung f aftertreatment; ladle treatment
Pfannenrestbildung f formation of skull in ladle
Pfannensinterversuch m box testing
Pfannenstein m ladle brick
Pfannenstopfen m ladle stopper
Pfannentrocknungsanlage f ladle drying plant
Pfannenwagen m ladle bogie; ladle car
Pfannenzusätze mpl ladle additions
Pfeiler m column
Pfeilhöhe f pitch
Pfeilzahn m herringbone tooth
Pflichtprüfung f audit
Phänomen n phenomenon

Phase f phase
Phasenentmischung f phase separation
Phasengrenze f phase boundary
Phasengrenzreaktion f phase boundary reaction
Phasenkontrastmikroskopie f phase contrast microscopy
Phasenschieber m phase advancer; phase shifter
Phasenspannung f phase voltage
Phasenumwandlung f phase transformation
Phasenverschiebung f (elektr.) lag; phase displacement
Phasenwinkel m phase angle
Phasenzertrümmerung f phase disintegration
Phenolwasserbeseitigung f phenol water removal
Phenolwasserverwertung f phenol water disposal
phosphatieren phosphate coat
Phosphatieren n phosphate coating
phosphatiert phosphate treated
Phosphatierung f phosphating
Phosphidseigerungsstreifen m phosphide streak
Phosphor m phosphorus
phosphorhaltiges Roheisen n phosphoric pig iron
Phosphorsäure f phosporic acid
Photozelle f photoelectric cell
pH-Wert Regler m pH-value regulating instrument
Physik f physics
physikalische Chemie f physical chemistry
Picke f pick [axe]
Pickelbildung f pick-up
Pigmentierung f pigmentation
Pilgerdorn m piercer
pilgern put through a pilger mill
Pilgerschritt-Rohrwalzwerk n pilger mill of the Mannesmann type; pilger step-by-step-type seamless tube rolling mill
Pilgerschrittschweiße f step back welding
Pilgerschrittverfahren n reciprocating rolling process
Pilgerschrittwalzen n pilger mill rolling
Pilgerwalze f pilger roll
pipettieren pipette
PI-Regler m proportional plus reset action controller
Plan m device; lay-out; schedule
Planarbeit f schedule work
Planck-Konstante f Planck constant
plandrehen face
Planetenrad n carrier pinion; planet wheel
Planetenwalzen n planetary rolling
Planetenwalzwerk n planetary mill
plangemäß according to plan
Planheit f flatness; shape
Planheitsregelung f shape control
planieren level
Plankosten pl predetermined standard rates
planmäßig well planned
Planschleifen n face grinding; surface grinding
Planungsforschung f operational research
Planwirtschaft f planned economy
Planziel n target
Plasmalichtbogenschweißen n plasma arc welding
Plasmanitrieren n plasma nitriding
Plasmaschneidbrenner m plasma cutting torch
Plasmaspritzen n plasma spraying
Plasmastrahlschweißen n plasma jet welding
Plastifizierungsmittel n plasticiser
plastische feuerfeste Masse f refractory mouldable material
plastische Formänderung f plastic deformation
plastisches Gelenk n plastic articulation
Plastisol n plastisol
Plastizität f ductility; plasticity
Platine f mill bar; sheet bar

Platine für Weißblechherstellung 122

Platine f **für Weißblechherstellung** tinplate bar
Platinengewicht n sheet bar weight
Platinenstab m **mehrfacher Länge** sheet bar multiple
Platinenwalzwerk n sheet bar rolling mill
Platinenwärmofen m bar [heating] furnace; sheet bar reheating furnace
plättchenförmig flaky
Platten[förder]band n apron conveyor
Plattenkokille f plate mould
Plattenspeicher m **(EDV)** disc memory
Plattformlore f buggy (am.)
Plattformwaage f weighbridge
plattieren clad
Plattieren n sandwich rolling
Plattieren n **(durch Aufwalzen)** cladding
Plattierungsmetall n cladding metal
platzen burst
Platzwechsel m **(Atom)** change of site
Pleuelstange f connecting rod
Plombendraht m locking wire; seal wire
Plunger[kolben] m plunger
Pochschuh m boss; stamp shoe; stamp stem
Pochwerk n stamp mill
Poissonsche Zahl f Poisson's ratio
Pol m pole
Polarbindung f polar bond
polare Moleküle npl polar molecules
polares Molekül n polar molecule
Polarisation f **von Leitungselektronen** conduction electron polarisation
Polarkette f polar chain
Polarkopf m polar head
Polarographie f polarography
Polarverbindung f polar compound
Polfigur f pole figure
Polierbock m polishing frame
polieren buff; burnish; polish
Polieren und Handrichten n shafting
Poliergerüst n planishing stand
Poliermaschine f buffer
Polierscheibe f buff
poliert und geätzt polished and etched

micro section
Polierwalzengerüst n bull head
Polterwerk n **(Draht)** shaker
Polypengreifer m orange peel bucket
Polzwinge f work clamp (earthing clamp)
Pore f pore; void
Poren fpl **(Bandfehler)** pitting
Porenbildner m pore forming material
Poren fpl **mit Mineralöl schließen** seal coat
porig porous
porös porous
Porosität f porosity
Porosität f **unter der Oberfläche** subsurface porosity
Portalhubwagen m straddle carrier
Portalkran m portal crane
Position f item
Posten m lot
Potential n potential
Potentiometer n potentiometer
prägen engrave
Prägen n stamping
prägen (Münze) coin
Prägerichten n flattening; straightening in patterned dies
Prägestempel m coin; stamping tool
Prägewalzen n roll embossing
Prägung f embossing
Prallblech n baffle plate
Prallbrecher m coarse reduction impact crusher; impact crusher
Prallmühle f rebound crusher
Prämie f bonus
Prämienlohnsystem n premium bonus system
Pratzen n bracket
Präzisionsguß m precision investment casting
Präzisionsmaschinenteil n precision machine element
Präzisionsstahlrohr n precision steel tube
Präzisionswaage f analytical balance
P-Regeleinrichtung f proportional action controller
Preis m price; rate

Preisbindung f price maintenance
Preisherabsetzung f price cut; price reduction
Preisnachlaß m price allowance
Preissteigerung f price rise
Prellbock m bumper
Preßbarkeit f compressibility
Preßblech n sheet suitable for press work
Preßboden m dished head
Preßbolzen m **(Strangpressen)** extrusion billet
Preßdichte f green density
Preßdruck m compacting pressure
Preßdruckschmierung f pressure lubrication
Preßdüse f die; extrusion die
pressen briquette
Presse f press
Pressenhub m press stroke
Pressen n **mit schwebender Matrize** floating die pressing
Preßform f die
Preßformauskleidung f die lining
Preßformgehäuse n die body
Preßguß m die casting
Preßgüte f stamping quality
Preßhärten n press quenching
Preßkolben m ram
Preßkopf m crown
Preßkörper m compact
Preßling m blank; briquette; compact; drop stamping; green body; unsintered body
Preßluftmeißel m pneumatic chisel
Preßluftschleifmaschine f pneumatic grinder
Preßluftstampfer m pneumatic rammer
Preßluftzuleitung f compressed-air pipe
Preßnahtschweißen n mash seam welding
Preßrohlinge mpl stampings
preßschweißbar pressure weldable
Preßschweißen n pressure welding
Preßspannung f press fit
Preßstofflager n composition bearing

Preßstumpfschweißen n straight flash welding
Preßwasserpumpe f water pressure pump
Preßweg m press stroke
Preßwerkzeug n die set
Primärcarbid m primary carbide
Primärfleck m **(Röntgen)** primary point
Primärgefüge n primary structure
Primärteilchen n single [crystal] particle
Primärzunder m furnace scale
Prismenspektrum n prismatic spectrum
Probe f experiment; sample; specimen; test piece; test specimen; trial
Probe f **auf die Güte der Anpassung** test of quality of fit
Probeerhebung f exploratory survey
Probefahrt f trial; trial run
Probekörper m test piece; test specimen
Probelöffel m test spoon
Probenahme f sampling
Probenahme f **periodische systematische** periodic systematic sampling
Probenheber m sample thief
Probe f test
Probenlage f position of sample
Probennehmer m sampler
Probestab m test bar
Probestück n test piece; test specimen
Probezählung f test census
probieren assay
Produktion f production
Produktionsausfall m loss of production
Produktionsbeginn m production start
Produktionsbericht m production report
Produktionsmittel n production facility
Produktionsplanungsübersicht f survey of the production plan
Produktionssteuerung f production control
Produktionszahlen fpl output rates; production figures

Produktivität f productivity
Profil n profile; section; shape; steel section
Profile npl **für Bodenbeläge** floor covering sections
Profile npl **für Decken** ceiling sections
Profile npl **für Turbinenschaufeln** turbine blade sections
Profilglattwalzen n **von Hohlkörpern** smooth rolling of tubular shapes
Profil n **(Hochofen)** construction lines; outlines
profilieren shape
profilierte Walze f grooved roll; shaped roll
Profilierung f shaping
Profilkaliber n shaping groove
Profil-Längswalzen n longitudinal rolling of shapes
Profil-Querwalzen n cross rolling of shapes
Profilrohr n special section tube
Profilschere f section shearing machine
Profilschere und Lochstanze f shearing machine and power punching
Profil-Schrägwalzen n skew rolling of shapes
Profil-Schrägwalzen n **von Hohlkörpern** skew rolling of tubular shapes
Profil-Schrägwalzen n **von Vollkörpern** skew rolling of solid sections
Profilstahl m sectional steel; steel shapes; structural shapes; structural steel
Profilstahl-Walzwerk n section [rolling] mill; shape [rolling] mill; structural [steel rolling] mill
Profilstich m forming pass
Profilwalze f shape roll
Profilwalzen n **von Bändern** roll-forming of strips
Programmausrüstung f **(Computer)** software
Programmdokumentation f software documentation
programmieren program
Programmkarte f program card

Programmregelung f program control; time program control
Programmspeicher m program memory; program storage
Proportionalbereich m range of proportionality
Proportionalitätsgrenze f limit of proportionality
Protokollierung f reporting
prozentuale Längenzunahme f **(eines Bleches beim Kaltwalzen)** temper
Prozeßdaten npl process data
Prozeßidentifikation f process identification
Prozeßlenkung f process control
Prozeßsteuerung f process control
prozeßsynchrone Rechenarbeit f online computation
prüfbar assessable [properties]
Prüfbericht m **(Bilanz)** auditor's certificate
Prüfbescheinigung f test certificate
Prüfeinrichtung f testing facility
prüfen audit; determine; examinate; test; try; verify
Prüfen n **auf Richtigkeit** verification
Prüfen n **nach beiden Ausläufern der Prüfverteilung** double-tailed test
Prüfen n **nach einem Ausläufer der Prüfverteilung** single-tailed test
Prüfer m auditor
Prüfer m **(Arbeiter)** verifying machine operator
Prüfer m **(Maschine)** verifier
Prüfgerät n testing set
Prüfkopf m sensor
Prüflast f test load
Prüfmaschine f testing machine
Prüfmaschine f **mit Laufgewichtswaage** lever testing machine
Prüfstab m test bar
Prüfstück n test piece; test specimen
Prüfumfang m amount of inspection
Prüfung f check; control; determination; examination; inspection; test[ing]
Prüfung f **auf Abplatzverhalten** spalling test

Prüfung f auf Zufälligkeit test for randomness
Prüfung f der statistischen Sicherung significance test
Prüfverfahren n testing method
Prüfverteilung f standard distribution
Prüfwert m test value
Puddelluppe f mill bar; muck bar
Puddeln n im flüssigen Zustand wet-puddling
Puddelroheisen n puddle pig
Puddelstahl-Walzwerk n muck mill
Puddelverfahren n puddle process
Puffer m buffer; bumper
Pulsfrequenz f puls frequency; pulse frequency
Pulveraufkohlen n pack carburising; powder carburising
Pulverbrennschneiden n powder cutting
pulverisieren levigate; pulverise
Pulvermetallurgie f powder metallurgy
pulvern comminute; pulverise
Pulvernitrieren n powder nitriding
Pulverspritzen n powder spraying
Pulverteilchen n powder particle
Pumpenhaus n pumping house
Pumpenhauswärter m pump house attendant
Pumpenschalter m pump switch
Punkt m gemeinsamer Kupplung (Lichtbogenofen) point of common coupling (pcc)
Punktrasterverfahren n dot-scanning method
Punktschreiber m dotted line recorder
Punktschweißen n spot welding
Punktschweißmaschine f spot welder; spot welding machine
Punktschweißung f spot welding
Punktschweißzange f spot welding electrode holder
Purpurerz n blue billy
putzen burr; trim
Putzen n slug
putzen (Blöcke) chip; deseam
putzen (Gußstücke) clean; dress; fettle; snag
Putzer m fettler
Putzerei f cleaning shop; cleaning shop (fettling shop); dressing shop
Putzholz n burnishing stick
Putzmaschine f boshing machine
Putztrommel f tumbler
Pyritabbrand m pyrites cinders
Pyrometer n pyrometer
pyrometrischer Wirkungsgrad m pyrometric efficiency
pyrophorer Gichtstaub m pyroforic blast-furnace flue dust
Pyrophorität f degree of inflammability

Q

quadratisch square
quadratischer Mittenrauhwert m root mean square height (RMS)
quadratisches Mittel n quadratic mean
Quadratstahl m square bar steel
Quadratwurzel f square root
Qualitätsblech n quality sheet metal
Qualitätseisen n high-grade iron
Qualitätsguß m high-grade casting
Qualitätskontrolle f quality control
Qualitätsmerkmal n feature; quality characteristic
Qualitätsstahl m high-grade steel; quality steel
Qualitätsstelle f quality control point
Qualitätsüberwachung f quality control
Qualitätswerkstoff m high quality material
Qualm m dense smoke; fume; smoke
Quant n quantum
Quanten npl quanta
quantisieren quantize
quantitativ quantitative
Quartil n quartile
Quartogerüst n four-high stand
Quarz m quartz

Quarzit *m* quartzite
Quarzitfindling *m* boulder of quartzite
Quarzsand *m* silica sand
Quarz-Schamotte-Stein *m* quartz grog brick
quasi-binärer Schnitt *m* quasi-binary section
Quecksilber *n* mercury
Quellbinder *m* swelling binder
Quelle *f* source
Querbiegeversuch *m* transverse bending test
Querbruch *m* **(auf Feinblech)** cross break
Querdehnung *f* transverse strain
Querfalte *f* transverse lap
Querfaltversuch *m* cross folding test
Querfließpressen *n* transverse impact extrusion
Quergleiten *n* cross slip
Querhaupt *n* cross head
Querkraft *f* radial stress
querkraftfreies Biegen *n* bending without radial force
Querprobe *f* transverse test specimen
Querprobenahme *f* transverse sampling
Querriß *m* transverse crack
Querschlepper *m* skid
Querschliff *m* transverse microsection
Querschneiden *n* cutting to length
Querschnitt *m* cross section; section; transverse section
Querschnittsfläche *f* cross sectional area
Querschnittsverjüngung *f* tapering of the cross section
Quer-Strangpressen *n* transverse extrusion of rods and tubes
Querteilanlage *f* cut-to-length-line
Querträger *m* cross-girder
Querverankerung *f* cross supports
Querwalzen *n* cross rolling; transverse rolling
Querwölber *m* end arch brick
Querzugversuch *m* tensile test across the rolling direction
quetschen squeeze

Quetschgrenze *f* compressive yield point; crushing yield point
Quetschriß *m* **(Stranguß)** pinch roll crack
Quetschung *f* crushing
Quote *f* quota
Quotenauswahl *f* quota sampling
Quotenstichprobe *f* quota sampling

R

Räderfräsmaschine *f* gear milling machine
Rädergetriebe *n* gear train
Radersatzteil *n* spare part for wheel
Räderuntersetzung *f* gear reduction
Rädervorgelege *n* back gear
Radialbohrkern *m* trepanned core
Radialbohrmaschine *f* radial drilling machine
Radialprobe *f* radial test
radioaktiver Zerfall *m* radioactive decay
radioaktives Isotop *n* radioactive isotope
radioaktive Spurenelemente *npl* radioactive tracers
Radioaktivität *f* radioactivity
radiochemische Untersuchung *f* radio-chemical test
Radiographie *f* radiography
Radius *m* radius
Radkörper *m* wheel body
Radkranz *m* wheel rim
Radnabe *f* wheel hub
Radreifen *m* tyre; wheel tire
Radreifenblock *m* tire ingot
Radreifen-Gußblock *m* cheese
Radreifen-Walzwerk *n* tire rolling mill
Radsatz *m* wheel set
Radscheibe *f* wheel disc
Radstand *m* wheel base
Raffinerie *f* refinery
raffinieren refine
Rahmen *m* frame
Rahmenblech *n* frame plate

Rahmenprofil n cold formed light U-section
Rampe f wharf
RAM-Speicher m main memory
Rand m border; case; edge; rim
Randabschreckvorrichtung f edge-quenching apparatus
Randblase f subcutaneous blow hole
Randeinrollen n **durch Drücken** curling by spinning
Rändelknopf m knurled knob
rändeln border; knurl
Rändelschraube f knurled thumb screw
Randentkohlung f skin decarburisation; surface decarburisation
Randgängigkeit f **(Hochofen)** working up the wall
Randhärten n case hardening; hardening of carburised surface
Rand m **(Kaliber)** collar
Randschicht f case; skin
Randschichthärten n surface layer hardening
Randsystem n binary edge
Randsystem n **(Dreistoffphasen)** bounding system
Randwellen fpl **(Bandfehler)** wavy edges
Randwelligkeit f **(Band)** edge waviness
Randzone f surface zone
Rangieranlage f shunting siding
rangieren shunt
Rangkorrelation f rank correlation
Rangkorrelationskoeffizient m rank correlation coefficient
rasch wirkende Lösung f fast acting solution
Raseneisenerz n bog iron ore; lake iron ore; limonite; marsh ore; meadow ore
Rasenerz n brown hematite
Rast f bosh
Raster n screen
Rasterabstand m grid element spacing
Rasterelektronenmikroskop n **(REM)** scanning electron microscope (SEM)
Rasterweite f **(Rasterformat)** screen size
Rastform f bosh tuyre
Rast f **mit Stahlpanzer** bosh with steel jacket
Rastwinkel m bosh angle
Rattern n **(Drahtziehen)** jerky drawing
Ratterwellen fpl shatter marks
Ratterwellen fpl **(in Schienen)** corrugations
Raubbau m rob
Rauch m fume; smoke
Rauchabzug m flue
Rauchdichtemesser m smoke meter
Rauchfahne f smoke plume; smoke streamer
Rauchfang m chimney
Rauchkanal m flue
rauchlos smokeless
Rauchschaden m damage caused by smoke
Rauchschiff n converter aisle
rauhen rag
rauhe Oberfläche f **(durch Zunder)** scale-pitted surface
Rauhtiefe f depth of roughness
Raumausdehnung f volume expansion
Raumbeständigkeit f constancy of volume; volume stability
Raumdiagonale f cube diagonal
Raumdiagonale f **des Würfels** cube diagonal
Raumdichte f bulk density
räumen broach
Räumerarm m **(Sinterkühler)** plough for removing cooled sinter
Raumerfüllung f chip density; density ratio; volume ratio
Raumfahrtindustrie f aerospace industry
Raumformfaktor m **(Kristall)** three-dimensional shape factor
Raumgetriebe n spatial mechanism
Raumgewicht n bulk density
Raumgitter n space lattice

Rauminhalt m capacity; cubic content; volume
Raumkinematik f spatial kinematics
räumliche Anordnung f **(Metallographie)** spatial arrangement
räumlicher Winkel m solid angle
Räummaschine f broaching machine
Räumnadel f broach
Raumschalldämpfung f sound absorption in rooms
Raumtemperatur f ambient temperature
Raum m **zwischen großer und kleiner Gichtglocke** inter-bell area
Raupenbildung f formation of beads
Raupenblech n checker[ed] plate
Raupe[nkette] f caterpillar
Raupenziehmaschine f caterpillar drawing machine
Rauschen n background noise; broadband noise
Rauschen n **rosa** pink noise
Rauschen n **weißes** white noise
rautenförmig rhomb-shaped
Rautenkaliber n diamond pass
Reagenz n chemical agent
Reaktanz f reactance
Reaktionsfähigkeit f reactivity
Reaktionsgeschwindigkeit f rate of reaction
reaktionsträge inert; sluggish in reaction
Reaktor m pile
Reaktorbaustahl m structural steel for reactors
Reaktordruckgefäß n reactor pressure vessel
Realzeitbetrieb m real time processing
Rechenanlage f computer installation
Rechen m **für die Kühlwasserleitung** rake for cleaning the cooling water main
Rechenglied n computing element
Rechenkühlbett n rake type cooling bed
Rechenlocher m calculating punch
Rechenmaschine f calculating machine; computer
Rechenschaltung f set up for calculating machine
Rechenschieber m slide-rute
Rechenzentrum n computer bureau; computing centre
rechnen compute
Rechner m computer
rechnergestützte Betriebsdatenerfassung f production data aquisition
rechnergestützte Betriebsleitung f production control
rechnergestützte Prozeßleitung f process control
rechnergestützte Prozeß- und Anlagenüberwachung f process monitoring
Rechnersteuerung f computer control
Rechnungsabschluß m statement [of accounts]
Rechnungswesen n accounting
Rechteckhohlprofil n rectangular hollow section
rechteckig rectangular
Rechteckknüppel m rectangular billet
Rechtsgewinde n right-handed thread
Reckaltern n strain ag[e]ing; strain age hardening
Reckalterung f strain ag[e]ing
Reckdrücken n **(Drückwalzen)** roller spinning
recken draw; draw out; extend; strain; stretch
Recken n hammer forging; stretch forming
Recken n **von Flachstäben in der Halbzeugfertigung** straightening by stretching
Recken n **von Hohlkörpern** hollow forging
Reckgrad m tensile strain
Reckschmieden n hammer forging
Reckstauchen n gathering by die stretching
Reckwalzen n elongation rolling; stretch rolling
Reckwalzen n **(Schmiedewalzen)** forge rolling

Redoxpotential n redox potential
Reduktion f (Erz) beneficiation
Reduktion f in der Wirbelschicht fluid iron ore reduction
Reduktionsgrad m reduction ratio
Reduktionskohle f reducing carbon
Reduktionsmittel n reducing agent; reducing medium
Reduktionsschöpfung f end reduction degree; melting start reduction degree
Reduktionszone f smelting section
Reduktion f **von Draht mit Hammermaschinen** rotary hammer swaging
Reduzierbarkeit f reducibility
reduzieren reduce
Reduziergesenk n reducing die
Reduziermatritze f reducing die
Reduzierwalzwerk n sinking mill
Referat n review
Regal n shelf
Regelabweichung f deviation
Regelanlage f control equipment
Regelantrieb m regulating drive
regelbarer Brenner m adjustable burner
regelbarer Gleichstrommotor m adjustable speed direct current motor
Regelbereich m range of adjustment
Regeleinrichtung f control system; controlling means
Regelgröße f controlled condition; controlled variable
Regelkreis m automatic control loop; control system
regellos random
regeln adjust; check; control; govern; regulate; time
Regeln n control
regelnder Brenner m conditioning burner
Regelschieber m governor slide valve
Regelstrecke f controlled system
Regelumspanner m regulating voltage transformer
Regelung f adjustment; arrangement; check; close loop control; control
Regelung f **mit Rückführung** feedback control system
Regelverhalten n automatic controller action
Regelwiderstand m regulating resistance
Regenerativ-Flammofen m regenerative reverberatory furnace
Regenerator m regenerator
Regenerieranlage f **zum Regenerieren der Waschmedien** recovery plant for recovering the scrubbing agents
regenerieren regenerate
Register n damper
Regler m automatic controller; controller
Reglereingriff m corrective action
Regler m **mit Hilfsenergie** relay-operated controler
Regler m **ohne Hilfsenergie** self-operated controller
Regulierhahn m regulating cock
Reibahle f broach
reiben ream; rub
Reibkorrosion f fretting corrosion
Reibscheibe f friction disc
Reibschweißen n friction welding
Reibung f friction
Reibungsarbeit f frictional work
Reibungsbeiwert m coefficient of friction
Reibungsfläche f rubbing surface
Reibungskoeffizient m coefficient of friction; friction coefficient
Reibungskraft f frictional force
Reibungsmoment n frictional moment
Reibungswärme f frictional heat
Reibungszustand m frictional state
Reibwerkstoff m friction material (powder met.)
Reibwinkel m angle of friction
reichhaltiges Erz n high grade ore; rich ore
Reichweite f range; reach
Reifencorddraht m tyre cord wire
Reihe f array; series; tier
Reihenherstellung f duplicate production; multiple production

Reihenpunktschweißen n straight line spot welding
rein neat; straight
Reindichte f absolute density (powder met.); particle true density
Reineisen n Armco iron; technical pure iron
Reinergebnis n net result
reiner Stoff m pure substance
Reinhaltung f (Luft) pollution abatement
Reinheitsgrad m cleaness; cleanliness; degree of purity
reinigen purify
Reinigung f clarification
Reinigungsmaschine f boshing machine
Reinigungsmittel n detergent
Reinraumgerät n air conditioning for clean room conditions
Reinsteisen n high-purity iron
Reisezeit f (eines Blockes) track time
Reißbrett n draught ga[u]ge
reißen draw
Reißfestigkeit f fracture strength; true tensile stress
Reißgeschwindigkeit f cracking rate
Reißkegelbildung f (bei Draht) cupping
Reißspan m discontinuous chip; tearing chip
Reklamation f complaint
Rekristallisation f recrystallisation
Rekristallisationsglühen n recrystallisation annealing; subcritical annealing
Rekuperator m recuperator
relative Atommasse f relative atomic mass
relative Feuchtigkeit f relative humidity
relative Molekülmasse f relative molecular mass
relative Standardabweichung f relative standard deviation
Relaxationszeit f relaxation time
Relingstahl m bulwark rail section steel

Remanenz f remanence; residual magnetism
Rennverfahren n direct process for the production of wrought iron
Rentenanwartschaft f retirement pension expectancy
Reparaturbetrieb m repair shop
Resonanzverfahren n resonance method
Restaustenit m residual austenite
Restblock m butt ingot
Restgas n (Kohleveredlung) residual gas
Restkalk m residual lime
Restlänge f short length
Restsauerstoff m residual oxygen
Restsäure f (beim Schmieren) carry-over acid
Restspannung f residual stress
Reststoffe mpl recyclings
Restwert m residual
retardierter Ausgang m postponed output
Retorte f retort
Retortenkohle f gas retort carbon
Retuschieren n touch-up
Reversiergerüst n reversing mill; reversing stand
Revier n country
Revision f audit
Revisor m auditor
Revolverdrehbank f turret lathe
reziprokes Gitter n reciprocal lattice
Rheologie f rheology
Rheostat m rheostat
rhombisches Gitter n rhombic lattice
richten level; straighten
Richten v von Hand hand setting
Richtkosten pl predetermined standard rates
Richtmaschine f straightening machine
Richtmaschine f (Bleche) levelling machine
Richtmaschine f (Feinblech) stretcher leveller
Richtplatte f straightening plate
Richtpresse f gag press; straightening

Richtrolle f bending roll; mangle roll; straightening roll
Richt- und Istlinien fpl estimated and actual curves (X-rays)
Richtung f direction
Richtungsabhängigkeit f directionality
Richtungssinn m sense
Richtwirkung f directivity factor
Riefe f groove; scratch
Riefenbildung f scoring
Riegel m latch
Riemen m belt
Riemenklammer f belt fastener
Riemenscheibe f pulley
Riemenwickler m **(bei Bandwickelvorrichtung)** belt wrapper
Rieselkühlung f spray cooling
Riffel f groove
Riffelblech n channeled plate; checkered plate
Riffelblock m corrugated ingot; fluted ingot
Riffelstahl m riffler tool steel; steel for fluting tool
Riffelwalze f corrugated roll
Rille f gouge; groove
Rillenherd-Durchstoßofen m **zum Wärmen von Rundmaterialien** continuous furnace with grid hearth for annealing of round stock
Rillenrohr n grooved tube
Rillenschiene f girder rail; grooved rail; tram[way] rail
Ring m coil; collar; link
Ringaufdornversuch m ring expanding test
Ringbildung f **(Drahtziehen)** ringing
Ringdurchziehofen m roller hearth furnace for coils
Ringfaltversuch m flattening test on tubes
Ringkolbenzähler m rotary piston meter
Ringleitung f **(Wind)** bustle pipe
Ringleitung f **zum Abziehen der Ofengase** bustle pipe
Ringschmierlager n ring oilbearing

Ringwaage f ring balance
Ringwalzen n ring rolling
Rinne f channel; duct; gutter; launder; trench; trough
rinnen run
Rinneneisen n gutter sections; trough sections
Rinnenschutt m trough rubbish
Rippe f rib
Rippenbetonstahl m ribbed rebars
Rippengewölbe n ribbed roof
rippenloses Gewölbe n plane roof
Rippenplatte f ribbed sole plate
Rippenrohr n finned tube; gilled tube; ribbed pipe
Rippenscharen fpl compound ribs
Rippentorstahl m ribbed reinforcing bars
Riß m break; burst; crack; fissure; flaw
Rißauffangversuch m crack arresting test
Rißaufweitung f crack expansion; crack opening
Rißausbreitung f crack propagation
Rißausbreitungsgeschwindigkeit f crack growth velocity
Rißausläufer m edge of a crack
Rißauslösung f crack initiation
Rißbildung f crack initiation; cracking; fissuring; formation of cracks; tearing
Rißentstehung f crack initiation
Rißfestigkeit f fracture strength
Rißfläche f crack area
rißgeprüfter Lieferzustand m tested for cracks in the as delivered condition
rissig cracky; seamy
rissige Kanten fpl broken corners; checked edges; cracked edges
rissig werden burst
Rißmuster n crack pattern
Rißneigung f tendency to cracking
Rißprüfer m crack detector; flaw detector
Rißwachstum n crack propagation
Rißwachstumsberechnung f crack propagation calculation

Rißwachstumsgeschwindigkeit f rate of crack propagation
Rißzähigkeit f fracture toughness
Ritzel n pinion; trunnion
Ritzer m scratch
Ritzhärte f abrasive hardness; scratch hardness
Ritzhärteprüfung f abrasive hardness test; surface scratching test
Rockwell-Härteprüfung f Rockwell hardness test
roh coarse; crude
Rohblock m ingot
Rohbramme f slab ingot
Rohbramme f (der gegossene Rohstahlblock) ingot
Roheisen-Abstichrinne f iron runner
Roheisenabstich m (Roheisenabfluß) crude iron runout; pig iron runout
Roheisenbehälter m jumbo
Roheisenbehälter m auf Roheisentransportwagen jumbo
Roheisenerzeugung f iron making
Roheisen-Erz-Verfahren n pig and ore process; pig iron ore process
Roheisen n festes pig iron
Roheisen n flüssiges hot metal
Roheisen n für basischen Siemens-Martin-Ofenbetrieb basic pig iron
Roheisengießmaschine f pig casting machine
Roheisenmischer m hot metal mixer; pig iron mixer
Roheisenpfanne f hot metal ladle; pig iron ladle
Roheisenpfanne f mit Obenentleerung top-pouring pig iron ladle
Roheisen-Schrott-Verfahren n pig iron scrap process
Roheisensorte f pig iron grade
Roheisentransportwagen m pig iron ladle car
Roheisenübergabewagen m hot metal transfer car
Roheisen n weiß erstarrendes white pig iron
Roherz n crude ore
Roherzeugnis n primary product

Rohformen n blanking
Rohgang m cold working
Rohgasabzug m crude gas off-take
Rohgewicht n gross weight
Rohkaolin n china clay
Rohling m blank; slug; stock; tool blank; tube blank
Rohmaß n base size
Rohöl n petroleum
Rohölverarbeitungsbetrieb m crude oil processing plant
Rohphenolbehälter m crude phenol tank
Rohr n pipe; tube
Rohrabstechbank f tube cutting-off bench
Rohrabzweigstück n pipe branch
Rohrbiegemaschine f tube bending machine
Rohrbogen m tube bend
Rohrbündel n bank of tubes
Rohrdurchlaufofen m continuous furnace for tubes
Röhre f duct; tube
Röhrenblech n tube plate
röhrenförmiger zweigeteilter Nietedraht m tubular bifurcated rivet wire
Röhrenknüppel m tube billet
Röhrenradiator m tube radiator
Röhrenrekuperator m tubular recuperator
Röhrenrundstahl m tube rounds
Röhrenstreifen m skelp; tube strip
Röhrenstreifen-Walzwerk n skelp [rolling] mill; tube strip rolling mill
Röhren-Walzwerk n tube rolling mill
Rohrerzeugnis n tubular product
Rohrflansch m pipe socket
rohrförmig tubular
Rohr n für Konstruktionszwecke mechanical tube; structural tube
Rohrknüppelbohrmaschine f billet drilling machine
Rohrkokille f tubular mould
Rohrkrümmer m pipe bend; pipe elbow
Rohrkühler m tube cooler
Rohrleitung f conduit; duct

Rohrleitungsarmatur f pipeline fitting
Rohrleitungsbau m pipeline construction
Rohrluppe f tube blank
Rohr n **mit geringer Festigkeit** low tensile steel tube
Rohr n **mit offener Naht** open joint tube
Rohrmuffe f pipe socket
Rohrofen m tube furnace
Rohrpresse f extrusion press for tubes
Rohrreduzierwalzwerk n pipe reducing [rolling] mill
Rohrrohling m tube round; tube square
Rohrschlange f coil; pipe coil
Rohrschweißanlage f tube welding plant
Rohrstopfenzug m tube drawing with a plug
Rohrstoßbank f tube-piercing bench
Rohrstrang m run of piping
Rohrstreifen m **in Kalibern gewalzt** grooved skelp
Rohrstreifen-Vorwalzwerk n skelp roughing mill
Rohrverbinder m pipe connection
Rohrverseilmaschine f tubular strander
Rohrwalzwerk n pipe [rolling] mill; tube [rolling] mill
Rohrwickelmasse f pipe wrapping compound
Rohrziehbank f tube drawing bench; tube sinking bench
Rohrziehen n tube drawing; tube sinking; tubing
Rohschiene f mill bar; muck bar
Rohstahl m crude steel
Rohstahlblock m steel ingot
Rohstahlerzeugung f ingot tons
Rohstahlgewicht (RSG) n crude steel weight (CSW)
Rohstoffe mpl raw materials
Rohstoffquelle f raw material source
Rohstoffversorgung f raw material supply
Rohteerbehälter m crude tar tank

Rohvolumen n bulk volume
Rollbahn f gravity [roller] conveyor
Rollbiegen n curling
Rollbiegen n **(Blechumformen)** curling; edge rolling
Rolle f sheave
Rolle f **(Band oder Draht)** coil
Rolle f **mit Zufallsgewicht** catchweight coil
rollen roll
Rollenachslager n roller bearing axle box
Rollenbandbreite f wheel strip width
rollender Verschleiß m rolling wear
rollendes Material n rolling stock
Rollenförderer m roller-conveyor
Rollenherd-Durchlaufofen m continuous roller-hearth annealing furnace
Rollenherd-Kammerofen m roller hearth chamber furnace
Rollenherdofen m roller hearth furnace; roller-conveyor furnace
Rollenkette f roller chain
Rollenkühlbett n roller cooling bank; roller cooling bed
Rollenlager n roller bearing
Rollennahtschweißen n roller seam welding
Rollen n **(Reckstauchen)** gathering
Rollenrichten n roller flattening
Rollenrichtmaschine f roller leveller; roller levelling machine
Rollformen n rollforming
Rollgang m roller table
Rollgang m **angetriebener** life roller table
Rollgang m **hinter der Walze** back mill [roller] table
Rollgang m **nicht angetriebener** idle roller table
Rollgangsrahmen m roller rack
Rollgang m **vor der Walze** front mill [roller] table
Rollgeld n cartage
Rollknicke mpl **(Bandfehler)** coil breaks
Rollkugel f tracker ball
Rollmischer m barrel-shaped mixer

Rollofen *m* roll-over type furnace
Rommelfaß *n* shaking barrel; tumbler; tumbling barrel
Rommeln *n* tumbling
Ronde *f* circular blank
Rondenschneiden *n* circling
Röntgenanalyse *f* X-ray analysis
Röntgenbeugungsdiagramm *n* X-ray diffraction pattern
Röntgenfluoreszenzanalyse *f* X-ray fluorescence analysis
Röntgeninterferenz *f* X-ray interference
Röntgenographie *f* radiography
röntgenographische Untersuchung *f* X-ray investigation
Röntgenprüfeinrichtung *f* X-ray testing apparatus
Röntgenrasterbild *n* X-ray scan picture
Röntgenröhre *f* target tube
Röntgenstrahlenmeßgerät *n* X-ray radiometer
Rost *m* grid
Röstanlage *f* roasting plant
Röstanlage *f* **für Erze** ore roasting plant
Rostbelag *m* **(Sinter)** bedding layer
Rostbeschicker *m* underfeed stoker
rostbeständig corrosion resistant; rust resistant; stainless
rosten corrode
rösten calcine; roast
Rösten *n* **der Erze** calcining of ores; roasting of ores
Rösterz *n* calcined ore
Rostfeuerung *f* grate hearth
rostfrei stainless
rostfreier Stahl *m* stainless steel
Rost *m* **(Kessel)** grate
Röstofen *m* calcining kiln; roasting kiln; stack kiln
Rostschutzmittel *n* agent for protection against corrosion
Rostspat *m* roasted spathic carbonate; roasted spathic iron ore
Roststab *m* brate-bar
Röstung *f* calcination

Röstwagen *m* pallet
Rotationsvermögen *n* rotatory capacity
Rotbruch *m* red shortness
Roteisenstein *m* kidney ore
Rotglut *f* red heat
Rotguß *m* red brass
Rotgußlager *n* red brass bearing
rotierende Schere *f* rotary shear
Rotor *m* rotor
Rotschlamm *m* red mud
RS-Kippglied *n* RS bistable element
Rückansicht *f* rear view
Rückbiegeversuch *m* alternating bending test
Rückbildung *f* **einer kristallographischen Phase** reconstitution
Rückdehnung *f* elastic recovery
Rückfederung *f* elastic recovery; spring-back resilience
Rückfederungsdehnung *f* elastic recovery
rückführen return
Rückführung *f* feedback (automatic control)
Rückgang *m* decrease; return stroke; return travel
rückgewinnen reclaim; recover
Rückgewinnung *f* reclamation; recovery; recuperation; regeneration
Rückgewinnung *f* **von Beizsäure** pickling acid regeneration
Rückgut *n* oversize; return material; return[ed] fines; returning fines; returns
Rückgutband *n* return fines conveyor
rückkohlen recarburise
Rückkohlmittel *n* recarburising agent
Rückkohlung *f* recarburisation
Rückkühlanlage *f* recooling plant
Rücklauf *m* return stroke; return travel
rückläufig retrograde
Rücklaufschrott *m* arising interplant scrap; circulating scrap; mill scrap; own scrap; revert scrap; works scrap
Rückmeldevariable *f* input variable

Rückphosphorung f rephosphorisation
rückschlagsicher (Düsenmischbrenner) blow-back proof
Rückschlagventil n back pressure valve; non-return valve; retaining valve
Rückseitenlack m backing coat
Rücksprunghärte f scleroscope hardness
Rücksprunghärteprüfung f Shore scleroscope hardness test; scleroscope hardness test
Rückstand m **(Aufbereitung)** oversize product
Rückstände mpl tailings
Rückstau m backward slip [rolling]
Rückstich m return pass
Rückstrahlaufnahme f diffraction pattern
Rückstrahlung f **(Röntgen)** back reflection
Rückumwandlung f retransformation
Rückwand f back wall
Rückwandecho n bottom echo
Rückwand-Widerlager n back wall skew back
Rückwärtsfließpressen n backward extrusion; indirect impact extrusion
Rückwärts-Strangpressen n indirect extrusion of rods and tubes
ruhende Belastung f static load
ruhende Konten npl inactive accounts
Ruhepotential n equilibrium rest potential
rühren churn; stir
Rühren n stirring
Rührgerät n agitating apparatus; stirring gear
Rührquirl m agitator
Rührspule f stirring coil
Rührversuch m stirring test (corrosion)
Rumpfverteilung f truncated frequency distribution
Rundbiegen n circular bending
Runddraht m wire rod
Rundeisen n round bar
Runden n circular form bending
Rundfrage f survey
Rundheit f roundness
rundkantiger U-Stahl m normal U sections
Rundkerbprobe f test piece with a U notch
Rundkneten n rotary swaging (for reducing bars or tubes); round kneading
Rundkneten n **im Einstechverfahren** rotary swaging by the infeed method
Rundkneten n **im Vorschubverfahren** rotary swaging by the high-feed method
rundliches Pulver n spheroidal powder
Rundmischer m circular mixer
Rundnahtschweißen n circular seam welding; circumferential welding; orbital welding
Rundschleifen n cylindrical grinding
Rundstranggießanlage f round caster
Rund- und Verteilgesenk n edger; roller
Rungenstahl m stanchion steel
Ruß m carbon black; soot
Rüssel m tuyre snout
Rüssel m **eines Düsenstockes** blow pipe
rußhaltig sooty
Rüstzeit f **bei Arbeitsbeginn** start-up time
Rüstzeit f **nach Arbeitsschluß** shutdown time
Rüstzeit f **(zum Einrichten)** set-up time
Rutschbahn f gravity [roller] conveyor
Rutsche f chute; gravity chute
rutschen glide; slide; slip
Rutschkupplung f safety-friction clutch; slipping clutch
Rutschstelle f spreader mark (surface defect); tree (surface defect)
Rüttelformmaschine f jar-ram moulding machine; jolt moulding machine
Rüttelgerät n vibrating apparatus
rütteln jar; jolt; shake

Rüttelsieb *n* jigging screen; vibrating screen; vibrating sieve
Rüttler *m* vibrator

S

Säbel *m* **(Bandwalzen)** strip sabre
Sachkundiger *m* expert
Sack *m* bag
sacken sag
Sackfilter *m* bag filter
Sackloch *n* blind hole; bottom hole
Säge *f* saw
Sägeblatthalter *m* blade holder
Sägeblatt-Schärfmaschine *f* saw blade sharpening machine
Sägemaschine *f* sawing machine
sägen saw
Sägen *n* saw cutting
Sägenstahl *m* saw steel
Sägespäne *mpl* saw dust
Salpetersäure *f* nitric acid
Salzbadhärten *n* salt bath hardening
Salzbadnitrieren *n* salt bath nitriding
Salzbadofen *m* salt bath furnace
Salzbadpatentieren *n* salt bath patenting
Salzlösung *f* brine
Salzsäure *f* muriatic acid
Salzsprühversuch *m* salt spray test
Sammelbehälter *m* storage tank
Sammelkreuz *n* four arm capstan (for holding rod coils)
Sammelkristallisation *f* recrystallisation combined with grain growth
Sammelleitung *f* collecting main
Sammelschiene *f* bus bar
Sammelschiene *f* **(elektr.)** common bus arrangement
Sammelschrott *m* collected scrap; trade scrap
Sandabdichtung *f* sand seal
Sandeinschluß *m* sand inclusion
Sanden *n* grit blasting
Sandhaken *m* gagger
Sandhaltestift *m* dabber

Sandpapier *n* emery paper
Sandputzerei *f* sand blast cleaning shop
Sandputzmaschine *f* sand blasting machine
Sandstelle *f* sand [mark] (surface defect); silicate area
Sandstelle *f* **(Gußfehler)** scab
Sandstrahleinrichtung *f* sand blast apparatus
sandstrahlen sand blast
Sandstrahlgebläse-Arbeit *f* sand blasting work
Sattdampf *m* saturated steam; saturated vapour
Sattel *m* **(für Schmiededorn)** saddle
Sattelsegment *n* saddle segment
sättigen saturate
Sättiger *m* **(LD-Gasreinigung)** saturator
Sättigung *f* saturation
Sättigungsaktivierung *f* saturation activation
Sättigungsaktivität *f* saturated activity
Sättigungsdichte *f* saturation density
Sättigungsdruck *m* saturation pressure
sättigungsfähig saturable
Sättigungsgrad *m* **(Magnetisieren)** saturation intensity
Sättigungsgrenze *f* saturation limit
Sättigungskonzentration *f* saturation concentration
Sättigungslinie *f* saturation line
Sättigungsmagnetisierung *f* saturation magnetisation
Sättigungspunkt *m* saturation point
Sättigungsstufe *f* saturation degree
Sättigungstemperatur *f* saturation temperature
Sättigungszustand *m* saturation; saturation state
Satz *m* batch
satzweises Beschicken *n* batch charging; charging by batches
satzweise Wärmebehandlung *f* batch heat treatment
sauber neat

säubern skim
sauer acid
Sauerstoffabbau *m* oxygen removal
sauerstoffangereicherter Wind *m* oxygen enriched air blast
Sauerstoffaufblasstahlwerk *n* basic oxygen steel plant
Sauerstoff[auf]blasverfahren *n* basic oxygen steelmaking process
Sauerstoffblasstahl *m* basic oxygen steel; oxygen steel
Sauerstoff-Blasstahlwerk *n* oxygen converter steel plant
Sauerstoffblasverfahren *n* oxygen steelmaking process
Sauerstoff-Brennstoff-Brenner *m* oxy fuel burner
Sauerstofffrischen *n* oxygen refining
Sauerstoffgewinnungsanlage *f* oxygen production plant; tonnage oxygen plant
Sauerstofflanze *f* oxygen lance
Sauerstoffmeßsonde *f* oxygen probe; oxygen sensor
Sauerstoffpulverlanze *f* oxygen powder lance
Sauerstoffstahl *m* oxygen refined steel
Saugfläche *f* (Sinter) suction area
Saughaube *f* suction hood
Saugkasten *m* (Sinter) wind box
Saugkopf *m* suction basket
Saugzug *m* down draft; induced draught
Saugzuganlage *f* exhauster; induced draft installation
Saugzugsinterung *f* down draft sintering
Säule *f* column
Säulenchromatographie *f* column type chromatography
Säulenführungsgestell *n* (Feinstanzen) die set
Säulenstrukturzone *f* columnar crystal zone
Saum *m* border; edge; selvage
säumen border
Saum *m* (ungeschweißter) seam

Säure *f* acid
säurebeständig acid proof; acid resisting
säurebeständiger Guß *m* acid resisting castings
säurebeständiger Stahl *m* acid resisting steel
säurefest acid proof; acid resistant
säurefeste Auskleidung *f* acid proof lining
säurefestes Metall *n* acid proof metal
Säuregrad *m* acid value; effective acid
Säurekitt *m* acid resisting cement
saurer (Siemens-Martin-) Stahl *m* acid steel
saurer Stahl *m* acid steel
saure Schlackenführung *f* acid slag practice; working with an acid slag
Säureschutz *m* acid protection
Säureschutzmittel *n* anti acid protective
saures Futter *n* acid lining
saures Verfahren *n* acid process
säure- und laugenbeständiger Kitt *m* acid and lye resisting cement
säure- und laugenbeständiger Stein *m* acid and lye resisting brick
Säurewert *m* pH-value
Säurezahl *f* acid number
saure Zustellung *f* acid lining
schaben scrape
Schablone *f* template
Schablonenformerei *f* strickle moulding; template moulding
Schablonenschleifen *n* form grinding
Schabloniermasse *f* strickle moulding mixture
Schabotte *f* anvil block
schachbrettartig verlaufende Spannungen *fpl* tessellated stresses
Schacht *m* shaft; stack; well
Schachtausbau *m* casing
Schachtdurchmesser *m* stack diameter
Schachtkühlbalken *m* (Hochofen) stack cooling plate
Schachtmauerwerk *n* inwall; stack lining

Schachtofen *m* shaft furnace
Schadensverhütung *f* damage precaution; safety precaution
schädigend deteriorating
schädlich deteriorating
Schadstoffe *mpl* contaminants (air pollution)
Schaffplatte *f* fore plate
Schaft *m* shank
Schaftschraube *f* grub screw; shank threaded screw
Schale *f* cup; fish plate; scab; tray
Schälen *n* scalping; shafting
Schalenhartguß *m* chill casting
Schalenstreifen *mpl* **(Bandfehler)** rokes
Schale *f* **(Oberflächenfehler)** sliver; spill
Schale *f* **(Stranggießen)** casting shell
schalig scabby; shelly
Schallabstrahlung *f* sound radiation
Schallbild *n* ultrasonic image
Schallbündel *n* sound beam
Schalldämmung *f* sound insulation
Schalldämpfer *m* silencer
Schalldämpferkulisse *f* sound absorbant screen
Schalldämpfung *f* sound absorption
Schalldruckpegel *m* sound pressure level
Schalleistungspegel *m* sound power level
schallharter Raum *m* reverberant room
Schallminderung *f* noise reduction; sound attenuation
Schallpegelmesser *m* sound level meter
Schallschatten *m* acoustical shadow
Schallschirm *m* acoustic shielding
Schallschlucken *n* sound absorption
Schallschluckwand *f* sound absorbing wall
Schallschutzfenster *n* sound protecting window
Schallschutzhaube *f* sound isolating enclosure
Schallschwächung *f* wave attenuation

Schallsicht-Verfahren *n* sonic image method
Schallstrahl *m* sound ray
Schallstreuung *f* sound scattering
schalltoter Raum *m* dead room (free field condition)
Schallwelle *f* sound wave
Schälmesser *n* peeling tool
Schaltanlage *f* distributing plant; switch gear; switch installation
Schaltbrett *n* switch board; switch panel
schalten clutch; switch; trip
Schaltglied *n* connecting device
Schalthebel *m* control lever; switch lever
Schaltplan *m* circuitry
Schaltpult *n* operating desk; operating panel
Schaltrad *n* rack wheel
Schaltschrank *m* switch cupboard
Schaltung *f* clutch
Schaltwagentechnik *f* draw out switchgear design
Schaltwalze *f* controller
Schamotte *f* fire clay
Schamottemörtel *m* fire proof cement
Schamottestein *m* fire clay brick
Schar *f* course
scharf caustic; keen
Schärfe *f* accuracy
schärfen sharpen
scharfe Phase *f* wild phase
scharfe Schlacke *f* aggressive slag
scharfkantig sharp edged
scharfkantiger Schrott *m* grit
scharfkantiger Winkelstahl *m* acute angles
scharfkantige Vertiefung *f* **(Kaltwalzen)** pit (cold rolling)
scharf schneidendes Werkzeug *n* keen edge tool
Scharnier *n* hinge
Schattenlinie *f* ghost [line]
Schattenriß *m* ghost [line]
Schattenstreifen *m* ghost [line]
schätzen estimate
Schätzung *f* appreciation; estimation;

valuation
Schätzwert *m* estimate rate; statistic value
Schaubild *n* chart; diagram; graph
Schaufel *f* blade; bucket; scoop; shovel; vane
schaufeln shovel
Schaufelmischer *m* paddle mixer
Schaufelrad *n* impeller
schaukeln rock; swing
schaukelnd hunting
Schaukelofen *m* rocking type furnace; tilting furnace
Schaukelrinne *f* rocking runner; rocking spout; swinging launder
Schaukelverteiler *m* rocking distributor
Schauloch *n* eyehole; observation hole; sight hole
Schaum *m* dross; foam; froth; scum
Schaumaufbereitung *f* froth flotation
Schäumen *n* effervescence; foaming
Schaumflotation *f* foam flotation
Schaumrad *n* foaming wheel
Schaumschlacke *f* foamed slag
Schaumstelle *f* gas holes
Schaumwäscher *m* foam washer
Scheibe *f* disc; sheave
Scheibenantrieb *m* pulley drive
Scheibenbremse *f* disc brake
Scheibendichte *f* **(Pulvermet.)** apparent density
Scheibenfeder *f* woodruff key
Scheibenfräser *m* side milling cutter
Scheiben-Lochwalzwerk *n* disc piercer
Scheibenmembranventil *n* deformed membrane-type shut-off valve
Scheibenrad *n* disc wheel
Scheibenrad-Walzwerk *n* disc wheel rolling mill
Scheibenrollen-Kühlbett *n* disc type cooling bed
Scheibenwalze *f* disc roll
Scheideblech *n* baffle plate
Scheidewand *f* bridge wall; partition wall
Scheinlast *f* apparent load

Scheinleistung *f* apparent power
Scheinwiderstand *m* **(Lichtbogenofen)** impedance
Scheitelpunkt *m* **(eines Winkels)** vertex
Schemel *m* stool
Schenkel *m* **(U-Rohr)** branch
Scherbe *f* fragment
Scherbelastung *f* **zusätzliche dynamische** dynamic incremental shear loading
Schere *f* shears
scheren shear
Scherfestigkeit *f* cohesive strength; shearing strength
Scherkraft *f* shearing force
Scherleistung *f* shearing yield
Schermesser *n* cutoff; shear blade; shear knife
Scherschnitt *m* shearing cut
Scherspan *m* continuous chip; shearing chip
Scherversuch *m* shearing test
Scheuerfaß *n* shaking barrel; tumbler; tumbling barrel
Scheuern *n* chafing (e. g. laps in a coil during transport); tumbling
Schicht *f* batch; bed; layer; stratum
Schicht *f* **(Arbeiter)** gang
Schicht *f* **durchlässige** permeable formation
Schichtfestigkeit *f* layer strength
Schicht *f* **(geol.)** stratum
Schichtkörper *m* composite
Schichtkristall *m* layer crystal
Schicht *f* **(Lage)** layer
Schichtlinie *f* layer line (X-rays)
Schichtpreßkörper *m* compact in layers
Schicht *f* **(Steine)** course
Schichtung *f* lamination; stratification
Schichtwechsel *m* change of shift; changing shift
Schichtzeit *f* spell
Schiebebühne *f* transfer table [railway]
Schiebekupplung *f* sliding coupling
schieben shove; slide; slip

Schieber *m* damper; shutter; slide gate; slide valve; valve
Schieberumsteuerung *f* reversing valve gear
Schieberverschluß *m* slide gate nozzle
Schieberzunge *f* valve tongue
Schiedsprobe *f* arbitrary test; arbitration test
schief bevel; oblique; skewed
Schiefe *f* skewness
Schiefer *m* shale; slate
Schieferbruch *m* fibrous fracture; fish scale fracture; flaky fracture; slaty fracture
Schieferton *m* clay schist; clay slate
Schieferung *f* lamination (powder met.)
schiefwinklig oblique; skew
Schiene *f* rail
Schienenfahrzeug *n* rail vehicle
Schienenflachstich *m* edger
Schienenfuß *m* rail base; rail flange; rail foot
Schienenkopf *m* rail head
Schienennagel *m* dog spike; spike
Schienenschraube *f* coach screw
Schienenstahl *m* rail steel
Schienenstoß *m* rail joint
Schienenwalzwerk *n* rail [rolling] mill
Schiffchen *n* sagger
Schiffsblech *n* ship plate
Schilfer *mpl* stringers
Schlacke *f* ash[es]; cinder; dross
Schlacke *f* **abziehen** slagging
Schlacke *f* **für das Flicken von Schweißeisenöfen** bull dog
Schlackemitlaufen *n* slag carry-over
Schlackenabscheider *m* slag separator
Schlackenabstich-Gaserzeuger *m* wet bottom gas producer
Schlackenabstichloch *n* cinder notch; slag hole; slag notch
Schlackenaufbereitungsanlage *f* slag reduction plant
Schlackenbeständigkeit *f* slag resistance

Schlackenbeton *m* slag concrete
Schlackenbett *n* slag bed
Schlackenbildner *m* flux (for making slag); slag forming addition
Schlackendamm *m* **(in der Pfanne)** slag dam
Schlackendecke *f* slag blanket
Schlackeneinschluß *m* slag inclusion
Schlackenfang *m* slag skimmer
Schlackenfleck *m* slag patch
Schlackenform *f* monkey; slag notch; slag tuyre
Schlackenfrischreaktion *f* lime boil
Schlackenfuchs *m* slag skimmer
Schlackenführung *f* slag control; slagging practice
Schlackenglas *n* vitreous slag
Schlackengranulierung *f* slag granulation
Schlackenhalde *f* slag dump; slag tip
Schlackenkammer *f* slag chamber; slag pocket
Schlackenkippe *f* slag dump; slag tip
Schlackenkipppfanne *f* dump cinder car; slag dumping car
Schlackenkörnung *f* slag granulation
Schlackenkühler *m* monkey cooler
Schlackenlinie *f* slag line
Schlackenloch *n* monkey; slag hole; slag notch
Schlackenloch-Kühlring *m* **(Hochofen)** monkey cooler
Schlackenmühle *f* slag grinding plant
Schlackenpfanne *f* cinder pot; slag ladle; slag pot
Schlackenpfannenwagen *m* slag ladle car
Schlackenprobe *f* slag sample; slag specimen; slag test
Schlackenreinheit *f* cleanness of slag
Schlackenrinne *f* slag runner; slag spout
Schlackensand *m* slag sand
Schlackenschotter *m* coarse crushed slag
Schlackenspiegel *m* slag line
Schlackensplitt *m* slag gravel
Schlackenstand *m* slag line

Schlackenstein m slag brick
Schlackensteinpresse f slag brick press
Schlackenstelle f slaggy patch
Schlackentasche f slag pocket
Schlackenüberlauf m slag overflow
Schlackenwagen m slag ladle car
Schlackenwolle f slag wool
Schlackenzahl f slag ratio
Schlackenzeile f scale roke
Schlacke f übergeflossene boilings; overflow slag
Schlag m blow; impact; shock; stroke
Schlagarbeit f energy absorbed in fracturing
Schlagbiegefestigkeit f impact bending strength
Schlagbiegeversuch m impact bending test
Schlagbohrer m percussion drill
Schlagdrehversuch m impact torsion test; torsion impact test
schlagen knock
Schlagfestigkeit f impact strength
Schlaghärteprüfung f impact hardness test
Schlaghaspel f (Drahtziehen) flipper
Schlagkraft f impact force
Schlagmühle f beater mill
Schlagpanzer m throat armour
Schlagpresse f blow forging press
Schlagprobe f drop test; impact test specimen
Schlagschmiedemaschine f impacter
Schlagversuch m drop test; falling weight test; impact test
Schlagwellen fpl (Feinblech) shatter marks
Schlagwerk n (Schrottzerkleinerung) skull cracker
Schlagzerreißversuch m tensile shock test
Schlamm m sludge; slurry
Schlammbelebung f sludge activation
Schlammbelebungsverfahren n activated sludge process
Schlammeindicker m mud thickener
schlämmen elutriate; levigate

Schlämmen n elutriation
Schlammentwässerung f sludge dewatering
Schlamm m (Erzaufbereitung) ooze; tails
Schlammfaulung f sludge digestion
Schlammpumpe f sludge pump
Schlammräumer m mud remover
Schlämmspritzmasse f wet spraying mass
Schlammtrocknung f sludge drying
Schlammverwertung f sludge utilisation
Schlangenbohrer m twist drill
Schlankheitsgrad m slenderness ratio
Schlankheitsgrad m (Dendriten) fineness
Schlauch m flexible tube
Schlauchfilter m bag filter
Schlauchpressen n hydrostatic compacting
Schlaufenprobe f loop test bar
schlechte Qualität f poor quality
Schleifarbeit f grinding work
Schleife f loop
schleifen burnish; grind; sharpen; slide
Schleifenbildung f kinking
Schleifenprobe f snarl test
Schleifenspeicher m (EDV) tank
Schleiferei f grinding shop
Schleifleitung f electric contact line
Schleifleitungskanal m contact line duct
Schleifmaschine f grinder; grinding machine
Schleifmittel n abrasive; whetting material
Schleifmühle f grinding mill
Schleifpapier n emery paper
Schleifpulver n grit
Schleifriß m grinding check; grinding crack
Schleifscheibe f abrasive; grinding wheel
Schleifstaub m grinding dust
Schleifstein m grind[ing] stone; whetstone

Schleifweg *m* grinding wheel travel
Schleißwirkung *f* abrading action
Schleppbetrieb *m* crawl operation
schleppen drag
Schlepper *m* skid; tractor
Schlepper *m* **(Walzen)** drag over; skid transfer
Schleppthermoelement *n* trailing thermocouple
Schleppwalze *f* drag roll; idle roll; idler
Schleppzeiger *m* trailing pointer
Schleudergebläse *n* centrifugal blower
Schleudergießmaschine *f* **(für Rohre)** pipe spinning machine
Schleuderguß *m* centrifugal casting
Schleudergußkokille *f* centrifugal casting mould
Schleudergußrohr *n* spun iron pipe
Schleudergußverfahren *n* centrifugal casting process; spin casting
Schleudermaschine *f* slinger
Schleuderpulver *n* atomised powder
Schleuse *f* sluice
Schlich *m* slick
Schlichte *f* blackening; facing
schlichten face
Schlichtoval *n* **(Walzen)** leading oval
Schlickergießen *n* slip casting
Schlicker *m* **(Pulvermet.)** slurry
Schliere *f* feather (surface defect)
schließen close; lock
Schliff *m* cross section; cut; metallographic specimen
Schliffbild *n* micrograph
Schliff *m* **poliert und geätzt** polished and etched microsection
Schlinge *f* loop
Schlingenbildung *f* looping
Schlingengrube *f* looping pit
Schlingenheber *m* loop [lifter]
Schlingenkanal *m* looper; looping floor; sloping loop channel
Schlingenleitblech *n* release apron
Schlingenprobe *f* **(Draht)** snarl test
Schlingenspanner *m* looper
Schlingenwagen *m* looping car

Schlitten *m* carriage; pallet; slide; sliding frame
Schlittensäge *f* sliding frame hot saw
Schlitz *m* groove; slit
Schlitzabdeckung *f* slot cover
Schlitznahtschweiße *f* slot welding
Schlitzrohr *n* open seam tube; split tube
Schlitzschraube *f* slotted head screw
Schlosser *m* locksmith
Schlosserei *f* fitter's shop; locksmith's shop
Schlot- und Pfeilerbildung *f* **(Aufbereitung)** piping and piling
Schluckvermögen *n* swallowing capacity
Schlupf *m* slip
schlüpfen slip
Schlupfkupplung *f* slip clutch
Schlüssel *m* key
Schlüsselbuchstabe *m* **(bei Kurznamen)** key letter
Schlüsselergebnis *n* break-down
schlüsselfertig turnkey (mini plants)
Schlüssellochkerb *m* keyhole notch
Schlußstein *m* **(Giebel)** cap stone
schmal narrow
Schmalband *n* narrow strip
Schmalbandanalysator *m* narrow-band analyser
schmaler I-Träger *m* narrow flange I-beam; normal beam
schmelzbar fusible
Schmelzbarkeit *f* fusibility
Schmelzbereich *m* melting range
Schmelzbetrieb *m* **mit ausschließlich kaltem Einsatz** cold metal shop
Schmelzbetrieb *m* **mit heißem Einsatz** hot metal shop
Schmelzbühne *f* stage
Schmelzdauer *f* duration of [s]melting; melting period; time of [s]melting
Schmelze *f* blow; cast; melting bath
schmelzen melt; smelt
Schmelzenanalyse *f* ladle analysis
Schmelzenfolgezeiten *fpl* tap-to-tap times
Schmelzen *n* **mit flüssigem Einsatz** hot

metal process
Schmelzer *m* blower; melter
Schmelzfluß *m* complete fusion
Schmelzführung *f* conduct of a heat
schmelzgegossenes Erzeugnis *n* fusion cast product
Schmelzgeschwindigkeit *f* melting rate
Schmelzkessel *m* melting pot
Schmelzkorund *m* fused corundum
Schmelzkugeln *fpl* burnt out particles
Schmelzmagnesit *m* fused magnesite; sintered magnesite
Schmelzmittel *n* flux; fluxing agent
Schmelzofen *m* melting furnace
Schmelzpunkt *m* fusion point; melting point; softening point
Schmelzreduktion *f* smelting reduction
Schmelzschneiden *n* electric arc cutting
Schmelzschweißen *n* fusion welding
Schmelzsinterung *f* liquid phase sintering
Schmelztauchverfahren *n* hot dip metal coating
Schmelzung *f* cast; fusion; melt
Schmelzverlaufkarte *f* cast history sheet
Schmelzwärme *f* effective [latent] heat of fusion
Schmelzzone *f* zone of fusion
Schmidtsche Brille *f* goggle valve
Schmied *m* blacksmith; forger; smith
schmiedbar forgeable
Schmiedbarkeit *f* forgeability; malleability
Schmiede *f* forge
Schmiedeblock *m* bloom; forging grade ingot
Schmiedeeisen *n* forging grade steel; malleable iron; wrought iron
Schmiedefeuer *n* forge
Schmiedegesenk *n* drop forge die
Schmiedehammer *m* forging hammer
Schmiedekohle *f* forge coal
Schmiedelegierung *f* forge alloy
Schmiedemanipulator *m* forging manipulator
Schmiedemaschine *f* forging machine
schmieden forge
Schmieden *n* forging
Schmieden *n* **eines halbkreisförmigen Abschlusses** closing
Schmieden *n* **eines mittleren dünneren Teiles** middling
Schmieden *n* **mit befestigtem Werkzeug** fast tool forging
Schmieden *n* **mit unbefestigtem Werkzeug** loose tool forging
schmieden vom Stück forge from a billet
schmieden von der Stange forge from a bar
Schmiedeofen *m* forging furnace
Schmiedepresse *f* forging press
Schmiederohling *m* rough forging
Schmiedeschweißung *f* forge welding
Schmiedestahl *m* forging steel; wrought steel
Schmiedestück *n* forged piece; forging
Schmiedestück *n* **schweres** heavy forging
Schmiede- und Preßteile *npl* forged and pressed pieces
Schmiedewalzmaschine *f* forging roll
Schmiede[werkstatt] *f* forge
Schmiere *f* tallow
schmieren grease; lubricate; oil; smear
Schmierfähigkeit *f* lubricating power
Schmierfett *n* grease; lubricating grease
Schmiermittel *n* lubricant; lubricating grease
Schmiermittelträger *m* lubricant carrier
Schmieröl *n* lubricating oil
Schmierpumpe *f* lubricating pump
Schmierrückstände *mpl* lubricating residuals
Schmierstoffträger *m* **(Drahtziehen)** coating
Schmierung *f* lubrication; oiling
Schmierwirkung *f* lubricating action

Schmirgelleinen *n* emery cloth
Schmutzstoff *m* pollutant
Schmutzwasser *n* dirty water
Schnabelpfanne *f* spouted ladle
Schnapper *m* **(Blechwalzwerk)** catcher
Schnauze *f* lip; nose; nozzle
Schnecke *f* worm
Schneckenfräser *m* hob cutter
Schneckengetriebe *n* worm gear
Schneckenkranz *m* worm rim
Schneckenpresse *f* worm extruder
Schneckenrad *n* worm wheel
Schneidbarkeit *f* cuttability
Schneidbrenner *m* cutting blowpipe; cutting torch
Schneide *f* cutting edge
Schneideansatz *m* **(Bearbeitung)** built up edge
Schneideisen *n* screw die
Schneidekeramik *f* ceramic cutting material
schneiden cut
schneidend keen
schneiden (Gewinde) tap
Schneidentemperatur *f* cutting edge temperature
Schneidhaltigkeit *f* cutting power; cutting tool endurance; cutting tool life; life of cutting tool (between regrindings); maintenance of the cutting edge; maintenance of the cutting power
Schneidkante *f* cutting edge; cutting lip
Schneidöl *n* cutting compound; straight cutting oil
Schneidstahl *m* cutter; cutting tool steel
Schneidwerkzeug *n* cutting tool
Schnellabschrecken *n* rapid quenching
Schnellanalyse *f* express analysis
Schnellarbeitsstahl *m* high-speed steel
Schnellautomatenstahl *m* **kohlenstoffarm** low-carbon free-cutting steel
Schnellautomaten-Weichstahl *m* soft free-cutting steel; soft free-machining steel
Schnellbeheizung *f* quick heating; rapid heating
Schnellbeschickungsvorrichtung *f* **(SM-Ofen)** rapid charging machine
Schnellbestimmung *f* rapid determination
Schnellbestimmungs-Verfahren *n* accelerated method
Schnelldrehbank *f* high-speed lathe
Schnellerregung *f* field forcing device
Schnelligkeit *f* speed
Schnellkorrosionsversuch *m* accelerated corrosion test
Schnellkupplung *f* bayonet coupling
Schnellprüfverfahren *n* rapid testing procedure
Schnellschlußventil *n* rapid action valve
Schnelltauchthermoelement *n* quick immersion thermocouple
Schnelltrockner *m* flash baker
Schnellverseilmaschine *f* high-speed stranding machine
Schnitt *m* blanking tool; section
Schnittgeschwindigkeit *f* cutting speed
Schnittkante *f* cutting edge; cutting lip
Schnittkraft *f* **(beim Drehen)** cutting power
Schnittpunkt *m* intersection
Schnittstahl *m* steel for blanking or punching dies
Schnittwerkzeug *n* blanking tool; cutting tool; die
Schockschweißen *n* explosive welding
Schockumformung *f* explosive forming
Schockwellenumformung *f* shock wave forming
Schoopsches Metallspritzverfahren *n* Schoop's metal spraying process
schopfen crop
Schopfende *n* crop end
Schöpfprobe *f* ladle sample; spoon sample
Schopfschere *f* crop shears; end

shears
Schopfverlust *m* crop-loss
Schorf *m* scab
Schornstein *m* chimney
Schott *n* water-tight partition wall
Schotter *m* broken stones; gravel
Schotter-Teerungsanlage *f* tar macadam plant
schräg bevel; oblique
Schrägaufzug *m* inclined elevator; inclined hoist; inclined lift
Schrägaufzug *m* **(Gichtkübel)** skip incline
Schrägbedampfung *f* oblique sputtering
Schräge *f* batter; draft; skewness; taper
Schrägeinschallung *f* angular sound incidence
Schräggewölbe *n* ramp
Schrägrippe *f* oblique rif
Schrägrollen-Richtmaschine *f* cross-roll straightening machine
Schrägrollgang *m* skew roller table
Schrägrückwand *f* **(Siemens-Martin-Ofen)** sloping back wall
Schrägverzahnung *f* helical gearing
Schrägwalzwerk *n* cross rolling mill; rotary forge mill; skew-rolling mill; slant rolling mill
Schrägwalzwerk *n* **(Rohre)** rotary piercing mill (tubes)
Schram *m* cut
Schrämarbeit *f* working of trenches
Schram *m* **(Bergwerk)** trench
schrämen cut
Schrämen *n* coal-cutting
Schramme *f* scratch
Schränken *n* **(Säge)** setting
Schrankenverfahren *n* load bounding method
Schränken *n* **(Walzen)** crossing
Schränkung *f* offset
Schrapper *m* scraper
Schrapperlader *m* scraper loader
Schrappvorrichtung *f* scraping device
Schraube *f* **(mutternlose)** screw
Schraube *f* **(Mutternschraube)** bolt

schrauben screw
Schrauben-Anstellvorrichtung *f* screw down [gear]
Schraubenbolzen *m* bolt; screw bolt
Schraubendraht *m* bolt stock
Schraubenfeder *f* helical spring
schraubenförmig screw like
Schraubengewinde *n* screw thread
Schraubengewinde-Schneideisen *n* screw threading die
Schraubengleitband *n* screw slip band
Schraubenmutter *f* nut
Schraubennagel *m* screw nail
Schraubenrad *n* helical gear
Schraubenschlüssel *m* spanner
Schraubenstahl *m* bolt stock; screw steel
Schraubenversetzung *f* screw dislocation
Schrauben[walz]draht *m* wire rod for screws
Schraubenwerkstoff *m* screw stock
Schraubmuffenverbindung *f* screwed joint
Schraubstock *m* vice
Schraubverbindung *f* screw joint
Schreckschale *f* chill
Schreckschicht *f* chill; chilling layer
Schreckwirkung *f* **(von Wasser durch die Kupferkühler; Hochofen)** chilling effect
Schredderanlage *f* schredding plant; shredding plant
Schreiber *m* recorder; recording instrument
Schritt *m* pace
Schrittregelung *f* step control
Schrittregler *m* contact controller
Schrott *m* scrap; scrap iron; waste
Schrottaufbereitungsanlage *f* scrap preparation plant
Schrottaufkommen *n* scrap arising
Schrottgroßhandel *m* scrap wholesale traders
Schrotthacker *m* scrap chopper
Schrotthändler *m* scrap dealer
Schrottkohlungsverfahren *n* scrap carburisation process

Schrottlagerplatz *m* scrap yard
Schrottmuldenkran *m* scrap charging box handling crane
Schrottpaketierpresse *f* scrap baling press; scrap bundling press
Schrott-Roheisen-Verfahren *n* pig and scrap process
Schrottschere *f* scrap shear
Schrottschlagkran *m* scrap drop crane
Schrott *m* **schwerer** heavy scrap
Schrottzerkleinerungsanlage *f* scrap crushing plant
schrumpfen shrink
Schrumpfmaß *n* dimension to which a material is constrained by shrinkage forces
Schrumpfriß *m* check; check crack; cooling crack; draw; shrinkage crack
Schrumpfung *f* contraction; shrinkage
Schrumpfverbindung *f* slip joint
schruppen scrub
Schub *m* end thrust; shear; shove; thrust
Schubbeize *f* push pickler
Schubbewegung *f* translational motion
Schubfestigkeit *f* shearing strength
Schubfließspannung *f* yield stress in shear
Schubgelenk *n* rectilinear sliding gear
Schubmittelpunkt *m* shear centre
Schubmodul *m* modulus of rigidity; shear modulus
Schubspannung *f* shear[ing] stress
Schubstange *f* connecting rod
Schubumformen *n* shear forming
Schubwelle *f* **(Ultraschallprüfung)** shear wave; transverse wave
Schuko-Steckdose *f* safety socket
Schulden *fpl* debts
Schuldschein *m* bond
Schülpe *f* scab
Schulterbohrung *f* counter bored hole
Schulterwalzwerk *n* Assel mill
Schulter *f* **(Welle)** shoulder
Schuppe *f* flake; scab; scale
Schuppen *fpl* **bilden** scale

Schuppen und Schalen *fpl* scabbiness
schuppig flaky; scabby; scaly
Schüreisen *n* poker
schüren stir
schürfen explore
Schürflader *m* tractoloader
Schürfwagen *m* scraper
Schürloch *n* stirring hole
Schurre *f* chute; down spout
Schuß *m* shot
Schüssel *f* pan; tray
Schüttdichte *f* bulk density; packing density
schütteln shake
Schüttelrutsche *f* oscillating conveyor
Schüttelsieb *n* jigging screen; shaking screen; vibrating screen; vibrating sieve
Schüttelwerk *n* shaker
schütten charge; dump; feed
schütten (Hochofen) distribute
Schüttgewicht *n* bulk weight
Schüttgut *n* bulk material
Schüttguthöhe *f* packed height
Schüttgut-Stetigförderung *f* bulk material continuous conveyer
Schütttrichter *m* feed hopper
Schüttung *f* packed bed
Schüttwinkel *m* angle of repose
Schutzanstrich *m* protective coating; protective finish; protective paint
Schutzanstrichmittel *n* agent for protecting coats
Schutzbrille *f* eye protector; protecting goggles; safety goggles
Schutzfilm *m* protective film
Schutzgas *n* controlled atmosphere; inert gas
Schutzgasanlage *f* inert gas plant
Schutzgas *n* **(beim Gießen)** gas shrouding
Schutzgasofen *m* controlled atmosphere furnace
Schutzgasschweißung *f* inert gas shielded arc welding; shielded arc welding
Schutzhelm *m* protective helmet
Schutzkleidung *f* protective clothing

Schutzmarke f trade mark
Schutzrohr n **(für Tauchthermoelement)** sheath tube
Schutzschaltung f protective circuit
Schutzschicht f protective layer
Schutzüberzug m protective coating
Schutzvorrichtung f guard; safety appliance; safety device
Schwachfeld-Magnetscheidung f low intensity magnetic separation
Schwachgas n lean gas; weak gas
Schwachgasheizung f lean-gas firing; weak gas firing
schwach gebrannt soft fired
schwachkörnige Einformung f weak spheroidising
Schwachstellenprüfung f testing of weakest points in a design
Schwachstrom m minute current; weak current
Schwächung f impairment
Schwalbenschwanz m dovetail (joint between dummy bar and dummy bar head)
Schwammpulver n sponge powder
schwankend hunting
Schwankung f fluctuation; variation
Schwankungsbreite f measure of variation
Schwanz m tail end
Schwarzbeizen n black-pickling
Schwarzblech n black plate; black sheet
Schwarzblech n **in Weißblechgröße** tin mill black plate
Schwarzbruch m black shortness
Schwärzegrad m shade of blackness
schwarze Kanten fpl black edges
schwarzer Temperguß m black heart [malleable] castings
Schwärzung f shading (spectrum analysis)
Schwärzungskurve f density exposure curve (spectrum analysis)
Schwärzungsmaximum n **(Röntgen)** intensity maximum
Schwebe-Feststoffteilchen n suspended solid particle

Schwebemantelmatrize f floating die
schwebende Matrize f floating die
Schwebeschmelzen n levitation melting
Schwebstoff m suspended substance
Schwefel m sulphur
Schwefelabdruck m sulphur print
Schwefelelend n sulphur set; troubles due to an excess of sulphur
schwefelhaltig sulphur bearing
Schwefelkies m common iron pyrites
Schwefelkies m **(FeS$_2$)** iron pyrites
Schwefelpocken fpl sulphide scale efflorescence; sulphur pockmarks (corrosion)
Schwefelsäure f sulphuric acid
schweißbarer Stahl m weldable steel
Schweißbarkeit f weldability
Schweißbrenner m welding blowpipe; welding torch
Schweißdraht m filler rod; welding rod; welding wire
Schweißdraht m **blanker** bare welding rod
Schweiße f weld
Schweißeisen n mill bar; wrought iron
Schweißelektrode f welding electrode
schweißen weld
Schweißen n welding
Schweißer m welder
Schweißfuge f welding joint
Schweißgleichrichter m welding rectifier
Schweißgrat m flash; welding burr
Schweißherd m soaking chamber; soaking hearth
Schweißhitze f **(zum Abschweißen und Entzundern von Blöcken)** wash[ing] heat
Schweißkern m weld nugget
Schweißkörper m welded body
Schweißlage f layer; pass; weld position
Schweißmaschine f welding machine
Schweißnaht f weld; welding seam
Schweißnahtrissigkeit f susceptibility of welding seams to cracking
Schweißplattieren n cladding

Schweißraupe f bead; welding bead
Schweißrißempfindlichkeit f sensitivity to welding cracks
Schweißrissigkeit f susceptibility to welding fissures
Schweißschicht f pass
Schweißstahl m wrought steel
Schweißstoß m welding joint
Schweißumformer m welding transformer
Schweißung f weld; welding
Schweißverbindung f welded joint
Schweißvorrichtung f welding appliance
Schweißwerk n welding department; welding plant; welding shop
Schweißwerkstoff m welding material
Schweißwerkzeug n welding apparatus and tool
Schweißzusatzwerkstoff m filler metal
Schwelanlage f low temperature carbonising plant
schwelen smoulder
Schwelkoks m semi-coke
Schwellbeanspruchung f pulsating stress
Schwellbereich m range of pulsating stress
Schwelle f sleeper
Schwelle f **(Grenzwert)** threshold
schwellen swell
schwellende Belastung f pulsating load
Schwellen n **(Pellet)** swelling
Schwellenschraube f coach screw
Schwellenwert m threshold value
Schwellfestigkeit f fatigue strength under pulsating stresses
Schwelofen m low temperature carbonisation furnace
Schwelung f carbonisation; low temperature carbonisation
Schwengel m **(Chargiermaschine)** peel
schwenkbar swivelling
Schwenkdeckel m swivelling cover
Schwenkkonverter m swivelling vessel

Schwenkrinne f swivelling launder
schwerer Einzelblock m bull block
schwerer Formstahl m heavy sections; section
Schwerkraftabscheider m gravitational separator
Schwerkraftförderer m gravity conveyor
Schwerlastfahrzeug n lorry
Schwermetallguß m heavy metal casting
Schweröl n fuel oil
Schwerpunkt m centre of gravity
schwerschmelzbar high melting
Schwertrübe f dense medium
Schwimmaufbereitung f dressing by flotation; flotation
Schwimmaufbereitungsanlage f flotation plant
schwimmen float
schwimmender Abstichverschluß m floating taphole plug
schwimmender Stopfen m floating stopper
schwinden shrink
Schwindmaß n allowance for contraction; degree of shrinkage
Schwindungshaarriß m check
Schwindungshohlraum m shrink hole; shrinkage cavity
Schwindungsriß m shrinkage crack
Schwingbelastung f cyclic load
Schwinge f oscillating crank; rocker
schwingen rock; swing
schwingend aufgehängt freely suspended
Schwinger m **(Ultraschall)** vibrator
Schwingförderer m vibrating conveyor
Schwingmühle f vibratory mill
Schwingrinne f oscillating conveyor
Schwingsäge f oscillating saw
Schwingschere f pendulum shears
Schwingung f oscillation
Schwingungsdämpfer m vibration damper
Schwingungsmarke f **(Bruchfläche)** striation

Schwingungsprüfmaschine f vibration testing machine
Schwingungsrißkorrosion f vibrational corrosion
Schwingungszahl f number of alternations; number of oscillations
Schwitzwasserkorrosion f corrosion by condensation of moisture
Schwund m shrinkage
Schwungradumformer m Ilgner [type motor generator] set; flywheel equaliser set; flywheel motor-generator set
sechskantig hexagonal
Sechskantschraube f hex head screw
Sechskantstahl m hexagon bars
Sechsphasen-Lichtbogenofen m six phase arc furnace
Sechsstrang-Gießmaschine f six strand continuous casting machine
Sedimentationsanalyse f sedimentation analysis
See-Erz n lake iron ore
Seelenelektrode f cored electrode
Seelenschweißdraht m core welding wire
Segerkegel m Seger cone; standard pyrometric cone
Segerkegel-Fallpunkt m Seger cone softening point
Segment-Sägeblatt n segmental saw blade
Segmentverschlußkorb m orange-peel type charging basket
seidiger Bruch m silky fracture
seifegezogener Draht m soap drawn wire
Seifenknoten mpl **(Drahtziehen)** soap balls
seigern liquate; segregate
Seigerteufe f perpendicular depth
Seigerung f liquation; segregation
Seigerung f **in den Blockecken** ingot corner segregation
seigerungsarmer Stahl m steel with little segregation
Seigerungsausgleich m breakdown of segregations
Seigerungsstreifen m ghost [line]; segregation line; segregation streamer
Seigerungszeilen fpl segregation streaks
Seil n cable
Seilbahn f areal ropeway
Seilbetrieb m cable transmission
Seildraht m rope wire; stranding wire
Seilkausche f grummet thimble; thimble
Seilschlepper m rope drag
Seiltrieb m cable drive
Seitenansicht f side view
Seitendruck m end thrust; side thrust
Seitenkipper-Lastwagen m side dumping truck
Seitenriß m **(Zeichnung)** side view
Seitenteil n cheek
Seitenwände fpl **(E-Ofen)** side walls
Seitenwände fpl **(SM-Ofen)** branks
seitlich blasender Konverter m Tropenas converter; side blown converter
seitliche Führung f side guard
seitliches Blasen n lateral blow
sekundärer Lunker m secondary pipe
Sekundärhärten n secondary hardening
Selbstabstich m siphon tap
selbstausschaltend self disconnecting
Selbstbauprofil m slotted section
Selbstdiffusion f self diffusion
Selbstentladewagen m automatic discharge hopper car
selbstentschlackend self skimming
Selbstentzündung f spontaneous combustion
selbstgängiger Sinter m self fluxing sinter
selbstgehendes Erz n self fluxing ore
Selbsthärtestahl m self hardening steel
Selbstkosten pl first cost
Selbstschärfung f self sharpening
selbstschmierend self oiling
selbstsichernde Mutter f self locking nut

selbsttätig automatic; self acting
selbsttätig abgleichend self balancing
selbsttätige Regelung f automatic control
selbsttätige Winderhitzer-Umsteuerung f automatic hot blast; automatic hot blast stove reversing device; stove reversing gear
selektive Korrosion f selective corrosion
Selen-Gleichrichter m selenium rectifier
Seltene Erden fpl rare earths [elements]
senken lower; sag; sink
Senker m countersink
Senkloch n sink hole
senkrecht beschnittenes Rohrende n end squared
Senkrecht-Bohrmaschine f vertical turret boring machine
Senkrechteinschallung f normal sound incidence
senkrechter Gichtaufzug m vertical furnace charging hoist
senkrecht nach oben vertical up
senkrecht nach unten vertical down
Senkrechtschweißung f vertical welding
Senkrecht-Stranggießanlage f vertical continuous casting installation
senkrecht verstellbar vertically adjustable
Senkschraube f countersunk bolt
Sensenstahl m scythe steel
sensibilisieren sensitize
Sensibilisieren n sensitising
Sensibilisierung f sensitization
Separationstrommel f separating drum
Sequenzgießen n sequence casting
Setzdehnungsmesser m unbonded strain ga[u]ge
Setzen n **(Feder)** scragging
Setzkübel m drop bottom bucket; drop bottom tub
Setzmaschine f jigging machine; separator

Setzpacklage f **(Schlackenaufbereitung)** infill
Setzsieb n jigging screen
sherardisieren sherardise
Shorehärte f Shore hardness; scleroscope hardness
Shredder-Schrott m shredded scrap
Sicherheit f safety; significance
Sicherheitsbeauftragter m safety official
Sicherheitsbeiwert m safety factor
Sicherheitsbereich m safety area
Sicherheitsbrille f safety goggles
Sicherheitsfaktor m safety factor
Sicherheitsgrad m margin of safety
Sicherheitsschaltung f safety cut out
Sicherheitsschwelle f significance level
Sicherheitstechnik f safety technics
Sicherheitsventil n safety valve
Sicherheitsvorrichtung f safety appliance; safety device
Sicherung f **(elektr.)** fuse
Sicherungsblech n **(Schraube)** locking plate; tab washer
Sicherungsmutter f lock nut
sichten sift
Sicke f bead
Sicken n beading
Sickenmaschine f beading machine (for barrels etc.); flanging machine
sickern trickle
Sieb n riddle; screen; sieve
Siebanalyse f screen analysis; sieve analysis
Siebboden m sieve bottom
Siebdurchgang m sub sieve powder; through fraction; undersize
sieben screen [out]; sift
Sieben n screening; sifting
Sieb n **für die Kühlwasserreinigung** screen for cleaning the cooling water
Siebkern m strainer core
Siebmaschine f screening machine
Siebrost m grizzly
Siebrückstand m on-fraction; screenings; shorts

Siebweite f mesh size
Siedekühlung f hot cooling
sieden boil; bubble
Sieden n boiling; ebullition
Siedepunkt m boiling point
Siederohr n water boiler tube
Siedeverzug m retardation of boiling
Siemens-Martin-Ofen m open hearth furnace
Siemens-Martin-Ofenkopf m open hearth furnace port end
Siemens-Martin-Ofen m **saurer** acid open hearth furnace
Siemens-Martin-Stahl m open hearth steel
Siemens-Martin-Stahlwerk n open hearth steel plant
Siemens-Martin-Verfahren n open hearth process
Sigma-Phasen-Versprödung f sigma phase embrittlement
Signalanlage f signalling equipment
Signal (EDV) n signal
Signalflußplan m signal flow plan
Signalumformer m transducer
Signalumformer (EDV) m translating device
Signalverarbeitung f signal processing
Signifikanz f significance
Signifikanzschwelle f significance level
Silber n silver
Silberstahl m silver steel
Silicastein m silica brick
silicieren siliconise
Silicium n silicon
Siliciumcarbidstein m silicon carbide brick
Siliciumdioxid n **(SiO₂)** silica
Siliciumstahl m silicon steel
Silicophosphat n silico phosphate
Silikat n silicate
Silikose f silicosis
Sillimanitstein m sillimanite brick
Silo n silo
Simulation f simulation
Simulationsmodell n simulation model

Sinkgeschwindigkeit f sinking speed; velocity of descent
Sinkscheider m float and sink apparatus
sinnwidrige Korrelation f nonsense correlation
Sinteranlage f agglomerating plant; ore sintering plant; sintering plant
Sinterband n sintering belt; sintering strand
Sinterbronze f sintered bronze
Sinterbrunnen m **(Walzwerk)** scale pit
Sinterdichte f sinter density
Sinterdolomit m dead burned dolomite
Sintereisen n sintered iron
Sinterfestigkeit f strength of sinter
Sinterformteil n sintered compact
Sintergrube f scale pit
Sinterhartmetall n sintered hard metal
Sinterkasten m sintering box
Sinterkorund m fused corundum
Sinterkuchen m sinter cake
Sintermagnesit m dead burned magnesite; sintered magnesite
Sintermagnetwerkstoff m sinter magnet material
Sintermetall n sintered metal
sintern bake; cake; sinter; vitrify
Sintern von losem Pulver n pressureless sintering
Sinterofen m sintering furnace
Sinterpfanne f pallet; sintering pallet; sintering pan
Sinterpresse f sintering press
Sinterstahl m sintered steel
Sinterteil n metal powder part; sintered part
Sintertränktechnik f sintering and infiltration technique
Sinterung f **mit flüssiger Phase** sintering with a liquid phase
sinterungshemmend delaying the sintering process
Sinterwerkstoff m sinter material
Siphon m skimmer
Skala f graduated scale; scale
Skibildung f **am Walzgut** turn-down of rolling stock; turn-up of rolling stock

Skizzenblech *n* sketch plate
Smog *m* smog
Sockel *m* base
Soda *n* soda
Sohlenneigungswinkel *m* angle of hearth slope
Sohlkanal *m* sole flue
Sohlplatte *f* bottom plate
Solidusfläche *f* solidus area
Soliduslinie *f* solidus line
Soll *n* target
Soll-Ist-Vergleich *m* variance comparison
Soll-Leistung *f* scheduled production; standard production
Solltemperatur *f* nominal temperature
Sollwert *m* desired value; nominal value; set point; set-point; theoretic value
Sollwerte *mpl* **verfälschen** falsify set-point values
Sollwertsteller *m* set-point controller
Sondererzeugnisse *npl* specials
Sonderstahl *m* special steel
Sonderstahl *m* **leichter Zerspanbarkeit** easy machining steel
Sonderstahl *m* **und legierter Stahl** special and alloy[ed] steel
Sonderstein *m* special brick
Sondertiefziehgüte *f* extra deep drawing quality
sondieren sound
Sonntagsein *n* week-end iron
Sorbit *m* sorbite
Sorteneinteilung *f* classification
sortieren sort
Sortierer *m* sorter
Sortierförderanlage *f* sorting conveyor
Sortierzylinder *m* sorting out cylinder
soziale Lasten *fpl* social charges
Sozialertrag *m* social net return
Sozialprodukt *n* social net return
Spachtel *m* smoothing trowel; spatula
Spalt *m* break; fissure; gap
Spaltband *n* slit strip
Spaltbarkeit *f* cleaving property
Spaltbruch *m* cleavage fracture

Spaltbrüchigkeit *f* cleavage brittleness
Spalte *f* crack; flaw; slit
spalten break up; separate; split
Spalten *n* crack
Spalten *n* **(von Band)** slitting
Spaltermüdungsbruch *m* cleavage fatigue failure
Spaltfläche *f* cleavage plane
Spaltgas *n* cracked gas
Spaltkorrosion *f* crevice corrosion
Spaltprobe *f* spalling test
Spaltschere *f* slitter
Spaltung *f* splitting
Span *m* chip; splinter; swarf
spanabhebende Umformung *f* machining
Spanablauf *m* chip flow
Spanbrecher *m* chip breaker
Spandicke *f* depth of cut; thickness of chip
Spanen *n* cutting
Spanleistung *f* cutting capacity
spanlos swarfless
spanlose Formgebung *f* chipless forming; chipless shaping
Spannbeton *m* prestressed concrete
Spannbetonstahl *m* prestressed concrete steel
Spanne *f* span
spannen extend
Spannfutter *n* chuck
Spannkopf *m* clamping head; gripping head; specimen holder
Spannmaschine *f* stretcher leveller
Spannpatrone *f* split chuck
Spannrollensatz *m* tension bridle
Spannseil *n* suspension rope
Spannung *f* stress
Spannung *f* **(auch elektrisch)** tension
Spannung *f* **(elektr.)** voltage
Spannungsarmglühen *n* stress relieve heat treatment
Spannungsausgleich *m* relaxation of stress
Spannungsausschlag *m* alternating stress amplitude
Spannungs-Dehnungs-Schaubild *n*

Spannungsdurchschlag m **(Lichtbogenofen)** surge
Spannungsfeld n stress field
Spannungskorrosionsversuch m stress corrosion test
Spannungsmesser m strain ga[u]ge
spannungsoptische Untersuchung f photoelastic investigation
Spannungsregler m barretter; voltage regulator
Spannungsreihe f chain
Spannungsrelaxationsversuch m stress relaxation test
Spannungsriß m clink; flake crack; shatter crack; stress crack; tension crack
Spannungsriß m **(im abkühlenden Guß)** cold crack
Spannungsrißkorrosion f stress corrosion cracking
Spannungsstufe f voltage tap
Spannungs-Verzerrungs-Beziehung f stress strain relation
Spannungszustand m tensile state
Spannweite f span
Spanstauchung f chip upset; cutting ratio
Spanungsdicke f undeformed chip thickness
Spanwinkel m rake angle
Sparbeize f inhibitor
Sparbeizwirkung f inhibiting effect
Sparzinklegierung f economic zinc alloy
Spateisenstein m siderite; sparry iron ore; spathic iron ore
spatig spathic
Spätschicht f late shift
Speckstein m French chalk; soap stone
Speicher m store
Speicherbunker m storage bunker
Speicher m **(EDV)** memory
Speicherfähigkeit f storing capacity
Speichergrube f storage pit
speichern accumulate; store

Speichervermögen n storage capacity
Speicherwärme f stored heat (Cowper)
Speisekopf m feeder head
Speisekopf m **(Block)** dozzle
speisen feed
Speiserinne f sprue canal
Speisespannung f supply voltage
Speisevorrichtung f feeder; feeding device
Speisewasser n feed water
Speisung f feed
Spektralanalyse f spectrographic analysis; spectrum analysis
Spektralphotometrie f spectrophotometry
spektrochemische Prüfung f spectrochemical analysis
Spektrographie f spectrography
Spektrometer n spectrometer
Spektroskopie f spectroscopy
Sperrad n rack wheel; ratchet
Sperrbrücke f weir across ladle mouth (to retain slag)
sperren close
Sperrflüssigkeit f sealing liquid
sperriges Stück n gagger
Sperrschicht f **(Schmieren)** parting layer
Sperrschichtwirkung f **(Schmierung)** blocking effekt
Sperrschieber m gate valve
Spezialprofil n special steel section
spezifisches Gewicht n specific weight
spezifische Wärme f specific heat capacity; thermal capacity
sphärolithisches Gußeisen n nodular [graphite] cast iron; spheroidal [graphite] cast iron
Spiegel m meniscus; surface of metal (in a mould)
Spiegeleisen n spiegel iron
Spiegelschauloch n gas end peep hole; gas port peep hole
Spiegelwand f **(SM-Ofen)** bulkhead (of uptake)
Spiel n cycle; margin; tolerance

Spielraum *m* allowable variation; backlash; clearance; margin; tolerance
Spießkant *m* diamond
Spindel *f* arbor; shaft; spindle
Spindeldrehmoment *n* spindle torque
Spindel *f* **(in Druckschraube)** screw
Spindelpresse *f* screw press
Spindelstahl *m* spindle steel
spinodaler Zerfall *m* spinodal decomposition
Spinortskorrelation *f* **(Atome und Elektronen)** interaction of spins
Spinwellenspektrum *n* spin wave spectrum
Spiralbohrer *m* spiral drill; twist drill
Spiralfeder *f* coil[ed] spring; spiral spring
spiralförmig steigend beim Aufwinden (Drahtring) spiral cast
Spiralschweißen *n* spiral welding
Spiralseil *n* **geschlossenes** locked coil rope
Spitzbogenkaliber *n* gothic groove; gothic pass
Spitze *f* tip
Spitzeisen *n* broad tool
Spitzendrehbank *f* centre lathe
spitzenlose Gewindeschleifmaschine *f* centreless thread grinding machine
Spitzenwert *m* peak value
Spitzenwinkel *m* vertex angle
spitzer Winkel *m* acute angle
Spitzkeil *m* **(ff. Stein)** feather end
Spitzkerb *m* V-notch
Spitzkerbprobe *f* V-notch specimen
Splint *m* corter pin; split pin
Splitt *m* splinter
Splitter *m* sliver; splinter
Splitterbruch *m* spall fracture
Splittern *n* scaling; spalling
splittriges Pulver *n* acicular powder; angular powder
Spongiose *f* graphitic corrosion
spratziges Pulver *n* spattered powder
Spreizdorn *m* expanding mandrel
Spreizhaspel *f* expanding coil

Sprengarbeit *f* shooting and blasting
sprengen blow up
Sprengkraft *f* explosive force
Sprengladung *f* explosive charge
Sprenglanze *f* jet tapper
Sprengplattieren *n* explosive cladding
Sprengring-Einwalzmaschine *f* spring ring closing machine
Sprengung *f* blasting
Springduowalzwerk *n* jump roughing mill
springen burst; split
Spritzaluminieren *n* spray aluminising
Spritzanlage *f* spray unit
Spritzblech *n* splash board
Spritzdüse *f* spray nozzle
Spritze *f* squirt
spritzen squirt
Spritzguß *m* pressure die casting
Spritzkanone *f* fettling gun
Spritzmaschine *f* spraying machine
Spritzmasse *f* spraying mixture
Spritzpistole *f* spraying gun
Spritzüberzug *m* spray coating
Sprödbruchprüfung *f* testing for brittle fracture sensitivity
Sprödbruch-Übergangstemperatur *f* brittle fracture transition temperature
sprödbruchunempfindlich not susceptible to brittle fracture
spröde brittle
Sprödigkeit *f* brittleness
Sprudelbett *n* spouted bed
Sprühhärten *n* spray hardening
Sprühkühlung *f* spray cooling
Sprühprobe *f* spray test
Sprühröstverfahren *n* spray roasting system
Sprühversuch *m* spray test
Sprung *m* crack; fissure; flaw; jump; spring
Sprungantwort *f* step response
Sprungpunkt *m* superconducting transition temperature
Sprungpunkttemperatur *f* superconducting transition temperature
Sprungschaltung *f* intermittent feed

Spülanlage f rinsing plant
Spule f coil
spülen rinse
Spuler m spooler
Spulmaschine f winding machine
Spülversatz m flush
Spülversatzleitung f hydraulic stowing
Spund m bung
Spundprofil n piling section
Spundwand f sheet piling
Spundwandstahl m steel sheet piling
Spur f trace
Spurenelement n tramp element
Spurenelemente npl tagged atoms; tracers; tramp elements
Spurkranz m flange; rim
Spurstange f ga[u]ge rod; tie rod
Spurweite f ga[u]ge
Stab m bar; rod
Stabelektrode f welding rod
stabil consistent; stable
stabiles Gleichgewicht n stable equilibrium
Stabilglühen n stabilisation annealing; stabilising
Stabilisieren n stabilisation
Stabstahl m bar; merchant bars; steel bars
Stabstahl m **in Ringen** coiled bar
Stabstahlwalzwerk n bar mill; light section rolling mill; merchant mill; small section rolling mill
Stabwalzwerk n rod mill
Stabziehbank f rod drawing bench
Stabziehen n rod drawing
Stacheldraht m barbed wire
Stachelwalze f crusher; spiked roll
Stadtgas n town gas
Staffel f step
Staffelwalze f roll in steps; staggered roll; stepped roll
Staffelwalze f **(für Flachstahl)** squabbing roll
Stahl m steel
Stahlanwendungsgebiete npl fields of steel application
Stahlband n steel strip
Stahlbau m steel structural work; structural steel work
Stahlbaufirma f steel fabricator
Stahlbauprofil n steel structural section
Stahlbaustahl m steel for steel structural work
Stahlbauteil n **dünnwandiges** thin walled steel structural element
Stahlbegleitelement n companion element; trace element; tramp element
Stahlbehälter m **mit Glasauskleidung** glass lined steel container; glass lined steel tank
Stahlberatungsstelle f steel advisory centre
Stahl m **beruhigter** killed steel
Stahlbeton m ferroconcrete
Stahlbetonbau m reinforced concrete construction
Stahlbewehrung f steel reinforcement
Stahlblech n steel plate; steel sheet
Stahlbogen m steel arch
Stahlbohrer m steel drill
Stahlbolzenkette f bolted steel chain
Stahldraht m steel wire
Stahl m **durch Aufwalzen plattiert** clad steel
Stahl m **durch Verdrillen kaltgereckter** cold twisted steel bars
Stahleinsatzliste f list of steel applications
Stahleisen n basic pig iron; non phosphorous pig iron
Stahl-Eisen-Lieferbedingungen fpl steel supply conditions
Stahl-Eisen-Prüfblatt n steel test specification
Stahlentgasung f steel degassing
Stahlfeder f steel spring
Stahlfenster-Profil n steel window section
Stahlfolie f steel foil
Stahlformguß m cast steel; steel castings
Stahlformmasse f moulding mixture for steel castings; steel foundry moulding compound

Stahl *m* **für Flamm- und Induktionshärten** steel for flame and induction hardening
Stahl *m* **für Kernenergie-Erzeugungsanlagen** steel for nuclear power plant
Stahl *m* **für Randschichthärten** steel for surface hardening
Stahl *m* **für Tiefziehzwecke** steel for deep drawing
Stahlgelenkkette *f* steel link chain
Stahlgießerei *f* steel casting foundry
Stahlgießereierzeugnisse *npl* cast steel products
Stahlgießwagen *m* steel pouring ladle car
Stahl *m* **grobkörniger** coarse grained steel
Stahlguß *m* cast steel
Stahlguß *m* **(Erzeugnis)** steel casting
Stahlgüte *f* grade of steel
Stahl *m* **halbberuhigter** balanced steel; semi killed steel
Stahlhochbau *m* steel frame superstructure; steel structural engineering
Stahl[hoch]bau *m* steel structures
Stahl *m* **hochfester** high strength steel; high tensile steel
Stahl *m* **hochlegierter** high-alloy steel
Stahl *m* **kaltgewalzter und kaltgereckter** cold-worked steel
Stahlkies *m* steel shot
Stahlklasse *f* steel grade
Stahlkugel *f* steel ball
Stahlleichtbau *m* light steel structure
Stahlleichtprofil *n* light weight steel shape
Stahlmantelstein *m* steel cased brick
Stahl *m* **mit besonderer Wärmeausdehnung** steel having particular thermal expansion properties
Stahl mit eingewalztem Muster *m* pattern rolled steel
Stahl *m* **mit nadelartigem oder kristallinischem Gefüge** scorched steel
Stahl *m* **mit niedrigerem C-Gehalt** low carbon steel

Stahlpanzerrohr *n* steel armoured conduit
Stahlplättchen-Aufschweißen *n* steel facing
Stahlprobe *f* steel sample
Stahlpulver *n* steel powder
Stahlrammpfahl *m* sheet piling
Stahlregal *n* steel shelf
Stahlroheisen *n* non phosphorous pig iron
Stahlrohr *n* steel pipe; steel tube
Stahlrohrgerüst *n* tubular steel scaffolding
Stahlsaitenbeton *m* long line prestressed concrete
Stahlsand *m* steel shot
Stahlsandblasen *n* cloudburst treatment; shot peening
Stahlschmelzofen *m* steel melting furnace
Stahlschwelle *f* steel sleeper; steel tie (am)
Stahlskelettbau *m* structural steel framework
Stahlsorte *f* steel grade
Stahlspritzer *mpl* spattering; splashes
Stahlträger *m* **(gewalzt)** steel beam
Stahlübergabewagen *m* steel transfer car
Stahl *m* **unberuhigter** rimmed steel (am.); rimming steel
stahlverarbeitende Industrie *f* steel users
Stahlverbraucher *m* steel user
Stahlverwendungsgebiete *npl* fields of steel application
Stahlwasserbau *m* steel hydraulic engineering
Stahlwerk *n* melting shop; steel melting shop; steel works; steelmaking plant
Stahlwerker *m* steel maker
Stahlwerks-Frischerz *n* steel refining ore
Stahlwerksgebläse *n* steel work's blower; steel work's blowing engine
Stahlwerkshalle *f* melting shop
Stahlwerksteer *m* tar for steel making

purposes
Stahlwerksverschleißstoff m casting pit refractories
Stammbaum m flow sheet
Stammlösung f parent solution
Stampfdolomit m tamping dolomite
stampfen bank; tamp
Stampfherd m rammed bottom; rammed hearth
Stampfmaschine f ramming machine
Stampfmasse f tamping clay
Stampfschablone f ramming form
Standardabweichung f standard deviation
Standardgüte f standard quality
Standardkostenrechnung f standard costing
Ständer m column; upright
Ständerholm m mill housing post
Ständerrolle f breast roller
Standfestigkeit f stability
Standort m site
Standplatz m location
Standrohr n bleeder; standpipe
Standsicherheit f stability
Standversuch m static test; stationary test
Stand-Weg-Versuch m tool life/tool path test
Standzeit f exposure time; standing time; stay[ing time]; time elapsed; time in the mould; time of exposure
Standzeit f **(im Ofen)** standing time
Standzeit-Schnittgeschwindigkeit-Kurve f service life cutting speed curve
Standzeit f **(Werkzeug)** life
Stange f bar; rod; steel rod
Stangenpoliermaschine f rod polishing machine
Stangenschälerei f bar turing [peeling] shop
Stangenwiderlager n **(Rohrwalzwerk)** bar steadler
Stangenziehbank f bar drawing bench; rod drawing bench
Stangenziehmaschine f rod drawing machine

Stanzblech n punching sheet
Stanze f stamping die
stanzen blank; stamp
Stanzwerkzeug n blanking tool; stamping tool
Stapel m pile; stack
Stapelfehlerausscheidung f stacking fault precipitation
stapeln pile; stack
Stapelplatte f pallet
Stapelvorrichtung f stacker
Stapler m stacker
Stärke f thickness
Starkfeldmagnetscheidung f high intensity magnetic separation
Starkgasheizung f rich gas heating; strong gas heating
stark kochend high boiled
Starkverzinnung f heavy galvanising
starr rigid
Statik f statics
stationärer Zustand m steady state condition
Statistik f statistics
statistischer Rückschluß m statistical inference
statistische Sicherung f significance
statistische Sicherung f **von Mittelwerten** significance of means
statistisch gesicherter Unterschied m significant difference
Staubablagerung f dust deposit
Staubabscheider m dust separator
Staubanfeuchter m dust wetting plant
Staubauswurf m emission of dust
Staubbekämpfung f dust prevention measures
Staubbelag m dust layer
stauberzeugend dust evolving
Staubfänger m dust catcher
staubförmig dusty
Staubgehalt m atmospheric pollution; dust content
Staubkalk m lime powder
Staubniederschlag m dust deposit; dustfall
Staubpegelwert m dust deposit ga[u]ge; dust level

Staubprobenahme f dust sampling
Staubsack m dust catcher
Staubsauger m vacuum cleaner
Staubscheibe f measuring orifice
staubschleifen lap
Staubschutz m dust shield
Stauchdraht m upsetting wire
stauchen bulge; cobble
Stauchen n upset forging compression; upsetting
stauchen (Breite) edge
Stauchen n **(Breite)** edging
Stauchen n eines Halbzeuges (Gesenkschmiede) gathering
stauchen (schmieden) upset
Stauchkaliber n edging pass
Stauchmaschine f upsetting machine
Stauchstich m edging pass; upset pass
Stauchstich m **(bei Schienen)** dummy pass
Stauchversuch m bulging test; compression test; dump test; jump test; knock down test; slug test; up-bending test; upsetting test
Staumauer f retaining wall
Staurand m diaphragm; orifice
Stauscheibe f diaghragm; orifice
Stauung f choking
Stearat n stearate
Stechen n an der Kontrolluhr time keeping
Steckel-Walzwerk n Steckel mill
Stecker m plug
Steckschlüssel m box spanner
Steg m fixed link
Steghöhe f depth of web
Steg m **(Träger)** web
Stehlager n pedestal bearing; pillow block (am.); plummer block
Steifigkeit f rigidity; stiffness
steigender Guß m bottom pouring; rising casting
steigender Stahl m effervescent steel; rising steel
steigendes Gießen n up-running; uphill casting
steigend gießen bottom cast; bottom pour; cast uphill
steigen (Stahl) rise
Steiger m flow gate; riser
Steigkanal m ascension pipe; riser; standpipe
Steigleitung f ascension pipe; riser; standpipe
Steigrohr n ascension pipe; riser; standpipe
Steigtrichter m flow gate; riser
Steigung f inclination; slope
Steinfabrik f brick making plant
Steinkohle f pit coal
Steinkohlen-Bergbau m coal mining
Steinkohleneinheit f **(SKE)** coal unit
Steinkohlenteerpech n coal tar pitch
Steinpresse f brick press
Steinstrahlofen m multi-jet bricked burner furnace
Stelleinheit f **(Walzwerk)** setting increment
stellen adjust; point; set
Stellenbesetzungsplan m manning schedule
Stellgeschwindigkeit f **(Regelungstechnik)** control rate
Stellglied n correcting element; final control element
Stellgröße f correcting condition (automatic control); manipulated variable (am.) (automatic control)
Stellit m stellite
Stellmotor m servomotor
Stellschraube f adjusting screw
Stellung f location
Stellungsregler m position regulator
Stellwerk n correcting unit
Stempel m die; stamp
Stempelguß m die casting
stempeln mark
Stempelrichtpresse f gag press
Stengelgefüge n columnar structure; stalk like structure
Steppschweißen n stitch welding
stereographische Projektion f stereographic projection
Sternkeilwelle f multiple spline shaft
Stern m **(Rad)** spider

stetig continuous; steady
stetige Häufigkeitsfunktion f continuous frequency function
Stetigförderer m continuous conveyor
Steuer n steerage
Steuer f tax
Steuerbarkeit f manoeuverability
Steuerbühne f control platform; control pulpit; operating pulpit
Steuergerät n controller
Steuerhebel m control lever
Steuerkette f control chain
Steuermann m attendant; driver; machinist; operator
steuern control; steer
Steuerrolle f steering roll
Steuerstand m control stand; operating stand
Steuerstromimpuls m control current impulse
Steuerung f automatic operation; control; control gear; controlling device; steering
Steuerung f **offene** open loop control
Stich m pass; stroke
Stichabnahme f draught; draught per pass
Stichflamme f fine pointed flame; shooting flame; torch for lighting fuse
Stichfolge f pass sequence
Stichloch n tap hole
Stichlochstopfmaschine f blast furnace gun; clay gun; furnace gun; mud gun; tap hole gun
Stichlochstopfstange f tap bar
Stichmaß n template
Stichprobe f control sample; sample
stichprobenartige Überprüfung f spot Charlier check; spot check
Stichprobe f **nehmen** sampling
Stichprobenerhebung f sampling; survey
Stichprobenfehler m sampling error
Stichprobenmuster n sample design
Stichprobenparameter m statistic
Stichprobenplan m sample design
Stichprobenverfahren n sampling

Stichtabelle f pass sequence
Stichzeit f manipulation time
Stickstoff m nitrogen
stickstofflegierter austenitischer Stahl m nitrogen-alloyed austenitic steel
Stiefelschaft m bootleg; box hat; top hat
Stiefelsches Lochwalzwerk n Stiefel-type disc piercer
Stiefelsches Scheiben-Loch-Walzwerk n Stiefel-type disc piercer
Stielpfanne f hand shank
Stift m stud
Stiftschraube f stud; stud screw
stillsetzen shut down; stop
Stillstand m stoppage; shut down
Stillstandkorrosion f corrosion during shut down period of service; idle [boiler] corrosion
Stillstandzeit f idle time
Stippenbildung f stippling
Stirnabschreckprobe f Jominy test piece; end quench specimen
Stirnbrenner m end burner
Stirnfläche f face
Stirnfräsen n front milling
Stirnrad n spur wheel
Stirnschleifen n face grinding
Stirnseite f end face; face; front face
Stirnwand f end wall
Stocheisen n poker
stochen stir; stoke
Stocher m fireman; stoker
Stöchiometrie f stoichiometry
stöchiometrische Zahl f stoichiometric number
Stoffbilanz f materials balance
Stofffluß m flow of material
Stoffflußverfolgung f tracing
Stoffmangel m underfilling (ingot defect)
Stoffmenge f amount of substance
Stoffmengengehalt m mole fraction
Stoffmengenstrom m molar flux
Stoffpaar n combination of materials
Stoffübergang m mass transfer
Stoffüberschuß m overfilling
Stoffumsatz m mass reaction

Stopfbüchse f packing box; stuffing box
Stopfen m bot[t]; plug; stopper
Stopfenläufer m leaky stopper
Stopfenpfanne f bottom tap ladle; stopper ladle
Stopfenstange f botter rod; stopper rod; tapping rod
Stopfenstangenrohr n sleeve brick; stopper rod brick
Stopfenstangenverschluß m stopper rod control
Stopfenweg m stopper travel
Stopfenziehen n mandrel drawing
Störanfälligkeit f sensibility to disturbances; susceptibility to trouble
Storchschnabelgetriebe n pantograph
Störecho n spurious echo
Störgröße f disturbance
Störgrößenaufschaltung f disturbance feed forward
Störpegel m noise level
Störschwingung f disturbing wave
Störung f accident; delay; disturbance; interference; interruption; obstruction; stoppage; trouble
Störwertspeicher m off-normal memory
Stoß m blow; impact; shock; shove; stroke; thrust
Stoßanlassen n flash tempering; shock tempering
Stoßbank f push bench
Stoßbankkluppe f push bench bloom
Stoßbankverfahren n (**Ehrhardt-Verfahren**) rotary forge process
Stoßbelastung f impact load
Stoßblech n baffle plate
Stößel m ram
stoßen join; knock
stoßfrei impact free
stoßfreie Umschaltung f bumpless transfer
Stoßfuge f expansion joint
Stoßmaschine f slotting machine
Stoßofen-Hängedecke f suspended roof for pusher-type furnace
Stoßprobe f drop test

Stoßschweißung f butt welding
Stoßstange f bumper
Strahl m jet; spurt
Strahldüsenfrischverfahren n spray steelmaking
Strahlen n radiating
Strahlenbündel n brush
Strahlenbüschel n pencil of rays
Strahlenschaden m radiation damage
Strahlenschutz m radiation protection
Strahlentzundern n shot blasting
Strahlentzunderung f shot blasting
Strahl m (**Licht**) beam
Strahlmittel n abrasives; sand blasting shot; shot
Strahlputzen n sandblasting
Strahlrohr n lance
Strahlrohrbeheizung f radiant tube heating
Strahlrohr-Durchlauf-Blankglühofen m radiation-tube continuous bright-annealing furnace
Strahlung f **des schwarzen Körpers** black body radiation
Strang m casting; strand
Strangabdichtung f strand seal
Strangförderwalze f (**Strangguß**) withdrawal roll
Strangfuß m bottom of the casting
stranggegossen continuously cast
Stranggießanlage f continuous casting plant
Stranggießanlage f **vertikaler Bauart mit Strangabbiegung** vertical type continuous casting plant with bending of the strand
Stranggießen n continuous casting
Stranggießen n **zwischen endlosen Bändern** belt casting
Stranggieß-Kreisbogenanlage f **mit gebogener Kokille** curved mould continuous casting machine
Stranggieß-Kreisbogenanlage f **mit gerader Kokille** S-type continuous casting machine with straight mould
Stranggieß-Ovalbogenanlage f oval bow-type continuous casting machine

Stranggußverfahren *n* continuous casting method
Stranghaut *f* strand shell
Strangpresse *f* extruding press; trace press
strangpressen extrude
Strangpressen *n* extrusion; extrusion press
Strangpreßrohling *m* extrusion billet
Strangpreßwerkzeug *n* extrusion press tool
Strangquerschnitts-Direktreduktion *f* direct strand reduction
Strangschale *f* strand shell
Strangwalze *f* strand roll
Straße *f* train
Straßenbauschlacke *f* road building slag
Strebe *f* brace; truss
Streckbarkeit *f* extensibility
Streckdraht *m* strained wire; stretched wire
Strecke *f* distance; intervall; line; train
strecken draw; draw out; extend; straighten; stretch; yield
Streckformen *n* stretch forming
Streckgerüst *n* blooming [mill] stand
Streckgesenk *n* fuller; swager
Streckgrenze *f* yield point; yield strength
Streckgrenzenabfall *m* drop in yield strength
Streckgrenzenverhältnis *n* ratio of yield point to tensile strength
Streckgrenze *f* **obere** upper yield point
Streckgrenze *f* **untere** lower yield point
Streckkaliber *n* break[ing] down pass
Streckmaschine *f* stretcher leveller
Streckmetall *n* expanded metal
Streckplanieren *n* spinning
Streckreduzierwalzwerk *n* stretch reducing mill
Streckrichten *n* stretcher levelling
Streckrichtmaschine *f* stretch levelling machine; tension levelling machine
Streckschmieden *n* cogging back
Streckspannung *f* yield stress

Streckstahl *m* stretched steel
Streckstich *m* roughing pass
Streckwalze *f* break[ing] down roll; cogging [down] roll
Streckwerkzeug *n* fuller; swager
Streckziehen *n* stretch forming
Streifen *m* blade; strip
Streifenbildung *f* roping
streifengesteuerter Kartenlocher *m* tape to card converter
Streifenlocher *m* tape perforator
Streifenwalzwerk *n* strip [rolling] mill; strip [steel] mill
streifig lamellar in the form of lamellar streaks; lamellar streaks
Streubereich *m* scatter; scatter band
streuen scatter; spread
Streufeldenergie *f* stray field energy
Streufluß *m* stray flux
Streureaktanz *f* **(Lichtbogenofen)** leakage reactance
Streustrom-Korrosion *f* vagabond current corrosion
Streuung *f* dispersion; scatter; variation
Streuungszerlegung *f* analysis of scatter; analysis of variance; scatter analysis; variance analysis
Streuwert *m* erratic value; scatter value
Striemen *m* mark
strippen strip
Stripperkran *m* stripping crane
Strom *m* current; flow
Stromabnehmer *m* brush; current collector
Stromanschlußwert *m* overall power consumption
Stromausbeute *f* current yield
Stromausfall *m* power failure
Stromdichte *f* current density
Stromdurchgang *m* passage of current
Stromerzeugung *f* power generation
Stromkreis *m* circuit
Stromkreisregelung *f* **(Lichtbogenofen)** closed loop energy control
Stromkreis *m* **schließen** connect a circuit

Stromkreis *m* **unterbrechen** break a circuit
stromlos powerless
Stromnetz *n* electric circuit
Stromschiene *f* bus bar; conductor rail
Stromschienensäule *f* bus bar tower; conductor rail tower
Stromstärke *f* amperage; intensity of current
Strömungsbild *n* flow pattern
Strömungsmesser *m* current meter; flow meter
Strömungsmodellversuch *m* flow pattern test
Strömungssichten *n* **(Pulvermet.)** elutriation
Strömungstechnik *f* fluid mechanics
Strömungsverhältnisse *npl* flow conditions
Strömungsvorgänge *mpl* flow phenomena
Stromverbrauch *m* current consumption
Stromversorgung *f* current supply
Stromversorgungsnetz *n* power supply network system; supply network system
Stromwandler *m* current transformer
Struktur *f* articulation; structure
Stückanalyse *f* check analysis
Stückerz *n* lump ore
Stücke *npl* **(z.B. Erz)** lumps
Stückgewicht *n* single weight
Stückigkeit *f* lumpiness
stückigmachen agglomerate; briquette; sinter
Stückkohle *f* clod coal; lump coal
Stückschlacke *f* lump slag
Stückschrott *m* lump scrap
Stückzeit *f* piece rate
Stückzeitermittlung *f* piece rate setting
Stufe *f* step
Stufendrehversuch *m* step-down test; stepped torsion test
Stufenhärten *n* interrupted hardening; stepped hardening
stufenlose Geschwindigkeitsregelung *f* infinitely variable control of speed
stufenloser Antrieb *m* infinitely variable speed drive
Stufenpresse *f* multiple die press
Stufenrolle *f* erste breast roller
Stufenschaubild *n* histogram
Stufentrainieren *n* **(Dauerfestigkeit verbessern)** coaxing
Stufenversetzung *f* edge dislocation
Stufenversuche *mpl* graduated test; tests by progressive loadings
Stufenwalze *f* roll in steps; stepped roll
Stuhl *m* stool
Stuhlschiene *f* chair rail
Stülpziehen *n* reverse drawing
Stummelblock *m* butt ingot; ingot butt
stumpf aneinandersetzen butt
Stumpfnaht *f* geschweißte butt-welded joint
Stumpfschweißen *n* butt welding
stumpf (stumpfer Winkel) obtuse (angle)
Stundenleistung *f* hourly output
Stundenlohn *m* an hour's wages
Stundenlohntarif *m* time wage rate
Sturz *m* break-down; camber
stürzen dump; tip
Stürzen *n* **der Gicht** slip[ping]
Sturzenglühen *n* pack annealing
Stürzen *n* **(Hochofen)** slip
Sturzenwärmofen *m* pack heating furnace; sheet heating furnace
Sturzfestigkeit *f* **(Koks)** shatter strength
Sturz *m* **(Oberschwelle)** lintel
Stütze *f* support; truss
Stutzen *m* connecting piece; socket
Stützgewölbe *n* sprung roof
Stützlinie *f* **(SM-Ofen)** pressure line
Stützring *m* **(Pfanne)** stand ring
Stützrolle *f* **(Strang)** support roll
Stützwalze *f* back up roll
Stützweite *f* span
Sublimieren *n* sublimation
Substitutionsmischkristall *m* substitution solid solution
Sulfat *n* sulphate

sulfatsaures Verfahren *n* acid sulphate process
Sulfid *n* sulphide
Sulfit *n* sulphite
Sulfonitrieren *n* sulphonitriding
Summe *f* amount
Summe *f* **der Abweichungsquadrate** deviance
Summenkurve *f* cumulating curve
Summenkurve *f* **(bei Normalverteilung)** ogive curve
Summenregelung *f* integrating control
Summenregler *m* integrating controller
Summenwert *m* cumulant
Sumpferz *n* bog iron ore
Sumpf *m* **flüssiger** hot heel; liquid initial bath
Sumpf *m* **flüssiger (Strangguß)** liquid crater
Sumpfgas *n* marsh gas
Sumpf *m* **(Stranggießen)** crater
Supraleitfähigkeit *f* superconductivity
Supraleitung *f* superconductivity
Suszeptibilität *f* susceptibility (to)
Symmetrierung *f* symmetrisation
Szintillationszähler *m* scintillation counter

T

Tabelle *f* table
Tabelliermaschine *f* tabulator
Tafel *f* chart; panel; sheet; table
Tafelschere *f* gate shear; guillotine shear; plate shears
Tagebau *m* open cut; open pit; opencut mining; surface digging
Tagelohn *m* day rates; day's pay; day's wages
Tagschicht *f* day shift
Talg *m* tallow
Tallage *f* **(Atomreihe)** valley location
Tandembogen *m* tandem arc
Tandemwalzwerk *n* tandem mill
Tangentialprobe *f* tangential test

Tank- und Behälterblech *n* tank and container sheet
Tankwagen *m* tank truck
Tantal *n* tantalum
Tänzerrolle *f* dancer roll
Tarifabkommen *n* tarif agreement
Tariflohn *m* base rate; wage conforming to the tarif
Tarifvertrag *m* labour agreement
Tasche *f* bin; pocket
Tastatur *f* keyboard
Tast-Dehnungsmesser *m* feeling elongation meter
tasten feel; touch
Taster *m* **(Fühlersteuerung)** tracer
Tasthebel *m* feeling lever; touching lever
Tastnadel *f* feeler ga[u]ge
taub barren; sterile
tauber Kontakt *m* barren contact
tauber Kontaktgang *m* barren contact
Tauchaluminieren *n* dip coating with aluminium
Tauchbrenner *m* immersion gas burner
Tauchelektrode *f* coated electrode; dipped electrode
Tauchhärten *n* immersion hardening
Tauchkolben *m* plunger
Tauchlöten *n* dip brazing
Tauchpatentieren *n* bath patenting
Tauchprobe *f* **(für Metallüberzüge)** stripping test
Tauchrohrgießen *n* submerged pouring
Tauchschmierung *f* splash lubrication
Tauchthermoelement *n* immersion thermocouple
Tauchtränkung *f* infiltration by dipping
Tauchwalze *f* immersed roll
Taumelmischer *m* asymetric moved mixer; rocking mixer
Taumelscheibe *f* swash plate [tilting box]
Taupunkt *m* dew point
Taupunktmeßgerät *n* dew point hygrometer; humidity cell
Technik *f* techniques

technische Anlage f plant
Technische Hochschule f Polytechnic Institute
technische Messe f technical fair
technischer Sauerstoff m tonnage oxygen
technische Störung f technical breakdown
technisch reines Eisen n commercially pure iron
Technologie f technology
technologische Prüfung f technological test
Teer m tar
Teerdolomitstein m tar dolomite brick
teergebunden tar-bonded
teergetaucht tar-impregnated
Teermagnesit m tar-bonded magnesite
Teerverarbeitungsanlage f tar processing plant
Teer m zum Korrosionsschutz Angus Smith solution
teigig pasty; plastic
Teilabgeleitete f partial derivative
Teilabschreckung f selective quenching
Teilchen n particle
Teilchenform f particle shape
Teilchengröße f particle size; screen size
Teilchengrößenbestimmung f particle size determination
Teilchen npl je Minute (Geigerzähler) counts per min
Teilchenzahl f number of particles
Teildruck m partial pressure
Teil n eines Gesenkes bender; setter
teilen divide
Teilerhitzung f selective heating
Teilfuge f joint; parting line
Teilgesenkschmieden n incremental forging in closed die
Teilkreisdurchmesser m (Lichtbogenofen) pitch circle diameter
Teilkreislinie f pitch line
Teilkreis m (Mikroskop) graduated circle; graticule

teillegiertes Pulver n partially alloyed powder
Teillinie f parting line
Teilmenge f quota; set
Teilmenge f von in increments of
Teilmenge f (von Fähigkeiten) subset
Teilschere f dividing shears; parting shears
Teilstrahlungspyrometer n optical pyrometer; partial radiation pyrometer
Teilsystem n (elektr.) sub-system
Teilung f (Zahnrad) pitch
Teilwärmen n selective heating
T-Eisen m T-iron
tellerartiges Pulver n plate-like powder
Tellerfeder f cup spring
Tellerfedersäule f disc-spring column; saucer spring
Tellerventil n mushroom valve; poppet valve
Temperatur f temperature
Temperatur-Abbau-Randkoordinaten[-System] n temperature-reduction-marginal coordinates [system]
Temperaturabfall m drop of temperature
Temperatur-Abkühlungsdauer-Gefügeschaubild n temperature-cooling period-structure diagram
Temperaturanstieg m recalescence; temperature rise
Temperaturausgleich m thermal equilibrium
Temperatur-Austenitisierungs-Schaubild n time-temperature austenitisation diagram
Temperaturbeständigkeit f infusibility; temperature stability
Temperaturempfindlichkeit f sensitivity to temperature
Temperaturfühler m thermometer probe
Temperaturfühler m mit Schutzrohr pyrometric rod
temperaturgeregelte Warmumformung f temperature-controlled hot

forming
Temperaturgradient *m* temperature gradient
Temperaturleitfähigkeit *f* thermal diffusivity
Temperaturmeßgerät *n* temperature measuring instrument
Temperaturmeßkegel *m* standard pyrometric cone
Temperaturmessung *f* **durch Widerstandsmessung** resistometric measurement of temperature
Temperaturregler *m* temperature control apparatus
Temperaturstandzeit *f* tool life at elevated temperature
Temperaturstrahler *m* heat radiating lamp
Temperaturverlauf *m* temperature gradient
Temperaturverlust *m* loss of temperature; temperature loss
Temperaturwechselbeanspruchung *f* alternating temperature loading; thermal shock stress
Temperaturwechselbeständigkeit *f* resistance to thermal shocks; spalling resistance; thermal fatigue resistance
Tempererz *n* malleablising ore
Tempergießerei *f* malleable iron foundry
Temperguß *m* malleable [cast] iron
Temperkohle *f* temper carbon
tempern malleablise; temper
Temperofen *m* malleablising furnace
Tempo *n* pace
Termin *m* limit; time limit
termingemäß according to delivery promise
Terminierung *f* timing
Terminplan *m* time schedule
Terminverschiebung *f* time shifting
Terminwirtschaft *f* time planning
ternär ternary
Ternband *n* terne strip
Ternblech *n* terne plate
Terrassenbruch *m* lamellar tearing

Tetracalciumphosphat *n* tetracalcium phosphate
tetragonales Gitter *n* tetragonal lattice
Teufenanzeiger *m* charge level indicator; stock level indicator; stock line gauge; stock line indicator; stock line recorder
Textkommunikation *f* text communication
Textur *f* texture
Theisen-Wäscher *m* Theisen disintegrator
thermischer Hochgeschwindigkeits-Bildumwandler *m* high speed thermal image transducer
thermisches Spritzen *n* thermal spraying
Thermistor *m* thermistor
Thermitschweißung *f* thermite welding
Thermo-Bimetall *n* bi-metal
thermochemische Untersuchung *f* thermo-chemical test
Thermodynamik *f* thermodynamics
thermodynamische statistische Größe *f* thermodynamic statistical
thermoelektrische Kraft *f* thermoelectric force
Thermoelement *n* thermocouple
Thermokette *f* thermopile
thermomechanische Behandlung *f* thermomechanical treatment
Thermometer *n* **zur Feuchtigkeitsmessung** wet and dry bulb thermometer
Thermopaar *n* thermocouple
thermoplastisch thermoplastic
Thermosäule *f* thermopile
Thermoswagen *m* rail wagon with compartments for taking red hot ingots
Thomaskonverter *m* **(Thomasbirne)** Thomas converter; basic Bessemer [steel] converter
Thomasmehl *n* ground basic slag
Thomasroheisen *n* Thomas pig iron; basic Bessemer pig iron
Thomasschlacke *f* basic slag
Thomasschlackenmühle *f* basic slag grinding plant

Thomasstahl *m* Thomas steel; basic Bessemer steel; basic converter steel
Thomasstahlwerk *n* Thomas steel works; basic Bessemer steel works
Thomasverfahren *n* Thomas process; basic Bessemer process; basic converter process
Tiefätzen *n* deep etching
Tiefbau *m* **(Bergwerk)** deep mine
Tiefblasen *n* **(Hochofen)** blowing down
Tiefbunker *m* sunken hopper
Tiefe *f* depth
Tiefeinbrandschweißen *n* deep penetration welding
Tiefen *n* stretch forming
Tiefenstreuung *f* throwing power
Tiefenwirkung *f* throwing power
tiefer Einzelriß *m* roke
Tiefkühlen *n* subzero refrigeration
Tiefladewagen *m* well wagon
Tieflauf *m* looping floor; sloping loop channel
Tiefofen *m* pit; pit [type] furnace; soaking pit
Tiefofendeckel *m* pit furnace cover
Tiefofen *m* **(geheizt)** live [soaking] pit
Tiefofenkran *m* pit furnace crane; soaking pit crane
Tiefofen *m* **(ungeheizt)** dead [soaking] pit
Tiefofenzelle *f* cell; hole
Tiefung *f* depth indication; indentation
Tiefungsprobe *f* indentation test
Tiefungsprüfmaschine *f* cupping test machine
Tiefungsversuch *m* cupping test
Tiefungsversuch *m* **nach Erichsen mit fest eingespannter Probe** cupping test with clamped blanks
Tiefungswert *m* index of deep drawing
Tiefzementieren *n* deep cementing
Tiefziehband *n* deep drawing strip
Tiefziehbarkeit *f* Erichsen index; deep drawing property
Tiefziehblech *n* deep drawing sheet
tiefziehen cup
Tiefziehen *n* deep drawing

Tiefziehen *n* **im Anschlag** first-operation drawing
Tiefziehen *n* **im Weiterschlag** second-operation drawing
Tiefziehen *n* **(von Näpfchen)** cupping; ironing
Tiefziehfähigkeit *f* deep drawing property; deep drawing quality
Tiefziehgüte *f* deep drawing grade; drawing grade
Tiefziehstahl *m* deep drawing quality steel
Tiefziehverfahren *n* cupping process
Tiefzug *m* deep drawing
Tiegel *m* crucible; melting pot; pan
Tiegelgußstahl *m* cast steel
Tiegelofen *m* crucible furnace
Tiegelstahl *m* cast steel; crucible steel
tilgen redeem
Tilgung *f* redemption
Tisch *m* table
Tischbelag *m* bench covering of chamotte slabs
Tischlerei *f* joiner's shop; joinery
Tischrede *f* luncheon adress
Titan *n* titanium
Titancarbid *n* titanium carbide
Titandioxid *n* titanium dioxide
Titaneisen *n* titaniferous iron
Titansäureelektrode *f* ruttile electrode
Titration *f* titration
Titrimeter *n* titrimeter
titrimetrisch titrimetric
Toleranz *f* allowable variation; margin; off-size; permissible variation; rolling
Toleranzfeld *n* tolerance zone
Ton *m* clay; grog
Tonerde *f* alumina
tonerdehaltig aluminous
Tonerde-Schmelzzement *m* aluminous cement
Tonfrequenzsteuerung *f* audio-frequency control
tonhaltiger Spateisenstein *m* clay band iron ore
toniges Erz *n* argillaceous ore; clayey ore

Tonnenblech *n* arched plate
Tonnengewölbe *n* barrel arch; semicircular arch
Tonnenretortenofen *m* drum type retort furnace
Topfglühofen *m* pan type annealing furnace; pot annealing furnace
Topgase *npl* top gases (tops)
Tor *n* gate
Tordieren *n* twisting
Torfkoks *m* peat coke
Torpedopfanne *f* submarine ladle; torpedo ladle
Torsionssteifigkeit *f* torsion resistance
Torstahl *m* reinforcing bar; reinforcing steel
totbrennen dead burn
tote Phase *f* **(Lichtbogenofen)** cold phase
toter Gang *m* backlash
toter Mann *m* dead man
totes Spiel *n* backlash
Totlage *f* dead-centre position
totweich dead soft
Totweichglühen *n* dead soft annealing
Totzeit *f* dead time
tragbar portable
Tragblech *n* dummy sheet
Tragbolzen *m* supporting bolt
Tragbrett *n* pallet
träge possessed of inertia; sluggish
tragen carry
Träger *m* beam; carrier; girder; joist
Trägergas *n* carrier gas
Trägerwalzwerk *n* beam rolling mill; girder rolling mill; joist rolling mill
Trägerwerkstoff *m* substrate
Träger *mpl* **wieder verschweißte** castellated beam
Tragfähigkeit *f* bearing capacity; bearing strength; carrying capacity; load capacity
Tragfähigkeitsversuch *m* load bearing test
Traggabel *f* double handle [crutch]
Trägheitsmoment *n* moment of inertia
Trägheitsradius *m* radius of gyration
Tragkorb *m* **für Schlackenpfanne** support for slag ladle
Tragkranz *m* **(Hochofen)** lintel; lintel girder; mantle (am.)
Traglast *f* bearing load; strength
Traglast *f* **nach der Fließtheorie** squash load
Tragpfanne *f* hand shank
Tragring *m* mantle ring; trunnion ring
Tragring *m* **(Hochofen)** lip ring
Tragring *m* **(Schlackentopf)** baling ring
Tragrolle *f* supporting roller
Tragrost *m* carrying grid; supporting grid
Tragseil *n* mains cable; track cable
Tragstiel *m* carrying bar
Tragverhalten *n* bearing properties
Tragweg *m* drag distance
Tränenblech *n* bulb plate; checker plate with oval protrusions for gripping
Tränen *fpl* **(Blechfehler)** burst blisters
tränken infiltrate
Tränkung *f* impregnation; infiltration
Transferdruck *m* transfer printing
Transformator *m* transformer
Transformatorenstahl *m* transformer sheet steel
Transformatorstufe *f* **(sekundär)** transformer tap; voltage tap
transitorische Aktiva *npl* deferred assets
transitorische Passiva *npl* deferred liabilities
transitorische Rechnungsposten *mpl* deferred items
transkristalline Korrosion *f* transcrystalline corrosion; transgranular corrosion
transkristalliner Bruch *m* transcrystalline fracture
Transkristallisation *f* columnar crystallisation
Transmissionselektronmikroskopie *f* **(TEM)** conventional transmission electron microscopy
Transportanlage *f* transport and conveying plant

Transportband *n* conveyor belt
Transportbandwaage *f* scale for conveyor
Transportdauer *f* **(bei Blöcken)** track-time
Transportführung *f* transport guidance
Transportgerät *n* transporting appliance
Transportkasten *m* transport box
Transportkette *f* conveying chain
Transportrolle *f* **(Stranggießen)** pinch roll
Trapezstahl *m* trapezoids
Traube *f* cluster
Treffsicherheit *f* ability to achieve specifications setting accuracy
treiben drive; expand; puff out; swell
Treiben *n* driving; expansion; raisening
Treiben *n* **(der Blöcke)** rise
Treiberprogramm *n* driver
Treibriemen *m* belt
Treibrolle *f* driving roll; pulling [pinch] roll
Treibstoff *m* motor fuel; power fuel
Trennbruch *m* cleavage fracture
Trennbruchsicherheit *f* freedom from brittle fracture
Trenndraht *m* timing wire
trennen separate
Trennen *n* cutting; parting; separating
Trennfestigkeit *f* cohesive strength
Trennfläche *f* interface
Trennschalter *m* disconnecting switch
Trennschärfe *f* selectivity
Trennschere *f* separating shears
Trennschleifen *n* abrasive cut off; friction sawing
Trennungslinie *f* parting line
Trennverfahren *n* discriminatory analysis of variance; separation process
Trennwiderstand *m* cohesive resistance; resistance to rupture
Treppenleiter *f* steps
Tribologie *f* tribology
Tricalciumsilicat *n* tricalcium silicate
Trichter *m* bell; funnel; git; trumpet
Trichter *m* **(Gicht)** hopper

Trichter *m* **(Gießen)** gate
Trichterhaube *f* centre riser; centre runner
Trichterkübel *m* receiving hopper
Trichterrohr *n* centre riser; centre runner; centre runner brick; sleeve brick
Trichterwagen *m* hopper car
Trichter *m* **(Ziehen)** mouth
Triebstahl *m* free cutting steel for horological industry
Trinkwasser *n* drinking water
Triogerüst *n* three-high stand
Triostraße *f* three-high train
Triowalzwerk *n* three-high mill
Triplexverfahren *n* three furnace process
trocken dry
Trockenanlage *f* drying plant
Trockenbinder *m* dry binder
Trockenelektrofilter *m* dry electric filter
Trockenentstauber *m* dry dust catcher
Trockenfestigkeit *f* **(Pellet)** dry strength
Trockenfrittmasse *f* (ff.) dry fritting mix
Trockengasfilter *m* dry gas filter
Trockenkammer *f* baking oven; drying house
Trockenkühlturm *m* dry cooling tower
Trockenlöschen *n* dry cooling; dry quenching
trockenmagnetische Aufbereitung *f* dry magnetic dressing
Trockenmahlung *f* dry grinding
Trockenofen *m* baking oven; drying oven
Trockenpuddeln *n* **(im teigigen Zustand)** dry puddling
Trockenreinigung *f* dry cleaning
Trockenreinigung *f* **für Hochofengas** dry cleaning of blast furnace gas
Trockenverzinkung *f* dry galvanising
trocknen bake; dry
Trocknen *n* **durch Erwärmen** stoving
Trocknungsanlage *f* drying plant
Trogförderer *m* trough conveyor

Trogschwelle f tie (am.); trough shaped steel sleeper
Trommel f drum
Trommelbeize f drum type pickler
Trommelfestigkeit f drum strength; tumbler strength (am.)
Trommelofen m drum type furnace; drum type kiln
Trommelprobe f rattler test; trommel test
Trommelschere f **(Kaltband)** rotary shears
Trommelschreiber m drum-chart recorder
Trommelsinterofen m rotary sintering kiln
Trommelspeicher m drum memory; drum store
tropfen drop; trickle
Tropfenabrißverfahren n drop detachement method
Tropfengewichtsverfahren n drop weight method
Tropfenschlag m impingement of drops
Tropfkörper m **(Wasserreinigung)** trickling filter
Tropfpunkt m **(Gewölbe)** drip point (arch)
Trübe f clouding; pulp; slag clouds; slime
Trümmer pl debris
T-Träger m T-steel bar; tee-bar
Tuchfilter m cloth filter
Tundish m **vor Luftzutritt geschützter** atmosphere controlled tundish
Tunnelofen m continuous pusher type furnace; pusher type furnace
Tüpfelprobe f spot test
Tür f door
Türaufzugsvorrichtung f electric door-lifting mechanism
Türausmauerung f door lining
Türhebevorrichtung f **(beim Ofen)** door winch
Türkühlrahmen m door cooling frame
Türpfeiler m door jamb

U

überaltern overage
Überaltern n overag[e]ing
Überbeanspruchung f overstressing
Überbelasten n **(eines SM-Ofens)** overcharging
überblasen over blow
Überbleibsel n debris; residue
überdecken mask an effect; overlap
Überdicke f off ga[u]ge
Überdruck m excess pressure; overpressure
übereinanderlegen match
Übereinkommen n agreement
Übereinstimmung f consistence; consistency
übereutektisch hypereutectic
übereutektoidisch hypereutectoid
übereutektoidischer Stahl m hypereutectoid steel
Überfrischen n over-oxidation
überführen convert
Überführungszahl f transport number
überfüllen crowd; overfill
Überfüllung f overfilling
Übergabewalzwerk n pass over mill
Übergabezeit f **(von Blöcken)** track time
Übergangseisen n off grade iron
Übergangsfunktion f step function response; time response; transient response
Übergangsmetall n transition metal
Übergangspunkt m transition point
Übergangstemperatur f impact transition temperature
Übergangszone f **(beim Schweißen)** heat-affected zone
übergeflossene Schlacke f boilings; overflow slag [boilings]
übergeschlossenes Getriebe n overclosed gear; overclosed mechanism
Übergreifungsstoß m overlapping joint
Überhang m cantilever

Überhängen *n* overhang
überheben drag over; pull over
Überhebewalzwerk *n* pass over mill; pull over mill
Überhitzerrohr *n* superheater tube
Überhitzung *f* superheat; superheating
Überhitzungsempfindlichkeit *f* overheating sensitivity
überhöht (Schweißen) overfilled
Überhöhung *f* camber
überholen overhaul
überholt obsolete
überholt (veraltet) outmoded obsolete
Überkapazität *f* over capacity; surplus capacity
Überkohlung *f* supercarburisation
Überkopfablauf *m* overhead pay off; overhead take off
Überkopfschweißen *n* overhead [position] welding
Überkorn *n* oversize
überlagernde Wirkung *f* additive effect
überlagert superimposed
Überlagerung *f* coincidence; superposition
Überlandleitung *f* grid
Überlänge *f* surplus length
überlappen overlap
Überlappschweißverfahren *n* lapweld process
Überlappstoß *m* overlap joint
überlappter Stoß *m* lap joint
überlappte Stoßschweiße *f* overlapped joint weld
überlappt geschweißt lap welded
Überlappung *f* lap [joint]; overlap; shut
Überlappungsnietung *f* lap riveting
Überlaschung *f* splicing
Überlastbarkeit *f* overload capacity
Überlastsicherung *f* overload safety device
Überlastung *f* overloading
Überlaufbehälter *m* surge tank
Überlauf *m* **(beim Sieben)** oversize product; residues
Überlaufrohr *n* overflow tube

Überlegung *f* analysis
Übermaß *n* oversize
Übermöllerung *f* overburdening
überprüfen verify
Übersättigung *f* supersaturation
Überschallwelle *f* ultrasonic wave
überschmiedeter Grat *m* cold lap
überschneiden overlap
Überschußgas *n* surplus gas
Übersetzung *f* gear[ing]; transmission
Übersetzungsverhältnis *n* gear ratio; speed ratio
Übersetzungszahnrad *n* back gear; gear wheel
übersintert oversintered
Überspannung *f* excess voltage; overvoltage
Überstruktur *f* superlattice
über Tage above ground
übertragen transfer
Übertragerblech *n* electrical quality sheet; electrical quality steel
Übertragung *f* transfer; transmission
Übertragungsglied *n* transfer element
Übertragungswelle *f* line shaft; transmission shaft
Überverdichter *m* supercharger
überwachen control
Überwachung *f* control; inspection; monitoring; supervision; survey
Überwachungsanlage *f* control plant
Überwachungsgerät *n* control instrument
Überwallung *f* **(Oberflächenfehler)** bottom splash; curtaining; double skin
überwalzte Falte *f* cold lap; lap
überwalzte Naht *f* lap
überwalzter Grat *m* cold lap
Überwalzung *f* bottom splash; double skin; lamination; lap; overlapping; seam
Überwalzungsfehler *m* pincher; seam
Überwurfflansch *m* loose flange
Überzeiten *n* excessive holding; overtiming
überziehen coat; overdraft
überziehen mit einer Blei-Zinn-Legie-

rung terne
überziehen (mit Zink) sherardise
Überzug m casing; coat[ing]; facing
üblich (math. gemeinsam) common
U-Eisen n E-channel (channel iron)
U-förmige Häufigkeitsverteilung f U-shaped frequency distribution
Uhrzeigersinn m clockwise
U-Kerb m U notch
Ultraschallimpuls[prüf]gerät n ultrasonic testing apparatus
Ultraschallprüfung f supersonic test; ultrasonic testing
Ultraschallprüfverfahren n ultrasonic examination method
Ultraschall-Scherwelle f ultrasonic shear wave
Ultraschallschweißen n ultrasonic welding
Umbau m rebuilding; reconstruction; redesign; remodelling
umbauen redesign
umbauen [der Walzen] change [the rolls]
Umbauzeit f (Walzenwechsel) time required for roll changing
umbiegen fold
Umdrehung f revolution; turn
Umdrehung f **pro Minute** revolution per min
umfallen (im Kaliber) fall over; turn over; upset
Umfallen n **(im Kaliber)** tilting over
Umfang m extent; range; size
Umfang-Querschnitt-Verhältnis n circumference to cross sectional area ratio
Umfangsteilung f circular pitch
Umformbarkeit f ductility; forming property; malleability; plasticity
umformen convert; deform; reform; shape; transform
Umformen n deformation; forming; reforming; shaping
Umformer m converter; transformer
Umformerhaus n motor generator set house
Umformgeschwindigkeit f deformation rate
Umformtechnik f metal forming; metal working; plastic metal working
Umformvermögen n plasticity
Umfrage f inquiry; survey
umführen loop
Umführung f bypass[ing]; circulation; repeater
umfüllen reladle
umgebende Luft f ambient air
Umgebung f environment
Umgehungsleitung f bypass[ing]
Umgehungsmechanismus m **(bei Versetzungen)** looping
umgekehrte Seigerung f inverse segregation; negative segregation
Umgestaltung f remodelling
umhüllen case; envelop; jacket
umhüllte Elektrode f coated electrode; sheathed electrode; shielded electrode
Umhüllung f case; casing; jacket
Umkehr f reversal
Umkehrantrieb m reversible drive; reversing drive
umkehren invert; reverse
umkehrflammenbeheizter Tiefofen m U-fired soaking pit
Umkehrpunkt m arrest point
Umkehrstraße f reversing mill; reversing train
Umkehrwalzmotor m reversing mill motor
Umkehrwalzwerk n reversing rolling mill
Umklappen n **des Gitters** lattice shearing; lattice transformation
Umkörnen n regenerative annealing
Umkreis m perimeter
umkristallisieren anneal just below lower critical point
Umlauf m circulation; complete rotation
Umlaufbiegen n rotary straightening
Umlaufbiegeversuch m rotating bar fatigue test
umlaufen rotate
umlaufend rotary

umlaufendes Wasser *n* circulating water
Umlaufentgasung *f* **(RH-Verfahren)** circulation degassing
Umlaufschmierung *f* circulation oiling; circulation system lubrication
Umlaufschrott *m* process scrap
Umlaufvermögen *n* current assets
umlegen (Sauerstoffkonverter) turn down
Umleitungskanal *m* bypass[ing]
Umlenkrolle *f* guide pulley
ummanteln encase; jacket
ummantelte Elektrode *f* covered electrode; sheathed electrode
Umrechnungswert *m* conversion value
Umrißprofilschneider *m* contour profile cutter
Umroll-Rüttelformmaschine *f* jar ramming rollover moulding machine; jolt rollover moulding
umrühren agitate; stir
Umrühren *n* agitation
Umrüstzeit *f* resetting up time; time required for changing (the rolls)
Umsatzsteuer *f* sales tax
umschaltbare Stromzuleitung *f* power supply line with change-over switching
umschalten change over; throw over
Umschalter *m* change over switch; switch
umschlagen fall over; turn over
umschlagen (im Kaliber) turn over; upset
Umschlagen *n* **(im Kaliber)** tilting over
Umschlagleistung *f* handling capacity
Umschlag *m* **(von Gütern)** turn round (of goods)
Umschmelze *f* remelt heat
Umschmelzelektrode *f* remelting electrode
umschmelzen remelt
Umschmelzen *n* **unter Vakuum** vacuum remelting
Umschüttverfahren *n* **(Entschwefelung außerhalb des Hochofens)** readling method
umsetzen change over; react
Umsetzung *f* change over; conversion; reaction
Umspanner *m* transformer
umsponnener Draht *m* braided wire
Umsteckwalzwerk *n* looping [type] rolling mill
umstellen change over; shift
umstellen auf Gas (Winderhitzer) change on gas
Umstellspindel *f* housing screw
Umstellzeit *f* reversal time
umsteuern change over; reverse
Umsteuerschieber *m* reversing gear valve
Umsteuerung *f* reversal
Umsteuerventil *n* reversing valve
Umwälzbeheizung *f* radiator heating
umwalzen loop
Umwalzer *m* looper; looping roller
Umwälzung *f* circulation; convection; revolution
umwandeln convert
Umwandlung *f* conversion; transformation
Umwandlungsbereich *m* transformation range
Umwandlungsgeschwindigkeitskurve *f* reaction rate curve
Umwandlungskosten *pl* conversion costs
Umwandlungspunkt *m* change point; critical point; recalescence; transition point
Umwandlungstemperatur *f* transformation temperature
Umwandlungsuntergefüge *n* transformation substructure
Umweltbedingungen *fpl* environment conditions; surrounding conditions
umweltfreundlich antipollution; low pollution
Umweltschutz *m* protection of the environment
Umweltverhältnisse *npl* surrounding conditions
Umwickelanlage *f* recoiling line; re-

unstetige Veränderliche

winder
umwickeln tape; wrap
umwickelter Draht *m* braided wire
unbearbeitet non-machined; not machined; rough
unbedingte Abhängigkeit *f* clear cut relationship
unbeeinflußt unbiased
unbelastet unbiased
unberuhigter Stahl *m* effervescent steel; rimmed steel (am.); rimming steel; rising steel; unkilled steel
undichtes Rohr *n* blower
Undichtheit *f* leak[age]
Undurchlässigkeit *f* impermeability
undurchsichtig opaque
uneben (Blech) not flat (sheet)
unedles Thermopaar *n* base metal thermocouple
unendliche Verdünnung *f* infinite dilution
unendlich verdünnte Lösung *f* infinitely dilute solution
unerwünschtes Begleitelement *n* undesirable element
Unfallhäufigkeit *f* frequency of accidents
Unfallschutz *m* accident prevention; guard
Unfallstation *f* first aid dispensary
Unfallverhütung *f* prevention of accidents
Unfallverhütungskampagne *f* safety campaign
ungebeizt unpickled
ungefähre Länge *f* approximate length
ungeheizter Tiefofen *m* dead [soaking] pit
ungelernter Arbeiter *m* unskilled workman
Ungenauigkeit *f* inaccuracy
ungepreßtes Pulver *n* loose powder
ungereinigtes Gas *n* crude gas
ungeschweißter Oberflächenriß *m* roak; roke; seam
ungesteuerte Kühlung *f* uncontrolled cooling

ungleichachsige Körner *npl* non equiaxial grains
ungleichartig heterogeneous
ungleichförmiges Pulver *n* non uniform powder
Ungleichgewicht *n* disequilibrium
Ungleichmäßigkeit *f* heterogeneity; non uniformity
ungleichnamige Versetzungen *fpl* dislocations of opposite sign
ungleichschenkliger rundkantiger Winkelstahl *m* round edge unequal angles
ungleichschenkliges Winkeleisen *n* unequal angle
unhaltig (Bergbau) sterile
Universalabkantmaschine *f* universal bending off machine
Universalbrennschneidemaschine *f* universal cutting machine
universaler Rechner *m* universal computer
Universalstahl *m* universal [mill] plate
Universalstahlwalzwerk *n* universal mill
Universalwickler *m* universal coiling machine
unlegierter kohlenstoffarmer Stahl *m* low carbon steel
unlegierter kohlenstoffreicher Stahl *m* plain carbon steel
unlegierter Stahl *m* carbon steel; mild steel; unalloyed steel
unlösliche Phase *f* insoluble phase
unmittelbar direct
unparteiisch unbiased
unpassend inadequate; unsuitable
Unreinheit *f* impurity
unrund noncircular
Unrundheitstoleranz *f* circularity tolerance
unsaubere Abgratkante *f* fraze
unschädlich machen neutralise; render harmless
Unschärfe *f* inaccuracy
Unschlitt *m* tallow
unschmelzbar infusible
unstetige Veränderliche *f* discrete variable

Unterbär *m* lower ram
unterbrechen break
Unterbrecher *m* breaker; stop bath
Unterbrechung *f* interruption
unterbrochenes Altern *n* interrupted ag[e]ing
unterbrochene Schweißnaht *f* intermittent weld
Unterdicke *f* off ga[u]ge
Unterdruck *m* bottom roll pressure; depression; negative pressure; vacuum
unterdrückte Verbrennung *f* suppressed combustion
unterer Heizwert *m* **(Hu)** lower caloric value; net caloric power (am.)
unterer Schmiedesattel *m* lower die block
unteres Blockende *n* butt
unteres Kaliber *n* bottom pass; lower pass
untere Streckgrenze *f* lower yield point
unteres Zwischenstufengefüge *n* lower bainite structure
untereutektisch hypoeutectic
untereutektoidischer Stahl *m* hypoeutectoid steel
Unterfeuerung *f* undergrate firing
Unterflurleitung *f* underfloor duct
Untergesenk *n* lower die
Untergestell *n* base
Untergrundschwärzung *f* fog level (spectrum analysis)
Untergruppe *f* subdivision
Unterhaltung *f* upkeep
Unterhöhlung *f* **(Fräslöcher)** undercutting
Unterkasten *m* lower frame (drag)
Unterkolben *m* lower ram
Unterkorn *n* undersize
Unterkühlung *f* supercooling
Unterlagen *fpl* data; statistics [data]
Unterlagplatte *f* bottom plate; ground plate; stool; tie plate
Unterlagsblech *n* dummy sheet
Unterlänge *f* short; short length
unterlegen support

Unterlegscheibe *f* washer
Unterlieferant *m* subcontractor
Unterlizenz *f* sublicense
unter Luftabschluß *m* hermetically sealed
Untermaß *n* undersize
Untermöllerung *f* underburdening
Unternehmen *n* enterprise; undertaking
Unterofen *m* lower furnace
Unterprobe *f* sub-sample
Unter-Pulver-Schweißen *n* **(UP-Schweißen)** submerged arc welding
Unterrostung *f* filiform corrosion
Untersatz *m* base; base support
Unterschied *m* difference
unterschiedlich varying
Unter-Schiene-Schweißen *n* firecracker welding
Unterschubfeuerung *f* underfeed furnace; underfeed stocker
untersintert undersintered
Unterspannung *f* minimum stress
Unterstempel *m* bottom punch
Unterstützung *f* support
untersuchen search; sound search; test
Untersuchung *f* analysis; examination; investigation; research; testing
unter Tage below ground; underground
Untertagevergasung *f* **(von Kohle)** underground gasification (of coal)
Unterwalze *f* bottom roll; lower roll
Unterwindfeuerung *f* undergrate air firing
Unterzug *m* underdraft
ununterbrochen continuous
ununterbrochener Abstich *m* continuous tapping
unverbindliches Angebot *n* offer without obligation
unverfälscht unbiased
unverkokbar noncoking
unvermischtes Hochofengas *n* straight blast-furnace gas
unverzerrt unbiased

V

Vakuumbedampfen *n* vacuum deposition
Vakuumbehandlung *f* vacuum treatment
Vakuumblockguß *m* vacuum ingot casting
Vakuumdurchlaufentgasung *f* continuous vacuum degassing; ladle to ladle stream degassing
Vakuumfrischen *n* vacuum refining
Vakuumgießen *n* vacuum casting
Vakuumgießstrahlentgasung *f* vacuum stream degassing
Vakuumheberverfahren *n* **(DH-Verfahren)** vacuum lift process (DH-process)
Vakuumheißextraktion *f* vacuum hot extraction
Vakuumheißwandofen *m* vacuum hot wall furnace
Vakuuminduktionsschmelzen *n* vacuum induction melting
Vakuumlichtbogenschmelzen *n* vacuum arc melting
Vakuum-Lichtgeschwindigkeit *f* speed of light in vacuum
Vakuum-Pfannendurchlaufentgasung *f* vacuum ladle degassing
Vakuumplasmaschmelzen *n* vacuum plasma melting
Vakuumraffination *f* vacuum refining
Vakuumrinnenofen *m* vacuum channel-type furnace
Vakuumschmelzanlage *f* vacuum melting plant
Vakuumschwebeschmelzen *n* vacuum levitation melting
Vakuumsinterglocke *f* vacuum sintering bell
Vakuumumlaufverfahren *n* vacuum circulation process
Valenzelektron *n* valency electron
Vanadinstahl *m* vanadium steel
Vanadium *n* vanadium
Variationsbreite *f* range

Ventil *n* valve
Ventilator *m* blower; fan; ventilator
Ventilfederdraht *m* valve spring wire
Ventilsitz *m* valve seat
Ventilstahl *m* valve steel
veränderlich variable
Veränderliche *f* variable
veränderliche Kosten *pl* variable costs
Veränderliche *f* **zufällige** variate
Veränderlichkeit *f* variability
verändern variate; vary
Veränderungskoeffizient *m* coefficient of variation
verankern tie
Verankerungsdraht *m* stay wire
Verankerungsträger *m* buck-stay
Verankerung *f* **(von Versetzungen)** pinning (of dislocations)
Verarbeitbarkeit *f* machinability
Verarbeitbarkeit *f* **(spanlos)** workability
verarbeiten manufacture; process; treat; use
Verarbeitung *f* processing; use
Verarbeitungsfehler *m* processing defect
Verarbeitungskosten *pl* manufacturing costs
Verarbeitungsmodul *n* processing module
veraschen incinerate
verästelte Strukturen *fpl* feathery structures
Verband *m* join[t]
verbessern improve
Verbesserung *f* improvement
verbinden connect; join[t]; tie
verbindliches Angebot *n* binding offer
Verbindung *f* assembly; bond; composition; compound; junction; union
Verbindungskanal *m* **(zwischen Schlacken- und Regeneratorkammer)** fantail
Verbindungslinie *f* binary edge
Verbindungsmasse *f* packing
Verbindungsschweißen *n* joint welding

Verblasbarkeit f blowability
verblasen blow
Verblaserost m sintering grate
verbleien lead; lead-coat
Verblendstein m facing brick
verbogene Ecken fpl bent corners
verbrannt burnt
verbrannte Form f burnt tuyre
verbrannte Kante f burnt edge
Verbrauch m consumption
verbrauchtes Gas n waste gas
verbrennen burn
Verbrennen n burning; oxidation
Verbrenner m incinerator
Verbrennung f combustion
Verbrennungsgeschwindigkeit f rate of combustion
Verbrennungskammer f combustion chamber
Verbrennungskraftmaschine f combustion engine
Verbrennungsluft f combustion air
Verbrennungsrückstand m residue from combustion
verbrennungstechnisch combustion engineering
Verbrennungsverhältnisse npl combustion conditions
Verbrennungsvorgänge mpl combustion phenomena
Verbrennungswärme f combustion heat
Verbrennung f **unterdrückte** suppressed combustion
Verbundarbeit f combined-operation work
Verbundbeheizung f combination firing; combined firing; compound firing
verbundene Verteilung f joint distribution
verbunden mit Schraubmuffe f **(Rohr)** screwed and socketed (joint)
Verbundguß m composite casting; compound casting
Verbundgußwalze f composite cast roll
Verbundmetall n clad metal; composite metal; ply-metal
Verbundpulver n composite powder
Verbundrohr n composite tube
Verbundstahl m composite steel; compound steel
Verbundstein m bonder
Verbundträger m composite beam
Verbundwerkstoff m composite material
Verbundwiderstand m bond strength
Verbundwirtschaft f combined utilities
verchromen chromise
verdampfen evaporate; flash into steam; vaporise; vaporize; volatilise
Verdampfen n vaporisation
Verdampfungskühlung f evaporation cooling
Verdampfungswärme f heat of evaporation
verdeckte Lichtbogenschweißung f submerged arc welding
verdeckter Lichtbogen m submerged arc
Verdichtbarkeit f compressibility
verdichten boost; compress; concentrate
Verdichter m compressor
Verdichtung f compression; packing
Verdichtungseinlage f densener
Verdichtungsverhältnis n compression ratio
verdicken bulge; reinforce; thicken
Verdienst n **(anerkennenswerte Leistung)** merit
Verdienst m **(Gewinn)** gain
verdrallen twist
Verdrehbeanspruchung f torsional stress; twisting stress
Verdrehdauerfestigkeit f torsional fatigue endurance limit; torsional fatigue strength
verdrehen twist; wrench
Verdrehen n twisting with rotary tool movement
Verdrehfestigkeit f torsional strength; twisting strength
Verdrehung f twist

Verdrehungsbruch m torsion failure
Verdrehungswechselfestigkeit f torsional fatigue endurance limit
Verdrehversuch m torsion test
Verdrehwechselfestigkeit f torsional fatigue endurance limit; torsional fatigue strength
Verdrillen n torsion
verdünnen dilute; thin
verdünnte Lösung f dilute solution
verdünnte Zone f depleted zone
Verdunstungskühlung f evaporative cooling
Verdüsungspulver n atomized powder
Verecken n (von Pfannen) collision
veredeln improve; refine
vereinbarte Einsatzhärtetiefe f specified depth of case hardening
Vereinfachung f simplification
vereinheitlicht standardised
Vereinheitlichung f standardisation
Vereinigung f amalgamation
Verengung f constriction
Vererzung f metal penetration
verfahrbar displaceable; mobile; movable
Verfahren n cluster sampling; method; procedure; treatment
Verfahren n **der größten Wahrscheinlichkeit** method of maximum likelihood
Verfahren n **des ruhenden Tropfens** sessile drop method
Verfahrensdatenanzeige f process visualisation
Verfahrenssteuerung f process control
Verfahrenstechnik f process technology
Verfahren n **wiederholter Gleichversuche** replication
Verfall m decay
Verfälschung f bias
Verfeinerungsbetrieb m refining department
verfestigen strain harden; strengthen; work harden
Verfestigen n strengthening

verfestigende Phase f **(in Legierungen)** strengthening phase
verfestigtes Gefüge n work hardened structure
Verfestigung f work hardening
Verfestigung f **durch Kaltverformung** strain hardening; work hardening
verfeuern burn; fire
verflüchtigen volatilise
verflüssigen liquify; thin
Verflüssigung f fluidisation
verfolgen trace
Verfolgung f tracking
verformbar ductile
Verformbarkeit f formability
verformen deform
Verformung f deformation; forming; shaping; strain
verformungsarmer Bruch m low-ductility fracture
Verformungsbruch m fracture on working
Verformungsgeschwindigkeit f strain rate
Verformungsgrad m amount of working
Verformungsmartensit m strain-induced martensite
Verfügbarkeitskontrolle f on-hand-status check
vergasen gasify
Vergasen n **(von Schmelzen)** gassing
Vergaser m carburettor
Vergasung f gasification
Vergasungsanlage f gasifying plant
Vergasungsmaschine f gasifying machine
Vergasungstechnik f gasifying method
vergießen cast; pour; teem
Vergießen n casting; pouring; teeming
Verglasungs-T-Stahl m glasing tees
Vergleicher m comparing element
Vergleichsformänderung f equivalent strain
Vergleichsspannung f effective stress
Vergleichsspannung f **(elektr.)** reference voltage
Vergleichsstelle f **(Thermopaar)** reference junction

Vergleichsversuch *m* comparative test; comparison test
Vergleichswert *m* comparative value; control
vergrößern amplify; enlarge; increase
vergüten harden and temper
Vergüten *n* hardening with subsequent drawing; hardening with subsequent tempering
vergütet quenched and tempered; tempered
vergüteter Stahl *m* quenched and tempered steel (QT steel)
Vergütungsanlage *f* heat treating plant
Vergütungsstahl *m* heat treatable steel; steel for hardening and tempering; tempering steel
Vergütungsstahlguß *m* heat treatable steel casting
Verhalten *n* behaviour
Verhältnis *n* ratio
Verhältnis *n* **Bißbreite zu Werkstückhöhe** bite ratio
verhärten harden
verhütten smelt
Verhütten *n* smelting
Verhüttung *f* metallurgical process; metallurgical treatment
verjüngen chamfer; swage; taper
Verjüngung *f* batter; conicity; draught
Verkalkung *f* calcification
Verkantungsmoment *n* **(Walzen)** tilting moment
Verkauf *m* sale
Verkaufsabteilung *f* sales department
Verkaufsbüro *n* sales office
Verkaufskonto *n* sales account
Verkaufskosten *pl* selling costs
Verkaufspreis *m* selling price
Verkehr *m* traffic
Verkehrsmittel *n* transportation means
verkeilen key
verkettete Spannung *f* secondary voltage
Verklebung *f* sticking
verkleiden case; cover

Verkleidung *f* casing; lining
Verkohlung *f* carbonisation
Verkokbarkeit *f* cokability
Verkokung *f* carbonisation; coking
verkracken crack
Verkröpfung *f* cranking; offset
verkupfern copper-coat; copperplate
Verkürzung *f* linear contraction
Verladeanlage *f* loading plant; loading station
Verladebrücke *f* charging and discharging gantry crane; loading bridge
Verladeeinrichtung *f* loading installation
verladen load
Verladen *n* **des Konverterausbruchs** loading of broken out lining material
Verladerampe *f* loading ramp
verlagerte Seigerung *f* displaced segregation
Verlängerung *f* elongation; extension
Verlappen *n* lock forming; lock seaming
Verlauf *m* course; process; response; trend
verlorene Gießform *f* investment casting
verlorener Kopf *m* dead-head; dozzle; dozzle feeder [head]; header; hot top; rising head; shrink bob; sinkhead; sullage piece; top discard
vermaschter Regelkreis *m* multi-loop control system
vermauern brick up; line; wall up
Vermauerung *f* bricking up
vermengen blend
vermindern diminish; lower; reduce
Verminderung *f* decay; decline; decrement; reduction
Vermischung *f* amalgamation
Vernickeln *n* nickel plating
Vernickelung *f* flash nickel plating
Verpackungsband *n* baling hoop
Verpackungsblech *n* packing plate
Verpackungslinie *f* packaging line
Verpreßbarkeit *f* compressibility

Verputz *m* rendering plaster
Verriegelungsvorrichtung *f* locking device
Verringern *n* **des Durchmessers am Ende eines Hohlschmiedestücks** bottling
Verringerung *f* decrease
verrosten corrode; rust
Versagen *n* failure
Versammlung *f* assembly
Versand *m* dispatch
Versandhalle *f* despatch department
verschiebbar displaceable
verschieben displace; move; shift; shunt
Verschieben *n* displacement by shear parallel to adjacent surfaces
Verschieber *m* manipulator for shifting
verschiedenartig heterogeneous
Verschiedenartigkeit *f* heterogeneity
verschlacken scorify; slag; vitrify
Verschlackungsverhältnis *n* ratio of iron in slag to iron in bath
verschlammen silt up
Verschleiß *m* scuffing; wear [and tear]
Verschleiß *m* **der Ausmauerung** wear of the lining
verschleißen abrade; wear
verschleißfest wear resistant
verschleißfeste Oberfläche *f* hard wearing surface
verschleißfester Stahl *m* wear resisting steel
Verschleißfestigkeit *f* resistance to wear; wear resistance; wear-resistance
Verschleißfutter *n* inner lining; working lining
Verschleißlinien *fpl* scoring
Verschleißmarkenbreite *f* width of wear band
Verschleißprüfung *f* wear test
Verschleißring *m* wear resisting collar
Verschleißstandzeit *f* wear [resisting] life
Verschleißteil *n* wear resisting part
Verschleißwiderstand *m* resistance to wear
Verschleißzahl *f* wear index
Verschluß *m* closure; gate; lock; seal
Verschlußkegel *m* **(Gichtglocke)** bell
Verschlüßler *m* encoder
Verschlußschraube *f* screw plug
Verschmelzung *f* amalgamation
Verschmiedungsgrad *m* ratio of reduction by forging
verschmieren caulk; lute
verschmoren oxidise
verschmorte Oberfläche *f* swealed surface
verschmutztes Blech *n* dirty sheet
Verschmutzung *f* contamination; pollution
verschneiden blend
Verschnitt *m* **(Stanzen)** scrap
verschrauben bolt
Verschraubung *f* screwed joint
verschrotten scrap
Verschrotten *n* scrapping
Verschrottungsbetrieb *m* scrapping off plant
verschütten spill
Verschweißen *n* fouling; fusing; welding
Verseifung *f* saponification
Verseifungszahl *f* saponification number
Verseilmaschine *f* stranding machine
versenken countersink
versetzbar portable
versetzen move
versetzt off centre
versetzt angeordnet staggered
Versetzung *f* dislocation; offset; scaffold
Versinterung *f* fusion
versorgen supply
Versorgung *f* supply
verspannen brace
Verspannung *f* **eines Lagers** bearing distortion
verspritzen spill; splash
verspröden embrittle
Versprödung *f* brittleness
Verstählen *n* acierage

verstärken amplify; boost; reinforce; strengthen
Verstärker *m* amplifier; intensifier
Verstärkermaschine *f* **(Lichtbogenofen)** amplifying machine
Versteifungsdraht *m* guy wire
Versteifungsträger *m* buck stay
verstellbar adjustable
Verstellweg *m* setting range [of screw-down]; slideways
Verstellweg *m* **der Stopfenstange** distance over which stopper is moved to control teeming rate
verstemmen caulk
verstopfen choke; clog; plug
Verstopfung *f* choking; clogging; obstruction; stopping
verstreben brace; strut
Versuch *m* experiment; test; trial
Versuchauswertung *f* interpretation of test results
versuchen test; try
Versuchsanlage *f* experimental plant; pilot plant; trial plant
Versuchsanstalt *f* laboratory; research lab[oratory]; testing laboratory
Versuchsbetrieb *m* pilot plant
Versuchsblech *n* test sheet
Versuchsfehler *m* experimental error
Versuchsplan *m* design [of an experiment]
Versuchsraum *m* laboratory
Verteilanlage *f* switch cupboard
verteilen distribute; divide
Verteiler *m* tundish
Verteilergetriebe *n* power drive transmission
Verteilerglocke *f* distributing bell
Verteilertrichter *m* revolving top
Verteilerwagen *m* tundish car
Verteilung *f* allocation; distribution; repartition
Verteilung *f* **in zwei Veränderlichen** bivariate distribution
Verteilungskoeffizient *m* distribution coefficient
Verteilungsnetz *n* grid

vertiefen dish
Vertiefung *f* cavity; depression; impression; indent
Vertikalschneiden *n* vertical cutting
Vertrag *m* agreement; contract; paper
Vertrauen *n* confidence
Vertrauensabstand *m* confidence interval
Vertrauensbereich *m* confidence interval
Vertrauensgrenze *f* confidence limit
Vertriebssystem *n* distribution system
verunreinigtes Eisen *n* contaminated iron
Verunreinigung *f* contamination; contamination impurity; impurity; pollution
Verwachsung *f* anchoring; bonding; intergrowth
Verwaltungsgebäude *n* administration building
Verwandlung *f* conversion
verweigern reject
Verweilzeit *f* dwell time; holding time; residence time; stay[ing] time; time of exposure
verwenden use
Verwendung *f* application; use
Verwendungszweck *m* range of application
Verwerfen *n* **nach Beanspruchung** flatting; kniking
Verwerfung *f* distortion; distortion fault; fault; trouble; warping
Verwertung *f* use; utilisation
Verwindemaschine *f* twisting machine
verwinden torsion
Verwinden *n* torsion
Verwindeversuch *m* single torsion test
Verwindung *f* gear cutting; twist
verwindungsfrei free from twist effects
verwittern weather
Verzahnung *f* gear cutting; gearing
Verzahnungsmaschine *f* gear cutting machine
verzapfen mortise
Verzapfung *f* mortising
Verzeichnis *n* schedule; table

verzerren strain
Verzerrung f bias; strain
verziehen distort; warp
Verziehen n distortion
verzinken galvanise
Verzinken n fluxes for pickling; galvanising; zinc coating
Verzinkerei f galvanising plant; galvanising shop; zinc coating shop
Verzinkereizink m zinc for [zinc] coating
verzinktes Band n galvanised strip
verzinktes Blech n galvanised sheet; zinc coated sheet
Verzinkung f galvanising; hot dip galvanising; zinc coating
Verzinkungsanlage f zinc coating plant
Verzinkungsblech n sheet for galvanising
Verzinkungsofen m galvanising furnace; zinc coating furnace
Verzinkungspfanne f galvanising kettle; galvanising pot; zinc coating kettle
verzinnen tin
Verzinnen n tinning
Verzinnerei f tinning department; tinning house
verzinnter Bandstahl m tin strip
verzinntes Band n tinned strip
Verzinnung f tinning
Verzinnungsanlage f tinning plant
Verzinnungsherd m tinning pot; tinning stack
Verzinnungswalze f tinning roll
verzogenes Band n twisted strip
verzögern delay; retard
Verzögerung f delay; lag; retardation; retarding; time consuming lag
Verzögerungsglied n lag element
Verzug m distortion; warping
verzugsbeständiger Stahl m non deforming steel
verzugsfreier Stahl m non deforming steel; non distorting steel; non warping steel
verzundern oxidise at high temperatures; scale
Verzunderung f high temperature oxidation; scaling
verzweigte Kette f branched chain
Vibrationsmühle f vibratory mill
Vibrationsverdichten n compacting by vibration
Vickershärte f Vickers hardness; diamond pyramid hardness number; pyramid hardness number
Vielfachprüfung f sequential analysis of variance
vielgipflige Verteilung f multimodal distribution
Vielkeilwelle f multiple spline shaft
Viellochstein m multi hole brick
Vielprobenmaschine f multiple testing machine
vielseitig versatile
Vielwalzengerüst n cluster mill
Viergelenkgetriebe n four bar linkage
viergerüstige Grobblechstraße f four-stand plate mill
Vierkantblock m square ingot
Vierkanteisen n square iron
Vierkantschraube f square head cap screw
Vierkantstahl m square [bar] steel; squares
Vierstoffsystem n quaternary system
Vierstranggießmaschine f four strand continuous casting machine
Viertaktgasmaschine f four stroke gas engine
viertelhart quarter hard
Viertelkreisdüse f quadrant nozzle
Vierwalzengerüst n four high rolling stand
Vignolschiene f flat bottom rail; vignol rail
virtueller Eingang m virtual input
Visioplastizität f visioplasticity
Viskosität f viscosity
volle Kehlnahtschweiße f convex weld
volle Schweiße f rounded weld
Vollfließpressen n rod extrusion; solid extrusion
Vollgas n **bei Leerlauf** high idle [run]

völlig gar (Koks) fully carbonised
vollkontinuierliches Stranggießen n continuous casting; sequence casting
Vollprägen n closed die coining
Voll-Quer-Fließpressen n transverse rod [impact] extrusion
Vollrad n solid wheel
Voll-Rückwärts-Fließpressen n indirect rod impact extrusion
Voll-Rückwärts-Strangpressen n indirect extrusion of rods
Vollstab m unnotched specimen
vollstopfen crowd
Voll-Vorwärts-Fließpressen n direct impact extrusion of rods
Voll-Vorwärts-Strangpressen n direct extrusion of rods
Vollwandträger m plate girder; web girder
Volumen n volume
Volumenänderung f volume change
Volumenbruch m volume fraction
Volumenkonzentration f volume concentration
volumetrischer Flüssigkeitszähler m volumetric liquid counter
Vorabscheider m preliminary separator
Vorabscheidungsbecken n pre-settling basin
Vorabsiebung f (Erz) pre-screening
Vorarbeiter m first helper
vorbearbeitet rough-machined
Vorbehandlung f pretreatment
Vorbehandlungsschicht f conversion layer
Vorbeizen n black pickling
vorbelastet prestressed
vorbereiten prepare
vorbereitetes Ende n **eines Schmiedestückes** bar hold; tong hold
Vorbiegemaschine f cambering machine
vorblasen fore blow; preblow
Vorblasezeit f fore blow time
Vorblech n sheet bar
Vorblock m bloom; cog; cogged ingot

Vorblock-Drillingsguß m triple cast bloom
vorblocken bloom; cog down
Vorblocken n **vor Zwischenaufheizung** saddening
Vorblockputzerei f bloom conditioning yard
Vorbramme f roughed slab
Vorbrechen n coarse breaking; coarse crushing
Vorcarbidausscheidung f carbide precipitated during quenching
vorderes Ende n leading end
Vorderwalzer m roller on the entry side of rolls
voreilen lead; slip forward
Voreilung f (Walzen) forward slip
voreutektisch preeutectic
voreutektoidischer Ferrit m preeutectoid ferrite
Vorevakuator m booster ejector; quick-start ejector
Vorfertigstich m leader
Vorfertigung f prefabrication
Vorformgebung f prior plastic deformation
Vorfrischen n preliminary oxidation
Vorfrischmischer m active hot metal mixer; metal mixer; preliminary refining mixer
Vorfunkzeit f (Spektralanalyse) presparking time
Vorgabe f allowance; rate
Vorgang m operation; process
vorgefertigt prefabricated
vorgeformte dünne Metallschicht f wad
vorgefrischt semi finished
Vorgelege n back gear; reduction gear; transmission gear
Vorgerüst n break[ing] down stand; cogging stand; rougher; roughing [down] stand
vorgeschmiedetes Stück n use
Vorgesetzter m supervisor
vorgespannte Diode f biassed diode
vorgespanntes Walzgerüst n prestressed rolling stand

vorgestauchter weicher Stahl *m* precompressed mild steel
vorgewalzter Block *m* blank; bloom; cogged ingot
vorgezogener Draht *m* processed wire
Vorglühen *n* preliminary annealing
Vorhalt *m* derivative action; rate action
Vorhaltezeit *f* derivation action time
Vorhaltzeit *f* rate time
vorhandene Korngröße *f* actual grain size
Vorheber *m* lifting rod
Vorherd *m* breast pan; forehearth
Vorholvorrichtung *f* advancing device; feeding device
Vorkaliber *n* blooming pass; breaking-down pass; preceding pass
Vorkalkulation *f* preliminary calculation
vorkalkulieren estimate
Vorkommen *n* occurence in beds; occurence in floors; occurence in veins
Vorkröpfgesenk *n* snaker
Vorlage *f* **(Koksofen)** gas collecting pipe
Vorlast *f* initial load
Vorlaufbehälter *m* **(Gasreinigung)** presettling tank
vorläufiges Mittel *n* working mean
Vorlaufschlacke *f* flush slag; flushing cinder
Vorlegierung *f* hardening alloy
Vorlegierungspulver *n* prealloyed powder
Vormann *m* foreman
Vormetall *n* blown metal; feed metal
vormischen premix
Vornorm *f* tentative standard
Vorpressen *n* prepressing
Vorprobe *f* pilot test; preliminary test
Vorprofil *n* preliminary section
Vorrat *m* stock; supply
Vorratsbehälter *m* stock bin; storage bunker
Vorratstrichter *m* hopper

Vorreduktion *f* prereduction
Vorreinigung *f* preliminary purification; primary cleaning; rough cleaning
Vorrichtung *f* apparatus; appliance; arrangement; set-up; device; equipment; jig; setup
Vorschlag *m* proposal; suggestion
Vorschlagswesen *n* **betriebliches** suggestion scheme; suggestion system
Vorschleifen *n* **(Gußputz)** rough grinding
Vorschmelzeisen *n* first smelting pig iron; premelted iron
Vorschmiedegesenk *n* blanker; blocker; rougher
vorschmieden cog down; hammer-cog; rough-forge; use
Vorschmieden *n* blocking
Vorschub *m* advance; feed
Vorschubhärten *n* progressive hardening
Vorschubschalthebel *m* feed control lever
Vorschubumsteuerung *f* feed reverse
Vorsinterung *f* presintering
vorspannen prestress
Vorspannstahl *m* reinforcing steel for prestressed concrete
Vorspannung *f* initial set; initial tension; preliminary stress; prestraining
Vorsprung *m* lug; projection
Vorsteuerung *f* pilot control
Vorstich *m* blooming pass; breaking down pass; cogging pass; roughing pass
Vorstoß *m* buffer; bumper; ga[u]ge
Vorstrahlbereich *m* **(Röntgen)** transmission range
Vorstraße *f* blooming train; break[ing] down train; cogging train; roughing
vorstrecken bloom; break down; cog; rough; roughdown
Vorstreckgerüst *n* pony rougher
Vorstreckkaliber *n* cogging pass; roughing pass
Vorstreckwalze *f* break[ing] down roll

Vorsturz *m* breakdown; mo[u]lder; scaler
vorsturzen break down
Vorsturzwalzwerk *n* jump roughing mill
Vorumwandlung *f* preliminary transformation
Vorvernicklung *f* flash nickel plating
Vorversuch *m* pretest
Vorwählschalter *m* preselector
vorwärmen preheat
Vorwärmer *m* economiser
Vorwärmer *m* **für Gas** preheater for gas
Vorwärmer *m* **für Luft** preheater for air
Vorwärmer *m* **für Wasser** preheater for water
Vorwärmer *m* **(SM-Ofen)** bank
Vorzerkleinerung *f* coarse breaking

W

Waage *f* analytical balance; balance
Waagebalken *m* balance beam
Waagerechtfräsmaschine *f* horizontal milling machine
Waagschale *f* scale
Wabenbruch *m* dimpled fracture
Wabenträger *m* castellated beam; open-web girder
Wachsausschmelzguß *m* lost-wax casting; precision investment casting
Wachsausschmelzverfahren *n* cire perdu process; waste-wax process
wachsen expand; grow; swell
Wachsen *n* expansion
Wachstumsgeschwindigkeit *f* **der Spannungsrisse** cracking rate
Waffelblech *n* goffered plate
wägbar ponderable
Wagen *m* car; cart; wagon
Wagenaufzug *m* wagon hoist
Wagenbaustahl *m* steel for wagon construction
Wagen *m* **für Massengut** bulk traffic wagon
Wagenguß *m* bogie casting; buggy casting; car casting
Wagenherdofen *m* bogie type [reheating] furnace; car bottom furnace (am.); car hearth furnace
Wagenladung *f* carload
Waggon *m* wagon
Waggonbauanstalt *f* railway wagon plant
Waggonladung *f* carload
Waggonwaage *f* freight car scales
wahrer Mittelwert *m* true mean
Wahrscheinlichkeit *f* empirical probability; probability
Wahrscheinlichkeitsdichte *f* probability density
Wahrscheinlichkeitspapier *n* probability paper
Wahrscheinlichkeitsrechnung *f* theory of probability
Wahrscheinlichkeitsverhältnisprobe *f* probability ratio test
wahrscheinlichster Wert *m* mode
Währung *f* currency
Walken *n* **(Blechumformen)** flex levelling
wallen boil; bubble
Walzanfangstemperatur *f* initial temperature of rolling; start temperature of rolling
Walzarbeit *f* rolling horsepower; torque
Walzbalken *m* rest bar for carrying guides and guards
Walzbarkeit *f* aptitude for rolling; rollability
Walzbeschichtung *f* roll coating
Wälzbewegung *f* combined rolling and sliding motion
Walzbiegen *n* roll bending
Walzblock *m* billet; bloom; ingot suitable for rolling
Walzbördeln *n* roll flanging
Walzdorn *m* mandrel
Walzdraht *m* wire rod
Walzdruck *m* draft; pressure of rolling; roll pressure
Walze *f* roll

Walze f (Halbstahl) steel-base roll
Walze f (Hartguß) clear chill roll
Walze f (Indefinitguß) indefinite chill roll
Walze f (Kohlenstoffstahl) carbon steel roll
Walze f (Lehmguß) loam iron roll
Walze f (Mildhart) high-Si chilled iron roll; mild-hard roll
Walze f mit gehärteten Kalibern chill pass roll
walzen mill; roll
wälzen roll
Walzen n lamination; rolling
Walzenabplattung f flattening of periphery of a roll (by pressure); roll flattening
Walzenanstellung f roll adjustment
Walzenbacke f (Brecher) roll jaw
Walzenballen m roll barrel; roll body
Walzenballigkeit f roll crown
Walzenbiegungsverfahren n (zur Einhaltung der Balligkeit) roll bending method (of crown control)
Walzenbrecher m giratory crusher; roll type crusher; rolling crusher
Walzenbürste f roll brush
Walzendrehbank f roll lathe
Walzendreherei f roll turning shop
Walzendtemperatur f final temperature of rolling; finish rolling temperature
Walzendurchbiegung f deflection of the rolls
Walzen f (Flockengraphitguß) flake graphite roll
Walzenfräser m plain milling cutter
Walzen fpl hauen rag
Walzenkalibrieren n roll drafting; roll pass design
Walzenkalibriermaschine f roll drafting machine
Walzenlager n cylinder [roll] bearing; roll bearing
Walzen n mit geteiltem Kaliber knifing
Walzenmühle f roller mill
Walzennarbe f roll mark
Walzenöffnung f roll clearance

Walzenprofil n roll profile
Walzensatz m set of roll[er]s
Walzenschlag m eccentricity of the rolls
Walzenschleifmaschine f roll grinding machine
Walzenschmierung f lubricating grease for rolls
Walzensinter m mill scale
Walzensprung m mill spring; roll spring
Walzenständer m housing; mill housing; roll housing
Walzenstrang m strand of rolls
Walzenstrecke f strand of rolls
Walzentreffer m coupling sleeve
Walzenvergüteofen m roll heat-treating furnace
Walzenverschleiß m roll wear
Walzen n von Band (Blech) rolling of strip (sheet)
Walzen n von Profilstäben rolling of sectional bars
Walzen n von Rohren über Stange rotary piercing of tubes over a plug
Walzen n von Stäben (Draht) rolling of bars (wire)
Walzen n von Vielnut-Wellen rolling of multiple-spline shafts
Walzen n von Vierkantrohren rolling of square tubes
Walzen fpl wechseln change the rolls
Walzenwechsel m roll changing
Walzenwechselschlitten m roll changing sledge
Walzenzapfen m roll neck
Walzenzapfenlager n roll neck bearing
Walzer m roller
Walzerzeugnis n rolled product
Walze f (Schalenguß) clear or plain chilled iron roll
Walze f (Sphäroguß) ductile iron roll; nodular iron roll; spheroidal graphite [iron] roll
Walze f (Stahlersatz) grain roll
Walze f (Verbundguß) overflowed roll
Walzfalte f lamination

Walzfehler *m* rolling defect
Walzfolge *f* rolling sequence
Wälzfräser *m* hob cutter
Walzgerüst *n* mill stand; rolling stand; stand of rolls
Walzgerüste *npl* **hintereinander angeordnet** stands in tandem
Walzgerüste *npl* **nebeneinander angeordnet** train of stands
Walzgeschwindigkeit *f* rolling speed
walzgrade straight as in the rolled condition
Walzgut *n* piece; rolled piece; rolling stock; stock
Walzgut *n* **(Walzstück)** workpiece
Walzhaut *f* roll scale; rolling skin; skin
Wälzhebelgetriebe *n* direct-contact mechanism
Walzkante *f* rolled [mill] edge
Walzkassette *f* mill stand of a forging-rolling unit
Walzkeil *m* tapered section entering the rolls
Walzknüppel *m* billet
Walzkraft *f* roll [separating] force; roll force
Walzkraftlager *n* main rollneck bearing
Wälzlager *n* anti-friction bearing; ball and roller bearing
Wälzlagerstahl *m* anti-friction bearing steel; roller bearing steel
Walzleistung *f* rolling load
Walzlinie *f* **(Bandwalzen)** pass line
Walzmannschaft *f* rolling mill crew
Walzmeister *m* boss roller; head roller; rolling-mill foreman
Walzmitte *f* centre line; pass line
Walzmoment *n* roll torque
Walznaht *f* rolling fin; seam
Walznarbe *f* roll pick-up
Walzöl *n* rolling oil
Walzplan *m* rolling program; rolling schedule
Walzplattieren *n* cladding by rolling
Wälzprägen *n* roller marking
Walzprofil *n* rolled section
Walzprofilieren *n* roll forming to shape
Walzprogramm *n* rolling program; rolling schedule
Walzrichten *n* roll[er] straightening; roller levelling
Walzrichten *n* **mit mehreren Walzen** mangling
Walzrichtung *f* direction of rolling; direction of the fiber; rolling direction
Walzriefe *f* mark from the roll; roll scratch
Walzring *m* roll ring; sleeve
Walzrunden *n* crimping; roll rounding
Walzscheibe *f* disc roll
Walzschlacke *f* mill scale
Walzschweißverfahren *n* sealed assembly rolling process
Walzsicken *n* roll beading
Walzsinterpulver *n* mill scale powder
Walzspalt *m* mill bite; roll gap; roll nip
Walzspaltaustritt *m* delivery side of roll gap
Walzsplitter *mpl* sleavers
Walzstahl *m* rolled steel
Walzständer *m* housing
Walzstichplan *m* rolling schedule; schedule
Walzstraße *f* mill train; rolling mill; rolling train
Walzstraße *f* **erster Hitze** primary mill
Walzstraße *f* **zur Herstellung von Bandstahl** manufacture of strip
Walzstrieme *f* roll pick-up
walztechnisch glatte Oberfläche *f* commercially smooth rolled surface
Walztextur *f* rolling texture
Walztisch *m* feed rollers
Walzwerk *n* mill; rolling mill
Walzwerk *n* **erster Hitze** primary mill
Walzwerk *n* **für kleine Bestellungen** jobbing mill
Walzwerksantrieb *m* rolling mill drive
Walzwerkserzeugnis *n* rolling mill product
Walzwerkshilfsantriebe *mpl* mill auxiliaries
Walzwerksingenieur *m* rolling mill superintendent

Walzwerksofen *m* rolling mill furnace
Walzwerksumlaufschrott *m* mill revert scrap
Walzwerk *n* **zweiter Hitze** secondary mill
Walzzeit *f* in roll time
Walzziehbiegen *n* roll draw bending to shape in a multiple-roll unit
Walzziehen *n* roll drawing
Walzziehen *n* **über festen Stopfen (Dorn)** roll drawing over stationary mandrel (plug)
Walzziehen *n* **über losen Stopfen (Dorn)** roll drawing over floating mandrel (plug)
Walzziehen *n* **über mitlaufende Stange** roll drawing over travelling [live] rod
Walzziehen *n* **von Bändern** roll drawing of strip
Walzzunder *m* mill scale; roll[ing] scale; secondary scale
Walzzunge *f* sliver
Walzzustand *m* as rolled; as rolled condition
Wand *f* wall
Wandauskleidung *f* panel lining
Wanddicke *f* wall thickness
Wanddicken-Empfindlichkeit *f* section sensitivity
Wanddickenmesser *m* wall thickness tester
Wanderfeldpumpe *f* travelling field pump
wandernde Versetzung *f* mobile dislocation
Wanderrost *m* travelling [fire] grate
Wanderrostbeschicker *m* chain grate stoker
Wandreibung *f* skin friction
Wandverlust *m* wall loss
wanken rock
Wanne *f* bath; tub
Wannenlage *f* flat position [welding]
Warenprobe *f* sample of commodities
Warenzeichen *n* registered trade mark; trade mark
Warmarbeitsstahl *m* hot forming tool steel; hot working steel; hot-work tool steel
Warmauslagern *n* artificial ag[e]ing
Warmbadhärten *n* delayed martensitic hardening; martempering
Warmband *n* hot [rolled] strip
Warmbandkratzer *m* hot strip scratch
Warmbett *n* hot bank; hot bed
Warmbiegeversuch *m* hot bend test
Warmbildsamkeit *f* ductility at elevated temperatures
Warmblechrichtmaschine *f* hot plate straightening machine
Warmblockschere *f* hot bloom shears
Warmbreitband *n* hot [rolled] wide strip
warmbrüchig hot short
Warmbrüchigkeit *f* hot shortness; red shortness
Wärmdauer *f* heating time
Wärme *f* quantity of heat
wärmeabgebende Mittel *npl* exothermic feeding materials
Wärmeangebot *n* heat evolved
Wärmeausdehnung *f* thermal expansion
Wärmeausnutzung *f* thermal efficiency
Wärmeaustauscher *m* heat exchanger
Wärmebedarf *m* heat required
wärmebeeinflußte Zone *f* heat-affected zone (HAZ)
Wärmebehandelbarkeit *f* capacity for heat treating
Wärmebehandlung *f* heat treatment; thermal treatment
Wärmebehandlung *f* **diskontinuierliche** batch heat treatment
Wärmebehandlung *f* **kontinuierliche** continuous heat treatment
Wärmebehandlungsofen *m* heat treating furnace
wärmebeständig heat resisting
Wärmebilanz *f* calorific balance; heat balance; thermal balance
wärmedämmender feuerfester Stoff insulating refractory
Wärmedämmung *f* heat insulation

Wärmedehnung f dilatation; heat expansion
Wärmedehnzahl f coefficient of thermal expansion
Wärmedurchgang m heat transition
Wärmedurchgangskoeffizient m coefficient of heat transition
Wärmeeinflußzone f **(WEZ)** heat-affected zone (HAZ)
Wärmeeinheit f heat unit; thermal unit; unit of heat
Wärmeentwicklung f recalescence
wärmeerzeugend heat producing
Wärmefluß m heat flow; heat flux; thermal flux
Wärmegefälle n temperature gradient; thermal head
wärmehärtend thermosetting
Wärmehaushalt m heat balance
Wärmeingenieur m fuel and heating engineer
Wärmeinhalt m heat capacity; heat contents
Wärmekapazität f heat capacity
Wärmekapazität f **bei konstantem Volumen (Druck)** heat capacity at constant volume (pressure)
Wärmekraftwerk n thermal power plant
Wärmeleitfähigkeit f conductivity of heat; heat conductivity; thermal conductivity
Wärmeleitplatte f convector; heat-conducting plate
Wärmeleitscheibe f convector
Wärmeleitwiderstand m thermal inertia; thermal resistivity
Wärmemenge f amount of heat; fuel energy; quantity of heat
Wärmemessung f calorimetry; heat measurement
Wärmen n heating
Wärmenutzen m thermal effect
Wärmeofen m **für satzweisen Einsatz** in-and-out reheating furnace
Wärmer m heater
Wärmeriß m heat crack; hot crack; hot tear; pull

Wärmeschutz m heat relief; protection against heat
Wärmeschutzglas n glass for protection against heat
Wärmeschutzmasse f heat insulation composition
Wärmespannung f temperature stress
Wärmespannungsriß m thermal stress crack
Wärmespeicher m heat accumulator; regenerator
Wärmespeicherung f accumulation of heat
Wärmestauung f accumulation of heat
Wärmestelle f fuel and power department
Wärmestrom m heat current; heat flow rate
Wärmestromdichte f heat current density
Wärmestufenschaubild n **(Hochofen)** Reichhardt heat diagram
Wärmetauscherabgas n exchanger exhaust
Wärmetauscheranlage f **(der Zyklonwärmetauscher)** heat exchanger (cyclone heat exchanger)
wärmetechnische Größe f thermic value
Wärmetönung f absorption of heat; evolution of heat; recalescence
Wärmeübergang m heat transfer; heat transmission; transfer of heat
Wärmeübergangskoeffizient m coefficient of heat transfer
Wärmeübergangswiderstand m resistance to heat transfer
Wärmeübergangszahl f heat transfer coefficient
Wärmeübertragung f heat transmission; transfer of heat
Wärmeumwälzung f heat convection
Wärmeverbrauch m heat consumption
Wärmeverlust m calorific loss; heat loss
Wärmewirkungsgrad m thermal efficiency

Wärmewirtschaft *f* fuel economy; heat economy
Wärmezunahme *f* recalescence
warm fertiggewalztes Rohr *n* hot finished tube
warmfest resistant to deformation at elevated temperatures
warmfester Baustahl *m* high-temperature structural steel
warmfester Stahl *m* creep resistant steel; high temperature steel
Warmfestigkeit *f* high-temperature strength; strength at elevated temperatures; strength at high temperatures
Warmformänderungsvermögen *n* hot forming property
Warmformgebung *f* hot forming; hot shaping; hot working
Warmformgebungshitze *f* working heat
Wärmgeschwindigkeit *f* rate of heating
warmgewalzter Flachstahl *m* hot rolled flats
warmgewalzter kleiner U-Stahl *m* hot rolled small U-section
warmgewalzter Rundstahl *m* hot rolled rounds
warmgewalzter Vierkantstahl *m* hot rolled squares
warmgewalzter Zustand *m* hot rolled condition
warmgewalztes Band *n* hot rolled strip
warmgezogenes Rohr *n* hot drawn tube
Warmhalteofen *m* holding furnace
Warmhärte *f* red hardness
warmharter Stahl *m* steel with a high degree of hardness at elevated temperatures
Warm-Kalt-Verfestigen *n* warm work hardening
Warmlager *n* cooling bed; hot bed
Wärmofen *m* reheating furnace
Wärmofen *m* **für satzweisen Einsatz** in-and-out reheating furnace

Warmpressen *n* die pressing; hot pressing
Warmrichten *n* hot straightening
Warmriß *m* chill crack; clink; fire check
warmrißanfällig hot short
Warmrissigkeit *f* hot shortness
Warmrundlaufversuch *m* thermal stability test
Warmsäge *f* hot saw
Warmsprödigkeit *f* hot brittleness
Warmstahl-Schlittenschere *f* sliding hot saw
Warmstrangpressen *n* hot extrusion
Warmstraße *f* hot rolling train
Warmstreckgrenze *f* yield point at elevated temperature
Warmumformbarkeit *f* hot forming property
Warmumformung *f* hot forming; hot shaping
Warmverarbeitkarkeit *f* hot forming property
Warmversprödung *f* hot embrittlement
warmwalzen hot roll[ing]
Warmwalzen *n* hot rolling
Warmwalzen *n* hot rolling
Warmwalzen *n* hot rolling
Warmwalzen *n* hot rolling
Warmwalzen *n* hot rolling
Warmwalzen *n* hot rolling
Warmwalzwerk *n* hot rolling mill
Wärmzeit *f* heating time
Warmziehbank *f* **(für Hohlkörper)** push-bench
Warmzugversuch *m* hot tensile test
Warngerät *n* monitor
Warten *n* servicing
Warteschlange *f* line-up; queue
Wartezeit *f* holding time
Wartung *f* attendance; servicing; upkeep
Wartungszeit *f* maintenance time
Warzenblech *n* nipple plate
Waschberge *mpl* refuse slate; washery slag
waschen (Gas) purify
Wäscher *m* scrubber; washer
Waschöltank *m* scrubbing oil tank

Waschturm *m* scrubber tower
Wasser *n* water
Wasserabscheider *m* water separator
Wasserarmaturen *fpl* water fittings
Wasserbad *n* water bath
Wasserdampf *m* steam; water vapour
Wasserdampfspaltung *f* decomposition of water-vapour (corrosion)
wasserdicht water-tight
Wasserdraht *m* water hardened wire rod
Wasserdruckversuch *m* hydraulic [pressure] test; hydrostatic test
Wasserfangkasten *m* water wheel
Wasserfläche *f* sheet of water
wasserführende Schicht *f* water bearing stratum
Wassergas *n* water gas
wassergehärteter Federstahl *m* water-hardened spring steel
wassergehärteter Walzdraht *m* water-hardened wire rod
wassergekühltes Kabel *n* water cooled cable
Wasserglas *n* waterglass
wassergranulierter Schlackensand *m* water-spray granulated slag sand
Wasserhaltungspumpe *f* draining pump
Wasserhärte *f* hardness of water
Wasserhärten *n* water harden; water hardening
Wasserhärter *m* water hardening steel
Wasserkasten *m* water tank
Wasserklärung *f* water clearing
Wasserkraft *f* hydraulic power; water power
Wasserkreislauf *m* water circulation
Wasserkühlrad *n* water [cooling] wheel; wet cooler
Wasserkühlung *f* water cooling; water-cooling system
Wasserleute *pl* men who control coolers and check water flow (on a blast furnace)
wasserlöslich water based; water borne

wasserlösliche Bindung *f* watersoluble binding
Wasserprobe-Entnahmegerät *n* water sampling device
Wasserreinigung *f* water purifying
Wassersäule *f* water ga[u]ge
Wasserschenkelstahl *m* window drip section
Wasserstandsanzeiger *m* water ga[u]ge
Wasserstandsregler *m* water level regulator
Wasserstoff *m* hydrogen
Wasserstoffaufnahme *f* hydrogen absorption
wasserstoffinduzierte Rißbildung *f* hydrogen-induced cracking (HIC)
Wasserstoffperoxid *n* hydrogen peroxide
Wasserstoffsprödigkeit *f* hydrogen embrittlement
Wasserturbine *f* water turbine
Wasserturm *m* water tower
wasser- und aschefrei (waf) dry and ash free (daf)
Wasservergüten *n* water quenching followed by tempering
Wasserverschmutzung *f* water pollution
Wasserversorgung *f* water feeding; water supply
Wasserwaage *f* spirit level
Wasserwert *m* water equivalent
Wasserzerstäubung *f* water atomising
Wechselbeanspruchung *f* alternating stress; cyclic stress
Wechselduo *n* three-high stand with two-high roll set
Wechselfestigkeit *f* endurance strength; fatigue resistance; fatigue strength
Wechselfestigkeit *f* **unter pulsierender Belastung** fatigue limit under pulsating stress
Wechselfolge *f* sequence of vessel changing
Wechselgerüst *n* change stand; interchangeable stand; spare stand

Wechselgetriebe *n* change speed gear
Wechselkanal *m* reversal conduit
Wechselkonverter *m* change vessel converter
wechselnde Belastung *f* alternating load
wechseln (Walzen) change
wechselseitig mutual
wechselseitige Beziehung *f* interrelationship
Wechselstrom *m* A.C.; alternating current
Wechselstromschweißmaschine *f* AC-welding machine
Wechselstromschweißverfahren *n* AC-welding technique
Wechseltauchversuch *m* alternate immersion test
Wechselverwindeversuch *m* alternating torsion test; reverse torsion test
Wechselwirkungskoeffizient *m* interaction coefficient
Wechselwirkungsparameter *m* interaction parameter
Weg *m* distance; path; way
wegfressen cut off; scour
wegnehmen remove
weichblankgeglühter Draht *m* bright soft wire
Weiche *f* siding; switch
Weiche *f* **für Zahnradbahn** cog-rail type switch; switch for cog-rail type
Weicheisen *n* Armco iron; soft iron
Weichensteller *m* switch man; switcher
Weichenzunge *f* switch blade
weicher Stahl *m* low carbon steel; mild steel; soft steel
weicher unlegierter Stahl *m* low-carbon steel
weiches Erz *n* soft ore
weiches Ferrochrom *n* low carbon ferro-chrome
Weichfleckigkeit *f* formation of soft spots; liability to harden with soft spots
weichgeglüht soft annealed; spheroidised
weichgeglüht und nicht entzundert black softened
Weichglühen *n* dead soft annealing; soft annealing; spheroidise annealing
Weichhaut *f* soft skin
Weichkohle *f* bituminous coal
Weichlot *n* soft solder
weichlöten solder
Weichmachen *n* softening
weichmagnetischer metallischer Sinterwerkstoff *m* soft magnetic sintered material
weichmagnetischer Stahl *m* electrical quality steel; soft magnetic steel
Weichnitrieren *n* salt bath nitriding
Weißband *n* tin strip
Weißbandzerteilanlage *f* tin plate shearing line
Weißbeize *f* white pickler
Weiß[blech]band *n* tinplate strip
Weißblech *n* **mit dickerer Zinnschicht** charcoal tinplate
Weißblech *n* **mit dünnerer Zinnschicht** coke tinplate
Weißblechtafel *f* tinplate sheet
Weißblechwalzwerk *n* tinplate mill
weißer Temperguß *m* white heart malleable [cast] iron
weißes Gußeisen *n* white cast iron
weißes Rauschen *n* white noise
weißes Roheisen *n* forge pigs; white pig [iron]
weißglühend incandescent
Weißglühen *n* white annealing
weißglühend white hot
Weißglut *f* incandescense; white heat
Weißguß *m* chilled cast iron; white heart malleable [cast] iron
Weißkalk *m* white lime
Weißmetall *n* babbitt [metal]
Weißmetall-Ausguß *m* anti friction metal lining; babbitt bearing lining; lining
Weißrost *m* wet storage stain; white rust
Weite *f* diameter; range

weiten extend; widen
Weiten n expanding
Weiten n **durch Drücken** expanding by spinning
Weite f **(Öffnung)** aperture
Weiterschlag m **(Tiefziehen)** second draw
Weiterverarbeitung f further treatment; subsequent processing
Wellbiegen n corrugating
Wellblech n corrugated sheet
Wellblechmaschine f corrugated sheet machine
Wellblechpresse f press for corrugated sheets
Wellblechwalzwerk n corrugating sheet rolling mill
Welle f arbor; corrugation; flopper; shaft; shape wave
Wellenbildung f **auf Schienen** rail corrugation
Wellenlänge f wave length
Wellenschälen n peeling shafts
Wellenschaubild n periodogram
Wellenwiderstand m capacitance
Wellenzahl f wave number
Wellenzerlegung f periodogram analysis
wellige Oberfläche f rippled surface
Welligkeit f waviness
Wellrohr n corrugated tube
Wendehaspel f reverse coiler
Wendekühlbett n rollover cooling bed
Wendelrohr n helical tube
wenden turn over
Wendevorrichtung f roll-over device; turn-over gear
weniger leicht schmelzbar less fusible
werfen distort; warp
Werk n achievement; mill; plant; works
Werkbank f work-bench
Werkmeister m foreman; master-mechanic
Werksbahn f works railway
Werksbescheinigung f statement of compliance with the order
Werksmarke f trade mark

Werksprüfzeugnis n works' test certificate
Werkstatt f shop; workshop
Werkstattbeleuchtung f workshop lighting
Werkstätte f workshop
Werkstätteneinrichtung f workshop installation
Werkstattschweißung f shop welding
Werkstattzusammenbau m shop assembly
Werkstoff m material
Werkstoffausschuß m Committee for Materials
Werkstoffdatenbank f material data bank
Werkstoffermüdung f material fatigue
Werkstoffhöhe f height
Werkstoffkunde f material science
Werkstoffnummer f number of materials
Werkstoffpaarung f mating material
Werkstoffprüfmaschine f material testing machine
Werkstoffprüfung f testing of materials
Werkstofftrennung f discontinuity
Werkstoffübergang m **(Lichtbogen)** material transfer
Werkstoffverlust m **durch Verzundern** fire waste; heat waste
Werkstück n work[ing] part; workpiece
Werkszeugnis n works' certificate
Werktransport m works' transport
Werkzeug n tool
Werkzeugausrüstung f tooling
Werkzeug-Hohlstahl m steel for fluting tool
Werkzeugmaschine f machine-tool
Werkzeugmaschinenguß m castings for machine-tools
Werkzeugsatz m tool set
Werkzeugschleifbock m tool grinder; tool-grinding machine
Werkzeugschneide f cutting edge; cutting lip
Werkzeugschrank m tool cupboard
Werkzeugstahl m tool steel
Werkzeugstahl m **für Kaltarbeit** cold

forming tool steel
Wert m quartile; value
Wert m **der Veränderlichen** variate
Wertefluß m flow of cost values
werten evaluate
Wertigkeit f valency
Wertminderung f depreciation
Wertpapier n bond
Wertung f evaluation
Wertzahl f rating
wesentlich significant
Wettbewerbsfähigkeit f competitive position
Wetterbeständigkeit f resistance to weathering
wetterfester Stahl m patinable steel; weathering steel
Wichte s. spezifisches Gewicht
Wickelanlage f **für Draht und Band** coiling apparatus for steel wire and strip
Wickeldorn m mandrel
Wickelhaspel f winding reel
Wickelhülse f sleeve
Wickelmantel m lay forming rim
Wickelmaschine f coiling machine; pouring reel; recoiler; reel
wickeln wrap
Wickeln n multi-turn coiling
wickeln von oben overcoiling; overwinding
wickeln von unten undercoiling; underwinding
Wickelplatte f front flange; rotary coil plate
Wickeltrommel f coiling drum
Wickelverhältnis n **(Feder)** spring index
Wickelversuch m wrapping test
Wickelwerk n **(Trafo)** coil former
Wickler m **für Draht** dead block
Widerlager n skew back; support; thrust bearing
Widerlagerbalken m skewback channel
Widerlagerstein m bevel brick; first brick out
Widerlagerstütze f skewback channel

Widerstand m **(elektr.)** resistor
Widerstandsbolzenschweißen n resistance stud welding
Widerstandsfähigkeit f resistivity
Widerstandslegierung f steel for electric resistance
Widerstandsmoment n moment of resistance; section modulus
Widerstandspatentieren n resistance patenting
Widerstandsschmelzschweißen n resistance fusion welding
Widerstandsstumpfschweißen n resistance butt welding
Widerstandsthermometer n resistance thermometer
Widerstandswerkstoff m heating resistor material; resistance material
Widerstandszahl f resistance number
widerstehen stand
Wiederanblasen n putting in blast again; restarting
Wiederanlassen n restarting
Wiederaufarbeitung f recutting (of a die)
Wiederaufbau m rebuilding; reconstruction
wiederaufkohlen recarburise
Wiederaufkohlung f carbon restoration
wiederaufnehmen resume
wiedereinschmelzen remelt
wiedererhitzen reheat
wiedererwärmen reheat
Wiedergewinnung f recovery; regeneration
wiederherstellen repair; restore
wiederholen (EDV) rerun
Wiederholungsversuch m retest
Wiederholung f **von Gleichversuchen** replication
wiederinstandsetzen recondition; repair
Wiege f cradle
Wiegebrücke f wagon weighbridge
Wiegebunker m weighing hopper
Wiegemeister m weighman
wiegen rock

Wiesenerz n brown hematite; meadow ore
WIG-Aufschmelzen n TIG-dressing
WIG-Schweißen n TIG-welding (tungsten isolating gas)
Wildmaßlänge f random length
Wind m blast; blow; vent; wind
Winddruck m blast pressure
Winde f crab; hoist; whim; winch; windlass
Winden n winding
Windenhaus n winch house
Winderhitzen n blast heating
Winderhitzer m Cowper; air preheater; blast preheater; hot blast stove
Winderhitzer m auf Gas (auf Wind) hot blast stove on gas (on blast)
Winderhitzerstein m Cowper brick; hot blast stove brick
Windform f blast tuyre; tuyre
Windfrischen n air refining; converting [with air]; purifying
Windfrischstahl m air refined steel
Windkasten m air box; air chamber; blast box; wind box
Windleitung f blast inlet; blast main; blast pipe
Windloch n blast inlet
Windmenge f volume of blast
Windring m air chamber
Windschieber m blast gate
Windsichten n air classification
Windsichter m cyclone; cyclone dust catcher; dust catcher
Windstock m blast connection
Windung f coil; lay; turn of a coil; wap
Windungsdurchmesser m lay diameter
Windungsleger m layer; laying head or unit
Windungssammler m coil accumulating station
Windungstransportgerüst n vibrating frame; vibrating lay conveyor
Windverteilungsregler m (Hochofen) blast distribution controller
Winkel m angle; plane angle; solid angle
Winkelbeschleunigung f angular acceleration
Winkeleisen n angle iron (angle)
Winkelgeschwindigkeit f angular velocity
Winkelgetriebe n bevel gearing
Winkelkopf m (zerstörungsfreie Prüfung) angle probe
Winkellage f angular position
Winkelmesser m protractor
Winkelprüfung f fillet weld break test
Winkelstahl m angle steel; round edge equal angles; round edge unequal angles; square edge equal angles
Winkelstahl m mit Leichtprofil light section angle
Winkelstahl m mit ungleichen Schenkeln unequal [leg] angle
Winkelzahn m herringbone tooth
Wippe f depressing table (up-cut shear); tilting chute
wippen whip
Wippen n luffing
Wippkran m luffing crane
Wipptisch m rising table; tilting table
Wirbel m vortex; whirl
Wirbelbrenner m turbulent burner
Wirbeldüse f eddy nozzle; swirl nozzle
Wirbeleinguß m whirl gate
wirbelig turbulent
Wirbelreduktionsverfahren n turbulence reduction method
Wirbelschicht f fluidised bed
Wirbelschichtofen m fluidised bed kiln
Wirbelschicht-Röstverfahren n fluid bed roasting process
Wirbelschlagpulver m eddy-mill powder
Wirbelsintern n fluidised bed sintering
Wirbelstrom m eddy current
Wirbelstrombremse f eddy current brake
Wirbler m cyclone dust catcher; cyclone gas washer; whirler
Wirklaststoß m active load impact
Wirkleistung f active power
Wirkleistung f (elektr.) real output capacity

wirksam efficient
Wirksamkeit f efficiency
Wirkschaltbild n wiring diagram
Wirkungsgrad m efficiency
Wirkungskoeffizient m interaction coefficient
Wirkungsparameter m interaction coefficient; interaction parameter
Wirkungsweise f blade action; mode of operation
Wirkwiderstand m effective resistance
Wirkwinkel m **(Spanen)** working angle
Wirtgitter n matrix lattice; solvent lattice
Wirtschaftlichkeit f economy efficiency
Wirtschaftlichkeitsrechnung f economics calculation
Wirtschaftsgeschichte f economic history
Wirtschaftspolitik f economic policy
Wirtschaftsprüfer m certified public accountant
Wirtschaftsvereinigung f Economic Union
Wismuth n bismuth
witterungsbeständig resistant to atmospheric conditions; resistant to atmospheric corrosion
Witterungsbeständigkeit f resistance to weathering
Wobbeleinrichtung f wobbling device
Wochendurchschnitt m average rate per week
Wochenendpendler m weekend commuter
Wöhlerlinie f SN curve; Woehler diagram; stress cycle; stress number curve
Wölber m arch brick
Wölbnaht f convex fillet weld
Wölbstein m end arch; roof brick; skew; wedge
Wölbung f arch; camber; crown
Wolfram n tungsten
Wolfram-Inertgas-Schweißen n tungsten inert gas arc welding
Wolfram-Lichtbogenpunktschweißen n tungsten arc spot welding
Wolfram-Schutzgasschweißen n TIG welding
Wolframstahl m tungsten steel
Wolfram-Wasserstoff-Schweißen n atomic hydrogen [arc] welding
Wood-Metall n Wood's metal
Wrackblock m scrap ingot
wrackgewalztes Stück n cobble; reject
Wrackguß m spoiled casting
Wrackwalzen n cobbling
Wringwalzenabstreifer m scrubbing unit
Wuchtsieb n **(Erzvorbereitung)** reciprocating screen
Wulst m bead; build-up; bulb
Wulstflachstahl m beaded flats; blub flats
Wulstflachstahl m **mit doppelseitigem Wulst** plain bulb
Wulst m **(Kaltband)** ridge
Würdigung f appreciation
Würfelfläche f cube face
Würfelkante f cube edge
Würfelmischer m cube mixer
Würste fpl **(beim Drahtziehen)** balling up
Wüstit m wustite

X

Xeroradiographie f xeroradiography
X-Naht geschweißte Probe f double-vee butt welded specimen

Z

Zähbruch m ductile fracture
zäher Bruch m ductile fracture
zähflüssig viscous
Zähigkeit f tenacity; toughness; viscosity
Zählblatt n schedule
Zahl f **der Fälle** volume of cases
Zahlentafel f table
Zahlenverhältnis n ratio

Zähler *m* integrator; numerator
Zählrohr *n* counter tube
Zahlzeichen *n* digit
Zahn *m* cog
Zahnflanke *f* flank of a tooth
Zahnfräsen *n* gear cutting; gear tooth milling
Zahnfuß *m* dedendum
Zahnkranz *m* toothed rim
Zahnrad *n* cog[ged] wheel; gear[ing]; toothed wheel
Zahnräder-Formmaschine *f* gear wheel moulding machine
Zahnräderwerk *n* cogged gear
Zahnstange *f* gearing
Zahnradstahl *m* gear wheel steel
Zahnradübertragung *f* gear transmission
Zahnspindel *f* gear-type spindle
Zahnspitze *f* tip of a tooth
Zahnstange *f* rack; spur rack; toothed bar rack
Zahnwelle *f* serrated shaft; toothed shaft
Zange *f* dogs; pincers; pliers tongs; tongs
Zangenkanter *m* tongs-type manipulator
Zangenkran *m* dogging crane; ingot [tong] crane
Zäpfchen *n* (**ff. Stoffe**) stalactite
Zapfen *m* hollow; journal; roof drip; shaft; stalactites; stud
Zapfen *m* (**Konverter**) trunnion
Zapfenlager *n* bearing; bush; journal bearing; journal box
Zapfenloch *n* mortise
Zapfenlochmaschine *f* mortising machine
Zapfen *m* (**Strangguß**) pivot
Zapfen *m* (**Walze**) neck
Zapfen *m* (**Welle**) pin
Zargenreißer *m* cup wall fracture
Zaundraht *m* fence wire
Zeche *f* coal mine; mine; pit
Zechenhalde *f* mine dump
Zeichen *n* mark
Zeichenbrett *n* drawing board

Zeichendreieck *n* set square
Zeichen *n* (**Steuerzeichen**) character
zeichnen draw
Zeichnung *f* drawing; plan
Zeiger *m* pointer
Zeilen *f*pl bands (structure)
Zeilenbildung *f* banding
Zeilendrucker *m* line printer
Zeilengefüge *n* banded structure; banding structure
Zeilen *f*pl (**Gußgefüge**) bands
Zeit *f* time
Zeit-Abbau-Randkoordinaten[System] *n* time-reduction-marginal coordinates
Zeitbilanz *f* time utilisation schedule
Zeitdehngrenze *f* creep limit; stress to produce a given creep in a given time
Zeitdehnung *f* creep
Zeit-Dehnungs-Kurve *f* creep curve
Zeit-Dehnungs-Schaubild *n* creep-time-diagram
Zeitdehnverhalten *n* creep characteristics
Zeitfestigkeit *f* fatigue strength for finite life
Zeitglied *n* time function element; timer
Zeitintervall *n* time interval
zeitlich einstellen time
Zeitlohntarif *m* time wage rate
Zeit *f* messen time
Zeitplanregelung *f* programmed control; time pattern control; time program control
zeitraubend time consuming
Zeitregistrierinstrument *n* time recorder
Zeitschalter *m* time limit switch
Zeitschaltung *f* timer circuit
Zeitstandbruch *m* creep fracture
Zeitstandbruchdehnung *f* elongation after fracture in creep rupture test
Zeitstand-Brucheinschnürung *f* reduction of area after fracture in creep rupture test
Zeitstandbruchlinie *f* stress rupture

curve
Zeitstandfestigkeit f creep rupture strength; creep strength depending on time
Zeitstandprüfanlage f creep strength testing plant; creep strength testing rig
Zeitstandversuch m creep rupture test; creep test
Zeitstauchgrenze f compression stress to produce a given creep in a given time
Zeitstudien fpl time keeping; time study
Zeit-Temperatur-Anlaßdiagramm n time-temperature-tempering diagram
Zeit-Temperatur-Austenitisierungs-Diagramm n **(ZTA-Diagramm)** time-temperature-austenitisation diagram (TTA-curve)
Zeit-Temperatur-Umwandlungs-Diagramm n **(ZTU-Diagramm)** time-temperature-transformation curve (TTT-curve)
Zeitverschiebung f lag
Zeitvorgabe f **(beim Akkord)** system of time allowance; system of time allowing; time allowed in advance
Zeitwirtschaft f time study
Zellentiefofen m cell pit furnace; cell type soaking pit
Zementfabrik f cement plant
zementieren caburise
Zementitzerfall m cementite breakdown
Zementmörtel m cement mortar
Zementstahl m blister bar; cemented bar; converted bar
Zentraleinheit f **mit Hauptspeicher und Rechenwerk** central processor with main memory and arithmetic unit
zentrieren center; locate
Zentriervorrichtung f centring device; side guide
Zentrifugalseparator m centrifugal separator

zentrifugieren centrifuge
zerbrechen break
Zerfall m break-up; degeneration; disintegration
zerfallen decompose; disintegrate; dissociate; slake
Zerfallschlacke f disintegrating slag; slaking slag
Zerfallsprüfung f collapsibility test; degradation test; disintegration test
zerfressen bite
zerkleinern comminute; crush; pulverise
Zerkleinerung f comminution; crushing; disintegration; pulverising
zerknallbares Gas n explosive gas; sharp gas
zerlegen decompose
Zerlegen n dismembering
Zerlegung f break-down; dissection
zerreiben levigate; pulverise
zerreißen tear
Zerreißfestigkeit f fracture strength; tearing strength
Zerreißprobe f tensile test [specimen]
Zerreiß[prüf]maschine f tensile testing machine
Zerreißstab m tensile test bar
Zerreißung f tear
Zerreißversuch s. **Zugversuch**
zerschneiden cut up
Zerschneiden n cutting up
zersetzen break up; decompose; dissociate
Zersetzung f decay; decomposition; dissociation
Zerspanbarkeit f cutting property; free machining property; machinability
zerspanen cut; machine
zerspanende Bearbeitbarkeit f machinability
zerstäuben atomise; pulverise
Zerstäuben n atomisation
zerstören destroy
zerstörende Werkstoffprüfung f destructive testing
zerstörungsfreie Prüfung f non-destructive test[ing]

Zerteilanlage f cut-up line; shearing and slitting line
zerteilen divide; section
Zerteilen n severing
Zertropfen n splittering
Zettel m schedule
Zickzackduo n staggered mill
Zickzacknahtschweiße f staggered weld
Zickzackschweiße f staggered weld
Zickzackstraße f staggered mill
Zickzacktrio n cross-country mill
Ziegel m block; brick
Ziegelbrennofen m brick kiln
ziegeln brick; briquette
Ziegeln n brick making; briquetting
Ziegelpresse f brick press
Ziegelstein m brick; clay brick
Ziehangel f drawing point
Ziehbank f drawing bench
Ziehbarkeit f drawability; ductility
Ziehblech n drawing sheet; sheet metal of deep drawing quality; sheet metal suitable for drawing
Ziehbonderflüssigkeit f bonder drawing lubricant
Ziehdorn m mandrel
Ziehdüse f die; die plate; draw plate; plate
Zieheisen n die; die plate; draw plate; plate; wortle
Zieheisenhalter m die holder
Zieheisenkopf m draw head
ziehen drag; draw; pull; sink
Ziehen n drawing; traction
ziehender Schnitt m oblique shearing
Ziehen n über kurzen Stopfen rodding
Zieherei f drawing plant
Ziehfähigkeit f drawing quality
Ziehfeder f drawing pen
Ziehfett n drawing grease
Ziehgüte f drawing quality
Ziehherd m discharging end of furnace
Ziehhol n drawing hole; drawing pass
Ziehhol-Neigungswinkel m angle of inclination of drawing hole
Ziehhol-Öffnungswinkel m angle of aperture of drawing hole
Ziehkopf m drawn head
Ziehkraft f drawing stress
Ziehlochplatte f draw plate; wortle plate
Ziehmatrize f draw-die
Ziehpresse f drawing press
ziehreif ready for drawing
Ziehriefe f die mark; die scar; die scratch
Ziehriefen fpl **(im Innern eines über den Stopfen gezogenen Rohres)** plug lines
Ziehring m drawing die
Ziehrohmaß n common draw size
Ziehschleifen n honing
Ziehsorte f deep drawing quality
Ziehstein m wire die
Ziehstempel m drawing punch
Ziehtrichter m bell; die; drawing nozzle; forming bell
Ziehtrommel f capstan
Ziehwalzen n drawing with roller dies
Ziehwalzwerk n **(Steckel)** coiler tension rolling mill
Ziehwerkzeug n drawing tool
Ziehwerkzeugfertigstellung f set
Ziel n aim; target
Ziffer f digit
Zink n spelter; zinc
Zinkasche f dross
Zinkblech n zinc plate; zinc sheet
Zinkblumen fpl flowers of zinc; spangle pattern
Zinkstearat n zinc stearate
Zinn n tin
Zinnrückgewinnung f scruff recovery
Zinnverbrauch m tin yield
Zipfel m distortion wedge; ear
Zipfelbildung f earing; formation of distortion wedges; tip formation
Zipfelzugprobe f wedge-draw test
Zirkel m compasses; pair of compasses
Zirkon[ium] n zircon[ium]
Zirkonsilicat n zirconium silicate
Zitronensäure f citric acid
zögern lag

Zolltarif m customs tarif
Zonenbildung f zoning
Zonengitterung f checkerwork arranged in stages
Zonenschmelzen n zone melting
Z-Stahl m Z-sections; zeds; zees (am.)
ZTU-Kennwerte mpl TTT characteristics
Zubehör n appliance; auxiliaries
Zubehörteile npl accessories; fittings
zubereiten condition; prepare
Zubrand m pickup
zubringen add; feed
Zubringer m feeder
Zubringerwagen m larry car; transfer car; travelling hopper
Zufall m chance
zufällig random
zufällig ausgewählte Gruppen fpl groups selected at random
zufällige Veränderliche f variate
Zufälligkeit f contingency
Zufallsanordnung f randomness
Zufallsfehler m accidental error
Zufallsfehlerbereich m confidence interval
Zufallsherstellung f randomisation
Zufallsstreuung f chance variation
Zufallszahl f sampling number
Zufuhr f supply
zuführen feed
Zufuhrrollgang m approach roller table; entry table; feed[ing] roller table; ingoing table
Zufuhrrollgang m **zum Walzwerk** mill approach table
Zuführungstisch m feeding table
Zuführung f **von Stahlkies oder Sand** steel grit or sand delivery pipe
Zufuhrvorrichtung f feeding device
Zug m downtake; draught; draw; flue; lift; pass; pull; stress; tension; train; uptake
Zugänglichkeit f accessibility
Zugband n tie member
Zugbeanspruchung f tensile stress
Zug-Druck-Schwingfestigkeit f alternating tensile and compression stress fatigue strength
Zug-Druck-Umformen n push-pull forming; tenso-compressive reforming
Zug-Druck-Wechselfestigkeit f fatigue limit under reversed tension-compression stresses
zugekehrt facing
Zugfeder f tension spring
Zugfestigkeit f tensile strength; ultimate strength
Zugfließspannung f yield stress under tensile load
Zughaken m drag bar; draw-hook
Zughaspel f tension reel
zügiger Regler m continuous controller
Zugkraft f drawing stress
Zugkraftmesser m die load meter
Zugluft f draft
Zugmesser m draught ga[u]ge
Zugregler m draft regulating damper
Zugriffshäufigkeit f access frequency
Zugriffszeit f access cycle
Zugrollengerüst n tension bridle; tension rolls
Zugschwellbereich m range of fatigue under pulsating tensile stresses
Zugschwellfestigkeit f fatigue strength under pulsating tensile stresses
Zugseil n hauling cable
Zugspannung f tensile stress
Zugspannungsmesser m tensile strain ga[u]ge
Zugspindel-Drehbank f screw cutting lathe
Zugstange f **(Hochofen)** bell lifting rod
Zugstärke f draught pressure
Zugumformen n tensile reforming
Zugverformung f tensile strain
Zugversuch m pulling test; tensile test
Zukaufschrott m bought scrap; external scrap
zulässige Abweichung f allowable variation; tolerance
zulässige Beanspruchung f safe working stress
Zulässigkeitsgrenze f allowable limit

Zulauf *m* inlet
zumutbar tolerable
Zunahme *f* increase
Zündbarkeit *f* inflammability
Zunder *m* cinder; drawn-in scale; oxide
Zunderabspritzvorrichtung *f* descaling sprays; high-pressure scale sprays
Zunderarmglühen *n* bright annealing
Zunderausblühungen *fpl* scale efflorescence
zunderbeständig non-scaling; resistant to scaling
zunderbeständiger Stahl *m* scale resisting steel
Zunderbeständigkeit *f* non-scaling property; scaling resistance
Zunderbrecher *m* processor
Zunderbrechgerüst *n* descaling mill; processor; scale breaker [stand]
Zunderbrech- und Abrollvorrichtung *f* **(für Blechbunde)** processing uncoiler; processing unit; processor
Zundereinsprenkelung *f* **(durch unvollständiges Beizen)** pickle sticker
Zunderfleck *m* black patch; fleck scale; kisser
Zunderflecken *mpl* flashing
zunderfrei free from scale
zundern scale
Zundern *n* high temperature oxidation; scaling
Zunderschicht *f* layer of scale; oxide layer
Zunderspülrinne *f* scale flume
Zunderstreifen *m* breaker roll scale; scale pattern
Zunderwäscher *m* descaling sprays
Zündflamme *f* pilot flame
Zündhaube *f* **(Sinter)** ignition hood
Zündtemperatur *f* ignition temperature
Zündung *f* firing; ignition
Zunge *f* **(Bandfehler)** sliver
Zuordner *m* translator
Zuordnung *f* co-ordination
Zurichterei *f* conditioning department; dressing shop; finishing department; finishing shop
Zurichtung *f* arrangement
zurückfordern reclaim
zurückhalten check; retain
zurückleiten reconduct
zurückstrahlen reflect
zurückweisen reject
zusammenballen cake; coalesce
Zusammenballung *f* balling; cluster; coalescence
Zusammenbau *m* assembly
zusammenbauen assemble; fabricate
zusammendrückbare Metalleinlage *f* crushable metal insertion
zusammengebogenes Rohr *n* **ohne Nahtschweißen** close-joint tube
zusammengesetzter Träger *m* built-up section; girder
zusammengesetzte Wahrscheinlichkeit *f* compound probability
zusammensetzen build up
Zusammensetzung *f* average chemical composition; composition; compound
Zusammenstellung *f* compilation
Zusammentreffen *n* coincidence
zusammenziehen contract; neck; shrink; swage
Zusatz *m* addition
Zusätze *mpl* additions
Zusätze *mpl* **zum Fertigmachen (Schmelze)** finishing additions
Zusatzfeuerung *f* additional firing; supplementary firing
zusätzliche dynamische Scherbelastung *f* dynamic incremental shear loading
zusätzliche Wirkung *f* additive effect
Zusatzmetall *n* added metal; alloying metal
Zuschlag *m* admixture; extra; fluxing agent
Zuschläge *mpl* additions; auxiliaries; fluxes
Zuschlagskosten *pl* controllable burden; overhead charges; overhead expenses

Zuschlag *m* **(zu Lohn oder Zeit)** allowance
Zuschneiden *n* **(von Feinblech)** resquaring; reshearing
zuschweißen weld up
zuspitzen point; scarf
Zustand *m* condition; state
Zustandsfeld *n* phase field
Zustandsgleichung *f* equation of state
Zustandsschaubild *n* constitutional diagram; equilibrium diagram; phase diagram
zu stark over-pickled
zu stark gebeizt overpickled
zustellen line
Zustellung *f* relining
Zustellungskosten *pl* lining cost
Zuteilung *f* allocation
Zuverlässigkeit *f* reliability
zuviel excess
Zuvollgehen *n* **(eines Kalibers)** overfilling (of a pass)
Zwanglauf *m* constrained motion; positive movement
Zwangsschnittgröße *f* sectional constraining values
Zwanzigwalzengerüst *n* stand with 20 rolls; twenty-roll stand
Zweckforschung *f* applied research
zweiachsig biaxial
zweiachsiger Spannungszustand *m* biaxial stress device
Zweierschritt *m* binary digit; bit
zweifelhafte Forderung *f* bad debt
zweigipflig bimodal
Zweilagenblech *n* clad sheet
Zweipunktregler *m* on-off controller; two-position controller; two-step action
Zweisäulen-Presse *f* double column press
Zweischichtbetrieb *m* two shifts operation
Zweischlackenverfahren *n* two-slag practice
zweiseitige Kehlnaht[schweiße] *f* double fillet weld
Zweiständerschere *f* closed shear; double-standard shear
Zweistofflegierung *f* binary alloy
Zweistoffsystem *n* binary system
Zweistrang-Gießmaschine *f* twin strand casting machine
Zweistufenauslagern *n* two step ag[e]ing
zweistufig two-stage
Zweitakt-Gasmaschine *f* two-stroke cycle gas engine
zweite Wahl *f* second quality
Zweitluft *f* secondary air
Zweiwalzen-[Duo]-Walzwerk *n* two-high mill
Zweiwalzengerüst *n* two-high [rolling] mill; two-high [rolling] stand; two-high stand of rolls
Zwei-Walzen-Richtmaschine *f* two-roll straightening machine
Zweiweg-Tiefofen *m* two way soaking pit
Zwillingsachsbüchse *f* twin journal box
Zwillingsantrieb *m* twin drive
Zwillingsbildung *f* twinning
Zwillingszug-Verbundkoksofen *m* twin draught compound coke oven
Zwischenblende *f* aperture
Zwischenblock *m* spacers
Zwischenbunker *m* intermediate hopper
Zwischenecho *n* intermediate echo
Zwischenentspannen *n* intermediate stress relieving
Zwischenerzeugnis *n* intermediate product
Zwischenformgebung *f* **(Walzen)** intermediate shaping
Zwischengefäß *n* **(Stranggießen)** pony ladle; tundish
zwischengeglühter Draht *m* interannealed wire; process annealed wire
zwischengeglühtes Feinblech *n* intermediate annealed sheet
Zwischengitteratom *n* interstitial atom
Zwischengitter-Mischkristall *m* interstitial solution
Zwischengitterplatz *m* ion in interstitial position

Zwischenglühen *n* intermediate annealing; process annealing; work annealing
Zwischengut *n* **(erzhaltiges Gestein)** middlings
Zwischenkorngrößen *fpl* intermediates
Zwischenkreis *m* intermediate circuit
Zwischenkreisumrichter *m* intermediate circuit
Zwischenpfanne *f* atmosphere controlled tundish; trough; tundish
Zwischenphase *f* intermediate phase
Zwischenraum *m* channel
Zwischenraum *m* **(Gitter)** interstitial space
Zwischenspindel *f* intermediate shaft
Zwischenstück *n* **des Hammersattels** bolster
Zwischenstufengefüge *n* bainite
Zwischenstufenhärtung *f* bainitic hardening
Zwischenstufen-Vergütung *f* austempering
Zwischenstufe s. Bainitstufe
Zwischenwand *f* bridge wall
Zwischenwärmofen *m* intermediate reheating furnace

II. Teil:
Englisch/Deutsch

Part II:
English/German

A

A.C. Wechselstrom *m*
abate bekämpfen; beruhigen; niederschlagen
abatement Bekämpfung *f*
abatement (of furnace) Abgänge *mpl*
ability to achieve specifications setting accuracy Treffsicherheit *f*
able to work arbeitsfähig
above ground über Tage
abrade abreiben; abschleifen; verschleißen
abrading action Schleißwirkung *f*
abrasion Abnutzung *f*; Abrieb *m*
abrasion resistance Abriebfestigkeit *f*
abrasive Schleifmittel *n*; Schleifscheibe *f*
abrasive cut off Trennschleifen *n*
abrasive hardness Ritzhärte *f*
abrasive hardness test Ritzhärteprüfung *f*
abrasives Strahlmittel *n*
abscissa axis Abszisse *f*
absence Abwesenheit *f*; Fehlen *n*
absenteeism Abwesenheit *f* (von Arbeitern); Fehlschicht *f*
absolute density (powder met.) Reindichte *f*
absorb aufnehmen (z. B. Kohlenstoff)
absorbed energy per cross sectional area Kerbschlagzähigkeit *f*
absorbent aufsaugefähig
absorption Absorption *f*; Aufnahme *f*
absorption capacity Aufsaugevermögen *n*
absorption of heat Wärmetönung *f*
abundance of isotopes Isotopenhäufigkeit *f*
accelerate beschleunigen
accelerated corrosion test Schnellkorrosionsversuch *m*
accelerated method Schnellbestimmungs-Verfahren *n*
accelerated test Kurzprüfverfahren *n*
accelerating incentive Leistungslohn *m*

acceleration Beschleunigung *f*
acceleration due to gravity Fallbeschleunigung *f*
acceleration of free fall Fallbeschleunigung *f*
accelerator Beschleunigungsmittel *n*
acceptable quality level (AQL) annehmbare Qualitätsgrenzlage *f*
acceptance Abnahme *f*; Akzeptanz *f*
acceptance report Abnahmeprotokoll *n*
acceptance-sampling Abnahmestichprobe *f*, Abnahmestichproben-Verfahren *n*
acceptance test Abnahmeprüfung *f*
access cycle Zugriffszeit *f*
access door Einsteigtür *f*
access frequency Zugriffshäufigkeit *f*
accessibility Zugänglichkeit *f*
accessories Armaturen *fpl*; Zubehörteile *npl*
accessory minerals Mineralien *npl*
accident Störung *f*
accidental error Zufallsfehler *m*; möglicher Fehler *m*
accident prevention Unfallschutz *m*
accompanying element Begleitelement *n*
according to delivery promise termingemäß
according to plan plangemäß
account Konto *n*
accounting Rechnungswesen *n*
accounts of movements within the business Konten *npl* der innerbetrieblichen Vorgänge
accounts receivable Forderungen *fpl*
accretions Ansätze *mpl*
accumulate häufen; speichern
accumulation Ansammlung *f* (Drahtziehen)
accumulation of heat Wärmespeicherung *f*; Wärmestauung *f*
accumulator Akkumulator *m*
accuracy Genauigkeit *f*; Schärfe *f*
accuracy to ga[u]ge Maßhaltigkeit *f*
accuracy to size Maßhaltigkeit *f*
acetylene cutting Acetylen-Schneid-

verfahren *n*
acetylene production plant Acetylen-Erzeugungsanlage *f*
achievement Ausführung *f*; Werk *n*
acicular feinnadelig; nadelförmig
acicular cast iron Gußeisen *n* mit Zwischenstufengefüge
acicular crystal Nadelkristall *m*
acicular powder nadeliges Pulver *n*; splittriges Pulver *n*
acicular structure Kristallbildung *f*; nadelförmige Struktur *f* (Stahlblock)
acid Säure *f*; sauer
acid and lye resisting brick säure- und laugenbeständiger Stein *m*
acid and lye resisting cement säure- und laugenbeständiger Kitt *m*
acid Bessemer process Bessemerverfahren *n*
acid Bessemer steel Bessemerstahl *m*
acid converter process Bessemerverfahren *n*
acid lining saure Zustellung *f*; saures Futter *n*
acid number Säurezahl *f*
acid open hearth furnace Siemens-Martin-Ofen *m* (saurer)
acid process saures Verfahren *n*
acid proof säurebeständig; säurefest
acid proof lining säurefeste Auskleidung *f*
acid proof metal säurefestes Metall *n*
acid protection Säureschutz *m*
acid resistant säurefest
acid resisting säurebeständig
acid resisting castings säurebeständiger Guß *m*
acid resisting cement Säurekitt *m*
acid resisting steel säurebeständiger Stahl *m*
acid slag practice saure Schlackenführung *f*
acid steel saurer (Siemens-Martin-) Stahl *m*
acid sulphate process sulfatsaures Verfahren *n*
acid value Säuregrad *m*

acierage Verstählen *n*
acoustical shadow Schallschatten *m*
acoustic irradiation Beschallung *f*
acoustic shielding Schallschirm *m*
acoustographic imaging system akustographisches Bildwandler-Verfahren *n*
Ac-point Ac-Punkt *m*; Haltepunkt *m*
activated carbon Aktivkohle *f*
activated sludge process Schlammbelebungsverfahren *n*
activability Aktivierbarkeit *f* (Reaktorstähle)
activating agent Aktivierungsmittel *n*; Beschleunigungsmittel *n*
activation energy Ablöseenergie *f*; Aktivierungsenergie *f*
active accounts bewegte Konten *npl*
active element aktives Glied *n* (EDV)
active hot metal mixer Vorfrischmischer *m*
active load impact Wirklaststoß *m*
active power Wirkleistung *f*
actual costs Ist-Kosten *pl*
actual grain size vorhandene Korngröße *f*
actual production Ist-Leistung *f*
actual section Ist-Profil *n*
actual value Ist-Wert *m*
actuator Kraftschalter *m*
acute angle spitzer Winkel *m*
acute-angle bulging Knickbauchen *n*
acute angles scharfkantiger Winkelstahl *m*
AC-welding machine Wechselstromschweißmaschine *f*
AC-welding technique Wechselstromschweißverfahren *n*
adapt angleichen; anpassen
adapt[at]ion Angleichung *f*
adapting program logic logische Programmanpassung *f*
add hinzufügen; zubringen
added metal Zusatzmetall *n*
addition Zusatz *m*
additional firing Zusatzfeuerung *f*
additions Zuschläge *mpl*; Zusätze *mpl*
additive effect zusätzliche Wirkung *f*; überlagernde Wirkung *f*

adhere haften; kleben
adherence Haftfähigkeit *f*
adhesion Haftung *f*
adhesive Haftmittel *m*; Klebmittel *n*
adhesive bonding Klebeverbindung *f*
adhesive power Adhäsionskraft *f*
adhesive strength Haftfestigkeit *f*; Haftfähigkeit *f*; Klebekraft *f*
adjacent anliegend
adjust anpassen; ausrichten; einrichten; einstellen; justieren; nachstellen; regeln; stellen
adjustable nachstellbar; verstellbar
adjustable speed direct current motor regelbarer Gleichstrommotor *m*
adjustible burner regelbarer Brenner *m*
adjusting control Anstellsteuerung *f*
adjusting equipment Anstellvorrichtung *f*
adjusting screw Druckschraube *f*; Stellschraube *f*
adjustment Einstellung *f*; Regelung *f*
administration building Verwaltungsgebäude *n*
admission Einlaß *m*
admixture Beimengung *f*; Zuschlag *m*
adsorptive capacity Adsorptionsvermögen *n*
adsorptive properties Adsorptionseigenschaften *fpl*
adult training Erwachsenenschulung *f*
advance Vorschub *m*; angeben
advancing device Vorholvorrichtung *f*
advice centre for steel use Beratungsstelle *f* für Stahlverwendung
aeration cell (corrosion) Belüftungselement *n*
aerial railway Drahtseilbahn *f*; Hängebahn *f*
aerial ropeway Drahtseilbahn *f*; Hängebahn *f*
aerosiderite Meteoreisenstein *m*
aerospace industry Raumfahrtindustrie *f*
affinity Affinität *f*
after-blow nachblasen
after-contraction Nachschwindung *f*

after-expansion Nachwachsen *n* (ff. Steine)
after first pass nach der ersten Überschmiedung *f*
after-pour nachgießen
aftertreatment Nachbehandlung *f*; Pfannennachbehandlung *f*
age altern; auslagern
ag[e]ing Alterung *f*
ag[e]ing brittleness Alterungssprödigkeit *f*
ageing crack Alterungsriß *m*
ageing treatment Alterungsbehandlung *f*; Auslagerungsbehandlung *f*
agent Mittel *n*
agent for protecting coats Schutzanstrichmittel *n*
agent for protection against corrosion Rostschutzmittel *n*
age of the furnace Ofenalter *n*
agglomerate Agglomerat *n*; stückigmachen
agglomerating plant Sinteranlage *f*
aggregate state Aggregatzustand *m*
aggressive medium Angriffsmittel *n*
aggressive slag scharfe Schlacke *f*
aggressivity Angriffsfreudigkeit *f*
agitate bewegen; umrühren
agitating apparatus Rührgerät *n*
agitation Bewegung *f*; Umrühren *n*
agitator Rührquirl *m*
agreement Vertrag *m*; Übereinkommen *n*
aim Ziel *n*
air blast Luftschleier *m*
air blast quenching Drucklufthärten *n*; Gebläselufthärten *n*
air box Windkasten *m*
air break contact Luftschütz *n*
air chamber Luftkammer *f*, Windkasten *m*; Windring *m*
air classification Windsichten *n*
air cleaner Luftreiniger *m*
air conditioning Klimatisierung *f*
air conditioning for clean room conditions Reinraumklima *n*
air conditioning plant Klimaanlage *f*
air-cooled luftgekühlt

air cooler Luftkühler *m*
air cooling Luftabkühlung *f*
air cushion Luftkissen *n*
air damping Luftdämpfung *f*
air disintegration plant Luftzerlegungsanlage *f*
air draft Luftzug *m*
air dry lufttrocken
air duct Luftkanal *m*; Luftschacht *m*; Luftweg *m*; Luftzug *m*
air filter Luftfilter *m*
air flap valve Luftklappe *f*
air flue Luftkanal *m*; Luftzug *m*
air freight traffic Luftfrachtverkehr *m*
air furnace Flammofen *m*
air gap relay Luftschütz *n*
air hammer Lufthammer *m*
air hardening Lufthärten *n*
air hardening steel Lufthärtestahl *m*
air heater Lufterhitzer *m*; Luftvorwärmer *m*
air inlet pipe Lufteinblasrohr *n*
air interchange Luftaustausch *m*
air jet Luftstrahl *m*
air lift gravity hammer Lufthammer *m*
air lift pump Druckluftheber *m*
air lubrication Luftschmierung *f*
air patenting Luftpatentieren *n*
air pipeline Luftführung *f*
air pollutant Luftverunreiniger *m*
air pollution Luftverunreinigung *f*
air pollution abatement Luftverunreinigungs-Bekämpfung *f*
air pollution control Luftreinhaltung *f*
air preheater Luftvorwärmer *m*; Winderhitzer *m*
air pressure test Innendruckversuch *m* mit Luft *f*
air quenching Luftabschrecken *n*
air raid precautions Luftschutz *m*
air raid protection Luftschutz *m*
air refined steel Windfrischstahl *m*
air refining Windfrischen *n*
air regenerator chamber Luftheizkammer *f*
air transport Luftfrachtverkehr *m*
air uptake Luftkanal *m*; Luftzug *m*; Luftzuggewölbe *n*

air washer Luftwäscher *m*
alcoholic nitric acid alkoholische Salpetersäure *f* (Ätzen)
alignment Fluchtlinie *f*
alkali measuring alkalimetrisch
alkaline alkalisch
alkaline solution Lauge *f*
all basic ganzbasisch
alligator cracking netzartige Rißbildung *f*
allocation Verteilung *f*; Zuteilung *f*
allotropy Allotropie *f*
allowable limit Zulässigkeitsgrenze *f*
allowable variation Abmaß *n*; Abweichung *f* zulässige; Spielraum *m*; Toleranz *f*
allowance Bearbeitungszugabe *f*; Vorgabe *f*; Zuschlag *m* (zu Lohn oder Zeit)
allowance coal Deputatkohle *f*
allowance for contraction Schwindmaß *n*
alloy Legierung *f*; legieren
alloyant hopper Legierungsbunker *m*
alloy[ed] steel legierter Stahl *m*
alloying addition Legierungszusatz *m*
alloying metal Zusatzmetall *n*
alloy ore Legierungserz *n*
alloy strip legiertes Band *n*
alloy up auflegieren
all purpose furnace Mehrzweckofen *m*
alpha iron Alpha-Eisen *n*
alpha solid solution Alpha-Mischkristall *m*
alternate immersion test Wechseltauchversuch *m*
alternating bending test Hin-und-Her-biegeversuch *m*; Rückbiegeversuch *m*
alternating bend test Biegeversuch *m* (Hin-und-Her-Biegeversuch)
alternating current Drehstrom *m*; Wechselstrom *m*
alternating load wechselnde Belastung *f*
alternating stress Wechselbeanspruchung *f*
alternating stress amplitude Spannungsausschlag *m*

alternating stress test Dauerversuch *m* mit Wechselbeanspruchung
alternating temperature loading Temperaturwechselbeanspruchung *f*
alternating tensile and compression stress fatigue strength Zug-Druck-Schwingfestigkeit *f*
alternating torsion fatigue test Dauerwechseldrehversuch *m*
alternating torsion test Wechselverwindeversuch *m*
alumina Aluminiumoxid *n* (Tonerde); Tonerde *f*
aluminium plating Alumetieren *n*; Aluminiumplattieren *n*
aluminium silicate Aluminiumsilicat *n*
aluminizing furnace Aluminierungsofen *m*
aluminous tonerdehaltig
aluminous cement Tonerde-Schmelzzement *m*
amalgamation Vereinigung *f*; Vermischung *f*; Verschmelzung *f*
ambient air Außenluft *f*; umgebende Luft *f*
ambient atmosphere Außenluft *f*
ambient temperature Raumtemperatur *f*
ammonia Ammoniak *n*
ammonia recovery plant Ammoniakgewinnungsanlage *f*; Ammoniakwäscherei *f*
ammonia water Ammoniakwasser *n*
ammonium solution Ammoniaklösung *f*
amount Anteil *m*; Betrag *m*; Menge *f*; Summe *f*
amount of heat Wärmemenge *f*
amount of inspection Prüfumfang *m*
amount of substance Stoffmenge *f*
amount of substance concentration Molarität *f*
amount of working Verformungsgrad *m*
amperage Stromstärke *f*
amplifier Verstärker *m*
amplify ergänzen; vergrößern; verstärken

amplifying machine Verstärkermaschine *f* (Lichtbogenofen)
amplitude Ausschlag *m*
analogue computer Analogrechner *m*
analogue-digital-converter Analog-Digital-Umformer *m*
analysis Analyse *f*; Auswertung *f*; Befund *m*; Untersuchung *f*; Überlegung *f*
analysis of scatter Streuungszerlegung *f*
analysis of variance Streuungszerlegung *f*
analytical balance Analysenwaage *f*; Präzisionswaage *f*; Waage *f*; chemische Waage *f*
analytical chemistry analytische Chemie *f*
analytic equipment Analysengerät *n*
anchor bolt Ankerbolzen *m*; Ankerschraube *f*
anchoring Verwachsung *f*
angle Winkel *m*
angle iron (angle) Winkeleisen *n*
angle of aperture of drawing hole Ziehhol-Öffnungswinkel *m*
angle of beam spread Öffnungswinkel *m* (Ultraschall)
angle of bite Greifwinkel *m* (Walze)
angle of contact Greifwinkel *m* (Walze)
angle of die taper Düseneintrittswinkel *m*
angle of friction Reibwinkel *m*
angle of hearth slope Sohlenneigungswinkel *m*
angle of incidence Einfallswinkel *m* (Ultraschall); Einstellwinkel *m* (Spanen)
angle of inclination of drawing hole Ziehhol-Neigungswinkel *m*
angle of repose Böschungswinkel *m* (einer Schüttung); Schüttwinkel *m*
angle of rotation transducer Drehwinkel-Meßumformer *m*
angle of sonic radiation Einschallwinkel *m* (Ultraschallprüfung)
angle probe Winkelkopf *m* (zerstö-

rungsfreie Prüfung)
angle sections with webs of unequal thickness Domflansch-Winkelstahl *m*
angle steel Winkelstahl *m*
angular acceleration Winkelbeschleunigung *f*
angularity Eckigkeit *f*
angular position Winkellage *f*
angular powder splittriges Pulver *n*
angular sound incidence Schrägeinschallung *f*
angular velocity Kreisfrequenz *f*; Winkelgeschwindigkeit *f*
Angus Smith solution Teer *m* zum Korrosionsschutz
an hour's wages Stundenlohn *m*
anhydrous sodium carbonate calcinierte Soda *f*
anihilation of dislocations Auflösung *f* von Versetzungen
anisotropy Anisotropie *f*
anneal anlassen; glühen
annealed geglüht
annealed powder geglühtes Pulver *n*
annealed stained edge Glührand *m* (Bandfehler)
annealed tensile strength Glühfestigkeit *f*
annealing Glühen *n*
annealing bell Glühhaube *f*
annealing box Glühbehälter *m*; Glühkiste *f*
annealing colour Anlauffarbe *f*
annealing furnace Glühofen *m*
annealing hood Glühhaube *f*
annealing muffle Glühmuffel *f*
annealing plant Glühanlage *f*
annealing pot Glühtopf *m*
annealing time Glühdauer *f*
annealing tube Glührohr *n*
anneal just below lower critical point umkristallisieren
annoyance (noise) Lästigkeit *f* (Lärm)
annual report Geschäftsbericht *m*
annular holder Faltenhalter *m*
annular jet discharge electron gun Elektronen-Ringstrahlkanone *f*
annular ring Faltenhalter *m*
anode Anode *f*
anodic protection anodischer Schutz *m* (Korrosion)
anodic voltametry anodische Amalgamvoltametrie *f*
anthracite Glanzkohle *f*
anthracite [glance coal] Anthrazit *m*
anthropometry Anthropometrie *f*
anti acid protective Säureschutzmittel *n*
anticipate a claim Patentanspruch *m* vorwegnehmen
anti corrosion mixture Korrosionsschutzmasse *f*
anti corrosive compound Korrosionsschutzmittel *n*
antifreezing quality Kältebeständigkeit *f*
anti-friction bearing Wälzlager *n*
anti-friction bearing steel Wälzlagerstahl *m*
anti-friction bonderising bath Gleitbonderflüssigkeit *f*
anti friction metal lining Weißmetall-Ausguß *m*
antimony Antimon *n*
anti-pipe compound Lunkerabdeckmasse *f*
antipollution umweltfreundlich
anvil Amboß *m*
anvil block Schabotte *f*
aperture Maschenweite *f*; Weite *f* (Öffnung); Zwischenblende *f*; Öffnung *f*
apparatus Einrichtung *f*; Gerät *n*; Vorrichtung *f*
apparatus to economise oil Ölspargerät *n*
apparent density Fülldichte *f*; Scheibendichte *f* (Pulvermet.)
apparent load Scheinlast *f*
apparent power Nennscheinleistung *f*; Scheinleistung *f*
apparent rating Nennscheinleistung *f*
appearance of corrosion Korrosionsform *f*
appearance potential Auftrittspotential *n*

appliance Einrichtung *f*; Gebrauch *m*; Gerät *n*; Mittel *n*; Vorrichtung *f*; Zubehör *n*
applicability Anwendungsmöglichkeit *f*
application Anmeldung *f* (Patent); Anwendung *f*; Auftragen *n*; Verwendung *f*
application of load Kraftangriff *m*
applicator roll Beschichtungswalze *f*
applied chemistry angewandte Chemie *f*
applied research Zweckforschung *f*
applied statistics angewandte Statistik *f*
apply (a protective coat) auftragen (Schutzüberzug)
apply by dropping auftropfen
apply for a patent Patent *n* anmelden
appreciation Bewertung *f*; Schätzung *f*; Würdigung *f*
apprentice Auszubildender *m*; Lehrling *m*
approach annähern
approach angle Konuswinkel *m*; Öffnungswinkel *m* (Ziehdüse)
approach roller table Zufuhrrollgang *m*
approval note Abnahmebescheinigung *f*
approximate length ungefähre Länge *f*
approximation Näherung *f*
apron conveyor Platten[förder]band *n*
aptitude for rolling Walzbarkeit *f*
aqua regia Königswasser *n*
aqueous ammonia Ammoniak *n* wäßriges
aqueous corrosion Feuchtigkeitskorrosion *f*
arbitrary test Schiedsprobe *f*
arbitration test Schiedsprobe *f*
arbor Achse *f*; Bolzen *m*; Dorn *m*; Spindel *f*; Welle *f*
arc Bogen *m*; Kreisbogen *m*; Lichtbogen *m*
arc cutting Lichtbogenschneiden *n*
arc discharge Bogenentladung *f*

arc flare region Lichtbogenbereich *m*
arc furnace Lichtbogenofen *m*
arch Bogen *f*, *m*; Gewölbe *n*; Gewölbebogen *m*; Wölbung *f*
arch brick Wölber *m*
arched plate Tonnenblech *n*
arched roof Deckengewölbe *n*; Gewölbe *n*
arched roof of hearth Herdgewölbe *n*
arched soaking pit lid gewölbter Tiefofendeckel *m*
arching Brückenbildung *f* (Bunker)
arch of a chamber Kammergewölbe *n*
arch rings Gewölbescharen *fpl*
arcing Brückenbildung *f* (Ultraschall)
arcing zone Brennfleck *m*
arc pressure welding Lichtbogen-Preßschweißen *n*
arc welder Elektroschweißer *m*
arc welding Lichtbogenschweißen *n*
ardometer Gesamtstrahlungspyrometer *n*
area Fläche *f*; Flächeninhalt *m*; Flächenraum *m*; Oberfläche *f*
areal ropeway Seilbahn *f*
area of contact Berührungsfläche *f*
area relation law Flächenbeziehungsgesetz *n*
argillaceous ore toniges Erz *n*
argon ladle purging Argonpfannenspülung *f*
argon oxygen decarburization process AOD-Verfahren *n*
arising interplant scrap Rücklaufschrott *m*
arithmetic mean arithmetisches Mittel *n*
armature load Ankerbelastung *f* (einer elektr. Maschine)
Armco iron Armco-Eisen *n*; Reineisen *n*; Weicheisen *n*
armoured glass Drahtglas *n*
armour plate Panzerplatte *f*
armour plate rolling mill Panzerplatten-Walzwerk *n*
Ar-point Ar-Punkt *m*
arrange anordnen
arranged in steps gestaffelt

arrange in order einordnen
arrangement Anordnung f; Einrichtung f; Regelung f; Vorrichtung f; Zurichtung f
array Ordnung f; Reihe f
arresting device Anschlagvorrichtung f; Ausschlagvorrichtung f; Feststellvorrichtung f
arrest point Haltepunkt m; Umkehrpunkt m
arsenic pyrites Arsenkies m
arsenious acid arsenige Säure f
art Fertigkeit f
articulated dummy bar Gliederkaltstrang m; Kettenkaltstrang m; biegsamer Kaltstrang m
articulated spindle Gelenkspindel f
articulation Gelenk n; Struktur f
artificial künstlich
artificial ag[e]ing Warmauslagern n; künstliches Altern
artificial weathering künstliche Bewitterung f
as annealed tensile strength Glühfestigkeit f
asbestos Asbest m
as cast im gegossenen Zustand m
ascension pipe Steigkanal m; Steigleitung f; Steigrohr n
as drawn im gezogenen Zustand m
ashes Asche f
ash[es] Schlacke f
ash removal [device] Entaschungsanlage f
ash removal plant Entaschungsanlage f
ash residue Aschenrückstand m
asphalt sheeting Asphaltüberzug m (warm aufgetragen)
as quenched hardness Härte f im abgeschreckten Zustand
as rolled Walzzustand m
as rolled condition Walzzustand m
assay probieren
assay office Laboratorium n
Assel mill Asselwalzwerk n; Schulterwalzwerk n
assemble montieren; zusammenbauen

assembling Montage f
assembly Aufstellung f; Einbau m; Montage f; Verbindung f; Versammlung f; Zusammenbau m
assembly engineer Montageingenieur m
assembly line Fließband n
assess bewerten
assessable [properties] prüfbar
assessment Beurteilung f; Bewertung f
assets Aktiva npl (Bilanz)
as tempered hardness Anlaßhärte f
as tempered tensile strength Anlaßfestigkeit f
asymetric moved mixer Taumelmischer m
athermal transformation athermische Umwandlung f
atmosphere controlled tundish vor Luftzutritt geschützter Tundish m
atmospheric corrosion atmosphärische Korrosion f
atmospheric pollution Staubgehalt m
atomic absorption spectrometer Atomabsorptions-Spektrometer n
atomic-fluorescence spectroscopy Atomfluoreszenzspektrometrie f
atomic hydrogen [arc] welding Wolfram-Wasserstoff-Schweißen n
atomic nucleus Atomkern m
atomic number Ordnungszahl f
atomic power plant Atomkraftwerk n
atomic weight Atomgewicht n
atomisation Zerstäuben n
atomise zerstäuben
atomised powder Druckverdüsungspulver n; Schleuderpulver n; Verdüsungspulver n
atrament process (see phosphate coating) Atramentverfahren n
attachment of bricks Aufhängevorrichtung f für Steine
attendance Bedienung f; Wartung f
attendant Bedienungsmann m; Steuermann m
attenuated air space gedämpfter Luftraum m

attenuation Dämpfung f
attractive force Anziehungskraft f
attribute Eigenschaft f; Kennzeichen n; Merkmal n
audio-frequency control Tonfrequenzsteuerung f
audio monitoring Gehörüberwachung f
audit Pflichtprüfung f; Revision f; prüfen
auditor Prüfer m; Revisor m
auditor's certificate Prüfbericht m (Bilanz)
Auger electron spectroscopy Auger Elektronenspektroskopie f
ausforming Austenitformhärten n
ausformpatenting Austenitformpatentieren n
austempering Zwischenstufen-Vergütung f
austenite Austenit m
austenitic manganese steel Manganhartstahl m
austenitic steel austenitischer Stahl m
austen[it]ize austenitisieren
austen[it]izing Austenitisierung f
autobody Karosserie f
autobody sheet Karosserieblech n; Kraftwagenblech n
autocorrelation Autokorrelation f; Eigenkorrelation f
automate automatisieren
automated process automatisiertes Verfahren n
automatic selbsttätig
automatic control selbsttätige Regelung f
automatic controller Regler m
automatic controller action Regelverhalten n
automatic control loop Regelkreis m
automatic coupling automatische Kupplung f (Eisenbahn)
automatic discharge hopper car Selbstentladewagen m
automatic ga[u]ge control Dickenregelung f; automatische Banddickenregelung f

automatic hot blast stove reversing device selbsttätige Winderhitzer-Umsteuerung f
automatic lathe component Drehautomatenteil n
automatic operation Steuerung f
automatic power peak limitation Leistungsspitzen-Begrenzungs-Automatik f (LBA)
automatic slow down Bremsautomatik f
automatic steel level control automatische Badspiegelregelung f (Stranggruß)
automatic welding Automatenschweißung f
automation Automatisierung f
automobile-body sheet Karosserieblech n
automotive crane Autokran m
autoradiography Autoradiographie f
auxiliaries Nebenbetriebe mpl; Zubehör n; Zuschläge mpl
auxiliary crane hoist Hilfskranzug m
auxiliary data Anhaltszahlen fpl
auxiliary department Hilfsbetrieb m
auxiliary material for iron and steel works Hüttenbedarf m
auxiliary metal alloy Hilfsmetallegierung f
auxiliary metal (powder met.) Bindemetall n
auxiliary plants and shops Nebenbetriebe mpl
auxiliary tuyere Notform f
auxiliary variable Hilfsgröße f
availability for use Einsatzfähigkeit f
average Mittelwert m
average chemical composition mittlere chemische Zusammensetzung f
average data recorder Mittelwertschreiber m
average rate per week Wochendurchschnitt m
aviation material Luftfahrtwerkstoff m
award Belohnung f
axial conduit Ankerrohr n

axial [fine] porosity Fadenlunker *m*
axial load Axialbeanspruchung *f*
axial ratio Achsenverhältnis *n*
axial stress mittige Beanspruchung *f*
axis Achse *f*
axle Achse *f*
axle bearing inside the wheels Innenachslager *n*
axle bearing outside the wheels Außenachslager *n*
axle box Achsbüchse *f*; Achskasten *m*; Achslager *n*; Lagerschale *f*
axle journal grinding machine Achsschenkelschleifmaschine *f*

B

babbitt Lagerfutter *n*
babbitt bearing lining Weißmetall-Ausguß *m*
babbitt [metal] Lagermetall *n*; Weißmetall *n*
baby Bessemer converter Kleinbessemerbirne *f*
back gear Rädervorgelege *n*; Vorgelege *n*; Übersetzungszahnrad *n*
background noise Geräuschgrundpegel *m*; Rauschen *n*
backing Hinterstampfung *f*
backing coat Rückseitenlack *m*
backlash Spielraum *m*; toter Gang *m*; totes Spiel *n*
back lining Dauerfutter *n*
back mill [roller] table Rollgang *m* hinter der Walze
back-pressure turbine Gegendruckturbine *f*
back pressure valve Rückschlagventil *n*
back pull Gegenzug *m*
back pull wire drawing Drahtziehen *n* mit Gegenzug
back reflection Rückstrahlung *f* (Röntgen)
back scatter of beta rays Beta-Rückstrahlung *f*

back tension Bremszug *m*
back twist Gegendrall *m*
back up roll Stützwalze *f*
back-up roll bending Andruckrollen-Biegeverfahren *n*
back-up rolls Andruckrollen *fpl*
back wall Rückwand *f*
back wall skew back Rückwand-Widerlager *n*
backward extrusion Rückwärtsfließpressen *n*
backward slip (rolling) Nacheilung *f* (Walzen)
backward slip [rolling] Rückstau *m*
bad debt zweifelhafte Forderung *f*
baffle plate Leitblech *n*; Prallblech *n*; Scheideblech *n*; Stoßblech *n*
bag Sack *m*
bag filter Beutelfilter *m*; Sackfilter *m*; Schlauchfilter *m*
bainite Bainit *m*; Bainitstufe *f*; Zwischenstufengefüge *n*
bainitic hardening Bainithärten *n*; Zwischenstufenhärtung *f*
bake backen; brennen; sintern; trocknen
baking Einbrennen *n*
baking oven Brennofen *m*; Trockenkammer *f*; Trockenofen *m*
balance Gleichgewicht *n*; Waage *f*; ausgleichen; technische Bilanz *f*
balance beam Waagebalken *m*
balanced sample kontrollierte ausgeglichene Stichprobe *f*
balanced station Hybridstation *f*
balanced steel halbberuhigter Stahl *m*
balance (sheet) Bilanz *f* (kaufm.)
balance weight Gegengewicht *n*
balancing machine Ausrichtmaschine *f*; Auswuchtmaschine *f*
bale Ballen *m*
baled scrap paketierter Eisenschrott *m*
baling hoop Verpackungsband *n*
baling press Ballenpresse *f*
baling ring Tragring *m* (Schlackentopf)
baling wire Bindedraht *m*

ball

ball Ballen *m*; Kugel *f*
ball and roller bearing Wälzlager *n*
ball bearing Kugellager *n*
ball bearing steel Kugellagerstahl *m*
ball hardness test Kugeldruck-Härteprüfung *f*; Kugeldruckversuch *m*
ball indentation test Kugeldruck-Härteprüfung *f*; Kugeldruckversuch *m*
balling Zusammenballung *f*
balling disc Pelletierteller *m*
balling up Würste *fpl* (beim Drahtziehen)
ball joint Kugelgelenk *n*
ball mill Kugelmühle *f*
band dent Beschädigung *f* durch Bandagieren
banded structure Zeilengefüge *n*
banding Zeilenbildung *f*
banding structure Zeilengefüge *n*
bands Zeilen *fpl* (Gußgefüge)
band saw Bandsäge *f*
bands (structure) Zeilen *fpl*
bank Vorwärmer *m* (SM-Ofen); dämmen; dämpfen; stampfen
banked blast furnace gedämpfter Hochofen *m*
bank (furnace) dämpfen
bank of tubes Rohrbündel *n*
bank (of tubes) Bündel *n* (Rohrbündel)
bar Stab *m*; Stabstahl *m*; Stange *f*
barbed wire Stacheldraht *m*
bar-cutting machine Blockschere *f*
bar drawing bench Stangenziehbank *f*
bare welding rod blanker Schweißdraht *m*
bare wire Blankdraht *m*
bare wire electrode nackte Elektrode *f*
bargain Abschluß *m*; Gedinge *n*
bar [heating] furnace Platinenwärmofen *m*
bar hold vorbereitetes Ende *n* eines Schmiedestückes
bar mill Stabstahlwalzwerk *n*
barrel Ballen *m*; Faß *n*
barrel arch Tonnengewölbe *n*
barrel length Ballenlänge *f*

barrel-shaped mixer Rollmischer *m*
barren taub
barren contact tauber Kontakt *m*; tauber Kontaktgang *m*
barren gangue taubes Gestein *n*
barretter Spannungsregler *m*
bar steadler Stangenwiderlager *n* (Rohrwalzwerk)
bar turing [peeling] shop Stangenschälerei *f*
bascule bridge Hubbrücke *f*
base Base *f*; Grundfläche *f*; Grundlage *f*; Grundlinie *f*; Lauge *f*; Sockel *m*; Untergestell *n*; Untersatz *m*
base box (sheets) Normalkiste *f*
base-exchanger Basenaustauscher *m*
base material Grundstoff *m*; Grundwerkstoff *m*
base metal Grundmetall *n*
base metal thermocouple unedles Thermopaar *n*
base-plate Grundplatte *f*
base rate Tariflohn *m*
base size Rohmaß *n*
base speed of mill Grunddrehzahl *f* (Walzwerk)
base steel Grundstahl *m*
base support Untersatz *m*
base thickness Bodendicke *f* (Fließpressen)
basic Bessemer pig iron Thomasroheisen *n*
basic Bessemer process Thomasverfahren *n*
basic Bessemer steel Thomasstahl *m*
basic Bessemer [steel] converter Thomaskonverter *m* (Thomasbirne)
basic Bessemer steel works Thomasstahlwerk *n*
basic converter process Thomasverfahren *n*
basic converter steel Thomasstahl *m*
basicity Basengrad *m*; Basizität *f*
basic lining basische Zustellung *f*, basisches Futter *n*
basic open hearth furnace basischer Siemens-Martin-Ofen *m*
basic oxygen furnace (BOF) Blas-

stahlkonverter *m*
basic oxygen furnace steel Konverterstahl *m*
basic oxygen steel Sauerstoffblasstahl *m*
basic oxygen steelmaking plant Blasstahlwerk *n*
basic oxygen steelmaking process Sauerstoff[auf]blasverfahren *n*
basic oxygen steel plant Sauerstoffaufblasstahlwerk *n*
basic pig iron Roheisen *n* für basischen Siemens-Martin-Ofenbetrieb; Stahleisen *n*; basisches Roheisen *n*
basic principle Grundlage *f*
basic refractory [product] basisches feuerfestes Erzeugnis *n*
basic slag Thomasschlacke *f*, basische Schlacke *f*
basic slag grinding plant Thomasschlackenmühle *f*
basic slag practice basische Schlackenführung *f*
basic type Grundsorte *f*
basic wage rate Grundlohn *m*
basket Korb *m*
basket charging Korbbeschickung *f*, Kübelbegichtung *f*
batch Einzellos *n*; Gemenge *n*; Gicht *f*, Haufen *m*; Satz *m*; Schicht *f*
batch charging satzweises Beschicken *n*
batch furnace Ofen *m* für satzweisen Einsatz
batch heat treatment diskontinuierliche Wärmebehandlung *f*, satzweise Wärmebehandlung *f*
batch operated furnace Einsatzofen *m*; Einsetzofen *m*
batch [type] furnace Kammerofen *m*
bath Bad *n*; Wanne *f*
bath agitation Badbewegung *f*
bath carburizing Badaufkohlen *n*
bath cyaniding Cyanbadhärten *n*
bath furnace Badofen *m*
bath patenting Badpatentieren *n*; Tauchpatentieren *n*
batter Ausbauchung *f* (eines Ofenschachtes); Verjüngung *f*, Neigung *f*; Schräge *f*
battery of coke ovens Koksofenbatterie *f*
battery of cylinders Flaschenbündel *n*
bauxite Bauxit *m*
bay Halle *f*
bayonet coupling Schnellkupplung *f*
bead Einlagedraht *m* (für Gummibereifung); Schweißraupe *f*, Sicke *f*; Wulst *m*; bördeln; falzen
bead bend test Aufschweißbiegeprobe *f*
bead chain Kugelkette *f*
beaded flats Wulstflachstahl *m*
beading Sicken *n*
bead bördeln
beading machine (for barrels etc.) Sikkenmaschine *f*
beam Strahl *m* (Licht); Träger *m*
beam rolling mill Trägerwalzwerk *n*
bean ore Bohnerz *n*
beans Kohlengrus *m*
bearing Lager *n* (Maschinenelement); Zapfenlager *n*; haltig
bearing area Auflagefläche *f*
bearing box Lagerbüchse *f*, Lagergehäuse *n*
bearing bush[ing] Lagerschale *f*
bearing capacity Lagertragfähigkeit *f*, Tragfähigkeit *f*
bearing collar Lagerkragen *m*
bearing distortion Verspannung *f* eines Lagers
bearing face Lauffläche *f*
bearing friction Lagerreibung *f*
bearing length Führungslänge *f*
bearing lining Lagerausgießung *f*, Lagerschale *f*
bearing load Traglast *f*
bearing pedestal Lagerständer *m*
bearing play Lagerspiel *n*
bearing pressure Lagerdruck *m*
bearing properties Tragverhalten *n*
bearing strength Tragfähigkeit *f*
bearing surface Auflage *f*, Lauffläche *f*
beater mill Schlagmühle *f*

beck aufweiten
becking mill Aufweitwalzwerk *n* (Rohre)
bed Flöz *n*; Lage *f*; Schicht *f*
bed coke Füllkoks *m*
bedding layer Rostbelag *m* (Sinter)
bed pig Masselform *f*
bed-plate Grundplatte *f*
beehive (coke) oven Bienenkorb-(Koks)ofen *m*
before going on nach der 1. Probe *f* (beim SM-Ofen)
behaviour Verhalten *n*
be laid out ausgelegt sein
bell Gießtrichter *m*; Glocke *f*; Trichter *m*; Verschlußkegel *m* (Gichtglocke); Ziehtrichter *m*
bell and hopper [arrangement] Gichtverschluß *m*
bell and spigot pipe Muffenrohr *n*
bell lifting rod Hubstange *f* für Glocke; Zugstange *f* (Hochofen)
bell mouth Eingangsschlüssel *m*; Eingangsschlüssel *m* (des Ziehsteins)
bellows Dehnungsausgleicher *m*
bellows expansion joint Kompensator *m*; Kompensator *m* (Dehnungsausgleicher)
bellshaped curve Glockenkurve *f* (Gaußsche)
bell type annealing furnace Haubenglühofen *m*
bell type furnace Haubenofen *m*
belly Bauch *m* (Konverter); Kohlensack *m*; Konvertermittelstück *n*; ausbauchen
below ground unter Tage
belt Anker *m* (eines Hochofens); Band *n*; Gurt *m*; Riemen *m*; Treibriemen *m*
belt casting Stranggießen *n* zwischen endlosen Bändern
belt conveyor Bandförderer *m*; Fließband *n*; Förderband *n*; Gurtförderer *m*
belt fastener Bandverbinder *m*; Riemenklammer *f*
belt idler Bandrolle *f*

belt wrapper Riemenwickler *m* (bei Bandwickelvorrichtung)
bench covering of chamotte slabs Tischbelag *m*
bend Biegung *f*; Bogen *m*; Krümmer *m*; abbiegen (Strangguß); biegen (Strangguß)
bend at right angles kröpfen
bender Teil *n* eines Gesenkes
bending and straightening Biegerichten *n*
bending apparatus Biegeapparat *m*
bending crack Biegeriß *m*
bending cycles Biegewechselzahl *f*
bending force Biegekraft *f*
bending impact test Biegeschlagversuch *m*
bending machine Biegemaschine *f*
bending moment Biegemoment *n*
bending-off press Abkantpresse *f*
bending press Biegepresse *f*
bending roll Biegewalze *f*; Richtrolle *f*
bending rolls Biegerollen *fpl*
bending strain Biegedehnung *f*
bending strength Biegefestigkeit *f*
bending stress Biegebeanspruchung *f*; Biegespannung *f*
bending test Biegeversuch *m*; Faltversuch *m*
bending without radial force querkraftfreies Biegen *n*
bend test ductility Biegefähigkeit *f*
beneficiation Reduktion *f* (Erz)
bent corners verbogene Ecken *fpl*
bentonite binder Bentonitbinder *m*
bent steel ring gebogener Stahlring *m*
benzene Benzol *n*
benzol Benzol *n*
beryllium Beryllium *n*
Bessemer process Bessemerverfahren *n*
Bessemer steel Bessemerstahl *m*
best fit line Ausgleichsgerade *f*
betatron Betatron *n*
bethanising elektrolytische Durchlaufverzinkung *f*
bevel Abflachung *f*; Abschrägung *f*; abkanten; abschrägen; schief;

schräg
bevel brick Widerlagerstein *m*
bevel gear Kegelrad *n*; konisches Getriebe *n*
bevel gear drive Kegeltrieb *m*
bevel gearing Winkelgetriebe *n*
bevelled abgeschrägt
bias Belastung *f* (= Überhang); Einseitigkeit *f*; Fehlerquelle *f*; Verfälschung *f*, Verzerrung *f*, einseitige Neigung *f*
bias of sampling Einseitigkeit *f* der Probenahme
biassed diode vorgespannte Diode *f*
biaxial zweiachsig
biaxial stress device zweiachsiger Spannungszustand *m*
bifurcated launder Hosenrinne *f*
big end up mould Kokille *f* mit dem weiten Ende oben; Massekopfkokille *f* (mit dem weiten Ende oben)
billet Barren *m*; Knüppel *m*; Walzblock *m*; Walzknüppel *m*
billet bank Knüppelputzerei *f*
billet chute Ausfallrutsche *f*
billet drilling machine Rohrknüppelbohrmaschine *f*
billet mill Knüppelwalzwerk *n*
billet sequence Knüppelfolge *f*
billet shears Knüppelschere *f*
billet unscrambler Knüppelordner *m*
bi-metal Thermo-Bimetall *n*
bimodal zweigipflig
bin Behälter *m*; Bunker *m*; Füllrumpf *m*; Tasche *f*
binary alloy Zweistofflegierung *f*, binäre Legierung *f*
binary-coded decimal system binärdekadisches System *n*
binary digit Binärziffer *f*, Zweierschritt *m*
binary edge Randsystem *n*; Verbindungslinie *f*
binary system Dualsystem *n*; Zweistoffsystem *n*; binäres System *n*
binder (powder met.) Bindemetall *n*
binding Bindemittel *n*; Bindung *f*
binding agent Bindemittel *n*

binding offer verbindliches Angebot *n*
binding power Bindefähigkeit *f*
binding wax Bindemittel *n*
binding wire Bindedraht *m*
birefringence Doppelbrechung *f*
birefringent doppelbrechend
bismuth Wismuth *n*
bit Binärziffer *f*, Zweierschritt *m*
bite Biß *m*; Kaliberdruck *m*; angreifen; greifen; zerfressen
bite mark Anstichwelle *f* (Bandrichten)
bite ratio Bißverhältnis *n*; Verhältnis *n* Bißbreite zu Werkstückhöhe
bitumen-asbestos-mastic Bitumen-Asbest-Überzug *m* (Korrosionsschutz)
bitumen lining Bitumenkorrosionsschutz *m* (Rohrinnenseite)
bituminization Bituminierung *f*
bituminous coal Gaskohle *f*, Kokskohle *f*, Weichkohle *f*, backende Kohle *f*
bivariate distribution Verteilung *f* in zwei Veränderlichen
black annealed wire dunkelgeglühter Draht *m*
black band Kohleneisenstein *m*
black body radiation Strahlung *f* des schwarzen Körpers
black edge Glührand *m* (Bandfehler)
black edges schwarze Kanten *fpl*
blackening Schlichte *f*
black heart [malleable] castings schwarzer Temperguß *m*
black hematite Hartmanganerz *n*
blacking Formschwärze *f*
black mould dressing Formschwärze *f*
black patch Zunderfleck *m*
black-pickling Schwarzbeizen *n*
black pickling Vorbeizen *n*
black plate Feinstblech *n*; Schwarzblech *n*
black sheet Schwarzblech *n*
black shortness Schwarzbruch *m*
blacksmith Schmied *m*
black softened weichgeglüht und nicht entzundert

black strip nicht entzundertes Band n
black wash Formschwärze f
blade Blatt n; Flügel m; Klinge f; Messer n; Schaufel f; Streifen m
blade action Wirkungsweise f
blade holder Messerhalter m; Sägeblatthalter m
blank Formling m; Preßling m; Rohling m; ausgestanztes Stück n; blank machen; stanzen; vorgewalzter Block m
blank carburizing Blindaufkohlen n (ohne Aufkohlungsmittel)
blanker Vorschmiedegesenk n
blank hardening Blindhärten n
blank hardness test Blindhärtungsversuch m
blank holder Blechhalter m; Niederhalter m
blanking Rohformen n
blanking tool Schnitt m; Schnittwerkzeug n; Stanzwerkzeug n
blank nitriding Blindnitrieren n (ohne Nitriermittel)
blank test Blindversuch m
blank [value] Blindwert m
blast Gebläse n; Gebläseluft f; Wind m
blast box Windkasten m
blast cleaning Abblasen n (mit Schrot oder mit Sand)
blast connection Düsenstock m; Windstock m
blast distribution controller Windverteilungsregler m (Hochofen)
blast engine Gebläsemaschine f
blast engine house Gebläsehaus n
blast furnace Hochofen m
blast-furnace blast Hochofenwind m
blast-furnace blower Hochofengebläse n
blast-furnace brickwork Hochofenmauerwerk n
blast-furnace campaign Hochofenreise f
blast-furnace coke Hochofenkoks m
blast-furnace flue dust Gichtstaub m
blast-furnace foamed slag Hochofenschaumschlacke f

blast-furnace framework Hochofengerüst n
blast-furnace gas Gichtgas n; Hochofengas n
blast furnace gasdriven blowing engine Gichtgasgebläse n
blast-furnace gas main Gichtgasleitung f
blast furnace gun Stichlochstopfmaschine f
blast-furnace hopper Hochofenbunker m
blast-furnace lines Hochofenprofil n
blast furnace man Hochöfner m
blast-furnace masonry Hochofenmauerwerk n
blast-furnace operation Hochofenbetrieb m
blast furnace operator Hochöfner m
blast-furnace output Hochofenerzeugung f
blast furnace plant Hochofenanlage f
blast furnace practice Hochofenbetrieb m
blast-furnace product Hochofenerzeugnis n
blast-furnace shaft Hochofenschacht m
blast-furnace shell Hochofenmantel m
blast-furnace slag Hochofenschlacke f
blast-furnace slag cement Hochofenschlackenzement m; Hüttenzement m
blast-furnace stack Hochofenschacht m
blast-furnace steel jacket Hochofenpanzer m
blast-furnace steel structure Hochofengerüst n
blast furnace top closing device Gichtverschluß m
blast gate Windschieber m
blast heating Winderhitzen n
blasting Sprengung f
blast inlet Windleitung f; Windloch n
blast main Hauptblasrohr n; Hauptwindleitung f; Luftzuleitung f; Windleitung f

blast pipe Blasrohr *n*; Düsenrohr *n*; Windleitung *f*
blast preheater Winderhitzer *m*
blast pressure Gebläsedruck *m*; Winddruck *m*
blast tuyre Windform *f*
bleach bleichen
bled ingot Gußblock *m* mit flüssigem Kern; ausgelaufener Block *m*
bleed abfackeln; anzapfen; auslaufen
bleeder Standrohr *n*
bleeder valve Anzapfventil *n* (Hochofen); Entlastungsventil *n*; Gasauslaßventil *n*
blend Mischung *f*; mischen; möllern; vermengen; verschneiden
blending (of powder grain size) Ausgleichen *n*
blind hole Sackloch *n*
blind load impulse (arc furnace) Blindlaststoß *m*
blind pass Blindstich *m*; blindes Kaliber *n*
blind tuyre gestopftes Windloch *n*
blister Blase *f*; Naht *f*
blister bar Zementstahl *m*
blistering Blasenbildung *f* (Block)
bloat aufblähen (Steine)
block Ziegel *m*; abfangen (Schmelze)
blocker Vorschmiedegesenk *n*
blocking Vorschmieden *n*
blocking effekt Sperrschichtwirkung *f* (Schmierung)
block slag Klotzschlacke *f*
bloom Schmiedeblock *m*; Vorblock *m*; Walzblock *m*; vorblocken; vorgewalzter Block *m*; vorstrecken
bloom conditioning yard Vorblockputzerei *f*
blooming mill Blockwalzwerk *n*; Grobwalzwerk *n*
blooming [mill] stand Blockgerüst *n*; Streckgerüst *n*
blooming pass Blockkaliber *n*; Vorkaliber *n*; Vorstich *m*
blooming roll Blockwalze *f*
blooming train Blockstraße *f*; Vorstraße *f*

bloom scrap Blockschrott *m*
bloom shears Blockschere *f*
blow Schlag *m*; Schmelze *f*; Stoß *m*; Wind *m*; abschäumen; anblasen; blasen; durchbrechen; erblasen; frischen; verblasen
blowability Blaseigenschaft *f*; Blaseignung *f*; Verblasbarkeit *f*
blow-back proof rückschlagsicher (Düsenmischbrenner)
blow down ausblasen; herunterfrischen; niederblasen
blower Blasemeister *m*; Gasbrenner *m*; Gebläse *n*; Gebläsemaschine *f*; Schmelzer *m*; Ventilator *m*; undichtes Rohr *n*
blower house Gebläsehaus *n*
blow forging press Schlagpresse *f*
blow full fertigblasen
blow hole Blase *f*; Gasblase *f*; Gaseinschluß *m*; Gußblase *f*; Luftblase *f*; Lunker *m*
blowing Blasen *n*
blowing down Tiefblasen *n* (Hochofen)
blowing engine Gebläse *n*; Gebläsemaschine *f*
blowing engine house Gebläsehaus *n*
blowing operation Blasarbeit *f*
blowing period Blasezeit *f*
blow into einblasen
blown ingot Block *m* mit ausgeprägten Gasblasen
blown metal Vormetall *n*
blow-off valve (cowper) Abblaseschieber *m*
blow out ausblasen; niederblasen
blow pipe Blasrohr *n*; Lötrohr *n*; Brenner *m*; Rüssel *m* eines Düsenstokkes
blow pipe flame Lötrohrflamme *f*
blow up aufblasen; aufpumpen; heißblasen; sprengen
blowy ingot Block *m* mit ausgeprägten Gasblasen
blub flats Wulstflachstahl *m*
blue annealing Blauglühen *n*
blue billy Purpurerz *n*
blue brittle bend specimen Blaubiegeprobe *f*

blue brittleness Blaubruch *m*; Blausprödigkeit *f*; Blaubrüchigkeit *f*
blued plate gebläutes Blech *n*
blu[e]ing Erwärmen *n*
blu[e]ing (e.g. sheet) Bläuen *n*
blu[e]ing furnace Bläuofen *m*
blue print Blaupause *f*; Pause *f*
blue shortness Blaubruch *m*; Blaubrüchigkeit *f*; Blausprödigkeit *f*
blunted abgestumpft
board [of directors] Aufsichtsrat *m*
body Bahn *f* (Kaliber); Ballen *m* (Walze); Bauch *m* (Konverter)
body centred cubic lattice kubischraumzentriertes Gitter *n*
body length Ballenlänge *f*
BOF shop Blasstahlwerk *n*
BOF steel Aufblasstahl *m*
bogie casting Wagenguß *m*
bogie frame Drehgestell *n*
bogie hearth furnace Herdwagenofen *m*
bogie type [reheating] furnace Wagenherdofen *m*
bog iron ore Brauneisenerz *n*; Raseneisenerz *n*; Sumpferz *n*
boil kochen; sieden; wallen
boiler Kessel *m*
boiler accessories Kesseltrommel *f*; Kesselzubehör *n*
boiler and fittings Kessel *m* und Kesselarmatur
boiler bottom Kesselboden *m*
boiler connections Kesselanschlüsse *mpl*
boiler drum Kesseltrommel *f*
boiler end Kesselboden *m*
boiler feed water Kesselspeisewasser *n*
boiler feed water preparation Kesselspeisewasseraufbereitungsanlage *f*
boiler feed water softening plant Kesselspeisewasseraufbereitungsanlage *f*
boiler firing Kesselfeuerung *f*
boiler furnace Kesselfeuerung *f*
boiler house Kesselhaus *n*
boiler house control plant Kesselhaus-Überwachungsanlage *f*
boiler mountings Kesselanschlüsse *mpl*
boiler plant Kesselanlage *f*
boiler plate Kesselblech *n*
boiler scale Kesselstein *m*
boiler scale removal Kesselsteinentfernung *f*
boiler scale solvent Kesselstein-Lösungsmittel *n*
boiler setting Kesseleinmauern *n*
boiler tube Kesselrohr *n*
boiling Kochen *n*; Sieden *n*
boiling point Siedepunkt *m*
boilings Abzugsschlacke *f*; übergeflossene Schlacke *f*
boiling test Kochversuch *m*
bolster Zwischenstück *n* des Hammersattels
bolt Bolzen *m*; Dorn[bolzen] *m*; Laschenbolzen *m*; Schraube *f* (Mutternschraube); Schraubenbolzen *m*; verschrauben
bolted steel chain Stahlbolzenkette *f*
bolt-head forging machine Bolzenkopf-Schmiedemaschine *f*
bolt stock Schraubendraht *m*; Schraubenstahl *m*
bond Bindemittel *n*; Obligation *f*; Schuldschein *m*; Verbindung *f*; Wertpapier *n*
bonder Verbundstein *m*
bonder drawing lubricant Ziehbonderflüssigkeit *f*
bonderize (see phosphate coating) bondern (siehe Phosphatieren)
bonding Verwachsung *f*
bonding agent Bindemittel *n*
bonding clay Bindeton *m*
bonding force Adhäsionskraft *f*
bonding of metals Metallkleben *n*
bonding strength Haftvermögen *n*
bond strength Verbundwiderstand *m*
bonus Gewinnanteil *m*; Prämie *f*
boom truck Dornhubwagen *m*
boom type jib crane Auslegerkran *m*
boost verdichten; verstärken
booster ejector Vorevakuator *m*

boot leg Düsenstock *m*; Kniestück *n* (des Düsenstocks)
bootleg Stiefelschaft *m*
border Fassung *f*; Kante *f*; Rand *m*; Saum *m*; bördeln; einfassen; flanschen; rändeln; säumen
bore Bohrung *f*; bohren
bore hole Bohrloch *n*; Bohrung *f*
bore out ausbohren
boric acid Borsäure *f*
boric oxide Boroxid *n*
boriding Borieren *n*
boring Bohren *n*
boring and milling machine Bohr- und Fräsmaschine *f*
boring bar Bohrspindel *f*; Bohrstange *f*
boring machine Bohrbank *f*; Bohrmaschine *f*
boring machine with revolving table Karusselldrehbank *f*
boring oil Bohröl *n*
borings Bohrspäne *mpl*
boring tools Bohrstahl *m*
boring tools Bohrgestänge *n*
boron Bor *n*
boron steel Borstahl *m*
borrowed capital Fremdkapital *n*
bosh Rast *f*
bosh angle Rastwinkel *m*
boshing machine Putzmaschine *f*; Reinigungsmaschine *f*
bosh parallels Kohlensack *m*
bosh tuyere Rastform *f*
bosh with steel jacket Rast *f* mit Stahlpanzer
boss Aufseher *m*; Betriebsleiter *m*; Erweiterung *f*; Gesenk *n*; Meister *m*; Nabe *f*; Pochschuh *m*
boss roller Walzmeister *m*
bot[t] Stopfen *m*
botter rod Stopfenstange *f*
botting Einhalsen *n*
bottle-neck Engpaß *m*; engster Querschnitt *n*
bottle top mould Flaschenkokille *f*
bottling Durchmesserverringerung *f* am Ende eines Hohlschmiedestücks
bottom block Bodenstein *m*
bottom blown converter bodenblasender Konverter *m*
bottom cast steigend gießen
bottom casting Gespannplatte *f*
bottom echo Bodenecho *n* (Ultraschall); Rückwandecho *n*
bottom fin Bodenbart *m* (Block)
bottom fin (ingot) Bodenbart *m*
bottom flash Bodenbart *m* (Block)
bottom flash (ingot) Bodenbart *m*
bottom [hearth] maintenance Herdpflege *f*
bottom hole Sackloch *n*
bottoming material Packlage *f*
bottom of the casting Strangfuß *m*
bottom pass unteres Kaliber *n*
bottom plate Bodenblech *n*; Bodenplatte *f*; Gespann *n*; Sohlplatte *f*; Unterlagplatte *f*
bottom pour gießen; steigend gießen
bottom pouring steigender Guß *m*
bottom pouring masonry mixture Gespann-Mauermasse *f*
bottom pouring plate Gespannplatte *f*
bottom punch Unterstempel *m*
bottom ramming machine Bodenstampfmaschine *f*
bottom roll Matrizenwalze *f*; Unterwalze *f*
bottom roll pressure Unterdruck *m*
bottom side of the strip Bandunterseite *f*
bottom splash Überwallung *f* (Oberflächenfehler); Überwalzung *f*
bottom splash (surface defect) Blockschale *f*
bottom tap ladle Stopfenpfanne *f*
bought scrap Fremdschrott *m*; Zukaufschrott *m*
boulder Geröll *n*
boulder crusher Grobbrecher *m*
boulder of quartzite Quarzitfindling *m*
boundary diffusion Korngrenzendiffusion *f*
boundary friction Grenzflächenreibung *f*; Grenzreibung *f*

boundary layer Grenzschicht *f*
boundary lubrication Grenzschmierung *f*
bounding system Randsystem *n* (Dreistoffphasen)
bow Bombierung *f* (Blech)
Bowden wire Bowdenzug *m*
bowlder Geröll *n*
bow type continuous casting machine Bogengießanlage *f*
bow-type continuous casting machine Bogenstranggießmaschine *f*
bow type continuous casting machine Kreisbogen-Stranggießmaschine *f*
box Buchse *f*; Gehäuse *n*; Kasten *m*; Kiste *f*; Lagerbock *m*; Paket *n*
box annealed sheet kistengeglühtes Feinblech *n*
box annealing Kastenglühen *n*
box annealing furnace Kastenglühofen *m*; Kistenglühofen *m*
box groove Flachkaliber *n*; Kaliber *n*; Kastenkaliber *n*; geschlossenes Kaliber *n*
box hat Stiefelschaft *m*
box hole Flachkaliber *n*; Kaliber *n*; Kastenkaliber *n*; geschlossenes Kaliber *n*
box pass Flachkaliber *n*; Kaliber *n*; Kastenkaliber *n*
box spanner Steckschlüssel *m*
box testing Pfannensinterversuch *m*
brace Strebe *f*; klammern; verspannen; verstreben
bracing Abstützung *f*
bracket Lagerblech *n*; Pratzen *n*
braided wire umsponnener Draht *m*; umwickelter Draht *m*
brake Bremse *f*; bremsen
brake drum Bremstrommel *f*
braking incline Bremsberg *m*
braking power Bremskraft *f*
branch Schenkel *m* (U-Rohr)
branched chain verzweigte Kette *f*
branks Seitenwände *fpl* (SM-Ofen)
branning machine Kleie-Putzmaschine *f* (Weißblech)
brass Lagerfutter *n*; Lagerschale *f*; Messing *n*
brass bearing Messinglager *n*
brate-bar Roststab *m*
braze hartlöten; löten
brazeability Lötbarkeit *f*
brazed joint Lötstelle *f*
brazing Löten *n*
brazing furnace Hartlötofen *m*
brazing solder Hartlot *n*; Lötmetall *n*
brazing torch Lötbrenner *m*
breadth Breite *f*
break Bruch *m*; Knick *m*; Riß *m*; Spalt *m*; abschalten; ausschalten; knikken; unterbrechen; zerbrechen
break a circuit Stromkreis *m* unterbrechen; ausschalten
breakage Bruch *m*
break-down Betriebsstörung *f*; Betriebsunterbrechung *f*; Bruch *m*; Fazit *n*; Schlüsselergebnis *n*; Sturz *m*; Vorsturz *m*; Zerlegung *f*
break down herunterwalzen; vorstrekken; vorsturzen
breakdown of segregations Seigerungsausgleich *m*
break-down test Bruchprobe *f*
breaker Ausschalter *m*; Brecher *m*; Mahlwerk *n*; Unterbrecher *m*
breaker bar Brechstange *f*
breaker block Brechtopf *m*
breaker roll scale Zunderstreifen *m*
breaking by twisting Drehbrechen *n*
break[ing] down pass Streckkaliber *n*
breaking down pass Vorstich *m*
breaking-down pass Vorkaliber *n*
break[ing] down roll Streckwalze *f*; Vorstreckwalze *f*
break[ing] down stand Vorgerüst *n*
break[ing] down train Vorstraße *f*
breaking stress Bruchspannung *f*
break-out Durchbruch *m*
break out Gestelldurchbruch *m*
break through durchbrechen
break-up Zerfall *m*
break up abbrechen; abwracken; spalten; zersetzen
breast pan Vorherd *m*
breast roller Ständerrolle *f*; erste Stu-

fenrolle f
breather Entlüftung f
breather (am.) Gasmaske f
breathing apparatus Atemschutzgerät n
breeze Kohlengrus m; Koksgrus m; kleinstückiger Koks m
breeze oven Grusofen m
brick Ziegel m; Ziegelstein m; mauern; ziegeln
brick backing Hintermauerung f
brick inclusions Einschlüsse mpl von Feuerfeststoffen
bricking up Ausmauerung f; Vermauerung f
brick kiln Ziegelbrennofen m
bricklayer Maurer m
brick lined ladle gemauerte Pfanne f
brick making Ziegeln n
brick making plant Steinfabrik f
brick press Steinpresse f; Ziegelpresse f
brick up vermauern
brickwork Mauerwerk n
bridge conveyor Förderbrücke f
bridge rail Brückengleis n
bridge wall Scheidewand f; Zwischenwand f
bright annealing Blankglühen n; Zunderarmglühen n
bright-annealing furnace Blankglühofen m
bright-drawing Blankziehen n
bright-drawing shop Blankzieherei f
bright drawn blankgezogen (Draht)
bright field image Hellfeldaufnahme f
bright hardening Blankhärten n
bright-luster sheet Hochglanzblech n
bright pickle blank beizen
bright [polished] sheet Glanzblech n
bright soft wire weichblankgeglühter Draht m
bright steel Blankstahl m
bright turned blankgedreht
bright turning Blankdrehen n
bright wet drawn wire naßblank gezogener Draht m
brine Salzlösung f

Brinell hardness Brinellhärte f
Brinell hardness test Brinell-Kugeldruckprobe f
bring down herunterschmelzen
bring up erhöhen
briquette Brikett n; Preßling m; brikettieren; pressen; stückigmachen; ziegeln
briquetting Paketieren n; Ziegeln n
briquetting plant Brikettieranlage f
briquetting property Brikettierfähigkeit f
brittle brüchig; bröckelig; faul; morsch; mürbe; spröde
brittle fracture transition temperature Sprödbruch-Übergangstemperatur f
brittleness Brüchigkeit f; Sprödigkeit f; Versprödung f
broach Reibahle f; Räumnadel f; räumen
broach (e.g. finish plate bolt holes) aufdornen
broaching machine Räummaschine f
broadband noise Rauschen n
broad beam electron gun Elektronen-Flachstrahlkanone f
broad flanged breitfüßig
broad flanged beam Breitflanschträger m
broad jet burner Breitstrahlbrenner m
broadsiding pass Breitungsstich m
broad tool Breiteisen n; Spitzeisen n
broken back Folge f von Querrissen auf gezogenem Draht
broken castings Gußbruch m
broken corners rissige Kanten fpl
broken line (curve) gestrichelte Linie f (Kurve)
broken oxide Oxideinsprenkelung f (Kaltwalzen)
broken ring segment Anpaßstein m (Lichtbogenofengewölbe)
broken scrap Bruchschrott m
broken stones Schotter m
bronze bearing Bronzelager n
brown-coal briquette Braunkohlenbrikett n

brown fume brauner Rauch *m*
brown hematite Brauneisenstein *m*; Limonit *m*; Rasenerz *n*; Wiesenerz *n*
brown iron ore Brauneisenstein *m*
bruised surface mechanisch beschädigte Oberfläche *f*
brush Bürste *f*; Strahlenbündel *n*; Stromabnehmer *m*; bürsten; leitendes Gleitstück *n*
brushing machine Bürstmaschine *f*
bubble Blase *f*; brodeln; sieden; wallen
bubble chain Blasenkette *f*
bubble memory Magnetblasenspeicher *m*
bubbling Blasenbildung *f* (Flüssigkeit)
bucket Eimer *m*; Gefäß *n*; Korb *m*; Kübel *m*; Löffel *m*; Schaufel *f*
bucket car Kübelwagen *m*
bucket charging Korbbeschickung *f*
bucket charging (am.) Kübelbegichtung *f*
bucket conveyor Becherwerk *n*; Kettenförderer *m*; Kübelaufzug *m*
bucket elevator Becherwerk *n*; Kettenförderer *m*; Kübelaufzug *m*
buckle knicken
buckled plate Buckelblech *n*
buckled sheet Buckelblech *n*; gebogenes Blech *n*; geknicktes Blech *n*
buckling Ausbeulen *n*
buckling line Beulenbahn *f*
buckling (of coil) Einknicken *n* (Kaltwalzen)
buckling resistance Knickfestigkeit *f*
buckling strength Knickfestigkeit *f*
buckling stress Knickbeanspruchung *f*; Knickspannung *f*
buckling test Knickversuch *m*
buck-stay Ankersäule *f*; Verankerungsträger *m*
buck stay Versteifungsträger *m*
budgetary control Budgetrechnung *f*
buff Polierscheibe *f*; polieren
buffer Poliermaschine *f*; Puffer *m*; Vorstoß *m*
bug Mündungsbär *m*

buggy (am.) Lore *f*; Plattformlore *f*
buggy casting Wagenguß *m*
build bauen; erbauen; konstruieren
build in einbauen
building block principle Baukastenprinzip *n*
building costs Baukosten *pl*
building material Baustoff *m*
building trade Hochbau *m*
build-up Wulst *m*
build up aufbauen; aufschweißen; auftragen; zusammensetzen
build-up heat Aufbauschmelze *f*
build-up metal Auftragsmetall *n*
build-up welding Auftragschweißung *f*
built-up edge Aufbauschneide *f*; Schneideansatz *m* (Bearbeitung)
built-up section zusammengesetzter Träger *m*
bulb Glühlampe *f*; Wulst *m*
bulb plate Flachwulststahl *m*; Tränenblech *n*
bulge Ausbuchtung *f*; Beule *f*; aufblähen; aufweiten; ausbauchen; stauchen; verdicken
bulge profil Nasenprofil *n*
bulging Ausbauchen *n*; Knickbiegen *n*
bulging test Aufweitversuch *m*; Stauchversuch *m*
bulk Hauptmasse *f*; Masse *f*
bulk density Raumdichte *f*; Raumgewicht *n*; Schüttdichte *f*
bulk ferrite massiver Ferrit *m*
bulk handling Massengutumschlag *m*
bulkhead Außenwand *f* des aufsteigenden Gas- oder Luftkanals (SM-Ofen)
bulkhead (of uptake) Spiegelwand *f* (SM-Ofen)
bulk material Schüttgut *n*
bulk material continuous conveyer Schüttgut-Stetigförderung *f*
bulk production Massenerzeugung *f*
bulk traffic wagon Wagen *m* für Massengut
bulk volume Rohvolumen *n*
bulk weight Schüttgewicht *n*
bull block Einzelblock *m*; schwerer

Einzelblock *m*
bull dog Schlacke *f* für das Flicken von Schweißeisenöfen
bullet Kugel *f*
bull head Polierwalzengerüst *n*
bullhead pass Flachbahnkaliber *n* (Walzwerk)
bull head rail Doppelkopfschiene *f*
bull ladle Gabelpfanne *f*; Handpfanne *f*; Mischpfanne *f*
bulwark rail section steel Relingstahl *m*
bumper Prellbock *m*; Puffer *m*; Stoßstange *f*; Vorstoß *m*
bumpless transfer stoßfreie Umschaltung *f*
bunch Ballen *m*; Bund *n*; Bündel *n*; Haufen *m*; häufen
bundle Bund *n*; bündeln
bundle of wire Drahtbund *n*
bundling plant Bündelanlage *f*
bung Spund *m*
bunker Behälter *m*; Bunker *m*
bunker C-standard oil Heizöl *n*
buoyancy Auftrieb *m* (Gas)
buoyancy plume Auftriebsfreistrahl *m*
burden Beschickung *f*; Einsatz *m*; Last *f*; Möller *m*; beeinflußbare Zuschlagskosten *pl*; begichten; beschicken; gattieren; möllern
burden calculation Gattierung *f*; Möllerberechnung *f*
burden chain Krankette *f*
burden charge Gicht *f*
burdening Begichtung *f*; Belastung *f*; Möllerberechnung *f*; Möllerung *f*
burden overhead cost Gemeinkosten *pl*
burden preparation plant Möllervorbereitungsanlage *f*
burden ratio Möllergewicht *n*
burden yield Möllerausbringen *n*
burn backen; brennen; flammen; verbrennen; verfeuern
burner Brenner *m*
burner mouth Brennermaul *n*
burner port Brennerstein *m*
burner tip Brennerkopf *m*

burn in einbrennen
burning Brennen *n*; Verbrennen *n*
burning [in] Einbrennen *n*
burning kiln Brennofen *m*
burning out the tap hole with the oxygen lance Aufbrennen *n* des Stichloches mit der Sauerstofflanze
burning period Brenndauer *f*
burnish brünieren; bräunen; glätten; polieren; schleifen
burnished chroming Glanzverchromen *n*
burnishing Brünieren *n*
burnishing stick Putzholz *n*
burn off Abrand *m* (Elektroden); abbrennen
burnt gebrannt; heißbrüchig; verbrannt
burnt edge verbrannte Kante *f*
burnt lime gebrannter Kalk *m*
burnt magnesite Magnesiumoxid *n*
burnt out particles Schmelzkugeln *fpl*
burnt tuyere verbrannte Form *f*
burr Bart *m*; Grat *m*; abgraten; putzen
burr removing machine Abgratmaschine *f*
burst Bruch *m*; Riß *m*; aufreißen; aufspalten; bersten; platzen; rissig werden; springen
burst blisters Tränen *fpl* (Blechfehler)
bursting Abplatzung *f*
bursting pressure Berstdruck *m*
bus bar Sammelschiene *f*; Stromschiene *f*
bus bar tower Stromschienensäule *f*
bush Büchse *f*; Zapfenlager *n*; ausbuchsen; füttern
bush chain Buchsenkette *f*
bushelling Paketieren *n*
bushing Büchse *f*
bush[ing] Lagerschale *f*; Laufbüchse *f*
bushing metal Lagermetall *n*
bustle pipe Ringleitung *f* (Wind); Ringleitung *f* zum Abziehen der Ofengase
butt stumpf aneinandersetzen; unteres Blockende *n*
butterfly valve Drosselklappe *f*; Drosselventil *n*

butt ingot Restblock *m*; Stummelblock *m*; kurzer Flußstahlblock *m*
butt-joint riveting Laschennietung *f*
button Bär *m*; Knopf *m*; Pfannenbär *m*
butt-welded joint Stumpfnaht *f* geschweißte
butt welding Stoßschweißung *f*; Stumpfschweißen *n*
bypass[ing] Umführung *f*; Umgehungsleitung *f*; Umleitungskanal *m*
by-product Abfallerzeugnis *n*; Nebenerzeugnis *n*

C

cable Drahtseil *n*; Leitung *f*; Seil *n*
cable drive Drahtseilbetrieb *m*; Drahtseiltrieb *m*; Seiltrieb *m*
cable duct Kabelkanal *m*
cable joint Drahtseilschloß *m*
cable protection Kabelschutz *m*
cable protection pipe Kabelschutzrohr *n*
cable railway Drahtseilbahn *f*
cable-stranding machine Kabelverseilmaschine *f*
cable tape Kabelband *n*
cable tape steel Kabelbandstahl *m*
cable transmission Drahtseilbetrieb *m*; Seiltrieb *m*
cable wire Kabeldraht *m*
cage Fördergestell *n*; Förderkorb *m*; Gehäuse *n*; Korb *m*
cage rotor Käfigläufer *m*
cage stranding machine Korbverseilmaschine *f*
cake Kuchen *m*; backen; sintern; zusammenballen
caking capacity Backfähigkeit *f*
caking coal Fettkohle *f*; Pechkohle *f*; backende Kohle *f*
calamine Galmei *m*
calcareous kalkhaltig
calcareous ore kalkiges Erz *n*
calciferous kalkhaltig
calcification Verkalkung *f*

calcination Brennen *n*; Calcinierung *f*; Oxidation *f*; Röstung *f*
calcine brennen; calcinieren; glühen; rösten
calcined ore Rösterz *n*
calcined pyrites Kiesabbrand *m*
calcining kiln Brennofen *m*; Calcinierofen *m*; Röstofen *m*
calcining of ores Rösten *n* der Erze
calcio-wustite Calciowüstit *m*
calcium carbide Calciumcarbid *n*
calcium ferrite Calciumferrit *m*
calcium precipitation Kalkabscheidung *f*
calculate berechnen
calculate the burden gattieren
calculating machine Rechenmaschine *f*
calculating punch Rechenlocher *m*
calculation Berechnung *f*
calibrate eichen; kalibrieren
calibrated standard defect size Ersatzfehlergröße *f* (zerstörungsfreies Prüfen)
calibration curve Eichkurve *f*
calibration solution Eichlösung *f*
calibration test piece Eichprobe *f*
callipering Messen *n*
calorific balance Wärmebilanz *f*
calorific loss Wärmeverlust *m*
calorific power Heizkraft *f*; Heizwert *m*
calorific value Heizkraft *f*
calorimeter Kalorimeter *n*
calorimetry Wärmemessung *f*
calorising Calorisieren *n*
calorized steel alitierter Stahl *m*
cam Kamm *m*; Knagge *f*; Kurvenscheibe *f*; Mitnehmer *m*; Nase *f*; Nocken *m*
camber Balligkeit *f*; Bombierung *f*; Bombierung *f* (Walzen); Krümmung *f*; Sturz *m*; Wölbung *f*; Überhöhung *f*
cambered girder gebogener Träger *m*
cambering machine Vorbiegemaschine *f*
camera scanning Kameraabtastung *f*
campaign Ofenreise *f*

camshaft Nockenwelle f
cam-type bed Klinkenbett n
cannel coal Fettkohle f
cantilever Ausleger m; Kragarm m; Überhang m
capacitance Wellenwiderstand m
capacitor Kondensator m
capacity Fassungsvermögen n; Leistung f; Leistungsfähigkeit f; Rauminhalt m
capacity adjustment Kapazitätsabgleich m
capacity for cold shearing Kaltscherbarkeit f
capacity for decomposition Aufschließbarkeit f
capacity for heat treating Wärmebehandelbarkeit f
capacity for passivation Passivierbarkeit f
capacity for pickling Beizbarkeit f
capacity for retaining hardness Härtebeständigkeit f
capacity for soldering Lötbarkeit f
capacity to withstand stresses Beanspruchbarkeit f
capacity utilisation Kapazitätsauslastung f
capillary tube Kapillarrohr n
capital costs Anlagekosten pl
capital goods Investitionsgüter npl
capital scrap Altschrott m
capping Abdecken n
capping (ingot) Deckelbildung f (Block)
capstan Drehkreuz n; Ziehtrommel f
cap stone Schlußstein m (Giebel)
car Fahrzeug n; Karre f; Wagen m
carbide Carbid n
carbide alloy Hartmetall-Legierung f
carbide bending Carbidzeiligkeit f
carbide cutting tool Hartmetallwerkzeug n
carbide precipitated during quenching Vorcarbidausscheidung f
carbide precipitation Carbidausscheidung f
carbide spacing Carbidanordnung f

carbide strengthening Carbidverstärkung f
carbide tipped tool hartmetallbestücktes Werkzeug n
car body sheet Karosserieblech n
carbon Kohle f; Kohlenstoff m
carbonaceous Kohlenstoff enthaltend; kohlehaltig
carbonaceous ironstone Kohleneisenstein m
carbon analyser Kohlenstoffbestimmungsgerät n
carbon arc welding Kohle-Lichtbogenschweißen n
carbon bearing Kohlelager n
carbon black Ruß m
carbon block Kohlenstoffstein m
carbon brick Kohlenstoffstein m
carbon brush Kohlebürste f
carbon crucible Kohletiegel m
carbon dioxide Kohlensäure f
carbon drop Entkohlungswirkung f; Frischen n; Kohlenstoffabfall m
carbon electrode Kohleelektrode f
carbon elimination Frischen n
carbonisation Abgarung f (Koks); Schwelung f; Verkohlung f; Verkokung f
carbonisation chamber Kokskammer f
carbonising period Garungsdauer f
carbonising time Garungsdauer f
carbonitriding Carbonitrieren n
carbonization Aufkohlung f
carbonize aufkohlen; ausgaren lassen
carbon lining Kohlenstoffzustellung f
carbon monoxide Kohlenmonoxid n
carbon monoxide poisoning Kohlenmonoxidvergiftung f
carbon network Kohlenstoffgerüst n
carbon pickup Kohlenstoffaufnahme f
carbon replica technique Kohleaufdampfverfahren n
carbon restoration Wiederaufkohlung f
carbon rod furnace Kohlestabofen m
carbon saturated iron kohlenstoffgesättigtes Eisen n

carbon sliding contact Kohleschleifkontakt m
carbon slip piece Kohleschleifstück n
carbon slip stirrup Kohleschleifbügel m
carbon smut Beizrückstände mpl
carbon steel unlegierter Stahl m
carbon steel roll Walze f (Kohlenstoffstahl)
carbon trolley shoe Kohleschleifstück n
carbonyl iron Carboneisen n
car bottom furnace Herdwagenofen m
car-bottom hearth ausfahrbarer Herd m
carburation Carburierung f
carburetted water gas installation Kohlenwassergasanlage f
carburetting Carburierung f (im SM-Ofen)
carburettor Vergaser m
carburisation Carburierung f; Einsatzhärtung f
carburise Kohlenstoff m zugeben; einsetzen; zementieren
carburiser Einsatzmittel n (für Einsatzhärten)
carburization Aufkohlen n
carburization by pig iron Aufkohlen n mit Roheisen
carburize aufkohlen; anreichern mit Kohlenstoff
carburizing agent Aufkohlungsmittel n
carburizing powder Aufkohlungspulver n
car casting Wagenguß m
card Karte f
Cardan joint Kardangelenk n
card-controlled tape punch kartengesteuerter Streifenlocher m
card punch Kartenlocher m
card wire Kratzendraht m
care of the hearth Herdpflege f
car hearth furnace Wagenherdofen m
carload Wagenladung f; Waggonladung f
carriage Schlitten m
carrier Bote m; Drehbankherz n; Fördergefäß n; Mitnehmer m; Träger m
carrier gas Trägergas n
carrier pinion Planetenrad n
carry leiten; tragen
carrying bar Tragstiel m
carrying capacity Tragfähigkeit f
carrying grid Tragrost n
carry-over acid Restsäure f (beim Schmieren)
cart Karre f; Wagen m
cartage Rollgeld n
cartridge Kartusche f
cascade control [system] Folgeregler m
case Außenschicht f; Behälter m; Einsatzschicht f; Gehäuse n; Härteschicht f; Kasten m; Mantel f; Rand m; Randschicht f; Umhüllung f; umhüllen; verkleiden
case depth Härtetiefe f
case harden einsatzhärten; einsetzen; hartgießen; oberflächenhärten
case hardening Einsatzhärten n; Randhärten n
case hardening carburiser Einsatzmittel n (für Einsatzhärtung)
case hardening compound Einsatzmittel n (für Einsatzhärtung)
case hardening steel Einsatzstahl m
caseing Herstellung f von Gehäusen
casement section Einfassungseisen n
casing Armierung f; Fassung f; Gehäuse m; Kapsel f; Mantel m; Panzer m; Schachtausbau m; Umhüllung f; Verkleidung f; Überzug m
cask hoop Bordeisen n
cast Abguß m; Guß m; Schmelze f; Schmelzung f; abgießen; gießen; vergießen
cast annealing pot gegossener Glühtopf m
cast blank gegossener Rohling m
cast chromium steel Chromstahlguß m (Werkstoff)
cast chromium steel [material] Chromstahlguß m
castellated beam Träger mpl wieder verschweißte; Wabenträger m

castellated nut Kronenmutter f
caster Gießer m
cast history sheet Schmelzverlaufkarte f
casting Abguß m; Gießen n; Guß m; Strang m; Vergießen n; gegossener Rohling m
casting bay Gießhalle f
casting bogie Gießwagen m
casting car Gießwagen m
casting crane Gießkran m
casting cycle Abstichfolge f
casting defect Gießfehler m
casting drum Gießtrommel f
casting flux Gießpulver n
casting for machine construction Maschinenguß m
casting ladle Gießkelle f; Gießlöffel m; Gießpfanne f
casting machine Gießmaschine f
casting pit Gießgrube f; Gießplatz m; Gießstelle f
casting pit operative Gießer m
casting pit refractories Stahlwerksverschleißstoff m
casting plate Gießplatte f
castings for general engineering Maschinenguß m
castings for hydraulic structures Hydraulikguß m
castings for machine-tools Werkzeugmaschinenguß m
casting shell Schale f (Stranggießen)
casting speed Gießgeschwindigkeit f
casting team Gießkolonne f
cast in one with angegossen
cast integral with angegossen
cast iron Eisenguß m; Gußeisen n
cast-iron products Eisengießerei-Erzeugnisse npl
cast-iron scrap Gußbruch m
cast-on angegossen
cast steel Stahlformguß m; Stahlguß m; Tiegelgußstahl m; Tiegelstahl m
cast steel products Stahlgießerei-Erzeugnisse npl
cast through the cinder notch Notabstich m (Hochofen)

cast up-hill gießen; steigend gießen
cast welding Gießschweißen n
catalyst Beschleunigungsmittel n; Katalysator m
catch Mitnehmer m; abfangen (Schmelze)
catch carbon heat Abfangschmelze f; Auffangschmelze f
catcher Greifvorrichtung f; Hinterwalzer m; Mann hinter der Walze m; Schnapper m (Blechwalzwerk)
catcher's side (of rolls) Austrittsseite f (an der Walze); Auslaufseite f (der Walzen)
catchweight coil Rolle f mit Zufallsgewicht
category Merkmalsklasse f
caterpillar Raupe[nkette] f
caterpillar drawing machine Raupenziehmaschine f
cathode ray tube Kathodenstrahlröhre f
cathode sputtering Kathodenzerstäubung f
cathodic oxide coating kathodischer Schutzüberzug m
cathodic protection Kathodenschutz m; kathodischer Schutz m
catwolk Laufsteg m
caulk abdichten; dichten; verschmieren; verstemmen
caulk welding Dichtschweißen f; Dichtungsschweißen f
caustic beizend
caustic cracking Laugensprödigkeit f
caustic embrittlement Laugensprödigkeit f
caustic soda Natronlauge f
cavitation Auswaschung f; Kavitation f
cavitation corrosion Kavitationskorrosion f
cavity Hohlraum m; Höhlung f; Innenlunker m; Vertiefung f
ceiling sections Profile npl für Decken
cell Tiefofenzelle f
cell pit furnace Zellentiefofen m
cell type soaking pit Zellentiefofen m

cemented bar Zementstahl *m*
cemented carbide Hartlegierung *f*
cemented carbide alloy Hartmetall *n*; Hartmetall-Legierung *f*
cemented carbide [alloy] tip Hartmetallplättchen *n*
cementite breakdown Zementitzerfall *m*
cement joint Mörtelfuge *f*
cement mortar Zementmörtel *m*
cement plant Zementfabrik *f*
center Kern *m*; einstellen; körnen; zentrieren
center of rotation Drehpol *m*
center [point] Mittelpunkt *m*
center punching Körnen *n*
central gate Einflußrohr *n*; Eingußrohr *n*
central heating of large rooms Großraumheizung *f*
central limiting value theorem Grenzwertsatz *m* (Statistik)
central porosity Fadenlunker *m*
central processor with main memory and arithmetic unit Zentraleinheit *f* mit Hauptspeicher und Rechenwerk
central roll Mittelwalze *f*
centre ankörnen
centre brick Mittelstein *m* (eines Blockgespannes)
centre frequency Mittelfrequenz *f*
centre lathe Spitzendrehbank *f*
centreless thread grinding machine spitzenlose Gewindeschleifmaschine *f*
centre line Walzmitte *f*
centre line average height (CLA) Mittenrauhwert *m*
centre of gravity Schwerpunkt *m*
centre punching Butzen *n* (beim Walzen von Stahlringen)
centre riser Gießtrichter *m*; Trichterhaube *f*; Trichterrohr *n*
centre roll Mittelwalze *f*
centre runner Gießtrichter *m*; Trichterhaube *f*; Trichterrohr *n*
centre runner brick Trichterrohr *n*
centrifugal blower Schleudergebläse *n*
centrifugal casting Schleuderguß *m*
centrifugal casting mould Schleudergußkokille *f*
centrifugal casting process Schleudergußverfahren *n*
centrifugal compressor Kreiselverdichter *m*
centrifugal dust separator Fliehkraft-Staubabscheider *m*
centrifugal force Fliehkraft *f*
centrifugal separator Fliehkraftabscheider *m*; Zentrifugalseparator *m*
centrifuge zentrifugieren
centring device Zentriervorrichtung *f*
ceramic keramisch
ceramic cutting material Schneidekeramik *f*
cerium Cer *n*
cermet Cermet *n*; Metall-Keramik-Werkstoff *m*
certified public accountant Wirtschaftsprüfer *m*
chafing (e. g. laps in a coil during transport) Scheuern *n*
chain Aufzug *m*; Kette *f*; Spannungsreihe *f*
chain block Kettenflaschenzug *m*
chain curtain Kettenschleier *m*
chain grate stoker Kettenrost-Beschickvorrichtung *f*; Wanderrostbeschicker *m*
chain gripper bar Greiferbrücke *f*
chain hoist Kettenflaschenzug *m*
chain link Kettenglied *n*
chain section Flacheisen *n* mit abgerundeten Kanten
chain shaft Kettenachse *f*
chain sling with hook Hakenkette *f*
chain steel Kettenstahl *m*
chain type dummy bar Gliederkaltstrang *m*; Kettenkaltstrang *m* (Stranggießen)
chain wheel Kettenrad *n*
chair rail Stuhlschiene *f*
chalking Kreidung *f*
chamber furnace Kammerofen *m*
chamfer Abrundung *f*; Abschrägung *f*;

Faser f; abkanten; abrunden; abschrägen; verjüngen
chamfered abgeschrägt
chamfering machine Anfasmaschine f
chance Möglichkeit f; Zufall m
chance variation Zufallsstreuung f
change wechseln (Walzen)
change in dimension Maßänderung f
change of shift Schichtwechsel m
change of site Platzwechsel m (Atom)
change on gas umstellen auf Gas (Winderhitzer)
change over Umsetzung f; umschalten; umsetzen; umstellen; umsteuern
change over switch Umschalter m
change point Haltepunkt m; Umwandlungspunkt m
change speed gear Wechselgetriebe n
change stand Wechselgerüst n
change the rolls Walzen fpl wechseln
change [the rolls] umbauen [der Walzen]
change vessel converter Wechselkonverter m
changing shift Schichtwechsel m
channel Kerb m; Rinne f; Zwischenraum m
channeled plate Riffelblech n
channel wheel pump Kanalradpumpe f
chaplet Kernbock m; Kernnagel m; Kernstütze f
character Zeichen n (Steuerzeichen)
character encoder Klarschriftcodierer m
characterisation Kennzeichnung f
characteristic data Kennzahlen fpl
characteristic value Kennzahl f
charcoal Holzkohle f
charcoal breeze Holzkohlengrieß m
charcoal hearth process Herdfrischverfahren n; Holzkohlenfrischverfahren n
charcoal pig iron Holzkohlen-Roheisen n
charcoal tinplate Weißblech n mit dickerer Zinnschicht

charge Belastung f; Beschickung f; Einsatz m; Gicht f (Möller); belasten; beschicken; chargieren; einsetzen; schütten
charge into eingießen (füllen)
charge level [indicator] Gichtsonde f; Möllersonde f; Teufenanzeiger m
charge number Ladungszahl f
charge point Haltepunkt m
charging Ofenbegichtung f
charging and discharging gantry crane Verladebrücke f
charging basket (am.) Gichtkübel m
charging box Beschickungsmulde f; Einsetzmulde f
charging bucket (am.) Gichtkübel m
charging by aerial ropeway Begichtung f mit Hängebahn
charging by batches Beschickungskran m; satzweises Beschicken n
charging by trolley conveyor Begichtung f mit Hängebahn
charging car Füllwagen m
charging crane Beschickungskran m
charging device Beschickvorrichtung f
charging floor Einsetzbühne f
charging gear Begichtungsvorrichtung f
charging hole Einfüllöffnung f
charging larry Füllwagen m
charging platform Beschickungsbühne f; Gichtbühne f; Ladebühne f
charging position for lime Füllstellung f für Kalk
charging position for molten pig iron Füllstellung f für flüssiges Roheisen
charging rate Beschickungsgeschwindigkeit f (Ofen)
charging sequence Gichtenfolge f
charging side Beschickungsseite f
Charlier check Charlier-Probe f
charpy Kerb m
Charpy-V-notch (CVN) Kerbschlagarbeit f an Spitzkerbproben nach ISO-V
chart Diagramm n; Karte f; Schaubild n; Tafel f

chaser Gewindeschneider *m*; Gewindestahl *m*
chassis Gestell *n*
check Haarriß *m*; Prüfung *f*; Regelung *f*; Schrumpfriß *m*; Schwindungshaarriß *m*; absperren; hemmen; hindern; nachmessen; nachprüfen; regeln; zurückhalten
check analysis Kontrollanalyse *f*, Stückanalyse *f*
check crack Schrumpfriß *m*
checked edges rissige Kanten *fpl*
checker brick Gitterstein *m*
checker chamber Gitterkammer *f*
checker[ed] plate Raupenblech *n*; Riffelblech *n*
checker heating surface Gitterheizfläche *f*
checker plate with oval protrusions for gripping Tränenblech *n*
checkers Gitterwerk *n*
checker work Ausgitterung *f*
checkerwork Gitterpackung *f*
checker work Gitterwerk *n*
checkerwork arranged in stages Zonengitterung *f*
checking dimensions Nachmessen *n*
checking test Kontrollversuch *m*
check test Gegenprobe *f*
cheek Seitenteil *n*; mittlerer Formkasten *m*
cheek brake Backenbremse *f*
cheese Radreifen-Gußblock *m*
chemical agent Reagenz *n*
chemical composition chemische Zusammensetzung *f*
chemically bonded brick chemisch gebundener Stein *m*
chemical metallurgy Metallurgie *f*
chemical potential chemisches Potential *n*
chemical technology chemische Technologie *f*
chemico-technological test chemischtechnologische Prüfung *f*
chemistry Chemie *f*
chestnut im Abstichloch erstarrtes Eisen *n*

Chief Engineer leitender Ingenieur *m*
chill Abschreckung *f*; Kokille *f*; Kopfkühlungselement *n* (an Kippöfen); Schreckschale *f*; Schreckschicht *f*; abkühlen; abschrecken; einfrieren
chill cast hartgießen
chill casting Hartguß *m*; Kokillenguß *m*; Schalenhartguß *m*
chill cast roll Mantelwalze *f*
chill crack Warmriß *f*
chill crystal zone globulitische Randzone *f*
chilled casting Kokillenhartguß *m*
chilled cast iron Hartguß *m*; Weißguß *m*
chilled roll Hartgußwalze *f*
chilling layer Schreckschicht *f*
chill pass roll Walze *f* mit gehärteten Kalibern
chimney Kamin *m*; Rauchfang *m*; Schornstein *m*
chimney cooler Kühlturm *m*
chimney damper Kaminschieber *m*
chimney effect Kaminwirkung *f*
chimney slide valve Kaminschieber *m*
chimney type checkers Glattschachtgitter *n*
china clay Rohkaolin *n*
chip Span *m*; abspänen; meißeln; putzen (Blöcke)
chip breaker Spanbrecher *m*
chip density Raumerfüllung *f*
chip flow Spanablauf *m*
chipless nichtspanabhebend
chipless forming spanlose Formgebung *f*
chipless shaping spanlose Formgebung *f*
chip off abblättern; abplatzen
chipping Blockputzen *n*
chipping [shop] Blockputzerei *f*
chip upset Spanstauchung *f*
chisel Meißel *m*; meißeln
chisel steel Meißelstahl *m*
chi-square test Chi-Quadrat-Probe *f*
chloridise abbinden (Ti); chlorieren
chlorinate chlorieren; chlorieren (z. B. Kalk)

chock Bremskeil m; Einbaustück n
choke drosseln; verstopfen
choker valve Drosselventil n
choking Stauung f; Verstopfung f
choking coil Drossel f (elektr.)
chopper bar Fallbügel m
chopper bar controller Fallbügelregler m
chopper type monitoring Fallbügelüberwachung f
chromating chromatieren; chromatisieren
chromatographic analysis chromatographische Prüfung f
chrome brick Chromitstein m; Chromstein m
chrome coating Chromüberzug m
chrome iron ore Chromeisenerz n; Chromeisenstein m
chromemagnesite brick Chrom-Magnesit-Stein m
chrome nickel steel Chrom-Nickel Stahl m
chrome steel Chromstahl m
chromise inchromieren; verchromen
chromising chromieren
chromite Chromeisenerz n
chromium-bearing slag Blasschlacke f
chromium coating Chromüberzug m
chromium depleted-zone theory Chromverarmungstheorie f (interkristalline Korrosion)
chromium diffusion coating Diffusionschromieren n
chromium nickel steel Chrom-Nickel Stahl m
chromium recovery Chromausbringen n
chromium steel casting [product] Chromstahlguß m
chuck Aufspannvorrichtung f; Spannfutter n; einspannen
chuck jaw Einspannbacke f
chunky graphite Knotengraphit m
churn rühren
chute Rutsche f; Schurre f
chute charging Einsetzen n mit Rutschen

cinder Schlacke f; Zunder m
cinder notch Schlackenabstichloch n
cinder pot Schlackenpfanne f
circling Rondenschneiden n
circuit Kreislauf m; Stromkreis m
circuit breaker Ausschalter m
circuitry Schaltplan m
circular aperture Kreisblende f
circular bending Rundbiegen n
circular blank Ronde f
circular-chart recorder Kreisblattschreiber m
circular flanging press Kümpelpresse f
circular form bending Runden n
circularity tolerance Unrundheitstoleranz f
circular mixer Rundmischer m
circular pitch Umfangsteilung f; Umfangstellung f
circular saw Kreissäge f
circular seam welding Rundnahtschweißen n
circular shears Kreisschere f
circular template Kreisführung f
circulating scrap Rücklaufschrott m
circulating water umlaufendes Wasser n
circulation Umführung f; Umlauf m; Umwälzung f
circulation degassing Umlaufentgasung f (RH-Verfahren)
circulation oiling Umlaufschmierung f
circulation system lubrication Umlaufschmierung f
circumference to cross sectional area ratio Umfang-Querschnitt-Verhältnis n
circumferential welding Rundnahtschweißen n
cire perdu process Wachsausschmelzverfahren n
citric acid Zitronensäure f
city gas Leuchtgas n
clack valve Klappe f
clad plattieren
cladding Plattieren n (durch Aufwalzen); Schweißplattieren n

cladding by rolling Walzplattieren *n*
cladding metal Plattierungsmetall *n*
clad metal Verbundmetall *n*
clad sheet Zweilagenblech *n*
clad steel Stahl *m* durch Aufwalzen plattiert
clamping device Aufspannvorrichtung *f*
clamping head Einspannkopf *m*; Spannkopf *m*
clamping plate Klemmplatte *f*
clamping ring Faltenhalter *m*
clamshell type charging bucket Halbschalenkorb *m*
clarification Reinigung *f*
clarify klären
clarifying plant Kläranlage *f*
class Klasse *f*; klassieren
class centre Klassenmitte *f*
class frequency Klassenhäufigkeit *f*
classification Sorteneinteilung *f*
classification by dimensions Größenklassierung *f*
classification of ores Klassierung *f* der Erze
classifying jigging screen Klassierrüttelsieb *n*
classifying screen Klassiersieb *n*
class limit Klassengrenze *f*
class range Klassenbreite *f*
clay Lehm *m*; Ton *m*
clay band iron ore tonhaltiger Spateisenstein *m*
clay brick Ziegelstein *m*
clayey ore toniges Erz *n*
clay gun Stichlochstopfmaschine *f*
clay schist Schieferton *m*
clay slate Schieferton *m*
clean putzen (Gußstücke)
clean air regulations Gesetzgebung *f* zur Reinhaltung der Luft
cleaness Reinheitsgrad *m*
cleaning plant Klärwerk *n*
cleaning shop Putzerei *f*
cleaning shop (fettling shop) Putzerei *f*
cleanliness Reinheitsgrad *m*
cleanness of slag Schlackenreinheit *f*

clear eindeutig
clearance Aussparung *f*; Spielraum *m*; freier Druchgang *m*; freier Druchlaß *m*; lichte Weite *f*
clearance angle Freiwinkel *m*
clearance between collars Kaliberöffnung *f*
clear chill roll Walze *f* (Hartguß)
clear coat Klarlack *m*
clear cut relationship unbedingte Abhängigkeit *f*
clear or plain chilled iron roll Walze *f* (Schalenguß)
clear with oxygen durchbrennen mit Sauerstoff
cleavage brittleness Spaltbrüchigkeit *f*; interkristalline Brüchigkeit *f*
cleavage fatigue failure Spaltermüdungsbruch *m*
cleavage fracture Spaltbruch *m*; Trennbruch *m*
cleavage plane Bruchfläche *f*; Spaltfläche *f*
cleavage (X-rays) Aufspaltung *f*
cleaving property Spaltbarkeit *f*
climb of dislocations Klettern *n* von Versetzungen
clink Heißriß *m*; Spannungsriß *m*; Warmriß *m*
clinkered dolomite Dolomitklinker *m*
clip Ausschnitt *m*; Klemmplatte *f*; abgraten; klammern
clipping Abgraten *n*
clockwise im Uhrzeigersinn *m*
clod coal Stückkohle *f*
clog verstopfen
clogging Verstopfung *f*
close dicht; genau; schließen; sperren
close annealing Kastenglühen *n*
close annealing furnace Kistenglühofen *m*
closed die coining Massivprägen *n*; Vollprägen *n*
closed die forming Gesenkformen *n* mit ganz umschlossenem Werkstück
closed-die press forming with flash Formpressen *n* mit Grat

closed-die press forming without flash Formpressen *n* ohne Grat
closed-die upsetting Formstauchen *n*
closed loop energy control Stromkreisregelung *f* (Lichtbogenofen)
closed moulding box geschlossener Formkasten *m*
closed pass Kaliber *n*; geschlossenes Kaliber *n*
closed shear Zweiständerschere *f*
closed top type housing geschlossener Walzenständer *m*
close grained pig feinkörniges Roheisen *n*
close grained steel Feinkornstahl *m*
close-joint tube zusammengebogenes Rohr *n* ohne Nahtschweißen
close loop control Regelung *f*
closeness (estimation) Güte *f*
closing Schmieden *n* eines halbkreisförmigen Abschlusses (am Behälterende)
closing device Gichtverschluß *m*
closure Verschluß *m*
cloth filter Tuchfilter *m*
cloudburst treatment Stahlsandblasen *n*
clouding Trübe *f*
clover leaf neck Kleeblattzapfen *m*
clover leaf sleeve Kleeblattmuffe *f*
cluster Klumpen *m*; Nest *n*; Traube *f*; Zusammenballung *f*
cluster bottom mould Königsstein *m*
cluster mill Vielwalzengerüst *n*
cluster sampling Klumpenauswahlverfahren *n*; Klumpenstichprobenverfahren *f*; Neststichprobe *f*; Neststichprobenverfahren *n*; Verfahren *n*
clutch Kupplung *f*; Schaltung *f*; schalten
coach screw Schienenschraube *f*; Schwellenschraube *f*
coagulate erstarren; gerinnen
coal Glanzkohle *f*; Kohle *f*
coal by-product Kohlenwertstoff *m*
coal by-products recovery plant Kohlenwertstoffgewinnungsanlage *f*

coal charging device Kohlenaufgabeeinrichtung *f*
coal crushing plant Kohlenbrechanlage *f*
coal-cutting Schrämen *n*
coal dust Kohlenstaub *m*
coal dust firing plant Kohlenstaubfeuerung *f*
coalesce zusammenballen
coalescence Koaleszenz *f*; Zusammenballung *f*
coal gas Leuchtgas *n*
coal gasification Kohlevergasung *f*
coal mine Grube *f*; Kohlenbergwerk *n*; Zeche *f*
coal mining Steinkohlen-Bergbau *m*
coal mixing plant Kohlenmischanlage *f*
coal storage tower Kohlenturm *m*
coal tar extraction Dickteerabscheidung *f*
coal tar pitch Steinkohlenteerpech *n*
coal-to-gas plant Kohlevergasungsanlage *f*
coal tower Kohlenturm *m*
coal tower conveyor Kohlenturmgurtförderer *m*
coal unit Steinkohleneinheit *f* (SKE)
coal washing and grading plant Kohlenaufbereitungsanlage *f*
coal washing plant Kohlenwäsche *f*
coarse grob; roh
coarse breaking Grobzerkleinerung *f*; Vorbrechen *n*; Vorzerkleinerung *f*
coarse crushed slag Schlackenschotter *m*
coarse crushing Grobzerkleinerung *f*; Vorbrechen *n*
coarse draft Grobzug *m*
coarse drafting Grobzug *m*
coarse grain Grobkorn *n*
coarse grain annealing Grobkornglühen *n*
coarse-grained steel grobkörniger Stahl *m*
coarse grain steel Grobkornstahl *m*
coarse grinding Grobzerkleinerung *f*
coarsening of carbides Carbidvergröberung *f*

coarse powder Grobpulver n
coarse reduction impact crusher Prallbrecher m
coat Anstich m; Auftrag m (Schicht); Belag m; Decke f; überziehen
coated electrode Tauchelektrode f; umhüllte Elektrode f
coating Beschichtung f; Schmierstoffträger m (Drahtziehen)
coat[ing] Überzug m
coat[ing] material Anstrichmittel n
coating sheet Bekleidungsblech n
coaxing Stufentrainieren n (Dauerfestigkeit verbessern)
cobalt Kobalt n
cobalt steel Cobaltstahl m
cobble Fehlwalzung f; Kleber m; stauchen; wrackgewalztes Stück n
cobble-baller Drahtschrott-Wickler m
cobbling Kleben n (des Walzgutes an der Walze); Wrackwalzen n
COD = crack opening displacement COD = crack opening displacement
coefficient Beiwert m; Koeffizient m
coefficient of friction Reibungsbeiwert m; Reibungskoeffizient m
coefficient of heat transfer Wärmeübergangskoeffizient m
coefficient of heat transition Wärmedurchgangskoeffizient m
coefficient of thermal expansion Wärmedehnzahl f
coefficient of variation Veränderungskoeffizient m
coercitive force Koerzitivkraft f
cog Kamm m; Mitnehmer m; Vorblock m; Zahn m; vorstrecken
cog down herunterwalzen; vorblokken; vorschmieden
cogged gear Zahnräderwerk n
cogged ingot Vorblock m; vorgewalzter Block m
cog[ged] wheel Kammrad n; Zahnrad n
cogging back Streckschmieden n
cogging [down] roll Streckwalze f
cogging mill Blockwalzwerk n
cogging [mill] stand Blockgerüst n
cogging pass Blockkaliber n; Vorstich m; Vorstreckkaliber m
cogging roll Blockwalze f
cogging stand Vorgerüst n
cogging train Blockstraße f; Vorstraße f
cog-rail type switch Weiche f für Zahnradbahn
cohesive resistance Trennwiderstand m
cohesive strength Scherfestigkeit f; Trennfestigkeit f
cohesive Zone kohäsive Zone f
coil Bandring m; Bund n; Ring m; Rohrschlange f; Rolle f (Band oder Draht); Spule f; Windung f; aufspulen; aufwickeln; haspeln
coil accumulating station Windungssammler m
coil break Knick m
coil breaks Rollknicke mpl (Bandfehler)
coil build-up Bundbildlinie f
coiled bar Stabstahl m in Ringen
coil[ed] spring Spiralfeder f
coiler Auflaufhaspel f; Haspel f
coiler tension rolling mill Ziehwalzwerk n (Steckel)
coil former Wickelwerk n (Trafo)
coiling Aufhaspeln n in Ringen (Bandstahl)
coil Rohrschlange f; Bandring m
coiling apparatus for steel wire and strip Wickelanlage f für Draht und Band
coiling device Aufrollvorrichtung f
coiling drum Wickeltrommel f
coiling machine Wickelmaschine f
coil lift truck Bundhubwagen m
coil of strip Bandstahlbund n
coil packing line Bundverpackungslinie f
coil patenting Bundpatentieren n
coil preparation Bundvorbereitung f
coil weight Bundgewicht n
coil winder Bundwickelmaschine f
coil wrench mark Knickstelle f im

Band
coin Prägestempel *m*; prägen (Münze)
coincidence Zusammentreffen *n*; Überlagerung *f*
coining Kalibrieren *n*; Massivpressen *n*; Massivprägen *n*
cokability Verkokbarkeit *f*
coke Koks *m*
coke breeze Koksgrus *m*
coke bunker Koksbunker *m*
coke by-product Kokereinebenerzeugnis *n*
coke consumption Koksverbrauch *m*
coke crushing plant Koksbrechanlage *f*
coke derivative Kokereinebenerzeugnis *n*
coke dust Kokslösche *f*
coke fines Feinkoks *m*
coke guide Kokskuchenführungswagen *m*
coke loading Koksverladung *f*
coke loading bay Koksrampe *f*
coke network Koksgerüst *n*
coke-oil rate Koks-Ölverbrauch *m*
coke oven Koksofen *m*
coke oven door Koksofentür *f*
coke oven gas Koksofengas *n*
coke-oven gas processing Kokereigasbehandlung *f*
coke oven plant Kokerei *f*
coke preparation plant Koksaufbereitungsanlage *f*
coke pusher machine Koksausdrückmaschine *f*
coke quenching car Kokslöschwagen *m*
coke quench tower Kokslöschturm *m*
coke rate Kokssatz *m*
coke screening plant Kokssiebanlage *f*
coke side bench Koksrampenband *n*
coke storage bin Koksbunker *m*
coke strength Koksfestigkeit *f*
coke tinplate Weißblech *n* mit dünnerer Zinnschicht
coke wharf Koksrampe *f*
coking Verkokung *f*

coking capacity Backfähigkeit *f*
coking chamber Kokskammer *f*
coking coal Fettkohle *f*; Kokskohle *f*
coking coal tower Kokskohlenturm *m*
coking fines Koksfeinkohle *f*
coking plant Kokerei *f*
coking time Garungszeit *f*
coky centre Fadenlunker *m*
cold bending Kaltbiegen *n*
cold-blast kalt erblasen
cold blast furnace Kaltwindofen *m*
cold blast sliding valve Kaltwindschieber *m*
cold bonderising Kaltbonderverfahren *n*
cold brittleness Kaltsprödigkeit *f*
cold compacting Kaltpressen *n*
cold compression strength Kaltdruckfestigkeit *f* (ff. Steine)
cold crack Spannungsriß *m* (im abkühlenden Guß)
cold cracking under the weld Kaltrißbildung *f* unter der Naht
cold draw Kaltzug *m*; kaltziehen
cold drawing tool Kaltziehmatrize *f*
cold drawn blankgezogen (Draht)
cold drawn steel Blankstahl *m*; kaltgezogener Stahl *m*
cold edge trimming Kaltabkanten *n*
cold extruding Kaltstrangpressen *n*
cold extrusion Fließpressen *n* (kalt); Kaltfließpressen *n*
cold extrusion finish Oberflächenvorbehandlung *f* für das Kaltfließpressen
cold formed light U-section Rahmenprofil *n*
cold forming Kaltformgebung *f*; Kaltumformen *n*; Kaltverformung *f*
cold forming tool steel Werkzeugstahl *m* für Kaltarbeit
cold headed wire kaltgestauchter Draht *m*
cold heading Kaltstauchen *n*
cold heading steel Kaltschlagstahl *m*
cold heading wire Kaltschlagdraht *m*
cold impact forging Kaltschlagschmieden *n*

cold junction Kaltlötstelle f
cold lap Falte f (überwalzte); Grat m (überwalzt oder überschmiedet); überwalzte Falte f
cold metal shop Schmelzbetrieb m mit ausschließlich kaltem Einsatz
cold phase tote Phase f (Lichtbogenofen)
cold phosphating Kaltphosphatieren n
cold pilgered tube kaltgepilgertes Rohr n
cold pilger rolling Kaltpilgern n
cold pressing Kaltpressen n
cold-press nut-iron Kaltpreßmuttern-Eisen n
cold reduction Kaltverformung f
cold reduction mill Kaltwalzwerk n
cold reforming Kaltumformen n
cold repressing Kaltnachpressen n
cold rerolling Kaltnachwalzen n
cold rinse tank Kaltspritzbehälter m
cold roll Kaltwalze f; kaltwalzen
cold [rolled] strip Kaltband n
cold-rolled strip kaltgewalztes Band n
cold roll forming machine Einrollmaschine f (für Rohrstreifen); Kaltband-Profilwalzwerk n
cold rolling Kaltwalzen n
cold rolling cluster mill Mehrrollen-Kaltwalzwerk n
cold rolling mill Kaltwalzgerüst n; Kaltwalzwerk n
cold run trial Kaltlaufversuch m
cold saw Kaltsäge f
cold shaping Kaltumformen n
cold shear Kaltblechschere f
cold short kaltbrüchig
cold shortness Kaltbruch m
coldshortness Kaltbrüchigkeit f
cold shut Falte f; Falte f (beim Schmieden); Kaltschweiße f; Mattschweiße f (Blockfehler)
cold shuts Kaltläufer mpl
cold straining Kaltbeanspruchung f; Kaltrecken n; Kaltverformung f
cold twisted reinforcing steel kaltverwundener Bewehrungsstahl m

cold twisted steel bars Stahl m durch Verdrillen kaltgereckter
cold twisting Kaltverwinden n
cold upsetting Kaltstauchen n
cold upsetting steel Kaltschlagstahl m
cold wall vacuum furnace Kaltwand-Vakuumofen m
cold water test pressure Kaltwasser-Prüfdruck m
cold welding Kaltpreßschweißen n
cold workability Kaltumformbarkeit f
cold-worked steel Stahl m kaltgewalzter und kaltgereckter
cold working Kaltbeanspruchung f; Kaltrecken n; Kaltumformen n; Kaltverarbeitung f; Kaltverformung f, Rohgang m
cold work steel Kaltarbeitsstahl m
collapse einstürzen
collapsibility test Zerfallsprüfung f
collapsible mandrel Klappdorn m
collar Bund m (Schraube); Kaliberrand m; Rand m (Kaliber); Ring m
collar forming Kragenziehen n
collaring holes by drawing Kragenziehen n
collar mould (ESR) Kragenkristallisator m (ESU)
collect (a gas) auffangen (ein Gas)
collected scrap Sammelschrott m
collecting main Sammelleitung f
colliery Grube f; Kohlenbergwerk n
colliery arches Grubenausbaustahl m
collision Verecken n (von Pfannen)
colloidal solution Kolloidlösung f
colorimetric pyrometer Farbpyrometer n
colorimetry Kolorimetrie f
columbium Niob n
column Pfeiler m; Ständer m; Säule f
columnar crystallisation Transkristallisation f
columnar crystal zone Säulenstrukturzone f
columnar structure Stengelgefüge n
column strength Knickfestigkeit f
column type chromatography Säulenchromatographie f

combat Bekämpfung f; bekämpfen
combination blanking and piercing Gesamtschneiden n
combination firing Verbundbeheizung f
combination of materials Stoffpaar n
combine abbinden
combined burner kombinierter Brenner m
combined carbon gebundener Kohlenstoff m
combined drawing gemeinsames Ziehen n
combined firing Verbundbeheizung f
combined-operation work Verbundarbeit f
combined rolling and sliding motion Wälzbewegung f
combined station Hybridstation f
combined utilities Verbundwirtschaft f
combustion Verbrennung f
combustion air Verbrennungsluft f
combustion chamber Brennkammer f; Brennschacht m; Feuerraum m (Ofen); Heizschacht m; Verbrennungskammer f
combustion coke Heizkoks m
combustion conditions Verbrennungsverhältnisse npl
combustion engine Verbrennungskraftmaschine f
combustion engineering verbrennungstechnisch
combustion heat Verbrennungswärme f
combustion phenomena Verbrennungsvorgänge mpl
command variable Führungsgröße f
commercial großtechnisch; handelsüblich
commercial grade Handelsgüte f; einfache Handelsgüte f
commercial grade sheet Handelsfeinblech n
commercially pure iron technisch reines Eisen n
commercially smooth rolled surface walztechnisch glatte Oberfläche f

commercial quality Handelsgüte f; Handelssorte f; einfache Handelsgüte f
commercial quality sheet Handelsfeinblech n
comminute pulvern; zerkleinern
comminution Zerkleinerung f
comminution of solid metals Feinzerkleinerung f fester Metalle
Committee for Materials Werkstoffausschuß m
Committee of Mechanical Engineers Maschinenausschuß m
common gemeinsam; üblich (math. gemeinsam)
common bus arrangement Sammelschiene f (elektr.)
common draw size Ziehrohmaß n
common iron pyrites Schwefelkies m
Common Market gemeinsamer Markt m
common salt Kochsalz n
communication process Kommunikationsprozess m
compact Preßkörper m; Preßling m
compact continuous annealing process Kompakt-Durchlaufglühverfahren n
compactibility Formbarkeit f
compacting by swaging Hämmerverdichten n
compacting by vibration Vibrationsverdichten n
compacting pressure Preßdruck m
compact in layers Schichtpreßkörper m
compact tensile specimens Kompaktzugproben fpl
companion element Eisenbegleitelement n; Stahlbegleitelement n
company management Geschäftsleitung f
comparative test Gleichversuch m; Vergleichsversuch m
comparative value Vergleichswert m
comparing element Vergleicher m
comparison test Vergleichsversuch m
compasses Zirkel m

compensate ausgleichen
compensation leads Ausgleichsleitung f
competitive position Wettbewerbsfähigkeit f
compilation Zusammenstellung f
complaint Beanstandung f; Beschwerde f; Einspruch m; Reklamation f
complete ergänzen
complete decarburisation Gesamtentkohlung f
complete fusion Schmelzfluß m
complete rotation Umlauf m
component (part) Bestandteil m
composite Schichtkörper m
composite beam Verbundträger m
composite casting Verbundguß m
composite cast roll Verbundgußwalze f
composite material Verbundwerkstoff m
composite metal Verbundmetall n
composite powder Verbundpulver n
composite steel Verbundstahl m
composite tube Verbundrohr n
composition Aufbau m; Verbindung f; Zusammensetzung f
composition bearing Preßstofflager n
composition of forces Kräftezusammensetzung f
compound Bindung f; Mischung f; Mittel n; Verbindung f; Zusammensetzung f
compound casting Verbundguß m
compound drawing die Mehrfachziehstein m
compound firing Verbundbeheizung f
compound probability zusammengesetzte Wahrscheinlichkeit f
compound ribs Rippenscharen fpl
compound steel Duplexstahl m; Verbundstahl m
compress verdichten
compressed air Druckluft f
compressed air container Druckluftkessel m
compressed air drop hammer Druckluft-Gesenkhammer m

compressed air hammer Drucklufthammer m
compressed air line Druckluftleitung f
compressed-air pipe Preßluftzuleitung f
compressed-air system Druckluftanlage f
compressed air tank Druckluftkessel m
compressed air tool Druckluftwerkzeug n
compressibility Preßbarkeit f; Verdichtbarkeit f; Verpreßbarkeit f
compression Druck m; Verdichtung f
compression load Druckbeanspruchung f
compression member Druckstab m
compression pulsating fatigue strength Druckschwellfestigkeit f
compression ratio Verdichtungsverhältnis n
compression strain Druckverformung f
compression strength Druckfestigkeit f
compression stress Druckbeanspruchung f; Druckspannung f
compression stress to produce a given creep in a given time Zeitstauchgrenze f
compression surface finishing Glattprägen n
compression test Druckversuch m; Stauchversuch m
compressive force Druckkraft f (Pressen)
compressive reforming Druckumformen n
compressive stress Druckbeanspruchung f
compressive yield point Quetschgrenze f
compressor Verdichter m
compressor for grid gas transmission Ferngasverdichter m
compressor for long distance gas transmission Ferngasverdichter m
computation Berechnung f

compute berechnen; rechnen
computer Rechenmaschine *f*; Rechner *m*
computer bureau Rechenzentrum *n*
computer control Rechnersteuerung *f*
computer installation Rechenanlage *f*
computing centre Rechenzentrum *n*
computing element Rechenglied *n*
concave fillet weld Hohlkehlnaht *f* (Schweißen)
concave milling cutter Halbkreisfräser *m*
concavity Hohlung *f*
concentrate Konzentrat *n*; anreichern; aufbereiten; verdichten
concentrated konzentriert
concentration Anreicherung *f*; Gehalt *m*; Konzentration *f*
concertina-type expansion joint Dreiwellenkompensator *m*
concrete Beton *m*
concrete product Betonware *f*
concrete reinforcing steel bars Betonstahl *m*; Moniereisen *n*
concrete reinforcing [steel] mat Betonstahlmatte *f*
concrete sealing agent Betondichtungsmittel *n*
concrete testing machine Betonprüfmaschine *f*
concrete ware Betonware *f*
concussion Erschütterung *f*
condensation Kondensieren *n*
condenser Kühler *m*
condenser plant Kondensationsanlage *f*
condition Beschaffenheit *f*; Lage *f*; Zustand *m*; aufbereiten; instand setzen; zubereiten
conditioner Konditionierer *m* (LD-Gasreinigung)
conditioning burner regelnder Brenner *m*
conditioning department Zurichterei *f*
condition of delivery Lieferzustand *m*
condition of treatment Behandlungszustand *m*
conduct führen; leiten

conductibility Leitfähigkeit *f* (magnet.)
conduction Leitung *f* (elektr.)
conduction electron polarisation Polarisation *f* von Leitungselektronen
conductivity Leitfähigkeit *f*
conductivity of heat Wärmeleitfähigkeit *f*
conduct of a heat Schmelzführung *f*
conductor Leiter *m* (elektr.)
conductor rail Stromschiene *f*
conductor rail tower Stromschienensäule *f*
conduit Kanal *m*; Rohrleitung *f*
cone Konus *m*
cone cooling system Hutkühlung *f*
cone crusher Kegelbrecher *m*
cone hardness test Kegelhärteprüfung *f*
cone impression Kegeleindruck *m*
cone thrust test Kegeldruckprobe *f*; Kegeldruckversuch *m*
cone upset test Kegelstauchversuch *m*
confidence Vertrauen *n*
confidence interval Fehlerbereich *m*; Vertrauensabstand *m*; Vertrauensbereich *m*; Zufallsfehlerbereich *m*
confidence limit Vertrauensgrenze *f*
confluence analysis Konfluenzanalyse *f*
congeal fest werden; gerinnen
congealing Gerinnen *n*
congelation geronnene Masse *f*
conical compression [upsetting] test Kegelstauchversuch *m*
conical converter top Konverterhut *m*
conical roller bearing Kegelrollenlager *n*
conicity Konizität *f*; Verjüngung *f*
coning Kümpeln *n*
connect verbinden
connect a circuit Stromkreis *m* schließen; einschalten
connected load Anschlußwert *m* (elektr.)
connecting device Schaltglied *n*
connecting piece Stutzen *m*

connecting rod Pleuelstange f; Schubstange f
connecting terminal Anschlußklemme f
connect into circuit einschalten
connection Anschluß m
consideration Diskussion f; Erörterung f
consistence Dichte f; Festigkeit f; Konsistenz f; Übereinstimmung f
consistency Folgerichtigkeit f; Konsistenz f; Übereinstimmung f
consistent folgerichtig; stabil
consolidated statement Bilanz f; Konzernbilanz f
consolidation roll Abquetschrolle f
constancy of volume Raumbeständigkeit f
constant Konstante f; beständig; fest; gleichbleibend
constituent Bestandteil m (Gefüge)
constitutional diagram Zustandsschaubild n
constitutional supercooling konstitutionelle Unterkühlung f
constrained motion Zwanglauf m
constriction Einschnürung f; Verengung f
construct aufbauen; errichten
construction Aufbau m; Bauwesen n
constructional feature Konstruktionsmerkmal n
construction lines Profil n (Hochofen)
construction of apparatus (plant manufacture) Apparatebau m
consulting engineer beratender Ingenieur m
consulting engineer's Ingenieurbüro n
consumable-arc furnace Abschmelzofen m
consumable electrode Abbrandelektrode f
consumption Verbrauch m
contact controller Schrittregler m
contact force Anpreßkraft f; Anstellkraft f (Stranggießen)
contact line duct Schleifleitungskanal m

contact material (powder met.) Kontaktwerkstoff m
contact power Haftvermögen n
contact pressure Anpreßdruck m
contact spot Klebestelle f (Oberflächenfehler)
contact welding Kontaktschweißen n
contact wire suspension (electric traction) Fahrdrahtaufhängung f
contain enthalten; fassen
container Behälter m
containing enthaltend; haltig
contaminants (air pollution) Schadstoffe mpl
contaminated iron verunreinigtes Eisen n
contamination Verschmutzung f; Verunreinigung f
contamination impurity Verunreinigung f
content Gehalt m
contingency Zufälligkeit f
continuous durchgehend; laufend; stetig; ununterbrochen
continuous casting Stranggießen n; vollkontinuierliches Stranggießen n
continuous casting method Stranggußverfahren n
continuous casting plant Stranggießanlage f
continuous chip Scherspan m
continuous controller zügiger Regler m
continuous conveyor Stetigförderer m
continuous cooling transformation curve (CCT) kontinuierliches ZTU-Diagramm n; kontinuierliches Kühlungs-Umwandlungsschaubild n
continuous degassing Durchlaufentgasung f
continuous electrode Dauerelektrode f
continuous flow test Dauerflußversuch m
continuous frequency function stetige Häufigkeitsfunktion f
continuous furnace Fließofen m
continuous furnace for tubes Rohr-

durchlaufofen *m*
continuous furnace with grid hearth for annealing of round stock Rillenherd-Durchstoßofen *m* zum Wärmen von Rundmaterialien
continuous heat treatment kontinuierliche Wärmebehandlung *f*
continuously cast stranggegossen
continuous muffle type furnace Muffel-Durchziehofen *m*
continuous operation Dauerbetrieb *m*
continuous oxygen refining process kontinuierliches Sauerstofffrischverfahren *n*
continuous process Fließvorgang *m*
continuous pusher type furnace Durchstoßofen *m*; Tunnelofen *m*
continuous roller-hearth annealing furnace Rollenherd-Durchlaufofen *m*
continuous [rolling] mill kontinuierliches Walzwerk *n*
continuous running Dauerbetrieb *m*
continuous service Dauerbetrieb *m*
continuous strand furnace Banddurchziehofen *m*
continuous strip annealing line Banddurchlauf-Glühanlage *f*
continuous tapping ununterbrochener Abstich *m*
continuous vacuum degassing Vakuumdurchlaufentgasung *f*
continuous wave transmission method Dauerschallverfahren *n*
contour of hole Düsenform *f*
contour profile cutter Umrißprofilschneider *m*
contract Gedinge *n*; Vertrag *m*; zusammenziehen
contracting by spinning Einhalsen *n* durch Drücken; Engen *n* durch Drücken
contraction Schrumpfung *f*
contract rate Akkordlohn *m*
contract spot Klebestelle *f* (Oberflächenfehler)
contra effect Gegenläufigkeit *f*; Gegenwirkung *f*

contributor Mitarbeiter *m* (Mitverfasser)
control Bewirtschaftung *f*; Kontrolle *f*; Prüfung *f*; Regeln *n*; Regelung *f*; Steuerung *f*; Vergleichswert *m*; nachprüfen; regeln; steuern; überwachen; Überwachung *f*
control chain Steuerkette *f*
control chart Kontrollschaubild *n*
control current impulse Steuerstromimpuls *m*
control equipment Regelanlage *f*
control gear Steuerung *f*
control instrument Überwachungsgerät *n*
controllable burden Zuschlagskosten *pl*
controllable [extras] beeinflußbare Zuschlagskosten *pl*
controlled atmosphere Schutzgas *n*; geregelte Atmosphäre *f*
controlled atmosphere furnace Schutzgasofen *m*
controlled condition Regelgröße *f*
controlled cooling gesteuerte Kühlung *f*
controlled cooling conveyor Kühlband *n*
controlled directional solidification gelenkte Erstarrung *f*
controlled feed belt weigher Dosierbandwaage *f*
controlled oxidation gelenkte Oxidation *f*
controlled system Regelstrecke *f*
controlled variable Regelgröße *f*
controlled volume pumpe Dosierpumpe *f*
controller Regler *m*; Schaltwalze *f*; Steuergerät *n*
control lever Schalthebel *m*; Steuerhebel *m*
controlling device Steuerung *f*
controlling means Regeleinrichtung *f*
controlling sizes Nachmessen *n*
control of level in a bin Füllstandsregelung *f*
control plant Überwachungsanlage *f*

control platform

control platform Steuerbühne f
control pulpit Steuerbühne f
control rate Stellgeschwindigkeit f (Regelungstechnik)
control sample Stichprobe f
control sequence Befehlsfolge f
control stand Steuerstand m
control system Leitsystem n; Regeleinrichtung f; Regelkreis m
control with fixed set-point Festwertregelung f
convection Konvektion f; Umwälzung f
convection cooling Konvektionskühlung f
convector Konvektor m; Wärmeleitplatte f; Wärmeleitscheibe f
conventional milling Gegenlauffräsen n
conventional transmission electron microscopy Transmissionselektronenmikroskopie f (TEM)
conversion Umsetzung f; Umwandlung f; Verwandlung f
conversion costs Umwandlungskosten pl
conversion layer Vorbehandlungsschicht f
conversion value Umrechnungswert m
convert umformen; umwandeln; überführen
converted bar Zementstahl m
converted to bezogen auf
converter Birne f; Konverter m; Umformer m
converter aisle Rauchschiff n
converter bearing Konverterlager n
converter bottom Konverterboden m
converter bottom mounting car Konverterboden-Einsetzwagen m
converter bottom tamping machine Konverterboden-Stampfmaschine f
converter casing Konvertereinhausung f
converter chimney Konverterkamin m
converter drive Konverterantrieb m
converter drying plant Konverter-Trocknungsanlage f
converter hood Konverterhut m
converter lining Konverterfutter n
converter mouth Konvertermündung f
converter shape Birnenform f
converter shell Konvertermantel m
converter shop Konverterbetrieb m
converter slopping and spatter Konverterauswurf m
converter steel Konverterstahl m
converter vessel Konvertergefäß n
converting [with air] Windfrischen n
convex fillet weld Wölbnaht f
convex milling cutter Halbkreisfräser m
convex weld volle Kehlnahtschweiße f
convey befördern; fördern; leiten
conveyer belt burdening installations Bandmöllerungsanlage f
conveying appliance Fördermittel n; Fördermittel npl
conveying belt Förderband n
conveying bridge Förderbrücke f
conveying chain Transportkette f
conveying device Fördermittel n; Fördermittel npl
conveying plant Förderanlage f
conveyor Förderer m
conveyor belt Förderband n; Transportband n
conveyor belt charging Bandbegichtung f (Hochofen)
conveyor belt furnaces Förderbandöfen mpl
conveyor chain Förderkette f
conveyor-type bucket loader Bandschaufellader m
conveyor type weigher Bandwaage f
cool abkühlen; erkalten
coolant Abkühlung f; Abkühlungsmittel n; Kühlmittel n
coolant supply pipe Kühlmittelzuführung f
coolers Kühlkasten m
cooling Erkaltung f; Kühlung f
cooling air Kühlluft f
cooling bank Kühlbett n

cooling basin Kühlwasserbecken n
cooling bed Kühlbett n; Warmlager n
cooling box Kühlkasten m
cooling cover Kühlhaube f
cooling crack Kühlspannungsriß m; Schrumpfriß m
cooling curve Abkühlkurve f
cooling hood Kühlhaube f
cooling in a static fluid Kühlung f in ruhender Flüssigkeit
cooling in a static liquid Kühlung f in ruhender Flüssigkeit
cooling jacket Kühlschale f
cooling plate Kühlplatte f
cooling rate Abkühlungsgeschwindigkeit f
cooling ring Kühlring m
cooling tower Kühlturm m
cooling tube roll bearing (bronze) Kühlrohr-Walzenlager n (Bronze)
cooling vat Abkühlungsbottich m
cooling water pipe Kühlwasserleitung f
cool melt matte Schmelze f
cooperative research Gemeinschaftsforschung f
co-ordinate Koordinate f
coordinates Ortskoordinaten fpl
co-ordination Zuordnung f
coping machine Ausklinkmaschine f
copperas Eisenvitriol n
copper bearing kupferhaltig
copper bit Lötkolben m
copper-coat verkupfern
coppering Kupferüberzug m
copperplate verkupfern
copper steel Kupferstahl m
copper sulphate test Kupfersulfatprüfung f
core Kern m
core baking oven Kerntrockenkammer f
core blower Kernblasmaschine f
cored electrode Seelenelektrode f
core hardenability Kernhärtbarkeit f
core hardening Kernhärten n
coreless induction furnace Hochfrequenz-Induktionsofen m; Hochfrequenzofen m; kernloser Induktionsofen m
core memory Kernspeicher m (EDV)
core mixture Kernmasse f
core oil Kernöl n
core print Kernmarke f
core refining Kernrückfeinen n; Kernrückfeinung f
core rod Dorn m
core segregation Kernseigerung f
core store Kernspeicher m (EDV)
core structure Kerngefüge n
core type induction furnace Induktionsrinnenofen m
core welding wire Seelenschweißdraht m
corner casting (on freight container) Eckbeschlag m
corner crack Kantenriß m
corpuscular pollution korpuskulare Verunreinigung f
corpuscular radiation Korpuskularstrahlung f
correcting condition (automatic control) Stellgröße f
correcting element Stellglied n
correcting unit Stellwerk n
corrective action Regeleingriff m
correlation coefficient Korrelationskoeffizient m
correlogram Beziehungsschaubild n
corrode anfressen; angreifen; korrodieren; rosten; verrosten
corrosion Korrosion f
corrosion by condensation of moisture Schwitzwasserkorrosion f
corrosion by condensed water Kondenswasserkorrosion f
corrosion cell Korrosionselement n
corrosion crack Korrosionsriß m
corrosion creep Korrosionsunterwanderung f
corrosion during shut down period of service Stillstandkorrosion f
corrosion erosion Erosionskorrosion f
corrosion fatigue Korrosionsermüdung f
corrosion inhibition Korrosionshemmung f

corrosion pit Korrosionsnarbe f
corrosion protection Korrosionsschutz m
corrosion resistance Korrosionsbeständigkeit f; Korrosionswiderstand m
corrosion resistant rostbeständig
corrosion under deposits Korrosion f unter Ablagerungen
corrosion under mechanical stress Korrosion f unter mechanischer Beanspruchung
corrosive fressend; korrosiv; ätzend
corrugated ingot Riffelblock m; mehrkantiger Block m (mit eingezogener Seitenfläche)
corrugated mould gewellte Kokille f
corrugated roll Riffelwalze f
corrugated sheet Wellblech n
corrugated sheet machine Wellblechmaschine f
corrugated tube Wellrohr n
corrugating Wellbiegen n
corrugating sheet rolling mill Wellblechwalzwerk n
corrugation Welle f
corrugations Ratterwellen fpl (in Schienen)
corter pin Splint m
corundum brick Korundstein m
cost account Kostenkonto n
cost accounting Kostenrechnung f
cost accounting department Betriebsbuchhaltung f
cost allocation on the basis of equipment life Kostenumlage f nach Gebrauchsdauer
cost allocation on the basis of floor space Kostenumlage f nach Raumgröße
cost allocation on the basis of material cost Kostenumlage f nach Stoffverbrauch
cost allocation on the basis of sales volume Kostenumlage f nach Umsatz
cost analysis Kostenanalyse f
cost bearer Kostenträger m

cost calculation guidelines Kostenrechnungs-Richtlinien fpl
cost center Kostenstelle f
cost comparison Kostenvergleich m
cost [factory] accounting betriebliches Rechnungswesen n
cost finding Kostenermittlung f
costing Kostenrechnung f
cost price Kostenpreis m
cost[s] Kosten pl
cost saving Kostenersparnis f
costs department Kostenabteilung f
costs of construction Baukosten pl
costs of installation Anlagekosten pl
cost type Kostenart f
cotter Keil m
coulometer Coulometer n
counterblow hammer Gegenschlaghammer m
counter bored hole Schulterbohrung f
counterclockwise gegen den Uhrzeigersinn m
counter-current heat exchanger Gegenstrom-Wärmeaustauscher m
counter electrode Gegenelektrode f
counterflow Gegenstrom m
counterflow heat exchanger Gegenstrom-Wärmeaustauscher m
countersink Senker m; versenken
countersunk bolt Senkschraube f
counter tube Zählrohr n
counterweight Gegengewicht n
country Feld n; Revier n
country rock Nebengestein n
counts per min Teilchen npl je Minute (Geigerzähler)
coupling Kupplung f
coupling box Kuppelmuffe f; Muffe f
coupling bush Kupplungsbüchse f
coupling shaft Kupplungswelle f
coupling sleeve Walzentreffer m
coupling spindle Kuppelspindel f
course Gang m (des Hochofens); Lage f; Lauf m; Schar f; Schicht f (Steine); Verlauf m
course of curve Kurvenverlauf m
co-variation Mitveränderlichkeit f
cover Belag m; Decke f; Deckel m; be-

decken; verkleiden
cover carriage Deckelwagen m
cover coat enamel Deckemail n
covered electrode ummantelte Elektrode f
covering ability Deckfähigkeit f; Deckvermögen n
covering agent for melts Abdeckmasse f
cover lid Deckel m
cover lifting bogie for pit furnaces Deckelabhebewagen m für Tieföfen
cowper Cowper m
Cowper Heißwindofen m; Winderhitzer m
cowper brick Cowperstein m
Cowper brick Winderhitzerstein m
crab Klauenkupplung f; Kupplung f; Laufkatze f; Winde f
crack Riß m; Spalte f; Spalten n; Sprung m; cracken; kracken; verkracken
crack area Rißfläche f
crack arresting test Rißauffangversuch m
crack detector Rißprüfer m
cracked ammonia Ammoniakspaltgas n
cracked back Folge f von Querrissen auf gezogenem Draht
cracked edges rissige Kanten fpl
cracked gas Spaltgas n
cracker Brechwalze f
crack expansion Rißaufweitung f
crack growth velocity Rißausbreitungsgeschwindigkeit f
cracking Rißbildung f
cracking rate Rißgeschwindigkeit f; Wachstumsgeschwindigkeit f der Spannungsrisse
crack initiation Rißauslösung f; Rißbildung f; Rißentstehung f
crack opening Rißaufweitung f
crack pattern Rißmuster n
crack propagation Rißausbreitung f; Rißwachstum n
crack propagation calculation Rißwachstumsberechnung f

crack superficially anreißen (= Risse bekommen)
cracky rissig
cradle Ablage f (für Kaltstrang); Bündeltasche f; Gestell n; Hürde f; Wiege f
cramp Klammer f; klammern
crane Kran m
crane dent Beschädigung f durch Krantransport
crane driver Kranführer m
crane gear Krangetriebe n
crane hook Kranhaken m
crane-operated ladle Kranpfanne f
crane operator Kranführer m
crane rail Kranschiene f
crane travel safety device Kranfahrsicherung f
crane trolley Krankatze f
crank Kurbel f; kröpfen
cranking Kröpfen n; Verkröpfung f
crank pin Kurbelzapfen m
crank press Kurbelpresse f
crankshaft Kurbelwelle f; gekröpfte Kurbelwelle f
crater Sumpf m (Stranggießen)
cratering Auskolkung f; Kolkung f
cratering lip Kolklippe f
crawing shaft Förderschacht m
crawl operation Schleppbetrieb m
crazing Brandriß m (in Kokillen); Netzwerk n
creep Zeitdehnung f; fließen; kriechen
creep behaviour Dauerstandverhalten n; Kriechverhalten n
creep buckling test Knick-Dauerstandversuch m
creep characteristics Zeitdehnverhalten n
creep curve Zeit-Dehnungs-Kurve f
creep fracture Zeitstandbruch m
creeping Fließen n
creep limit Zeitdehngrenze f
creep rate Kriechgeschwindigkeit f
creep resistance Kriechwiderstand m
creep resistant steel warmfester Stahl m
creep rupture strength Dauerstandfestigkeit f; Zeitstandfestigkeit f

creep rupture test Dauerstandversuch *m*; Zeitstandversuch *m*
creep speed Kriechgeschwindigkeit *f*
creep strength depending on time Zeitstandfestigkeit *f*
creep strength testing plant Zeitstandprüfanlage *f*
creep strength testing rig Zeitstandprüfanlage *f*
creep test Dauerstandversuch *m*; Zeitstandversuch *m*
creep-time-diagram Zeit-Dehnungs-Schaubild *n*
crest Gewindespitze *f*
crest line Hüllinie *f*
crevice corrosion Spaltkorrosion *f*
crevice corrosion at contact Berührungskorrosion *f*
crew Arbeitsgruppe *f*; Besatzung *f*; Mannschaft *f*
crimped leather Ledermanschette *f*
crimping Walzrunden *n*
crimping machine Krippmaschine *f* (für das Drahtweben)
crinkle falten; knicken
critical cooling rate kritischer Abkühlungsverlauf *m*
critical grain growth kritisches Kornwachstum *n*
critical point Haltepunkt *m*; Umwandlungspunkt *m*
critical range kritisches Feld *n*
critical shear stress kritische Schubspannung *f*
crocodile skin Netzwerk *n*
crop Blockende *n*; abschneiden; abschopfen; schopfen
crop coal Kohle *f* minderwertige
crop end Schopfende *n*; abgeschnittenes Ende *n*
crop-loss Schopfverlust *m*
cropping tool Abschneidstempel *m* (Umformen)
crop shears Endenschere *f*; Schopfschere *f*
cross break Querbruch *m* (auf Feinblech)
cross classification Mehrfachauftei- lung *f*
cross-country mill Zickzacktrio *n*
crossed nicols gekreuzte Nicols *pl*
cross flow heat exchanger Kreuzstrom-Wärmeaustauscher *m*
cross folding test Querfaltversuch *m*
cross-girder Querträger *m*
cross head Querhaupt *m*
crossing Kreuzung *f*; Schränken *n* (Walzen)
cross joint Kreuzungsstoß *m*
cross recessed screw Kreuzschlitzschraube *f*
cross roll friemeln
cross rolling Querwalzen *n*
cross rolling mill Schrägwalzwerk *n*
cross rolling of shapes Profil-Querwalzen *n*
cross-roll straightening machine Schrägrollen-Richtmaschine *f*
cross section Querschnitt *m*; Schliff *m*
cross sectional area Querschnittsfläche *f*
cross slip Quergleiten *n*
cross supports Querverankerung *f*
cross tabulation mehrfach gegliederte Tabelle *f*
crowd vollstopfen; überfüllen
crown Balligkeit *f*; Bombierung *f* (Blech); Preßkopf *m*; Wölbung *f*
crown bow Bombierung *f*
crown control Balligkeitssteuerung *f*
crucible Tiegel *m*
crucible furnace Muldenofen *m*; Tiegelofen *m*
crucible steel Tiegelstahl *m*
crude roh
crude gas ungereinigtes Gas *n*
crude gas off-take Rohgasabzug *m*
crude iron runout Roheisenabstich *m* (Roheisenabfluß)
crude oil processing plant Rohölverarbeitungsbetrieb *m*
crude ore Fördererz *n*; Roherz *n*
crude phenol tank Rohphenolbehälter *m*
crude steel Rohstahl *m*
crude steel weight (CSW) Rohstahl-

crude tar tank Rohteerbehälter *m*
crude zinc Hüttenrohzink *n*
crumbly bröckelig
crush brechen; mahlen; zerkleinern
crushable metal insertion zusammendrückbare Metalleinlage *f*
crushed coke Breckkoks *m*
crusher Brecher *m*; Stachelwalze *f*
crusher ball Mahlkörper *m*
crusher roll Brechwalze *f*
crushing Quetschung *f*; Zerkleinerung *f*
crushing plant Brechanlage *f* (Erzaufbereitung); Mahlanlage *f*
crushing strength Druckfestigkeit *f*
crushing test Druckversuch *m*
crushing yield point Quetschgrenze *f*
cryogenic steel kaltzäher Stahl *m*
cryogenic steel casting kaltzäher Stahlguß *m*
cryogenic strength Kältebeständigkeit *f*
crystal grain Kristallkorn *n*
crystal growth Kristallwachstum *n*
crystal lattice Kristallgitter *n*
crystalline kristallin
crystalline fracture kristalliner Bruch *m*
crystallisation Kristallbildung *f*; Kristallisation *f*
crystal orientation Kristallorientierung *f*
crystal recovery Kristallerholung *f*
crystal segregation Kristallseigerung *f*
crystal structure Kristallstruktur *f*
cube diagonal Raumdiagonale *f*; Raumdiagonale *f* des Würfels
cube edge Würfelkante *f*
cube face Würfelfläche *f*
cube face diagonal Flächendiagonale *f* des Elementarwürfels
cube mixer Würfelmischer *m*
cubic body centered lattice kubischraumzentriertes Gitter *n*
cubic content Rauminhalt *m*
cubic face centered lattice kubischflächenzentriertes Gitter *n*
cumulant Summenwert *m*; gehäufter Wert *m*
cumulating curve Summenkurve *f*
cumulative load curve Leistungssummenkurve *f*
cumulative value gehäufter Wert *m*
cup Näpfchen *n* (Tiefzug); Schale *f*; hohlziehen; tiefziehen
cup and cone arrangement Gichtverschluß *m*
cup-and-cone fracture Becherbruch *m*
cup base fracture Bodenreißer *m*
cup leather Ledermanschette *f*
cupola [furnace] Kupolofen *m*
cupping Becherbruch *m*; Höhlung *f*; Reißkegelbildung *f* (bei Draht); Tiefziehen *n* (von Näpfchen)
cupping index Erichsen-Tiefung *f*
cupping process Tiefziehverfahren *n*
cupping test Napfziehversuch *m*; Tiefungsversuch *m*
cupping test machine Tiefungsprüfmaschine *f*
cupping test with clamped blanks Tiefungsversuch *m* nach Erichsen mit fest eingespannter Probe
cup spring Tellerfeder *f*
cup wall fracture Zargenreißer *m*
curing Einbrennen *n*; Härten *n*
curl kräuseln
curling Einrollen *n*; Rollbiegen *n*; Rollbiegen *n* (Blechumformen)
curling by spinning Randeinrollen *n* durch Drücken
currency Währung *f*
current Strom *m*
current assets Umlaufvermögen *n*
current collector Stromabnehmer *m*
current consumption Stromverbrauch *m*
current density Stromdichte *f*
current financial strength Liquidität *f*
current from external source (corrosion) Fremdstrom *m*
current liabilities kurzfristige Verbindlichkeiten *fpl*
current meter Strömungsmesser *m*

current supply Stromversorgung f
current transformer Stromwandler m
current yield Stromausbeute f
curtaining Überwallung f (Oberflächenfehler)
curtaining (surface defect) Blockschale f
curtain wall plate Bekleidungsblech n
curtain wall sheet Bekleidungsblech n
curvature Krümmung f
curve Kurve f; Linie f
curved bogenförmig
curved groove ausgerundetes Kaliber n
curved mould gebogene Kokille f
curved mould casting machine Bogengießanlage f
curved mould continuous casting machine Bogengießanlage f; Bogenstranggießanlage f; Stranggießkreisbogenanlage f mit gebogener Kokille
curved roller table Kurvenrollgang m
curved teeth coupling Bogenzahnkupplung f
curve fitting Anpassen n von Kurven; Kurvenanpassung f
curve template Kurvenlineal n
curvilinear gekrümmt
curvilinear correlation nichtlineare Korrelation f
customs tarif Zolltarif m
cut Gravur f; Schliff m; Schram m; abtrennen; fressen; fräsen; schneiden; schrämen; zerspanen
cut edge geschnittene Kante f
cut [in a die] Gravur f
cut length geschnittene Länge f
cutlery steel Messerstahl m
cutoff Schermesser n
cut off abscheren; wegfressen
cut-off devices (e. g.: valves) Absperrteile npl
cut off [die] Abschneidegesenk n
cut out ausschalten
cut out torque Abschaltmoment n
cuttability Schneidbarkeit f
cutter Fräser m; Messer n; Schneidstahl m
cutter blade Fräsermesser n
cutter head grinding machine Messerkopf-Schleifmaschine f
cutting Spanen n; Trennen n
cutting alloy Hartlegierung f
cutting blowpipe Schneidbrenner m
cutting capacity Spanleistung f
cutting compound Schneidöl n
cutting edge Schneide f; Schneidkante f; Schnittkante f; Werkzeugschneide f
cutting edge of hard metal Hartmetallschneide f
cutting edge temperature Schneidentemperatur f
cutting fluid emulsion Bohrölwasser n
cutting lip Schneidkante f; Schnittkante f; Werkzeugschneide f
cutting power Schneidhaltigkeit f; Schnittkraft f (beim Drehen)
cutting property Zerspanbarkeit f
cutting ratio Spanstauchung f
cutting speed Schnittgeschwindigkeit f
cutting to length Querschneiden n
cutting tool Drehstahl m; Schneidwerkzeug n; Schnittwerkzeug n
cutting tool endurance Schneidhaltigkeit f
cutting tool life Schneidhaltigkeit f
cutting tool steel Schneidstahl m
cutting torch Schneidbrenner m
cutting up Zerschneiden n
cut-to-length-line Querteilanlage f
cut up zerschneiden
cut-up line Zerteilanlage f
cut wire Drahtkorn n
CVN-toughness Kerbschlagzähigkeit f (ISO-V)
cyanide hardening Cyanbadhärten n
cyaniding Badcarbonitrieren n; Cyanbadhärten n
cycle Periode f (elektr.); Spiel n; pendeln
cycle annealing Pendelglühen n
cycle of charges Gichtenfolge f
cycles per second Perioden fpl je Se-

kunde
cyclic load Schwingbelastung f
cyclic stress Dauerschwingbeanspruchung f; Wechselbeanspruchung f
cyclone Windsichter m
cyclone dust catcher Windsichter m; Wirbler m
cyclone dust collector Drallabscheider m; Fliehkraft-Staubabscheider m
cyclone gas washer Wirbler m
cyclone separator Drallabscheider m
cylinder [roll] bearing Walzenlager n
cylinder trolley Flaschenwagen m
cylindrical grinding Rundschleifen n

D

dab abklatschen; betupfen
dabbed spout ausgekleideter Auslauf m
dabber Kernhaltestift m; Sandhaltestift m
damage Beschädigung f
damage caused by smoke Rauchschaden m
damaged edge beschädigte Kante f
damage precaution Schadensverhütung f
damp dämpfen; feucht
damp down dämmen
damped-down blast furnace gedämpfter Hochofen m
damper Luftschieber m; Register n; Schieber m
damping Dämpfung f (Schwingungskreis)
damping capacity Dämpfungsfähigkeit f
dancer roll Tänzerrolle f
dark field image Dunkelfeldaufnahme f
dashed line gestrichelte Kurve f
data Angaben fpl; Kennzahlen fpl; Meßwerte mpl; Unterlagen fpl
data access method Datenzugriffsmethode f
data acquisition Datenerfassung f
data bank Datenbank f
data base Datenbank f
data circuit-terminating equipment Datenübertragungseinrichtung f
data collection Datensammlung f; Meßwerterfassung f
data file Datei f
data file access module Datenzugriffsmodul n
data flow Datenfluß m
data logger Meßwertschreiber m
data logging Datenerfassung f
data processing Meßwertverarbeitung f
data processing system EDV-System n
data processing task Datenverarbeitungsaufgabe f
data recall Datenabruf m
data recording Datenaufschreibung f
data recovery Datenerfassung f
data storage Meßwertspeicherung f
data structure concept Datenstrukturierung f
data system adjusted application EDV-technische Anpassung f
data transfer Datenübertragung f
date granted Genehmigungsdatum n (Patent)
date of delivery Lieferfrist f
datum (pl.: data) Größe f (EDV)
daub beschmieren
day's pay Tagelohn m
day's wages Tagelohn m
day rates Tagelohn m
day shift Tagschicht f
DC-welding machine Gleichstromschweißmaschine f
DC-welding techniques Gleichstromschweißverfahren n
dead block Wickler m für Draht
dead burn totbrennen
dead burned dolomite Sinterdolomit m
dead burned magnesite Sintermagnesit m

dead cast wire coil Drahtring *m* ohne Spannungen aufgewickelt
dead-centre position Totlage *f*
dead-drawn wire biegungsfrei gezogener Draht *m*
deaden (flotation) passivieren
dead-flat eben
dead-head verlorener Kopf *m*
dead man toter Mann *m*
dead melt abstehen lassen (Schmelze)
dead room (free field condition) schalltoter Raum *m*
dead [soaking] pit ungeheizter Tiefofen *m*
dead soft totweich
dead soft annealing Totweichglühen *n*; Weichglühen *n*
dead stock Immobilien *fpl*
dead time Totzeit *f*
dead weight Eigengewicht *n*
debenzoling by cooler and heat exchanger Entbenzolung *f* mit Kühler und Wärmetauscher
debris Bergversatz *m*; Trümmer *pl*; Überbleibsel *n*
debt Forderung *f*
debts Schulden *fpl*
debur entgraten
deburring Abgraten *n*
deburring machine Abgratmaschine *f*
decalescence Dekaleszenz *f*
decanting of the strand Auswaschen des Stranges *n* (Strangguß)
decarburise entkohlen
decarburising effect Entkohlungswirkung *f*
decay Verfall *m*; Verminderung *f*; Zersetzung *f*; abklingen
decay constant Abklingkonstante *f* (innere Reibung)
dechroming Entchromen *n*
decline Abfall *m*; Abnahme *f*; Verminderung *f*
decoder Entschlüßler *m*
decompose auflösen; zerfallen; zerlegen; zersetzen
decomposition Abbau *m*; Zersetzung *f*

decomposition of water-vapour (corrosion) Wasserdampfspaltung *f*
decontamination Entgiftung *f*
decrease Abfall *m*; Abnahme *f*; Rückgang *m*; Verringerung *f*
decrement Abnahme *f*; Verminderung *f*

dedendum Zahnfuß *m*
deduct ableiten
deep cementing Tiefzementieren *n*
deep drawing Tiefziehen *n*; Tiefzug *m*
deep drawing grade Tiefziehgüte *f*
deep drawing property Tiefziehbarkeit *f*; Tiefziehfähigkeit *f*
deep drawing quality Tiefziehfähigkeit *f*; Ziehsorte *f*
deep drawing quality steel Tiefziehstahl *m*
deep drawing sheet Tiefziehblech *n*
deep drawing strip Tiefziehband *n*
deep etching Tiefätzen *n*
deep mine Tiefbau *m* (Bergwerk)
deep penetration welding Tiefeinbrandschweißen *n*
deep pierce im Gesenk *n* hohlschmieden
deep webbed hochstegig
defect Fehler *m*; Fehlstelle *f*; Mangel *m*
defect arising in annealing (ingots) Glühfehler *m*
defect depth Halbwertsbreite *f*
defect echo Fehlerecho *n*
defect electron Defektelektron *n*
defective fehlerhaft
defects detecting device Fehlerprüfgerät *n*
deferred assets transitorische Aktiva *npl*
deferred items transitorische Rechnungsposten *mpl*
deferred liabilities transitorische Passiva *npl*
deficiency Mangel *m*
deficiency of gas Gasmangel *m*
deflection Ausschlag *m* (Ultraschall); Durchbiegung *f* (elastisch)

deflection indicator Durchbiegungsmesser *m*
deflection of the rolls Walzendurchbiegung *f*
deflector plate Leitblech *n*
deflector table Abwurftisch *m* (Sinter)
deform umformen; verformen
deformability Formänderungsvermögen *n*
deformation Formänderung *f*; Umformen *n*; Verformung *f*
deformation at low temperatures Kaltverformung *f*
deformation due to hardening Härteverzug *m*
deformation rate Umformgeschwindigkeit *f*
deformation resistance Formänderungswiderstand *m*
deformation work Formänderungsarbeit *f*
deformed membrane-type shut-off valve Scheibenmembranventil *n*
degas entgasen
degasify entgasen
degassing Entgasung *f* (von Schmelzen)
degenerate pearlite entarteter Perlit *m*
degeneration Zerfall *m*
degradation test Zerfallsprüfung *f*
degrease entfetten
degreasing Entfettung *f*
degreasing agent Entfettungsmittel *n*
degree Grad *m*; Maß *n*
degree of chemical utilisation of gas Gasausnutzung *f*
degree of disorder Fehlordnungsgrad *m*
degree of dissociation Dissoziationsgrad *m*
degree of dust extraction Entstaubungsgrad *m*
degree of dust removal Entstaubungsgrad *m*
degree of freedom from coarse non-metallic inclusions makroskopischer Reinheitsgrad *m*

degree of grain coarsening Körnung *f*
degree of inflammability Pyrophorität *f*
degree of purity Reinheitsgrad *m*
degree of sealing Dichtigkeit *f* (Ofen)
degree of shrinkage Schwindmaß *n*
delay Störung *f*; Verzögerung *f*; verzögern
delayed martensitic hardening Warmbadhärten *n*
delaying the sintering process sinterungshemmend
deliver abliefern
delivery Ablieferung *f*; Auslaß *m*; Beförderung *f*; Fördermenge *f* (Pumpe); Lieferung *f*
delivery beam Austrittsbalken *m*
delivery guide Ausführmeißel *m*
delivery pipe Auslaufrohr *n*
delivery promise Liefertermin *m*
delivery roller table Abfuhrrollgang *m*; Auslaufrollgang *m*
delivery side of roll gap Walzspaltaustritt *m*
delivery side (of rolls) Auslaufseite *f* (der Walzen)
delivery speed Austrittsgeschwindigkeit *f*
delta connection Dreieckschaltpunkt *m*
delta-gamma transformation Delta-Gamma-Umwandlung *f*
delta iron Delta-Eisen *n*
delta solid solution Delta-Mischkristall *m*
demagnetising Entmagnetisieren *n*
demolition scrap Abbruchschrott *m*
demurrage Liegegeld *n*
dendrite Dendrit *m*
dendrite arm spacing Dendritenarmabstand *m*
dendritic dendritisch
dendritic zone Dendritenstrukturzone *f*
denitriding Denitrieren *n*
denominator Nenner *m*
dense dicht
dense medium Schwertrübe *f*
densener Verdichtungseinlage *f*

dense smoke Qualm *m*
density Dichte *f*
density defect Dichtenfehler *m*
density exposure curve (spectrum analysis) Schwärzungskurve *f*
density ratio Raumerfüllung *f*
dent Beule *f*
de-oil entölen
deoxidant Desoxidationsmittel *n*
deoxidation alloy Desoxidationslegierung *f*
deoxidise desoxidieren
deoxidiser Desoxidationsmittel *n*
deoxidising agent Desoxidationsmittel *n*
deoxidising slag Desoxidationsschlacke *f*
deoxidize beruhigen; feinen
deoxidizing Beruhigung *f*
departmental manager Abteilungsleiter *m*; Betriebsleiter *m*
departure Abweichung *f*
dependence Abhängigkeit *f*
dependent on abhängig von
dependent variable abhängige Veränderliche *f*
dephosphorisation Entphosphorung *f*
depleted zone verdünnte Zone *f*
deposit Flöz *n*; Lager *n*; Lagerstätte *f*; Niederschlag *m*; abscheiden; absetzen; auftragen; niederschlagen
deposit attack Belagskorrosion *f*
deposit metal Auftragsmetall *n*
deposit (of contaminants) Ablagerung *f* (von Schadstoffen)
deposit welding Auftragschweißung *f*
depot Materiallagerplatz *m*
depreciation Abschreibung *f*; Wertminderung *f*
depreciation allocation kalkulatorische Abschreibung *f*
depressing table (up-cut shear) Wippe *f*
depression Unterdruck *m*; Vertiefung *f*
depth Tiefe *f*
depth indication Tiefung *f*
depth of case Härtetiefe *f*

depth of chill Abschrecktiefe *f*; Härtetiefe *f*
depth of cut Spandicke *f*
depth of electrode immersion Elektrodeneintauchtiefe *f*
depth of nitration Nitrierhärtetiefe *f*
depth of penetration Einbrandtiefe *f*; Eindringtiefe *f*
depth of roughness Rauhtiefe *f*
depth of the hearth Herdtiefe *f*
depth of web Steghöhe *f*
derivation Ableitung *f*
derivation action time Vorhaltezeit *f*
derivative Nebenerzeugnis *n*; abgeleitet; abgeleiteter Wert *m*
derivative action Vorhalt *m*
derive ableiten
derust entrosten
derusting agent Entrostungsmittel *n*
desalinated water entsalztes Wasser *n*
desalination Entsalzen *n* (Meerwasser)
desalting Entsalzen *n*
descale entzundern (bei Blöcken)
descale (in acid) dekapieren
descaling Entzunderung *f*
descaling mill Zunderbrechgerüst *n*
descaling plant Entzunderungsanlage *f*
descaling sprays Zunderabspritzvorrichtung *f*; Zunderwäscher *m*
descent of charge Absenken *n* der Gicht (Hochofen)
deseam Flämmputzen *n*; brennputzen; putzen (Blöcke)
design Bauart *f*; Entwurf *m*; Gestaltung *f*; Konstruktion *f*
design curve Gestaltungskurve *f*
designer Konstrukteur *m*
design of an experiment Anlage *f* eines Versuches
design [of an experiment] Versuchsplan *m*
design roll passes kalibrieren
desiliconize entsilicieren
desired value Sollwert *m*
deslag abschlacken; entschlacken

deslagging agent Entschlackungsmittel *n*
deslime entschlämmen
desorption Desorption *f*
despatch department Versandhalle *f*
destroy zerstören
destructive testing zerstörende Werkstoffprüfung *f*
desulphurisation Entschwefelung *f*
desulphurisation agent Entschwefelungsmittel *n*
desulphurisation of pressure gas Druckgasentschwefelung *f*
desulphurisation plant Entschwefelungsanlage *f*
detach ablösen; abnehmen; abschalten
detachable abnehmbar; lösbar
detaching mill Lösewalzwerk *n*
detail Einzelheit *f*
detarring plant Entteerungsanlage *f*; Entteerungsanlage *f*
detecting element Meßfühler *m*
detergent Reinigungsmittel *n*
deteriorating schädigend; schädlich
determination Bestimmung *f*; Prüfung *f*
determination of actual size Ist-Messen *n*
determination of iron Eisenbestimmung *f*
determination of total iron Gesamteisenbestimmung *f*
determine bestimmen; feststellen; prüfen
detoxication Entgiftung *f*
development of gas Gasentwicklung *f*
deviance Abweichungssumme *f*; Summe *f* der Abweichungsquadrate
deviate abweichen
deviation Abweichung *f*; Regelabweichung *f*
device Einrichtung *f*; Entwurf *m*; Gerät *n*; Mittel *n*; Plan *m*; Vorrichtung *f*
dewater entwässern
dewatering Entwässerung *f*
dewax entfetten
dewax (powder met.) abbrennen

dew point Taupunkt *m*
dew point hygrometer Taupunktmeßgerät *n*
dewpoint recorder Feuchtigkeitsmeßgerät *n*
dezincification Entzinkung *f*
diagram Schaubild *n*
dial error Ablesefehler *m*
dialogue program generator Dialogprogrammgenerator *m*
diameter Dicke *f*; Weite *f*
diameter of bore Bohrung *f*; Lochdurchmesser *m*
diameter of wire Drahtdurchmesser *m*
di-ammonium sulphate Ammoniumsulfat *n*
diamond Spießkant *m*
diamond bearing alloy Diamantmetallegierung *f*
diamond cone Diamantkegel *m*
diamond drawing die Diamantziehstein *m*
diamond knurling Kordeln *n*
diamond pass Rautenkaliber *n*
diamond pyramid hardness number Vickershärte *f*
diaphragm Blende *f*; Staurand *m*; Stauscheibe *f*
diaphragm measurement Messung *f* mit Staurand
dicalcium ferrite Dicalciumferrit *m*
dicalcium silicate Dicalciumsilicat *n*
die Düse *f*; Lochstempel *m*; Matrize *f*; Preßdüse *f*; Preßform *f*; Schnittwerkzeug *n*; Stempel *m*; Ziehdüse *f*; Zieheisen *n*; Ziehtrichter *m*
die angle Büchsenwinkel *m* (Fließpressen)
die aperture Düsenöffnung *f*
die approach angle Düseneintrittswinkel *m*; Düsenwinkel *m*
die beading Gesenksicken *n*
die bending Gesenkbiegen *n*
die [block] Gesenk *n*
die block Matrizenblock *m*
die body Preßformgehäuse *n*
die bolster Matrizenmantel *m*

die casting Dauerform-Gußstück *n*; Dauerformguß *m*; Druckguß *m*; Kokillenguß *m*; Preßguß *m*; Stempelguß *m*
die channel Düsenkanal *m*
die channel surface Düsenwand *f*
die entrance Düseneinlauf *m*
die entrance angle Düseneintrittswinkel *m*
die exit Düsenausgang *m*; Düsenauslauf *m*
die fill Füllhöhe *f*
die flanging Gesenkbördeln *n*
die forging Gesenkschmieden *n*
die formed part Gesenkschmiedestück *n*
die forming Gesenkformen *n*
die forming by drawing Formstanzen *n*; Formziehen *n* im Gesenk; Gesenkziehen *n*
die forming with partly enclosed work Gesenkformen *n* mit teilweise geschlossenem Werkstück *n*
die heading Kopfanstauchen *n* im Gesenk
die hobbing Einsenken *n*
die holder Düsenhalter *m*; Fassung *f* (bei Ziehsteinen); Zieheisenhalter *m*
dielectric coefficient Dielektrizitätskonstante *f*
die lining Preßformauskleidung *f*
die load meter Zugkraftmesser *m*
die mark Ziehriefe *f*
die mouth Düseneinlauf *m*; Düseneintritt *m*; Holeintritt *m*
die plate Ziehdüse *f*; Zieheisen *n*
die pressing Warmpressen *n*
die reduction zone Düsenarbeitsfläche *f*
die ring Matrizenarmierung *f* (Fließpressen)
die rolling periodisches Walzen *n* (im Gesenk)
die scar Ziehriefe *f*
die scratch Ziehriefe *f*
diesel engine Dieselmotor *m*
die set Preßwerkzeug *n*; Säulenführungsgestell *n* (Feinstanzen)
die shape Düsenform *f*
die sinking Gravieren *n*
die squeezing Gesenkdrücken *n*
die steel Matrizenstahl *m*
die straightening Gesenkrichten *n*
die tonnage Düsenleistung *f*
die typing press Kalteinsenkpresse *f*
die upsetting Gesenkstauchen *n*
die wall Düsenwand *f*
die wall taper Düsenwand-Neigungswinkel *m*
die working zone Düsenarbeitsfläche *f*
difference Abweichung *f*; Differenz *f*; Unterschied *m*
differential flame photometry Differential-Flammenphotometrie *f*
differential gear Ausgleichgetriebe *n*
differentially coated tinplate differenzverzinntes Weißblech *n*
differential pressure Differenzdruck *m*
differential thermal analysis Differentialthermoanalyse *f* (DTA)
diffraction Beugung *f*
diffraction pattern Rückstrahlaufnahme *f*
diffractometer Diffraktometer *n*
diffuse diffundieren
diffusion Diffusion *f*
diffusion coating Diffusionsverfahren *n* für Metallüberzüge
diffusion coefficient Diffusionskoeffizient *m*
diffusion welding Diffusionsschweißen *n*
digit Zahlzeichen *n*; Ziffer *f*
digital computer Digitalrechner *m*
digital data processing digitale Informationsverarbeitung *f*
digital data storage digitale Datenspeicherung *f*
digital display Digitalanzeige *f*
digital input unit Digitaleingabe-Einheit *f*
digitally operating installation digital arbeitende Anlage *f*
digital output unit Digitalausgabe-Ein-

heit f
digital state digitaler Zustand m
dilatation Ausdehnung f; Dehnung f; Wärmedehnung f
dilute verdünnen
dilute solution Lösung f (dissoziierte); verdünnte Lösung f
dimension Abmessung f; Maß n
dimensional accuracy Maßgenauigkeit f; Maßhaltigkeit f
dimensional variation Maßabweichung f
dimensioning Bemessung f
dimensioning basis Bemessungsgrundlage f
dimensionless parameter dimensionslose Kennzahl f
dimension to which a material is constrained by shrinkage forces Schrumpfmaß n
diminish abklingen; vermindern
dimpled fracture Grübchenbruch m; Wabenbruch m
dinas brick Dinasstein m
ding Beule f
dip eintauchen
dip brazing Tauchlöten n
dip coating with aluminium Tauchaluminieren n
dipole moment Dipolmoment n
dipped electrode Tauchelektrode f
direct unmittelbar
direct casting Fallendgießen n
direct-contact mechanism Wälzhebelgetriebe n
direct-current arc plasma jet excitation source Gleichstrom-Plasmabogen-Generator m
direct current (D.C.) Gleichstrom m
direct current motor Gleichstrommotor m
direct extrusion of rods Voll-Vorwärts-Strangpressen n
direct hardening Direkthärten n
direct impact extrusion of rods Voll-Vorwärts-Fließpressen n
direction Leitung f; Richtung f
directionality Richtungsabhängigkeit f

directional solidification gerichtete Erstarrung f
direction of rolling Walzrichtung f
direction of the fiber Walzrichtung f
directivity factor Richtwirkung f
director Leiter m
direct process for the production of wrought iron Erzfrischverfahren n; Rennverfahren n
direct reduction Direktreduktion f
direct strand reduction Gießwalzen n; Strangquerschnitts-Direktreduktion f
direct teem fallend; fallend [ver]gießen
direct tubular impact extrusion Hohl-Vorwärts-Fließpressen n
dirty sheet verschmutztes Blech n
dirty water Schmutzwasser n
disappearance of network pattern Netzzerfall m
disappearing filament optical pyrometer (D.F.) Glühfaden-Pyrometer n
disc Scheibe f
discard Abfall m; Ausschuß m; Entfall m
disc brake Scheibenbremse f
disc clutch Lamellenreibungskupplung f
disc for recorder Diagrammscheibe f
discharge Abgänge mpl; Ablaß m; Ausfluß m; Ausguß m; Auslaß m; Ausstoß m (Gas); Austrag m; Auswurf m; Entlassung f; ablassen; abschütten; ausfließen; austragen; entkuppeln; entladen; entlassen; löschen
discharge duct Abzugsrohr n
discharge (or: release) of gas from the coke ovens Gasaustritt m aus den Koksöfen m
discharge pipe Abflußrohr n
discharge plough Austragschieber m
discharging end of furnace Ziehherd m
disc memory Plattenspeicher m (EDV)
disconnect abkuppeln; ausrücken; ausschalten

disconnecting switch Trennschalter *m*
discontinuity Auftrennung *f*; Lockerstelle *f*; Werkstofftrennung *f*; gelokkerte Stelle *f* (Gefüge)
discontinuous chain type of carbide precipitation perlenschnurartige Carbidausscheidung *f*
discontinuous chip Reißspan *m*
disc piercer Scheiben-Lochwalzwerk *n*
discrepancy in weight Gewichtsabweichung *f*
discrete variable unstetige Veränderliche *f*
discriminatory analysis of variance Trennverfahren *f*
disc roll Scheibenwalze *f*; Walzscheibe *f*
disc-spring column Tellerfedersäule *f*
disc store Magnetplattenspeicher *m*
disc type cooling bed Scheibenrollen-Kühlbett *n*
discussion Diskussion *f*; Erörterung *f*
disc wheel Scheibenrad *n*
disc wheel rolling mill Scheibenrad-Walzwerk *n*
disengage auslösen; ausrücken; entkuppeln
disengagement point Ausklinkpunkt *m*
disequilibrium Ungleichgewicht *n*
dish einbeulen, einbuchten; kümpeln; vertiefen
dished head Kesselboden *m*; Preßboden *m*; gekümpelter Kesselboden *m*; gewölbter Kesselboden *m*
dished products Kümpelerzeugnisse *npl*
dishing Kümpeln *n*
dishing press Kümpelpresse *f*
disintegrate zerfallen
disintegrating slag Zerfallschlacke *f*
disintegration Zerfall *m*; Zerkleinerung *f*
disintegration test Zerfallsprüfung *f*
disintegrator Desintegrator *m*
dislocation Versetzung *f*
dislocations of opposite sign ungleichnamige Versetzungen *fpl*

dismantle abbrechen; ausbauen; demontieren
dismantling Abbrucharbeiten *fpl*; Demontage *f*
dismembering Zerlegen *n*
disordered alloy fehlgeordnete Legierung *f*
disorder (structure) Fehlordnung *f*
dispatch Kommissionierung *f*; Versand *m*
dispatching Lastverteilung *f* (Strom)
dispatch warehouse Kommissionierungslager *n*
dispenser Druckförderer *m*
dispersing agent Dispersionsmittel *n*
dispersion Einlagerung *f*; Streuung *f*
dispersion hardening Dispersionshärten *n*
dispersion kneader Dispersionskneter *m*
displace verschieben
displaceable verfahrbar; verschiebbar
displaced segregation verlagerte Seigerung *f*
displacement by shear parallel to adjacent surfaces Verschieben *n*
display (computer) Anzeige *f*
disposable head Aufsteckkopf *m* (Thermoelement)
disposal Absatz *m*
dissection Zerlegung *f*
dissociate zerfallen; zersetzen
dissociated dislocation aufgespaltene Versetzung *f*
dissociation Zersetzung *f*
dissolution Auflösung *f*; Lösung *f*
dissolve auflösen; lösen
distance Strecke *f*; Weg *m*
distance between supports Auflagerentfernung *f*
distance over which stopper is moved to control teeming rate Verstellweg *m* der Stopfenstange
distill destillieren
distillate fuel Benzin *n*
distillation Destillation *f*
distort verziehen; werfen

distortion Verwerfung *f*; Verziehen *n*; Verzug *m*
distortion due to hardening Härteverzug *m*
distortion fault Verwerfung *f*
distortion wedge Zipfel *m*
distribute schütten (Hochofen); verteilen
distributing bell Verteilerglocke *f*
distributing plant Schaltanlage *f*
distribution Verteilung *f*
distribution coefficient Verteilungskoeffizient *m*
distribution of voids Lückengradverteilung *f*
distribution plant for electric current elektrische Verteileranlage *f*
distribution system Vertriebssystem *n*
district heating plant Fernheizungsanlage *f*
disturbance Störgröße *f*; Störung *f*
disturbance feed forward Störgrößenaufschaltung *f*
disturbed structure gestörtes Gefüge *n*
disturbing wave Störschwingung *f*
ditch Graben *n*
diverge abweichen (= unterscheiden)
divergence Divergenz *f*
divide teilen; verteilen; zerteilen
dividing shears Teilschere *f*
dog Anschlag *m*; Knagge *f*
dog-bar type conveyor Daumenschlepper *m*; Knaggenschlepper *m*
dogging crane Zangenkran *m*
dog leg mechanische Oberflächenbeschädigung *f*
dogs Zange *f*
dog spike Schienennagel *m*
dog-type bed Klinkenbett *n*
dole Arbeitslosenunterstützung *f*
dolly bar Gegenhalter *m* (beim Nieten)
dolomite Dolomit *m*
dolomite brick Dolomitstein *m*
dolomite brick press Dolomitsteinpresse *f*

dolomite calcining kiln Dolomitbrennofen *m*
dolomite centrifuging machine Dolomit-Schleudermaschine *f*
dolomite plant Dolomitanlage *f*
dolomitic lime[stone] dolomitischer Kalk *m*
domain structure Bereichstruktur *f* (Kristall)
dome Kuppel *f*; Kuppelgewölbe *n*
dome-shaped kalottenförmig
dome temperature Kuppeltemperatur *f*
donkey arms Aufgabeapparat *m*
door Klappe *f*; Tür *f*
door cooling frame Türkühlrahmen *m*
door jamb Türpfeiler *m*
door lining Türausmauerung *f*
door winch Türhebevorrichtung *f* (beim Ofen)
dope dotieren
doping material kristallwachstumshemmender Zusatz *m*
dore Kern *m*
dotscanning method Punktrasterverfahren *n*
dotted line gepunktete Kurve *f*
dotted line recorder Punktschreiber *m*
double doppeln; falten
double action pressing beidseitiges Pressen *n*
double-block drawing machine Doppelscheiben-Ziehmaschine *f*
double cold reducing mill Doppelreduzierstraße *f*
double column press Zweisäulen-Presse *f*
double disc wedge valve Doppelplattenkeilschieber *m* (Winderhitzer)
double draw Dopplung *f*
double-duo Doppelduowalzwerk *n*
double fillet weld Kehlnaht *f*; zweiseitige Kehlnaht[schweiß] *f*
double-flanged joint Bördelnaht *f*
double galvanising Doppelverzinken *n*
double handle [crutch] Traggabel *f*
double hardening Doppelhärten *n*

double head pay-off reel Doppelkopf-Ablaufhaspel f

double press[ing] technique Doppelpreßtechnik f

doubler Doppler m

doubles paarweise gewalzte Bleche npl

double skin (surface defect) Blockschale f; Überwalzung f

double-standard shear Zweiständerschere f

double-tailed test Prüfen n nach beiden Ausläufern der Prüfverteilung

double teem (surface defect) Absatz m

double tempering Doppelanlassen n

double two-high mill Doppelduowalzwerk n

double-vee butt welded specimen X-Naht geschweißte Probe f

double walking beam furnaces Gleichschrittöfen mpl

dovetail (joint between dummy bar and dummy bar head) Schwalbenschwanz m

dowel Dübel m

downcomer Fallrohr n; Gasabfang m; Gasabzug m; Gasfang m; Gichtgasabzugsrohr n; geneigter Hochofen m

downcut milling Gleichlauffräsen n

down draft Saugzug m

down draft sintering Saugzugsinterung f

down gate Eingußtrichter m; Gießtrichter m

down-hill teem fallend [ver]gießen

downpipe Fallrohr n

down spout Auslauf m; Schurre f

downtake Abzugsrohrleitung f; Gichtgasabzug m; Zug m

downtime Ausfallzeit f; Nebenzeit f

dozzle Blockaufsatz m; Gießaufsatz m; Speisekopf m (Block); verlorener Kopf m

dozzle feeder [head] verlorener Kopf m

draft Abnahme f (je Stich); Anzug m (Kaliber); Kaliberdruck m; Schräge f; Walzdruck m; Zugluft f

draft regulating damper Zugregler m

drag bremsen; hemmen; schleppen; ziehen

drag bar Zughaken m

drag distance Tragweg m

drag-line excavator Greifbagger m

drag-link mechanism Doppelkurbel f

drag over Schlepper m (Walzen); überheben

drag reel Bremshaspel f

drag roll Schleppwalze f

drain Ablaß m; Ausguß m; abtropfen; entwässern

drainage pipe Entwässerungsrohr n

draining of the strand Auswaschen des Stranges m (Strangguß)

draining plant Entwässerungsanlage f

draining pump Wasserhaltungspumpe f

drain [pipe] Abflußrohr n

draught Anzug m; Stichabnahme f; Verjüngung f; Zug m

draught ga[u]ge Reißbrett n; Zugmesser m

draught per pass Stichabnahme f

draught pressure Zugstärke f

draw Schrumpfriß m; Zug m; abheben; anlassen; recken; reißen; strecken; zeichnen; ziehen

drawability Ziehbarkeit f

draw bench with chains Kettenziehbank f

draw-die Ziehmatrize f

draw down abziehen

draw head Zieheisenkopf m

draw-hook Zughaken m

drawing Zeichnung f; Ziehen n

drawing bench Ziehbank f

drawing board Zeichenbrett n

drawing (by a sliding action) Gleitziehen n

drawing device Ausziehvorrichtung f

drawing die Ziehring m

drawing down properties Herunterzieh-Eigenschaften fpl

drawing engine Fördermaschine f;

Göpel *m*
drawing grade Tiefziehgüte *f*
drawing grease Ziehfett *n*
drawing hole Ziehhol *n*
drawing nozzle Ziehtrichter *m*
drawing of tubular bodies Hohl-Gleitziehen *n*
drawing over mandrel Dornziehen *n*
drawing pass Ziehhol *m*
drawing pen Ziehfeder *f*
drawing plant Zieherei *f*
drawing point Ziehangel *f*
drawing press Ziehpresse *f*
drawing punch Ziehstempel *m*
drawing quality Ziehfähigkeit *f*; Ziehgüte *f*
drawing shaft Förderschacht *m*
drawing sheet Ziehblech *n*
drawing stress Ziehkraft *f*; Zugkraft *f*
drawing tool Ziehwerkzeug *n*
drawing with roller dies Ziehwalzen *n*
drawn head Ziehkopf *m*
drawn-in scale Zunder *m*
drawn steel bar gezogener Stabstahl *m*
draw off ableiten; absaugen; abziehen
draw out herausziehen; recken; strekken
draw out switchgear design Schaltwagentechnik *f*
draw plate Ziehdüse *f*; Zieheisen *n*; Ziehlochplatte *f*
draw [up] a list Liste *f* aufstellen
draw with back pull Gegenzugziehen *n*
draw with back tension Gegenzugziehen *n*
dredger Bagger *m*
dredging slag Baggerschlacke *f*
dress abrichten; aufbereiten; dressieren; nachdrehen; putzen (Gußstücke)
dressed edges nachgearbeitete Kanten *fpl*
dressing Nacharbeiten *n*
dressing and straightening machine Adjustagemaschine *f*
dressing by flotation Schwimmaufbereitung *f*
dressing by magnetic separation Aufbereitung *f* durch magnetische Trennung
dressing by screening Aufbereitung *f* durch Absieben (Erz)
dressing by washing Aufbereitung *f* durch Auswaschen
dressing shop Putzerei *f*; Zurichterei *f*
DRI (=direct reduced iron) Eisenschwamm *m*
drift Dorn *m*
drift test Aufweitversuch *m*
drill bohren
drill-bit Drehbohrschneide *f*
driller Bohrer *m* (Facharbeiter)
drill hole Bohrloch *n*
drilling Bohren *n* (mit Spiralbohrer)
drilling machine Bohrmaschine *f*
drilling shaft Bohrwelle *f*
drillings sampler Bohrprobenehmer *m*
drill manufacture Bohrerherstellung *f*
drill pipe Gestängerohr *n*
drill steel Bohrstahl *m*
drill tube Bohrrohr *n*
drinking water Trinkwasser *n*
drip point Tropfpunkt *m* (Gewölbe)
drip point (arch) Tropfpunkt *m*
drive Getriebe *n*; treiben
driver Steuermann *m*; Treiberprogramm *n*
driver's compartment Führerstand *m*
driving Treiben *n*
driving band Führungsring *m*
driving elements Antriebselemente *npl*
driving gear Getriebe *n*
driving motor Antriebsmotor *m*
driving pinion Antriebsritzel *n*
driving power Antriebskraft *f*
driving roll Treibrolle *f*
driving shaft Antriebswelle *f*
drop Abnahme *f*; Fallbär *m*; Gefälle *n*; tropfen
drop bottom bucket Setzkübel *m*
drop bottom tub Setzkübel *m*

drop detachement method Tropfenabrißverfahren n
drop forge die Schmiedegesenk n
drop forging Gesenkschmieden n; Gesenkschmiedestück n
drop forging die steel Gesenkschmiedestahl m
drop forging press Gesenkschmiedepresse f
drop hammer Fallhammer m
drop hardness test Fallhärteprüfung f
drop in yield strength Streckgrenzenabfall m
drop of temperature Temperaturabfall m
dropping in Eintröpfelung f
drop plate-type moulding machine Absenkformmaschine f
drop press Fallhammer m
drop stamper Fallhammer m
drop stamping Preßling m
drop test Schlagprobe f; Schlagversuch m; Stoßprobe f
drop weight Fallbirne f
drop weight method Tropfengewichtsverfahren n
drop weight test Fallversuch m (DWT)
drop-weight trial Drop-Weight-Probe f
dross Abstrich m; Gekrätz n; Schaum m; Schlacke f; Zinkasche f
drum Kesselschuß m; Trommel f
drum-chart recorder Trommelschreiber m
drum for recorder Diagrammrolle f
drum memory Trommelspeicher m
drum of a boiler Kesselschuß m
drum store Trommelspeicher m
drum strength Trommelfestigkeit f
drum type furnace Trommelofen m
drum type kiln Drehtrommelofen m; Trommelofen m
drum type pickler Trommelbeize f
drum type retort furnace Tonnenretortenofen m
dry trocken; trocknen
dry and ash free (daf) wasser- und aschefrei (waf)
dry binder Trockenbinder m

dry burning coal Magerkohle f
dry cleaning Trockenreinigung f
dry cleaning of blast furnace gas Trockenreinigung f für Hochofengas
dry cooling Trockenlöschen n
dry cooling tower Trockenkühlturm m
dry dust catcher Trockenentstauber m
dry electric filter Trockenelektrofilter m
dry fritting mix Trockenfrittmasse f (ff.)
dry galvanising Trockenverzinkung f
dry gas filter Trockengasfilter m
dry grinding Trockenmahlung f
drying house Trockenkammer f
drying hurdle Hordentrockner m
drying of building Bautentrocknung f
drying oven Trockenofen m
drying plant Trockenanlage f; Trocknungsanlage f
dry magnetic dressing trockenmagnetische Aufbereitung f
dry nitriding Gasnitrieren n
dry puddling Trockenpuddeln n (im teigigen Zustand)
dry quenching Trockenlöschen n
dry-sand moulding Masseformerei f
dry strength Trockenfestigkeit f (Pellet)
dual-hearth furnace Doppelherdofen m
dual phase steel Dualphasenstahl m
duct Kanal m; Rinne f; Rohrleitung f; Röhre f
ductile bildsam; formbar; verformbar
ductile cast iron Gußeisen n mit Kugelgraphit
ductile fracture Zähbruch m; zäher Bruch m
ductile iron roll Walze f (Sphäroguß)
ductility Bildsamkeit f; Dehnbarkeit f; Geschmeidigkeit f; Plastizität f; Umformbarkeit f; Ziehbarkeit f
ductility at elevated temperatures Warmbildsamkeit f
dulled abgestumpft
dull finish matte Oberfläche f
dull-finish sheet Mattblech n
dummy Gesenkschmiederohling m

dummy bar Anfahrstrang m; Anfahrstück n; Kaltstrang m (Stranggießen)
dummy bar head Anfahrkopf m (Strangguß)
dummy pass Stauchstich m (bei Schienen); blindes Kaliber n
dummy roll Blindwalze f
dummy sheet Tragblech n; Unterlagsblech n
dump Abladeplatz m; Halde f; abkippen; kippen; schütten; stürzen
dump cart Kippwagen m
dump cinder car Schlackenkipppfanne f
dumper Abladeanlage f
dumping device (am.) Kippvorrichtung f
dumping of coking coal Kokskohlenentladung f
dumping [refuse] Deponie f
dump test Stauchversuch m
duplex[ing] process Duplexverfahren n
duplex steel Duplexstahl m
duplicate production Reihenherstellung f
durability Dauerhaftigkeit f; Haltbarkeit f
duralumin Duraluminium n
duration of burning Brenndauer f
duration of [s]melting Schmelzdauer f
dust catcher Entstauber m; Entstaubungsanlage f; Staubfänger m; Staubsack m; Windsichter m
dust-collecting machine Entstaubungsanlage f
dust content Staubgehalt m
dust deposit Staubablagerung f; Staubniederschlag m
dust deposit ga[u]ge Staubpegelwert m
dust evolving stauberzeugend
dust extraction Entstaubung f
dustfall Staubniederschlag m
dust layer Staubbelag m
dust level Staubpegelwert m
dust off entstauben

dust prevention measures Staubbekämpfung f
dust removal Entstaubung f
dust removing plant Entstaubungsanlage f
dust sampling Staubprobenahme f
dust separator Staubabscheider m
dust shield Staubschutz m
dust wetting plant Staubanfeuchter m
dusty staubförmig
dwell period Haltedauer f
dwell time Verweilzeit f
dye-penetrant farbdurchdringend
dynamic incremental shear loading zusätzliche dynamische Scherbelastung f
dynamic load dynamische Belastung f
dynamometer Kraftmeßglied n; Meßdose f

E

E.P. (= **extreme pressure**) Höchstdruck m
ear Zipfel m
earing Zipfelbildung f
early disability Frühinvalidität f
early shift Frühschicht f
ear protection Gehörschutz m
earth connection Erdschluß m; Erdung f
earthed kurzgeschlossen (Stromkreis)
earth fault Erdschluß m
earthing Erdung f
earth lead Erdungskabel n
earth leakage Erdschluß m
earthy ore Erz n mulmiges; erdiges Erz n
easily reducible ore leicht reduzierbares Erz n
easy-machining steel Automatenstahl m; Sonderstahl m leichter Zerspanbarkeit
ebullition Aufwallen n; Kochen n; Sieden n
eccentric abgesetzt (Welle)

eccentric bearing load außermittige Lagerlast f
eccentricity außermittige Lage f
eccentricity of the rolls Walzenschlag m
E-channel (channel iron) U-Eisen n
economic history Wirtschaftsgeschichte f
economic policy Wirtschaftspolitik f
economics calculation Wirtschaftlichkeitsrechnung f
Economic Union Wirtschaftsvereinigung f
economic zinc alloy Sparzinklegierung f
economiser Luftvorwärmer m; Vorwärmer m
economy Energie- und Stoffwirtschaft f
economy efficiency Wirtschaftlichkeit f
eddy current Wirbelstrom m
eddy current brake Wirbelstrombremse f
eddy diffusion Diffusion f bei turbulenter Strömung
eddy-mill powder Wirbelschlagpulver n
eddy nozzle Wirbeldüse f
edge Kante f; Rand m; Saum m; hochkant stellen; kanten; stauchen (Breite)
edge break Kantenriß m
edge dislocation Stufenversetzung f
edge mill Kollergang m
edge of a crack Rißausläufer m
edge positioner Bandkantensteuerung f
edge-quenching apparatus Randabschreckvorrichtung f
edger Rund- und Verteilgesenk n; Schienenflachstich m
edge rolling Rollbiegen n (Blechumformen)
edge runner Kollergang m
edge strength Kantenfestigkeit f
edge tearing Einreißen n der Kante
edge trimming Beschneiden von Kanten
edge wave Kantenwelle f (Kaltband)
edge waviness Randwelligkeit f (Band)
edging Beschneiden von Kanten (Band); Stauchen n (Breite)
edging pass Stauchkaliber n; Stauchstich m
effect Einwirkung f
effective acid Säuregrad m
effective coefficient of friction in the groove Kaliberreibungsbeiwert m
effective cutting angle Eckenwinkel m (Spanen)
effective [latent] heat of fusion Schmelzwärme f
effective length Fertiglänge f; Knicklänge f
effective resistance Wirkwiderstand m
effective stress Vergleichsspannung f
effective value Effektivwert m
effervescence Aufbrausen n; Aufwallen n; Schäumen n
effervescent steel steigender Stahl m; unberuhigter Stahl m
efficiency Brauchbarkeit f; Leistung f; Leistungsfähigkeit f; Leistungsgrad m; Wirksamkeit f; Wirkungsgrad m
efficiency factor Leistungsgrad m
efficient brauchbar; leistungsfähig; wirksam
effluent Auswurf m
effluent (of furnace) Abgänge mpl
effusiometer Gasdichtemesser m
eight-strand continuous casting machine Achtstrang-Gießmaschine f
eject ausheben; ausstoßen; auswerfen
ejector Auswerfer m
elastic deformation elastische Formänderung f
elastic energy of deformation elastische Formänderungsarbeit f
elastic limit Elastizitätsgrenze f
elastic modulus Elastizitätsmodul m
elastic recovery Erholung f; Rückdehnung f; Rückfederung f; Rückfede-

rungsdehnung f
elbow Kniestück n; Krümmer m
electrical conductivity elektrische Leitfähigkeit f
electrical engineering Elektrotechnik f
electrical field elektrisches Feld n
electrical machinery elektrische Maschinen fpl
electric[al] quality sheet Elektroblech n
electrical quality sheet Übertragerblech n
electrical quality steel weichmagnetischer Stahl m
electric arc Lichtbogen m
electric arc cutting Schmelzschneiden n
electric arc furnace Lichtbogenofen m elektrischer
electric arc melting Erschmelzung f im Lichtbogen
electric arc reduction furnace Elektroreduktionsofen m
electric circuit Stromnetz n
electric contact line Schleifleitung f
electric control elektrische Steuerung f
electric displacement elektrische Verschiebung f
electric door-lifting mechanism Türaufzugsvorrichtung f
electric driven tool Elektrowerkzeug n
electric field strength elektrische Feldstärke f
electric furnace Elektroofen m
electric furnace iron Elektroroheisen n
electric [furnace] steel Elektrostahl m
electric fusion welding Elektroschmelzschweißen n
electric heating elektrische Beheizung f
electric heating plant elektrische Beheizung f
electric hoist Elektrozug m
electrician Elektriker m; Elektromechaniker m

electric low shaft furnace Elektroniederschachtofen m
electric ore reduction furnace Elektroreduktionsofen m
electric overhead trolley Elektrohängebahn f
electric power house elektrische Zentrale f
electric pulley block Elektroflaschenzug m
electric rectifier Gleichrichter m
electric shaft furnace Elektrohochofen m
electric storage battery Akkumulator m; elektrische Batterie f
electric truck Elektrokarren m
electric turbo blower Elektroturbogebläse n
electric vehicle Elektrofahrzeug n
electrochemical mobility elektrochemische Beweglichkeit f
electrochemical potential elektrochemisches Potential n
electro-chemical series elektrochemische Spannungsreihe f
electro-chemical stripping elektrochemisches Ablösen n (Zinküberzug)
electrochemistry Elektrochemie f
electrocoating galvanisches Überziehen n
electrode Elektrode f
electrode arm Elektrodenarm m
electrode case Elektrodenköcher m
electrode consumption Elektrodenverbrauch m
electrode control system Elektrodenregelung f
electrode holder Elektrodenhalter m
electrode joining Elektrodenaufbau m
electrode joining and lifting nipple equipment Annippelvorrichtung f für Elektroden
electrodeposited nickel undercoat elektrolytische Nickelunterschicht f (bei Weißblech)
electrode-pressure cylinder Elektrodenkraftzylinder m
electrodes arranged in a circle Elektroden fpl kreisförmig angeordnet

electrode scrap Elektrodenbruch *m*
electrodes off-furnace assembling Elektrodenaufbau *m* neben dem Ofen
electrodes on-furnace assembling Elektrodenaufbau *m* auf dem Ofen
electrode waste Elektrodenbruch *m*
electrode with basic sheath kalkbasisch umhüllte Elektrode *f*
electro dry filter Elektro-Trockenfilter *m*
electro forming Elysieren *n*
electrogalvanised elektrolytisch verzinkt
electro [gas] filter Elektrofilter *m*
electro gas welding Elektrogasschweißen *n*
electrolysis Elektrolyse *f*
electrolytic polishing elektrolytisches Polieren *n*
electrolytic powder Elektrolytpulver *n*
electrolytic tinning elektrolytisches Verzinnen *n*
electrolytic tinplate elektrolytisch verzinntes Weißblech *n*
electromagnet Elektromagnet *m*
electromagnetic elektromagnetisch
electromagnetic counter current elektromagnetischer Gegenstrom *m*
electromagnetic inverse current elektromagnetischer Gegenstrom *m*
electromagnetic stirring of the bath induktive Badbewegung *f*; induktives Rühren der Schmelze *f*
electromotive force (EMF) elektromotorische Kraft *f* (EMK)
electron attenuation process Elektronendämpfungsverfahren *n*
electron beam cutting Elektronenstrahlschneiden *n*
electron beam melting process Elektronenstrahl-Schmelzverfahren *n*
electron beam welding Elektronenstrahlschweißen *n*
electron diffraction Elektronenbeugung *f*
electron emission microscope Emissions-Elektronenmikroskop *n*

electron gun Elektronenstrahler *m*
electron gun with built-in self-acceleration Elektronenkanone *f* mit Selbstbeschleunigung
electron gun with external acceleration Elektronenkanone *f* mit Fremdbeschleunigung
electronic computer Elektronenrechner *m*
electronic data processing Datenverarbeitung *f*; elektronische Datenverarbeitung *f*
electronic valve Elektronenröhre *f*
electron-micrograph elektronenmikroskopische Aufnahme *f*
electron microscope Elektronenmikroskop *n*
electron probe microanalysis Elektronenstrahl-Mikroanalyse *f*
electron shell Elektronenschale *f*
electrophoresis Elektrophorese *f*
electroplate elektroplattieren
electroplating elektrolytisches Veredeln *n*
electroslag refining (ESR) Elektroschlackeumschmelzen *n* (ESU)
electroslag remelting (ESR) Elektroschlackeumschmelzen *n* (ESU)
electro slag remelting (ESR) Elektroschlackeumschmelzverfahren *n* (ESU)
electro slag welding Elektroschlacke-Schweißen *n*
electrostatic precipitator Elektrofilter *m*
electrotechnics Elektrotechnik *f*
electrothermal elektrothermisch
electro thermal upsetting Elektroanstauchen *n*
element Glied *n*
elementary charge elektrische Elementarladung *f*
elementary substance Grundstoff *m*
elevated inclined chute Dachrutsche *f*; Hochlauf *m*
elevated road Hochstraße *f*
elevated tank Hochbehälter *m*
elevated temperature höhere Tem-

peratur f
elevating platform Hebebühne f
elevation Aufriß m; Aufsteigen n; Erhebung f
elevator (am.) Aufzug m; Hebevorrichtung f
elevator tee [guide] Aufzugführungsschiene f
elliptic spring Kegelfeder f
elongating Dehnen n
elongation Dehnung f, Längsstrecken n; Längsstreckung f, Verlängerung f
elongation after fracture Bruchdehnung f
elongation after fracture in creep rupture test Zeitstandbruchdehnung f
elongation rolling Reckwalzen n
elongation step Dehnungsstufe f
elongation with necking Einschnürdehnung f
elongation without necking Gleichmaßdehnung f
elucidation Aufklärung f; Erklärung f; Erläuterung f
elutriate schlämmen
elutriation Schlämmen n; Strömungssichten n (Pulvermet.)
embed einbetten
embossed sheet geprägtes Blech n
embossing Hohlprägen n; Prägung f
embrittle verspröden
embryo Keim m
emergency Notfall m
emergency brake Notbremse f
emergency power unit Notstromaggregat n
emery cloth Schmirgelleinen n
emery paper Sandpapier n; Schleifpapier n
EMF cell EMK-Sonde f
emf (cell voltage) EMK f (Zellspannung)
emission Ausstoß m (Gas); Auswurf m; Emission f
emission flame photometry Emissions-Flammenphotometrie f
emission of dust Staubauswurf m

emission (of furnace) Abgänge mpl
empirical probability Erfahrungswahrscheinlichkeit f; Wahrscheinlichkeit f
employee Angestellter m
employers' liability insurance association Berufsgenossenschaft f
employment bureau Arbeitsamt n
employment factor Beschäftigungsgrad m
emptiness Leere f
empty entladen; entleeren; leer
emulsion Emulsion f
enamel emaillieren
enamel[ing] oven Emaillierofen m
enameling sheet Emaillierblech n
encase einkapseln; ummanteln
enclosed resistance welding Kammerschweißen n
enclosure protective walls Konvertereinhausung f
encoder Verschlüßler m
end arch Ganzwölber m (ff. Stein); Wölbstein m
end arch brick Querwölber m
end burner Stirnbrenner m
end cutting edge Nebenschneide f
end dumping truck Hinterkipper m
end face Stirnseite f
ending machine Adjustagemaschine f
endothermic endotherm
end quench specimen Stirnabschreckprobe f
end reduction degree Reduktionsschöpfung f
end shears Schopfschere f
end squared senkrecht beschnittenes Rohrende n
end thrust Schub m; Seitendruck m
endurance limit Dauerfestigkeit f
endurance strength Dauerfestigkeit f; Wechselfestigkeit f
endurance test Dauerversuch m; Ermüdungsversuch m
endure aushalten; dauern
end wall Kopfwand f; Stirnwand f
energizer in carburizing Aufkohlungsbeschleuniger m

energy Arbeit *f*; Energie *f*
energy absorbed in fracturing Schlagarbeit *f*
energy consumption Energieverbrauch *m*
energy efficiency Arbeitswirkungsgrad *m*
energy expended Arbeitsaufwand *m*
energy flow Energiefluß *m*
energy manager Energiewirtschaftsingenieur *m*
energy source Energiequelle *f*
engine Lokomotive *f*
engineer in charge Betriebsingenieur *m*
engineering Bauwesen *n*
engineering castings Maschinenguß *m*
engineering consultancy Ingenieurberatung *f*
engineering department Maschinenbetrieb *m*
engineering steel Maschinenbaustahl *m*
engine fuel Kraftstoff *m*
engine house Maschinenhaus *n*
engine manufacture Motorenbau *m*
engrave gravieren; prägen
enlarge aufweiten; erweitern; vergrößern
enlargement Aufweitung *f* (Ziehstein); Erweiterung *f*
enrich anreichern
enriched matte Konzentrationsstein *m*
enrichment Anreicherung *f*
enrichment of gas Gasanreicherung *f*
enter einführen; einstecken; eintreten
entering angle Eintrittswinkel *m* (Walzen)
entering guide Einlaßführung *f*
enterprise Unternehmen *n*
enthalpy Bildungswärme *f*; Enthalpie *f*
entrained air Falschluft *f*
entrainment loss Ausschleppverlust *m* (beim Beizen)
entrance angle Konuswinkel *m*
entropy Entropie *f*

entropy of mixing Mischungsentropie *f*
entry guide Einführung *f*; Einlaßführung *f*
entry section Einlaufteil *n*
entry side of rolls Einsteckseite *f* (vor der Walze)
entry speed Einfahrgeschwindigkeit *f*
entry table Zufuhrrollgang *m*
envelop umhüllen
environment Umgebung *f*
environment conditions Umweltbedingungen *fpl*
epitaxial oxide epitaxiales Oxid *n*
epoxy Epoxid *n*
equalize abgleichen; ausgleichen
equal-leg angle gleichschenkliger Winkel *m*
equation Gleichung *f*
equation of state Zustandsgleichung *f*
equiaxed crystal Globularkristall *m*; kugeliger Kristall *m*
equiaxed crystal core zone globulitische Kernzone *f*
equiaxed crystals gleichgerichtete Kristalle *mpl*
equilibrium Gleichgewicht *n*; Gleichgewichtszustand *m*
equilibrium constant Gleichgewichtskonstante *f*
equilibrium diagram Gleichgewichtsschaubild *n*; Zustandsschaubild *n*
equilibrium index Gleichgewichtskennzahl *f*
equilibrium rest potential Ruhepotential *n*
equilibrium temperature Gleichgewichtstemperatur *f*
equilibrium value Gleichgewichtswert *m*
equip einrichten
equipment Anlage *f*; Ausrüstung *f*; Einrichtung *f*; Vorrichtung *f*
equipment for large open cast brown coal mining Braunkohlen-Großabbauanlage *f*
equivalence coefficient Gleichwertigkeitskoeffizient *m*

equivalent conductivity Äquivalentleitfähigkeit f
equivalent spherical drop diameter kugeläquivalenter Durchmesser m
equivalent strain Vergleichsformänderung f
erect aufbauen; errichten; montieren
erection Aufbau m; Aufstellung f
erection (of a mill) Errichtung f (eines Werkes)
erector of industrial plant Montageunternehmer m
ergonomics Arbeitswissenschaft f, Ergonomie f
Erichsen index Tiefziehbarkeit f
erode anfressen; erodieren; fressen
erosion Erosion f
erosion characteristics Erosionsverhalten f
erratic value Streuwert m
error Abweichung f; Fehler m
escape valve Auslaßventil n
establishment Aufstellung f, Einrichtung f
establishment charges Anlagekosten fpl
estimate Kostenvoranschlag m; bewerten; schätzen; vorkalkulieren
estimated and actual curves (X-rays) Richt- und Istlinien fpl
estimate rate Schätzwert m
estimation Schätzung f
etch ätzen
etchant Ätzmittel n
etching Anätzung f (Fehler beim Kaltwalzen)
etching figure Ätzbild n
etching medium Ätzmittel n
etching [re]agent Ätzmittel n
etch pit Ätzgrübchen n
European Communities Commission (ECC) Kommission f der Europäischen Gemeinschaften (KEG)
European Community for Steel and Coal (ECSC) Europäische Gemeinschaft für Kohle und Stahl (EGKS)
evaluate bestimmen; bewerten; werten

evaluation Auswertung f; Bestimmung f; Wertung f
evaporate entgasen; verdampfen
evaporation cooling Verdampfungskühlung f
evaporative cooling Verdunstungskühlung f
evolution Ausstoß m (von Gasen)
evolution of heat Wärmetönung f
evolve entwickeln (Rauch)
exact genau
exact length feste Länge f
examinate prüfen
examination Prüfung f; Untersuchung f
excavation Ausschachtung f
excess zuviel
excess air Luftüberschuß m
excess blast-furnace gas burner Gichtgasfackel f
excess burner Abgasfackel f
excess costs Mehrkosten pl
excess free energy freie Überschußenthalpie f
excess gas burner Fackel f (Abgas)
excessive hardening Aufhärtung f
excessive holding Überzeiten n
excess pressure Überdruck m
excess voltage Überspannung f
exchange current density Austauschstromdichte f
exchanger exhaust Wärmetauscherabgas n
excite anregen; erregen
exclusion of air Luftabschluß m
exfoliation Abblättern n
exhaust absaugen
exhaust air Abluft f
exhauster Saugzuganlage f
exhaust gas Abgas n; Auspuffgas n
exhausting plant Absaugeanlage f
exhaustion Erschöpfung f
exhaustive erschöpfend
exhibiting internal cracks kernrissig
exit Ausgang m; Austritt m
exit guide Auslaßführung f
exit pipe Abflußrohr n
exit roller table Abfuhrrollgang m

exit section Auslaufteil n
exit thickness to roll diameter ratio in % Dickenverhältnis n (beim Walzen)
exit tube Abflußrohr n
exothermic exotherm
exothermic feeder head mixture Haubenmasse f
exothermic feeding materials wärmeabgebende Mittel npl
expand aufblähen; aufgehen (Pulvermet.); ausdehnen; erweitern; treiben; wachsen
expandability Aufdornbarkeit f (Rohre)
expanded metal Streckmetall n
expanding Weiten n
expanding by spinning Weiten n durch Drücken
expanding coil Spreizhaspel f
expanding mandrel Spreizdorn m
expanding mill Aufweitwalzwerk n
expanding test Aufweitversuch m (Rohr)
expansion Ausdehnung f; Dehnung f (s. a. Bruchdehnung); Treiben n; Wachsen n
expansion coefficient Ausdehnungskoeffizient m
expansion joint Dehnfuge f; Stoßfuge f
expansion of the base of the crack Aufweitung f im Rißgrund
expansion pipe Kompensator m; Kompensator m (Dehnungsausgleicher)
expansion pipe bellows Dehnungsausgleicher m
expansion test Aufweitversuch m
expectation Erwartung f
expectation value Erwartungswert m
expenditure Aufwand m
expense Gemeinkosten pl
experiment Probe f; Versuch m
experimental error Versuchsfehler m
experimental plant Versuchsanlage f
expert Fachmann m; Sachkundiger m
expert workman Facharbeiter m

exploit betreiben; gewinnen
exploitation of coal Kohlengewinnung f
exploration Abbau m
exploratory survey Probeerhebung f
explore schürfen
explosion forming Formen n durch Stoßwellen
explosive charge Sprengladung f
explosive cladding Sprengplattieren n
explosive force Sprengkraft f
explosive forming Schockumformung f
explosive gas zerknallbares Gas n
explosive welding Schockschweißen n
expose (phot.) belichten
exposure Belichtung f
exposure time Belichtungszeit f; Liegezeit f; Standzeit f
express analysis Schnellanalyse f
extend ausdehnen; erweitern; recken; spannen; strecken; weiten
extended dislocation aufgespaltene Versetzung f
extender element Erweiterungsglied n
extender function Erweiterungsfunktion f
extending Dehnen n
extending by stretching Längen n
extensibility Streckbarkeit f
extension Anbau m; Ausdehnung f; Dehnung f; Erweiterung f; Verlängerung f
extensometer Dehnungsmesser m
extent Maß n; Umfang m
externally fired hot blast heater fremdbeheizter Rekuperator m
external power supply Fremdstrombezug m
external pressure Außendruck m
external scrap Fremdschrott m; Zukaufschrott m
external sound level Fremdschallpegel m
extinguish löschen (Feuer)
extra Zuschlag m

fatigue failure

extra deep drawing quality Sondertiefziehgüte *f*
extraneous rust Fremdrost *n*
extreme case Grenzfall *m*
extreme pressure additive Füllmittel *n* (Schmierung); Hochdruckzusatz *m* (Schmieren)
extrude strangpressen
extruding Durchdrücken *n*
extruding press Ausstoßpresse *f*; Strangpresse *f*
extrusion Strangpressen *n*
extrusion billet Preßbolzen *m* (Strangpressen); Strangpreßrohling *m*
extrusion die Preßdüse *f*
extrusion press Strangpressen *n*
extrusion press for tubes Rohrpresse *f*
extrusion press tool Strangpreßwerkzeug *n*
extrusion rate Fließpreßgeschwindigkeit *f*
eye Öse *f*
eyehole Schauloch *n*
eye protection Augenschutz *m*
eye protector Schutzbrille *f*

F

fabricate herstellen; zusammenbauen
fabricated steel sheet products and structures Blechkonstruktionen *fpl*
fabrication Erzeugung *f*
fabric wire Gewebedraht *m*
face Bahn *f*; Fläche *f*; Stirnfläche *f*; Stirnseite *f*
face centered cube space lattice kubisch-flächenzentriertes Gitter *n*
face grinding Planschleifen *n*; Stirnschleifen *n*
face length Ballenlänge *f*
facilities Betriebsanlagen *fpl*
facility Einrichtung *f*
facing Belag *m*; Schlichte *f*; zugekehrt; Überzug *m*
facing brick Verblendstein *m*

facing sand Modellsand *m*
factor Beiwert *m*
factorial analysis Einflußuntersuchung *f*
factorial design faktorielle Versuchsplanung *f*
factorial experiment Einflußversuch *m*
factory accounting Betriebsbuchhaltung *f*
factory building Fabrikgebäude *n*
fag[g]oting Paketieren *n*
fag[g]oting furnace Paketwärmofen *m*
fag[g]oting scrap Paketierschrott *m*
fag[g]ot iron Paketierschrott *m*
fagotted iron [scrap] paketierter Eisenschrott *m*
failure Bruch *m*; Fehlschlag *m*; Versagen *n*
falling weight test Fallgewichtsversuch *m*; Fallprobe *f*; Schlagversuch *m*
fall over umfallen (im Kaliber); umschlagen
false air Falschluft *f*
falsify set-point values Sollwerte *mpl* verfälschen
family of curves Kurvenschar *f*
fan Gebläse *n*; Lüfter *m*; Ventilator *m*
fantail Verbindungskanal *m* (zwischen Schlacken- und Regeneratorkammer)
Faraday constant Faraday-Konstante *f*
fast acting solution Kurzzeitlösung *f*; rasch wirkende Lösung *f*
fast coating festhaftender Überzug *m*
fasten befestigen
fast tool forging Schmieden *n* mit befestigtem Werkzeug
fatigue Ermüdung *f*
fatigue bend test Dauerbiegeversuch *m*
fatigue corrosion Ermüdungskorrosion *f*
fatigue crack Ermüdungsriß *m*
fatigue endurance limit Dauerschwingfestigkeit *f*
fatigue failure Dauerbruch *m*; Ermüdungsbruch *m*

fatigue fracture Dauerbruch m; Dauerschwingbruch m; Ermüdungsbruch m

fatigue limit Gesamtlebensdauer f

fatigue limit under pulsating stress Wechselfestigkeit f unter pulsierender Belastung

fatigue limit under reversed tension-compression stresses Zug-Druck-Wechselfestigkeit f

fatigue loading alternating stress Dauerschwingbeanspruchung f

fatigue notch factor Kerbwirkungszahl f

fatigue ratio Dauerfestigkeitsverhältnis n

fatigue resistance Dauerfestigkeit f; Wechselfestigkeit f

fatigue strength Dauerfestigkeit f; Dauerschwingfestigkeit f; Wechselfestigkeit f

fatigue strength for finite life Zeitfestigkeit f

fatigue strength reduction factor Kerbwirkungszahl f

fatigue strength test Dauerfestigkeitsversuch m

fatigue strength under bending stress Biegedauerfestigkeit f

fatigue strength under completely reversed stress Dauerwechselfestigkeit f

fatigue strength under pulsating stresses Schwellfestigkeit f

fatigue strength under pulsating tensile stresses Zugschwellfestigkeit f

fatigue strength under repeated bending stresses Biegedauerfestigkeit f im Schwellbereich

fatigue strength under reversed bending stresses Biegewechselfestigkeit f

fatigue stress Dauerbeanspruchung f; Dauerfestigkeit f

fatigue test Dauerschwingversuch m; Dauerversuch m; Ermüdungsversuch m

fatigue testing machine Dauerprüfmaschine f

fatigue test in one load stage Einstufen-Dauerschwingversuch m

fatigue test under actual service conditions Betriebsschwingversuch m

fatigue test under operational stresses Betriebsfestigkeitsversuch m

fatigue test under reversed bending stresses Biegewechselfestigkeitsversuch m

fat lime Fettkalk m

fattening Aufbauchung f (Ziehstein)

fatty oil Fettöl f

faucet pipe (am.) Muffenrohr n

fault Fehler m; Fehlererscheinung f; Gangspalte f; Verwerfung f

faulty fehlerhaft

faulty cast Fehlguß m

feather end Spitzkeil m (ff. Stein)

feathering Dressierblumen fpl

feather key Federkeil m

feather (surface defect) Schliere f

feathery structures verästelte Strukturen fpl

feature Merkmal n; Qualitätsmerkmal n

feebly caking coal Magerkohle f

feed Beschickung f; Speisung f; Vorschub m; beschicken; nachgießen; schütten; speisen; zubringen; zuführen

feedback (automatic control) Rückführung f

feedback control system Regelung f mit Rückführung

feed control lever Vorschubschalthebel m

feeder Gießaufsatz m; Hebevorrichtung f; Speisevorrichtung f; Zubringer m

feeder head Blockaufsatz m; Gießkopf m; Speisekopf m

feeder table Aufgabeteller m

feed hopper Beschickungstrichter m; Fülltrichter m; Schütttrichter m

feeding Einspeisen n; Nachsaugen n (Blöcke)

feeding device Beschickungsvorrich-

tung f; Zufuhrvorrichtung f; Speisevorrichtung f; Vorholvorrichtung f; Beschickvorrichtung f
feeding rate Beschickungsgeschwindigkeit f
feed[ing] roller table Zufuhrrollgang m
feeding side Beschickungsseite f
feeding table Zuführungstisch m
feed metal Vormetall n
feed ore Frischerz n
feed reverse Vorschubumsteuerung f
feed rollers Walztisch m
feed runner Eingußrinne f
feed water Speisewasser n
feel fühlen; tasten
feeler ga[u]ge Fühler m; Meßnadel f; Tastnadel f
feeling elongation meter Tast-Dehnungsmesser m
feeling lever Fühlhebel m; Tasthebel m
fence bar Hespenstahl m
fence wire Gitterdraht m; Zaundraht m
fencing iron Hespenstahl m
ferric oxide Eisenoxid n
ferric oxide briquette Eisenerzbrikett n
ferriferous eisenhaltig
ferris wheel Aufbereitungs-Heberad n
ferrite Ferrit m
ferrite grain Ferritkorn n
ferrite lath Ferritspieß m
ferritic steel ferritischer Stahl m
ferro alloy Ferrolegierung f
ferrocarbide brick Ferrocarbidstein m
ferroclad brick blechummantelter Stein m
ferroclip brick Ferroclipstein m
ferro-coke Ferrokoks m
ferroconcrete Stahlbeton m
ferromagnetic ferromagnetisch
ferro-manganese Ferromangan n
ferro-molybdenum Ferromolybdän n
ferro-silicon Ferrosilicium n
ferrostatic pressure ferrostatischer Druck m
ferro-titanium Ferrotitan n

ferro-tungsten Ferrowolfram n
ferrous material Eisenwerkstoff m
ferrous metallurgy Eisenhüttenkunde f; Eisenhüttenwesen n
ferrous oxide Eisenoxidul n
ferrous sulfate Eisensulfat n
ferruginous lime eisenschüssiger Kalk m
fettle ausfüttern; flicken
fettler Abschläger m (Gießerei); Putzer m
fettling gun Spritzkanone f
fiber Faser f
fibering Faserstruktur f
fibre reinforced material Faserverbundwerkstoff m
fibre reinforced metal faserverstärktes Metall n
fibre reinforcement Faserverstärkung f
fibrous fracture Schieferbruch m; faseriger Bruch m
fibrous powder faseriges Pulver n
fibrous structure Faserstruktur f
field definition Feldanweisung f
field electron microscope Feldelektronenmikroskop n
field forcing device Schnellerregung f
field intensity Feldstärke f
field ion microscopy Feldionenmikroskopie f
field of application Anwendungsbereich m
fields of steel application Stahlanwendungsgebiete npl; Stahlverwendungsgebiete npl
field test Naturversuch m (Korrosion)
field variable Feldvariable f
field welding Baustellenschweißung f
filament Faden m; Faser f
file Datei f; Feile f; feilen
file steel Feilenstahl m
filiform corrosion Unterrostung f
filing date Anmeldetag m (Patent)
filings Feilspäne mpl
fill Füllgewicht n; beladen
filler Dichtungsmasse f (für Mauerwerk); Füllmasse f; Füllstoff m

filler brick Besatzstein *m*; Nachsetzstein *m* (für SM-Ofengewölbe)
filler metal Aufschweißlegierung *f*; Schweißzusatzwerkstoff *m*
filler rod Schweißdraht *m*
fillet Abrundung *f*; Hohlkehle *f*
fillet ga[u]ge Kehlnahtmeßlehre *f*
fillet weld Kehlnahtschweißen *n*
fillet weld break test Keilprüfung *f*; Keilprüfung *f* (schmelzgeschweißter Stumpfnähte); Winkelprüfung *f*
fillet welded connection Kehlnahtschweiße *f*
filling brick Füllstein *m*
filling hole Einfüllöffnung *f*
filling space Füllraum *m*
filling volume Füllvolumen *n*
film Folie *f*
film-boiling Filmverdampfung *f*
film of paint Farbschicht *f*
filter Filter *m*; filtern; filtrieren
filter bag Filterschlauch *m*
filter plant Filteranlage *f*
fin Grat *m*; Gratrippe *f*; Naht *f*
final accounts Abschlußkonten *npl*
final annealing Fertigglühung *f*
final control element Stellglied *n*
final density Fertigdichte *f* (Pulvermet.)
final pass Decklage *f* (Schweißen)
final position Endstellung *f*
final run Decklage *f* (Schweißen)
final sample Endprobe *f*
final sintering operation Fertigsinterung *f*
final slag Feinungsschlacke *f*; Fertigschlacke *f*
final temperature of rolling Walzendtemperatur *f*
final trimming Nachschneiden *n*
finance accounts Finanzkonten *pl*
financial accounts department Finanzbuchhaltung *f*
fin crack Gratriß *m*
fine Naht *f*
fine cleaning Feinreinigung *f*
fine-edge blanking Feinschneiden *n*
fine-grained feinkörnig

fine-grained fracture feinkörniger Bruch *m*
fine grained low pearlite structural steel perlitarmer Sonderbaustahl *m* (PAS)
fine-grained mag Magnesitmehl *n*
fine grained steel Feinkornstahl *n*
fine-grained structure feinkörniges Gefüge *n*
fine grinding (powder met.) Feinzerkleinerung *f*
fineness Schlankheitsgrad *m* (Dendriten)
fine ore Feinerz *n*
fine pointed flame Stichflamme *f*
fine powder Feinpulver *n*
fine purification Feinreinigung *f*
fines bed Mischungsbett *n*
fine silicon Feinsilicium *n*
finest ga[u]ge feinste Abmessung *f*
fine structure Feingefüge *n*
finish fertigmachen; nacharbeiten
finish as turned gedreht (Oberflächenzustand)
finished goods Fertigerzeugnis *n*
finished length Fertiglänge *f*
finished part Fertigteil *n*
finished product Fertigerzeugnis *n*
finished size Fertigmaß *n*
finisher Fertiggerüst *n*; Fertiggesenk *n*
finishing Oberflächenveredelung *f*
finishing additions Zusätze *mpl* zum Fertigmachen (Schmelze)
finishing department Adjustage *f*; Zurichterei *f*
finishing die (drawing) Endstein *m* (Ziehen)
finishing groove Fertigkaliber *n*
finishing lathe Fertigdrehbank *f*
finishing pass Feinzug *m*; Fertigkaliber *n*
finishing [rolling] mill Fertigwalzwerk *n*
finishing shop Adjustage *f*; Zurichterei *f*
finishing slag Fertigschlacke *f*
finishing stand Fertiggerüst *n*
finishing train Fertigstraße *f*

finish-machined fein bearbeitet
finish machining Fertigbearbeitung *f*
finish quality Oberflächenzustand *m*
finish [roll] fertigwalzen
finish rolling by the infeed method Glattwalzen *n* im Einstechverfahren
finish rolling of bar stock by the through-feed method Glattwalzen *n* von Stäben im Durchlaufverfahren
finish rolling temperature Walzendtemperatur *f*
finish shaving Nachschneiden *n*
finite element method (FEM) Finite-Elemente-Verfahren *n*
finned tube Flossenrohr *n*; Rippenrohr *n*
fire anheizen; beheizen; brennen (Pellets); verfeuern
fire box Brennkammer *f* (Glühofen)
firebrick feuerfester Stein *m*
fire-bridge Feuerbrücke *f*
fire check Brandriß *m*; Warmriß *m*
fire clay Schamotte *f*; feuerfester Ton *m*
fire clay brick Schamottestein *m*
fire crack Brandriß *m*
firecracker welding Elin-Hafergut-Verfahren *n*; Unter-Schiene-Schweißen *n*
fire crack transfer mark Brandrißabdruck *m* (Walzdrahtfehler)
fire detector Feuermelder *m*
fire-engine Feuerspritzenwagen *m*
fire extinguisher Feuerlöscher *m*
fireman Heizer *m*; Stocher *m*
fire place Feuerung *f*; Herd *m*
fire proof feuerfest
fire proof cement Schamottemörtel *m*
fireproof lining feuerfeste Ausmauerung *f*
fire-proof wall Brandmauer *f*
fire protection Brandschutz *m*
fire resisting feuerbeständig; feuerfest
fire-resisting casting feuerbeständiger Guß *m*
fire spot Brennfleck *m*
fire-tube boiler Flammrohrkessel *m*

fire waste Werkstoffverlust *m* durch Verzundern
firing Beheizung *f*; Feuerung *f*; Heizung *f*; Zündung *f*
firing expansion Brennwachsen *n* (ff. Steine)
firing in Einbrennen *n*
firing plant Feuerungsanlage *f*
firing shrinkage Brennschwinden *n* (ff. Steine)
firmly adhering festhaftend
firmly bonded to festhaftend
firmness Haftfestigkeit *f*
first aid dispensary Unfallstation *f*
first brick out Widerlagerstein *m*
first cost Selbstkosten *pl*
first draw Anschlag *m* (Drahtziehen)
first helper Vorarbeiter *m*
first-operation drawing Tiefziehen *n* im Anschlag
first smelting pig iron Vorschmelzeisen *n*
fish eye Fischauge *n*
fish-plate Lasche *f*
fish plate Schale *f*
fish scale Fischschuppe *f*
fish scale fracture Schieferbruch *m*
fish tails Fischschwänze *mpl*
fissure Gangspalte *f*; Riß *m*; Spalt *m*; Sprung *m*
fissuring Rißbildung *f*
fit Passung *f*; anpassen; justieren
fit in einbauen
fitter Maschinenschlosser *m*; Monteur *m*
fitter's shop Schlosserei *f*
fitting key Federkeil *m*
fitting piece Paßstück *n*
fittings Fittings *pl*; Zubehörteile *npl*
fix abbinden; abbinden (Ti); befestigen
fixation Abbinden *n* (des Stickstoffs)
fixed feststehend
fixed assets Anlagevermögen *n*
fixed carbon gebundener Kohlenstoff *m*
fixed costs feste Kosten *pl*
fixed flange Flansch *m*

fixed link Steg *m*
fixed price Festpreis *m*
fixed set point control Festwertregelung *f*
fixing bath Fixierbad *n*
fixing pin Haltestift *m*
fixture Aufspannvorrichtung *f*
flake Flocke *f*; Flockenriß *m*; Schuppe *f*; abblättern; abplatzen
flake crack Spannungsriß *m*
flake formation Flockenbildung *f*
flake graphite Lamellengraphit *m*
flake graphite roll Walzen *f* (Flockengraphitguß)
flaking Abblättern *n*; Abplatzung *f*
flaky blättchenförmig; plättchenförmig; schuppig
flaky fracture Schieferbruch *m*
flaky powder flittriges Pulver *n*
flame Flamme *f*
flame chipping Brennputzen *n*
flame cutting Brennschneiden *n*
flame-cutting machine Brennschneidmaschine *f*
flame descaling Brennputzen *n*; Flämmen *n*
flame deseaming Brennputzen *n*; Flammstrahlen *n*; Flämmen *n*
flame gouging Flämmhobeln *n*
flame hardening Brennhärten *n*; Flammenhärten *n*
flame-hardening machine Brennhärtemaschine *f*
flame ionization detector Flammenionisationsdetektor *m*
flame out ausflammen
flame scarfing Brennputzen *n*; Flämmen *n*; Heißflämmen *n*
flange Flansch *m*; Spurkranz *m*; krempen; kümpeln
flanged beam Flanschträger *m*
flanged head bolt Flanschverschraubung *f*
flanged pipe Bördelrohr *n*
flanged products Kümpelerzeugnisse *npl*
flanged profile Abkantprofil *n*
flange joint Flanschverbindung *f*

flange rail Breitfußschiene *f*
flange tube Flanschenrohr *n*
flanging machine Bördelmaschine *f*; Sickenmaschine *f*
flanging press Kümpelpresse *f*
flanging test Bördelversuch *m*
flank of a tooth Zahnflanke *f*
flap valve Klappe *f*
flare aufweiten; erweitern; flackern
flare flicker flackern
flash Bart *m*; Grat *m*; Schweißgrat *m*
flash annealing Glühen *n*
flash baker Blitztrockner *m*; Schnelltrockner *m*
flash [butt] welding Abbrenn[stumpf]schweißung *f*
flash butt welding Abbrennstumpfschweißen *n*
flash heat kurze Anwärmhitze *f*
flashing Zunderflecken *mpl*
flash into steam verdampfen
flash nickel plating Vernickelung *f*; Vorvernicklung *f*
flash off abschmelzen
flash point Flammpunkt *m*
flash steam boiler Dampferzeuger *m*
flash tempering Stoßanlassen *n*
flash trim entgraten
flash trimmer Abgratmaschine *f*
flask annealing Kastenglühen *n*
flask conveyor Kastenförderer *m*
flat Flachprägen *n*
flat bar Flacheisen *n*; Flachstab *m*
flat-bending test Flachbiegeversuch *m*
flat bottom rail Breitfußschiene *f*; Vignolschiene *f*
flat-die thread rolling Gewinderollen *n*
flat drawing Flachziehen *n*
flat face fillet weld Flachnaht *f*
flat half rounds Flachhalbrundstahl *m*
flat-hearth type mixer Flachherdmischer *m*
flat joint Flachlasche *f*
flat longitudinal rolling Flach-Längswalzen *n*
flat longitudinal rolling of hollow items Flach-Längswalzen *n* von Hohlkörpern

flat longitudinal rolling of solid bodies Flach-Längswalzen *n* von Vollkörpern
flatness Planheit *f*
flat pass Flachstich *m*
flat position [welding] Wannenlage *f*
flat product Flachzeug *n*
flat roll Flachbahnwalze *f*
flat rolled products flachgewalzte Erzeugnisse *npl*
flat rolled steel Flachstahl *m*
flat rolling flachwalzen
flat rolling of round wire Flachwalzen *n* von Runddraht
flats Flachstahl *m*
flat sheet gerichtetes Blech *n*
flat sided oval gedrungenes Oval *n*
flat skew rolling Flach-Schrägwalzen *n*
flat slab Flachbramme *f*
flat steel bar Flachstahl *m*
flattened abgeflacht
flattening Prägerichten *n*
flattening of periphery of a roll (by pressure) Walzenabplattung *f*
flattening (of sheets) Glätten *n*
flattening test Faltversuch *m*
flattening test on tubes Ringfaltversuch *m*
flat tensile test bar Flachzerreißstab *m*
flatting Verwerfen *n* nach Beanspruchung
flat transverse rolling Flach-Querwalzen *n*
flat wire Flachdraht *m*
flaw Anriß *m*; Einriß *m*; Fleck *m*; Riß *m*; Spalte *f*; Sprung *m*
flaw detector Rißprüfer *m*
flaw echo Fehlerecho *n*
flawless surface finish oberflächenrein
flaw location scale Fehlerortungsstab *m* (Ultraschall)
fleck scale Zunderfleck *m*
flexibility Anpassungsfähigkeit *f*; Biegsamkeit *f*; Dehnbarkeit *f*
flexible biegsam

flexible belt sander Bandschleifmaschine *f*
flexible connection nachgiebige Verbindung *f*
flexible dummy bar biegsamer Kaltstrang *m*
flexible joint bewegliche Kupplung *f* (Rohr)
flexible tube Schlauch *m*
flexible tubing biegbare Röhren *fpl*
flex levelling Walken *n* (Blechumformen)
flexural rigidity Biegesteifigkeit *f*
flexural strength Biegefestigkeit *f*
flexure Biegung *f*; Durchbiegung *f* (quer)
flexure fatigue test Dauerbiegeversuch *m*
flexure test Biegeversuch *m*
flicker flackern
flickering Flimmern *n*
flipper Schlaghaspel *f* (Drahtziehen)
flip-up window hochklappbares Schutzglas *n*
float schwimmen
float and sink apparatus Sinkscheider *m*
floating die Schwebemantelmatrize *f*; gefederte Matrize *f*; schwebende Matrize *f*
floating die pressing Pressen *n* mit schwebender Matrize
floating stopper schwimmender Stopfen *m*
floating taphole plug schwimmender Abstichverschluß *m*
flocculation Ausflockung *f*; Flockenausbildung *f*
flood a mine with water Grube *f* unter Wasser setzen
floor cover angle sections Bodenbelag-Winkelstahl *m*
floor covering sections Profile *npl* für Bodenbeläge
floor plate Belagblech *n*
flopper Welle *f*
floppy disc drive Floppy disk-Laufwerk *n*

floppy disc reader Leseeinheit f für Disketten f
flotation Flotation f; Schwimmaufbereitung f
flotation plant Schwimmaufbereitungsanlage f
flow Durchfluß m; Fluß m; Strom m; fließen
flowability Fließvermögen n
flowbien Container m
flow boiling cooling Kühlung f in strömender Flüssigkeit
flow characteristics Fließverhalten n
flow chip Fließspan m
flow conditions Strömungsverhältnisse npl
flow diagram Flußbild n
flowers of zinc Zinkblumen fpl
flow gate Steiger m; Steigtrichter m
flow-harden kaltverfestigen
flow limit Fließgrenze f
flow lines Fließfiguren fpl (Bleche)
flow meter Durchflußmesser m; Fließzeit-Meßgerät n; Strömungsmesser n
flow of cost values Wertefluß m
flow of material Stoffluß m
flow out ausfließen
flow pattern Strömungsbild n
flow pattern test Strömungsmodellversuch m
flow phenomena Strömungsvorgänge mpl
flow rate Fließdauer f; Fließgeschwindigkeit f; Fließzeit f
flow sheet Stammbaum m
flow stress Fließwiderstand m
flow turning Abstreckdrücken n; Fließdrücken n
fluctuation Schwankung f
fluctuation in the mains voltage Netzspannungsschwankung f
flue Abzugskanal m; Rauchabzug m; Rauchkanal m; Zug m
flue ash Flugasche f
flue boiler Flammrohrkessel m
flue cinder Abgaskanal-Schlacke f (Wärmeofen)

flue dust Flugstaub m; Gichtstaub m
flue dust briquetting plant Gichtstaubbrikettierungsanlage f
flue gas Abgas n
flue gas tester Abgasprüfer m
flue gas thermometer Abgasthermometer n
flue gas valve Abgasschieber m
flue uptake Fuchs m
fluid Flüssigkeit f; flüssig
fluid bed roasting process Wirbelschicht-Röstverfahren n
fluid film friction Flüssigkeitsreibung f
fluid flow meter Mengenmesser m
fluid gear Flüssigkeitsgetriebe n
fluid iron ore reduction Reduktion f in der Wirbelschicht
fluidisation Verflüssigung f
fluidised bed Wirbelschicht f
fluidised bed kiln Wirbelschichtofen m
fluidised bed sintering Wirbelsintern n
fluidity Dünnflüssigkeit f; Fluidität f
fluidized bed Fließbett n
fluid mechanics Strömungstechnik f
fluorescent strip lamp Leuchtstoffröhre f
fluorometallic intensifying screen fluormetallische Verstärkungsfolie f
fluorspar Flußspat m
flush Spülversatz m
flushing cinder Abstichschlacke f; Vorlaufschlacke f
flush slag Abstichschlacke f; Vorlaufschlacke f
fluted ingot Riffelblock m; mehrkantiger Block m (mit eingezogener Seitenfläche)
flux Flußmittel n; Schmelzmittel n
fluxed electrode Elektrode f mit Flußmittel
fluxes Zuschläge mpl
fluxes for pickling Flußmittel npl für das Beizen; Verzinken n
flux (for making slag) Schlackenbildner m
fluxing Fluxen n
fluxing agent Flußmittel n; Schmelzmittel n; Zuschlag m

fly ash Flugasche f
flyball governor Fliehkraftregler m
flying change fliegender Wechsel m
flying shears fliegende Schere f
flyover Hochstraße f
flywheel equaliser set Schwungradumformer m
flywheel motor-generator set Schwungradumformer m
foam Schaum m
foamed slag Hüttenbims m; Schaumschlacke f
foamed slag brick Hüttenschwemmstein m
foam flotation Schaumflotation f
foaming Schäumen n
foaming wheel Schaumrad n
foam washer Schaumwäscher m
focal point of power economy Energiewirtschafts-Schwerpunkt m
focal radius Leitstrahl m
focusing current Fokalisierungsstrom m
fog level (spectrum analysis) Untergrundschwärzung f
fog quenching Nebelhärten n
foil Folie f
foil butt seam welding Foliennahtschweißen n
foil rolling mill Folienwalzwerk n
fold Falte f; doppeln; falten; falzen; umbiegen
fold crack Faltungsriß m
fold crevice Faltungsriß m
folded bundle Faltbund n
folding test Faltversuch m
follow-die cutting Folgeschneiden n
follower control device Nachlaufregler m
follow-up control Folgeregelung f
follow up draft Nachzug m
force Kraft f
forced draft fan Druckgebläse n
forced lubrication Druckschmierung f
forcing pump Druckpumpe f
fore blow vorblasen
fore blow time Vorblasezeit f
forehearth Vorherd m

foreign atom Fremdatom n
foreign labour ausländische Arbeitskraft f
foreign substance Fremdstoff m (Luftverunreinigung)
foreign trade Außenhandel m
foreign trade policy Handelspolitik f
foreman Meister m; Vormann m; Werkmeister m
fore plate Schaffplatte f
forge Hammerwerk n; Schmiede f; Schmiede[werkstatt] f; Schmiedefeuer n; schmieden
forgeability Bildsamkeit f; Schmiedbarkeit f
forgeable schmiedbar
forgeable alloy Knetlegierung f
forge alloy Schmiedelegierung f
forge coal Schmiedekohle f
forged and pressed pieces Schmiede- und Preßteile npl
forged piece Schmiedestück n
forge from a bar schmieden von der Stange
forge from a billet schmieden vom Stück
forge-on anschmieden
forge pigs weißes Roheisen n
forger Schmied m
forge rolling Reckwalzen n (Schmiedewalzen)
forge welding Feuerschweißen n; Hammerschweißung f; Schmiedeschweißung f
forging Schmieden n; Schmiedestück n
forging and sizing press Gesenkschmiede- und Kalibrierpresse f
forging burst Kernzerschmiedung f
forging furnace Schmiedeofen m
forging grade ingot Schmiedeblock m
forging grade steel Schmiedeeisen n
forging hammer Schmiedehammer m
forging machine Schmiedemaschine f
forging manipulator Schmiedemanipulator m
forging press Schmiedepresse f
forging roll Schmiedewalzmaschine f

forging steel Schmiedestahl m
fork Gabel f
forked runner Hosenrinne f
forked tapping spout Hosenrinne f
fork lift truck Gabelstapler m; Hubstapler m
fork piler Gabelstapler m
fork-test bar Gabelprobe f
form Ausbildung f; Formblatt n; formen; gestalten
formability Verformbarkeit f
formation of beads Raupenbildung f
formation of cracks Rißbildung f
formation of distortion wedges Zipfelbildung f
formation of skull in ladle Pfannenrestbildung f
formation of soft spots Weichfleckigkeit f
formation of wrinkles Faltenbildung f
form bending Formbiegen n
form bending by a sliding-action draw Gleitziehbiegen n
formed coke Formkoks m
formfactor (sphericity) Formfaktor m (Sphärizität)
form grinding Schablonenschleifen n
forming Gestaltung f; Umformen n; Verformung f
forming bell Ziehtrichter m
forming by bending Biegeumformen n
forming gas Formiergas n
forming limit curve Grenzformänderungskurve f
forming operation Formgebung f
forming pass Profilstich m
forming property Umformbarkeit f
form turning Formdrehen n
forward slip Voreilung f (Walzen)
fouling Verschweißen n
foundation Gründung f
foundation screw Ankerschraube f
founder Gießer m
foundry Gießerei f
foundry auxiliary material Gießereihilfsstoff m
foundry coke Gießereikoks m
foundry crane Gießereikran m

foundryman Gießer m
foundry materials Gießereibedarf m
foundry pig iron Gießereiroheisen n
foundry plants and equipments Gießereianlagen und -einrichtungen fpl
foundry product Gießereierzeugnis n
four arm capstan (for holding rod coils) Sammelkreuz n
four bar linkage Viergelenkgetriebe n
four high rolling stand Vierwalzengerüst n
four-high stand Quartogerüst n
fourstand plate mill viergerüstige Grobblechstraße f
four strand continuous casting machine Vierstranggießmaschine f
four stroke gas engine Viertaktgasmaschine f
fracture Bruch m; Bruchgefüge n
fracture appearance Bruchaussehen n
fracture face Bruchstelle f
fracture initiation Brucheinleitung f
fracture load Abreißkraft f (Tiefziehen)
fracture mechanics Bruchmechanik f
fracture on working Verformungsbruch m
fracture strength Reißfestigkeit f; Rißfestigkeit f; Zerreißfestigkeit f
fracture test Bruchprobe f
fracture toughness Rißzähigkeit f
fragment Scherbe f
frame Bock m; Gerüst n; Gestell n; Hammerständer m; Rahmen m
framed structure Gitterfachwerk n
frame of accounts Kontenrahmen m
frame plate Rahmenblech n
frame section Einfassungseisen n
framework Fachwerk n
framework knote Fachwerkknoten m
fraze unsaubere Abgratkante f
freak value (data) Ausreißer m
free bending freies Biegen n
free-cutting steel Automatenstahl m
free cutting steel for horological industry Triebstahl m
freedom from brittle fracture Trennbruchsicherheit f

free electron (conduction electron) freies Elektron *n* (Leitungselektron)
free energy in standard state freie Energie *f* im Normalzustand
free energy of reaction Bildungsenergie *f*
free from mud entschlämmen
free from scale zunderfrei
free from twist effects verwindungsfrei
free jet burner Freistrahlbrenner *m*
freely suspended schwingend aufgehängt
free machining property Zerspanbarkeit *f*
free-machining steel Automatenstahl *m*
freeze einfrieren; erstarren; gefrieren
freezing Erstarren *n*
freezing point Erstarrungspunkt *m*; Gefrierpunkt *m*
freight car Güterwagen *m*
freight car scales Waggonwaage *f*
freight elevator Lastenaufzug *m*
freight space Laderaum *m*
French chalk Speckstein *m*
French curves Kurvenlineal *n*
frequency Frequenz *f*; Häufigkeit *f*
frequency analysis Geräuschspektrum *n*
frequency break Frequenzeinbruch *m*
frequency curve Häufigkeitskurve *f*
frequency diagram Häufigkeitsschaubild *n*
frequency distribution Häufigkeitsverteilung *f*
frequency of accidents Unfallhäufigkeit *f*
frequency of load alternations Lastwechselfrequenz *f*
frequency of load cycles Lastwechselfrequenz *f*
frequency research Großzahlforschung *f*
frequency response Frequenzgang *m*
frequent häufig; in geringer Entfernung *f* voneinander
fretting corrosion Abriebkorrosion *f*; Reibkorrosion *f*

friable iron ore Erz *n* mulmiges
friction Reibung *f*
frictional force Reibungskraft *f*
frictional heat Reibungswärme *f*
frictional loss Gleitverlust *m*
frictional moment Reibungsmoment *n*
frictional state Reibungszustand *m*
frictional work Reibungsarbeit *f*
friction coefficient Reibungskoeffizient *m*
friction disc Reibscheibe *f*
friction-grip type gleitfester Typ *m*
friction material (powder met.) Reibwerkstoff *m*
friction sawing Trennschleifen *n*
friction welding Reibschweißen *n*
front cutting edge Nebenschneide *f*
front face Stirnseite *f*
front flange Wickelplatte *f*
front milling Stirnfräsen *n*
front mill [roller] table Rollgang *m* vor der Walze
froth Schaum *m*
froth flotation Schaumaufbereitung *f*
fuel Brennstoff *m*
fuel and heating engineer Wärmeingenieur *m*
fuel and power department Wärmestelle *f*
fuel coke Heizkoks *m*
fuel consumption Brennstoffverbrauch *m*
fuel economy Wärmewirtschaft *f*
fuel energy Wärmemenge *f*
fuel gas Brenngas *n*; Heizgas *n*
fuel gas conduit Heizgasleitung *f*
fuel oil Brennöl *n*; Heizöl *n*; Schweröl *n*
fuel particle Brennstoffteilchen *n*
fugacity Fugazität *f*
fugacity coefficient Fugazitätskoeffizient *m*
fulcrum Drehpunkt *m*
full annealing Ausglühen *n*
full center Mittenwelle *f* (Kaltband)
fuller Abschreckwerkzeug *n*; Streckgesenk *n*; Streckwerkzeug *n*
full-length durchgehend

full scale fatigue test Dauerschwingversuch *m*
full strip gewölbtes Band *n*
fully carbonised völlig gar (Koks)
fully galvanised wire Draht *m* mit galvanischem Überzug
fully killed steel beruhigter Stahl *m*
fume Dampf *m*; Qualm *m*; Rauch *m*
funicular railway Drahtseilbahn *f*
funnel Trichter *m*
furnace Ofen *m*
furnace atmosphere Ofenatmosphäre *f*
furnace bleeder Gichtgasfackel *f*
furnace campaign Ofenreise *f*
furnace casing Ofengefäß *n*; Ofenmantel *m*
furnace chamber Ofenraum *m*
furnace control station Ofenwarte *f*
furnace door Ofentür *f*
furnace gun Stichlochstopfmaschine *f*
furnace lining Ofenauskleidung *f*; Ofenfutter *n*; Ofenmauerung *f*
furnace operation Ofenbetrieb *m*
furnace practice Ofenbetrieb *m*
furnace pressure control Ofenraum-Druckregelung *f*
furnace scale Ofenzunder *m*; Primärzunder *m*
furnace shell Ofengefäß *n*
furnace sow Bodensau *f*
furnace throat Gicht *f*, Gichtöffnung *f*
furnace top Gicht *f*, Gichtöffnung *f*
furnace top bell Gichtglocke *f*
furnace top hopper Gichttrichter *m*
furnace vessel Ofengefäß *n*
furnace working Ofengang *m*
further treatment Weiterverarbeitung *f*
fuse Sicherung *f* (elektr.); abschmelzen
fused corundum Schmelzkorund *m*; Sinterkorund *m*
fused-in extraneous matter eingeschmolzener Fremdstoff *m*
fused magnesite Schmelzmagnesit *m*
fusibility Schmelzbarkeit *f*
fusible schmelzbar

fusing Aufschmelzen *n*; Verschweißen *n*
fusion Schmelzung *f*; Versinterung *f*
fusion cast product schmelzgegossenes Erzeugnis *n*
fusion point Erweichungspunkt *m*; Schmelzpunkt *m*
fusion welding Abschmelzschweißverfahren *n*; Schmelzschweißen *n*

G

gab Ausladung *f*
gagger Sandhaken *m*; sperriges Stück *n*
gag press Richtpresse *f*, Stempelrichtpresse *f*
gain Verdienst *m* (Gewinn)
gall anfressen; festfressen; fressen; klemmen; klemmen (sich)
Gall's chain Gallsche Gelenkkette *f*
galling fressender Verschleiß *m*
galling rust Passungsrost *m*
galvanic cell galvanische Kette *f*, galvanisches Element *n*
galvanic corrosion galvanische Korrosion *f*
galvanise galvanisieren; verzinken
galvanised sheet verzinktes Blech *n*
galvanised strip verzinktes Band *n*
galvanising Flußmittel *npl* für das Beizen; Verzinken *n*; Verzinkung *f*
galvanising furnace Verzinkungsofen *m*
galvanising kettle Verzinkungspfanne *f*
galvanising plant Verzinkerei *f*
galvanising pot Verzinkungspfanne *f*
galvanising shop Verzinkerei *f*
galvannealed wire nach dem Verzinken wärmebehandelter Draht *m*
galvanostatic pulse method galvanostatische Impulsmethode *f*
gamma iron Gamma-Eisen *n*
gamma solid solution Gamma-Mischkristall *m*

gang Schicht f (Arbeiter)
gangue Gangart f
ganister brick Dinasstein m
ganister brick (am.) Kalkdinasstein m
gantry [crane] Bockkran m
gap Lücke f; Spalt m
gas Gas n; Gas n (auf einen Ofen) geben (= anheizen)
gas analysis Gasanalyse f
gas aspirator Gassauger m
gas bell Gasglocke f
gas bubble Gasblase f
gas burner Gasbrenner m
gas carbonitriding Gascarbonitrieren n
gas carburising Gaseinsatzhärtung f; Gaszementieren n
gas carburising furnace Gasaufkohlungsofen m
gas chamber Gaskammer f
gas cleaning Gasreinigung f
gas cleaning plant Gasreinigungsanlage f
gas coal Fettkohle f; Gaskohle f
gas coke Gaskoks m
gas collecting hood Gasfanghaube f
gas collecting main Gassammelleitung f (Vorlage)
gas collecting pipe Vorlage f (Koksofen)
gas compressor Gaskompressor m
gas conduit Gasleitung f
gas cooler Gaskühler m
gas cooling Gaskühlung f
gas cooling plant Gaskühlanlage f
gas cracking Gasspaltung f
gas cutting Brennschneiden n; Gasschneiden n
gas cylinder manifold Flaschenbatterie f
gas density ga[u]ge Gasdichtemesser m
gas detector Gasprüfer m; Gasspürer m
gas drying Gastrocknung f
gas duct Gaskanal m
gas end peep hole Spiegelschauloch n

gas engine power house Gasmaschinenzentrale f
gaseous inclusion Gaseinschluß m
gas extractor Gassauger m
gas-fired calcining kiln Gasröstofen m (Erze)
gas fired furnace Muffelofen m (Härteofen)
gas [fired] furnace gasbeheizter Schmiedeofen m
gas firing Gasbeheizung f
gas flue Gasabzug m; Gaskanal m
gas furnace Gasofen m
gas [fusion] welding Gasschmelzschweißung f; autogenes Schweißen n
gas grid Ferngasnetz n
gas holder Gasbehälter m; Gasglocke f; Gassammelbehälter m
gas holes Schaumstelle f
gas hose Gasschlauch m
gasification Vergasung f
gasify vergasen
gasifying machine Vergasungsmaschine f
gasifying method Vergasungstechnik f
gasifying plant Vergasungsanlage f
gas in bottles (for welding) Flaschengas n (zum Schweißen)
gas jet Gasbrenner m; Gasdüse f
gasket Dichtungsring m
gas line Gasleitung f
gas main Hauptgasleitung f
gas mask Gasmaske f
gas meter Gaszähler m
gas nitriding Gasnitrieren n
gas off-take Gasabzug m; Gasfang m
gasometer Gasbehälter m; Gasometer m
gasometric gasvolumetrisch
gas permeability Gasdurchlässigkeit f
gas phase Gasphase f
gas pickling Gasbeizen n
gas pick-up Gasaufnahme f
gas pipe Gasleitung f; Gasrohr n; Gaszufuhr f
gas pipeline Gasleitung f

gas pipeline accessories and fittings Gasarmaturen *fpl*
gas piston blower Kolbengebläse *n*
gas poker Gasstocher *m*
gas port Gasbrenner *m*
gas port block Brennerkopf *m*
gas port end Brennerkopf *m*
gas port peep hole Spiegelschauloch *n*
gas processing plant Gasverarbeitungsanlage *f*
gas producer Gaserzeuger *m*; Gasgenerator *m*
gas purification Gasreinigung *f*
gas purifying plant Gasreinigungsanlage *f*
gas reformer Gasumsetzer *m*
gas reforming Gasspaltung *f*
gas regenerator chamber Gasheizkammer *f*
gas retort carbon Retortenkohle *f*
gas sampling device Gasprobe-Entnahmevorrichtung *f*
gas scrubber Gaswäscher *m*
gas seal Gasschleuse *f*
gas separating plant Gastrennanlage *f*
gas separator Gasabscheider *m*
gas shrouding Schutzgaß *n* (beim Gießen)
gassing Vergasen *n* (von Schmelzen)
gas-tight gasdicht
gas tuyre Gasdüse *f*
gas-type reduction Gasreduktion *f*
gas valve Gasventil *n*
gas water removal Gaswasserbeseitigung *f*
gas welding blow pipe Injektorbrenner *m*
gate Eingußtrichter *m*; Fenster *n* (EDV); Klappe *f*; Tor *n*; Trichter *m* (Gießen); Verschluß *m*; anschneiden
gate shear Tafelschere *f*
gate valve Absperrschieber *m*; Sperrschieber *m*
gathering Rollen *n* (Reckstauchen); Stauchen *n* eines Halbzeuges (Gesenkschmiede)
gathering by die stretching Reckstauchen *n*
gating (of moulds) Anschneiden *n* (von Formen); Anschnitt-Technik *f*
ga[u]ge Abmessung *f*; Dicke *f*; Lehre *f*; Maß *n*; Meißel *m*; Pegel *m* (air pollution); Spurweite *f*; Vorstoß *m*
ga[u]ge length Meßlänge *f*
gauge marks Körnereinschläge *mpl*
ga[u]ge measuring device Banddikken-Meßgerät *n*
ga[u]ge reading (air pollution) Pegelwert *m*
ga[u]ge rod Spurstange *f*
ga[u]ging Messen *n*
gear Haspel *f*
gear cutting Verwindung *f*; Verzahnung *f*; Zahnfräsen *n*
gear cutting machine Verzahnungsmaschine *f*
geared motor Getriebemotor *m*
gear[ing] Getriebe *n*; Zahnrad *n*; Übersetzung *f*
gearing Verzahnung *f*; Zahnradgetriebe *n*
gear milling machine Räderfräsmaschine *f*
gear ratio Übersetzungsverhältnis *n*
gear reduction Räderuntersetzung *f*
gear speed Getriebestufe *f*
gear tooth milling Zahnfräsen *n*
gear train Rädergetriebe *n*
gear transmission Zahnradübertragung *f*
gear-type spindle Zahnspindel *f*
gear wheel Übersetzungszahnrad *n*
gear wheel moulding machine Zahnräder-Formmaschine *f*
gear wheel steel Zahnradstahl *m*
general expense Gemeinkosten *pl*
general symbol Grundschaltzeichen *n*
generation Erzeugung *f* (Strom)
geological research procedure geologisches Untersuchungsverfahren *n*
geology Geologie *f*
geometric mean geometrisches Mittel *n*

geophysics Geophysik f
German Industrial Standards Institute DIN (Deutsches Institut für Normung)
getter Getter m
getter (powder met.) Fangstoff m
ghost [line] Schattenlinie f; Schattenriß m; Schattenstreifen m; Seigerungsstreifen m
Gibbs free energy freie Enthalpie f (Gibbs)
gilled tube Rippenrohr n
giratory crusher Walzenbrecher m
girder Doppel-T-Träger m; Träger m; zusammengesetzter Träger m
girder pole Gittermast m
girder rail Rillenschiene f
girder rolling mill Trägerwalzwerk n
git Gießtrichter m; Trichter m
glance coal Anthrazit m; Magerkohle f
glasing tees Verglasungs-T-Stahl m
glass fiber filter Glasfaserfilter m
glass for protection against heat Wärmeschutzglas n
glass hard glashart
glass lined steel container Stahlbehälter m mit Glasauskleidung
glass lined steel tank Stahlbehälter m mit Glasauskleidung
glass lubrication Glasschmierung f
glaze Glasur f; glasieren
glazing Glasur f
glide gleiten; rutschen
globe valve Kugelventil n
globular kugelig
globular powder kugeliges Pulver n
gloss Glanz m
glow Glut f; glimmen; glühen
glow discharge Glimmentladung f
glow nitriding Glimmnitrieren n
goffered plate Waffelblech n
goggle valve Brillenschieber m; Schmidtsche Brille f
go-no-go gauge Betriebslehre f
goodness of [best] fit Güte f der Anpassung
goods in conveying plant Fördergut n

goods wagon Güterwagen m
gooseneck Anschlußstück n; Kniestück n
gothic groove Spitzbogenkaliber n
gothic pass Spitzbogenkaliber n
gouge Hohlbeitel m; Hohlmeißel m; Rille f
govern regeln
governor slide valve Regelschieber m
grab [bucket] Greifer m
grab crane Greiferkran m
gradation Abstufung f; Eichstrich m
grade Güte f; Gütestufe f; abstufen; einteilen; klassieren
grade of steel Stahlgüte f
gradient Gefälle n
grading Einstufung f
grading jigging screen Klassierrüttelsieb n
grading of ores Klassieren n der Erze
grading screen Klassiersieb n
graduated circle Teilkreis m (Mikroskop)
graduated flask Meßkolben m
graduated scale Skala f
graduated test Stufenversuche mpl
graduation Gradeinteilung f
grain Korn n
grain boundary Korngrenze f
grain boundary attack Korngrenzenangriff m
grain boundary hardening Korngrenzhärtung f
grain boundary migration Korngrenzenwanderung f
grain boundary network Korngrenzennetzwerk n
grain classification Korngrößeneinteilung f
grain coarsening Kornvergrößerung f; Körnung f
grain growth Kornwachstum n
grain oriented sheet kornorientiertes Blech n
grain refined C-Mn steel kornverfeinerter unlegierter Manganstahl m
grain refinement Kornfeinung f (Wärmebehandlung)

grain refining Kornfeinen *n*
grain roll Walze *f* (Stahlersatz)
grain size control by deoxidizing practice Feinkorn-Desoxidation *f*
grain size distribution Korngrößenverteilung *f*
grain size fraction Korngrößenfraktion *f*
grain size [number] Korngröße *f*
grain size range Korngrößenbereich *m*
grain sizing Kornklassierung *f*
grain structure Kornaufbau *m*; Korngefüge *n*
grant a patent Patent *n* erteilen
granular structure körniges Gefüge *n*
granulate körnen
granulated blast-furnace slag Hüttensand *m*
granulated material Granulat *n*
granulated slag gekörnte Schlacke *f*; granulierte Schlacke *f*
granulated slag brick Hüttenstein *m*
granulating of sinter mix Krümeln *n*
granulating plant Granulationsanlage *f*
granulating spout Granulierrinne *f*
granulation Kornbildung *f*; Körnung *f*
granulation characteristica [curve] Kornverteilungskurve *f*, Körnungskennlinie *f*
graph Diagramm *n*; Graph *m*; Netzplan *m*; Schaubild *n*
graphical representation graphische Darstellung *f*
graphite Graphit *m*
graphite bearing Graphitlager *n*
graphite electrode Graphitelektrode *f*
graphite nodule Graphitknötchen *n*
graphite rod furnace Graphitstabofen *m*
graphitic graphitisch
graphitic carbon Graphitkohle *f*, Graphitkohlenstoff *m*
graphitic corrosion Spongiose *f*
graphitisation Graphitisierung *f*
graph paper Koordinatenpapier *n*
grapple bucket Greifer *m*

grasp ergreifen; fassen
grate Rost *m* (Kessel)
grate hearth Rostfeuerung *f*
grate plane Netzebene *f*
graticule Teilkreis *m* (Mikroskop)
grating Gitter *n*
grating spectrograph Gitterspektrometer *n*
gravel Grieß *m*; Kies *m*; Schotter *m*
gravimetric gewichtsanalytisch
gravitational separator Schwerkraftabscheider *m*
gravity chute Rutsche *f*
gravity conveyor Schwerkraftförderer *m*
gravity die casting Dauerform-Gußstück *n*; Dauerformguß *m*; Kokillenguß *m*
gravity [roller] conveyor Rollbahn *f*; Rutschbahn *f*
grease schmieren
grease gun Fettschmierpresse *f*
grease or dirt marks (surface defect) Fett- oder Schmutzgrübchen *npl*
grease or dirt pits Fett- oder Schmutzgrübchen *npl*
grease packed in Fett arbeitend (Lager)
grease pump Fettschmierpumpe *f*
greasing Abschmieren *n*
green ball Grünpellet *n*
green body Preßling *m*
green coal Förderkohle *f*
green compact Grünling *m*
green density Preßdichte *f*
green pellet Grünpellet *n*
green sand Grünsand *m*
green sand core Grünsandkern *m*
green strength Grünfestigkeit *f*; Kantenbeständigkeit *f* (Pulvermet.)
green vitriol Eisenvitriol *n*
grey [cast] iron Grauguß *m*
grey cast iron Gußeisen *n* mit Lamellengraphit
grey pig graues Roheisen *n*
grid Ferngasnetz *n*; Gitter *n*; Rost *m*; Verteilungsnetz *n*; Überlandleitung *f*

grid element spacing Rasterabstand *m*
grid gas Ferngas *n*
grid gas supply Ferngasversorgung *f*
grid point Gitterpunkt *m*
grid welding machine Gitterschweißmaschine *f*
grind mahlen; schleifen
grindability Mahlbarkeit *f*
grinder Schleifmaschine *f*
grinding check Schleifriß *m*
grinding crack Schleifriß *m*
grinding dust Schleifstaub *m*
grinding machine Schleifmaschine *f*
grinding mill Schleifmühle *f*
grinding shop Schleiferei *f*
grind[ing] stone Schleifstein *m*
grinding wheel Schleifscheibe *f*
grinding wheel travel Schleifweg *m*
grinding work Schleifarbeit *f*
grind off abschleifen
grind with emery abschmirgeln
grip einspannen; fassen; greifen
gripping head Einspannkopf *m*; Spannkopf *m*
gripping tongs Greifzange *f*
grip type tilter Greifkanter *m* (Walzen)
grit Grieß *m*; Schleifpulver *n*; scharfkantiger Schrott *m*
grit-blasting Ablasen *n*; Sanden *n*
grizzly Siebrost *m*
grog Ton *m*; gebrannter Ton *m*; gemahlene Schamotte *f*
groove Auskehlung *f*; Einbrandkerbe *f*; Kaliber *n*; Keilwellennut *f*; Kerb *m*; Riefe *f*; nuten *f*; Riffel *f*; Rille *f*; Schlitz *m*
grooved rail Rillenschiene *f*
grooved roll Kaliberwalze *f*; kalibrierte Walze *f*; profilierte Walze *f*
grooved skelp in Kalibern gewalzter Rohrstreifen *m*
grooved tube Rillenrohr *n*
grooving Kerben *n*
gross caloric power (am.) Heizwert *m*; oberer Heizwert *m*
gross sample Großprobe *f*
gross weight Rohgewicht *n*

ground geschliffen
ground bar geschliffener Stab *m*
ground basic slag Thomasmehl *n*
grounded (am.) kurzgeschlossen (Stromkreis)
ground finish geschliffener Zustand *m*
ground level charging machine Einsetzmaschine *f*
ground level transportation gear Flurfördereinrichtung *f*
ground-plate Bodenplatte *f*; Grundplatte *f*; Unterlagplatte *f*
ground powder gemahlenes Pulver *n*
ground vibration Bodenerschütterung *f*
group casting Gespannguß *m*
grouping Einstufung *f*; Gruppenbildung *f*; Gruppierung *f*
group of curves Kurvenschar *f*
groups selected at random zufällig ausgewählte Gruppen *fpl*
group teeming bottom plate Gespannplatte *f*
group teeming stool (am.) Gespannplatte *f*
grow wachsen
grub screw Gewindestift *m*; Schaftschraube *f*
grummet thimble Seilkausche *f*
guarantee range Gewährleistungsumfang *m*
guard Abstreifmeißel *m*; Schutzvorrichtung *f*; Unfallschutz *m*
guidance Führung *f*
guide Führung *f*; Führung *f* (Maschinenteil)
guide box Führungskasten *m*
guide bush Führungsbüchse *f*
guide mark Führungskratzer *m*
guide pulley Umlenkrolle *f*
guide rail Leitschiene *f*
guide scar Führungskratzer *m*
guide scratch Führungskratzer *m*
guillotine shear Tafelschere *f*
gusset [plate] Knotenblech *n*
gutter Gesenkrinne *f* zur Aufnahme des Grates; Rinne *f*
gutter sections Rinneneisen *n*

guy wire Versteifungsdraht *m*
gypsum Gips *m*
gyratory crusher Kreiselbrecher *m*
gyro-frequency Kreisfrequenz *f*
gyratory crusher Kreiselbrecher *m*
gyro-frequency Kreisfrequenz *f*

H

habit plane Habitusebene *f*
hack saw Bügelsäge *f*; Kaltsäge *f*
hair hygrometer Haarhygrometer *n*
hair [line] crack Haarriß *m*
hair line pointer Fadenzeiger *m*
half flat semifinished product halbflaches Halbzeug *n*
half gas firing Halbgasfeuerung *f*
half hard halbhart
half life Halbwertzeit *f*
half line width Halbwertsbreite *f*
half roasted lumps of iron ore Eisenerzstücke *npl*; halbgeröstete Eisenerzstücke *npl*
half rounds Halbrundstahl *m*
half round wire rod halbrunder Walzdraht *m*
half time width Halbwertsbreite *f*
half wedge brick Halbwölber *m* (ff. Stein)
hammer Hammer *m*; hämmern
hammer-cog vorschmieden
hammer crusher (hammer mill) Hammerbrecher *m*
hammer forging Flachstauchen *n*; Freiformschmieden *n*; Recken *n*; Reckschmieden *n*
hammer head Hammerkopf *m*
hammer mill Hammerwerk *n*
hand chisel Handmeißel *m*
handle bewegen; handhaben
hand lever Handhebel *m*
handling break Kantenbeschädigung *f*
handling capacity Umschlagleistung *f*
handling (material) Bewegung *f*
hand rammer Handstampfer *m*
hand setting Richten *n* von Hand

hand shank Stielpfanne *f*; Tragpfanne *f*
hand tight handfest geschraubt
hanger crack Haubenriß *m*
hanger-on Anschläger *m* (Kran)
hanging Hängen *n* (der Gicht)
hanging guard Hängemeißel *m*
hard chromium plating Hartverchromen *n*
hard drawn wire hartgezogener Draht *m*
harden härten; verhärten
hardenability Härtbarkeit *f*
hardenable härtbar
harden and temper vergüten
hardened casting Guß *m* gehärteter
hardeness increase Aufhärtung *f*
hardening Härtearbeit *f*; Härten *n*; Härtung *f*
hardening alloy Vorlegierung *f*
hardening and heat treating plant Härte- und Vergüteanlage *f*
hardening crack sensitivity Härtungsrißempfindlichkeit *f*
hardening crucible Härtetiegel *m*
hardening flaw Härteriß *m*
hardening fracture sensitivity Härtungsrißempfindlichkeit *f*
hardening from hot forming temperature Härten *n* aus der Warmumformhitze
hardening furnace Härteofen *m*
hardening machine Härtemaschine *f*
hardening of carburised surface Randhärten *n*
hardening shop Härterei *f*
hardening stock Härtegut *n*
hardening test Härteprüfung *f*
hardening with subsequent drawing Vergüten *n*
hardening with subsequent tempering Vergüten *n*
hard-facing Aufschweißen *n* (oder Auflöten) von Hartmetallplättchen; Hartauftragsschweißung *f*
hard-facing alloy Aufschweißlegierung *f*
hard magnetic sintered material hart-

magnetischer metallischer Sinterwerkstoff *m*
hard material powder Hartstoffpulver *n*
hard metal Hartlegierung *f*
hard metal alloy Hartmetall *n*; Hartmetall-Legierung *f*
hard metal draw die Hartmetall-Ziehstein *m*
hardness Härte *f*
hardness drop tester Fallhärteprüfer *m*
hardness of water Wasserhärte *f*
hardness penetration Härtetiefe *f*
hardness penetration [depth] Einhärtetiefe *f*
hardness scatter band Härtestreuband *n*
hardness testing machine Härteprüfmaschine *f*
hard rubber Hartgummi *m*
hard solder Hartlot *n*
hard spots Härtungsgefüge *n* (Drahtfehler)
hardware configuration Gerätekonfiguration *f* (EDV)
hard wearing surface verschleißfeste Oberfläche *f*
harmonic distortion factor Klirrfaktor *m*
harmonic mean harmonisches Mittel *n*
harmonic oscillation Oberschwingung *f*
harmonic reponse Frequenzgang *m*
haulage gear Haspel *f*
hauling cable Zugseil *n*
hauling installation Förderanlage *f*
hauling plant Förderanlage *f*
haze dome Dunstglocke *f*
H-beam Doppel-T-Eisen *n*
head Druckhöhe *f*; Kopf *m*; anstauchen
header verlorener Kopf *m*
head frame Förderturm *m*
headgear Fördergerüst *n*
headless screw Gewindestift *m*
head office Generaldirektion *f*, Hauptverwaltungsbüro *n*

head of metal Metallsäule *f*
head roller Walzmeister *m*
headroom Kopfhöhe *f*
heap Halde *f*; Haufen *m*; häufen
hearing impairment Gehörschädigung *f*
hearth Gestell *n*; Herd *m*; Hochofengestell *n*; Ofenraum *m*
hearth area Herdfläche *f*
hearth block Bodenstein *m*
hearth bottom Herdsohle *f*
hearth casing Gestellpanzer *m*
hearth jacket Gestellpanzer *m*
hearth load Gestellbelastung *f*
hearth refining Herdfrischen *n*
hearth type furnace Herdofen *m*
hearth type melting process Herdschmelzverfahren *n*
hearth type steelmaking plant Herdstahlwerk *n*
heat Hitze *f*; beheizen; einheizen; erhitzen; erwärmen
heat accumulator Wärmespeicher *m*
heat-affected zone (HAZ) Übergangszone *f* (beim Schweißen); Wärmeeinflußzone *f* (WEZ); wärmebeeinflußte Zone *f*
heat at constant volume (pressure) Molwärme *f* bei konstantem Volumen (Druck)
heat balance Wärmebilanz *f*; Wärmehaushalt *m*
heat capacity Wärmeinhalt *m*; Wärmekapazität *f*
heat capacity at constant volume (pressure) Wärmekapazität *f* bei konstantem Volumen (Druck)
heat-conducting plate Konvektor *m*; Wärmeleitplatte *f*
heat conductivity Wärmeleitfähigkeit *f*
heat consumption Wärmeverbrauch *m*
heat contents Wärmeinhalt *m*
heat convection Wärmeumwälzung *f*
heat crack Wärmeriß *m*
heat current Wärmestrom *m*
heat current density Wärmestromdichte *f*
heat cycle Glühzyklus *m*

heat economy Wärmewirtschaft f
heater Heizer m; Wärmer m
heat evolved Wärmeangebot n
heat exchanger Wärmeaustauscher m
heat expansion Wärmedehnung f
heat flow Wärmefluß m
heat flow rate Wärmestrom m
heat flux Wärmefluß m
heat hardening Hartbrennen n
heating Beheizung f; Feuerung f; Heizung f; Wärmen n
heating by arc Lichtbogenbeheizung f
heating conductor material Heizleiter-Werkstoff m
heating flue Heizgas-Sammelkanal m; Heizung f
heating installation Beheizungseinrichtung f
heating resistor material Widerstandswerkstoff m
heating surface Lichtfläche f
heating time Erwärmdauer f; Wärmdauer f; Wärmzeit f
heat insulation Wärmedämmung f
heat insulation composition Wärmeschutzmasse f
heat loss Wärmeverlust m
heat measurement Wärmemessung f
heat of evaporation Verdampfungswärme f
heat of formation Bildungswärme f
heat of mixture Mischungswärme f
heat of solution Lösungswärme f
heat producing wärmeerzeugend
heat radiating lamp Temperaturstrahler m
heat relief Wärmeschutz m
heat required Wärmebedarf m
heat resistance Hitzebeständigkeit f
heat resistant hitzebeständig
heat resisting wärmebeständig
heat-resisting casting feuerbeständiger Guß m
heat resisting steel hitzebeständiger Stahl m
heat transfer Wärmeübergang m
heat transfer coefficient Wärmeübergangszahl f

heat transition Wärmedurchgang m
heat transmission Wärmeübergang m; Wärmeübertragung f
heat treatable steel Vergütungsstahl m
heat treatable steel casting Vergütungsstahlguß m
heat treating furnace Wärmebehandlungsofen m
heat treating plant Vergütungsanlage f
heat treatment Wärmebehandlung f
heat treatment crack Härteriß m
heat unit Wärmeeinheit f
heat waste Werkstoffverlust m durch Verzundern
heavy current conductors Hochstrombahn f
heavy duty spring Hochleistungsfeder f
heavy forging Schmiedestück n schweres
heavy galvanising Starkverzinnung f
heavy metal casting Schwermetallguß m
heavy plate Grobblech n
heavy scrap Blockschrott m; Schrott m schwerer
heavy sections schwerer Formstahl m
height Höhe f; Werkstoffhöhe f
helical gear Schraubenrad n
helical gearing Schrägverzahnung f
helical spring Schraubenfeder f
helical tube Wendelrohr n
Helmholtz free energy freie Energie f (Helmholtz)
hematite Hämatit m
hematite pig iron Hämatitroheisen n
hemisphere temperature Halbkugelpunkt m (Schmelzbarkeit von Kohle)
hemp rope Hanfseil n
hermetically sealed unter Luftabschluß m
herringbone tooth Pfeilzahn m; Winkelzahn m
heterogeneity Ungleichmäßigkeit f; Verschiedenartigkeit f

heterogeneous heterogen; ungleichartig; verschiedenartig
hexagonal sechskantig
hexagonal socket head cap screw Innensechskantschraube *f*
hexagon bars Sechskantstahl *m*
hex head screw Sechskantschraube *f*
H-girder Doppel-T-Eisen *n*
hierarchical process computing system hierarchisches Prozeßrechnersystem *n*
high alloy steel hochlegierter Stahl *m*
high angle tilt boundaries Großwinkelkorngrenzen *fpl*
high-bay warehouse Hochregallager *n*
high boiled stark kochend
high carbon steel Hartstahl *m* (unlegiert); hochgekohlter Stahl *m*; kohlenstoffreicher Stahl *m*
high carbon steel casting Hartstahlguß *m*
high centrifugal force cyclone Drallabscheider *m*
high current arc Hochleistungslichtbogen *m*
high duty cast iron hochfestes Gußeisen *n*
high energy rate forming Hochenergieumformung *f*
high energy scrubber Hochleistungswäscher *m*
high-frequency induction furnace Hochfrequenz-Induktionsofen *m*; kernloser Induktionsofen *m*
high-grade casting Qualitätsguß *m*
high-grade iron Qualitätseisen *n*
high grade ore reichhaltiges Erz *n*
high-grade steel Edelstahl *m*; Qualitätsstahl *m*
high humidity and condensation test Feuchtigkeitslagerversuch *m*
high idle [run] Vollgas *n* bei Leerlauf
high intensity magnetic separation Starkfeldmagnetscheidung *f*
high level storage bunker Hochbunker *m*
high level tank Hochbehälter *m*

highly refractory brick hochfeuerfester Stein *m*
high melting schwerschmelzbar
high-mirror-finished sheet Hochglanzblech *n*
high output burner Hochleistungsbrenner *m*
high power leistungsstark
high pressure accessories and fittings Hochdruckarmaturen *fpl*
high pressure boiler Druckkessel *m*
high pressure container Druckkessel *m*
high pressure die casting Druckguß *m*
high pressure gas main Hochdruckgasleitung *f*
high pressure lubricant Hochdruckschmiermittel *n*
high pressure manometer Hochdruckmanometer *n*
high pressure part Hochdruckteil *n*
high-pressure scale sprays Zunderabspritzvorrichtung *f*
high pressure tank Druckkessel *m*
high-purity iron Reinsteisen *n*
high quality hochwertig
high quality material Qualitätswerkstoff *m*
high-Si chilled iron roll Walze *f* (Mildhart)
high sintering Nachsintern *n*
high speed forming Hochgeschwindigkeitsumformen *n*
high-speed lathe Schnelldrehbank *f*
high-speed steel Schnellarbeitsstahl *m*
high-speed stranding machine Schnellverseilmaschine *f*
high speed thermal image transducer thermischer Hochgeschwindigkeits-Bildumwandler *m*
high spot dicke Stelle *f*
high-strength cast iron Edelguß *m*
high strength patented wire rope patentierter Seildraht *m* mit besonders hoher Zugfestigkeit
high strength steel hochfester Stahl *m*
high strength structural steel hochfester Baustahl *m*

high temperature alloy hochwarmfeste Legierung f
high temperature brittleness Hochtemperaturversprödung f
high temperature oxidation Verzunderung f; Zundern n
high temperature properties Hochtemperatureigenschaften fpl
high temperature steel warmfester Stahl m
high-temperature strength Warmfestigkeit f
high-temperature structural steel warmfester Baustahl m
high tensile steel hochfester Stahl m
high top pressure operation Hochdruckverfahren n (Hochofen)
high top pressure operation of blast furnace Hochofenbetrieb m mit Gegendruck an der Gicht
hight top ressure Gichtgegendruck m
high-vacuum arc furnace Hochvakuumlichtbogenofen m
high-vacuum electron beam welding Hochvakuum-Elektronenstrahlschweißen n
high-vacuum melting furnace Hochvakuumofen m
high velocity burner Hochgeschwindigkeitsbrenner m
high-voltage lines and equipment Hochspannungsanlagen fpl
high voltage spark generator Hochspannungsfunkenerzeuger m
hinge Gelenk n; Gelenk-Scharnier n; Scharnier n
hinge profile Gelenkbandprofil n
hire rolling Lohnwalzen n
histogram Stufenschaubild n
historical costing Nachkalkulation f
hob Gesenkmatrize f; Obergesenk n
hobbing Einsenken n (kalt)
hobbing press Kalteinsenkpresse f
hob cutter Schneckenfräser m; Wälzfräser m
hoist Fördermaschine f; Hebezeug n; Winde f; fördern; heben; hochwinden

hoisting apparatus Hebezeug n
hoisting cage Fördergestell n
hoisting speed Hubgeschwindigkeit f
hoist shaft Förderschacht m
hold a ladle Pfanne f abstehen lassen
holding Halten n
holding capacity Fassungsvermögen n
holding down member (open hearth furnace) Gewölbeniederhalter m
holding furnace Warmhalteofen m
holding period Haltedauer f
holding time Haltezeit f; Liegezeit f; Verweilzeit f; Wartezeit f
hole Kaliber n; Loch n; Tiefenzelle f
holes Löcher npl (Bandfehler)
holidays Ferien pl
hollow Höhlung f; Zapfen m
hollow axle Hohlachse f
hollow [body] Hohlkörper m
hollow brick Hohlblockstein m; Hohlstein m; Hohlziegel m
hollow casting Hohlguß m
hollow checker brick Gitterhohlstein m
hollow drill Hohlbohrer m
hollow drill steel Hohlbohrstahl m
hollow electrode Hohlelektrode f
hollow extrusion Hohlstrangpressen n
hollow forging Hohlschmieden n; Lochen n; Recken n von Hohlkörpern
hollow-punch piercing Hohldornen n
hollow roll Hohlwalze f
hollow section Hohlprofil n
hollow shape Hohlblockstein m; Hohlstein m; Hohlziegel m
hollow weld Kehlnaht f; leichte Kehlnaht f
home port Heimathafen m
home scrap Eigenschrott m
homogeneity Gleichartigkeit f
homogeneous gleichartig; gleichmäßig; homogen
homogeneousness Homogenität f
homogenised ore burden Möller m vorbereiteter
homogenising Diffusionsglühen n

homogenize homogenisieren
honeycomb type erosion löcherartige Ausfressung f
honing Honen n; Ziehschleifen n
honing machine Honmaschine f
hood Abzug m; Abzugshaube f; Kappe f; Kessel m
hood cooling Haubenkühlung f
hood type annealing furnace Haubenglühofen m
hook Haken m
hook conveyer Hakenbahn f (für Drahtringe)
Hooke's law Hooke'sches Gesetz
Hooke's universal joint Kardangelenk n; Kreuzgelenk n
hooked tie plate Hakenplatte f
hook in einhaken
hook on einhaken
hoop mill Bandstahlwalzwerk n
hopper Behälter m; Füllrumpf m; Klärsumpf m; Trichter m (Gicht); Vorratstrichter m
hopper car Trichterwagen m
horizontal milling machine Waagerechtfräsmaschine f
horizontal position welding horizontales Schweißen n
host computer Fremdrechner m
hot air duct Heißluftleitung f
hot bank Warmbett m
hot bed Warmbett n; Warmlager n
hot bend test Warmbiegeversuch m
hot blast Heißwind m
hot blast cupola Heißwind-Kupolofen m
hot blast furnace Heißwindofen m
hot blast pipe Heißwindleitung f
hot blast [slide] valve Heißwindschieber m
hot blast stove Cowper m; Heißwindofen m; Winderhitzer m
hot blast stove brick Cowperstein m; Winderhitzerstein m
hot blast stove on gas (on blast) Winderhitzer m auf Gas (auf Wind)
hot bloom shears Warmblockschere f
hot box Haspelofen m

hot brittleness Warmsprödigkeit f
hot compression strength Heißdruckfestigkeit f (ff. Steine)
hot cooling Heißkühlung f; Siedekühlung f
hot crack Wärmeriß m
hot dip aluminising Feueraluminieren n
hot [dip] galvanised feuerverzinkt
hot dip galvanising Feuerverzinken n
hot [dip] galvanising Feuerverzinken n
hot dip galvanising Verzinkung f
hot dip metal coating Schmelztauchverfahren n
hot-dipped tinplate feuerverzinntes Weißblech n
hot drawn tube warmgezogenes Rohr n
hot embrittlement Warmversprödung f
hot extrusion Fließpressen n (warm); Warmstrangpressen n
hot finished tube warm fertiggewalztes Rohr n
hot forming Warmformgebung f; Warmumformung f
hot forming property Warmformänderungsvermögen n; Warmumformbarkeit f; Warmverarbeitbarkeit f
hot forming tool steel Warmarbeitsstahl m
hot heel Sumpf m flüssiger
hot immersion tank Heißspülbehälter m
hot material conveyor Heißgutförderer m
hot metal flüssiges Roheisen n
hot metal ladle Roheisenpfanne f
hot metal mixer Mischer m; Roheisenmischer m
hot metal process Schmelzen n mit flüssigem Einsatz
hot metal shop Schmelzbetrieb m mit heißem Einsatz
hot metal transfer car Roheisenübergabewagen m
hot plate straightening machine Warmblechrichtmaschine f

hot press heißpressen
hot pressing Warmpressen *n*
hot repressing Heißnachpressen *n*
hot rolled condition warmgewalzter Zustand *m*
hot rolled flats warmgewalzter Flachstahl *m*
hot rolled rounds warmgewalzter Rundstahl *m*
hot rolled small U-section warmgewalzter kleiner U-Stahl *m*
hot rolled squares warmgewalzter Vierkantstahl *m*
hot [rolled] strip Warmband *n*
hot rolled strip warmgewalztes Band *n*
hot [rolled] wide strip Warmbreitband *n*
hot rolling Warmwalzen *n*
hot roll warmwalzen
hot rolling mill Warmwalzwerk *n*
hot rolling of flats Flachstahl-Warmwalzen *n*
hot rolling train Warmstraße *f*
hot saw Warmsäge *f*
hot shaping Warmformgebung *f*; Warmumformung *f*
hot short warmbrüchig; warmrißanfällig
hot shortness Heißbruch *m*; Warmbrüchigkeit *f*; Warmrissigkeit *f*
hot stage microscope Heiztischmikroskop *n*
hot straightening Warmrichten *n*
hot strip scratch Warmbandkratzer *m*
hot tear Wärmeriß *m*
hot tensile test Warmzugversuch *m*
hot tinning Feuerverzinnung *f*
hot top Blockaufsatz *m*; Gießaufsatz *m*; Gießkopf *m*; Kokillenhaube *f*; verlorener Kopf *m*
hot top ingot Haubenblock *m*
hot top mould Massekopfkokille *f*
hot topping feeder head heating Blockkopfbeheizung *f*
hot water part Heißwasserteil *n*
hot working Warmformgebung *f*
hot working steel Warmarbeitsstahl *m*

hot-work tool steel Warmarbeitsstahl *m*
hourly output Stundenleistung *f*
housing Gehäuse *n*; Walzenständer *m*
housing of the close top type geschlossener Walzenständer *m*
housing of the open top type Kappenständer *m*
housing screw Umstellspindel *f*
hub Nabe *f*
humidity Feuchtigkeit *f*
humidity cell Feuchtigkeitsgeber *m*; Taupunktmeßgerät *n*
hump plate Höckerplatte *f*
hunting pendelnd; schaukelnd; schwänkend
hurdle type scrubber Hordenwäscher *m*
hurdle washer Hordenwäscher *m*
hurdle washing tower Hordenwäscher *m*
hybrid computer Hybridrechner *m*
hydraulic accumulator hydraulischer Akkumulator *m*
hydraulically operated bell type furnace hydraulischer Haubenofen *m*
hydraulic control hydraulische Steuerung *f*
hydraulic descaling hydraulische Entzunderung *f*
hydraulic drive hydraulischer Antrieb *m*
hydraulic fluid Druckflüssigkeit *f*
hydraulic forging press hydraulische Schmiedepresse *f*
hydraulic jack hydraulische Winde *f*
hydraulic machine hydraulische Maschine *f*
hydraulic piston Hydraulikkolben *m*
hydraulic power Wasserkraft *f*
hydraulic press hydraulische Presse *f*
hydraulic [pressure] test Wasserdruckversuch *m*
hydraulic stowing Spülversatzleitung *f*
hydraulic test Innendruckversuch *m* mit Wasser
hydraulic water Druckwasser *n*

hydride powder Hydridpulver *n*
hydrocarbon Kohlenwasserstoff *m*
hydrodynamic drawing hydrodynamisches Ziehen *n*
hydrodynamic friction hydrodynamische Reibung *f*
hydrodynamics Hydrodynamik *f*
hydrodynamic theory of rolling hydrodynamische Walztheorie *f*
hydrofluoric acid Flußsäure *f*
hydrogen Wasserstoff *m*
hydrogen absorption Wasserstoffaufnahme *f*
hydrogenate hydrieren
hydr[ogen]ation works Hydrierwerk *n*
hydrogen embrittlement Wasserstoffsprödigkeit *f*
hydrogen induced corrosion (HIC) Korrosion *f* durch Wasserstoff
hydrogen-induced cracking (HIC) wasserstoffinduzierte Rißbildung *f*
hydrogen peroxide Wasserstoffperoxid *n*
hydromatic drawing tool hydromatisches Ziehwerkzeug *n*
hydrometallurgy Hydrometallurgie *f*
hydrosparking Formen *n* durch Stoßwellen
hydrostatic compacting Schlauchpressen *n*; hydrostatisches Pressen *n*
hydrostatic direct impact extrusion hydrostatisches Vorwärts-Fließpressen *n*
hydrostatic direct impact extrusion of rods hydrostatisches Voll-Vorwärts-Fließpressen *n*
hydrostatic direct rod extrusion hydrostatisches Vorwärts-Strangpressen *n*
hydrostatic direct tubular impact extrusion hydrostatisches Hohl-Vorwärts-Fließpressen *n*
hydrostatic test Abpreßversuch *m*; Wasserdruckversuch *m*
hygrometer Luftfeuchtigkeitsmesser *m*
hypereutectic übereutektisch

hypereutectoid übereutektoidisch
hypereutectoid steel hypereutektoidischer Stahl *m*; übereutektoidischer Stahl *m*
hypoeutectic untereutektisch
hypoeutectoid steel untereutektoidischer Stahl *m*
hypothetical postulate Erscheinungsbild *n*
hysteresis loop Hysteresisschleife *f*
hysteresis loss Hysteresisverlust *m*

I

I-beam Doppel-T-Träger *m*
iceberg Eisberg *m* (Eisenschwammberg im Ofen)
ideal ideal
ideal solution ideale Lösung *f*
identation Eindruck *m*
identification Erkennung *f*; Feststellung *f*; Identifizierung *f*
identification marking Kennzeichnung *f* (von Erzeugnissen)
idle [boiler] corrosion Stillstandkorrosion *f*
idle operation Leerlauf *m*
idle period Nebenzeit *f*
idler Schleppwalze *f*
idle roll Blindwalze *f*; Schleppwalze *f*
idle roller table nichtangetriebener Rollgang *m*
idle-running period Leerlaufzeit *f*
idle-running time Leerlaufzeit *f*
idle time Stillstandzeit *f*
ignite anzünden; entzünden
ignition Entzündung *f*; Zündung *f*
ignition hood Zündhaube *f* (Sinter)
ignition loss Glühverlust *m*
ignition residue Glührückstand *m*
ignition temperature Zündtemperatur *f*
Ilgner [type motor generator] set Schwungradumformer *m*
illuminate beleuchten

illuminated dial balance Leuchtbildwaage f
illuminated mimic panel Leuchtschaltbild n
immerse eintauchen
immersed roll Tauchwalze f
immersion electrode Eintauchelektrode f
immersion gas burner Tauchbrenner m
immersion hardening Tauchhärten n
immersion pouring Metallzuführung f unter dem Gießspiegel
immersion thermocouple Tauchthermoelement n
impact Anstoß m; Schlag m; Stoß m
impact ball hardness test Fallhärteprüfung f
impact bending strength Schlagbiegefestigkeit f
impact bending test Schlagbiegeversuch m
impact crusher Prallbrecher m
impact endurance test Dauerschlagfestigkeitsversuch m
impacter Schlagschmiedemaschine f
impact extrusion Fließpressen n
impact extrusion press Fließdruckpresse f
impact extrusion with action media Fließpressen n mit Wirkmedien
impact extrusion with rigid tool Fließpressen n mit starrem Werkzeug
impact force Schlagkraft f
impact free stoßfrei
impact hardness test Schlaghärteprüfung f
impacting Kaltschlagschmieden n
impact load Stoßbelastung f
impact noise Impulslärm m
impact strength Schlagfestigkeit f
impact test Kerbschlagbiegeversuch m; Kerbschlagversuch m; Schlagversuch m
impact test specimen Schlagprobe f
impact torsion test Schlagdrehversuch m
impact transition temperature Übergangstemperatur f
impairment Schwächung f
impedance Impedanz f; Scheinwiderstand m (Lichtbogenofen)
impedance voltage Nennkurzschlußspannung f
impeller Schaufelrad n
impermeability Undurchlässigkeit f
impetus Anstoß m; Antrieb m
impinge anprallen; aufschlagen; auftreffen
impingement Brennfleck m
impingement of drops Tropfenschlag m
impinging face Auftrefffläche f
implant method Implantmethode f
implant test Implantversuch m
imported workers ausländische Arbeitskräfte fpl
impregnate imprägnieren
impregnating agent Imprägnierungsmittel n
impregnation Tränkung f
impressing Eindrücken n
impression Eindruck m; Vertiefung f
impression [of finished drop forging] Gravur f
improve verbessern; veredeln
improvement Verbesserung f
impulse Impuls m
impulse counter Impulszähler m
impulse reflection method Impuls-Echo-Verfahren n
impulse sender Impulsgeber m
impulse type remote control Impuls-Fernsteuerung f
impurity Beimengung f; Unreinheit f; Verunreinigung f
inaccuracy Ungenauigkeit f; Unschärfe f
inactive accounts ruhende Konten npl
inadequate unpassend
in-and-out reheating furnace Wärmofen m für satzweisen Einsatz
incandescence Weißglut f
incandescent weißglühend
incentive operator Akkordarbeiter m
incidental element Eisenbegleitele-

incidental light microscopy Auflichtmikroskopie f
incinerate veraschen
incinerator Abfallverbrennungsanlage f; Verbrenner m
incipient crack Anriß m
incipient tear Anriß m
inclination Gefälle n; Neigung f (Steigung); Steigung f
inclination balance Neigungswaage f
inclined geneigt
inclined elevator Schrägaufzug m
inclined hoist Schrägaufzug m
inclined lift Schrägaufzug m
include in a list in eine Liste f eintragen
inclusion Einlagerung f; Einschluß m
in comparison with im Vergleich m mit (oder: zu)
incomplete decarbonizing Abkohlung f (Kokerei)
incorporated eingearbeitet
increase Ertrag m; Zunahme f; erhöhen; vergrößern
increase of grain size Kornwachstum n
increase of ouput Leistungssteigerung f
incremental forging partielles Stauchen n
incremental forging in closed die Teilgesenkschmieden n
increment division method Inkrement-Teilungsverfahren n
increment sampling Inkrement-Probenahme f
incubation time Anlaufzeit f (Gamma-Alpha-Umwandlung)
indefinite chill roll Walze f (Indefinitguß)
indent Vertiefung f
indentation Einschnitt m; Tiefung f
indentation test Tiefungsprobe f
indenting Eindrücken n
index Kenngröße f
index card cabinet [library] Karteischrank m
index number Meßzahl f
index of deep drawing Tiefungswert m
indicate anzeigen
indicating instrument Anzeigegerät n
indication Anzeige f
indicator Fühler m; Gichtsonde f
indicator board Anzeigetafel f
indirect mittelbar
indirect extrusion of rods Voll-Rückwärts-Strangpressen n
indirect extrusion of rods and tubes Rückwärts-Strangpressen n
indirect impact extrusion Rückwärts-fließpressen n
indirect impact extrusion of hollow items Massiv-Lochen n
indirect rod impact extrusion Voll-Rückwärts-Fließpressen n
indirect tubular impact extrusion Hohl-Rückwärts-Fließpressen n
indirect tubular rod extrusion Hohl-Rückwärts-Strangpressen n
individual drive Einzelantrieb m
individual journal box Einzelachsbüchse f
induced draft installation Saugzuganlage f
induced draught Saugzug m
inductance Induktivität f
induction furnace Induktionsofen m
induction hardening Induktionshärten n
induction heating Induktionserhitzen n
induction stirring induktive Badbewegung f; induktives Rühren n
induction welding induktives Schweißen n
induration Hartbrennen n
industrial großtechnisch
industrial budgetary control Budgetrechnung f
industrial engineering Betriebswirtschaft f
Industrial Engineering Committee Ausschuß m für Betriebswirtschaft
industrial furnace Industrieofen m
industrial garbage Gewerbemüll m
industrial hygiene Arbeitshygiene f; Gewerbehygiene f

industrial legal protection gewerblicher Rechtsschutz *m*
industrial management Betriebswirtschaft *f*
industrial medicine Arbeitsmedizin *f*
industrial noise Industrielärm *m*
industrial operation Industriebetrieb *m*
industrial psychology Betriebspsychologie *f*
industrial structures Industriebauten *mpl*
industrial undertaking Industriebetrieb *m*
industrial waste Industrieabfall *m*
industrial waste sintering plant Industriemüll-Sinteranlage *f*
industrial waste water Industrieabwasser *n*
industrial workshop Lehrwerkstatt *f*
industry control office Gewerbeaufsichtsamt *n*
inert reaktionsträge
inert gas Edelgas *n*; Inertgas *n*; Schutzgas *n*
inert gas metal arc welding Metall-Inertgasschweißen *n*; Metall-Schutzgasschweißen *n*
inert gas plant Schutzgasanlage *f*
inert gas shielded arc welding Schutzgasschweißung *f*
inert materials Ballast *m* (Hochofen)
infill Setzpacklage *f* (Schlackenaufbereitung)
infiltrate einziehen; tränken
infiltrated air Falschluft *f*; Frischluft *f*
infiltration Tränkung *f*
infiltration by capillary force Kapillartränkung *f*
infiltration by dipping Tauchtränkung *f*
infiltration (powder met.) Auflagetränkung *f*
infinite dilution unendliche Verdünnung *f*
infinitely dilute solution unendlich verdünnte Lösung *f*
infinitely variable control of speed stufenlose Geschwindigkeitsregelung *f*
infinitely variable speed drive stufenloser Antrieb *m*
inflammability Zündbarkeit *f*
inflammable feuergefährlich
information demand Informationsbedarf *m*
information flow Informationsfluß *m*
information path Informationsweg *m*
information processing device informationsverarbeitendes Gerät *n*
infrared control system Infrarotsteueranlage *f*
infrared radiation furnace Infrarotstrahlungsofen *m*
infringement of a patent Patentverletzung *f*
in furnace sizes chargierfähig
infusibility Temperaturbeständigkeit *f*
infusible unschmelzbar
ingate Anschnitt *m*; Einguß *m*
ingoing table Zufuhrrollgang *m*
ingoing wire Einspannlänge *f*
ingot Block *m*; Rohblock *m*; Rohbramme *f* (der gegossene Rohstahlblock)
ingot breaker Blockbrecher *m*
ingot buggy Blockfähre *f*; Blockwagen *m*
ingot butt Blockrest *m*; Stummelblock *m*
ingot charging crane Blockeinsetzkran *m*
ingot chariot Blockwagen *m*
ingot corner segregation Seigerung *f* in den Blockecken
ingot crusher Blockbrecher *m*
ingot dog Blockzange *f*
ingot drawing crane Blockausziehkran *m*
ingot [handling] crane Blockkran *m*
ingot iron Armco-Eisen *n*
ingotism Blockseigerung *f*
ingot lathe Blockdrehbank *f*
ingot mold stool (am.) Kokillenuntersatz *m*
ingot mould Blockform *f*; Blockkokille *f*; Kokille *f*
ingot mould blackening Kokillen-

schlichte f
ingot mould bottom plate Kokillenuntersatz m
ingot mould coating Kokillenlack m
ingot mould coating material Kokillenanstrichmittel n
ingot mould dressing material Kokillenanstrichmittel n
ingot mould glasing Kokillenglasur f
ingot mould scrap Kokillenbruch m
ingot mould varnish Kokillenlack m
ingot mould washing plant Kokillenspritzeinrichtung f
ingot parting machine Blockabstechmaschine f
ingot pusher Blockdrücker m
ingot scum Blockschaum m
ingot segregation Blockseigerung f
ingot slab mill Block-Brammen-Walzwerk n
ingot steel Flußstahl m
ingot stripper Blockabstreifer m
ingot stripping crane Blockabstreifkran m
ingot suitable for rolling Walzblock m
ingot tilter Blockkipper m
ingot tipping device Blockkipper m
ingot [tong] crane Zangenkran m
ingot tongs Blockzange f
ingot tons Rohstahlerzeugung f
ingot top crust Deckelbildung f (Block)
ingot [transfer] car Blockfähre f; Blockwagen m
in handy sizes chargierfähig
inherent arteigen
inhibit hemmen; hindern
inhibiting effect Sparbeizwirkung f
inhibitor Beizzusatz m; Inhibitor m; Sparbeize f
inhomogeneity Inhomogenität f
in increments of in Teilmengen fpl von
initial corrosion rate Anfangskorrosionsgeschwindigkeit f
initial costs Anlagekosten pl; Anschaffungskosten pl
initial easily removable rust Flugrost m
initial load Vorlast f

initial material Ausgangswerkstoff m
initial [pass] section Anfangsquerschnitt m; Anstichquerschnitt m
initial set Vorspannung f
initial size Ausgangsgröße f
initial temperature of rolling Walzanfangstemperatur f
initial tension Vorspannung f
initial thickness Ausgangsdicke f
initiation of a fatigue crack Einschwingen n eines Ermüdungsanrisses
inject einblasen
injected eingeblasen
injection fan Einspritzventilator m
injection (of blast furnace flue dust) Einblasen n (von Gichtstaub)
injection pump Einspritzpumpe f
inleaked air Falschluft f
inlet Einführung f; Einlaß m; Zulauf m
inner lining Verschleißfutter n
inoculant Impfstoff m (Gußeisen)
inoculate (cast iron) impfen
inoculating agent Impfstoff m
inoculation Impfung f (Gußeisen)
input Antrieb m
input connection Eingangsverbindung f
input information Eingangsinformation f
input primary status (IPS) Eingabe-Primärstatus m
input resolution (automatic control) Ansprechwert m
input secondary status (ISS) Eingabe-Sekundärstatus m
input shaft Antrieb m
input (signal) Eingangsgröße f
input time interval Eingabezeit f
input value Eingangswert m
input variable Eingangsgröße f; Rückmeldevariable f
inquiry Anfrage f; Umfrage f
in roll time Walzzeit f
in series hintereinander (geschaltet)
insert Einbaustück n; Einlage f; einbauen; einsetzen; einstecken
insertion Einbau m; Einfügung f; Einspannung f; Einstich m

inside diameter lichte Weite f
insoluble phase Bodenkörper m; unlösliche Phase f
inspection Abnahme f; Abnahme f (von Maschinen); Kontrolle f; Prüfung f; Überwachung f
inspection certificate Abnahmeprüfzeugnis n
inspection report Abnahmeprüfprotokoll n
inspector Abnahmebeamter m
install einbauen; einrichten
installation Anlage f; Aufstellung f; Einrichtung f
installing Einrichtung f (z. B. einer Versuchsstation)
instructional workshop Lehrwerkstatt f
insulated wire isolierter Draht m
insulating brick Isolierstein m
insulating material Dämmstoff m; Dämmstoff m (Isolierstoff); Isolierstoff m
insulating refractory wärmedämmender feuerfester Stoff m
insulating tube Isolierrohr n
insulation Isolierung f
insulator Isolator m
intake Einlaßöffnung f; Einströmungsrohr n
in tandem with im Anschluß m an (Walzwerk)
integer ganze Zahl f
integral action time Nachstellzeit f
integral J J-Integral n
integrated iron and steel plant gemischtes Hüttenwerk n
integrated level measurement integrierende Pegelmessung f
integrated power system Energieverbundwirtschaft f
integrated system Gesamtkonzeption n
integrating control Summenregelung f
integrating controller Summenregler m
integration Einbindung f

integrator Zähler m
intensifier Verstärker m
intensity maximum Schwärzungsmaximum n (Röntgen)
intensity of current Stromstärke f
intensity of light Lichtstärke f
interaction coefficient Wechselwirkungskoeffizient m; Wirkungskoeffizient m; Wirkungsparameter m
interaction of spins Spinortskorrelation f (Atome und Elektronen)
interaction parameter Wechselwirkungsparameter m; Wirkungsparameter m
interannealed wire zwischengeglühter Draht m
interatomic bond interatomare Verbindung f
inter-bell area Raum m zwischen großer und kleiner Gichtglocke
intercept method Linienschnittverfahren n (Korngröße)
interchangeable stand Wechselgerüst n
intercom [system] Gegensprechanlage f
intercritical [heat]treatment interkritische [Wärme]behandlung f
intercrystalline corrosion interkristalline Korrosion f
intercrystalline fracture interkristalliner Bruch m
interdendritic interdendritisch
interdendritic graphite interdendritischer Graphit m
interdiffusion Interdiffusion f
interface Grenzfläche f; Kopplung f; Trennfläche f
interfacial corrosion Messerschnittkorrosion f
interfacial diffusion Korngrenzendiffusion f
interfacial tension Grenzflächenspannung f
interference Störung f
interference coating microscopy Interferenzschichten-Mikroskopie f
intergranular attack Korngrenzenan-

griff *m*
intergranular corrosion Korngrenzenkorrosion *f*; interkristalline Korrosion *f*
intergranular fracture Korngrenzenbruch *m*
intergrowth Verwachsung *f*
interior innen
interlinked gas grid system Gasverbundnetz *n*
interlocking [suspended] bricks ineinandergreifende Sondersteine *mpl* mit Aufhängung
intermediate annealed sheet zwischengeglühtes Feinblech *n*
intermediate annealing Zwischenglühen *n*
intermediate circuit Zwischenkreis *m*; Zwischenkreisumrichter *m*
intermediate echo Zwischenecho *n*
intermediate hopper Zwischenbunker *m*
intermediate mill Mittelstraße *f*
intermediate phase Zwischenphase *f*; intermediäre Phase *f*
intermediate product Zwischenerzeugnis *n*
intermediate reheating furnace Zwischenwärmofen *m*
intermediate rolling mill Mittelwalzwerk *n*
intermediate roll stand Mittelgerüst *n*
intermediates Zwischenkorngrößen *fpl*
intermediate shaft Zwischenspindel *f*
intermediate shaping Zwischenformgebung *f* (Walzen)
intermediate stress relieving Zwischenentspannen *n*
intermetallic compound intermetallische Verbindung *f*
intermittent feed Sprungschaltung *f*
intermittent operation intermittierende Betriebsweise *f*
intermittent weld unterbrochene Schweißnaht *f*
internal consumption Eigenverbrauch *m*

internal crack Innenriß *m*
internal energy innere Energie *f*
internal evacuation Innenabsaugung *f*
internal exhaust Innenabsaugung *f*
internal fissure Innenriß *m*
internal oxidation innere Oxidation *f*
internal stress Eigenspannung *f*
internal welding Innenschweißen *n*
inter-pass annealing Glühen *n* zwischen zwei Zügen (Kaltziehen)
interpenetrating lattices (X-rays) ineinandergeschachtelte Gitter *npl*
interpretation of test results Versuchsauswertung *f*
interrelationship wechselseitige Beziehung *f*
interrupted ag[e]ing unterbrochenes Altern *n*
interrupted hardening Härten *n*; Stufenhärten *n*
interrupted segment method Linienschnittverfahren *n* (Korngröße)
interruption Störung *f*; Unterbrechung *f*
intersection Schnittpunkt *m*
interstitial atom Zwischengitteratom *n*
interstitial solid solution Einlagerungsmischkristall *m*
interstitial solution Zwischengitter-Mischkristall *m*
interstitial space Zwischenraum *m* (Gitter)
interval Strecke *f*
in the form of lamellar streaks streifig lamellar
in the hot rolled condition im warmgewalzten Zustand *m*
intimate mixing innige Vermischung *f*
introduce einführen; einstecken
introduce into an equation in eine Gleichung *f* einführen
introduction Einführung *f*; Einstich *m*
introduction of dummy bar Kaltstrangeinfahren *n*
Invar steel Invarstahl *m*
inventory on-hand quantity Inventurbestand *m*
inventory stock Inventurbestand *m*

inverse feedback Gegenkopplung f
inverse segregation umgekehrte Seigerung f
invert umkehren
investigation Erforschung f; Untersuchung f
investment casting Genauguß m; Gießen n mit verlorener Gießform; verlorene Gießform f
invoice typewriter Fakturiermaschine f
inwall Schachtmauerwerk n
iodine number Jodzahl f (Schmieren)
ion exchange Ionenaustausch m
ionic bonding Ionenbindung f
ionic defect Ionenstörstelle f
ionic strength Ionenstärke f
ion in interstitial position Zwischengitterplatz m
ionisation state Ionisierungszustand m (Spektralanalyse)
ionitriding Ionitrieren n
IPE-beam (European section) IPE-Träger m (IPE-Reihe)
iron Eisen n
iron and steel manufacture Eisenhüttenwesen n
iron and steel plant Eisenhüttenwerk n
iron and steel producing industry eisenschaffende Industrie f
iron and steel products Eisen- und Stahlerzeugnisse npl
iron and steel trade Eisen- und Stahlhandel m
iron and steel works Eisenhüttenwerk n
iron and steel works crane Hüttenwerkskran m
iron bath Eisenbad n
iron carbide Eisencarbid n
iron carbon diagram Eisen-Kohlenstoff-Schaubild n
iron casting Eisenguß m
iron castings gußeiserne Formstücke npl
iron content Eisengehalt m
iron foundry Eisengießerei f

iron glance Eisenglanz m; Hämatit m
iron hoop Bandstahl m
ironing Abstrecken n; Tiefziehen n (von Näpfchen)
iron making Roheisenerzeugung f
iron mine Eisenbergwerk n
iron nickel pyrites Eisennickelkies m
iron notch Eisenabstichloch n
iron ore Eisenerz n
iron ore briquette Eisenerzbrikett n
iron ore deposit Eisenerz-Lagerstätte f
iron oxide fume Eisenoxidrauch m
iron phosphide Eisen-Phosphor n
iron Portland cement Eisenportlandzement m
iron powder Eisenpulver n
iron precipitation Eisenausscheidung f
iron pyrites Eisenkies m (FeS_2); Schwefelkies m (FeS_2)
iron recovery plant Eisenrückgewinnungsanlage f
iron runner Roheisen-Abstichrinne f
iron saturated eisengesättigt
iron soap Eisenseife f
iron sulphate Eisenvitriol n
iron wire Eisendraht m
ironworker Hüttenmann m
ironworks Eisenhütte f; Eisenwerk n; Hüttenwerk n
iron works chemistry Eisenhüttenchemie f
irradiate bestrahlen
isochronous curve Isochrone f
ISO draft ISO-Entwurf m
isolation Isolierung f
ISO rough draft ISO-Vorentwurf m
isosceles triangle gleichschenkliges Dreieck n
isothermal annealing Perlitisieren n
isothermal transformation isotherme Umwandlung f
isotope Isotop n
issue Ausgang m; Ergebnis n
item Einheit f; Einzelheit f; Gegenstand m; Position f; einzelner Posten m

J

jack Hebebock *m*; Hebel *m*
jacket Mantel *m*; Panzer *m* (Hochofen); Umhüllung *f*; umhüllen; ummanteln
jacketed jet pipe Mantelstahlrohr *n*
jam festfressen; festklemmen; klemmen
jar rütteln
jar ramming rollover moulding machine Umroll-Rüttelformmaschine *f*
jar-ram moulding machine Rüttelformmaschine *f*
jaw chuck Backenfutter *n*
jaw crusher Backenbrecher *m*
Jenkin's bend test Jenkin-Biegeversuch *m*
jerky drawing Rattern *n* (Drahtziehen)
jet Düse *f*; Gießloch *n*; Gießrinne *f*; Strahl *m*
jet process Düsenabstreifverfahren *n*
jet tapper Sprenglanze *f*
jet tapper (am.) Abstichladung *f*
jib crane Auslegerkran *m*
jig Aufspannvorrichtung *f*; Einspannvorrichtung *f*; Vorrichtung *f*
jigging Haltevorrichtung *f*
jigging machine Setzmaschine *f*
jigging screen Rüttelsieb *n*; Schüttelsieb *n*; Setzsieb *n*
job Arbeit *f*
job analysis Arbeitsanalyse *f*
jobbing casting Handelsguß *m*; Kundenguß *m*
jobbing mill Walzwerk *n* für kleine Bestellungen
jobbing plate mill Mittelblech-Walzwerk *n*
jobbing [sheet] Mittelblech *n*
jobbing sheet mill Mittelblech-Walzwerk *n*
job description Arbeitsbeschreibung *f*
job evaluation Arbeits[platz]bewertung *f*
job requirement Arbeitsanforderung *f*
job rolling Lohnwalzen *n*
job work Akkordarbeit *f*
joggling machine Maschine *f* zum Verkröpfen und Ab- oder Durchsetzen
join stoßen
joiner's shop Tischlerei *f*
joinery Tischlerei *f*
joining Fügen *n*
joining by flanging Fügen *n* durch Bördeln
join[t] Dichtung *f*; Verband *m*; anschließen; verbinden
joint Gelenk *n*; Teilfuge *f*; dichten
joint bars and fishplates Laschen und Platten *fpl* (Eisenbahn-Oberbau)
joint distribution Mehrfachteilung *f*; verbundene Verteilung *f*
jointing Bindemittel *n*; Dichten *n*
join[t]ing Dichtung *f*
jointing compound Dichtungsmasse *f* (für Mauerwerk)
jointing compounds for furnace masonry Ofenmauer-Dichtungsmasse *f*
jointing mixture Ausfugmasse *f*
joint of the bed Lagerfuge *f*
joint welding Verbindungsschweißen *n*
joist Doppel-T-Träger *m*; Träger *m*
joist rolling mill Trägerwalzwerk *n*
jolt rütteln
jolt moulding machine Rüttelformmaschine *f*
jolt rollover moulding Umroll-Rüttelformmaschine *f*
Jominy curve Jominy-Kurve *f*
Jominy test Jominy-Versuch *m*
Jominy test piece Stirnabschreckprobe *f*
journal Laufzapfen *m*; Zapfen *m*
journal bearing Achslager *n*; Zapfenlager *n*
journal box Achslager *n*; Zapfenlager *n*
jumbo Roheisenbehälter *m*; Roheisenbehälter *m* auf Roheisentransportwagen
jump Sprung *m*

jump roughing mill Springduowalzwerk *n*; Vorsturzwalzwerk *n*
jump test Stauchversuch *m*
junction Verbindung *f*

K

kaolin sand Kaolinsand *m*
keen scharf; schneidend
keen edge tool scharf schneidendes Werkzeug *n*
key Keil *m*; Keilstein *m*; Schlüssel *m*; verkeilen
key bar Keilstahl *m*
keyboard Tastatur *f*
keyed in eingekeilt
keyhole notch Schlüssellochkerb *m*
key letter Schlüsselbuchstabe *m* (bei Kurznamen)
keyway Keilnut *f*
kidney ore Eisenglanz *m*; Glaskopf *m* (Roteisenstein); Hämatit *m*; Roteisenstein *m*
kieselguhr Kieselgur *f*
kill abstehen lassen; beruhigen
killed steel beruhigter Stahl *m*; entgaster Stahl *m*
kiln Brennofen *m*; Ofen *m* (Brennofen)
kindling point Flammpunkt *m*
kinematic viscosity kinematische Viskosität *f*
kinetic energy kinetische Energie *f*
kinetics Kinetik *f*
king brick Königsstein *m*
kink Knick *m*
kinking Schleifenbildung *f*
kish Garschaum *m*
kish graphite Garschaumgraphit *m*
kisser Zunderfleck *m*
knead durcharbeiten; kneten
kneadable knetbar
knife-edge corrosion Messerschnittkorrosion *f*
knife pass Kneifstich *m*; geteiltes Kaliber *n*
knifing Walzen *n* mit geteiltem Kaliber

kniking Verwerfen *n* nach Beanspruchung
knock schlagen; stoßen
knock down test Stauchversuch *m*
knock out ausstoßen (von Gasen)
knuckle Gelenk *n*; Herdgewölbe *n*; Knie *n*; Knochen *m* (Gießen); Krümmung *f*
knuckle (open hearth furnace) Einschnürung *f* an beiden Enden des Hauptgewölbes (SM-Ofen)
knuckle (reheat furnace) Höcker *m*
knurl rändeln
knurled knob Rändelknopf *m*
knurled thumb screw Rändelschraube *f*

L

labile labil
laboratory Laboratorium *n*; Versuchsanstalt *f*; Versuchsraum *m*
laboratory apparatus Laboratoriumsgerät *n*
laboratory appliance Laboratoriumsgerät *n*
laboratory assistant Laborant *m*
laboratory research Laboratoriumsforschung *f*
labour agreement Tarifvertrag *m*
labour costs Lohnkosten *pl*
labour efficiency Arbeitsleistung *f*
labour element of cost Kostenanteil *m* des Arbeitslohnes
labourer Hilfsarbeiter *m*
labo[u]r office Arbeitsamt *n*
lack Fehlen *n*; Mangel *m*
lack of gas Gasmangel *m*
lacquer Lack *m*; lackieren; lackieren (Band)
lacquer drawn wire naß gezogener Draht *m* (mit heller Oberfläche)
lacquered lackiert
lacquer print Lackabdruck *m*
ladder Leiter *f*
ladle Pfanne *f*

ladle additions Pfannenzusätze *mpl*
ladle analysis Schmelzenanalyse *f*
ladle bogie Pfannenwagen *m*
ladle brick Pfannenstein *m*
ladle car Pfannenwagen *m*
ladle casing Pfannengehäuse *n*
ladle covering compound Pfannenabdeckmasse *f*
ladle degassing Pfannenentgasung *f*
ladle drying plant Pfannentrocknungsanlage *f*
ladle emptying time Pfannenausgießzeit *f*
ladle heating plant Pfannenaufheizanlage *f*
ladle lining Pfannenausmauerung *f*
ladle lip Pfannenausguß *m*
ladle metallurgy aftertreatment pfannenmetallurgische Nachbehandlung *f*
ladle operator Pfannenbedienungsmann *m*
ladle pouring time Pfannengießzeit *f*
ladle sample Schöpfprobe *f*
ladle shank Pfannengabel *f*
ladle shell Pfannengehäuse *n*
ladle skull Pfannenbär *m*
ladle stand Pfannenbock *m*
ladle stopper Gießstopfen *m*; Pfannenstopfen *m*
ladle to ladle stream degassing Vakuumdurchlaufentgasung *f*
ladle treatment Pfannenbehandlung *f*; Pfannennachbehandlung *f*
lag Phasenverschiebung *f* (elektr.); Verzögerung *f*; Zeitverschiebung *f*; hemmen; zögern
lag element Verzögerungsglied *n*
lagging Nacheilung *f* (Walzen)
lake iron ore Raseneisenerz *n*; See-Erz *n*
lamella pump Lamellenpumpe *f*
lamellar graphite Lamellengraphit *m*
lamellar streaks streifig lamellar
lamellar tearing Terrassenbruch *m*
laminate Kunststoffolien *fpl* aufwalzen; laminieren
laminated spring Blattfeder *f*

lamination Dopplung *f*; Dopplung *f* (im Stahlblock); Kaschierung *f*; Schichtung *f*; Walzen *n*; Walzfalte *f*; Überwalzung *f*
lamination (powder met.) Schieferung *f*
lance Lanze *f*; Strahlrohr *n*
lance carriage Lanzenschlitten *m*
lance carrier Lanzenwagen *m*
lance cost Lanzenkosten *pl*
lance safety gear Lanzenfangvorrichtung *f*
lancing Einschneiden *n*
landing skid Gleitkufe *f*
Lang's lay rope Gleichschlagseil *n*
lap Dopplung *f*; Mattschweiße *f*; Naht *f* (überwalzte); läppen (Oberfläche); staubschleifen; überwalzte Falte *f*; überwalzte Naht *f*; Überwalzung *f*
lap joint überlappter Stoß *m*
lap [joint] Überlappung *f*
lap riveting Überlappungsnietung *f*
lap welded überlappt geschweißt
lapweld process Überlappschweißverfahren *n*
large boiler plant Großkesselanlage *f*
large compartment soaking pit Großraum-Tiefofen *m*
large-scale production trial Großversuch *m*
larry [car] Füllwagen *m*; Möllerwagen *m*; Zubringerwagen *m*
laser beam Laserstrahl *m*
laser microprobe Laser-Mikrosonde *f*
laser welding Lichtstrahlschweißen *n*
last aushalten; dauern
latch Klinke *f*; Riegel *m*
latent heat latente Wärme *f*
lateral blow seitliches Blasen *n*
laterally sprung axle bearing Achslager *n* mit seitlichen Federabstützungen
late shift Spätschicht *f*
lathe Drehbank *f*
lattice Gitter *n*; Netzwerk *n*
lattice defect Gitterbaufehler *m*; Gitterstörung *f*
latticed girder pole Gittermast *m*

lattice distortion Gitterstörung f
lattice girder Fachwerkträger m
lattice grate Gitterrost m
lattice grate (for lighting) Lichtgitter n
lattice mast Gittermast m
lattice shearing Umklappen n des Gitters
lattice structure Gitterstruktur f
lattice transformation Gitterumwandlung f; Umklappen n des Gitters
lattice vacant site Gitterleerstelle f
launch in Betrieb m setzen
launder Abstichrinne f; Gießrinne f; Rinne f
lay Windung f
lay a course of (bricks) Lage f verlegen (von Steinen)
lay diameter Windungsdurchmesser m
lay down ablegen
layer Flöz n; Lage f; Metallschicht f; Schicht f (Lage); Schweißlage f; Windungsleger m
layer crystal Schichtkristall m
layer line (X-rays) Schichtlinie f
layer of air Luftschicht f
layer of scale Zunderschicht f
layer strength Schichtfestigkeit f
lay forming rim Wickelmantel m
laying head or unit Windungsleger m
laying reel Drehkorbhaspel f; Edenbornhaspel f
lay off workman Arbeiter m zeitweilig entlassener
lay-out Anlage f; Anordnung f; Plan m
lay out auslegen
LD-AC process LD-AC-Verfahren n
LD lip ring Mündungsring m
LD process LD-Verfahren n
leach Lauge f
lead Blei n; Ganghöhe f (Steigung); Leitung f; führen; leiten; verbleien; voreilen
lead bath vat Bleibadkessel m
lead-coat verbleien
leader Vorfertigstich m
lead froth Bleischaum m (Feuerverzinken)

lead hardening Bleibadhärten n
leading dimensions Hauptabmessungen fpl
leading end vorderes Ende n
leading oval Schlichtoval n (Walzen)
leading pass section Anstichquerschnitt m
leading spindle Leitspindel f
lead patenting Bleipatentieren n
lead screw Leitspindel f
leaf Blatt n; Folie f
leaf aluminium rolling mill Aluminiumfolien-Anlage f
leaf spring Blattfeder f
leak Leck n; auslaufen; lecken
leak[age] Undichtheit f
leakage reactance Streureaktanz f (Lichtbogenofen)
leaker Ausläufer m; Läufer m
leaking tuyre leckende Form f
leak-proof dicht
leaky stopper Stopfenläufer m
lean coal Magerkohle f
lean gas Schwachgas n
lean-gas firing Schwachgasheizung f
learner Anlernling m
least square kleinstes Quadrat n
ledeburite Ledeburit m
ledeburitic steel ledeburitischer Stahl m
left-handed thread Linksgewinde n
left hand welding Linksschweißung f
length Länge f; gerade Länge f (Draht)
lengthen längen
lengthening Dehnen n (Längen)
length of parallel Führungslänge f (Ziehstein)
length of the hearth Herdlänge f
length of wire drawn per unit of power consumed Kraftausbeute f beim Drahtziehen
less fusible weniger leicht schmelzbar
letters patent Patentschrift f
let well carbonize ausgaren lassen
level Höhe f; Niveau n; dressieren; ebnen; planieren; richten
level height Höhe f
level indicator for bunker Bunkerfüll-

standanzeiger m
levelling machine Richtmaschine f (Bleche)
level of factors Abstufung f der Einflußgrößen
level of filling in a hopper Bunkerfüllstand m
level of significance Irrtumswahrscheinlichkeit f
level rule Hebelgesetz n
lever Hebel m
lever factor Hebelarmbeiwert m (Walzen)
lever principle Hebelgesetz n
lever relationship rule Hebelbeziehung f
lever testing machine Prüfmaschine f mit Laufgewichtswaage
levigate pulverisieren; schlämmen; zerreiben
levitation melting Schwebeschmelzen n
liabilities Passiva npl; ausstehende Verpflichtungen fpl
liability to Anfälligkeit f (für)
liability to harden with soft spots Weichfleckigkeit f
liability to the formation of soft spots Neigung f zu Weichfleckigkeit
license Lizenz f
license agreement Lizenzvertrag m
licensee Lizenznehmer m
licenser Lizenzgeber m
lid Deckel m
life Haltbarkeit f; Lebensdauer f; Standzeit f (Werkzeug)
life durability Haltbarkeit f
life of arched roof Gewölbehaltbarkeit f
life of cutting tool (between regrindings) Schneidhaltigkeit f
life roller table Rollgang m angetriebener
life-time Lebensdauer f
lift Aufzug m; Hub m; Last f (Ventil); Zug m; heben; hochheben
lifting apparatus Hebezeug n
lifting device Hebebühne f

lifting magnet Hubmagnet m; Lasthebemagnet m
lifting movement Hubbewegung f (Kran)
lifting rod Vorheber m
lifting table Hebetisch m
lift[ing] truck Hubwagen m
light beleuchten
light barrier Lichtschranke f
light-gage spring Feder f kleiner Abmessung
light ga[u]ge design Leichtbau m
light metal Leichtmetall n
light pen Lichtgriffel m
light petroleum distillate Benzin n
light plate Blech n (mittel); Mittelblech n
light print Ablichtung f; Lichtpause f
light section Leichtprofil n
light-section Lichtschnitt m
light section angle Winkelstahl m mit Leichtprofil
light section rolling mill Feinstahl-Walzwerk n; Stabstahlwalzwerk n
light sections leichter Formstahl m
light signal plant Lichtrufanlage f
light source Lichtquelle f
light steel structure Stahlleichtbau m
light up anheizen
light-weight brick Leichtstein m
light weight refractory feuerfester Leichtstoff m
light-weight refractory brick Feuerleichtstein m
light-weight scrap Kleinschrott m
light weight steel shape Stahlleichtprofil n
lignite Braunkohle f
lignite briquette Braunkohlenbrikett n
lime Kalk m
lime-alumina mixture Kalk-Tonerde-Gemisch n
lime-basic covering kalkbasische Umhüllung f (Schweißdraht)
lime boil Schlackenfrischreaktion f
lime-bonded silica brick kalkgebundener Silicastein m
lime bunker Kalkbunker m

lime-burning kiln Kalkbrennofen *m*
lime dinas brick Kalkdinasstein *m*
lime injection equipment Kalkblasanlage *f*
lime powder Staubkalk *m*
lime set Kalkelend *n*
limestone Kalkstein *m*
limestone chips Kalksplitt *m*
limey ore kalkiges Erz *n*
liming Kälken *n* (Draht)
limit Grenze *f*; Termin *m*; abgrenzen; beschränken; bestimmen
limiting characteristic value Grenzmerkmal *n*
limiting creep stress Kriechgrenze *f*
limiting density Grenzpreßdichte *f*
limiting drawing ratio Grenzziehverhältnis *n*
limiting size Grenzmaß *n*
limiting spread factor Begrenzungsgrad *m* der Breitung (Walzen)
limit of error Fehlergrenze *f*
limit of proportionality Proportionalitätsgrenze *f*
limit switch Begrenzungsschalter *m*; Endschalter *m*
limonite Brauneisenerz *n*; Limonit *m*; Raseneisenerz *n*
line Leitung *f*; Linie *f*; Strecke *f*; ausfüttern; vermauern; zustellen
linear contraction Verkürzung *f*
linear expansion Längen[aus]dehnung *f*; Längsdehnung *f*
linear expansion coefficient Längenausdehnungskoeffizient *m*
linear programming lineares Programmieren *n*
line assembly work Fließarbeit *f*
line frequency (am.) Netzfrequenz *f*
line frequency induction crucible melting furnace Netzfrequenz-Induktions-Tiegelschmelzofen *m*
line of best fit Mittelwertsgerade *f*
line of magnetic force Magnetisierungskraftlinie *f*
line pipe Leitungsrohr *n*
line printer Zeilendrucker *m*

liner Laufbüchse *f*
line reactor (am.) Drosselspule *f* (Lichtbogenofen)
line shaft Längswelle *f*; Übertragungswelle *f*
lines of stress Fließfiguren *fpl* (Bleche)
line-up Warteschlange *f*
line wire Leitungsdraht *m*
lining Ausgießen *n* (Lager); Auskleidung *f*; Ausmauerung *f*; Belag *m*; Büchse *f*; Garnitur *f*; Verkleidung *f*; Weißmetall-Ausguß *m*
lining cost Zustellungskosten *pl*
lining sheet Bekleidungsblech *n*
link Gelenk *n*; Glied *n*; Ring *m*
linkage Bindemittel *n*; Bindung *f*
linkage of bars Gestänge *n*
linking primer Bindemittel *n*
lintel Sturz *m* (Oberschwelle); Tragkranz *m* (Hochofen)
lintel girder Tragkranz *m* (Hochofen)
lip Ausguß *m*; Schnauze *f*
lip angle Keilwinkel *m* (Spanen)
lip ring Mündungsring *m*; Tragring *m* (Hochofen)
liquate seigern
liquation Seigerung *f*
liquation cracking Aufschmelzriß *m* (Schweißen)
liquid Flüssigkeit *f*; flüssig
liquid ammonia Ammoniakwasser *n*
liquid crater flüssiger Sumpf *m*
liquid gas Flüssiggas *n*
liquid initial bath flüssiger Sumpf *m*
liquid metal level [in mould] Gießspiegel *m*
liquid phase sintering Schmelzsinterung *f*
liquid solubility Löslichkeit *f* im flüssigen Zustand
liquid stage flüssige Phase *f*
liquidus [area] Liquidusfläche *f*
liquidus [line] Liquiduslinie *f*
liquify verflüssigen
list Liste *f*; in eine Liste eintragen
list of steel applications Stahleinsatzliste *f*

lithium Lithium *n*
live roller table angetriebener Rollgang *m*
live [soaking] pit geheizter Tiefofen *m*
llgner [type motorgenerator] set llgnersatz *m*
load Arbeitsbelastung *f*; Beanspruchung *f*; Belastung *f*; Beschickung *f*; Last *f*; aufladen; beschicken; verladen
loadability Belastbarkeit *f*
load bearing test Tragfähigkeitsversuch *m*
load bounding method Schrankenverfahren *n*
load capacity Tragfähigkeit *f*
load (carrying) capacity Belastungsfähigkeit *f*
load cell Kraftmeßdose *f*
load deflection curve for spring Federkennlinie *f*
load deflection measurement Kraft-Durchbiegungs-Messung *f*
loader Beladevorrichtung *f*
load extension curve Kraft-Verlängerungskurve *f*
load factor Auslastung *f*
load hook Lasthaken *m*
loading Aufladen *n*; Beschicken *n*; Ladung *f*
loading beam Lasttraverse *f*
loading bridge Ladebrücke *f*; Verladebrücke *f*
loading bunker Ladebehälter *m*
loading capability Belastbarkeit *f* (Elektroden)
loading capacity Besatzgewicht *n*; Ladefähigkeit *f*
loading curve Belastungskurve *f*
loading device Beladevorrichtung *f*
loading diagram Belastungskurve *f*
loading installation Verladeeinrichtung *f*
loading of broken out lining material Verladen *n* des Konverterausbruchs
loading plant Verladeanlage *f*
loading ramp Laderampe *f*; Verladerampe *f*

loading station Verladeanlage *f*
load lug Lastbolzen *m*
load swing Belastungsschwankung *f* (Lichtbogenofen)
load [up] beladen
loam Lehm *m*
loam iron roll Walze *f* (Lehmguß)
loamy sand Formsand *m*; Klebsand *m*
local buckling Knickung *f*
local cell Lokalelement *n* (Korrosion)
local element Lokalelement *n* (Korrosion)
local hardening Härten *n* örtliches
locate lagern; zentrieren
location Lage *f*; Standplatz *m*; Stellung *f*
lock Verschluß *m*; absperren; schließen
lock die Gesenk *n* mit gebrochener Teilfuge
locked coil rope geschlossenes Spiralseil *n*
lock forming Verlappen *n*
lock forming by twisting Drehverlappen *n*
locking device Verriegelungsvorrichtung *f*
locking plate Sicherungsblech *n* (Schraube)
locking wire Plombendraht *m*
lock nut Sicherungsmutter *f*
lock seaming Verlappen *n*
locksmith Schlosser *m*
locksmith's shop Schlosserei *f*
locomotive Lokomotive *f*
log Betriebsbericht *m* (Zahlenaufstellung)
logical connective Grundverknüpfung *f*; logische Grundverknüpfung *f*
logic element digitales Verknüpfungsglied *n*
log sheet Aufschreibung *f* (Blatt)
long chain molecules langgestreckte Moleküle *npl*; langkettige Moleküle *npl*
long-distance gas Ferngas *n*
long-distance gas supply Ferngasversorgung *f*

long distance heating Fernheizung f
long-distance pipeline Fernleitung f
longitudinal corner crack Kantenlängsriß m
longitudinal crack Längsriß m
longitudinal facial crack Flächenlängsriß m
longitudinal force Längskraft f
longitudinal pass Längsstich m
longitudinal rolling Längswalzen n
longitudinal rolling of shapes Profil-Längswalzen n
longitudinal sampling Längsprobenahme f
longitudinal section Längsschnitt m
longitudinal thrust of the roof Gewölbelängsschub m
long line prestressed concrete Stahlsaitenbeton m
long range antiferromagnetic order antiferromagnetische Fernbereichsordnung f (in Einkristall)
long range order Fernordnung f
long test bar Langstab m
long-time test Langzeitversuch m
loop Schleife f; Schlinge f; umführen; umwalzen
looper Schlingenkanal m; Schlingenspanner m; Umwalzer m
looping Schlingenbildung f; Umgehungsmechanismus m (bei Versetzungen)
looping car Schlingenwagen m
looping floor Schlingenkanal m; Tieflauf m
looping pit Schlingengrube f
looping roller Umwalzer m
looping [type] rolling mill Umsteckwalzwerk n
loop [lifter] Schlingenheber m
loop test bar Schlaufenprobe f
loose flange Überwurfflansch m
loosen lockern; losmachen; lösen
loosening Lösung f
loose powder ungepreßtes Pulver n
loose tool forging Schmieden n mit unbefestigtem Werkzeug
lorry Schwerlastfahrzeug n

loss Abbrand m
loss by burning Abbrand m
loss of energy Energieverlust m
loss of power Energieverlust m
loss of pressure Druckverlust m
loss of production Produktionsausfall m; Produktionsausfall m
loss of temperature Temperaturverlust m
lost-wax casting Wachsausschmelzguß m
lot Kollektiv n (Großzahlforschung); Los n; Posten m
lot size Losgröße f
loudness level (dB) Lautstärke f
low alloy steel niedriglegierter Stahl m
low carbon ferro-chrome weiches Ferrochrom n
low carbon free-cutting steel kohlenstoffarmer Schnellautomatenstahl m
low carbon steel Stahl m mit niedrigerem C-Gehalt; kohlenstoffarmer Stahl m; kohlenstoffarmer weicher Stahl m; niedrig gekohlter Stahl m; unlegierter kohlenstoffarmer Stahl m; weicher Stahl m; weicher unlegierter Stahl m
low cycle fatigue Ermüdung f bei niedriger Lastspielzahl
low density refractory feuerfester Leichtstoff m
low-ductility fracture verformungsarmer Bruch m
low energy electron diffraction Beugung f langsamer Elektronen
lower senken; vermindern
lower bainitic structure unteres Zwischenstufengefüge n
lower caloric value unterer Heizwert m (Hu)
lower die Matrize f (Untergesenk); Untergesenk n
lower die block unterer Schmiedesattel m
lower frame (drag) Unterkasten m
lower furnace Unterofen m

lower pass unteres Kaliber *n*
lower ram Unterbär *m*; Unterkolben *m*
lower roll Unterwalze *f*
lower yield point untere Streckgrenze *f*
low frequency induction furnace Niederfrequenzofen *m*
low frequency welding Niederfrequenzschweißen *n*
low grade minderwertig
low grade coal Kohle *f* minderwertige
low idle [run] niedrigster Leerlauf *m*
low in arm an
low intensity magnetic separation Schwachfeld-Magnetscheidung *f*
low pollution umweltfreundlich
low pressure cylinder Niederdruckzylinder *m*
low pressure gas main Niederdruckgasleitung *f*
low pressure manometer Niederdruckmanometer *n*
low pressure torch Injektorbrenner *m*
low shaft [blast] furnace Niederschachtofen *m*
low-surface tension water entspanntes Wasser *n*
low temperature break LTB Niedrigtemperaturzerfall *m* NTZ
low temperature carbonisation Schwelung *f*
low temperature carbonisation furnace Schwelofen *m*
low temperature carbonising plant Schwelanlage *f*
low-temperature steel kaltzäher Stahl *m*
low tensile steel tube Rohr *n* mit geringer Festigkeit
low tension automatic circuit breaker Niederspannungsautomat *m*
low tension plant Niederspannungsanlage *f*
low voltage generator Niederspannungsgenerator *m*
lubricant Gleitmittel *n*; Schmiermittel *n*

lubricant carrier Schmiermittelträger *m*
lubricate einfetten; schmieren
lubricating Abschmieren *n*
lubricating action Schmierwirkung *f*
lubricating grease Schmierfett *n*; Schmiermittel *n*
lubricating grease for rolls Walzenschmierung *f*
lubricating oil Schmieröl *n*
lubricating power Schmierfähigkeit *f*
lubricating pump Schmierpumpe *f*
lubricating residuals Schmierrückstände *mpl*
lubrication Schmierung *f*
lubrication machine Einölmaschine *f*
Lüders' lines Fließfiguren *fpl*
luffing Wippen *n*
luffing crane Wippkran *m*
lufting Auf- und Abbewegung *f*
lug Ansatz *m*; Nase *f* (Vorsprung); Nocken *m*; Vorsprung *m*; Öse *f*
luminous flame Flamme *f*
luminous source Lichtquelle *f*
lump coal Stückkohle *f*
lumpiness Stückigkeit *f*
lumping Klumpenbildung *f* (Schlacke)
lump ore Stückerz *n*
lumps Stücke *npl* (z.B. Erz)
lump scrap Bruchschrott *m*; Stückschrott *m*
lump slag Stückschlacke *f*
luncheon adress Tischrede *f*
lute dichten; kitten; verschmieren
lye Lauge *f*; laugen
lye-resisting laugenbeständig

M

machinability Verarbeitbarkeit *f*; Zerspanbarkeit *f*; zerspanende Bearbeitbarkeit *f*
machine bearbeiten; zerspanen
machine casting Maschinenguß *m*
machine construction steel Maschinenbaustahl *m*

machine for forming screws Maschine f zur spanlosen Herstellung von Schrauben
machine for structural engineering Baumaschine f
machine house Maschinenhaus n
machine master file Maschinenstamm m
machinery steel Maschinenbaustahl m
machine shop mechanische Werkstätte f
machine tight maschinell festgeschraubt
machine-tool Werkzeugmaschine f
machining mechanische Bearbeitung f; spanabhebende Umformung f
machining oil Metallbearbeitungsöl n
machining step Bearbeitungsstufe f
machining time Arbeitszeit f; Bearbeitungsdauer f; Bearbeitungszeit f
machinist Maschinist m; Steuermann m
macro-etching Grobätzung f
macro hardness test Makrohärteprüfung f
macropore Grobpore f
macrostructure Makrogefüge n
Maerz-Boelens furnace Maerz-Boelens-Ofen m
Maerz checkers Maerz-Gitter n
magazine elevator feeder Hebe- und Zufuhrvorrichtung f
magnaflux testing method Magnetpulver-Prüfverfahren n
magnesia Magnesia f
magnesia-limestone Dolomit m
magnesidon special brick Magnesidon-Spezialstein m
magnesio-wustite Magnesiowüstit m
magnesite brick Magnesitstein m
magnesite chrome brick Magnesit-Chromerz-Stein m
magnesite ramming mass Magnesit-Stampfmasse f
magnesium Magnesium n
magnet crane Magnetkran m
magnetic ag[e]ing magnetisches Altern n
magnetic anisotropy magnetische Anisotropie f
magnetic annealing Magnetfeldglühen n
magnetic change magnetische Störung f
magnetic core memory Magnetkernspeicher m
magnetic disc memory Magnetplattenspeicher m
magnetic drum Magnettrommel f
magnetic field strength magnetische Feldstärke f
magnetic flaw detection magnetische Rißprüfung f
magnetic flow detection Durchflutungsprüfung f
magnetic flow meter Magnetmesser m
magnetic flux magnetischer Fluß m
magnetic grader Magnet[ab]scheider m
magnetic hammer Magnethammer m
magnetic iron ore Magneteisenstein m; Magnetit m
magnetic particle method Fluoreszenz-Magnetpulver-Verfahren n
magnetic particle testing Fluxen n
magnetic powder testing method Magnetpulver-Prüfverfahren n
magnetic pyrites Magnetkies m
magnetic roasting magnetisierende Röstung f
magnetic roll for strip magnetische Bandumlenkwalze f
magnetic rotating field magnetisches Drehfeld n
magnetic separator Magnet[ab]scheider m
magnetic sheet Elektroblech n
magnetic steel Magnetstahl m
magnetic structure examination apparatus Magneto-Strukturprüfgerät n
magnetic tape Magnetband n
magnetic tape control Magnetbandsteuerung f

magnetic tape memory Bandspeicher *m*
magnetic tape reel Magnetbandeinheit *f*; Magnetbandspule *f*
magnetisation axis Magnetisierungsachse *f*
magnetite Magnetit *m*
magnetizability Magnetisierbarkeit *f*
magnetostriction Magnetostriktion *f*
magnetostrictive ultrasonic test magnetostriktive Ultraschallprüfung *f*
magnet yoke Joch *n*; magnetisches Joch *n*
magnitude Betrag *m*
main memory RAM-Speicher *m*
main production department Hauptbetrieb *m*
main rollneck bearing Walzkraftlager *n*
main roof Hauptgewölbe *n*
mains cable Tragseil *n*
mains circuit connection Netzanschluß *m*
main screw Druckschraube *f*
mains frequency Netzfrequenz *f*
mains water Leitungswasser *n*
maintaining Halten *n*
maintenance Instandhaltung *f*
maintenance department Erhaltungsbetrieb *m*
maintenance of the cutting edge Schneidhaltigkeit *f*
maintenance of the cutting power Schneidhaltigkeit *f*
maintenance time Wartungszeit *f*
major diameter Außendurchmesser *m*
major segregation Blockseigerung *f*
making the mixture Gattieren *n*
maladjustment falsche Einstellung *f*
malleability Bildsamkeit *f*; Hämmerbarkeit *f*; Schmiedbarkeit *f*; Umformbarkeit *f*
malleable [cast] iron Temperguß *m*
malleable iron Schmiedeeisen *n*
malleable iron foundry Tempergießerei *f*
malleablise tempern
malleablising furnace Temperofen *m*

malleablising ore Tempererz *n*
malleablize by graphitisation glühfrischen
management Betriebsführung *f*; Führung *f*; Leitung *f* (Betriebsleitung)
manager Leiter *m* (eines Unternehmens)
mandrel Dorn *m*; Lochdorn *m*; Walzdorn *m*; Wickeldorn *m*; Ziehdorn *m*
mandrel drawing Stopfenziehen *n*
mandrel piler Dornstapler *m*
mandrel thrust block Dornwiderlager *n*
manganese ore Braunstein *m*; Manganerz *n*
manganese steel Manganhartstahl *m*; Manganstahl *m*
manganese steel casting Mangan-Stahlguß *m*
manganiferous manganhaltig
mangle roll Richtrolle *f*
mangling Walzrichten *n* mit mehreren Walzen
man hole Mannloch *n*
man hour Arbeitsstunde *f*
manifold mehrfach
manipulated variable (am.) (automatic control) Stellgröße *f*
manipulation time Stichzeit *f*
manipulator Kantvorrichtung *f*; Manipulator *m*
manipulator for shifting Verschieber *m*
manipulator for turning-over and shifting Kant- und Verschiebevorrichtung *f*
manipulator for turnover Kanter *m*
manipulator mark mechanische Oberflächenbeschädigung *f*
manned time Betriebszeit *f*
manning schedule Stellenbesetzungsplan *m*
manoeuverability Steuerbarkeit *f*
manometer Druckmesser *m*
man-power Arbeitseinsatz *m*; Arbeitskraft *f*
mantle Ofenstock *m*
mantle (am.) Tragkranz *m* (Hochofen)

mantle ring Tragring *m*
manual control Handregelung *f*
manual operation Handarbeit *f*
manual welding Handschweißen *n*
manual work Handarbeit *f*
manufacture Anfertigung *f*; Herstellung *f*, verarbeiten
manufacture of strip Walzstraße *f* zur Herstellung von Bandstahl
manufacturing Erzeugung *f*
manufacturing costs Herstellungskosten *pl*; Verarbeitungskosten *pl*
manufacturing of crank shaft Kurbelwellenfertigung *f*
manufacturing time Fertigungszeit *f*
marag[e]ing Martensitaushärten *n*
marag[e]ing steel martensitaushärtender Stahl *m*
margin Gewinnspanne *f*; Spiel *n*; Spielraum *m*; Toleranz *f*
margin of safety Sicherheitsgrad *m*
mark Marke *f*; Narbe *f*; Oberflächeneindruck *m* (Kaltwalzen); Striemen *m*; Zeichen *n*; ankörnen; bezeichnen; kennzeichnen; stempeln
marker Markiervorrichtung *f*
mark from the roll Walzriefe *f*
marking Anzeichnen *n* (von Blechen)
marl Mergel *m*
marsh gas Sumpfgas *n*
marsh ore Raseneisenerz *n*
martempering Warmbadhärten *n*
martensite Martensit *m*
martensite breakdown Martensitzerfall *m*
martensite hardening martensitische Härtung *f*
martensite tempering Martensitanlassen *n*
martensite transformation point Martensitpunkt *m*
martensitic martensitisch
martensitic steel martensitischer Stahl *m*
mash seam welding Preßnahtschweißen *n*
mask an effect überdecken
mason Maurer *m*

masonry Ausmauerung *f*
mass Masse *f*
mass absorption coefficient Massenschwächungskoeffizient *m*
mass action law Massenwirkungsgesetz *n*
mass attenuation coefficient Massenschwächungskoeffizient *m*
mass [bulk] flux Massenstrom *m*
mass concentration Massenkonzentration *f*; Partialdichte *f*
mass flux density Massenstromdichte *f*
mass fraction Massenbruch *m*; Massengehalt *m*
mass production Massenherstellung *f*
mass reaction Stoffumsatz *m*
mass spectrometry Massenspektrometrie *f*
mass storage device Massenspeicher *m*
mass transfer Stoffübergang *m*
mast Mast *m*
master controller Führungsregler *m*
master-mechanic Werkmeister *m*
master switch Hauptschalter *m*
match anpassen; aufeinanderlegen (Bleche); übereinanderlegen
material Material *n*; Werkstoff *m*
material data bank Werkstoffdatenbank *f*
material fatigue Werkstoffermüdung *f*
material for aircraft industry Luftfahrtwerkstoff *m*
material level in a bin Bunkerfüllstand *m*
material management Materialwirtschaft *f*
material master file Materialstamm *m*
materials balance Stoffbilanz *f*
material science Werkstoffkunde *f*
materials testing Materialprüfung *f*
material testing machine Werkstoffprüfmaschine *f*
material tracking Materialverfolgung *f*
material transfer Werkstoffübergang *m* (Lichtbogen)
material withdrawal Materialentnah-

me *f*
mathematical model mathematisches Modell *n*
mathematics Mathematik *f*
mating material Werkstoffpaarung *f*
matrix Gefügegrundmasse *f*; Grundmasse *f*
matrix lattice Wirtgitter *n*
mattress wire Matratzendraht *m*
maverick Ausreißer *m*
maximum allowable concentration höchstzulässiger Konzentrationswert *m*
maximum concentration at the work place maximale Arbeitsplatzkonzentration *f* MAK (an Schadstoffen)
maximum hardness obtainable Aufhärtbarkeit *f*
maximum torque Höchstdrehmoment *n*
McQuaid grain size McQuaid-Ehn-Korngröße *f*
meadow ore Raseneisenerz *n*; Wiesenerz *n*
mean Mittel *n* (mathem.)
mean error mittlerer Fehler *m*
mean free path mittlere freie Weglänge *f*
means of transportation Fördermittel *npl*
mean square deviation mittlere quadratische Abweichung *f*
mean value Mittelwert *m*
measure Maß *n*; messen
measured profile Ist-Profil *n*
measured value Meßwert *m*
measured variable Meßgröße *f*
measurement Messung *f*
measurement of sound conducted through solids Körperschallmessung *f*
measure of variation Schwankungsbreite *f*
measuring Messen *n*
measuring arm Meßschenkel *m*
measuring device Meßeinrichtung *f*
measuring error Meßfehler *m*
measuring instrument Meßgerät *n*

measuring instrument cupboard Meßgeräteschrank *m*
measuring junction Meßstelle *f*
measuring leads Meßleitung *f*
measuring line Eichstrich *m*
measuring means Meßglied *n*
measuring orifice Meßblende *f*; Staubscheibe *f*
measuring pipe Meßleitung *f*
measuring point Meßort *m*; Meßstelle *f*
measuring point change-over switch Meßstellenumschalter *m*
measuring probe Meßnadel *f*
measuring rail Meßschiene *f*
measuring range Meßbereich *m*
measuring station Meßwarte *f*
measuring stop Maßvorstoß *m*
measuring tool Meßwerkzeug *n*
measuring transmitter Meßumformer *m*
measuring unit Meßglied *n*
mechanic Mechaniker *m*
mechanical assembly technique (MAT) Baukastenprinzip *n*
mechanical engineering Maschinenbau *m*; Maschinenwesen *n*
mechanical engineering department Maschinenbetrieb *m*
mechanical focussing mechanism mechanisches Einstellglied *n*
mechanical properties Festigkeitseigenschaften *fpl*
mechanical technology mechanische Technologie *f*
mechanical tube Rohr *n* für Konstruktionszwecke
mechanical workshop Bearbeitungswerkstatt *f*, mechanische Werkstätte *f*
median Mittelwert *m*
medium drawing Mittelzug *m*
medium frequency converter Mittelfrequenz-Umformer *m*
medium frequency transformer Mittelfrequenz-Umformer *m*
medium ga[u]ge wire Mitteldraht *m*

medium high vacuum electron beam welding Feinvakuum-Elektronenstrahlschweißen n
medium plate Blech n (mittel)
medium sheet Blech n (mittel); Mittelblech n
medium waviness Mittenwelligkeit f (Band)
medium wide strip Mittelband n
melt Schmelzung f; schmelzen
melt down einschmelzen; herunterschmelzen; niederschmelzen; niederschmelzen (umschmelzen)
melt-down carbon Anlaufkohlenstoff m; Einlaufkohlenstoff m; Einschmelzkohlenstoff[gehalt] m
meltdown rate Aufschmelzgeschwindigkeit f
melt down slag Einlaufschlacke f
melt-down slag Einschmelzschlacke f
melter Schmelzer m
melting bath Schmelze f
melting down Einschmelzen n (Umschmelzen)
melting furnace Schmelzofen m
melting loss condition Abbrandverhältnis n
melting loss (in a liquid medium) Abbrand m
melting on Aufschmelzen n
melting out Herausschmelzen n
melting period Schmelzdauer f
melting point Schmelzpunkt m
melting pot Schmelzkessel m; Tiegel m
melting process Erschmelzungsart f
melting range Schmelzbereich m
melting rate Schmelzgeschwindigkeit f
melting shop Stahlwerk n; Stahlwerkshalle f
melting start reduction degree Reduktionsschöpfung f
melt off abschmelzen
membranar residual stress Längsspannung f
membrane valve Membranventil n
memory Speicher m (EDV)

mender Blech n zweiter Wahl
meniscus Gießspiegel m; Spiegel m
men who control coolers and check water flow (on a blast furnace) Wasserleute pl
merchant bars Handelsstabstahl m; Stabstahl m
merchant mill Stabstahlwalzwerk n
merchant sheet Handelsblech n
mercury Quecksilber n
merit Verdienst n (anerkennenswerte Leistung)
merit rating Leistungseinstufung f
mesh Maschenweite f (Sieb)
mesh screen Maschensieb n
mesh sieve Maschensieb n
mesh size Siebweite f
message storage unit Nachrichtenspeicher m
metal bath Metallbad n
metal bonding Metallkleben n
metal cased brick blechummantelter Stein m
metal dent Beschädigung f durch metallischen Überzug
metal forming Umformtechnik f
metal goods Metallwaren fpl
metal insertion Metallblecheinlage f
metal jacket Blechmantel m
metallic-arc welding Metall-Lichtbogenschweißen n
metallic charge Metalleinsatz m
metallic coating Metallüberzug m
metallic insert metallische Einlage f
metallic resistance material Heizleiterlegierung f
metallised iron ore Eisenschwamm m
metalographic specimen Schliff m
metallography Metallkunde f; Metallographie f
metallurgical coke Hüttenkoks m
metallurgical load on a furnace Herdbelastung f
metallurgical plant Hütte f; Hüttenwerk n
metallurgical process Verhüttung f; metallurgischer Vorgang m
metallurgical test metallkundliche

Prüfung f
metallurgical treatment Verhüttung f
metallurgical works Hütte f
metallurgist Hüttenmann m
metallurgy Hüttenkunde f; Metallhüttenkunde f; Metallurgie f
metallurgy of iron Eisenhüttenwesen n
metal mixer Vorfrischmischer m
metal penetration Vererzung f
metal physics Metallphysik f
metal plate insert Innenblech n; Innenblech n (ff. Steine)
metal plate insert (arch) Innenblech n (Gewölbe)
metal powder part Sinterteil n
metal residues Metallrückstände mpl
metal runner Eisenrinne f
metal sheet Feinblech n
metal soap Metallseife f
metal spinning Drücken n (Blechumformen)
metal spraying Metallspritzen n
metal ware Metallwaren fpl
metal working Umformtechnik f
metalworking industry metallverarbeitende Industrie f
metal working oil Metallbearbeitungsöl n
metastable metastabil
meteoric iron Meteoreisenstein m
meter Messer m; dosieren
metering Messen n
metering pump Dosierpumpe f
metering-type belt scales Dosierbandwaage f
methane Methan n
method Verfahren n
method of evalution Beurteilungsmaßstab m; Beurteilungsverfahren n
method of maximum likelihood Verfahren n der größten Wahrscheinlichkeit
method of working Arbeitsmethode f
micaceous iron ore Eisenglimmer m
micro alloyed structural steel mikrolegierter Baustahl m

micro-duplex structure Duplex-Mikro-Struktur f
micro etching Mikroätzen n
microfinishing Feinstbearbeitung f
micrograph Gefügebild n; Schliffbild n
microhardness Mikrohärte f
micrometer ga[u]ge Mikrometerschraube f
micromotion analysis Mikrobewegungsanalyse f
micro pelletising Mikropelletieren n
micropore Feinpore f; Mikropore f
microprobe Mikrosonde f
microprobe analyser Elektronenmikrosonde f
microscalping Nadelfräsen n (zur Beseitigung von entkohlten Schichten)
microscopic degree of purity mikroskopischer Reinheitsgrad
microsection Mikroschliff m; metallographischer Schliff m
microsegregation Kristallseigerung f
microstructure Feingefüge n; Gefüge n; Mikrogefüge n
micro-train measurement Feindehnungsmessung f
microvoid Mikropore f
middle roll Mittelwalze f
middling Schmieden n eines mittleren dünneren Teiles
middlings Zwischengut n (erzhaltiges Gestein)
MIG welding Metall-Inertgasschweißen n
mild drawn wire Draht m mit geringer Querschnittsabnahme gezogen
mild-hard roll Walze f (Mildhart)
mild steel kohlenstoffarmer weicher Stahl m; unlegierter Stahl m; weicher Stahl m
milk of lime Kalkmilch f
mill Betriebsanlage f; Hütte f; Mühle f; Walzwerk n; Werk n; fräsen; mahlen; walzen
mill accident Betriebsunfall m
mill annealed geglüht vom Lieferanten
mill approach table Zufuhrrollgang m zum Walzwerk

mill auxiliaries Walzwerkshilfsantriebe *mpl*
mill bar Platine *f*; Puddelluppe *f*; Rohschiene *f*; Schweißeisen *n*
mill bite Walzspalt *m*
milled edge gerändelte Kante *f*
mill edge Naturkante *f*
milled powder gemahlenes Pulver *n*
mill floor level Hüttenflur *m*
mill housing Walzenständer *m*
mill housing post Ständerholm *m*
milling and boring machine Fräs- und Bohrmaschine *f*; Fräs- und Bohrwerk *n*
milling cutter Fräser *m*
milling machine Fräsmaschine *f*
millings Frässpäne *mpl*
mill length Lagerlänge *f* (Walzstäbe)
mill revert scrap Walzwerksumlaufschrott *m*
mill scale Glühzunder *m*; Walzensinter *m*; Walzschlacke *f*; Walzzunder *m*
mill scale powder Walzsinterpulver *n*
mill scrap Rücklaufschrott *m*
mill shearing Paketschneiden *n* (Blech)
mill spring Walzensprung *m*
mill stand Walzgerüst *n*
mill stand of a forging-rolling unit Walzkassette *f*
mill train Walzstraße *f*
mine Zeche *f*
mine car Förderwagen *m*
mine dump Zechenhalde *f*
mine kibble Drahtseilkübel *m*
mineral component Mineralbestandteil *m* (Kohle)
mineral matter Mineralbestandteil *m* (Kohle)
mineralogy Mineralogie *f*
mineral oil Mineralöl *n*
miner summation Miner-Summierung *f*
mine tram Förderwagen *m*
minette Minette *f*
minimum stress Unterspannung *f*
minimum tensile strength Mindestzugfestigkeit *f*
mining Bergbau *m*
mining activity Bergwirtschaft *f*
mining by deep level workings Gewinnung *f* im Tiefbau
mining by open-cast method Gewinnung *f* im Tagebau
mining drill steel Gesteinsbohrstahl *m*
mining equipment Bergbauausrüstung *f*
mining industry Montanindustrie *f*
minor constituent Eisenbegleitelement *n*
minor diameter Kerndurchmesser *n* (Gewinde)
minor segregation Kristallseigerung *f*
minute current Schwachstrom *m*
miscible mischbar
misfit cast Fehlschmelze *f*
mismatch Fehler *m* durch nicht genau übereinander sitzende Gesenkhälften
mis-run [casting] Fehlguß *m*
mist lubrication Nebelschmierung *f*
mitre gear Kegelrad *n*
mix mischen
mixable mischbar
mixed coke oven gas-oxygen burner Koksgas-Sauerstoff-Brenner *m*
mixed crystal Mischkristall *m*
mixed friction Mischreibung *f*
mixed gas Mischgas *n*
mixed logic gemischte Logik *f*
mixed ore pellet Mischerzpellet *n*
mixed phase Mischphase *f*
mixer Mischer *m*
mixer metal Mischerroheisen *n*
mixer type hot metal car fahrbarer Roheisenmischer *m*
mixing ratio Mischungsverhältnis *n*
mixture Gemisch *n*; Mischung *f*
mobile beweglich; fahrbar; verfahrbar
mobile dislocation wandernde Versetzung *f*
mobile drum type ladle fahrbare Trommelpfanne *f*
mobile hearth Herd *m*; ausfahrbarer Herd *m*

mobile prime costs bewegliche Herstellungskosten *pl*
mode Art und Weise *f*; dichtester Wert *m*; wahrscheinlichster Wert *m*
mode echo Nebenecho *n*
model Modell *n*
model chart of accounts Kontenrahmen *m*
mode of operation Betriebsweise *f*; Wirkungsweise *f*
moderate mäßig
modification Modifikation *f*
modular building brick principle Baukastenprinzip *n*
modulus Modul *m*
modulus of compression Kompressionsmodul *m* (K-Modul)
modulus of elasticity E-Modul *m*; Elastizitätsmodul *m*; Gleitmodul *m*
modulus of rigidity Schubmodul *m*
Mohr circle [of stresses] Mohrscher Spannungskreis *m*
moisture Feuchtigkeit *f*
moisture content Nässegehalt *m* (Probenahme)
moisture meter Feuchtigkeitsgradmesser *m* (bei festen Stoffen)
moisture sample Nässeprobe *f*
molality Molalität *f*
molar flux Stoffmengenstrom *m*
molar heat capacity molare Wärmekapazität *f*
molarity Molarität *f*
molar mass molare Masse *f*
mold Gießsturz *m*
molecular heat at constant volume (pressure) Molwärme *f* bei konstantem Volumen (Druck)
molecular sieve Molekularsieb *n*
mole fraction Molenbruch *m*; Stoffmengengehalt *m*
molten iron flüssiges Eisen *n*
molten level measurement system Gießspiegelmeßsystem *n*
molten metal pressure welding Gießpreßschweißen *n*
molybdenum Molybdän *n*
moment of inertia Trägheitsmoment *n*

moment of resistance Widerstandsmoment *n*
monitor Warngerät *n*
monitoring Überwachung *f*
monkey Fallhammer *m*; Kühlkasten *m*; Schlackenform *f*, Schlackenloch *n*
monkey cooler Schlackenkühler *m*; Schlackenloch-Kühlring *m* (Hochofen)
monocrystal Einkristall *m*
monolithic roll housing einteiliger Walzständer *m*
monorail Einschienenbahn *f*
monotonic state Monotonie *f*
mordant Beize *f*; Ätzmittel *n*
mortar Mörtel *m*
mortise Zapfenloch *n*; einzapfen; verzapfen
mortising Verzapfung *f*
mortising machine Zapfenlochmaschine *f*
motion Bewegung *f*
motor Motor *m*
motor car Kraftfahrzeug *n*
motorcar body sheet Karosserieblech *n*
motor-car body sheet Kraftwagenblech *n*
motor-car engine Kraftwagenmotor *m*
motor construction Motorenbau *m*
motor fuel Treibstoff *m*
motor generator set house Umformerhaus *n*
motor scraper Motorschürfwagen *m*
mottled fleckig; gesprenkelt; halbiert; meliert
mould Blockform *f*; Kokille *f*; Kristallisator *m*; Kühlschale *f*
mo[u]ld Form *f*; Gießform *f*; formen
mould cooling jacket Kühlschale *f*
mo[u]lder Vorsturz *m*
mould frame Kokillenhubtisch *m*
moulding blackening Formschwärze *f*
moulding machine Formmaschine *f*
moulding material Formstoff *m*
moulding mixture for steel castings Stahlformmasse *f*

moulding sand Formsand *m*
mould level control Gießspiegelregelung *f*
mould scrap Kokillenbruch *m*
mould sticker in der Kokille steckengebliebener Block *m*
mould wall Kokillenwand *f*
mould wash Formschlichte *f*; Kokillenanstrichmittel *m*
mount Fassung *f*; Fassung *f* (Ziehstein); einbauen; einspannen; montieren
mountain railway Bergbahn *f*
mounting Aufstellung *f*; Einbau *m*; Einspannung *f*
mouth Mündung *f* (Konverter); Trichter *m* (Ziehen)
mouth of die Eingangsschlüssel *m*
mouth skull Mündungsbär *m*
movable beweglich; fahrbar; verfahrbar
move bewegen; verschieben; versetzen
movement Bewegung *f*
moving average gleitender Durchschnitt *m*
moving-coil measuring system Drehspulmeßwerk *n*
moving in opposite directions gegenläufig
moving load bewegte Last *f*
Ms point Martensitpunkt *m*
muck bar Puddelluppe *f*; Rohschiene *f*
muck mill Puddelstahl-Walzwerk *n*
mud gun Stichlochstopfmaschine *f*
mud remover Schlammräumer *m*
mud thickener Schlammeindicker *m*
muffle furnace Muffelofen *m*
muliple disk brake Lamellenbremse *f*
muller Kollergang *m*; Mahlläufer *m*
multi-axial stress condition mehrachsiger Spannungszustand *m*
multicolour plotter Mehrfarbenschreiber *m*
multicolour recorder Mehrfarbenschreiber *m*
multicomponent system Mehrstoffsystem *n*
multi-fuel annular burner system Mantelbrenner *m*
multi hole brick Viellochstein *m*
multi-jet bricked burner furnace Steinstrahlofen *m*
multi-loop control system vermaschter Regelkreis *m*
multimodal distribution vielgipflige Verteilung *f*
multiple mehrfach
multiple blow [impact] test Mehrfachschlagversuch *m*
multiple cropping Mehrfachabschneiden *n*
multiple die press Stufenpresse *f*
multiple disc clutch Mehrscheibenkupplung *f*
multiple drafting Mehrfachzug *m*
multiple drawing Mehrfachzug *m*
multiple drawing bench Mehrfachziehmaschine *f*
multiple drawing machine Mehrfachziehmaschine *f*
multiple drill pass Gelenkspindel-Bohrmaschine *f*
multiple factor experiment Mehreinflußversuch *m*
multiple folding Mehrfachabbiegen *n*
multiple gas jet brazing Flammenfeldlöten *n*
multiple nozzle lance Mehrdüsenlanze *f*
multiple pressing Mehrfachpreßtechnik *f*
multiple production Reihenherstellung *f*
multiple recorder Mehrfachschreiber *m*
multiple spline shaft Sternkeilwelle *f*; Vielkeilwelle *f*
multiple stage gas cleaning mehrstufige Gasreinigung *f*
multiple stand rolling mill mehrgerüstiges Walzwerk *n*
multi[ple] strand casting machine mehrsträngige Gießmaschine *f*
multiple testing machine Vielproben-

maschine *f*
multiple V-form bending Mehrfachkeilbiegen *n*
multiple zone furnace Mehrzonenofen *m*
multi stage cooling Mehrstufenkühlung *f*
multi stage fatigue test Mehrstufen-Dauerschwingversuch *m*
multi strand line Mehrbandanlage *f*
multi-turn coiling Wickeln *n*
multi variate distribution mehrdimensionale Verteilung *f*
muriatic acid Salzsäure *f*
mushroom valve Tellerventil *n*
mushy zone heterogene Zone *f*
mutual wechselseitig
mutual repulsion gegenseitiges Ausweichen *n*

N

nail Nagel *m*; nageln
name plate Firmenschild *n*; Namensschild *n*
name plate rating Nennleistung *f* (Ofentransformator)
narrow eng; schmal
narrow-band analyser Schmalbandanalysator *m*
narrow flange I-beam schmaler I-Träger *m*
narrow strip Schmalband *n*
natural natürlich
natural ag[e]ing Kaltauslagern *n*; natürliches Altern *n*
natural circulation Naturumlauf *m*
natural gas Erdgas *n*; Naturgas *n*
naturally hard naturhart
natural oscillation Eigenschwingung *f*
nature Beschaffenheit *f*
near contact friction Epilamenreibung *f*
neat rein; sauber
neat's foot oil Klauenfett *n*

neck Laufzapfen *m*; Zapfen *m* (Walze); einschnüren; einziehen
necked-down bolt Dehnschraube *f*
necking [down] Einschnürung *f*
needle Nadel *f*
needle bearing Nadellager *n*
needle bottom Nadelboden *m*
needle wire Nadeldraht *m*
negative correlation gegensinniger Kurvenverlauf *m*
negative feedback Gegenkopplung *f*
negative pressure Unterdruck *m*
negative segregation umgekehrte Seigerung *f*
net caloric power (am.) unterer Heizwert *m* (Hu)
net heat consumption Netto-Wärmeverbrauch *m*
net result Fazit *n*; Reinergebnis *n*
netting wire Maschendraht *m*
net wage Nettolohn *m*
network plan Netzplan *m*
neutralise neutralisieren; unschädlich machen
neutral point Fließscheide *f* (beim Walzen)
neutron absorption cross section Absorptionsquerschnitt *m*
neutron activation Neutronenaktivierung *f*
neutron radiation Neutronenbestrahlung *f*
new lining Neuzustellung *f*
new shape Form *f* neue
nibbling Knabberschneiden *n* (Blech); Nibbeln *n* (Blech)
nick Kerb *m*; einkerben
nick bend test Kerbbiegeprobe *f*; Kerbbiegeversuch *m*
nicked fracture test Kerbbiegeprobe *f*; Kerbbiegeversuch *m*
nickel Nickel *n*
nickel plating Vernickeln *n*
nickel silver Alpacca *n*; Neusilber *n*
nickel steel Nickelstahl *m*
nicopyrite Eisennickelkies *m*
night-gang Nachtschicht *f*
night shift Nachtarbeit *f*; Nachtschicht *f*

night turn Nachtarbeit f; Nachtschicht f
niobium Niob n
nipple Anschlußstück n; Nippel m
nipple plate Warzenblech n
nitric acid Salpetersäure f
nitride Nitrid n
nitrided case nitrierte Schicht f
nitride former Nitridbildner m
nitriding Aufsticken n; Nitrieren n; Nitrierhärten n
nitriding agent Nitridbildner m
nitriding steel Nitrierstahl m
nitrogen Stickstoff m
nitrogen-alloyed austenitic steel stickstofflegierter austenitischer Stahl m
nitrogen hardening Nitrierhärten n
nitrogen pick-up Aufsticken n
nitrogen removal Denitrieren n
nodular [graphite] cast iron Gußeisen n mit Kugelgraphit; sphärolithisches Gußeisen n
nodular iron roll Walze f (Sphäroguß)
nodulising Kugelsintern n
noise abatement Lärmbekämpfung f
noise level Geräuschpegel m; Störpegel m
noise reduction Lärmminderung f; Schallminderung f
nominal capacity Nennleistung f
nominal rating Nennscheinleistung f
nominal size Nennmaß n; Paßmaß n
nominal speed Nenndrehzahl f
nominal temperature Solltemperatur f
nominal value Nennwert m; Sollwert m
nomogram Nomogramm n
non automatic control nichtselbsttätige Regelung f
non-caking coal Magerkohle f
noncircular unrund
non-coke charge Leergicht f (Hochofen)
noncoking unverkokbar
non-conducting nicht leitend
non corroding nichtrostend
non deforming steel verzugsbeständiger Stahl m; verzugsfreier Stahl m

non-destructive test[ing] zerstörungsfreie Prüfung f
non distorting steel verzugsfreier Stahl m
non equiaxial grains ungleichachsige Körner npl
non-ferrous metal Buntmetall n; NE-Metall n; Nichteisenmetall n
non-linear member nichtlineares Glied n
non-load time Leerlaufzeit f
non-machined unbearbeitet
non-magnetizable steel nichtmagnetisierbarer Stahl m
non metallic inclusion nichtmetallischer Einschluß m
non-operating expenditure neutraler Aufwand m
non-operating income and expenditure accounts neutrale Aufwands- und Ertragskonten npl
non-ore charge Leergicht f (Hochofen)
non phosphorous pig iron Stahleisen n; Stahlroheisen n
non-pressure thermit welding Gießschmelzschweißen n
non-propagating fatigue crack nicht fortschreitender Dauerbruch m
non-return valve Rückschlagventil n
non-scaling feuerbeständig; zunderbeständig
non-scaling property Zunderbeständigkeit f
nonsense correlation sinnwidrige Korrelation f
non-sizing nicht maßhaltig
non slip drawing gleitloses Ziehen n
no[n]slip point Fließscheide f
non swirl nozzle nichtwirbelnde Düse f (Stranggießen)
non uniformity Ungleichmäßigkeit f
non uniform powder ungleichförmiges Pulver n
non warping steel verzugsfreier Stahl m
normal beam schmaler I-Träger m
normal distribution Normalverteilung f

normal force Normalkraft f
normalise glühen; normalglühen
normalising Normalglühen n
normalising forming normalisierendes Umformen n
normal sound incidence Senkrechteinschallung f
normal stress Normalspannung f
normal U sections rundkantiger U-Stahl m
nose Mündung f; Nase f; Schnauze f
nosing Anspitzen n (Stauchen)
not blistered (steel) blasenfrei
notch Einbrandkerbe f; Kerb m; einkerben; falzen
notch bending test Kerbfallprüfung f
notch bend test Kerbbiegeprobe f; Kerbbiegeversuch m
notch brittleness Kerbsprödigkeit f
notch diameter Kerbdurchmesser m
notched bar impact bend test Kerbschlagbiegeversuch m
notched bar impact fatigue test Dauerkerbschlagversuch m
notched bar impact test Kerbschlagprüfung f
notched creep test Kerbdauerstandversuch m
notched hearth furnace Nockenherdofen m
notched sample Kerbprobe f
notched tension test Kerbzugversuch m
notched torsion test Kerbverdrehversuch m
notch effect Kerbwirkung f
notch impact energy Kerbschlagarbeit f
notch sensitivity Kerbempfindlichkeit f
not cut to pattern nicht maßhaltig geschnitten
not determined nicht nachgewiesen (in Tabellen: n. n.)
not flat (sheet) uneben (Blech)
not machined unbearbeitet
not susceptible to brittle fracture sprödbruchunempfindlich
novel object of invention neuer Erfindungsgedanke m (Patent)
novelty neuer Erfindungsgedanke m (Patent)
nozzle Ausguß m; Düse f; Schnauze f
nozzle cross sectional area Düsenquerschnitt m
nozzle of a ladle Pfannenausguß m
nozzling Herstellen n eines Ziehendes (Rohr)
nuclear energy Atomenergie f; Kernenergie f
nuclear fission Kernspaltung f
nuclear physics Kernphysik f
nuclear power Kernenergie f
nuclear power plant Atomkraftwerk n
nuclear power station Kernkraftwerk n
nuclear reactor Atomreaktor m; Kernreaktor m
nucleate-boiling Blasenverdampfung f
nucleation Keimbildung f
nucleous Kern m
nucleus Keim m
nuisance from odours Geruchsbelästigung f
number of alternations Schwingungszahl f
number of alternations to fracture Bruchlastspielzahl f
number of cycles Lastspielzahl f
number of cycles to fracture Bruchlastspielzahl f
number of data places Datenstellenzahl f
number of materials Werkstoffnummer f
number of operatives Personalbestand m
number of oscillations Schwingungszahl f
number of particles Teilchenzahl f
number of revolutions Drehzahl f
numerator Zähler m
nut Schraubenmutter f

O

object Gegenstand m
objection Beanstandung f
oblique geneigt; schief; schiefwinklig; schräg
oblique rif Schrägrippe f
oblique shearing ziehender Schnitt m
oblique sputtering Schrägbedampfung f
oblong länglich
oblong hole Langloch n
obnoxious odour Geruchsbelästigung f
observation hole Schauloch n
observe feststellen
obsolet überholt
obstruction Störung f; Verstopfung f
obtaining of equilibrium Gleichgewichtseinstellung f
obtuse (angle) stumpf (stumpfer Winkel)
occluded gases Gase npl im Stahl
occlusion Gaseinschluß m
occupational disease Berufskrankheit f
occupational group Berufsgruppe f
occurence in beds Vorkommen n
occurence in floors Vorkommen n
occurence in veins Vorkommen n; gangförmiges Vorkommen n
octagons Achtkantstahl m
octave analysis Oktavspektrum n
ocular micrometer Okularmikrometer n
off-cast Fehlguß m
off centre außermittig; versetzt
offer Angebot n
offer without obligation unverbindliches Angebot n
off-ga[u]ge Fehlabmessung f (beim Kaltwalzen); Unterdicke f; nicht maßhaltig; Überdicke f
off grade iron Übergangseisen n
off-hand forming under compression conditions Freiformen n
off-hand grinding Freihandschleifen n
off-hand piercing Dornen n
off-hand rounding freies Runden n
off-heat Fehlschmelze f
office Büro n
off-loader Abheber m
off-normal memory Störwertspeicher m
offset Absatz m; Biegung f; Fehler m durch nicht genau übereinander sitzende Gesenkhälften; Schränkung f; Verkröpfung f; Versetzung f; absetzen; geschränkt; kröpfen
offsetting Kröpfen n
offset tool depth ga[u]ge Drehstrahltaster m
off-size Abmaß n; Toleranz f; nicht formhaltig
off-take Abzug m; Abzugskanal m
ogive curve Summenkurve f (bei Normalverteilung)
ohmic resistance ohmscher Widerstand m
oil schmieren; ölen; Öl n
oil burner Ölbrenner m
oil carburising plant Ölkarburierungsanlage f
oil change Ölwechsel m
oil contaminated soil ölverseuchtes Erdreich n
oil cooler Ölkühler m
oiled finish eingeölt
oil emulsive ölhaltig
oil filled cable Öldruckkabel n
oil film Ölfilm m
oil film bearing Ölflutlager n
oil firing Ölfeuerung f
oil hardening Ölhärten n
oil hardening steel Ölhärter m
oil hydraulics Ölhydraulik f
oil impregnation Öltränkung f
oiling Schmierung f
oil mist lubrication Ölnebelschmierung f
oil mist spray Ölnebelschmierung f
oil quenched and tempered wire ölvergüteter Draht m
oil quenching Ölhärten n
oil-retaining layer ölhaltende Schicht f

oil seal Ölabdichtung *f*
oil separator Entöler *m*; Ölabscheider *m*
oil shale Ölschiefer *m*
oil spray lubrication Ölnebelschmierung *f*
oil tempering Ölanlassen *n*
oil wedge Ölkeil *m*
oily ölhaltig
oligiste iron ore Eisenglanz *m*; Glanzeisenstein *m*
one circuit lance Einkreislanze *f*
on edge hochkantig
one hand burner Einhandbrenner *m*
one tube welded across on top of another im Kreuzstoß *m* geschweißte Rohre
one-way top-fired soaking pit Einwegaufblas-Tiefofen *m*
on-fraction Siebrückstand *m*
on-hand-status check Verfügbarkeitskontrolle *f*
on-line direkt prozeßgekoppelt
on-line computation prozeßsynchrone Rechenarbeit *f*
on-line enquiry Dialogauskunft *f*
on-line open loop offen prozeßgekoppelt
on-line processing Dialogverarbeitung *f*
oolitic [iron] ore Minette *f*
oolitic limonite Brauneisenoolith *m*
ooze Schlamm *m* (Erzaufbereitung)
opaque undurchsichtig
open annealing Blauglühen *n*
open-coil annealing furnace Offenbundglühofen *m*
open cut Tagebau *m*
open-cut mining Gewinnung *f* im Tagebau; Tagebau *m*
open die offenes Gesenk *n*
open die forging Freiformschmieden *n*
open die forming Freiformen *n*
open grain Grobkorn *n*
open groove offenes Kaliber *n*
open hearth furnace Siemens-Martin-Ofen *m*
open hearth furnace port end Siemens-Martin-Ofenkopf *m*
open hearth process Herdfrischverfahren *n*; Siemens-Martin-Verfahren *n*
open hearth steel Siemens-Martin-Stahl *m*
open hearth steel plant Siemens-Martin-Stahlwerk *n*
opening Öffnung *f*
opening up of crack by rolling Aufwalzung *f* (Stranggießen)
open joint tube Rohr *n* mit offener Naht
open loop control offene Steuerung *f*
open moulding box geöffneter Formkasten *m*
open pass offenes Kaliber *n*
open pit Gießgrube *f*; Tagebau *m*
open seam tube Schlitzrohr *n*
open top mould offene Kokille *f*
open-web girder Wabenträger *m*
operate betreiben
operating in Betrieb *m*
operating characteristics Betriebskennzahlen *fpl*
operating costs Betriebskosten *pl*
operating desk Schaltpult *n*
operating equipment Betriebseinrichtung *f*
operating figures Betriebszahlen *fpl*
operating lever Bedienungshebel *m*
operating material Betriebsstoff *m*
operating numbers Betriebszahlen *fpl*
operating panel Schaltpult *n*
operating pulpit Steuerbühne *f*
operating report Betriebsbericht *m*
operating result Betriebsergebnis *n*
operating results Betriebsergebnisse *npl*
operating safety Betriebssicherheit *f*
operating sequence control Betriebsablaufsteuerung *f*
operating stand Steuerstand *m*
operating time Arbeitszeit *f*
operating trouble Betriebsstörung *f*
operating voltage Arbeitsspannung *f*

operation

operation Arbeitsvorgang m; Bedienung f; Betrieb m; Einwirkung f; Führung f (Ofen); Vorgang m
operational computer Betriebsrechner m
operational data Betriebsdaten npl
operational experience Betriebserfahrung f
operational facility Arbeitsmittel n
operational means Arbeitsmittel n
operational plant Betriebsanlage f
operational record[ing] Betriebsaufschreibung f
operational research Planungsforschung f
operation and error indicators Operations- und Fehleranzeigen f
operation characteristic (OC) Kennkurve f
operation first costs Betriebsselbstkosten pl
operation prime costs Betriebsselbstkosten pl
operation rate Leistung f
operations research Ablauf- und Planungsforschung f
operative Arbeiter m; Bedienungsmann m
operator Arbeiter m; Bedienungsmann m; Steuermann m
operator's platform Bedienungsbühne f
oppose a patent Einspruch m einlegen gegen ein Patent
opposite pole Gegenpol m
opposition to a patent Patenteinspruch m
optical microscopy Lichtmikroskopie f
optical pyrometer Teilstrahlungspyrometer n; optisches Pyrometer n
optimisation Optimierung f
orange peel Orangenhaut f (Bandfehler)
orange peel bucket Polypengreifer m
orange-peel type charging basket Segmentverschlußkorb m
orbital welding Rundnahtschweißen n
order Auftrag m; Ordnung f

ordered weight Bestellgewicht n
order of magnitude Größenordnung f
order transformation Ordnungs-Umwandlung f
order transmitting device Befehlsgerät n
ordinary gewöhnlich
ordinary lay rope Kreuzschlagseil n
ordinary quality einfache Handelsgüte f
ore Erz n
ore bearing erzführend; erzhaltig
ore beneficiation Eisenerzvorbereitung f
ore bin Erzbunker m
ore burden Erzgicht f
ore coke pellet Eisenerz-Koks-Pellet n
ore committee Erzausschuß m
ore concentrate Erzkonzentrat n
ore concentration Erzaufbereitung f
ore crusher Erzbrecher m
ore dressing Erzaufbereitung f
ore dressing facility Erzaufbereitungsanlage f
ore dressing plant Erzaufbereitungsanlage f
ore fines Feinerz n
ore freighter Erzfrachter m
ore preparation plant Erzaufbereitungsanlage f
ore roasting plant Röstanlage f für Erze
ore sintering plant Sinteranlage f
ore storage bunker Erzbunker m
ore up erzen (Erz zusetzen)
ore vein Erzader f
organic matter organischer Stoff m
organisation of power and material supply Energie- und Stoffwirtschaft f
organosol Organosol n
orientation dependence Orientierungsabhängigkeit f
orientation index Ausrichtungsgrad m (Kristall)
orifice Ausflußöffnung f; Blende f; Staurand m; Stauscheibe f; Öffnung f

orifice measurement Differenzdruck *m*; Messung *f* mit Staurand
original cost Gestehungskosten *pl*
orthosilicate Orthosilicat *n*
oscillating conveyor Schwingrinne *f*; Schüttelrutsche *f*
oscillating crank Schwinge *f*
oscillating saw Pendelsäge *f*; Schwingsäge *f*
oscillation Oszillation *f*; Pendelung *f*; Schwingung *f*
oscillation marks Hubmarken *fpl* (Stranggießen)
oscillograph Oszillograph *m*
osmotic pressure osmotischer Druck *m*
outage Ausfall *m* (Generator)
outdoor transformer Freilufttransformator *m*
outer lining Dauerfutter *n*
outgoing side (of rolls) Auslaufseite *f* (der Walzen)
outlet Abfluß *m*; Ausgang *m*; Ausguß *m*; Auslauf *m*
outlet gate Auslaßschütz *n*
outlet pipe Abflußrohr *n*; Auslaß *m*
outlier Ausreißer *m*
outlines Profil *n* (Hochofen)
outmoded obsolete überholt (veraltet)
out of straightness Durchbiegung *f*
output Ausbeute *f*; Ausbringen *n*; Ertrag *m*; Erzeugung *f*; Erzeugungsmenge *f*; Fördermenge *f*; Leistung *f*; Menge *f*
output data Erzeugungsangaben *fpl*
output of coal Kohlengewinnung *f*
output of hearth surface Herdflächenleistung *f*
output rates Produktionszahlen *fpl*
output shaft Abtrieb *m* (Stranggießen)
output variable Ausgangsgröße *f*
output yield Ertrag *m*
outside diameter Außendurchmesser *m*
oval bow-type continuous casting machine Stranggieß-Ovalbogenanlage *f*
oval groove Ovalkaliber *n*

oval pass Ovalkaliber *n*
oven Ofen *m* (Kokerei)
overage überaltern
overag[e]ing Überaltern *n*
overall deflexion Durchbiegung *f* gesamte
overall noise Gesamtschallpegel *m*
overall power consumption Stromanschlußwert *m*
overall precision Gesamtpräzision *f* (Probenahme)
overall reduction Gesamtquerschnittsabnahme *f*
overarm Gegenhalter *m* (Fräsmaschine)
over blow überblasen
overburden Abraum *m*
overburdening Übermöllerung *f*
over capacity Überkapazität *f*
overcharging Überbelasten *n* (eines SM-Ofens)
overclosed gear übergeschlossenes Getriebe *n*
overclosed mechanism übergeschlossenes Getriebe *n*
overcoiling wickeln von oben
overdraft überziehen
overextended current liabilities Kreditanspannung *f*
overfill überfüllen; Überfüllung *f*
overfilled überhöht (Schweißen)
overfilling Stoffüberschuß *m*
overfilling (of a pass) Zuvollgehen *n* (eines Kalibers)
overflowed roll Walze *f* (Verbundguß)
overflow slag [boilings] übergeflossene Schlacke *f*
overflow tube Überlaufrohr *n*
overhang Ausladung *f*; Überhängen *n*
overhaul überholen
overhead beam Deckenbalken *m*; Fahrschiene *f*
overhead charges Zuschlagskosten *pl*
overhead conveyor furnace Hängebahnofen *m*
overhead cost Gemeinkosten *pl*
overhead expense distribution sheet Betriebsabrechnungsbogen *m*

overhead expenses Zuschlagskosten *pl*
overhead hopper Hochbunker *m*
overhead pay off Überkopfablauf *m*
overhead [position] welding Überkopfschweißen *n*
overhead take off Überkopfablauf *m*
overhead travelling crane (OTC) Laufkran *m*
overhead trolley Hängebahn *f*
overheating sensitivity Überhitzungsempfindlichkeit *f*
overhung ausladend angeordnet; fliegend angeordnet
overlap überdecken; überlappen; überschneiden; Überlappung *f*
overlap joint Überlappstoß *m*
overlapped joint weld überlappte Stoßschweiße *f*
overlapping Überwalzung *f*
overlapping joint Übergreifungsstoß *m*
overlaying welding Auftragschweißung *f*
overload capacity Überlastbarkeit *f*
overloading Überlastung *f*
overload safety device Überlastsicherung *f*
over-oxidation Überfrischen *n*
overpickled zu stark gebeizt
overpressure Überdruck *m*
oversintered übersintert
oversize Rückgut *n*; Überkorn *n*; Übermaß *n*
oversized material Grobgut *n*
oversize product Rückstand *m* (Aufbereitung); Überlauf *m* (beim Sieben)
overstressing Überbeanspruchung *f*
overtiming Überzeiten *n*
overvoltage Überspannung *f*
overwinding wickeln von oben
own scrap Rücklaufschrott *m*
own scrap arisings Kreislaufschrott *m*
own use Eigenverbrauch *m*
oxacetylene welding Gasschmelzschweißung *f*

oxidant Oxidationsmittel *n*
oxidation Frischen *n*; Verbrennen *n*
oxide Zunder *m*
oxide film Oxidbelag *m*
oxide inclusion Oxideinschluß *m*
oxide layer Zunderschicht *f*
oxide skin Oxidhaut *f*
oxidise frischen; oxidieren; verschmoren
oxidise at high temperatures verzundern
oxidising period Frischperiode *f*
oxidising reaction Frischwirkung *f*
oxidising slag Frischschlacke *f*
oxidizing loss (in a gaseous medium) Abbrand *m*
oxyacetylene cutting Brennschneiden *n*
oxyacetylene welding autogenes Schweißen *n*
oxy fuel burner Sauerstoff-Brennstoff-Brenner *m*
oxygen consumption type of corrosion Korrosion *f* unter Sauerstoffverbrauch
oxygen converter steel plant Sauerstoff-Blasstahlwerk *n*
oxygen enriched air blast sauerstoffangereicherter Wind *m*
oxygen lance Sauerstofflanze *f*
oxygen lance powder converter OLP-Konverter *m*
oxygen powder lance Sauerstoffpulverlanze *f*
oxygen probe Sauerstoffmeßsonde *f*
oxygen production plant Sauerstoffgewinnungsanlage *f*
oxygen refined steel Sauerstoffstahl *m*
oxygen refining Blasfrischen *n*; Sauerstofffrischen *n*
oxygen removal Sauerstoffabbau *m*
oxygen sensor Sauerstoffmeßsonde *f*
oxygen steel Sauerstoffblasstahl *m*
oxygen steelmaking process Sauerstoffblasverfahren *n*

P

pace Schritt *m*; Tempo *n*
pack Bergeversatz *m*; Lage *f*; Pack *m*; Paket *n*; abdichten; packen
packaging Konfektionierung *f*
packaging control Konfektionierungssteuerung *f*
packaging line Verpackungslinie *f*
packaging planning Konfektionierungsplanung *f*
pack annealing Sturzenglühen *n*
pack carburising Kastenaufkohlen *n*; Pulveraufkohlen *n*
packed bed Schüttung *f*
packed height Schüttguthöhe *f*
pack heating furnace Paketwärmofen *m*; Sturzenwärmofen *m*
packing Dichtung *f*; Packung *f*; Verbindungsmasse *f*; Verdichtung *f*
packing box Stopfbüchse *f*
packing density Packungsdichte *f*; Schüttdichte *f*
packing machine Packmaschine *f*
packing material Einbettmaterial *n*
packing of a lattice direction (X-rays) Besetzung *f* einer Gittergeraden
packing of spheres Kugelpackung *f*
packing plate Verpackungsblech *n*
packing ring Dichtungsring *m*
pack rolling Paketwalzen *n*
paddle mixer Paddelmischer *m*; Schaufelmischer *m*
paint[ing] medium Anstrichmittel *n*
paint spraying process Farbspritzverfahren *n*
paint systems Lacksysteme *npl*
pair of compasses Zirkel *m*
pallet Fördergestell *n*; Gleitbahn *f*; Gleitfläche *f*; Palette *f*; Röstwagen *m*; Schlitten *m*; Sinterpfanne *f*; Stapelplatte *f*; Tragbrett *n*
palletised in Palettenverpackung *f*
pan Schüssel *f*; Tiegel *m*
panel Tafel *f*
panel lining Wandauskleidung *f*
pan grind kollern
pan grinder Kollergang *m*

pantograph Storchschnabelgetriebe *n*
pan type annealing furnace Topfglühofen *m*
paper Abhandlung *f*; Vertrag *m*
paper bag Papiersack *m*
parallel flanged beam Parallelflanschträger *m*
parallel flanged joist Parallelflanschträger *m*
paramagnetism Paramagnetismus *m*
parameter Kenngröße *f*; Parameter *m*
parcel Päckchen *n*
parent material Grundwerkstoff *m*
parent metal Grundmetall *n*
parent population Grundgesamtheit *f*
parent solution Stammlösung *f*
parity check Gleichheitsprüfung *f*
Parkerising Parkerverfahren *n*
Parry type cup and cone arrangement Parry-Kegel *m*; Parry-Verschluß *m*
partial decarbonizing Abkohlung *f* (Kokerei)
partial decarburization Abkohlung *f* (Stahl)
partial derivative Teilabgeleitete *f*; partielle Ableitung *f*
partially alloyed powder teillegiertes Pulver *n*
partial parting by chiseling Einschroten *n*
partial pressure Partialdruck *m*; Teildruck *m*
partial radiation pyrometer Teilstrahlungspyrometer *n*
partial regression line Ausgleichsgerade *f* (durch Korrelationsrechnung)
partial spreading Einspritzen *n*
particle Korn *n*; Teilchen *n*
particle shape Kornform *f*; Teilchenform *f*
particle size Korngröße *f*; Teilchengröße *f*
particle size determination Teilchengrößenbestimmung *f*
particle size distribution Korngrößenverteilung *f*
particle size fraction Korngrößenklasse *f*

particle-size network Körnungsnetz n
particle size range Korngrößenbereich m
particle sizing Kornklassierung f
particle true density Kompaktdichte f; Reindichte f
parting Trennen n
parting layer Sperrschicht f (Schmieren)
parting line Teilfuge f; Teillinie f; Trennungslinie f
parting-off tool Abstechstahl m
parting shears Teilschere f
partition wall Scheidewand f
pass Einstich m; Kaliber n; Schweißlage f; Schweißschicht f; Stich m; Zug m
passage Durchfluß m; Gang m (des Hochofens)
passage of current Stromdurchgang m
pass design Kaliberbauart f; Kalibrieren n
passenger lift Personenaufzug m
passing Glätten n
passivation Passivierung f
passive layer Passivschicht f
passivity Passivität f
pass-line Bandlaufebene f angestrebte
pass line Walzlinie f (Bandwalzen); Walzmitte f
pass over mill Übergabewalzwerk n; Überhebewalzwerk n
pass sequence Stichfolge f; Stichtabelle f
password protection Passwortsicherung f
paste carburising Pastenaufkohlen n
paste process Pastenverfahren n
pasty teigig
patch Flickmasse f (für Ofenherde); flicken
patent patentieren
patentable novelty patentschutzfähige Neuheit f
patent agent Patentanwalt m
patent application Patentanmeldung f

patent applied for Patent n angemeldet
patented steel wire patentierter Stahldraht m
patentee Patentinhaber m
patent flattening Glätten n
patent office Patentamt n
patent specification Patentbeschreibung f
patent (wire) patentieren
path Kurve f; Weg m
path length Kurvenlänge f; Laufweg m
path running Gang m (des Hochofens)
patinable steel wetterfester Stahl m
pattern Form f (der Modellabdruck); Modell n
pattern rolled steel Stahl mit eingewalztem Muster m
pattern sheet gemustertes Blech n
pattern shop Modellschreinerei f
pawl-type bed Klinkenbett n
pawl type skid Klinkenschlepper m
pay-off reel Abhaspelvorrichtung f; Ablaufhaspel f; Abspulgerät n
payroll Lohnliste f; Personalkosten pl
pea coke Perlkoks m
peak power Eckleistung f
peak to mean line height Glättungstiefe f
peak value Spitzenwert m
pearlite Perlit m
pearlite cast iron Perlitguß m
pearlite grain Perlitkorn n
pearlitic perlitisch
pearlitic steel perlitischer Stahl m
peas Kohlengrus m
peat coke Torfkoks m
pedestal bearing Stehlager n
peel Schwengel m (Chargiermaschine); abplatzen
peeling Abblättern n
peeling shafts Wellenschälen n
peeling tool Schälmesser n
peel off abschälen
peen hämmern; kalthämmern
peg Dübel m; Keil m
pellet Pellet n
pelletise pelletieren

pelletising Pelletierung *f*
pelletising disc Pelletierteller *m*
pelletising drum Pelletiertrommel *f*
pellet slide bar Gleitschiene *f*
pencil of rays Strahlenbüschel *n*
pendulum impact test machine Pendelhammerschlagwerk *n*
pendulum shears Schwingschere *f*
penetrating body Eindringkörper *m* (bei der Härteprüfung)
penetration Durchdringung *f*; Eindringen *n*
penetration zone Einbrandzone *f*
pen stock Düsenstock *m*; Kniestück *n*
pentlandite Eisennickelkies *m*
pepperbox Oberflächenporen *fpl*
percolate filtrieren
percussion drill Schlagbohrer *m*
perfectly plastic ideal plastisch
perforated brick Lochstein *m*
perforated card Lochkarte *f*
perforated plate Lochblech *n*; gelochtes Blech *n*
perforated tape Lochband *n*; Lochstreifen *m*
perforating machine Perforiermaschine *f*
perforation Lochung *f*
performance Leistung *f*
performance index Leistungsgrad *m*
perimeter Umkreis *m*
periodic system Periodensystem *n* der chemischen Elemente
periodic systematic sampling periodische systematische Probenahme *f*
periodogram Wellenschaubild *n*
periodogram analysis Wellenzerlegung *f*
peripheral recession Nacheilung *f* (Walzen)
peritectic Peritektikum *n*
peritectic transformation peritektische Umwandlung *f*
perlitic structure perlitische Struktur *f*
permanent limit of elongation Dehngrenze *f*
permanent magnet Dauermagnet *m*

permanent magnet material Dauermagnetwerkstoff *m*
permanent mould casting Dauerform-Gußstück *n*; Dauerformguß *m*
permanent set bleibende Durchbiegung *f*; bleibende Verformung *f*
permanent way material Oberbaumaterial *n*
permeability Permeabilität *f*
permeability to gas Gasdurchlässigkeit *f*
permeable formation durchlässige Schicht *f*
permissible variation Abmaß *n*; Toleranz *f*
permitted dimensional tolerance Maßabweichung *f*
permittivity Dielektrizitätskonstante *f*
perpendicular depth Seigerteufe *f*
persistent anhaltend
personnel management Menschenführung *f*
petrochemistry Petrochemie *f*
petrographic thin section petrographischer Dünnschliff *m*
petroleum Erdöl *n*; Petroleum *n*; Rohöl *n*
petroleum coke Petrolkoks *m*
pewter Hartzinn *n*; Lötmetall *n*
phase Phase *f*
phase advancer Phasenschieber *m*
phase angle Phasenwinkel *m*
phase boundary Phasengrenze *f*
phase boundary reaction Phasengrenzreaktion *f*
phase contrast microscopy Phasenkontrastmikroskopie *f*
phase diagram Zustandsschaubild *n*
phase disintegration Phasenzertrümmerung *f*
phase displacement Phasenverschiebung *f* (elektr.)
phase field Zustandsfeld *n*
phase separation Entmischung *f*; Phasenentmischung *f*
phase shifter Phasenschieber *m*
phase transformation Phasenumwandlung *f*
phase voltage Phasenspannung *f*

phenol extraction from the gas water
Entphenolung f des Gaswassers
phenol water disposal Phenolwasserverwertung f
phenol water removal Phenolwasserbeseitigung f
phenomenon Erscheinung f; Phänomen m
phosphate coat phosphatieren
phosphate coating Phosphatieren n
phosphate treated phosphatiert
phosphating Phosphatierung f
phosphide streak Phosphidseigerungsstreifen m
phosphoric pig iron phosphorhaltiges Roheisen f
phosphorus Phosphor m
phosporic acid Phosphorsäure f
photoelastic investigation spannungsoptische Untersuchung f
photoelectric amplifier lichtelektrischer Verstärker m
photoelectric cell Photozelle f
pH-value Säurewert m
pH-value regulating instrument pH-Wert-Regler m
physical chemistry physikalische Chemie f
physical metallurgy Metallkunde f
physics Physik f
piano wire Klavier[saiten]draht m
pick [axe] Picke f
picking plant Klaubanlage f
pickle Beize f; abbeizen; beizen; dekapieren
pickle brittleness Beizsprödigkeit f
pickle sticker Zundereinsprenkelung f (durch unvollständiges Beizen)
pickle test Beizprobe f
pickling acid regeneration Rückgewinnung f von Beizsäure
pickling acid waste Beizablauge f
pickling agent Beizmittel n
pickling agents Beizbedarf m
pickling basket Beizkorb m
pickling bath Beizbad n; Beize f
pickling blistering Beizblasen fpl
pickling blow holes Beizblasen fpl

pickling compound Beizzusatz m
pickling crade Beizkorb m
pickling department Beizerei f
pickling deposit Beizbast m
pickling equipment Beizausrüstung f
pickling fluid Beizflüssigkeit f
pickling inhibitor Beizinhibitor m
pickling line Beizstrecke f
pickling machine Beizmaschine f
pickling plant Beizanlage f
pickling residue Beizrückstand m
pickling section Beizstrecke f
pickling solution Beizlösung f
pickling tank Beizbottich m
pickling vat Beizbehälter m; Beizbottich m; Beizkasten f
pickup Abgriff m (EDV); Zubrand m
pick-up Meßwertgeber m; Pickelbildung f
pick up mitnehmen
piece Walzgut n
piece rate Stückzeit f
piece rate setting Stückzeitermittlung f
piece rate wages Akkordlohn m
pieces in handy sizes chargierfähige Stücke npl
piece work Akkordarbeit f; Gedingearbeit f
piece worker Akkordarbeiter m
pierce durchbrechen; lochen
piercer Dorn m; Lochdorn m; Lochwalzwerk n; Pilgerdorn m
piercing Lochen n
piercing die Kaltschlagmatrize f; Lochstempel m
piercing holes Lochen n
piercing mandrel Lochdorn m; Lochstempel m
piercing mill Lochwalzwerk n
pig Massel f
pig and ore process Roheisen-Erz-Verfahren n
pig and scrap process Schrott-Roheisen-Verfahren n
pig bed Masselbett n
pig breaker Masselbrecher m; Masselschläger m

pig-breaking travelling crane Massel-Schlagwerkskran *m*
pig casting machine Masselgießmaschine *f*; Roheisengießmaschine *f*
piggyback motors Huckepackmotoren *mpl*
pig iron festes Roheisen *n*
pig iron grade Roheisensorte *f*
pig iron ladle Roheisenpfanne *f*
pig iron ladle car Roheisentransportwagen *m*
pig iron mixer Roheisenmischer *m*
pig iron ore process Roheisen-Erz-Verfahren *n*
pig iron runout Roheisenabstich *m* (Roheisenabfluß)
pig iron scrap process Roheisen-Schrott-Verfahren *n*
pigmentation Pigmentierung *f*
pig mould Masselform *f*
pig moulding machine Masselformmaschine *f*
pile Reaktor *m*; Stapel *m*; häufen; stapeln
pile driver Pfahlramme *f*
pilger mill of the Mannesmann type Pilgerschritt-Rohrwalzwerk *n*
pilger mill rolling Pilgerschrittwalzen *n*
pilger roll Pilgerwalze *f*
pilger step-by-step-type seamless tube rolling mill Pilgerschritt-Rohrwalzwerk *n*
piling section Spundprofil *n*
pillow block (am.) Stehlager *n*
pilot halbtechnisch
pilot control Vorsteuerung *f*
pilot fire Lockfeuer *n*
pilot flame Zündflamme *f*
pilot plant Versuchsanlage *f*; Versuchsbetrieb *m*
pilot relay Kraftschalter *m*
pilot test Vorprobe *f*
pin Drahtstift *m*; Nadel *f*; Zapfen *m* (Welle)
pincers Zange *f*
pinch Längsüberwalzungsfehler *m*
pincher Falte *f*; Überwalzungsfehler *m*

pinch pass rolling mill Kaltnachwalzwerk *n*
pinch roll Abziehrolle *f*; Klemmrolle *f*; Transportrolle *f* (Stranggießen)
pinch roll crack Quetschriß *m* (Strangguß)
pinch rolling oberflächliches Walzen *n* mit geringem Druck
pin hole Gasblase *f*; Loch *n*
pinhole Nadelstichpore *f*
pinhole detector Lochsuchgerät *n*
pinhole plug Nadelboden *m*
pinholes Oberflächenporen *fpl*
pinion Kammwalze *f*; Ritzel *n*
pink noise rosa Rauschen *n*
pinning (of dislocations) Verankerung *f* (von Versetzungen)
pipe Lunker *m*; Rohr *n*
pipe bend Rohrkrümmer *m*
pipe branch Rohrabzweigstück *n*
pipe coil Rohrschlange *f*
pipe connection Rohrverbinder *m*
pipe elbow Rohrkrümmer *m*
pipe eliminator Lunkerabdeckmasse *f*
pipe eradicator Lunkerabdeckmasse *f*
pipeline construction Rohrleitungsbau *m*
pipeline fitting Rohrleitungsarmatur *f*
pipe-line pressure Leitungsdruck *m*
pipe reducing [rolling] mill Rohrreduzierwalzwerk *n*
pipe [rolling] mill Rohrwalzwerk *n*
pipe socket Rohrflansch *m*; Rohrmuffe *f*
pipe spinning machine Schleudergießmaschine *f* (für Rohre)
pipette pipettieren
pipe wrapping compound Rohrwickelmasse *f*
piping Lunkerbildung *f*
piping and piling Schlot- und Pfeilerbildung *f* (Aufbereitung)
piston Kolben *m*
piston pump Kolbenpumpe *f*
piston ring Kolbenring *m*
piston stroke Kolbenhub *m*
pit Grübchen *n*; Löcher *npl* bilden; Narbe *f*; Tiefofen *m*; Zeche *f*; anfressen; fressen

pit annealing Grubenglühen n
pit arch steel Kappenstahl m
pitch Pech n; Pfeilhöhe f; Teilung f (Zahnrad)
pitch circle Elektrodenteilkreis m
pitch circle diameter Teilkreisdurchmesser m (Lichtbogenofen)
pitch coal Pechkohle f
pitch line Teilkreislinie f; neutrale Linie f (eines Walzkalibers)
pit coal Steinkohle f
pit (cold rolling) scharfkantige Vertiefung f (Kaltwalzen)
pit furnace cover Tiefofendeckel m
pit furnace crane Tiefofenkran m
pithead frame Förderturm m
pithead gear Fördergerüst n
pit hoist Förderturm m
pit hole Blasenloch n
pit railway Grubenbahn f
pitted surface Oberflächenporen fpl
pitticite Eisenpecherz n
pitting Grübchenbildung f; Lochfraß m; Lochkorrosion f; Poren fpl (Bandfehler)
pitting corrosion potential Lochfraßpotential n
pit trench Grube f
pit [type] furnace Tiefofen m
pivot Drehpunkt m; Drehzapfen m; Zapfen m (Strangguß)
place on edge hochkant stellen
plain axle bearing Gleitachslager n
plain bearing Gleitlager n; offenes Gleitlager n
plain bulb Wulstflachstahl m mit doppelseitigem Wulst
plain carbon steel Kohlenstoffstahl m (unlegierter Stahl); unlegierter kohlenstoffreicher Stahl m
plain die offenes Gesenk n
plain end tube Glattendrohr n
plain milling cutter Walzenfräser m
plain roll Glattwalze f; glatte Walze f
plain roof glattes Gewölbe n
plain sheet Flachblech n
plain strain Flachverformung f
plain suface roll (am.) Flachbahnwalze f

plan Entwurf m; Zeichnung f
Planck constant Planck-Konstante f
plane Ebene f; Fläche f; hobeln
plane angle Winkel m; ebener Winkel m
plane roof rippenloses Gewölbe n
plane sided flachwandig (Kokillen)
planetary mill Planetenwalzwerk n
planetary rolling Planetenwalzen n
planet wheel Planetenrad n
planing machine Hobelmaschine f
planing tool Hobelmesser n
planish glätten
planishing Glattdrücken n
planishing stand Poliergerüst n
planned economy Planwirtschaft f
plano-milling Langtiastfräsen n
plant Anlage f; Betrieb m; Hütte f; Werk n; technische Anlage f
plant economics Betriebswirtschaft f
plant engineering Anlagentechnik f
plant management Betriebsführung f
plant scrap Eigenschrott m
plant superintendent Betriebsleiter m
plant techniques Anlagentechnik f
plan view Grundriß m
plasma arc welding Plasmalichtbogenschweißen n
plasma cutting torch Plasmaschneidbrenner m
plasma jet welding Plasmastrahlschweißen n
plasma nitriding Plasmanitrieren n
plasma spraying Plasmaspritzen n
plaster Gips m
plaster casting method Gipsabgußverfahren n
plastic Kunststoff m; bildsam; formbar; teigig
plastic articulation plastisches Gelenk n
plastic coated sheet and strip kunststoffbeschichtetes Stahlblech und -band n
plastic coating Kunstharzüberzug m
plastic deformation bildsame Formgebung f; plastische Formänderung f

plasticiser Plastifizierungsmittel *n*
plasticity Bildsamkeit *f*; Plastizität *f*; Umformbarkeit *f*; Umformvermögen *n*
plastic metal working Umformtechnik *f*
plastic shaping bildsame Formgebung *f*
plastisol Plastisol *n*
plate Blech *n*; Grobblech *n*; Ziehdüse *f*; Zieheisen *n*
plate bending machine Blechbiegemaschine *f*
plate brushing machine Blechbürstmaschine *f*
plate clippings Blechabfälle *mpl*
plate doubler Blechdoppler *m*
plate drying table Blechtrockentisch *m*
plate-edge bending press Blechkantenanbiegepresse *f*
plate ga[u]ge Blechlehre *f*
plate girder Blechträger *m*; Vollwandträger *m*
plate gripping tongs Blechzange *f*
plate-laying Gleisbau *m*
plate-like powder tellerartiges Pulver *n*
plate link chain Gallkette *f*
plate mould Plattenkokille *f*
plate roll Blechwalze *f*
plate [rolling] mill Blechwalzwerk *n* (grob); Grobblech-Walzwerk *n*
plate scrap Blechschrott *m*
plate shears Blechschere *f*; Tafelschere *f*
plate structures Blecharbeiten *fpl*
plate testing machine Blechprüfmaschine *f*
plate working machine Blechbearbeitungsmaschine *f*
pliable biegsam
pliers Drahtzange *f*
pliers tongs Zange *f*
plot graphische Darstellung *f*
plough for removing cooled sinter Räumerarm *m* (Sinterkühler)
plucking fressender Verschleiß *m*

plug Konverterboden *m*; Lochdorn *m*; Stecker *m*; Stopfen; verstopfen
plug bottom Düsenboden *m*
plug drawing Dornziehen *n*
plug lines Ziehriefen *fpl* (im Innern eines über den Stopfen gezogenen Rohrs)
plug ramming machine Bodenstampfmaschine *f*
plug weld Lochschweiße *f*; Nietschweiße *f*
plumbago Graphit *m*
plumbago [refractory] feuerfestes Graphit-Ton-Erzeugnis *n*
plummer block Stehlager *n*
plunge cut grinding Einstechschleifen *n*
plunger Plunger[kolben] *m*; Tauchkolben *m*
ply-metal Verbundmetall *n*
pneumatic chisel Preßluftmeißel *m*
pneumatic grinder Preßluftschleifmaschine *f*
pneumatic rammer Preßluftstampfer *m*
pneumatic refining Blasfrischen *n*
pneumatic tool Druckluftwerkzeug *n*
pocket Tasche *f*
point stellen; zuspitzen
pointed cobblestoning Drachenzähne *mpl* (im Konus einer Torpedopfanne)
pointer Zeiger *m*
point of [application of] load Lastangriffspunkt *m*
point of common coupling (pcc) Punkt *m* gemeinsamer Kupplung (Lichtbogenofen)
point of contact Griffstelle *f*
poison Gift *n*
poisonous giftig
Poisson's ratio Kontraktionszahl *f*; Poissonsche Zahl *f*
poker Schüreisen *n*; Stocheisen *n*
polar bond Polarbindung *f*
polar chain Polarkette *f*
polar compound Polarverbindung *f*
polar head Polarkopf *m*

polar molecule polares Molekül n
polarography Polarographie f
pole Mast m; Pol m
pole figure Polfigur f
polish glätten; polieren
polished and etched micro section poliert und geätzter Schliff m
polishing frame Polierbock m
pollutant Fremdstoff m (Luftverunreinigung); Schmutzstoff m
pollution Verschmutzung f; Verunreinigung f
pollution abatement Reinhaltung f (Luft)
pollution of in-house atmosphere Immission f
polyphase alloy mehrphasige Legierung f
Polytechnic Institute Technische Hochschule f
ponderable wägbar
pony ladle Zwischengefäß n (Stranggießen)
pony rougher Vorstreckgerüst n
poor quality schlechte Qualität f
pop marks Körnereinschläge mpl
poppet valve Tellerventil n
population Grundgesamtheit f
pore Pore f
pore forming material Porenbildner m
pork pie furnace Maerz-Boelens-Ofen m
porosity Gasdurchlässigkeit f; Porosität f
porous porig; porös
porous structure lockeres Gefüge n
portable tragbar; versetzbar
portable cover furnace Haubenofen m
portal crane Portalkran m
port block Ofenkopf m
port[end] Kopf m
port end Ofenkopf m
porter bar Lagerbock m
portion of the roof Gewölbeteil n
position Lage f
position of sample Probenlage f
position regulator Stellungsregler m
positive movement Zwanglauf m

possessed of inertia träge
possibility Möglichkeit f
postponed output retardierter Ausgang m
post sintering operations Nachbearbeitung f nach dem Sintern n
pot annealing furnace Topfglühofen m
potassium Kalium n
potassium soap Kaliseife f
potential Potential n
potential hardness increase Einhärtbarkeit f
potentiometer Potentiometer n
pour abgießen; abkippen; eingießen (füllen); vergießen
pouring Abguß m; Guß m; Vergießen n
pouring bay Gießhalle f
pouring car Gießwagen m
pouring crane Gießkran m
pouring end Eingießende n
pouring gate Gießtrichter m
pouring ladle Gießpfanne f
pouring ladle lip Gießpfannenschnabel m
pouring lip Gießschnauze f
pouring platform Gießbühne f
pouring reel Ablaufhaspel f; Wickelmaschine f
pouring spout Gießrinne f
pouring stream treatment Gießstrahlbehandlung f
powder carburising Pulveraufkohlen n
powder cutting Pulverbrennschneiden n
powdered blast-furnace slag Hüttenkalk m
powder metallurgy Pulvermetallurgie f
powder nitriding Pulvernitrieren n
powder particle Pulverteilchen n
powder spraying Pulverspritzen n
power Kraft f; Leistung f; Leistungsfähigkeit f
power and material Energie- und Stoffwirtschaft f
power cable Leistungskabel n
power consumption Energieverbrauch m

power conversion Energieumwandlung *f*
power drive Kraftantrieb *m*
power drive transmission Verteilergetriebe *n*
power factor Leistungsfaktor *m*
power failure Stromausfall *m*
power fuel Treibstoff *m*
power generation Stromerzeugung *f*
power house Kraftwerk *n*
powerless stromlos
power-on period Einschaltdauer *f*
power plant Krafterzeugungsanlage *f*
power required Energiebedarf *m*
power station Kraftwerk *n*; Maschinenhaus *n*; elektrische Zentrale *f*
power supply Energieversorgung *f*
power supply interlinked system energiewirtschaftliches Verbundsystem *n*
power supply line with change-over switching umschaltbare Stromzuleitung *f*
power supply network system Stromversorgungsnetz *n*
power-to-weight ratio Leistungsgewicht *n*
power transmission Kraftübertragung *f*
practical result Betriebsergebnis *n*
practice Betrieb *m*; Einarbeitung *f*; Führung *f*
prealloyed powder Vorlegierungspulver *n*
preblow vorblasen
preceding pass Vorkaliber *n*
precipitate Niederschlag *m*; ausscheiden; fällen; niederschlagen
precipitated powder Fällungspulver *n*; gefälltes Pulver *n*
precipitation Fällung *f*
precipitation deoxidation Fällungsdesoxidation *f*
precise genau
precision Genauigkeit *f*
precision casting Feinguß *m*
precision forging Genauschmieden *n*
precision ground feingeschliffen

precision investment casting Präzisionsguß *m*; Wachsausschmelzguß *m*
precision machine element Präzisionsmaschinenteil *n*
precision measurement Feinmessung *f*
precision of measurement Meßgenauigkeit *f*
precision steel tube Präzisionsstahlrohr *n*
precompressed mild steel vorgestauchter weicher Stahl *m*
predetermined standard rates Plankosten *pl*; Richtkosten *pl*
preeutectic voreutektisch
preeutectoid ferrite voreutektoidischer Ferrit *m*
prefabricated vorgefertigt
prefabricated member Fertigbauteil *n*
prefabrication Vorfertigung *f*
prefered direction of magnetisation magnetische Vorzugsrichtung *f*
preheat vorwärmen
preheat bore Heizdüse *f* (Gasschweißen)
preheater for air Vorwärmer *m* für Luft
preheater for gas Vorwärmer *m* für Gas
preheater for water Vorwärmer *m* für Wasser
preheat gas way Heizdüse *f* (Gasschweißen)
preheat orifice Heizdüse *f* (Gasschweißen)
preliminary annealing Vorglühen *n*
preliminary calculation Vorkalkulation *f*
preliminary dust extraction Grobentstaubung *f*
preliminary oxidation Vorfrischen *n*
preliminary purification Vorreinigung *f*
preliminary refining mixer Vorfrischmischer *m*
preliminary section Vorprofil *n*
preliminary separator Vorabscheider *m*

preliminary stress Vorspannung f
preliminary test Vorprobe f
preliminary transformation Vorumwandlung f
premelted iron Vorschmelzeisen n
premium bonus system Prämienlohnsystem f
premix vormischen
prepare vorbereiten; zubereiten
prepared ore burden vorbereiteter Möller m
prepressing Vorpressen n
prereduction Vorreduktion f
pre-screening Vorabsiebung f (Erz)
preselector Vorwählschalter m
pre-settling basin Vorabscheidungsbecken n
presettling tank Vorlaufbehälter m (Gasreinigung)
preshaped (blocked) workpiece freiformgeschmiedetes (vorgeschmiedetes) Werkstück n
presintering Vorsinterung f
presparking time Vorfunkzeit f (Spektralanalyse)
press Presse f
press die forming Formstanzen n
press fit Preßspannung f
press for corrugated sheets Wellblechpresse f
press forging in geschlossenem Gesenk in der Presse hergestellt
press quenching Preßhärten n
press rating Nennkraft f einer Presse
press stroke Pressenhub m; Preßweg m
pressure Druck m
pressure cell Druckmeßdose f
pressure die casting Druckguß m; Druckgußstück n; Spritzguß m
pressure drop Druckabfall m
pressure forming Druckumformen n
pressure ga[u]ge Druckluftmeßgerät n; Druckmesser m
pressure governor Druckregler m
pressureless sintering Sintern von losem Pulver n
pressure line Stützlinie f (SM-Ofen)

pressure lubrication Preßdruckschmierung f
pressure marking Druckmarkierung f
pressure of rolling Walzdruck m
pressure pad Drucktopf m (Walzen)
pressure per unit of area Flächendruck m
pressure per unit of surface Flächendruck m
pressure piece Drucktopf m (Walzen)
pressure pouring Druckguß m
pressure reducing valve Druckminderventil n
pressure shell Druckmantel m
pressure spray process Druckspritzverfahren n
pressure spring Druckfeder f
pressure thermit welding Gießpreßschweißen n
pressure vessel Druckbehälter m
pressure vessel test Druckgefäßversuch m
pressure water Druckwasser n
pressure weldable preßschweißbar
pressure welding Druckschweißung f; Preßschweißen n
pretraining Vorspannung f
prestress vorspannen
prestressed vorbelastet
prestressed concrete Spannbeton m
prestressed concrete steel Spannbetonstahl m
prestressed rolling stand vorgespanntes Walzgerüst n
pretest Vorversuch m
pretreatment Vorbehandlung f
prevention of accidents Unfallverhütung f
price Preis m
price allowance Preisnachlaß m
price cut Preisherabsetzung f
price maintenance Preisbindung f
price reduction Preisherabsetzung f
price rise Preissteigerung f
pricker Nadel f
primary air Frischluft f
primary arm Hauptast m (Dendriten)
primary carbide Primärcarbid m

primary cleaning Grobreinigung f; Vorreinigung f
primary element Meßwertgeber m
primary element (am.) Meßfühler m
primary industry Grundstoffindustrie f
primary mill Walzstraße f erster Hitze; Walzwerk n erster Hitze
primary point Primärfleck m (Röntgen)
primary product Roherzeugnis n
primary structure Primärgefüge n
primary voltage Oberspannung f
prime cost Gestehungskosten pl
primer Grundierung f
prime sheet Blech n erster Wahl
priming coat Grundanstrich m; Grundbeschichtung f
principal stress Hauptspannung f
printing machine Druckereimaschine f
printing office Druckerei f
print-out Druckerausgabe f (EDV)
printout Niederschrift f (EDV)
prior plastic deformation Vorformgebung f
prior use Patentvorbenutzung f
prismatic spectrum Prismenspektrum n
probability Wahrscheinlichkeit f
probability density Wahrscheinlichkeitsdichte f
probability paper Wahrscheinlichkeitspapier n
probability ratio test Wahrscheinlichkeitsverhältnisprobe f
probe Fühler m; fühlen
procedure Verfahren n
process Verlauf m; Vorgang m; verarbeiten
process annealed wire zwischengeglühter Draht m
process annealing Zwischenglühen n
process card Materialbegleitkarte f
process control Prozeßlenkung f; Prozeßsteuerung f; Verfahrenssteuerung f; rechnergestützte Prozeßleitung f

process data Prozeßdaten npl
processed wire vorgezogener Draht m
process identification Prozeßidentifikation f
processing Verarbeitung f
processing defect Verarbeitungsfehler m
processing line Betriebseinrichtung f
processing module Verarbeitungsmodul n
processing of semi finished product Halbzeugzurichtung f
processing uncoiler Zunderbrech- und Abrollvorrichtung f (für Blechbunde)
processing unit Zunderbrech- und Abrollvorrichtung f (für Blechbunde)
processing water Industriewasser n
process metallurgy Metallurgie f
process monitoring rechnergestützte Prozeß- und Anlagenüberwachung f
process of buckling Knickvorgang m
process of deformation Formänderungsverlauf m
processor Zunderbrech- und Abrollvorrichtung f (für Blechbunde); Zunderbrecher m; Zunderbrechgerüst n
process scrap Umlaufschrott m
process technology Verfahrenstechnik f
process visualisation Verfahrensdatenanzeige f
produce entwickeln (Rauch); erzeugen (Dampf); herstellen
producer Erzeuger m; Generator m (Gas)
producer coal Generatorkohle f
producer gas Generatorgas n
production Erzeugung f; Fertigung f; Herstellung f; Leistung f; Produktion f
production and evaluation review technique Netzplantechnik f
production cast Betriebsschmelze f

production control Fertigungssteuerung *f*; Produktionssteuerung *f*; rechnergestützte Betriebsleitung *f*
production data Erzeugungsangaben *fpl*
production data aquisition rechnergestützte Betriebsdatenerfassung *f*
production facility Produktionsmittel *n*
production figures Produktionszahlen *fpl*
production flow Fertigungsablauf *m*
production heat Betriebsschmelze *f*
production process Herstellungsverfahren *n*
production rate Erzeugungsleistung *f*
production report Produktionsbericht *m*
production start Produktionsbeginn *m*
production time Fertigungszeit *f*
production trial Betriebsversuch *m*
productivity Produktivität *f*
profile Gestalt *f*, Profil *n*
profile grinding Formschleifen *n*
profit Ertrag *m*; Gewinn *m*
profit and loss accounts Gewinn- und Verlustkonten *npl*
profit sharing Gewinnbeteiligung *f*
program programmieren
program card Programmkarte *f*
program control Folgeregelung *f*; Programmregelung *f*
programmed control Zeitplanregelung *f*
program memory Programmspeicher *m*
program storage Programmspeicher *m*
progressive ageing gestuftes Warmauslagern *n*
progressive flanging fortschreitendes Bördeln *n*
progressive hardening Vorschubhärten *n*
progress of refining Frischverlauf *m*
projection Vorsprung *m*
projection sphere Lagekugel *f* (Röntgen)
promote fördern

prop abstützen
properly proportioned for stress and strain festigkeitsgerecht
property Eigenschaft *f*
proportional action controller P-Regeleinrichtung *f*
proportional plus rate [derivative] action controller PD-Regler *m*
proportional plus reset action controller PI-Regler *m*
proportioning mixer Mischbrenner *m*
proposal Vorschlag *m*
protected crystal geschützter Schwinger *m* (Ultraschallprüfung)
protecting goggles Schutzbrille *f*
protection against corrosion Korrosionsschutz *m*
protection against heat Wärmeschutz *m*
protection against noise Lärmschutz *m*
protection of the environment Umweltschutz *m*
protective circuit Schutzschaltung *f*
protective clothing Schutzkleidung *f*
protective coating Schutzanstrich *m*; Schutzüberzug *m*
protective film Schutzfilm *m*
protective finish Schutzanstrich *m*
protective helmet Schutzhelm *m*
protective layer Deckschicht *f*; Schutzschicht *f*
protective paint Schutzanstrich *m*
protest Einspruch *m*
protractor Winkelmesser *m*
pseudocarburising Blindaufkohlen *n*
pseudonitriding Blindnitrieren *n*
psilomelane Hartmanganerz *n*
puddle pig Puddelroheisen *n*
puddle process Puddelverfahren *n*
puff out treiben
pull Wärmeriß *m*; Zug *m*; klaffender Querriß *m*; ziehen
pull crack Haarriß *m*
pulley Riemenscheibe *f*
pulley block Flaschenzug *m*
pulley drive Scheibenantrieb *m*
pulling-in dog Einziehzange *f*

pulling [pinch] roll Treibrolle f
pulling test Zugversuch m
pull over überheben
pull over mill Überhebewalzwerk n
pull slag abziehen
pulp Trübe f
pulsatance Kreisfrequenz f
pulsating bending fatigue limit Biegedauerfestigkeit f im Schwellbereich m
pulsating fatigue strength under bending stresses Biegeschwellfestigkeit f
pulsating load schwellende Belastung f; stoßweise Belastung f
pulsating stress Schwellbeanspruchung f
pulse echo technique Impuls-Echo-Verfahren n
pulse envelope Impulsform f (Ultraschall)
pulse frequency Pulsfrequenz f
pulse generator Impulsgeber m
pulse shaper Impulsformer m
puls frequency Pulsfrequenz f
pulverise pulverisieren; pulvern; zerkleinern; zerreiben; zerstäuben
pulverised coal Kohlenstaub m
pulverised coal/gas combined burner Kohlenstaubgasbrenner m
pulverised coal firing plant Kohlenstaub-Feuerungsanlage f
pulverising Zerkleinerung f
pulverize mahlen
pumice slag Hüttenbims m
pumice slag brick Hüttenschwemmstein m
pump house attendant Pumpenhauswärter m
pumping house Pumpenhaus n
pump switch Pumpenschalter m
punch Locher m; Lochstempel m; lochen
punch[ed] card Lochkarte f
punched-card control Lochkartensteuerung f
punched card reader and punch Lochkartenleser und -stanzer m

punched hole gestanztes Loch n
punched tape Lochband n; Lochstreifen m
punching and drawing press Loch- und Ziehpresse f
punching press Lochstanze f
punching sheet Stanzblech n
punching test Lochprobe f; Lochversuch m
punching tool Lochwerkzeug n
punch marking Körnen n
punch steel Döpperstahl m
purchasing department Einkauf m; Einkaufsabteilung f
pure substance reiner Stoff m
pure tone Einzelton m
purify feinen; reinigen; waschen (Gas)
purifying Windfrischen n
push drücken
push bench Stoßbank f
push-bench Warmziehbank f (für Hohlkörper)
push bench bloom Stoßbankluppe f
pusher Abschiebevorrichtung f; Drücker m; Einstoßvorrichtung f
pusher ram Koksausdrückmaschine f
pusher type billet heating furnace Knüppelstoßofen m
pusher type furnace Durchstoßofen m; Tunnelofen m
pushing device Abschiebevorrichtung f; Einstoßvorrichtung f
pushing through durchdrücken
push pickler Schubbeize f
push pull Gegentakt m
push-pull forming Zug-Druck-Umformen n
put into operation in Betrieb m setzen
put out ausbringen
put through a pilger mill pilgern
putting in blast again Wiederanblasen n
putty Kitt m
pyramid hardness number Vickershärte f
pyrites Kies m
pyrites cinders Pyritabbrand m
pyroforic blast-furnace flue dust pyrophorer Gichtstaub m

pyrometer Pyrometer *n*
pyrometric cone equivalent Kegelfallpunkt *m*
pyrometric efficiency pyrometrischer Wirkungsgrad *m*
pyrometric rod Temperaturfühler *m* mit Schutzrohr

Q

Q-BOP process OBM-Verfahren *n*
quadrant nozzle Viertelkreisdüse *f*
quadratic mean quadratisches Mittel *n*
qualification test Eignungsprüfung *f*
quality Güte *f*; Gütestufe *f*
quality characteristic Qualitätsmerkmal *n*
quality control Güteüberwachung *f*; Qualitätskontrolle *f*; Qualitätsüberwachung *f*
quality control point Qualitätsstelle *f*
quality group Gütegruppe *f* (von Stählen)
quality index Gütezahl *f*
quality of fit Güte *f* der Anpassung
quality sheet metal Qualitätsblech *n*
quality specification Gütevorschrift *f*
quality steel Qualitätsstahl *m*
quanta Quanten *npl*
quantile Mengenwert *m*
quantitative quantitativ
quantitative television microscope Fernsehmikroskop *n*
quantity Größe *f*; Menge *f*
quantity of heat Wärme *f*; Wärmemenge *f*
quantity production Massenherstellung *f*
quantize quantisieren
quantum Quant *n*
quarter hard viertelhart
quartile Quartil *n*; Wert *m*
quartz Quarz *m*
quartz grog brick Quarz-Schamotte Stein *m*

quartzite Quarzit *m*
quasi-binary section quasi-binärer Schnitt *m*
quaternary system Vierstoffsystem *n*
quench abschrecken; löschen (Koks)
quench ag[e]ing Abschreckalterung *f*
quench bending test [specimen] Abschreckbiegeprobe *f*
quenched and tempered vergütet
quenched and tempered steel (QT steel) vergüteter Stahl *m*
quench hardening Abschreckhärten *n*
quenching Abschrecken *n*; Löschen *n*
quenching car Löschwagen *m*
quenching medium Abschreckmittel *n*
quenching temperature Abschrecktemperatur *f*
quenching time Abschreckdauer *f*
quenching tower Löschturm *m*
quenching wharf Löschrampe *f*
questionnaire Fragebogen *m*
queue Warteschlange *f*
quick heating Schnellbeheizung *f*
quick immersion thermocouple Schnelltauchthermoelement *n*
quicklime Kalk *m* ungelöschter; gebrannter Kalk *m*
quick-start ejector Vorevakuator *m*
quota Kontingent *n*; Quote *f*; Teilmenge *f*
quota sampling Quotenauswahl *f*; Quotenstichprobe *f*

R

rabble Krätzer *m*
race Laufring *m*
raceway Laufbahn *f*
rack Gestell *n*; Zahnstange *f*
rack oil Erdnaphtha *f*
rack wheel Schaltrad *n*; Sperrad *n*
radial die forming Gesenkrunden *n*
radial drilling machine Radialbohrmaschine *f*
radial stress Querkraft *f*
radial test Radialprobe *f*

radiant tube bell type annealing furnace Haubenglühofen *m* mit Strahlheizrohren
radiant tube heating Strahlrohrbeheizung *f*
radiating Strahlen *n*
radiation damage Strahlenschaden *m*
radiation loss Abstrahlungsverlust *m*
radiation protection Strahlenschutz *m*
radiation-tube continuous bright-annealing furnace Strahlrohr-Durchlauf-Blankglühofen *m*
radiator heating Umwälzbeheizung *f*
radioactive decay radioaktiver Zerfall *m*
radioactive isotope radioaktives Isotop *n*
radioactive tracers radioaktive Spurenelemente *npl*
radioactivity Radioaktivität *f*
radio-chemical test radiochemische Untersuchung *f*
radiography Radiographie *f*; Röntgenographie *f*
radius Durchmesser *m*; Radius *m*
radius of gyration Trägheitsradius *m*
rag Walzen *fpl* hauen; einhauen (Walzen); einkerben; rauhen
ragging Hauen *n*
rail Eisenbahnschiene *f*; Schiene *f*
rail accessories Eisenbahnoberbaustoffe *mpl*
rail base Schienenfuß *m*
rail brake Gleisbremsanlage *f*
rail corrugation Wellenbildung *f* auf Schienen
rail flange Schienenfuß *m*
rail foot Schienenfuß *m*
rail head Schienenkopf *m*
rail joint Schienenstoß *m*
railmounted gleisgebunden
rail [rolling] mill Schienenwalzwerk *n*
rail steel Schienenstahl *m*
rail vehicle Schienenfahrzeug *n*
rail wagon with compartments for taking red hot ingots Thermoswagen *m*
railway loading installation Eisenbahn-Verladeanlage *f*
railway material Eisenbahnbedarf *m*; Eisenbahnzeug *n*
railway track Gleisanlage *f*
railway transport vessel Eisenbahn-Transportkessel *m*
railway tyre Eisenbahnradreifen *m*
railway wagon construction Eisenbahnwagenbau *m*
railway wagon plant Waggonbauanstalt *f*
raise erzeugen (Dampf); heben; hochheben
raisening Treiben *n*
raising delay Einschalt-Verzögerung *f*
raising of coal Kohlengewinnung *f*
rake Feuerkratze *f*
rake angle Neigungswinkel *m* (Spanen); Spanwinkel *m*
rake for cleaning the cooling water main Rechen *m* für die Kühlwasserleitung
rake type cooling bed Rechenkühlbett *n*
ram Preßkolben *m*; Stößel *m*
rammed and sintered bottom Hartherd *m*
rammed bottom Stampfherd *m*; gestampfter Boden *m*
rammed hearth Stampfherd *m*
ramming form Stampfschablone *f*
ramming machine Stampfmaschine *f*
ramp Herdgewölbe *n*; Schräggewölbe *n*
ramp roof Führungsbogen *m*
ram truck Dornhubwagen *m*
ram (tup) Hammerbär *m*
random regellos; zufällig
randomisation Zufallsherstellung *f*
randomised blocks zufällig ausgewählte Blöcke *mpl*
random length Wildmaßlänge *f*
randomness Zufallsanordnung *f*
range Bereich *m*; Reichweite *f*; Umfang *m*; Variationsbreite *f*; Weite *f*
range for pulsating compressive stresses Druckschwellbereich *m*
range of adjustment Regelbereich *m*

range of application Verwendungszweck m
range of fatigue under pulsating tensile stresses Zugschwellbereich m
range of proportionality Proportionalbereich m
range of pulsating stress Schwellbereich m
rank correlation Rangkorrelation f
rank correlation coefficient Rangkorrelationskoeffizient m
ranked data gegliederte Unterlagen fpl
rap klopfen (rütteln)
rapid action valve Schnellschlußventil n
rapid charging machine Schnellbeschickungsvorrichtung f (SM-Ofen)
rapid determination Schnellbestimmung f
rapid heating Schnellbeheizung f
rapid quenching Schnellabschrecken n; schnelles Abschrecken n
rapid testing procedure Schnellprüfverfahren n
rare earths [elements] Seltene Erden fpl
rare gas Edelgas n
rare metal seltenes Metall n
ratchet Sperrad n
rate Geschwindigkeit f; Maß n; Preis m; Vorgabe f
rate action Vorhalt m
rate constant Geschwindigkeitskonstante f
rated capacity Nennleistung f
rated power Nennleistung f
rate fixing standard Akkordvorgabe f
rate of attack Angriffsfreudigkeit f
rate of carbon drop Frischgeschwindigkeit f
rate of carbon elimination Frischgeschwindigkeit f
rate of combustion Verbrennungsgeschwindigkeit f
rate of cooling Abschreckgeschwindigkeit f
rate of corrosion Korrosionsgeschwindigkeit f
rate of crack propagation Rißwachstumsgeschwindigkeit f
rate of heating Wärmegeschwindigkeit f
rate of reaction Reaktionsgeschwindigkeit f
rate time Vorhaltzeit f
rating Nennzahl f; Wertzahl f
ratio Verhältnis n; Zahlenverhältnis n
ratio of iron in slag to iron in bath Verschlackungsverhältnis n
ratio of reduction by forging Verschmiedungsgrad m
ratio of yield point to tensile strength Streckgrenzenverhältnis n
rattler test Trommelprobe f
raw materials Rohstoffe mpl
raw material source Rohstoffquelle f
raw material supply Rohstoffversorgung f
rayotube pyrometer Gesamtstrahlungspyrometer n
reach Bereich m; Reichweite f
react umsetzen
reactance Blindwiderstand m; Reaktanz f
reactance coil Drossel f (elektr.)
reacting force Gegenkraft f
reaction Umsetzung f
reaction rate curve Umwandlungsgeschwindigkeitskurve f
reactive current Blindstrom m
reactive wire drawing Drahtziehen n mit Gegenzug
reactivity Reaktionsfähigkeit f
reactor pressure vessel Reaktordruckgefäß n
react with abbinden
readiness Einsatzfähigkeit f
reading Ablesung f
reading error Ablesefehler m
read in of information Informationsübernahme f
ready for drawing ziehreif
ready for industrial application betriebsreif
ready for operation betriebsfertig

ready (for operation) fertig
real estate Grundbesitz *m*; Immobilien *fpl*
real output capacity Wirkleistung *f* (elektr.)
real time processing Realzeitbetrieb *m*
ream reiben
reanneal nachglühen
rear axle Hinterachse *f*
rear view Rückansicht *f*
rebound crusher Prallmühle *f*
rebound loss Abprallverlust *m*
rebuilding Umbau *m*; Wiederaufbau *m*
recalescence Temperaturanstieg *m*; Umwandlungspunkt *m*; Wärmeentwicklung *f*; Wärmetönung *f*; Wärmezunahme *f*
recalescence point Haltepunkt *m*
recarburisation Rückkohlen *n*
recarburise rückkohlen; wiederaufkohlen
recarburising agent Rückkohlmittel *n*
receipt Annahme *f*; Eingang *m*; Empfang *m*
receiver Abnehmer *m*; Gefäß *n*
receiving hopper Gichtkübel *m*; Gichttrichter *m*; Trichterkübel *m*
receptacle Gefäß *n*
reception test Abnahmeprüfung *f*
recess Absatz *m*
recheck Nachprüfung *f*; nachprüfen (messen)
reciprocal lattice reziprokes Gitter *n*
reciprocal value Kehrwert *m*
reciprocating blowing engine Kolbengebläse *n*
reciprocating rolling process Pilgerschrittverfahren *n*
reciprocating screen Wuchtsieb *n* (Erzvorbereitung)
reciprocation marks Gießwellen *fpl*; Hubmarken *fpl* (Stranggießen)
reclaim rückgewinnen; zurückfordern
reclaimation Rückgewinnung *f*
reclaimed material Mischung *f* vom Mischbett
recoiler Haspel *f*; Wickelmaschine *f*

recoiling line Umwickelanlage *f*
recondition wiederinstandsetzen
reconditioning costs Instandsetzungskosten *pl*
reconduct zurückleiten
reconstitution Rückbildung *f* einer kristallographischen Phase
reconstruction Umbau *m*; Wiederaufbau *m*
recooling plant Rückkühlanlage *f*
recorder Schreiber *m*
recording instrument Schreiber *m*
recover rückgewinnen
recovery Rückgewinnung *f*; Wiedergewinnung *f*
recovery annealing Erholungsglühen *n*
recovery plant for recovering the scrubbing agents Regenerieranlage *f* zum Regenerieren der Waschmedien
recruits (for training) Nachwuchs *m*
recrystallisation Rekristallisation *f*
recrystallisation annealing Rekristallisationsglühen *n*
recrystallisation combined with grain growth Sammelkristallisation *f*
rectangular rechteckig
rectangular billet Rechteckknüppel *m*
rectangular hollow section Rechteckhohlprofil *n*
rectilinear sliding gear Schubgelenk *n*
recuperation Rückgewinnung *f*
recuperator Luftvorwärmer *m*; Rekuperator *m*
recurrent lap Anhäufung *f* von Mattschweißen
recutting (of a die) Wiederaufarbeitung *f*
recycled coal Kreislaufkohle *f*
recycling of top gas Gichtgasrückführung *f*
recyclings Reststoffe *mpl*
red brass Rotguß *m*
red brass bearing Rotgußlager *n*
redeem tilgen
redemption Tilgung *f*
redesign Umbau *m*; umbauen

red hardness Warmhärte f
red heat Rotglut f
redistribution of moments Momentumlagerung f
red mud Rotschlamm m
redox potential Redoxpotential n
red shortness Rotbruch m; Warmbrüchigkeit f
reduce einziehen; reduzieren; vermindern
reducibility Reduzierbarkeit f
reducing Einstoßen n
reducing agent Reduktionsmittel n
reducing carbon Reduktionskohle f
reducing die Reduziergesenk n; Reduziermatritze f
reducing medium Reduktionsmittel n
reduction Abnahme f; Verminderung f
reduction degradation index RDI Niedrigtemperaturzerfall m NTZ
reduction gear Vorgelege n
reduction of area Einschnürung f
reduction of area after fracture in creep rupture test Zeitstand-Brucheinschnürung f
reduction of solids Feststoffreduktion f
reduction per pass Abnahme f je Stich
reduction ratio Reduktionsgrad m
reel Haspel f; Wickelmaschine f; glätten; haspeln
reel break Kantenbeschädigung f (durch eine Haspel)
reeler Friemelwalzwerk n; Glättwalzwerk n
reel for strip Bandhaspel f
reel furnace Haspelofen m
reeling mill Glättwalzwerk n
reeling mill (for tubes) Friemelwalzwerk n
reeling of tubes by the through-feed method Glattwalzen n von Rohren im Durchlaufverfahren
reeling plant Haspelanlage f
reel tension Haspelzug f
reference data Anhaltszahlen fpl
reference input Führungsgröße f
reference junction Vergleichsstelle f (Thermopaar)
reference material Analysenkontrollprobe f
reference sample Belegstück n
reference test piece Bezugsprobe f
reference value Bezugswert m
reference voltage Vergleichsspannung f (elektr.)
refine feinen; frischen; garen; raffinieren; veredeln
refinery Raffinerie f
refining action Frischwirkung f
refining department Verfeinerungsbetrieb m
refining period Frischperiode f
refining slag Feinungsschlacke f; Fertigschlacke f
refining steel by top-blowing Lanzenfrischen n
refining vessel Frischgefäß n
reflect zurückstrahlen
reform umformen
reforming Umformen n
refractability Feuerfestigkeit f; Feuerbeständigkeit f (eines Steines)
refractories industry Feuerfest-Industrie f
refractoriness Feuerfestigkeit f; Hitzebeständigkeit f
refractoriness-under-load Druckfeuerbeständigkeit f
refractory feuerfest; hitzebeständig
refractory breaks Feuerfestausbruch m (Entfallstoff)
refractory brick feuerfester Stein m
refractory building material feuerfester Baustoff m
refractory cement feuerfester Mörtel m
refractory clay feuerfester Ton m
refractory coating feuerfeste Anstrichmasse f
refractory concrete Feuerbeton m
refractory lining feuerfeste Auskleidung f
refractory mixture feuerfeste Masse f
refractory mortar Feuerzement m
refractory mortar (am.) feuerfester

Mörtel *m*
refractory mouldable material plastische feuerfeste Masse *f*
refractory patching mass feuerfeste Flickmasse *f*
refractory quality Feuerbeständigkeit *f* (eines Steines)
refractory ramming mixture feuerfeste Stampfmasse *f*
refrigerate abkühlen; gefrieren
refrigerating machine Kältemaschine *f*
refuse Gekrätz *n*
refuse incineration plant Müllverbrennungsanlage *f*
refuse mixing plant Müllmischanlage *f*
refuse slate Waschberge *mpl*
regenerate nachschärfen (Beizbad); regenerieren
regeneration Rückgewinnung *f*; Wiedergewinnung *f*
regeneration of spent pickle liquor Abfallbeizen-Aufarbeitung *f*
regenerative annealing Umkörnen *n*
regenerative reverberatory furnace Regenerativ-Flammofen *m*
regenerator Regenerator *m*; Wärmespeicher *m*
region of homogeneity Homogenitätsbereich *m*
region of rejection Ablehnungsbereich *m*
registered design Gebrauchsmuster *n*
registered name gesetzlich geschützter Name *m*
registered pattern Gebrauchsmuster *n*
registered share Namensaktie *f*
registered trade mark Warenzeichen *n*
regrinding Nachschleifen *n*
regular lay rope Kreuzschlagseil *n*
regular power furnace Normalleistungsofen *m*
regulate regeln
regulating cock Regulierhahn *m*
regulating drive Regelantrieb *m*

regulating resistance Regelwiderstand *m*
regulating voltage transformer Regelumspanner *m*
reheat wiedererhitzen; wiedererwärmen
reheating furnace Nachwärmofen *m*; Wärmofen *m*
Reichhardt heat diagram Wärmestufenschaubild *n* (Hochofen)
reinforce abstützen; verdicken; verstärken
reinforced concrete construction Stahlbetonbau *m*
reinforcing bar Betonstahl *m*; Torstahl *m*
reinforcing steel Torstahl *m*
reinforcing steel for prestressed concrete Vorspannstahl *m*
reinforcing wire mesh Baustahlmatte *f*
reject beanstanden; verweigern; wrackgewalztes Stück *n*; zurückweisen
rejection Abnahmeverweigerung *f*; Beanstandung *f*
reladle umfüllen
reladling method Umschüttverfahren *n* (Entschwefelung außerhalb des Hochofens)
relative atomic mass relative Atommasse *f*
relative humidity relative Feuchtigkeit *f*
relative molecular mass relative Molekülmasse *f*
relative standard deviation relative Standardabweichung *f*
relative value Bezugswert *m*
relative wattless power Blindleistung *f*
relaxation of stress Spannungsausgleich *m*
relaxation time Relaxationszeit *f*
relay-operated controler Regler *m* mit Hilfsenergie
release Lösung *f* (einer Schraube); lösen

release apron Schlingenleitblech n
reliability Zuverlässigkeit f
reline flicken; neu zustellen
relining Neuzustellung f; Zustellung f
remanence Remanenz f
remelt umschmelzen; wiedereinschmelzen
remelt heat Umschmelze f
remelting electrode Umschmelzelektrode f
remodelling Umbau m; Umgestaltung f
remote control Fernsteuerung f
remote control device Nachlaufregler m
remote control[led] grab Ferngreifer m
remote transmitter Fernsender m
removable abnehmbar
removal of gangue Entfernen n der Gangart; Gangartentfernung f
removal of load Entlastung f
removal of nitrogen Entstickung f
removal of stress Entspannung f
removal of workhardening Entfestigung f
remove entfernen; wegnehmen
remove dust entstauben
remove slag entschlacken
render harmless unschädlich machen
rendering plaster Verputz m
render suitable geeignet machen
renew erneuern
repair flicken; instandsetzen; wiederherstellen; wiederinstandsetzen
repairing costs Instandsetzungskosten pl
repair shop Reparaturbetrieb m; mechanische Werkstätte f
repartition Verteilung f
repeated impact bending strength Dauerschlagbiegefestigkeit f
repeated impact bending test Dauerschlagbiegeversuch m
repeated impact tension test Dauerschlagzugversuch m
repeated impact test Dauerschlagfestigkeitsversuch m; Dauerschlagversuch m
repeated torsion test Dauerverdrehversuch m
repeater Umführung f
rephosphorisation Rückphosphorung f
replace ersetzen
replacement Ersatz m
replace stand Ersatzgerüst n
replenishing solution Ersatzbad n
replica technique Abdruckverfahren n
replication Parallelversuch m; Verfahren n wiederholter Gleichversuche; Wiederholung f von Gleichversuchen
reporting Protokollierung f
repour nachgießen
repress nachpressen (Pulvermet.)
repressing Nachpressen n
request Anfrage f
requirement Anforderung f
reroll nachwalzen
rerun wiederholen (EDV)
research Erforschung f; Forschung f; Untersuchung f
research lab[oratory] Versuchsanstalt f
reset abgleichen
reset time Nachstellzeit f
resetting up time Umrüstzeit f
reshearing Zuschneiden n (von Feinblech)
residence time Verweilzeit f
residual Restwert m
residual austenite Restaustenit m
residual coke Koksrückstand m
residual gas Restgas n (Kohleveredlung)
residual lime Restkalk m
residual magnetism Remanenz f
residual oxygen Restsauerstoff m
residual stress Eigenspannung f; Restspannung f
residuary product Abfallerzeugnis n
residue Überbleibsel n
residue from combustion Verbrennungsrückstand m
residues Überlauf m (beim Sieben)

resin Harz *n*
resintering Nachsintern *n*
resistance Festigkeit *f*
resistance-arc furnace Lichtbogen-Widerstandsofen *m*
resistance butt welding Widerstandsstumpfschweißen *n*
resistance flash welding Abbrennschweißung *f*
resistance fusion welding Widerstandsschmelzschweißen *n*
resistance material Widerstandswerkstoff *m*
resistance number Widerstandszahl *f*
resistance patenting Widerstandspatentieren *n*
resistance stud welding Widerstandsbolzenschweißen *n*
resistance thermometer Widerstandsthermometer *n*
resistance to ag[e]ing Alterungsbeständigkeit *f*
resistance to cold Kältebeständigkeit *f*
resistance to crushing Druckfestigkeit *f*
resistance to heat transfer Wärmeübergangswiderstand *m*
resistance to repeated impact Dauerschlagfestigkeit *f*
resistance to rupture Trennwiderstand *m*
resistance to scratching Kratzbeständigkeit *f*
resistance to slip Gleitwiderstand *m*
resistance to thermal shocks Temperaturwechselbeständigkeit *f*
resistance to wear Verschleißfestigkeit *f*; Verschleißwiderstand *m*
resistance to weathering Wetterbeständigkeit *f*; Witterungsbeständigkeit *f*
resistant to atmospheric conditions witterungsbeständig
resistant to atmospheric corrosion witterungsbeständig
resistant to caustic cracking laugenrißbeständig
resistant to caustic embrittlement laugenbeständig
resistant to cavitation kavitationsbeständig
resistant to corrosion korrosionsbeständig
resistant to deformation at elevated temperatures warmfest
resistant to heat hitzebeständig
resistant to scaling zunderbeständig
resistivity Widerstandsfähigkeit *f*
resistometric measurement of temperature Temperaturmessung *f* durch Widerstandsmessung
resistor Widerstand *m* (elektr.)
resizing Nachprägen *n*
resoluble lösbar
resolve erweichen
resonance method Resonanzverfahren *n*
response Verlauf *m*
response time Einstellzeit *f* (EDV)
re-squaring Zuschneiden *n* (von Feinblech)
resqueezing Nachdrücken *n*
rest lagern
restarting Wiederanblasen *n*; Wiederanlassen *n*
rest bar for carrying guides and guards Walzbalken *m*
restore erneuern; wiederherstellen
restraint stress Flanschstärke *f*
restriction Einschränkung *f*
restrictive beschränkend; einschränkend
restriking Nachschlagen *n*; kurzes Nachrichten *n*
result Ergebnis *n*; anfallen; ergeben
resume wiederaufnehmen
retain behalten; zurückhalten
retained austenite Abschreckaustenit *m*
retaining valve Absperrventil *n*; Rückschlagventil *n*
retaining wall Staumauer *f*
retard verzögern
retardation Verzögerung *f*
retardation of boiling Siedeverzug *m*

retardation time Haltezeit f
retarding Verzögerung f
retention of hardness Anlaßbeständigkeit f; Anlaßhärte f
retention of shape Formbeständigkeit f
retest Wiederholungsversuch m
reticular netzförmig
retirement pension expectancy Rentenanwartschaft f
retort Retorte f
retort oven Kammerofen m
retract einziehen
retractable höhenverstellbar
retracting die Abzugsmantelmatrize f (Pulvermet.)
retransformation Rückumwandlung f
retrograde rückläufig
return rückführen
return[ed] fines Rückgut n
return fines conveyor Rückgutband n
returning fines Rückgut n
return material Rückgut n
return pass Rückstich m
returns Rückgut n
return stroke Rückgang m; Rücklauf m
return travel Rückgang m; Rücklauf m
revamp ausbessern; flicken
reverberant room schallharter Raum m
reverberation Nachhall m
reverberatory flammenbeheizt
reverberatory furnace Flammofen m
reversal Umkehr f; Umsteuerung f
reversal conduit Wechselkanal m
reversal of stress Lastwechsel m
reversal time Umstellzeit f
reverse umkehren; umsteuern
reverse bend test Hin- und Herbiegeversuch m
reverse coiler Wendehaspel f
reverse drawing Stülpziehen n
reverse torsion test Hin- und Herverdrehversuch m; Wechselverwindeversuch m
reverse twist Kreuzschlag m
reversible drive Umkehrantrieb m
reversible switch Kippschalter m

reversing drive Umkehrantrieb m
reversing gear valve Umsteuerschieber m
reversing mill Reversiergerüst n; Umkehrstraße f
reversing mill motor Umkehrwalzmotor m
reversing rolling mill Umkehrwalzwerk n
reversing stand Reversiergerüst n
reversing train Umkehrstraße f
reversing valve Umsteuerventil n
reversing valve gear Schieberumsteuerung f
revertive signal panel Wartentafel f
revert scrap Rücklaufschrott m
review Referat n
revise a claim Patentanspruch m berichtigen
revolution Drehung f; Umdrehung f; Umwälzung f
revolution per min Umdrehung f pro Minute
revolvable drehbar
revolve drehen
revolving drehend
revolving cylindrical furnace Drehrohrofen m
revolving furnace Karussellofen m
revolving grate gas producer Drehrost-Gaserzeuger m
revolving hearth Drehgestell n (beim Drehofen zum Wiedererhitzen)
revolving table Drehtisch m
revolving top Verteilertrichter m
revolving tubular kiln Drehrohrofen m
re-weld nachschweißen
rewinder Umwickelanlage f
rheology Rheologie f
rheostat Rheostat m
rhombic lattice rhombisches Gitter n
rhomb-shaped rautenförmig
rib Rippe f
ribbed gerippt
ribbed flats Nasenprofil n
ribbed pipe Rippenrohr n
ribbed rebars Rippenbetonstahl m
ribbed reinforcing bars Betonrippen-

stahl *m*; Rippentorstahl *m*
ribbed roof Rippengewölbe *n*
ribbed sole plate Rippenplatte *f*
ribbon chip Bandspan *m*
rich gas Gas *n* starkes
rich gas heating Starkgasheizung *f*
rich ore reichhaltiges Erz *n*
riddle Sieb *n*
ridge Wulst *m* (Kaltband)
ridging plate Firstblech *n*
riffler Lochfeile *f*
riffler tool steel Riffelstahl *m*
right-handed thread Rechtsgewinde *n*
rigid starr
rigidity Steifigkeit *f*
rim Außenzone *f*; Felge *f*; Kranz *m* (Rad); Rand *m*; Spurkranz *m*
rimmed steel (am.) unberuhigter Stahl *m*
rimming steel unberuhigter Stahl *m*
ring balance Ringwaage *f*
ringed roof Kranzgewölbe *n*
ring expanding test Ringaufdornversuch *m*
ringing Ringbildung *f* (Drahtziehen)
ring inside a filter bag Kollapsring *m*
ring oilbearing Ringschmierlager *n*
ring rolling Ringwalzen *n*
rinse abspülen; spülen
rinsing plant Spülanlage *f*
ripped gerippt
ripping erster Zug *m* (beim Kaltziehen)
rippled surface wellige Oberfläche *f*
ripple marks Hubmarken *fpl* (Stranggießen)
rise Treiben *n* (der Blöcke); steigen (Stahl)
rise of crown Gewölbestich *m*
rise of the crown Gewölbestich *m*
riser Steiger *m*; Steigkanal *m*; Steigleitung *f*; Steigrohr *n*; Steigtrichter *m*
rise time (automatic control) Anlaufzeit *f*
rising casting steigender Guß *m*
rising flow Aufwärtsströmung *f*
rising head verlorener Kopf *m*

rising steel steigender Stahl *m*; unberuhigter Stahl *m*
rising table Wipptisch *m*
rivet Niet *m*; nieten
riveted joint Nietverbindung *f*
rivet hole Nietloch *n*
riveting machine Nietmaschiene *f*
rivet steel Nietstahl *m*
rivet test Nietprüfung *f*
road building slag Straßenbauschlacke *f*
roak ungeschweißter Oberflächenriß *m*
roast abrösten (Erze); rösten
roasted iron ore geröstetes Eisenerz *n*
roasted spathic carbonate Röstspat *m*
roasted spathic iron ore Röstspat *m*
roasting Brennen *n*
roasting kiln Röstofen *m*
roasting of ores Rösten *n* der Erze
roasting plant Röstanlage *f*
rob Raubbau *m*
rock schaukeln; schwingen; wanken; wiegen
rock drill Gesteinsbohrer *m*
rocked tube kaltgepilgertes Rohr *n*
rocker Kippwiege *f*, Schwinge *f*
rocker bar type furnace Balkenherdofen *m*; Hubbalkenofen *m*
rocker bearing Kipplager *n*
rocking distributor Schaukelverteiler *m*
rocking mixer Taumelmischer *m*
rocking runner Schaukelrinne *f*
rocking spout Schaukelrinne *f*
rocking type furnace Kippofen *m*; Schaukelofen *m*
rocksalt lattice Kochsalzgitter *n*
Rockwell hardness test Rockwell-Härteprüfung *f*
rod Stab *m*; Stange *f*
rodding Ziehen *n* über kurzen Stopfen
rod drawing Stabziehen *n*
rod drawing bench Stabziehbank *f*; Stangenziehbank *f*
rod drawing machine Stangenziehmaschine *f*

rod extrusion Vollfließpressen n
rod mats for concrete reinforcement Bewehrungsmatte f
rod mill Stabwalzwerk n
rod mill rougher Drahtvorwalzgerüst n
rod polishing machine Stangenpoliermaschine f
rod reel Drahthaspel f
rod [rolling] mill Drahtwalzwerk n
roke tiefer Einzelriß m; ungeschweißter Oberflächenriß m
rokes Schalenstreifen mpl (Bandfehler)
roll Walze f; rollen; walzen; wälzen
rollability Walzbarkeit f
roll adjustment Walzenanstellung f
roll barrel Walzenballen m
roll beading Walzsicken f
roll bearing Walzenlager n
roll bending Walzbiegen n
roll bending method (of crown control) Walzenbiegungsverfahren n (zur Einhaltung der Balligkeit)
roll body Walzenballen m
roll brush Walzenbürste f
roll camber Balligkeit f der Walze
roll changing Walzenwechsel m
roll changing sledge Walzenwechselschlitten m
roll clearance Walzenöffnung f
roll coating Walzbeschichtung f
roll crown Balligkeit f der Walze; Walzenballigkeit f
roll down herunterwalzen
roll drafting Kalibrieren n; Kalibrierung f; Walzkalibrieren n
roll drafting machine Walzenkalibriermaschine f
roll draw bending to shape in a multiple-roll unit Walzziehbiegen n
roll drawing Walzziehen n
roll drawing of hollow items without central tool Hohl-Walzziehen n
roll drawing of strip Walzziehen n von Bändern
roll drawing over floating mandrel (plug) Walzziehen n über losen Stopfen (Dorn)
roll drawing over stationary mandrel (plug) Walzziehen n über festen Stopfen (Dorn)
roll drawing over travelling [live] rod Walzziehen n über mitlaufende Stange
rolled diameter of stock gewalzter Durchmesser m des Walzgutes
rolled-in extraneous matter Einwalzung f
rolled-in scrap eingewalzter Splitter m
rolled [mill] edge Walzkante f
rolled piece Walzgut n
rolled product Walzerzeugnis n
rolled section Walzprofil n
rolled steel Walzstahl m
roll embossing Prägewalzen n
roller Rund- und Verteilgesenk n; Walzer m
roller's side Einsteckseite f (vor der Walze)
roller bearing Rollenlager n
roller bearing axle box Rollenachslager n
roller bearing steel Wälzlagerstahl m
roller chain Rollenkette f
roller-conveyor Rollenförderer m
roller-conveyor furnace Rollenherdofen m
roller cooling bank Rollenkühlbett n
roller cooling bed Rollenkühlbett n
roller flattening Rollenrichten n
roller hearth chamber furnace Rollenherd-Kammerofen m
roller hearth furnace Rollenherdofen m
roller hearth furnace for coils Ringdurchziehofen m
roller leveller Rollenrichtmaschine f
roller levelling Walzrichten n
roller levelling machine Rollenrichtmaschine f
roller marking Wälzprägen n
roller mill Walzenmühle f
roller on the entry side of rolls Vorderwalzer m

roller pug mill Kollergang *m*
roller rack Rollgangsrahmen *m*
roller seam welding Rollennahtschweißen *n*
roller spinning Drückwalzen *n*; Reckdrücken *n* (Drückwalzen)
roller spinning over conical mandrel Drückwalzen *n* über kegeligen Dorn
roller spinning over cylindrical mandrel Drückwalzen *n* über zylindrischen Dorn
roll[er] straightening Walzrichten *n*
roller straightening dent Beschädigung *f* durch Richtmaschine
roller table Rollgang *m*
roller twister units Drallrollen *fpl*
roll flanging Walzbördeln *n*
roll flattening Walzenabplattung *f*
roll force Walzkraft *f*
rollforming Rollformen *n*
roll forming of strips Profilwalzen *n* von Bändern
roll forming to shape Walzprofilieren *n*
roll gap Walzspalt *m*
roll grinding machine Walzenschleifmaschine *f*
roll [guide] mark Abdruck *m* (Walzdrahtfehler)
roll heat-treating furnace Walzenvergüteofen *m*
roll housing Walzenständer *m*
roll in einwalzen
rolling Toleranz *f*; Walzen *n*
rolling circle envelope Hüllprofil *n* (Rauheitsmessung)
rolling crusher Walzenbrecher *m*
rolling defect Walzfehler *m*
rolling direction Walzrichtung *f*
rolling fin Walznaht *f*
rolling horsepower Walzarbeit *f*
rolling load Walzleistung *f*
rolling mill Walzstraße *f*; Walzwerk *n*
rolling mill crew Walzmannschaft *f*
rolling mill drive Walzwerksantrieb *m*
rolling-mill foreman Walzmeister *m*
rolling mill for medium-sized products Mittelstahl-Walzwerk *n*

rolling mill for semi finished products Halbzeug-Walzwerk *n*
rolling mill furnace Walzwerksofen *m*
rolling mill product Walzwerkserzeugnis *n*
rolling mill superintendent Walzwerksingenieur *m*
rolling of bars (wire) Walzen *n* von Stäben (Draht)
rolling of multiple-spline shafts Walzen *n* von Vielnut-Wellen
rolling of sectional bars Walzen *n* von Profilstäben
rolling of square tubes Walzen *n* von Vierkantrohren
rolling of strip (sheet) Walzen *n* von Band (Blech)
rolling oil Walzöl *n*
rolling program Walzplan *m*; Walzprogramm *n*
roll[ing] scale Walzzunder *m*
rolling schedule Walzplan *m*; Walzprogramm *n*; Walzstichplan *m*
rolling sequence Walzfolge *f*
rolling skin Walzhaut *f*
rolling speed Walzgeschwindigkeit *f*
rolling stand Walzgerüst *n*
rolling stock Walzgut *n*; rollendes Material *n*
rolling texture Walztextur *f*
rolling train Walzstraße *f*
rolling train for heavy products Grobstraße *f*
rolling wear rollender Verschleiß *m*
roll in steps Staffelwalze *f*, Stufenwalze *f*
roll jaw Walzenbacke *f* (Brecher)
roll lathe Walzendrehbank *f*
roll mark Walzennarbe *f*
roll neck Walzenzapfen *m*
roll neck bearing Walzenzapfenlager *n*
roll nip Walzspalt *m*
rollover cooling bed Wendekühlbett *n*
roll-over device Wendevorrichtung *f*
roll-over type furnace Rollofen *m*
roll pass design Kalibrieren *n*; Kalibrierung *f*, Walzenkalibrieren *n*

roll pass dressing machine Kaliberbearbeitungsmaschine *f*
roll pick-up Walznarbe *f*; Walzstrieme *f*
roll pressure Walzdruck *m*
roll profile Walzenprofil *n*
roll ring Walzring *m*
roll rounding Walzrunden *n*
roll scale Walzhaut *f*
roll scratch Walzriefe *f*
roll [separating] force Walzkraft *f*
roll spring Auffederung *f*; Walzensprung *m*
roll torque Walzmoment *n*
roll turning shop Walzendreherei *f*
roll type crusher Walzenbrecher *m*
roll wear Walzenverschleiß *m*
roof Dach *n*; Decke *f*; Gewölbe *n*
roof (arc furnace) Deckel *m*
roof brick Deckenstein *m*; Gewölbestein *m*; Wölbstein *m*
roof drip Zapfen *m*
roofing sheet Dachblech *n*; Dachpfannenblech *n*; Pfannenblech *n*
roof life Gewölbehaltbarkeit *f*
roof panel Feld *n* (Gewölbe)
roof portion Gewölbeausschnitt *m*
roof rise Gewölbestich *m*
roof skewback Deckelauflage *f*
roof tile Dachziegel *m*
roof with fixed skewback Gewölbe *n* mit festem Widerlager
room temperature precipitation hardening Kaltaushärtung *f*
root Gewindegrund *m*
root-bead defect Grundnahtfehler *m*
root mean square height (RMS) Mittenrauhwert *m*; quadratischer Mittenrauhwert *m*
rope drag Seilschlepper *m*
rope wire Seildraht *m*
roping Streifenbildung *f*
rosted spathic carbonate Rostspat *m*
rosted spathic iron ore Rostspat *m*
rotary drehbar; umlaufend
rotary bit Drehbohrschneide *f*
rotary chute Drehschurre *f*
rotary coil plate Wickelplatte *f*

rotary converter Drehkonverter *m*
rotary crane Drehkran *m*
rotary crusher Kreiselbrecher *m*
rotary feed table Drehteller *m*
rotary forge mill Schrägwalzwerk *n*
rotary forge process Stoßbankverfahren *n* (Ehrhardt-Verfahren)
rotary furnace Drehofen *m*
rotary grate gas producer Drehrost-Gaserzeuger *m*
rotary hammer swaging Reduktion *f* von Draht mit Hammermaschinen
rotary hearth furnace Drehherdofen *m*
rotary kiln Drehrohrofen *m*
rotary piercing mill Hohlwalzwerk *n*
rotary piercing mill (tubes) Schrägwalzwerk *n* (Rohre)
rotary piercing of tubes over a plug Walzen *n* von Rohren über Stange
rotary piston blowing engine Drehkolbengebläse *n*
rotary piston meter Ringkolbenzähler *m*
rotary reverberatory furnace Drehflammofen *m*
rotary shear rotierende Schere *f*
rotary shears Kreisschere *f*; Trommelschere *f* (Kaltband)
rotary sintering kiln Drehrohr-Sinterofen *m*; Trommelsinterofen *m*
rotary [slide] valve Drehschieber *m*
rotary sputtering Drehbedampfung *f* (Elektronenmikroskop)
rotary straightening Umlaufbiegen *n*
rotary swaging Formrundkneten *n*
rotary swaging by the heat-feed method Rundkneten *n* im Vorschubverfahren
rotary swaging by the infeed method Rundkneten *n* im Einstechverfahren
rotary swaging (for reducing bars or tubes) Rundkneten *n*
rotary swaging of external shapes Formrundkneten *n* von Außenformen
rotary swaging of internal shapes Formrundkneten *n* von Innenformen
rotary table Drehtisch *m*

rotate drehen; umlaufen
rotating bar fatigue test Umlaufbiegeversuch *m*
rotating beam fatigue test Drehstabdauerfestigkeit *f*
rotating crystal photograph Drehkristallaufnahme *f*
rotating table press Drehtischpresse *f*
rotation Drehung *f*
rotational motion Drehbewegung *f*
rotatory capacity Rotationsvermögen *n*
rotor Läufer *m*; Rotor *m*
rotor wheel Laufrad *n*
rough unbearbeitet; vorstrecken
rough adjustment Grobeinstellung *f*
rough cleaning Vorreinigung *f*
rough down herunterwalzen; vorstrecken
rough draft of a standard Normenvorentwurf *m*
roughed slab Vorbramme *f*
roughen einhauen (Walzen); einkerben
rougher Vorgerüst *n*; Vorschmiedegesenk *n*
rough-forge vorschmieden
rough forging Schmiederohling *m*
rough grinding Vorschleifen *n* (Gußputz)
roughing Vorstraße *f*
roughing [down] stand Vorgerüst *n*
roughing [mill] stand Blockgerüst *n*
roughing pass Blockkaliber *n*; Streckstich *m*; Vorstich *m*; Vorstreckkaliber *n*
roughing slag Nachschlacke *f* (Hochofen)
rough-machined vorbearbeitet
round bar Rundeisen *n*
round caster Rundstranggießanlage *f*
round die thread rolling Gewindewalzen *n*
round edge equal angles Winkelstahl *m*; gleichschenkliger rundkantiger Winkelstahl *m*
round edge unequal angles Winkelstahl *m*; ungleichschenkliger rundkantiger Winkelstahl *m*
rounded weld Kehlnaht *f*; volle Schweiße *f*
rounding off Abrundung *f*
rounding off of the edges Kantenabrundung *f*
round kneading Rundkenten *n*
roundness Rundheit *f*
round off abrunden
route card Laufkarte *f*
royalty Lizenzgebühr *f*
rpm drop Drehzahlabfall *m*
RS bistable element RS-Kippglied *n*
rub reiben
rubber Gummi *m*
rubber drive belt Gummitreibriemen *m*
rubber gasket Gummidichtung *f*
rubber hose Gummischlauch *m*
rubber spring wheels gummigefederte Räder *npl*
rubbing surface Reibungsfläche *f*
rubble Abraum *m*
rubbly culm coke Feinkoks *m*; Perlkoks *m*
rub off abreiben
rule Maßstab *m*
rule of thumb Faustregel *f*
ruling section maßgeblicher Querschnitt *m*
rumpling erster Zug *m* (beim Kaltziehen)
run Gang *m* (des Hochofens); Lauf *m*; fließen; laufen; rinnen
run a hydraulic pressure test Abdrücken *n* (Rohre); abpressen (von Rohren)
run and guide bushes Lauf- und Führungsbüchsen *fpl*
run-in roller table Einlaufrollgang *m*
runner Abstichrinne *f*; Gießrinne *f*; Gleisrad *n*; Läufer *m*
runner brick Kanalstein *m*
runner core Königsstein *m*
runner gate Einguß *m*
runner head Gießkopf *m*
running-in period Einlaufperiode *f*
running out nicht maßhaltig

running slag Laufschlacke f
running surface Lauffläche f
run-off Abstich m
run-of-mine Fördererz n
run of piping Rohrstrang m
run-out roller table Abfuhrrollgang m
rupturing capacity Abschaltleistung f
rust verrosten
rust from external sources Fremdrost n
rustless nichtrostend
rust removal Entrostung f
rust resistant rostbeständig
rust resisting property Korrosionsbeständigkeit f
rutile electrode Titansäureelektrode f

S

sadden nachwärmen
saddening Vorblocken n vor Zwischenaufheizung
saddle Sattel m (für Schmiededorn)
saddle segment Sattelsegment n
safe end Anschweißende n (Rohre)
safety Sicherheit f
safety appliance Schutzvorrichtung f; Sicherheitsvorrichtung f
safety area Sicherheitsbereich m
safety campaign Unfallverhütungskampagne f
safety cut out Sicherheitsschaltung f
safety device Schutzvorrichtung f; Sicherheitsvorrichtung f
safety factor Sicherheitsbeiwert m; Sicherheitsfaktor m
safety-friction clutch Rutschkupplung f
safety goggles Schutzbrille f; Sicherheitsbrille f
safety lining Dauerfutter n
safety official Sicherheitsbeauftragter m
safety precaution Schadensverhütung f
safety socket Schuko-Steckdose f
safety technics Sicherheitstechnik f

safety valve Sicherheitsventil n
safe working stress zulässige Beanspruchung f
sag sacken; senken
sagger Schiffchen n
sagging point Erweichungspunkt m
sag resistance Eindruckbeständigkeit f
salamander Bodensau f; Ofenbär m; Ofensau f
salaried worker Angestellter m
salary Gehalt m
salary earner Gehaltsempfänger m
sale Absatz m; Verkauf m
sales account Verkaufskonto n
sales department Verkaufsabteilung f
sales office Verkaufsbüro n
sales tax Umsatzsteuer f
salt bath furnace Salzbadofen m
salt bath hardening Salzbadhärten n
salt bath nitriding Badnitrieren n; Salzbadnitrieren n; Weichnitrieren n
salt bath patenting Salzbadpatentieren n
salt spray test Salzsprühversuch m
salvage Erhaltung f (z.B. durch Ausbesserung)
sample Probe f; Stichprobe f; auswählen
sample design Anlage f eines Stichprobenverfahrens; Stichprobenmuster n; Stichprobenplan m
sample of commodities Warenprobe f
sampler Probennehmer m
sample thief Probenheber m
sampling Auswahl f; Auswahlverfahren n; Probenahme f; Stichprobe f nehmen; Stichprobenerhebung f; Stichprobenverfahren n
sampling error Stichprobenfehler m
sampling length Bezugsstrecke f
sampling number Zufallszahl f
sand blast abstrahlen; sandstrahlen
sand blast apparatus Sandstrahleinrichtung f
sand blast cleaning shop Sandputzerei f

sandblasting Strahlputzen n; Abblasen n (mit Sand)
sand blasting machine Sandputzmaschine f
sand blasting shot Strahlmittel n
sand blasting work Sandstrahlgebläse-Arbeit f
sand inclusion Sandeinschluß m
sand [mark] (surface defect) Sandstelle f
sand seal Sandabdichtung f
sandwich rolling Plattieren n
saponification Verseifung f
saponification number Verseifungszahl f
sappy fracture feinkörniger Bruch m
sappy structure feinkörniges Gefüge n
sash and casement sections Fensterstahl m
sash section Einfassungseisen n
satisfaction of energy requirement Energiebedarfsdeckung f
saturable sättigungsfähig
saturate sättigen
saturated activity Sättigungsaktivität f
saturated steam Sattdampf m
saturated vapour Sattdampf m
saturation Sättigung f, Sättigungszustand m
saturation activation Sättigungsaktivierung f
saturation concentration Sättigungskonzentration f
saturation degree Sättigungsstufe f
saturation density Sättigungsdichte f
saturation intensity Sättigungsgrad m (Magnetisieren)
saturation limit Sättigungsgrenze f
saturation line Sättigungslinie f
saturation magnetisation Sättigungsmagnetisierung f
saturation point Sättigungspunkt m
saturation pressure Sättigungsdruck m
saturation state Sättigungszustand m
saturation temperature Sättigungstemperatur f
saturator Sättiger m (LD-Gasreinigung)

saucer spring Tellerfedersäule f
saving Einsparung f; Ersparnis f
saw Säge f; sägen
saw blade sharpening machine Sägeblatt-Schärfmaschine f
saw cutting Sägen n
saw dust Sägespäne mpl
sawing machine Sägemaschine f
saw steel Sägenstahl m
scab Ansatz m (Hochofen); Ansatz m (Oberflächenfehler); Sandstelle f (Gußfehler); Schale f, Schorf m; Schuppe f, Schülpe f
scabbiness Schuppen und Schalen fpl
scabby schalig; schuppig
scaffold Ansatz m (Schachtofen); Gerüst n; Versetzung f
scaffolding Hängen n (der Gicht)
scale Gradeinteilung f; Hammerschlag m; Leiter f, Maßstab m; Schuppe f; Schuppen fpl bilden; Skala f, Waagschale f, abblättern; abbrennen; abbröckeln; abschuppen; verzundern; zundern
scale breaker [stand] Zunderbrechgerüst n
scale deposit Kesselsteinablagerung f
scale efflorescence Zunderausblühungen fpl
scale flume Zunderspülrinne f
scale for conveyor Transportbandwaage f
scale pattern Zunderstreifen m
scale pit Sinterbrunnen m (Walzwerk); Sintergrube f
scale-pitted surface rauhe Oberfläche f (durch Zunder)
scaler Vorsturz m
scale removal by bending Biegeentzundern n
scale-resisting feuerbeständig
scale resisting steel zunderbeständiger Stahl m
scale roke Schlackenzeile f
scaling Abblättern n; Bereichsanpassung f (EDV); Splittern n; Verzunderung f; Zundern n

scaling loss Abbrand *m*
scaling loss condition Abbrandverhältnis *n*
scaling resistance Zunderbeständigkeit *f*
scalping Schälen *n*
scaly schuppig
scan abtasten; genau prüfen
scanner Abtaster *m* (EDV)
scanning electron microscope (SEM) Rasterelektronenmikroskop *n* (REM)
scanning element Abtastglied *n*
scar Ansatz *m* (auf Ofenwänden); Narbe *f*
scarf abschrägen; zuspitzen
scarfing Flammstrahlen *n*
scatter Streubereich *m*; Streuung *f*; streuen
scatter analysis Streuungszerlegung *f*
scatter band Streubereich *m*
scatter band of Jominy hardenability Härtestreuband *n*
scatter value Streuwert *m*
schedule Formblatt *n*; Fragebogen *m*; Liste *f*; Liste *f* aufstellen; Plan *m*; Verzeichnis *n*; Walzstichplan *m*; Zettel *m*; Zählblatt *n*; in eine Liste *f* eintragen
scheduled production Soll-Leistung *f*
schedule work Planarbeit *f*
Schoop's metal spraying process Schoopsches Metallspritzverfahren *n*
schredding plant Schredderanlage *f*
scintillation counter Szintillationszähler *m*
scleroscope hardness Kugelfallhärte *f*; Rücksprunghärte *f*; Shorehärte *f*
scleroscope hardness test Rücksprunghärteprüfung *f*
scoop Schaufel *f*
scope Anwendungsbereich *m*
scorched steel Stahl *m* mit nadelartigem oder kristallinischem Gefüge
scorching nadelförmige Kristallbildung *f* (Stahlblock)
score einkerben; kratzen

scorify verschlacken
scoring Riefenbildung *f*; Verschleißlinien *fpl*
scotch abfangen (Schmelze); einkerben
scotch block Auswechselteil *n* an Generatorgasbrennern
scour festfressen; fressen; wegfressen
scouring of the valve seat Fressen *n* des Ventilsitzes
scragging Setzen *n* (Feder)
scragging machine for testing springs Federn-Schwingprüfmaschine *f*
scrap Abfall *m*; Ausschuß *m*; Schrott *m*; Verschnitt *m* (Stanzen); verschrotten
scrap arising Schrottaufkommen *n*
scrap baling press Schrottpaketierpresse *f*
scrap bundling press Schrottpaketierpresse *f*
scrap carburisation process Schrottkohlungsverfahren *n*
scrap charging box handling crane Schrottmuldenkran *m*
scrap chopper Schrotthacker *m*
scrap coke Abfallkoks *m*
scrap crushing plant Schrottzerkleinerungsanlage *f*
scrap dealer Schrotthändler *m*
scrap drop crane Schrottschlagkran *m*
scrape kratzen; schaben
scraper Ausdrückmaschine *f*; Schrapper *m*; Schürfwagen *m*
scraper loader Schrapperlader *m*
scrap for cooling Kühlschrott *m*
scraping device Schrappvorrichtung *f*
scrap ingot Wrackblock *m*
scrap iron Alteisen *n*; Schrott *m*
scrap mark Einwalzung *f*
scrap of blooms Blockschrott *m*
scrap of ingot moulds Kokillenbruch *m*
scrapping Verschrotten *n*
scrapping off plant Verschrottungsbetrieb *m*
scrap preparation plant Schrottaufbereitungsanlage *f*

scrap shear Schrottschere f
scrap wholesale traders Schrottgroßhandel m
scrap yard Schrottlagerplatz m
scratch Kratzer m; Riefe f; Ritzer m; Schramme f; kratzen
scratch hardness Ritzhärte f
screen Blende f; Raster n; Sieb n
screen analysis Siebanalyse f
screen for cleaning the cooling water Sieb n für die Kühlwasserreinigung
screening Sieben n
screening machine Siebmaschine f
screening of lump coal and culm Grob- und Feinkokssieberei f
screenings Siebrückstand m
screen [out] absieben; sieben
screen size Rasterweite f (Rasterformat); Teilchengröße f
screw Schraube f (mutternlose); Spindel f (in Druckschraube); schrauben
screw bolt Schraubenbolzen m
screw cutting lathe Zugspindel-Drehbank f
screw cutting tool Gewindeschneidwerkzeug n
screw die Schneideisen n
screw dislocation Schraubenversetzung f
screw down Anstellschraube f; Druckschraube f
screw down control Anstellsteuerung f
screw down [gear] Schrauben-Anstellvorrichtung f
screw-down nut Druckmutter f
screwed and socketed (joint) verbunden mit Schraubmuffe f (Rohr)
screwed flange Gewindeflansch m
screwed joint Schraubmuffenverbindung f; Verschraubung f
screw hook Hakenschraube f
screwing machine Gewindeschneidmaschine f
screw joint Schraubverbindung f
screw like schraubenförmig
screw nail Schraubennagel m
screw on anschrauben; aufnippeln (Elektrode)
screw pitch Gewindesteigung f
screw plug Verschlußschraube f
screw press Spindelpresse f
screw slip band Schraubengleitband n
screw steel Schraubenstahl m
screw stock Schraubenwerkstoff m
screw tap Gewindebohrer m
screw thread Gewinde n; Schraubengewinde n
screw threading die Schraubengewinde-Schneideisen n
scrub schruppen
scrubber Berieselungsturm m; Naßreiniger m; Wäscher m
scrubber tower Waschturm m
scrubbing oil tank Waschöltank m
scrubbing unit Wringwalzenabstreifer m
scruff recovery Zinnrückgewinnung f
scuff abnutzen
scuffing Verschleiß m
scum Abstrich m; Schaum m
scythe steel Sensenstahl m
seal Dichtung f; Verschluß m
seal coat Poren fpl mit Mineralöl schließen
sealed assembly rolling process Walzschweißverfahren n
seal gas Dichtgas n
sealing liquid Sperrflüssigkeit f
sealing ring Abschlußring m
sealing wire Glaseinschmelzdraht m
seal ring Dichtungsring m
seal welding Dichtschweißung f; Dichtungsschweißung f
seal wire Plombendraht m
seam Faltungsriß m; Flöz n; Gang m; Lager n; Naht f; Oberflächenriß m; Saum m (ungeschweißter); Walznaht f; ungeschweißter Oberflächenriß m; Überwalzung f; Überwalzungsfehler m
seaming Falzen n (Anlegen eines Bordes)
seaming by spinning Falzen n durch Drücken

seamless nahtlos
seamless tube nahtlos gewalztes Rohr *n*
seam welding Nahtschweißung *f*
seamy rissig
search forschen; untersuchen
seat grinding Einschleifen *n*
seating Auflagefläche *f*
secondary air Zweitluft *f*
secondary arm (dendrites) Nebenast *m* (Dendriten)
secondary cleaning Feinreinigung *f*; Nachreinigung *f*
secondary crushing Nachzerkleinern *n*
secondary dust removal Feinentstaubung *f*
secondary hardening Sekundärhärten *n*
secondary mill Walzwerk *n* zweiter Hitze
secondary pipe sekundärer Lunker *m*
secondary scale Walzzunder *m*
secondary stress Nebenspannung *f*
secondary voltage verkettete Spannung *f*
second draw Weiterschlag *m* (Tiefziehen)
second-operation drawing Tiefziehen *n* im Weiterschlag
second quality zweite Wahl *f*
section Formstahl *m*; Profil *n*; Querschnitt *m*; Schnitt *m*; schwerer Formstahl *m*; zerteilen
sectional area of hardening Härtequerschnitt *m*
sectional constraining values Zwangsschnittgröße *f*
section[al] steel Formstahl *m*
sectional steel Profilstahl *m*
sectional view Aufriß *m*
section modulus Widerstandsmoment *n*
section of the hearth Herdquerschnitt *m*
section [rolling] mill Formstahl-Walzwerk *n*; Profilstahl-Walzwerk *n*
section sensitivity Wanddicken-Empfindlichkeit *f*
section shearing machine Profilschere *f*
security against failure Bruchsicherheit *f*
sedimentation analysis Sedimentationsanalyse *f*
sedimentation basin Absetzbecken *n*
seed impfen
seeding Impfen *n*
Seger cone Segerkegel *m*
Seger cone softening point Segerkegel-Fallpunkt *m*
segmental saw blade Segment-Sägeblatt *n*
segregate aussortieren (Schrott); seigern
segregation Aussonderung *f*; Entmischung *f*; Seigerung *f*
segregation line Seigerungsstreifen *m*
segregation streaks Seigerungszeilen *fpl*
segregation streamer Seigerungsstreifen *m*
seize anfressen; fassen; festfressen; fressen; greifen; klemmen
seizing Fressen *n*; fressender Verschleiß *m*
select auswählen
selective corrosion Lochfraßkorrosion *f*; selektive Korrosion *f*
selective heating Teilerhitzung *f*; Teilwärmen *n*
selective quenching Teilabschreckung *f*
selectivity Trennschärfe *f*
selenium rectifier Selen-Gleichrichter *m*
self acting selbsttätig
self aligning bearings Pendellager *n*
self aligning roller bearing Pendelrollenlager *n*
self balancing selbsttätig abgleichend
self diffusion Selbstdiffussion *f*
self disconnecting selbstausschaltend
self fluxing ore selbstgehendes Erz *n*
self fluxing sinter selbstgängiger Sin-

ter *m*
self hardening steel Selbsthärtestahl *m*
self inspiration burner Einregelungsbrenner *m*
self locking nut selbstsichernde Mutter *f*
self oiling selbstschmierend
self-operated controller Regler *m* ohne Hilfsenergie
self sharpening Selbstschärfung *f*
self skimming selbstentschlackend
selling costs Verkaufskosten *pl*
selling price Verkaufspreis *m*
selvage Saum *m*
semiautomatic welding halbautomatische Schweißung *f*
semi-bituminous coal Magerkohle *f*
semi-circular arch Tonnengewölbe *n*
semi-coke Schwelkoks *m*
semi commercial halbtechnisch
semi conducter Halbleiter *m*
semicontinuous rolling mill halbkontinuierliches Walzwerk *n*
semi finished vorgefrischt
semi finished products Halbzeug *n*
semifluid dickflüssig
semi killed halbberuhigt
semi killed steel halbberuhigter Stahl *m*
semi product conditioning department Halbzeugputzerei *f*
semi rimming steel halbberuhigter Stahl *m*
semi-skilled worker angelernter Arbeiter *m*
semi-steel Gußeisen *n* mit Stahlschrottzusatz
semi suspended roof Hängestützgewölbe *n*
sense Richtungssinn *m*
sensibility to disturbances Störanfälligkeit *f*
sensible heat Eigenwärme *f*; fühlbare Wärme *f*
sensing device Meßfühler *m*
sensitising Sensibilisieren *n*
sensitive feed feinstufiger Vorschub *m*

sensitiveness (to) Anfälligkeit *f* (für); Ansprechempfindlichkeit *f*; Empfindlichkeit *f* (gegen)
sensitivity regulator Empfindlichkeitsregler *m*
sensitivity to ag[e]ing Alterungsempfindlichkeit *f*
sensitivity to hardening Härteempfindlichkeit *f*
sensitivity to temperature Temperaturempfindlichkeit *f*
sensitivity to welding cracks Schweißrißempfindlichkeit *f*
sensitization Sensibilisierung *f*
sensitize sensibilisieren
sensor Fühler *m*; Prüfkopf *m*
separate spalten; trennen
separating Trennen *n*
separating drum Separationstrommel *f*
separating shears Trennschere *f*
separation Entmischung *f*
separation process Trennverfahren *n*
separator Abscheider *m*; Setzmaschine *f*
sequence casting Sequenzgießen *n*; vollkontinuierliches Stranggießen *n*
sequence of vessel changing Wechselfolge *f*
sequential analysis of variance Folgeprüfung *f*; Vielfachprüfung *f*; fortschreitendes Stichprobenverfahren *n*
sequential control Ablaufprogrammsteuerung *f*; Folgesteuerung *f*
sequential method of sampling Folgestichprobenverfahren *n*
sequential program Ablaufprogramm *n*
sequential sampling Folgestichprobe *f*
sequential test Folgeprüfung *f*
series Reihe *f*; hintereinander (geschaltet)
series armature circuit Ankerreihenschaltung *f* (elektr. Antrieb)
series arranged according to magnitude Anordnung *f* nach der Größe

series of moulds Kokillenband n
series of reference diagrams Gefügerichtreihe f
serrated shaft Zahnwelle f
service Bedienung f; Betrieb m; Kundendienst m
serviceable brauchbar
service and secondary process department Hilfs- und Nebenbetrieb m
service bunker Kokskohlenkomponentenbunker m
service department Hilfsbetrieb m
service life Dauerhaltbarkeit f
service life cutting speed curve Standzeit-Schnittgeschwindigkeit-Kurve f
service stage Betriebsreife f
service test Betriebsversuch m
servicing Warten n; Wartung f
servo-mechanism Betriebsregelsatz m; Folgeregelung f
servomotor Stellmotor m
sessile drop method Verfahren n des ruhenden Tropfens
set Teilmenge f, Ziehwerkzeugfertigstellung f; ausrichten; bleibende Durchbiegung f, einbauen; einrichten; einstellen; erstarren; justieren; stellen
set alight entflammen
set (cement) abbinden (Zement)
set-down bucket Aufsetzkübel m
set of roll[er]s Walzensatz m
set point Festwertregelung f, Sollwert m
set-point controller Sollwertsteller m
set square Zeichendreieck n
setter Teil n eines Gesenkes
setting Schränken n (Säge)
setting angle Freiwinkel m
setting increment Stelleinheit f (Walzwerk)
setting range [of screw-down] Verstellweg m
setting up Einrichtung f (z. B. einer Versuchsstation)
settle out abscheiden; absetzen
settler Klärbecken n
settling basin Klärbecken n

settling chamber Absetzkammer f (Staub)
settling (of contaminants) Ablagerung f (von Schadstoffen)
settling slime Klärschlamm m
settling sludge Klärschlamm m
settling tank Klärbecken n
settling tank (gas cleaning) Absetzbecken n
settling time (automatic control) Anlaufzeit f
setup Vorrichtung f
set up for calculating machine Rechenschaltung f
set-up time Rüstzeit f (zum Einrichten)
setup angeheftet (zum Schweißen)
set value control Festwertregelung f
severing Zerteilen n
sewage Abwasser n
sewer castings Kanalguß m
shade of blackness Schwärzegrad m
shading (spectrum analysis) Schwärzung f
shadow line Härteader f (Bandfehler)
shaft Achse f; Hochofenschacht m; Schacht m; Spindel f; Welle f; Zapfen m
shaft furnace Schachtofen m
shafting Polieren und Handrichten n; Schälen n
shake rütteln; schütteln
shake out auspacken (Formen)
shaker Polterwerk n (Draht); Schüttelwerk n
shaking barrel Rommelfaß n; Scheuerfaß n
shaking screen Schüttelsieb n
shale Schiefer m
shank Gabel f; Gießlöffel m; Gießpfanne f, Schaft m
shank ladle Gabelpfanne f, Handpfanne f
shank threaded screw Schaftschraube f
shape Form f; Gestalt f; Planheit f; Profil n; formen; gestalten; profilieren; umformen
shape control Planheitsregelung f

shaped brick Formstein *m*
shaped roll profilierte Walze *f*
shape roll Profilwalze *f*
shape [rolling] mill Formstahl-Walzwerk *n*; Profilstahl-Walzwerk *n*
shape wave Welle *f*
shaping Formgebung *f*; Gestaltung *f*; Profilierung *f*; Umformen *n*; Verformung *f*
shaping groove Profilkaliber *n*
shaping pass Fertigstich *m*; Formstich *m*
share Aktie *f*; Anteil *m*
shareholder Aktionär *m*
sharp edged scharfkantig
sharpen anspitzen; schleifen; schärfen
sharp gas zerknallbares Gas *n*
shatter crack Haarriß *m*; Innenriß *m*; Nierenbruch *m* (Schiene); Spannungsriß *m*
shattering of grains Kornzertrümmerung *f*
shatter marks Ratterwellen *fpl*; Schlagwellen *fpl* (Feinblech)
shatter strength Sturzfestigkeit *f* (Koks)
shatter test Fallprobe *f*
shear Schub *m*; abscheren; scheren
shear blade Schermesser *n*
shear centre Schubmittelpunkt *m*
sheared edge beschnittene Kante *f*; geschnittene Kante *f*
shear forming Schubumformen *n*
shearing action Abscherwirkung *f*
shearing and slitting line Zerteilanlage *f*
shearing chip Scherspan *m*
shearing cut Scherschnitt *m*
shearing force Scherkraft *f*
shearing machine and power punching Profilschere und Lochstanze *f*
shearing strength Scherfestigkeit *f*; Schubfestigkeit *f*
shear[ing] stress Schubspannung *f*
shearing test Scherversuch *m*
shearing yield Scherleistung *f*

shear knife Schermesser *n*
shear modulus Gleitmodul *m*; Schubmodul *m*
shear off abscheren
shears Schere *f*
shear spinning Abstreckdrücken *n*
shear to length ablängen
shear wave Schubwelle *f* (Ultraschallprüfung)
sheathed electrode umhüllte Elektrode *f*; ummantelte Elektrode *f*
sheath tube Schutzrohr *n* (für Tauchthermoelement)
sheave Rolle *f*; Scheibe *f*
sheet Blatt *n*; Bogen *m*; Feinblech *n*; Fläche *f*; Metallplatte *f*; Tafel *f*
sheet bar Platine *f*; Vorblech *n*
sheet bar multiple Platinenstab *m* mehrfacher Länge
sheet bar reheating furnace Platinenwärmofen *m*
sheet bar rolling mill Platinenwalzwerk *n*
sheet bar weight Platinengewicht *n*
sheet clippings Blechabfälle *mpl*
sheet fabricating industry blechverarbeitende Industrie *f*
sheet for galvanising Verzinkungsblech *n*
sheet ga[u]ge Blechlehre *f*
sheet greasing machine Blecheinfettmaschine *f*
sheet heating furnace Paketwärmofen *m*; Sturzenwärmofen *m*
sheet metal Feinblech *n*
sheet metal container Blechbehälter *m*
sheet metal of commercial quality Handelsblech *n*
sheet metal of deep drawing quality Ziehblech *n*
sheet-metal stacking machine Blechstapler *m*
sheet metal suitable for drawing Ziehblech *n*
sheet of water Wasserfläche *f*
sheet pack Blechpaket *n*
sheet panel Blechtafel *f*

sheet piling Spundwand f; Stahlrammpfahl m
sheet [printing] Druckbogen m
sheet [rolling] mill Blechwalzwerk n (fein); Feinblech-Walzwerk n
sheets and plates Blech n (Oberbegriff)
sheet scrap Blechabfälle mpl; Blechschrott m
sheet straightening machine Blechrichtmaschine f
sheet suitable for press work Preßblech n
sheet sweep genaues Aufeinanderlegen n von Blechen (vor dem Glühen)
sheet with good bending properties Falzblech n
sheet wrench mark Knickstelle f im Blech
shelf Regal n
shell Becher m; Gehäuse n; Hohlgeschoß n; Hülse f; Kessel m; Mantel m; abplatzen
shell burner Mantelbrenner m
shelling Ausbrechen n von Teilchen (aus der Walzoberfläche)
shell mould Formmaske f
shell steel Granatenstahl m
shelly schalig
shelly spot Ausbruch m (Schienen)
sherardise sherardisieren; überziehen (mit Zink)
shielded arc welding Schutzgasschweißung f
shielded electrode umhüllte Elektrode f
shielding Abschirmung f
shift umstellen; verschieben
ship plate Schiffsblech n
shock Erschütterung f; Schlag m; Stoß m
shock proof erschütterungssicher
shock tempering Stoßanlassen n
shock wave forming Schockwellenumformung f
shooting and blasting Sprengarbeit f
shooting flame Stichflamme f

shop Halle f; Werkstatt f
shop assembly Werkstattzusammenbau m
shop committee Betriebsrat m
shop floor level Hüttenflur m
shop for steel structures Eisenbau-Werkstätte f
shop for structural engineering Eisenbau-Werkstätte f
shop manager Betriebsleiter m
shop morale Betriebsklima n
shop welding Werkstattschweißung f
Shore hardness Shorehärte f
Shore scleroscope hardness test Rücksprunghärteprüfung f
short Unterlänge f
shortage Knappheit f; Mangel m
short-brittle faulbrüchig
short-cut method abgekürztes Verfahren n
short distance conveying plant Nahförderanlage f
short end Abfallende n
short length Restlänge f; Unterlänge f
shortness Brüchigkeit f
short poured mould nichtausgefüllte Form f
short range order Nahordnung f
shorts Siebrückstand m
short-stroke drop hammer Kurzhubgesenkhammer m
shot Kies m; Schrot n; Schuß m; Strahlmittel n
shot blasting Strahlentzundern n; Strahlentzunderung f
shot peening Kugelstrahlen n; Stahlsandblasen n
shoulder Ansatz m; Bund n; Schulter f (Welle)
shouldered die Ansatzmatrize f
shoulder screw Paßschraube f
shove Schub m; Stoß m; schieben
shovel Schaufel f; schaufeln
shredded scrap Shredder-Schrott m
shredding plant Schredderanlage f
shrink schrumpfen; schwinden; zusammenziehen
shrinkage Schrumpfung f; Schwund m

shrinkage cavity Lunker *m*; Schwindungshohlraum *m*
shrinkage crack Schrumpfriß *m*; Schwindungsriß *m*
shrinkage in height Höhenschwund *m*
shrinkage in length Längsschwund *m*
shrink away abheben
shrink bob verlorener Kopf *m*
shrink head Gießkopf *m*
shrink head casing Blockaufsatz *m*
shrink hole Lunker *m*; Schwindungshohlraum *m*
shrinking Lunkerbildung *f*
shrink on aufschrumpfen
shrink point Abhebepunkt *m* (Stranggießen)
shunt Nebenschluß *m*; rangieren; verschieben
shunting siding Rangieranlage *f*
shunt wound motor Nebenschlußmotor *m*
shut Überlappung *f*
shut down stillsetzen
shut-down time Rüstzeit *f* nach Arbeitsschluß
shut off absperren (Leitung); abstellen
shut-off valve Abschlußventil *n*
shutter Schieber *m*
shuttle valve Pendelklappe *f*
side blown converter seitlich blasender Konverter *m*
side cut shear Besäumschere *f*
side dumping truck Seitenkipper-Lastwagen *m*
side guard seitliche Führung *f*
side guards manipulator Kant- und Verschiebevorrichtung *f*
side guide Zentriervorrichtung *f*
side milling cutter Scheibenfräser *m*
siderite Spateisenstein *m*
side shearing Beschneiden *n* von Kanten (Band)
side thrust Seitendruck *m*
side view Seitenansicht *f*; Seitenriß *m* (Zeichnung)
side walls Seitenwände *fpl* (E-Ofen)
siding Ausweichplatz *m*; Nebengleise *npl*; Weiche *f*

sieve Sieb *n*; absieben
sieve analysis Siebanalyse *f*
sieve bottom Siebboden *m*
sift absiebßen; sichten; sieben
sifting Sieben *n*
sight hole Schauloch *n*
sigma phase embrittlement Sigma-Phasen-Versprödung *f*
signal Signal (EDV) *n*
signal flow plan Signalflußplan *m*
signaling equipment Nachrichtenanlage *f*
signal light Leuchtmelder *m*
signalling equipment Signalanlage *f*
signal processing Signalverarbeitung *f*
significance Bedeutung *f*; Sicherheit *f*; Signifikanz *f*; statistische Sicherung *f*
significance level Sicherheitsschwelle *f*; Signifikanzschwelle *f*
significance of means statistische Sicherung *f* von Mittelwerten
significance test Prüfung *f* der statistischen Sicherung
significant aufschlußreich; bedeutungsvoll; bezeichnend; gesichert; wesentlich
significant difference statistisch gesicherter Unterschied *m*
significant digit gesicherte Dezimalstelle *f*
silencer Schalldämpfer *m*
silica Kieselsäure *f*; Siliciumdioxid *n* (SiO_2)
silica brick Dinasstein *m*; Silicastein *m*
silica sand Quarzsand *m*
silicate Silikat *n*
silicate area Sandstelle *f*
siliceous ore kieseliges Erz *n*
silicic acid Kieselsäure *f*
silico-manganese Mangan-Silicium *n*
silico-manganese steel Mangan-Silicium-Stahl *m*
silicon Silicium *n*
silicon carbide brick Siliciumcarbidstein *m*
siliconise silicieren

silicon steel Siliciumstahl m
silicon steel sheet Elektroblech n
silico phosphate Silicophosphat n
silicosis Silikose f
silky fracture seidiger Bruch m
sillimanite brick Sillimanitstein m
silo Bunker m; Silo m
silt up verschlammen
silver Silber n
silver steel Silberstahl m
simple einfach
simplification Vereinfachung f
simulation Nachbildung f; Simulation f
simulation model Simulationsmodell n
simulation test Modellversuch m
simulator Analogiemodell n
simultaneous gleichzeitig
single action pressing einseitiges Pressen n
single bending Einfachbiegen n
single block Einzelblock m
single cropping Einfachabschneiden n
single crystal Einkristall m
single [crystal] particle Primärteilchen n
single cylinder steam engine Einzylinder-Dampfmaschine f
single disc cartridge Einzelplattenkassette f (für Datenspeicherung)
single drive Einzelantrieb m
single fillet weld Kehlnaht f
single groove plug mill Einkaliber-Stopfenwalzwerk n
single hardening Einfachhärten n
single hole nozzle Einlochdüse f
single-layer enamelling Einschichtemaillieren n
single on-hand quantity Einzelbestand m (im Lager)
single or double shear lap joint Einzel- oder Doppelüberlappverbindung f
single or multiple spot welding specimen Einzel- oder Mehrpunktschweißprobe f
single pass welding Einlagenschweißung f

single press technique Einfachpreßtechnik f
single-purpose machine-tool Einzweckmaschine f
single slag process Einschlackenverfahren n
single stack furnace Ein-Stapel-Ofen m
single-stage einstufig
single strand Einstrangbetrieb m
single strand casting machine Einstrang-Gießmaschine f
single strand continuous furnace Einstrang-Durchlaufofen m
single strand process Einstrangverfahren n
single-tailed test Prüfen n nach einem Ausläufer der Prüfverteilung
single test Einzelversuch m
single torsion test Verwindeversuch m
single way furnace Einwegofen m
single weight Stückgewicht n
sink abteufen; senken; ziehen
sinkhead Gießaufsatz m; Gießkopf m; verlorener Kopf m
sinkhead mould Massekopfkokille f
sink hole Lunker m; Senkloch n
sink in eintauchen
sinking Hohl-Gleitziehen n; Hohlzug m (Rohr)
sinking mill Reduzierwalzwerk n
sinking speed Sinkgeschwindigkeit f
sinter sintern; stückigmachen
sinter cake Sinterkuchen m
sinter density Sinterdichte f
sintered bronze Sinterbronze f
sintered carbide alloy Hartmetall n; Hartmetall-Legierung f
sintered compact Sinterformteil n
sintered hard metal Sinterhartmetall n
sintered iron Sintereisen n
sintered magnesite Schmelzmagnesit m; Sintermagnesit n
sintered metal Sintermetall n
sintered metal-metaloid-material Metall-Metalloid-Sinterwerkstoff m
sintered part Sinterteil n
sintered steel Sinterstahl m

sintering Aufschmelzen *n*
sintering and infiltration technique Sintertränktechnik *f*
sintering belt Sinterband *n*
sintering box Sinterkasten *m*
sintering furnace Sinterofen *m*
sintering grate Verblaserost *m*
sintering pallet Sinterpfanne *f*
sintering pan Sinterpfanne *f*
sintering plant Sinteranlage *f*
sintering point Erweichungspunkt *m*
sintering press Sinterpresse *f*
sintering strand Sinterband *n*
sintering under pressure Drucksintern *n*
sintering with a liquid phase Sinterung *f* mit flüssiger Phase
sinter magnet material Sintermagnetwerkstoff *m*
sinter material Sinterwerkstoff *m*
siphon tap Selbstabstich *m*
site Standort *m*
site welding Baustellenschweißung *f*
situation Lage *f*
six phase arc furnace Sechsphasen-Lichtbogenofen *m*
six strand continuous casting machine Sechsstrang-Gießmaschine *f*
size Abmessung *f*; Größe *f*; Maschenweite *f* (Sieb); Maß *n*; Umfang *m*; kalibrieren; klassieren; maßprägen
size distribution Größenverteilung *f*; Kornband *n*
size factor Größenfaktor *m*
size grading Kornzusammensetzung *f*
size sample Größenprobe *f*
size variation Maßabweichung *f*
sizing Bemessung *f*; Kalibrieren *n*; Maßprägen *n*
sizing jigging screen Klassierrüttelsieb *n*
sizing mill Kalibrierwalzwerk *n*
sizing of ores Klassieren *n* der Erze
sizing [rolling] mill Maßwalzwerk *n*
sizing rolls Maßwalzwerk *n*
sizing screen Klassiersieb *n*
sizing stand Nachwalzgerüst *n*
skelp Röhrenstreifen *m*

skelp [rolling] mill Röhrenstreifen-Walzwerk *n*
skelp roughing mill Rohrstreifen-Vorwalzwerk *n*
sketch plate Skizzenblech *n*
skew Wölbstein *m*; schiefwinklig
skew back Widerlager *n*
skewback channel Widerlagerbalken *m*; Widerlagerstütze *f*
skewed abgeschrägt; schief
skewness Schiefe *f*; Schräge *f*
skew roller table Schrägrollgang *m*
skew-rolling mill Schrägwalzwerk *n*
skew rolling of shapes Profil-Schrägwalzen *n*
skew rolling of solid sections Profil-Schrägwalzen *n* von Vollkörpern
skew rolling of tubular shapes Profil-Schrägwalzen *n* von Hohlkörpern
skid Förderkasten *m*; Ladegestell *n*; Querschlepper *m*; Schlepper *m*
skid mark Kühlschatten *m*
skid pipe Gleitrohr *n*
skid [rail] Gleitschiene *f*
skid transfer Schlepper *m* (Walzen)
skilled worker Facharbeiter *m*
skilled workman Facharbeiter *m*
skim abstreichen; säubern
skimmer Fuchs *m*; Siphon *m*
skimmer rod Krammstock *m*
skin Glätten *n*; Randschicht *f*; Walzhaut *f*
skin decarburisation Randentkohlung *f*
skin friction Wandreibung *f*
skin hardness Oberflächenhärte *f*
skin holes Oberflächenporen *fpl*
skin passing Glätten *n* (von Feinblech)
skin pass mill Dressierwalzwerk *n*
skin pass mill stand Nachwalzgerüst *n*
skin pass roll Dressierwalze *f*
skin pass rolling Dressieren *n*; Kaltnachwalzen *n*; Nachwalzen *n*; oberflächliches Walzen *n* mit geringem Druck
skip Förderkorb *m*; Förderkübel *m*; Gichtkübel *m*

skip bridge Gichtbrücke f (Hochofen)
skip car Kippkübel m; Kübelwagen m
skip filling Kippkübel-Begichtung f
skip hoist Laufkatze f
skip incline Schrägaufzug m (Gichtkübel)
skull Bär m; Pfannenbär m
skull cracker Fallwerk n (Schrottzerkleinerung); Schlagwerk n (Schrottzerkleinerung)
slab Bramme f, flachwalzen
slab billet Flachknüppel m
slabbing mill Brammenwalzwerk n
slabbing pass Brammenkaliber n
slab cogging mill Brammenwalzwerk n
slab ingot Brammenblock m; Rohbramme f
slab shears Brammenschere f
slab turning device Brammendrehvorrichtung f
slab turn-over device Brammenwendevorrichtung f
slack Durchhang m
slag verschlacken
slag bed Schlackenbett n
slag blanket Schlackendecke f
slag brick Schlackenstein m
slag brick press Schlackensteinpresse f
slag carry-over Schlackemitlaufen n
slag chamber Schlackenkammer f
slag clouds Trübe f
slag concrete Schlackenbeton m
slag control Schlackenführung f
slag dam Schlackendamm m (in der Pfanne)
slag dump Schlackenhalde f, Schlackenkippe f
slag dumping car Schlackenkipppfanne f
slag forming addition Schlackenbildner m
slagging Schlacke f abziehen
slagging practice Schlackenführung f
slag granulation Schlackengranulierung f; Schlackenkörnung f
slag gravel Schlackensplitt m

slag grinding plant Schlackenmühle f
slaggy patch Schlackenstelle f
slag hole Schlackenabstichloch n; Schlackenloch n
slag inclusion Schlackeneinschluß m
slag ladle Schlackenpfanne f
slag ladle car Schlackenpfannenwagen m; Schlackenwagen m
slag lime Hüttenkalk m
slag line Schlackenlinie f; Schlackenspiegel m; Schlackenstand m
slag notch Schlackenabstichloch n; Schlackenform f; Schlackenloch n
slag off abschlacken
slag overflow Schlackenüberlauf m
slag patch Schlackenfleck m
slag pocket Schlackenkammer f; Schlackentasche f
slag Portland cement Eisenportlandzement m
slag pot Schlackenpfanne f
slag ratio Basizitätsgrad m; Basizitätsverhältnis n; Schlackenzahl f
slag reduction plant Schlackenaufbereitungsanlage f
slag resistance Schlackenbeständigkeit f
slag runner Schlackenrinne f
slag sample Schlackenprobe f
slag sand Schlackensand m
slag separator Schlackenabscheider m
slag skimmer Schlackenfang m; Schlackenfuchs m
slag specimen Schlackenprobe f
slag spout Schlackenrinne f
slag test Schlackenprobe f
slag tip Schlackenhalde f; Schlackenkippe f
slag tuyre Schlackenform f
slag wool Hüttenwolle f; Schlackenwolle f
slake ablöschen (Kalk); löschen (Kalk); zerfallen
slaked lime gelöschter Kalk m
slaking Löschen n (Kalk)
slaking slag Zerfallschlacke f
slant rolling mill Schrägwalzwerk n

slate Schiefer m
slaty fracture Schieferbruch m
sleavers Walzsplitter mpl
sleeper Schwelle f
sleeve Walzring m; Wickelhülse f
sleeve back-up roll Mantelstützwalze f
sleeve bearing Gleitlager n; geschlossenes Gleitlager n
sleeve brick Stopfenstangenrohr n; Trichterrohr n
sleeve coupling Muffenkupplung f
slenderness ratio Schlankheitsgrad m
slewing crane Drehkran m
slicing lathe Abstechdrehbank f
slick Schlich m
slide Gleitbahn f; Gleitfläche f; Schlitten m; gleiten; rutschen; schieben; schleifen
slide bearing geschlossenes Gleitlager n
slide gate Schieber m
slide gate nozzle Schieberverschluß m
slide (microscope) Deckglas n
slide-rute Rechenschieber m
slide valve Absperrschieber m; Schieber m
slideways Verstellweg m
sliding agent Gleitmittel n
sliding coupling Schiebekupplung f
sliding cutting lathe Leitspindel-Drehbank f
sliding feather key Gleitfeder f
sliding frame Schlitten m
sliding frame hot saw Schlittensäge f
sliding friction Gleitreibung f
sliding hot saw Warmstahl-Schlittenschere f
sliding plane Gleitebene f
sliding shoe Gleitschuh m
sliding weight Laufgewicht n
slime Trübe f
slinger Schleudermaschine f
slip Schlupf m; Stürzen n (Hochofen); gleiten; rutschen; schieben; schlüpfen
slip band Gleitlinienstreifen m

slip blackening Formschwärze f
slip casting Schlickergießen n
slip clutch Schlupfkupplung f
slip forward voreilen
slip joint Schrumpfverbindung f
slip line Gleitlinie f
slip line theory Gleitlinientheorie f
slip[ping] Stürzen n der Gicht
slipping clutch Rutschkupplung f
slip system Gleitsystem n
slip-type drawing Gleitziehen n
slit Schlitz m; Spalte f
slit strip Spaltband n
slitter Spaltschere f
slitting Längsschneiden n; Längsteilen n; Spalten n (von Band)
slitting shears Längsteilschere f
sliver Schale f (Oberflächenfehler); Splitter m; Walzzunge f; Zunge f; Zunge f (Bandfehler)
slope Gefälle n; Neigung f; Steigung f
slope angle Neigungswinkel m (Spanen)
sloping back wall Schrägrückwand f (Siemens-Martin-Ofen)
sloping flange geneigter Flansch m
sloping loop channel Schlingenkanal m; Tieflauf m
slop ingot durch Nachgießen in den Lunker ausgefüllter Block m
slopping Auswurf m
slot nuten
slot and groove Feder und Nut f
slot cover Schlitzabdeckung f
slotted head screw Schlitzschraube f
slotted section Selbstbauprofil n
slotting cutter Lochfräser m
slotting machine Stoßmaschine f
slot welding Schlitznahtschweiße f
slow acting bath Langzeitbad n
slow cooling Langsamkühlung f
slow down abbremsen
sludge Bodenkörper m; Schlamm m
sludge activation Schlammbelebung f
sludge dewatering Schlammentwässerung f
sludge digestion Schlammfaulung f
sludge drying Schlammtrocknung f

sludge pump Dickstoffpumpe f; Schlammpumpe f
sludge utilisation Schlammverwertung f
slug Metallklumpen m; Putzen n; Rohling m
sluggish träge
sluggish in reaction reaktionsträge
slug test Stauchversuch m
sluice Schleuse f
slurry Aufschlämmung f; Schlamm m; Schlicker m (Pulvermet.)
slurry pump Dickstoffpumpe f
slush casting Hohlguß m
slushed eingeölt
slush pump Dickstoffpumpe f
small angle grain boundary Kleinwinkelkorngrenze f
small coke kleinstückiger Koks m
small end up (S.E.U.) mould Kokille f mit dem dünnen Ende oben
small grained feinkörnig
small iron ware Kleineisenzeug n
small section mill Feinstraße f
small section rolling mill Feinstahl-Walzwerk n; Stabstahlwalzwerk n
small sections Feineisen n
smear bestreichen; schmieren
smelt schmelzen; verhütten
smelt down einschmelzen
smelting Verhütten n
smelting down Einschmelzen n
smelting reduction Schmelzreduktion f
smelting section Reduktionszone f
smith Schmied m
smith hammer forging Freiform-Schmiedestück n
smog Smog m
smoke Qualm m; Rauch m
smokeless rauchlos
smoke meter Rauchdichtemesser m
smoke plume Rauchfahne f
smoke streamer Rauchfahne f
smooth Glattprägen n; glätten
smoothing rolls Glättwalzwerk n
smoothing trowel Spachtel m
smooth roll Glattwalze f

smooth rolling of tubular shapes Profilglattwalzen n von Hohlkörpern
smoulder schwelen
snag putzen (Gußstücke)
snaker Biegegesenk n; Vorkröpfgesenk n
snaky edge Glührand m (Bandfehler)
snap riveting set Nietstempel m
snarl test Schleifenprobe f; Schlingenprobe f (Draht)
SN curve Wöhlerlinie f
soak ausgleichen
soaking chamber Ausgleichsherd m; Schweißherd m
soaking hearth Ausgleichsherd m; Schweißherd m
soaking pit Ausgleichsgrube f; Tiefofen m
soaking-pit cover carriage Deckelwagen m
soaking pit crane Tiefofenkran m
soaking time Haltedauer f
soaking zone Ausgleichszone f
soap balls Seifenknoten mpl (Drahtziehen)
soap drawn wire seifegezogener Draht m
soaping out Ausfällen n (Drahtziehen)
soap stone Speckstein m
social charges soziale Lasten fpl
social net return Sozialertrag m; Sozialprodukt n
socket Muffe f; Stutzen m
socket pipe Muffenrohr n
soda Soda m
sodium sulphate Natriumsulfat n
soft annealed weichgeglüht
soft annealing Weichglühen n
soft center steel sheet Dreilagenstahlblech n
soft drawn wire Draht m mit geringer Querschnittsabnahme gezogen
soften erweichen
softened water enthärtetes Wasser n
softener Enthärtungsanlage f
softening Weichmachen n
softening point Erweichungspunkt m; Schmelzpunkt m

softening under load (refractory bricks) Druckerweichung *f* (ff. Steine)
soft fired schwach gebrannt
soft free-cutting steel Automatenweichstahl *m*; Schnellautomaten-Weichstahl *m*
soft free-machining steel Automatenweichstahl *m*; Schnellautomaten-Weichstahl *m*
soft iron Weicheisen *n*
soft magnetic sintered material weichmagnetischer metallischer Sinterwerkstoff *m*
soft magnetic steel weichmagnetischer Stahl *m*
soft mill Feinblech-Vorwalzgerüst *n* mit ungehärteten Gußwalzen
soft ore weiches Erz *n*
soft skin Weichhaut *f*
soft solder Weichlot *n*
soft steel weicher Stahl *m*
software Programmausrüstung *f* (Computer)
software documentation Programmdokumentation *f*
soil corrosion test Bodenkorrosionsversuch *m*
solder Lötmetall *n*; weichlöten
solder brittleness Lötbrüchigkeit *f*
soldered joint Lötstelle *f*
soldered seam Lötnaht *f*
soldering Löten *n*
soldering burner Lötbrenner *m*
soldering fluid Lötwasser *n*
soldering iron Lötkolben *m*
soldering tin Lötzinn *n*
sole flue Sohlkanal *m*
solenoid valve Magnetventil *n*
sole plate (permanent way) Dachschwelle *f* (Eisenbahnoberbau)
solid Festkörper *m*; Feststoff *m*; fest
solid angle Winkel *m*; räumlicher Winkel *m*
solid converter bottom Konverterboden *m*
solid drawn tube nahtlos gezogenes Rohr *n*

solid electrolyte cell EMK-Sonde *f*
solid extrusion Vollfließpressen *n*
solidification Erstarrung *f*
solidification range Erstarrungsbereich *m*
solidify erstarren
solidifying pig erstarrender Metallblock *m*
solid length Blocklänge *f*
solid matter Feststoff *m*
solid solubility Löslichkeit *f* im festen Zustand
solid solution Mischkristall *m*; feste Lösung *f*
solid solution hardening Mischkristallhärtung *f*; Mischkristallverfestigung *f*
solid solution segregation Mischkristallseigerung *f*
solid solution strengthening Mischkristallverfestigung *f*
solid stage feste Phase *f*
solid state fester Zustand *m*
solid-state body Festkörper *m*
solid state reduction Direktreduktion *f*
solid steel beruhigter Stahl *m*
solidus area Solidusfläche *f*
solidus line Soliduslinie *f*
solid wheel Vollrad *n*
solubility Löslichkeit *f*
soluble oil Bohröl *n*; Kühlöl *n*
soluble oil emulsion Bohrölwasser *n*
solution Lösung *f*
solution annealing Lösungsglühen *n*
solution entropy Lösungsentropie *f*
solution [heat] treatment Lösungsbehandlung *f*
solution heat treatment (precipitation hardening) Lösungsglühen *n*
solvent Lösemittel *n*; Lösungsmittel *n*
solvent capacity Lösungsfähigkeit *f*
solvent lattice Wirtgitter *n*
solvent power Auflösungsfähigkeit *f*; Lösungsfähigkeit *f*
sonic image method Schallsicht-Verfahren *n*
soot Ruß *m*
sooty rußhaltig

sorbite Sorbit *m*
sort auslesen; aussondern; sortieren
sorter Sortierer *m*
sorting belt Klaubband *n*; Leseband *n*
sorting conveyor Sortierförderanlage *f*
sorting out Aussonderung *f*
sorting out cylinder Sortierzylinder *m*
sound gesund; sondieren
sound absorbant screen Schalldämpferkulisse *f*
sound absorbing wall Schallschluckwand *f*
sound absorption Schalldämpfung *f*; Schallschlucken *n*
sound absorption in rooms Raumschalldämpfung *f*
sound analyser Einzelton-Analysator *m*
sound attenuation Schallminderung *f*
sound beam Schallbündel *n*
sound insulation Schalldämmung *f*
sound isolating enclosure Schallschutzhaube *f*
sound level meter Schallpegelmesser *m*
sound power level Schalleistungspegel *m*
sound pressure level Schalldruckpegel *m*
soundproofing Geräuschdämpfung *f*
sound protecting window Schallschutzfenster *n*
sound radiation Schallabstrahlung *f*
sound ray Schallstrahl *m*
sound scattering Schallstreuung *f*
sound search untersuchen
sound test piece fehlerfreie Probe *f*
sound wave Schallwelle *f*
source Quelle *f*
source of air pollution Luftverunreiniger *m*
source of defect Fehlerquelle *f*
source of error Fehlerquelle *f*
source of ore Erzlager *n*
sow Ofensau *f*
space lattice Raumgitter *n*
spacers Zwischenblock *m*

spacer sheet Distanzblech *n*
spall abblättern; abplatzen; abspalten
spall fracture Splitterbruch *m*
spalling Abblättern *n* (Schienen); Absplittern *n*; Splittern *n*
spalling resistance Temperaturwechselbeständigkeit *f*
spalling test Prüfung *f* auf Abplatzverhalten; Spaltprobe *f*
span Spanne *f*; Spannweite *f*; Stützweite *f*
spangle pattern Zinkblumen *fpl*
spanner Schraubenschlüssel *m*
spare part Ersatzteil *n*
spare part for wheel Radersatzteil *n*
spare stand Ersatzgerüst *n*; Wechselgerüst *n*
spark erosion Elektroerosion *f*
spark gap Elektrodenabstand *m* (Spektralanalyse)
spark machining Elektroerosion *f*
sparry iron ore Spateisenstein *m*
spathic spatig
spathic iron Eisenspat *m*
spathic iron ore Spateisenstein *m*
spatial arrangement räumliche Anordnung *f* (Metallographie)
spatial kinematics Raumkinematik *f*
spatial mechanism Raumgetriebe *n*
spatter and slopping Auswurf *m*
spattered powder spratziges Pulver *n*
spattering Stahlspritzer *mpl*
spatula Spachtel *m*
special and alloy[ed] steel Sonderstahl *m* und legierter Stahl
special brick Sonderstein *m*
special cast iron Edelguß *m*
specialist Fachmann *m*
specials Sondererzeugnisse *npl*
special section tube Profilrohr *n*
special shape turned part Fassondrehteil *n*
special steel Edelstahl *m*; Sonderstahl *m*
special steel casting Edelstahlguß *m*
special steel section Spezialprofil *n*
specific bezogen
specific energy efficiency bezogener

Arbeitswirkungsgrad *m*
specific heat capacity spezifische Wärme *f*
specific inductive capacity Dielektrizitätskonstante *f*
specific weight spezifisches Gewicht *n*
specified depth of case hardening Einsatzhärtetiefe *f*; vereinbarte Einsatzhärtetiefe *f*
specified length fixe Länge *f*
specimen Probe *f*
specimen holder Objektträger *m* (Elektronenmikroskop); Spannkopf *m*
spectrochemical analysis spektrochemische Prüfung *f*
spectrographic analysis Spektralanalyse *f*
ectrography Spektrographie *f*
spectrometer Spektrometer *n*
spectrophotometry Spektralphotometrie *f*
spectroscopy Spektroskopie *f*
spectrum analysis Spektralanalyse *f*
specular iron ore Eisenglanz *m*
speed Drehzahl *f*; Geschwindigkeit *f*; Schnelligkeit *f*
speed characteristic Drehzahlverlauf *m*
speed drop Drehzahlabfall *m*
speed of light in vacuum Vakuum-Lichtgeschwindigkeit *f*
speed ratio Übersetzungsverhältnis *n*
spell Schichtzeit *f*
spelter Lötmetall *n*; Zink *n*
spent gas Abgas *n*
spent pickle liquor Beizablauge *f*
spent pickling solution Beizablauge *f*
sphere Kugel *f*
sphere of action Einwirkungsbereich *m* (Gas)
spherical powder kugeliges Pulver *n*
spheroidal kugelig
spheroidal graphite cast iron Gußeisen *n* mit Kugelgraphit; Kugelgraphit-Gußeisen *n*
spheroidal [graphite] cast iron sphärolithisches Gußeisen *n*

spheroidal graphite [iron] roll Walze *f* (Sphäroguß)
spheroidal powder rundliches Pulver *n*
spheroidise annealing Weichglühen *n*
spheroidised weichgeglüht
spheroidised carbide kugelförmiger Zementit *m*
spheroidising Glühen *n* auf kugeligen Zementit (GKZ); Kugelglühen *n*; Kugeligglühen *n*
spider Königstein *m*; Stern *m* (Rad)
spiegel iron Spiegeleisen *n*
spike Schienennagel *m*
spiked roll Stachelwalze *f*
spill Schale *f* (Oberflächenfehler); verschütten; verspritzen
spillage sand Haufensand *m*
spin drücken
spin casting Schleudergußverfahren *n*
spindle Antriebsspindel *f* (Walzen); Spindel *f*
spindle steel Spindelstahl *m*
spindle torque Spindeldrehmoment *n*
spin forming (tubes) Abstreckdrücken *n*
spinning Drücken *n*; Streckplanieren *n*
spinning of external flanges Drücken *n* von Außenborden
spinning of hollow items Drücken *n* von Hohlkörpern
spinning of inside beads Drücken *n* von Innenborden; Innenborden *n* durch Drücken
spinodal decomposition spinodaler Zerfall *m*
spin wave spectrum Spinwellenspektrum *n*
spiral cast spiralförmig steigend beim Aufwinden (Drahtring)
spiral drill Spiralbohrer *m*
spiral looper accumulator Aufwickler *m* mit spiralenförmiger Bandspeicherung
spiral [mould] Gießspirale *f*
spiral spring Spiralfeder *f*
spiral tooth bevel gear Kegelrad-Spiralverzahnung *f*

spiral welding Spiralschweißen n
spirit level Wasserwaage f
spittings Auswurf m
splash verspritzen
splash board Spritzblech n
splashes Stahlspritzer mpl
splash lubrication Tauchschmierung f
splice bar Lasche f
splicing Überlaschung f
spline[d] shaft Keilwelle f (aus dem Vollen herausgearbeitet)
splinter Span m; Splitt m; Splitter m; absplittern
split Längsriß m; brechen (von Emulsionen); spalten; springen
split away abplatzen
split chuck Spannpatrone f
split die geteilte Matrize f
split ends gespaltene Enden npl
split off abspalten; absplittern
split pin Splint m
splittering Zertropfen n
splitting Spaltung f
split tube Schlitzrohr n
spoiled casting Wrackguß m
sponge iron Eisenschwamm m
sponge iron made from lump ore Eisenschwamm m aus Stückerz
sponge iron pellet Eisenschwammpellet n
sponge powder Schwammpulver n
spongy surface brüchige Fläche f (Blockfehler)
spontaneous combustion Selbstentzündung f
spontaneous fracture Gewaltbruch m
spool aufspulen
spooler Spuler m
spoon Löffel m
spoon sample Schöpfprobe f
spoon test specimen Löffelprobe f
spot Charlier check stichprobenartige Überprüfung f
spot check stichprobenartige Überprüfung f
spot test Tüpfelprobe f
spot welder Punktschweißmaschine f
spot welding Punktschweißen n; Punktschweißung f
spot welding electrode holder Punktschweißzange f
spot welding machine Punktschweißmaschine f
spout Ausgußrinne f
spouted bed Sprudelbett n
spouted ladle Schnabelpfanne f
spray aluminising Spritzaluminieren n
spray coating Spritzüberzug m
spray cooling Rieselkühlung f; Sprühkühlung f
spray cooling tank Flächenberieselungskühler m
spray hardening Sprühhärten n
spraying gun Spritzpistole f
spraying machine Spritzmaschine f
spraying mixture Spritzmasse f
spray nozzle Spritzdüse f
spray roasting system Sprühröstverfahren n
spray scrubber Berieselungswäscher m
spray steelmaking Strahldüsenfrischverfahren n
spray test Sprühprobe f; Sprühversuch m
spray tower Berieselungsturm m
spray unit Spritzanlage f
spread Breitenänderung f; Breitung f; ausbreiten; breiten; streuen
spreader mark (surface defect) Rutschstelle f
spread fully contained vollkommen verhinderte Breitung f
spreading pass Breitungsstich m
spring Feder f; Sprung m; abstützen
spring-back resilience Rückfederung f
spring blade Federblatt n
spring factor (powder met.) Aufgehmaß n
spring housing Federführungshülse f
spring index Wickelverhältnis n (Feder)
spring leaf Federblatt n
spring-operated safety valve Feder-Sicherheitsventil n
spring plate Federblatt n

spring plate bend test Federblech-Biegeversuch *m*
spring pressure gauge Federdruckmesser *m*
spring ring closing machine Sprengring-Einwalzmaschine *f*
spring steel Federstahl *m*
spring steel wire Federstahldraht *m* ring-supported abgefedert
spring supported die Federmatrize *f*
spring suspension federnde Aufhängung *f*
spring testing machine Federprüfmaschine *f*
spring washer Federring *m*; Federscheibe *f* (screw)
spring wire Federdraht *m*
sprocket Kettenzahnrad *n*
sprue Eingußtrichter *m*; Gießtrichter *m*; Griff *m* (am Gesenkschmiedestück); Knochen *m* (Gießen)
sprue canal Speiserinne *f*
sprung abgefedert
sprung arch Gewölbebogen *m*; eingespanntes Gewölbe *n*
sprung roof Stützgewölbe *n*; abgestütztes Gewölbe *n*
sprung type roof Gewölbe *n* mit beweglichem Widerlager
spun iron pipe Schleudergußrohr *n*
spurious echo Störecho *n*
spur rack Zahnstange *f*
spurt Strahl *m*
spur wheel Stirnrad *n*
sputtering (electron microscope) Bedampfung *f*
squabbing roll Staffelwalze *f* (für Flachstahl)
square quadratisch
square [bar] steel Quadratstahl *m*; Vierkantstahl *m*
square edge equal angles Winkelstahl *m*; gleichschenkliger scharfkantiger Winkelstahl *m*
square head cap screw Vierkantschraube *f*
square ingot Vierkantblock *m*
square iron Vierkanteisen *n*

square root Quadratwurzel *f*
squares Vierkantstahl *m*
square thread Flachgewinde *n*
squaring shears Kopfschere *f*
squash load Traglast *f* nach der Fließtheorie
squatting test Erweichungsprobe *f*
squeeze durcharbeiten; kneten; quetschen
squeeze roll Abquetschrolle *f* (Bramme)
squirt Spritze *f*; ausspritzen; spritzen
stabilisation Stabilisieren *n*
stabilisation annealing Stabilglühen *n*
stabilising Stabilglühen *n*
stability Beständigkeit *f*; Haltbarkeit *f*; Standfestigkeit *f*; Standsicherheit *f*
stability of shape Formbeständigkeit *f*
stable beständig; stabil
stable equilibrium stabiles Gleichgewicht *n*
stack Hochofenschacht *m*; Kamin *m*; Schacht *m*; Stapel *m*; aufschichten; häufen; stapeln
stack batter Ausbauchung *f* (eines Ofenschachtes)
stack cooling plate Schachtkühlbalken *m* (Hochofen)
stack diameter Gichtdurchmesser *m*; Schachtdurchmesser *m*
stacker Stapelvorrichtung *f*; Stapler *m*
stack flue Fuchs *m*
stack gas Abgas *n*
stacking fault precipitation Stapelfehlerausscheidung *f*
stack kiln Röstofen *m*
stack lining Schachtmauerwerk *n*
stack of finished steel sheets Fertigstapel *m*
stack of sheets Blechpaket *n*
stack valve Kaminschieber *m*
staff department Personalbüro *n*
stage Objekttisch *m* (Mikroskop); Schmelzbühne *f*
staggered gestaffelt; versetzt angeordnet
staggered mill Zickzackduo *n*; Zickzackstraße *f*

staggered roll Staffelwalze f
staggered roll[ing] train gestaffelte Walzstraße f
staggered teeth milling cutter kreuzverzahnter Fräser m
staggered tooth pinion Kammrad n mit versetzten Zähnen
staggered weld Zickzacknahtschweiße f; Zickzackschweiße f
staging Gerüst n (Baugerüst)
stain Flecken m
stained sheet fleckiges Blech n
stainless nichtrostend; rostbeständig; rostfrei
stainless property Korrosionsbeständigkeit f
stainless steel chemisch beständiger Stahl m; nichtrostender Stahl m; rostfreier Stahl m
stalactite Zäpfchen n (ff. Stoffe)
stalactites Zapfen m
stalk like structure Stengelgefüge n
stamp Stempel m; stanzen
stamping Prägen n
stamping (characters into the surface of a workpiece) Einprägen n
stamping die Stanze f
stamping quality Preßgüte f
stampings Preßrohlinge mpl
stamping tool Prägestempel m; Stanzwerkzeug n
stamp mill Pochwerk n
stamp on aufstampfen
stamp shoe Pochschuh m
stamp stem Pochschuh m
stanchion steel Rungenstahl m
stand Gerüst n; aushalten; widerstehen
standard Maschinenständer m; Norm f, einheitlich
standard acceleration of free fall Normfallbeschleunigung f
standard beam Doppel-T-Träger m
standard costing Standardkostenrechnung f
standard deviation Standardabweichung f, mittlere Abweichung f
standard distribution Prüfverteilung f

standard error mittlerer Fehler m
standard free energy of reaction freie Standardreaktionsenthalpie f
standardisation Normung f, Vereinheitlichung f
standardised genormt; vereinheitlicht
standard length produced Herstellänge f
standard nozzle Normdüse f
standard orifice Normblende f
standard part Normteil n
standard production Soll-Leistung f
standard pyrometric cone Segerkegel m; Temperaturmeßkegel m
standard quality Standardgüte f
standard size Normgröße f
standard specification Normvorschrift f
standard specimen Normprobe f
standard square [brick] Normalstein m
standard steel Normstahl m
standard [structural] section Normalprofil n
standard [structural] shape Normalprofil n
standing time Standzeit f, Standzeit f (im Ofen)
stand of rolls Walzgerüst n
standpipe Standrohr n; Steigkanal m; Steigleitung f, Steigrohr n
stand ring Stützring m (Pfanne)
stands in tandem hintereinander angeordnete Walzgerüste npl
stand with 20 rolls Zwanzigwalzengerüst n
staple Öse f
start anfahren; anlassen
starting Ingangsetzen n
starting bar Anfahrstrang m; Kaltstrang m
starting material Ausgangswerkstoff m
starting moment Anlaufmoment n; Drehmoment n
starting section Anfangsquerschnitt m
start of casting Angießen n
start temperature of rolling Walzan-

fangstemperatur f
start-up graph Anfahrdiagramm n
start-up time Rüstzeit f bei Arbeitsbeginn
state Beschaffenheit f; Lage f; Zustand m; feststellen
state employment bureau Arbeitsamt n
statement [of accounts] Bilanz f; Rechnungsabschluß m
statement of compliance with the order Werksbescheinigung f
state of the atmosphere (at the workplace) Klima n (am Arbeitsplatz)
static bed Festbett n
static friction Haftreibung f
static load ruhende Belastung f
statics Statik f
static test Standversuch m
stationary feststehend; ortsfest
stationary test Standversuch m
statistic Kennzahl f; Parameter m; Stichprobenparameter m
statistical inference statistischer Rückschluß m
statistical interpretation Großzahlauswertung f
statistics Statistik f
statistics [data] Unterlagen fpl
statistic value Schätzwert m
staying Absteifung f
stay[ing] time Aufenthalt m; Liegezeit f; Standzeit f
stay[ing] time Verweilzeit f
stay wire Verankerungsdraht m
steady Gegenführung f; stetig
steady state condition stationärer Zustand m
steady state condition (automatic control) Beharrungszustand m
steam Dampf m; Wasserdampf m
steam atomising Dampfzerstäubung f
steam blowing engine Dampfkolbengebläse n
steam bluing Dampfanlassen n
steam boiler Dampfkessel m
steam boiler firing Dampfkesselfeuerung f

steam crane Dampfkran m
steam credit Dampfgutschrift f
steam drum Dampffaß n
steam engine Dampfmaschine f
steam fittings Dampfarmaturen fpl
steam generation plant Dampferzeugungsanlage f
steam hammer Dampfhammer m
steamjacket gas producer Dampfmantel-Gaserzeuger m
steam jet blower Dampfstrahlgebläse n
steam pipe Dampfrohr n
steam piston blowing engine Dampfkolbengebläse n
steam power station Dampf-Kraftwerk n
steam shovel Löffeldampfbagger m
steam test Dampfversuch m (Korrosion)
steam trap Kondenstopf m
steam turbine Dampfturbine f
stearate Stearat n
Steckel mill Steckel-Walzwerk n
steel Stahl m
steel advisory centre Stahlberatungsstelle f
steel arch Stahlbogen m
steel armoured conduit Stahlpanzerrohr n
steel ball Stahlkugel f
steel bars Stabstahl m
steel-base roll Walze f (Halbstahl)
steel beam Stahlträger m (gewalzt)
steel cased brick Stahlmantelstein m
steel casing Blechmantel m; Blechpanzer m
steel casting Stahlguß m (Erzeugnis)
steel casting foundry Stahlgießerei f
steel castings Stahlformguß m
steel castings having high impact strength at low temperature kaltzäher Stahlguß m
steel degassing Stahlentgasung f
steel die Gesenk n
steel drill Stahlbohrer m
steel fabricator Stahlbaufirma f

steel facing Auflöten *n* (von Stahlplättchen); Aufschweißen *n*; Stahlplättchen-Aufschweißen *n*
steel foil Stahlfolie *f*
steel for blanking or punching dies Schnittstahl *m*
steel for building construction Hochbaustahl *m*
steel for deep drawing Stahl *m* für Tiefziehzwecke
steel for electric resistance Widerstandslegierung *f*
steel for flame and induction hardening Stahl *m* für Flamm- und Induktionshärten
steel for fluting tool Riffelstahl *m*; Werkzeug-Hohlstahl *m*
steel for hardening and tempering Vergütungsstahl *m*
steel for high-pressure hydrogenation vessels druckwasserstoffbeständiger Stahl *m*
steel for mechanical engineering Maschinenbaustahl *m*
steel for nuclear power plant Stahl *m* für Kernenergie-Erzeugungsanlagen
steel for steel structural work Stahlbaustahl *m*
steel for structural steelwork Hochbaustahl *m*
steel for surface hardening Stahl *m* für Randschichthärten
steel for wagon construction Wagenbaustahl *m*
steel foundry moulding compound Stahlformmasse *f*
steel frame superstructure Stahlhochbau *m*
steel girder Eisenträger *m* (Baustahlträger)
steel grade Stahlklasse *f*; Stahlsorte *f*
steel grit or sand delivery pipe Zuführung *f* von Stahlkies oder Sand
steel having a high impact strength at low temperature kaltzäher Stahl *m*
steel having particular thermal expansion properties Stahl *m* mit besonderer Wärmeausdehnung
steel hoop Bandstahl *m*
steel hydraulic engineering Stahlwasserbau *m*
steel ingot Rohstahlblock *m*
steel jacket Blechmantel *m*; Panzer *m* (Hochofen)
steel link chain Stahlgelenkkette *f*
steel maker Stahlwerker *m*
steelmaking plant Stahlwerk *n*
steel man Eisenhüttenmann *m*
steel melting furnace Stahlschmelzofen *m*
steel melting shop Stahlwerk *n*
steel pipe Stahlrohr *n*
steel pit Grübchen *n* (Oberflächenfehler)
steel plate Stahlblech *n*
steel plate lining Panzer *m* (Hochofen)
steel pouring ladle car Stahlgießwagen *m*
steel powder Stahlpulver *n*
steel processing industry eisenverarbeitende Industrie *f*
steel refining ore Stahlwerks-Frischerz *n*
steel reinforcement Stahlbewehrung *f*
steel rod Stange *f*
steel sample Stahlprobe *f*
steel section Profil *n*
steels for cold upsetting and cold extrusion Kaltstauch- und Kaltfließpreßstähle *mpl*
steel shape Formstahl *m*
steel shapes Profilstahl *m*
steel sheet Stahlblech *n*
steel sheet casing Blechpanzer *m*
steel sheet piling Spundwandstahl *m*
steel shelf Stahlregal *n*
steel shell Blechpanzer *m*
steel shot Stahlkies *m*; Stahlsand *m*
steel sleeper Stahlschwelle *f*
steel spring Stahlfeder *f*
steel strip Stahlband *n*
steel structural engineering Stahlhochbau *m*
steel structural section Stahlbauprofil *n*

steel structural work Stahlbau m
steel structures Stahl[hoch]bau m
steel supply conditions Stahl-Eisen-Lieferbedingungen fpl
steel test specification Stahl-Eisen-Prüfblatt n
steel tie (am.) Stahlschwelle f
steel transfer car Stahlübergabewagen m
steel tube Stahlrohr n
steel user Stahlverbraucher m
steel users stahlverarbeitende Industrie f
steel window section Stahlfenster-Profil n
steel wire Stahldraht m
steel with a high degree of hardness at elevated temperatures warmharter Stahl m
steel with little segregation seigerungsarmer Stahl m
steel work's blower Stahlwerksgebläse n
steel work's blowing engine Stahlwerksgebläse n
steel works Stahlwerk n
steepening incentive Leistungslohn m
steer steuern
steerage Steuer n
steering Steuerung f
steering roll Steuerrolle f
stellite Stellit m
step Absatz m; Staffel f; Stufe f; absetzen; abstufen
step back welding Pilgerschritt-Schweiße f; Pilgerschrittschweiße f
step control Schrittregelung f
step-down test Stufendrehversuch m
step function response Übergangsfunktion f
stepped abgesetzt (Stempel)
stepped extrusion abgesetzte Verformung f
stepped hardening Härten n; Stufenhärten n
stepped roll Staffelwalze f; Stufenwalze f
stepped torsion test Stufendrehversuch m
step quenching gestuftes Abschrecken n
step response Sprungantwort f
steps Treppenleiter f
stereographic projection stereographische Projektion f
sterile taub; unhaltig (Bergbau)
stick kleben
sticker Blechpaket n; Kleber m; in der Kokille steckengebliebener Block m
sticker break Oberflächen-Aufreißung f (durch Zusammenkleben beim Walzen)
sticker mark Klebestelle f (Oberflächenfehler)
sticking Kleben n (dünner Bleche); Verklebung f
sticking in the guides (lamination) Festbrennen n auf den Führungen
sticking of dolomite during bottom fettling Ansintern n des bei Herdreparaturen aufgeworfenen Dolomits
sticky blast-furnace flue dust klebriger Gichtstaub
sticky sand Klebsand m
Stiefel-type disc piercer Stiefelsches Lochwalzwerk n; Stiefelsches Scheiben-Loch-Walzwerk n
stiffen absteifen
stiffening Absteifen n
stiffness Steifigkeit f
stiffener Längsträger m
stillage Huboffsatz m
stippling Stippenbildung f
stir rühren; schüren; stochen; umrühren
stirring Rühren n
stirring coil Rührspule f
stirring gear Rührgerät n
stirring hole Schürloch n
stirring test (corrosion) Rührversuch m
stitching wire Heftdraht m
stitch welding Heftschweiße f; Steppschweißen n
stock Material n; Möller m; Rohling m; Vorrat m; Walzgut n; lagern

stock bin Vorratsbehälter m
stock column Beschickungssäule f (Hochofen)
stock-control oriented materialflußorientiert
stocker Dampfkessel m
stockholder Aktionär m
stock [house] Lager n
stocking ground Lagerplatz m
stock level [indicator] Gichtsonde f; Teufenanzeiger m
stock line ga[u]ge Gichtsonde f; Möllersonde f; Teufenanzeiger m
stock line indicator Möllersonde f; Teufenanzeiger m
stock line recorder Gichtsonde f; Teufenanzeiger m; Möllersonde f
stock on-hand-quantity Materialbestand m
stock pile Lagerplatz m
stock plan Materialplan m
stock registration Bestandsführung f (EDV)
stock release Materialfreigabe f
stock requirement Materialbedarf m
stock size Lagergröße f
stock transfer Materialbewegung f
stock yard Lagerplatz m
stoichiometric number stöchiometrische Zahl f
stoichiometry Stöchiometrie f
stoke stochen
stoker Heizer m; Stocher m; Kohlenbeschickvorrichtung f
stool Schemel m; Unterlagplatte f; Stuhl m
stool for bottom casting Gespannplatte f
stopcock Absperrhahn m
stop anhalten; hemmen; stillsetzen
stop bath Unterbrecher m
stope filling Bergeversatz m
stop ingot durch Nachgießen in den Lunker ausgefüllter Block m
stoppage Betriebsunterbrechung f; Stillstand m; Störung f
stopper Keil m; Stopfen m
stopper bell Gichtglocke f

stopper ladle Stopfenpfanne f
stopper rod Stopfenstange f
stopper rod brick Stopfenstangenrohr n
stopper rod control Stopfenstangenverschluß m
stopper travel Stopfenweg m
stopping Halten n; Verstopfung f
storage Lagerung f
storage bunker Speicherbunker m; Vorratsbehälter m
storage capacity Speichervermögen n
storage pit Speichergrube f
storage tank Sammelbehälter m
storage yard Lagerplatz m
store Lager n; Speicher m; lagern; speichern
stored heat (Cowper) Speicherwärme f
store-keeping Lagerhaltung f
stores equipment Betriebslagereinrichtung f; Magazineinrichtung f
storing capacity Speicherfähigkeit f
stove Koksofen m; Ofen m
stove reversing gear selbsttätige Winderhitzer-Umsteuerung f
stoving Trocknen n durch Erwärmen
stowage Bergeversatz m
straddle carrier Portalhubwagen m
straight gerade; gewöhnlich; rein
straight as in the rolled condition walzgrade
straight bead welding Längsnahtschweißen n
straight blast-furnace gas unvermischtes Hochofengas n
straight cast gerade vom Ring m ablaufend
straight chained geradkettig (Moleküle)
straight coke oven gas ungemischtes Koksofengas n
straight cutting oil Schneidöl n
straighten ausrichten; geraderichten; richten; strecken
straightening by stretching Recken n von Flachstäben in der Halbzeugfertigung

straightening in patterned dies Prägerichten *n*
straightening machine Richtmaschine *f*
straightening plate Richtplatte *f*
straightening point Biegepunkt *m* (Stranggießen)
straightening press Richtpresse *f*
straightening roll Richtrolle *f*
straight flash welding Preßstumpfschweißen *n*
straight grate pellet Bandpellet *n*
straightline chart Nomogramm *n*
straight line drawing machine Geradeausziehmaschine *f*
straight line spot welding Reihenpunktschweißen *n*
straight manganese steel Manganhartstahl *m*
straight mineral oil Blankwalzöl *n*
straightness Geradheit *f*
straight tooth bevel gear Kegelrad-Geradverzahnung *f*
straight tooth bevels Geradverzahnung *f*
straight tubular rod extrusion Hohl-Vorwärts-Strangpressen *n*
strain Anforderung *f*; Anspannung *f*; Beanspruchung *f*; Dehnung *f* (s. a. Bruchdehnung); Verformung *f*; Verzerrung *f*; ansetzen (Bad); beanspruchen; dehnen; recken; verzerren
strain age hardening Reckaltern *n*
strain ag[e]ing Altern *n* nach Deformation; Reckaltern *n*; Reckalterung *f*
strained wire Streckdraht *m*
strainer Filter *m* (EDV)
strainer core Siebkern *m*
strain ga[u]ge Dehnungsmesser *m*; Dehnungsmeßstreifen *m*; Spannungsmesser *m*
strain harden kaltverfestigen; verfestigen
strain hardenability Kalthärtbarkeit *f*
strain hardened steel kaltverfestigter Stahl *m*

strain hardening Kalthärtung *f*; Kaltverfestigung *f*; Verfestigung *f* durch Kaltverformung
strain-induced martensite Verformungsmartensit *m*
strain line etching Kraftwirkungsfiguren-Ätzverfahren *n*
strain rate Verformungsgeschwindigkeit *f*
strand Ader *f*; Gießader *f*; Litze *f*; Strang *m*; flechten
stranded wire Litze *f*
stranding machine Verseilmaschine *f*
stranding wire Seildraht *m*
strand of rolls Walzenstrang *m*; Walzenstrecke *f*
strand roll Strangwalze *f*
strand seal Strangabdichtung *f*
strand shell Stranghaut *f*; Strangschale *f*
strand sintering Bandsintern *n*
strand sintering plant Bandsinteranlage *f*
strand wire Litzendraht *m*
strap joint assembly Laschenstoß *m*
stratification Schichtung *f*
stratum Schicht *f*; Schicht *f* (geol.)
stratum of air Luftschicht *f*
stray current Irrstrom *m*
stray field energy Streufeldenergie *f*
stray flux Streufluß *m*
strength Festigkeit *f*; Haltbarkeit *f*; Traglast *f*
strength at elevated temperatures Hochtemperaturfestigkeit *f*; Warmfestigkeit *f*
strength at high temperatures Hochtemperaturfestigkeit *f*; Warmfestigkeit *f*
strength characteristics Festigkeitseigenschaften *fpl*
strength depending on design Gestaltfestigkeit *f*
strength depending on shape Gestaltfestigkeit *f*
strengthen verfestigen; verstärken
strengthening Verfestigen *n*
strengthening by cold working Kaltverfestigung *f*

strengthening phase verfestigende Phase f (in Legierungen)
strength of sinter Sinterfestigkeit f
strength properties Festigkeitseigenschaften fpl
strength weld Festigkeitsschweiße f
stress Spannung f; Zug m
stress analysis Kräftebestimmung f
stress concentration factor Formzahl f
stress corrosion by molten zinc Lötbruch m (Feuerverzinken)
stress corrosion cracking Spannungsrißkorrosion f
stress corrosion test Spannungskorrosionsversuch m
stress crack Spannungsriß m
stress curve Belastungskurve f
stress cycle Wöhlerlinie f
stress diagram Belastungskurve f
stress field Spannungsfeld n
stress number curve Wöhlerlinie f
stress relaxation test Spannungsrelaxationsversuch m
stress relieve heat treatment Spannungsarmglühen n
stress relieving Entspannung f
stress relieving annealing Entspannungsglühen n
stress removal Entlastung f
stress rupture curve Zeitstandbruchlinie f
stress strain curve Fließkurve f
stress-strain curves Spannungs-Dehnungs-Schaubild n
stress-strain diagram Spannungs-Dehnungs-Schaubild n
stress strain relation Spannungs-Verzerrungs-Beziehung f
stress to produce a given creep in a given time Zeitdehngrenze f
stretch Dehnung f; Dehnung f (s. a. Bruchdehnung); recken; strecken
stretchability Abstreckbarkeit f
stretched steel Streckstahl m
stretched wire Streckdraht m
stretched zone Dehnungszone f
stretcher brick Läuferstein m (Kokerei)
stretcher leveller Richtmaschine f (Feinblech); Spannmaschine f; Streckmaschine f
stretcher levelling Streckrichten n
stretcher lines Fließfiguren fpl; Kraftwirkungsfiguren fpl
stretcher strains Kraftwirkungsfiguren fpl
stretch forming Formrecken n; Recken n; Streckformen n; Streckziehen n; Tiefen n
stretching Dehnen n
stretch levelling machine Streckrichtmaschine f
stretch reducing by roll drawing Nachziehen n
stretch reducing mill Streckreduzierwalzwerk n
stretch rolling Reckwalzen n
striation Schwingungsmarke f (Bruchfläche)
strickle moulding Schablonenformerei f
strickle moulding mixture Schabloniermasse f
striker Anschläger m (Kran)
striking the arc Lichtbogenzünden n
stringers Schilfer mpl
strip Band n; Streifen n; abstreifen (Kokillen oder Dorn); strippen
strip annealing furnace Bandstahl-Glühofen m
strip brake Bandbremse f
strip chart recorder Bandschreiber m
strip crown Bandwölbung f
strip cutting-off machine Bandabschneidmaschine f
strip flatness Ebenheit f des Bandes
strip mill Bandwalzwerk n
stripper [guide] Abstreifer m; Blockabstreifer m; Ausführhund m; Hund m (Abstreifmeißel)
stripper plate Abstreifplatte f
stripper pressure Niederhaltedruck m
stripping Abstreifen n
stripping bay Abstreifhalle f
stripping crane Abstreifkran m; Strip-

substitute material

perkran *m*
stripping plate Absteifmeißel *m*; Abstreifmeißel *m*
stripping test Tauchprobe *f* (für Metallüberzüge)
strip [rolling] mill Bandwalzwerk *n*; Streifenwalzwerk *n*
strip sabre Säbel *m* (Bandwalzen)
strip steel Bandstahl *m*
strip [steel] mill Bandstahlwalzwerk *n*; Bandwalzwerk *n*; Streifenwalzwerk *n*
strip stiffness Bandsteifigkeit *f*
strip straightening machine Bandrichtmaschine *f*
strip tension control Bandzugsteuerung *f*
strip thickness measuring device Banddicken-Meßgerät *n*
strip tinning Bandverzinnen *n*
strip winder Bandwickler *m*
stroke Hub *m*; Schlag *m*; Stich *m*; Stoß *m*
stroke arresting device Hubbegrenzer *m*
stroke length Hubhöhe *f*
strong gas heating Starkgasheizung *f*
structural difference Gefügeunterschied *m*
structural engineering workshop Eisenbahn-Werkstätte *f*
structural member Bauteil *n*
structural pipe Konstruktionsrohr *n*
structural shape Formstahl *m*
structural shapes Baustahl *m*; Profilstahl *m*
structural steel Baustahl *m*; Formstahl *m*; Profilstahl *m*
structural steel for reactors Reaktorbaustahl *m*
structural steel framework Stahlskelettbau *m*
structural steel plate Baublech *n*
structural [steel rolling] mill Formstahl-Walzwerk *n*; Profilstahl-Walzwerk *n*
structural steel work Stahlbau *m*
structural transformation Gefügeumwandlung *f*
structural tube Rohr *n* für Konstruktionszwecke
structure Aufbau *m*; Gefüge *n*; Struktur *f*
structure as tempered Anlaßgefüge *n*
structure rating chart Gefügerichtreihe *f*
strut abstützen; verstreben
stub column kurze Stützen *fpl*
stud Stift *m*; Stiftschraube *f*; Zapfen *m*
stud screw Stiftschraube *f*
stud welding Bolzenschweißung *f*
study group Arbeitsgemeinschaft *f*
stuffing Dichtung *f*; Dichtungsring *m*; Packung *f*
stuffing box Stopfbüchse *f*
subcontractor Unterlieferant *m*
subcritical annealing Rekristallisationsglühen *n*
subcutaneous blow hole Randblase *f*
subdivision Untergruppe *f*
subject Gegenstand *m*
subject to design certification bauartgenehmigungspflichtig
sublicense Unterlizenz *f*
sublimation Sublimieren *n*
submarine ladle Torpedopfanne *f*
submerged arc verdeckter Lichtbogen *m*
submerged arc welding Unter-Pulver-Schweißen *n* (UP-Schweißen); verdeckte Lichtbogenschweißung *f*
submerged pouring Metallzuführung *f* unter dem Gießspiegel; Tauchrohrgießen *n*
sub-sample Unterprobe *f*
subsequent charging Nachsetzen *n*
subsequent processing Weiterverarbeitung *f*
subset Teilmenge *f* (von Fähigkeiten)
subsidiary manufacturing company Betriebsgesellschaft *f*
sub-sieve powder Feinstpulver *n*; Siebdurchgang *m*
substitute gear Ersatzgetriebe *n*
substitute material Austauschwerkstoff *m*

substitute mechanism Ersatzgetriebe *n*
substitute steel Austauschstahl *m*
substitution Ersatz *m*
substitution solid solution Substitutionsmischkristall *m*
substrate Trägerwerkstoff *m*
sub-surface porosity Porosität *f* unter der Oberfläche
sub-system Teilsystem *n* (elektr.)
subterranean water Grundwasser *n*
subzero refrigeration Tiefkühlen *n*
sucking Kneifen *n*
sucking-off plant Absauganlage *f*
suck off absaugen
suction apparatus Absauggerät *n*
suction area Saugfläche *f* (Sinter)
suction basket Saugkopf *m*
suction hood Absaugehaube *f*; Saughaube *f*
suction line Ansaugleitung *f*
suction output Ansaugeleistung *f*
suction plant Absauganlage *f*
suction power Ansaugeleistung *f*
suction pyrometer Durchfluß-Thermoelement *n*
sufficient erschöpfend; hinreichend
suggestion Vorschlag *m*
suggestion scheme betriebliches Vorschlagswesen *n*
suggestion system betriebliches Vorschlagswesen *n*
sullage piece verlorener Kopf *m*
sull coat anlaufen lassen
sull coating Abbrausen *n* (Draht); Abspritzen *n*
sulphate Sulfat *n*
sulphide Sulfid *n*
sulphide scale efflorescence Schwefelpocken *fpl*
sulphite Sulfit *n*
sulphonitriding Sulfonitrieren *n*
sulphur Schwefel *m*
sulphur bearing schwefelhaltig
sulphuric acid Schwefelsäure *f*
sulphur pockmarks (corrosion) Schwefelpocken *fpl*
sulphur print Baumann-Abdruck *m*; Schwefelabdruck *m*
sulphur set Schwefelend *n*
sum total Fazit *n* (Schlüsselergebnis)
sunken hopper Tiefbunker *m*
supercarburisation Überkohlung *f*
supercharger Überverdichter *m*
superconducting transition temperature Sprungpunkt *m*; Sprungpunkttemperatur *f*
superconductivity Supraleitfähigkeit *f*; Supraleitung *f*
supercooling Unterkühlung *f*
supercritically annealed and quenched geglüht und gehärtet oberhalb des Umwandlungsbereiches *m*
superfines Feinstanteil *m*
superfinishing Feinstziehschleifen *n*
superheat Überhitzung *f*
superheater tube Überhitzerrohr *n*
superheating Überhitzung *f*
super high strength steel höchstfester Stahl *m*
superimposed überlagert
superintendent Abteilungsleiter *m*; Betriebschef *m*
superlattice Überstruktur *f*
superposition Überlagerung *f*
supersaturation Übersättigung *f*
supersonic test Ultraschallprüfung *f*
supervision Überwachung *f*
supervisor Aufsichtsbeamter *m*; Vorgesetzter *m*
supplementary firing Zusatzfeuerung *f*
supplementary reactor Drosselspule *f* (Lichtbogenofen)
supplementary reactor rating Drosselleistung *f* (Lichtbogenofen)
supplier Lieferwerk *n*
supply Lieferung *f*; Versorgung *f*; Vorrat *m*; Zufuhr *f*; liefern; versorgen
supply network system Stromversorgungsnetz *n*
supply system loading Netzbelastung *f*
supply transformer Einspeisetrafo *m*
supply voltage Speisespannung *f*
support Lager *n*; Stütze *f*; Unterstüt-

zung f; Widerlager n; lagern; unterlegen
support for slag ladle Tragkorb m für Schlackenpfanne
supporting bolt Tragbolzen m
supporting bracket Lagerbock m
supporting grid Tragrost m
supporting hoop for barrels Faßreifen-Bandstahl m
supporting roller Tragrolle f
support roll Stützrolle f (Strang)
suppressed combustion unterdrückte Verbrennung f
surface Fläche f; Oberfläche f
surface active agent oberflächenaktiver Stoff m
surface area Oberfläche f
surface bands Fließfiguren fpl (Bleche)
surface concentration Oberflächenkonzentration f
surface condition Oberflächenbeschaffenheit f
surface crack Oberflächenriß m
surface decarburisation Randentkohlung f
surface defect Oberflächenfehler m
surface digging Tagebau m
surface finish Oberflächenbeschaffenheit f
surface grinding Flachschleifen n; Planschleifen n
surface hardening Oberflächenhärten n
surface imperfection Oberflächenfehler m
surface layer Deckschicht f
surface layer hardening Randschichthärten n
surface-layer welding Auftragschweißung f
surface milling Flächenfräsen n
surface of fracture Bruchfläche f
surface of metal (in a mould) Gießspiegel m; Spiegel m
surface pressing Flächenpressung f
surface protective agent Oberflächenschutzmittel n

surface quality Oberflächenbeschaffenheit f; Oberflächenzustand m
surface replica Oberflächenabdruck m (Mikroskopie)
surface scratching test Ritzhärteprüfung f
surface tear Oberflächenriß m
surface tension Oberflächenspannung f
surface treatment Oberflächenbehandlung f; Oberflächenveredelung f
surface zone Randzone f
surfacing Auftragschweißung f; Flachprägen n
surfacing (am.) Hartauftragsschweißung f
surge Spannungsdurchschlag m (Lichtbogenofen)
surge hopper Ausgleichstrichter m
surge tank Druckausgleichbehälter m; Hochbehälter m; Überlaufbehälter m
surging lap Anhäufung f von Mattschweißen
surplus blast-furnace gas burner Gichtgasfackel f
surplus capacity Überkapazität f
surplus gas Überschußgas n
surplus gas burner Abgasfackel f; Fackel f (Abgas)
surplus length Überlänge f
surrounding conditions Umweltbedingungen fpl; Umweltverhältnisse npl
survey Rundfrage f; Stichprobenerhebung f; Umfrage f; Überwachung f
survey of the production plan Produktionsplanungsübersicht f
susceptibility Neigung f
susceptibility of welding seams to cracking Schweißnahtrissigkeit f
susceptibility (to) Anfälligkeit f (für); Empfindlichkeit f (gegen); Suszeptibilität f
susceptibility to ag[e]ing Alterungsempfindlichkeit f
susceptibility to grain coarsening Grobkornanfälligkeit f

susceptibility to hardening Härteempfindlichkeit f
susceptibility to trouble Störanfälligkeit f
susceptibility to welding fissures Schweißrissigkeit f
suspended arch Hängedecke f
suspended roof Hängedecke f
suspended roof for pusher-type furnace Stoßofen-Hängedecke f
suspended solid particle Schwebe-Feststoffteilchen n
suspended substance Schwebstoff m
suspended wall Hängewand f
suspension Aufhängung f
suspension of bricks Aufhängevorrichtung f für Steine
suspension rope Spannseil n
sustained deviation (am.) bleibende Regelabweichung f
swab anstreichen
swage Gesenk n; anspitzen; verjüngen; zusammenziehen
swage block Lochplatte f (Schmieden)
swaged and rolled high-purity steel im Gesenk geschmiedetes und gewalztes Reinsteisen n
swaged forging Gesenkschmiedestück n
swager Streckgesenk n; Streckwerkzeug n
swaging Gesenkschmieden n
swaging hammer Gesenkhammer m
swallowing capacity Schluckvermögen n
swallowing capacity of moulds Kokillenschluckvermögen n
swarf Drehspäne mpl; Span m
swarfiess spanlos
swarfless nichtspanabhebend
swash plate [tilting box] Taumelscheibe f
swealed surface verschmorte Oberfläche f
sweep Bogen m; Hohlung f (Walze); bestreichen
swell aufgehen; blähen; schwellen; treiben; wachsen
swelling Auffederung f (Draht); Schwellen n (Pellet)
swelling binder Quellbinder m
swelling index Blähgrad m (Koks)
swelling property Blähgrad m (Koks)
swift Abwickelgerüst n (z. B. für Drahtringe); Drehteller m
swill abspülen
swing Auslandung f; Ausschlag m; Kredithöhe f (bei Verrechnungsabkommen); schaukeln; schwingen
swing grinding machine Pendelschleifmaschine f
swinging launder Schaukelrinne f
swing roof arc furnace Lichtbogenofen m mit Schwenkdeckel
swing type arc furnace Lichtbogen-Schaukelofen m
swirl burner Drallbrenner m
swirl nozzle Wirbeldüse f
swirl promoter Drallrohr n
switch Einschalter m; Umschalter m; Weiche f; schalten
switch blade Weichenzunge f
switch board Schaltbrett n
switch cupboard Schaltschrank m; Verteilanlage f
switcher Weichensteller m
switch for cog-rail type Weiche f für Zahnradbahn
switch gear Schaltanlage f
switching period (motor) Einschaltdauer f
switch installation Schaltanlage f
switch lever Schalthebel m
switch man Weichensteller m
switch panel Schaltbrett n
swivel-joint Drehgelenk n
swivelling drehbar; schwenkbar
swivelling cover Schwenkdeckel m
swivelling launder Schwenkrinne f
swivelling vessel Schwenkkonverter m
symmetrisation Symmetrierung f
synchronism Gleichlauf m
synthetic resin bearing Kunstharzlager n
syphon Fuchs m

system-controlled netzgeführt
system of coordinates Liniennetz n
system of ore dressing Aufbereitungsstammbaum m
system of time allowance Zeitvorgabe f (beim Akkord)
system of time allowing Zeitvorgabe f (beim Akkord)
system used in calculating price extras on basic price list Anhängerverfahren n

T

table Liste f; Tabelle f; Tafel f; Tisch m; Verzeichnis n; Zahlentafel f
tabulator Tabelliermaschine f
tab washer Sicherungsblech n (Schraube)
tack Drahtstift m; Nagel m; heften
tackle Flaschenzug m; Haspel f
tack weld Heftschweiße f
tacky slag klebrige Schlacke f
tag Anhängeschild n; angeln (= mit Schwanzende versehen)
tagged atoms Spurenelemente npl
tail Ausläufer m
tail end Schwanz m; hinteres Ende n
tail end of strip Bandende n
tailings Berge mpl; Erzabfälle mpl; Gangart f, Rückstände mpl
tailoring Abrundung f
tails Schlamm m (Erzaufbereitung)
take off abheben; abnehmen; ausbauen (Walzen)
tallow Schmiere f, Talg m; Unschlitt m
tamp stampfen
tamp down aufstampfen
tamped bottom gestampfter Boden m
tamping clay Stampfmasse f
tamping dolomite Stampfdolomit m
tandem arc Tandembogen m
tandem mill Tandemwalzwerk n
tangential point Biegepunkt m (Stranggießen)
tangential test Tangentialprobe f

tank Behälter m; Bottich m; Schleifenspeicher m (EDV)
tank and container sheet Tank- und Behälterblech n
tank truck Tankwagen m
tantalum Tantal n
tap Abgriff m; Abstich m; Anzapfung f (EDV); Gewindebohrer m; Gewindeschneider m; Guß m; ablassen; abstechen; abziehen (Schlacke); schneiden (Gewinde)
tap bar Stichlochstopfstange f
tap changer Lastschalter m (Lichtbogenofen)
tap density Klopfdichte f
tape Band n; Bandmaß n; umwickeln
tape perforator Streifenlocher m
taper Anzug m (Kaliber); Konizität f; Konus m; Schräge f; verjüngen
tape reader Lochstreifenleser m
tape recorder Magnetbandspeicher m
tapered roller bearing Kegelrollenlager n
tapered section entering the rolls Walzkeil m
tapering of the cross section Querschnittsverjüngung f
taper of a groove Kaliberanzug m
taper pin Kegelstift m
tape to card converter streifengesteuerter Kartenlocher m
taphole Abstichloch n; Hut m (LD-Verfahren); Stichloch n
taphole gun Stichlochstopfmaschine f
taping machine Bandwickler m
tapping Abstechen n; Gewindebohren n; Innengewindeschneiden n; kurzes Nachrichten n
tapping machine Innengewinde-Schneidmaschine f
tapping rod Stopfenstange f
tapping screw Blechschraube f
tapping spout Abstichrinne f
tap slag abschlacken
tap-to-tap time Abstich-zu-Abstich-Zeit f
tap-to-tap times Schmelzenfolgezeiten fpl

tap volume Klopfvolumen *n*
tar Teer *m*
tar-bonded teergebunden
tar-bonded magnesite Teermagnesit *m*
tar dolomite brick Teerdolomitstein *m*
tar for steel making purposes Stahlwerksteer *m*
target Planziel *n*; Soll *n*; Ziel *n*
target tube Röntgenröhre *f*
tarif agreement Tarifabkommen *n*
tar-impregnated teergetaucht
tar macadam plant Schotter-Teerungsanlage *f*
tarnish anlaufen; beschlagen; mattieren
tar processing plant Teerverarbeitungsanlage *f*
task Kernprogramm *n*
task-work performance Akkordleistung *f*
tax Abgabe *f*; Steuer *f*
teaching workshop Lehrwerkstatt *f*
team Arbeitsgruppe *f*; Mannschaft *f*
team work Gruppenarbeit *f*
tear Zerreißung *f*; zerreißen
tearing Rißbildung *f*
tearing chip Reißspan *m*
tearing in Einreißen *n*
tearing strength Zerreißfestigkeit *f*
technical breakdown technische Störung *f*
technical fair technische Messe *f*
technical literature Fachliteratur *f*
technical pure iron Reineisen *n*
technical school for engineers Ingenieurschule *f*
techniques Technik *f*
technological test technologische Prüfung *f*
technology Technologie *f*
tee-bar T-Träger *m*
tee head bolt Hammerschraube *f*
teem abgießen; abstechen; gießen; vergießen
teem direct fallend [ver]gießen; gießen
teem down-hill fallend [ver]gießen

teeming Abguß *m*; Vergießen *n*
teeming arrest (surface defect) Absatz *m*
teeming ladle Gießpfanne *f*
teeming lap Mattschweiße *f* (Blockfehler)
teeming platform Gießbühne *f*
teeming rate Gießgeschwindigkeit *f*
teem off abgießen
telecommunication system Fernmeldeanlage *f*
telemeter Fernmeßgerät *n*
telemetering Fernmessung *f*
teleprinter Fernschreiber *m*
tele-transmission of measured values Fernübertragung *f* von Meßgrößen
teletransmitter Ferngeber *m*
television transmission Fernsehübertragung *f*
telewriter Fernschreiber *m*
telpher line Drahtseilbahn *f* (elektr.); Elektrohängebahn *f*; Hängebahn *f*
temper anfeuchten (Steine); anlassen; prozentuale Längenzunahme *f* (eines Bleches beim Kaltwalzen); tempern
temper air line Kaltwindzusatzleitung *f*
temperature Temperatur *f*
temperature control apparatus Temperaturregler *m*
temperature-controlled hot forming temperaturgeregelte Warmumformung *f*
temperature-cooling period-structure diagram Temperatur-Abkühlungsdauer-Gefügeschaubild *n*
temperature gradient Temperaturgradient *m*; Temperaturverlauf *m*; Wärmegefälle *n*
temperature loss Temperaturverlust *m*
temperature measuring instrument Temperaturmeßgerät *n*
temperature of quench Ablöschtemperatur *f*
temperature-reduction-marginal coordinates [system] Temperatur-

Abbau-Randkoordinaten [-System] *n*
temperature rise Temperaturanstieg *m*
temperature stability Temperaturbeständigkeit *f*
temperature stress Wärmespannung *f*
temper brittleness Anlaßprödigkeit *f*
temper carbon Temperkohle *f*
temper colour Anlaßfarbe *f*; Glühfarbe *f*
tempered vergütet
tempered hardness Anlaßhärte *f*
temper etch Anlaßätzung *f*
tempering furnace Anlaßofen *m*
tempering steel Vergütungsstahl *m*
tempering temperature Anlaßtemperatur *f*
tempering time Anlaßdauer *f*
temper mill Kaltnachwalzwerk *n*
temper [pass] mill Dressierwalzwerk *n*
temper [pass] rolling Dressieren *n*; oberflächliches Walzen *n* mit geringem Druck
temper [pass] rolling mill Dressierwalzwerk *n*; Kaltnachwalzwerk *n*
temper rolling Nachwalzen *n*
template Lehre *f*; Schablone *f*; Stichmaß *n*
template moulding Schablonenformerei *f*
tenacity Festigkeit *f*; Zähigkeit *f*
tendency Neigung *f* (Tendenz)
tendency to cracking Rißneigung *f*
tendency to edge corner Kantenrissigkeit *f*
tender Angebot *n*
tensile properties Festigkeitseigenschaften *fpl*
tensile reforming Zugumformen *n*
tensile shock test Schlagzerreißversuch *m*
tensile state Spannungszustand *m*
tensile strain Reckgrad *m*; Zugverformung *f*
tensile strain ga[u]ge Zugspannungsmesser *m*

tensile strength Festigkeit *f*; Zugfestigkeit *f*
tensile stress Zugbeanspruchung *f*; Zugspannung *f*
tensile test Zugversuch *m*
tensile test across the rolling direction Querzugversuch *m*
tensile test bar Zerreißstab *m*
tensile testing machine Zerreiß[prüf]maschine *f*
tensile test [specimen] Zerreißprobe *f*
tension Spannung *f* (auch elektrisch); Zug *m*
tension bridle Spannrollensatz *m*; Zugrollengerüst *n*
tension crack Spannungsriß *m*
tension levelling machine Streckrichtmaschine *f*
tension reel Zughaspel *f*
tension rolls Zugrollengerüst *n*
tension spring Zugfeder *f*
tenso-compressive reforming Zug-Druck-Umformen *n*
tentative standard Vornorm *f*
term Glied *n*
term of delivery Lieferfrist *f*
terms of delivery Lieferbedingungen *fpl*
terms of supply Lieferbedingungen *fpl*
ternary ternär
ternary system Dreistoffsystem *n*
terne überziehen mit einer Blei-Zinn-Legierung
terne plate Mattblech *n*; Ternblech *n*
terne strip Ternband *n*
tessellated stresses schachbrettartig verlaufende Spannungen *fpl*
test Versuch *m*; untersuchen; versuchen; erproben; prüfen
test bar Probestab *m*; Prüfstab *m*
test by free oscillations Ausschwingversuch *m*
test census Probezählung *f*
test certificate Prüfbescheinigung *f*
tested for cracks in the "as delivered" condition rißgeprüfter Lieferzustand *m*
test for randomness Prüfung *f* auf Zufälligkeit

test in boiling liquids Kochversuch *m*
test[ing] Prüfung *f*
testing Untersuchung *f*
testing facility Prüfeinrichtung *f*
testing for brittle fracture sensitivity Sprödbruchprüfung *f*
testing laboratory Versuchsanstalt *f*
testing machine Prüfmaschine *f*
testing method Prüfverfahren *n*
testing of materials Werkstoffprüfung *f*
testing of weakest points in a design Schwachstellenprüfung *f*
testing set Prüfgerät *n*
test load Prüflast *f*
test of quality of fit Probe *f* auf die Güte der Anpassung
test piece Probe *f*; Probestück *n*; Prüfstück *n*; Probekörper *m*
test piece with a U notch Rundkerbprobe *f*
test rod Meßschwert *n*
tests by progressive loadings Stufenversuche *mpl*
test sheet Versuchsblech *n*
test specimen Probe *f*; Probestück *n*; Prüfstück *n*; Probekörper *m*
test spoon Probelöffel *m*
test value Prüfwert *m*
tetracalcium phosphate Tetracalciumphosphat *n*
tetragonal lattice tetragonales Gitter *n*
text communication Textkommunikation *f*
texture Gefüge *n*; Textur *f*
The High Authority Hohe Behörde *f*
Theisen disintegrator Theisen-Wäscher *m*
theoretical to actual die pull ratio Formänderungswirkungsgrad *m* (beim Drahtziehen)
theoretic value Sollwert *m*
theory of probability Wahrscheinlichkeitsrechnung *f*
thermal balance Wärmebilanz *f*
thermal capacity spezifische Wärme *f*
thermal conductivity Wärmeleitfähigkeit *f*

thermal diffusivity Temperaturleitfähigkeit *f*
thermal effect Wärmenutzen *m*
thermal efficiency Wärmeausnutzung *f*; Wärmewirkungsgrad *m*
thermal equilibrium Temperaturausgleich *m*
thermal expansion Wärmeausdehnung *f*
thermal fatigue resistance Temperaturwechselbeständigkeit *f*
thermal flux Wärmefluß *m*
thermal head Wärmegefälle *n*
thermal inertia Wärmeleitwiderstand *m*
thermal load Hitzebelastung *f*
thermal power plant Wärmekraftwerk *n*
thermal resistivity Wärmeleitwiderstand *m*
thermal shock stress Temperaturwechselbeanspruchung *f*
thermal spraying thermisches Spritzen *n*
thermal stability test Warmrundlaufversuch *m*
thermal stress crack Wärmespannungsriß *m*
thermal treatment Wärmebehandlung *f*
thermal unit Wärmeeinheit *f*
thermic value wärmetechnische Größe *f*
thermistor Thermistor *m*
thermite welding Thermitschweißung *f*; aluminothermisches Schweißen *n*
thermo-chemical test thermochemische Untersuchung *f*
thermocouple Thermoelement *n*; Thermopaar *n*
thermodynamics Thermodynamik *f*
thermodynamic statistical thermodynamische statistische Größe *f*
thermoelectric force thermoelektrische Kraft *f*
thermomechanical treatment thermomechanische Behandlung *f*
thermometer probe Temperaturfühler

m
thermopile Thermokette *f*; Thermosäule *f*
thermoplastic thermoplastisch
thermosetting wärmehärtend
thicken absteifen; verdicken
thickening Eindicken *n*
thickness Dicke *f*; Stärke *f*
thickness ga[u]ge Dickenmeßgerät *n*
thickness measuring device using isotopes Isotopen-Dickenmeßanlage *f*
thickness of boundary layer Grenzschichtdicke *f*
thickness of case hardening Einsatzhärtetiefe *f*
thickness of chip Spandicke *f*
thimble Kausche *f*; Seilkausche *f*
thin dünn; verdünnen; verflüssigen
thin film lubrication Grenzschmierung *f*
thin foil technique Dünnschichtverfahren *n* (für Stahldrähte)
thinning Dengeln *n*
thin section Dünnschliff *m*
thin strip casting Bandgießen *n*
thin walled steel structural element dünnwandiges Stahlbauteil *n*
Thomas converter Thomaskonverter *m* (Thomasbirne)
Thomas low carbon steel kohlenstoffarmer Thomasstahl *m*
Thomas pig iron Thomasroheisen *n*
Thomas process Thomasverfahren *n*
Thomas steel Thomasstahl *m*
Thomas steel works Thomasstahlwerk *n*
thoroughly work durcharbeiten
thread Gewinde *n*; einführen (in Kaliber); einfädeln (in Kaliber)
thread cutting Gewindeschneiden *n*
threaded coupling Gewindekupplung *f*
threaded pin Gewindebolzen *m*
threaded pipe Gewinderohr *n*
threaded rod Gewindestange *f*
thread grooving Gewindefurchen *n*
threading Gewindeschneiden *n* (außen)

threading device Einfädelvorrichtung *f*
thread rolling Gewindedrücken *n*
thread rolling by the plungecut method Gewindewalzen *n* im Einstechverfahren
thread rolling by the throughfeed method Gewindewalzen *n* im Durchlaufverfahren
thread rolling machine Gewindewalzmaschine *f*
thread spinning Gewindedrücken *n*
three bell hopper arrangement Drei-Glocken-Gichtverschluß *m*
three-cornered dreieckig
three-dimensional shape factor Raumformfaktor *m* (Kristall)
threefold dreifach
three furnace process Triplexverfahren *n*
three-high mill Triowalzwerk *n*
three-high rolling stand Dreiwalzengerüst *n*
three-high stand Triogerüst *n*
three-high stand with two-high roll set Wechselduo *n*
three-high train Triostraße *f*
three-hole nozzle Dreilochdüse *f*
three-layer steel Dreilagenstahl *m*
three phase alternating current Drehstrom *m*
three phase current Drehstrom *m*
three phase [current] motor Drehstrommotor *m*
three-phase star inverse parallel connection Dreiphasen-Sterngegenparallelschaltung *f*
three phase to direct current motor generator set Drehstrom-Gleichstrom-Umformer *m*
three-ply plate Dreilagenblech *n*
three shift operation Dreischichtbetrieb *m*
three-stage dreistufig
three-stage transmission filter Dreistufenfilter *m* (Spektralanalyse)
three-step dreistufig
three strand machine Dreistrangmaschine *f*

threshold Schwelle *f* (Grenzwert)
threshold value Grenzwert *m*; Schwellenwert *m*
throat Ausladung *f* (Hochofen); Gicht *f*, Maul *n*
throat armour Schlagpanzer *m*
throat diameter Gichtdurchmesser *m*
throat dust Gichtstaub *m*
throat opening Gichtöffnung *f*
throat stopper Gichtverschluß *m*
throttle Drossel *f* (elektr.); drosseln
throttle valve Drosselklappe *f*, Drosselventil *n*
through durchgehend
through fraction Siebdurchgang *m*
throughhole Durchgangsloch *n*
throwing power Tiefenstreuung *f*, Tiefenwirkung *f*
throw out ausrücken
throw over umschalten
thrust Druck *m*; Schub *m*; Stoß *m*
thrust bearing Drucklager *n*; Widerlager *n*
thrust block bearing Druckwiderlager *n* (Rohrwalzwerk)
thrust of roof Gewölbeschub *m*
tie binden; verankern; verbinden
tie (am.) Trogschwelle *f*
tie bar Ankerschiene *f*
tie bolt Ankerbolzen *m*
tied rank gebundener Rang *m*
tie element Anker *m*
tie line Konode *f*
tie member Zugband *n*
tie plate Unterlagplatte *f*
tier Lage *f*, Reihe *f*
tiering truck Hubwagen *m*
tie rod Spurstange *f*
tie-wire Bandagendraht *m*
TIG-dressing WIG-Aufschmelzen *n*
tight dicht
tight coil table Festbundtisch *m*
tighten abdichten; anziehen
tightening material Dichtungsmasse *f* (für Mauerwerk)
tightness weld Dichtheitsschweiße *f*, Festigkeitsschweiße *f*
TIG welding WIG-Schweißen *n*; Wolfram-Schutzgasschweißen *n*
tile Dachziegel *m*; Hohlstein *m* (Rekuperator)
tilting chute Wippe *f*
tilting device Kantvorrichtung *f*, Kippstuhl *m*; Kippvorrichtung *f*
tilting fingers Hakenkanter *m*
tilting furnace Kippofen *m*; Schaukelofen *m*
tilting hearth Kippherd *m*
tilting ladle Kippfanne *f*
tilting moment Kippmoment *n*; Verkantungsmoment *n* (Walzen)
tilting over Umfallen *n* (im Kaliber); Umschlagen *n* (im Kaliber)
tilting skip Kippkübel *m*
tilting table Kipptisch *m*; Wipptisch *m*
tilting type [hot metal] receiver kippbarer Vorherd *m*
time Zeit *f*; Zeit *f* messen; einstellen; regeln; zeitlich einstellen
time allowed in advance Zeitvorgabe *f* (beim Akkord)
time and motion study Arbeitsstudie *f*
time consuming zeitraubend
time-consuming lag Bearbeitungsdauer *f*, Verzögerung *f*
time elapsed Standzeit *f*
time function element Zeitglied *n*
time interval Zeitintervall *n*
time in the mould Standzeit *f*
time keeping Stechen *n* an der Kontrolluhr; Zeitstudien *fpl*
time limit Termin *m*
time limit switch Zeitschalter *m*
time of exposure Standzeit *f*; Verweilzeit *f*
time of operation Betriebsdauer *f*, Betriebszeit *f*
time of [s]melting Schmelzdauer *f*
time pattern control Zeitplanregelung *f*
time planning Terminwirtschaft *f*
time program control Programmregelung *f*; Zeitplanregelung *f*
timer Zeitglied *n*
timer circuit Zeitschaltung *f*
time recorder Zeitregistrierinstru-

ment *n*
time-reduction-marginal coordinates Zeit-Abbau-Randkoordinaten [System] *n*
time required for changing (the rolls) Umrüstzeit *f*
time required for roll changing Umbauzeit *f* (Walzenwechsel)
time response Übergangsfunktion *f*
time schedule Terminplan *m*
time shifting Terminverschiebung *f*
time study Zeitstudien *fpl*; Zeitwirtschaft *f*
time-temperature-austenitisation diagram (TTA-curve) Temperatur-Austenitisierungs-Schaubild *n*; Zeit-Temperatur-Austenitisierungs-Diagramm *n* (ZTA-Diagramm)
time-temperature-tempering diagram Zeit-Temperatur-Anlaßdiagramm *n*
time-temperature-transformation curve (TTT-curve) Zeit-Temperatur-Umwandlungs-Diagramm *n* (ZTU-Diagramm)
time under load Belastungsdauer *f*
time utilisation schedule Zeitbilanz *f*
time wage rate Stundenlohntarif *m*; Zeitlohntarif *m*
timing Terminierung *f*
timing wire Trenndraht *m*
tin Zinn *n*; verzinnen
tin mill black plate Schwarzblech *n* in Weißblechgröße
tinned strip verzinntes Band *n*
tinning Verzinnen *n*; Verzinnung *f*
tinning department Verzinnerei *f*
tinning house Verzinnerei *f*
tinning plant Verzinnungsanlage *f*
tinning pot Verzinnungsherd *m*
tinning roll Verzinnungswalze *f*
tinning stack Verzinnungsherd *m*
tinplate alloy layer Legierungszwischenschicht *f* bei Weißblech
tinplate bar Platine *f* für Weißblechherstellung
tinplate mill Weißblechwalzwerk *n*
tinplate shearing line Weißbandzerteilanlage *f*
tinplate sheet Weißblechtafel *f*
tinplate strip Weiß[blech]band *n*
tin strip Weißband *n*; verzinnter Bandstahl *m*
tiny crack Haarriß *m*
tin yield Zinnverbrauch *m*
tip Ablageplatz *m*; Halde *f*; Spitze *f*; abkippen; bestücken; kippen (Pfanne); stürzen
tip formation Zipfelbildung *f*
tip of a tooth Zahnspitze *f*
tipping Kippen *n*
tipping bucket Kippkübel *m*
tipping device Kippstuhl *m*; Kippvorrichtung *f*
tipp[l]er Kipper *m*
tire ingot Radreifenblock *m*
tire rolling mill Radreifen-Walzwerk *n*
titaniferous iron Titaneisen *n*
titanium Titan *n*
titanium carbide Titancarbid *n*
titanium dioxide Titandioxid *n*
titration Titration *f*
titrimeter Titrimeter *n*
titrimetric titrimetrisch
to-and fro-bend test Biegeversuch *m* (Hin- und Her-Biegeversuch)
toggle Kniehebel *m*
tolerable zumutbar
tolerance Maßgrenze *f* (Spielraum); Spiel *n*; Spielraum *m*; zulässige Abweichung *f*
tolerance on size Maßtoleranz *f*
tolerance zone Toleranzfeld *n*
tong hold vorbereitetes Ende *n* eines Schmiedestückes
tongs Zange *f*
tongs-type manipulator Zangenkanter *m*
tongue Feder *f*
tongue and groove Feder und Nut *f*
tongue and groove pass geschlossenes Stauchkaliber *n*
tonnage oxygen technischer Sauerstoff *m*
tonnage oxygen plant Sauerstoffgewinnungsanlage *f*
tonnage production Massenherstellung *f*

tool   394

tool Werkzeug n
tool blank Rohling m
tool cupboard Werkzeugschrank m
tool cutting edge angle Einstellwinkel m (Spanen)
tool cutting edge inclination Neigungswinkel m (Spanen)
tool grinder Werkzeugschleifbock m
tool-grinding machine Werkzeugschleifbock m
tool [holder] bit Drehling m
tooling Werkzeugausrüstung f
tool life/tool path test Stand-Weg-Versuch m
tool life at elevated temperature Temperaturstandzeit f
tool set Werkzeugsatz m
tool steel Werkzeugstahl m
toothed bar rack Zahnstange f
toothed rim Zahnkranz m
toothed shaft Zahnwelle f
toothed wheel Zahnrad n
top Gicht f; Klappe f; oberes Blockende n; Kappe f; Kopf m; Kopfteil n; oberes Teil n
top blowing process Aufblasverfahren n; LD-Verfahren n
top-cast fallend [ver]gießen; gießen
top-charging hoist Begichtungsaufzug m
top coat Deckschicht f
top crust (in tundish or mould) Deckel m (in Gießwanne oder Form)
top discard verlorener Kopf m
top discard scrap Kopfschrott m
top fin Kopfbart m
top flash Kopfbart m
top freezing (ingot) Deckelbildung f (Block)
top gas Gichtgas n
top gases (tops) Topgase npl
top gas main Gichtgasleitung f
top hat Stiefelschaft m
top hat furnace Haubenofen m
topping Abschlagen n des verlorenen Kopfes
top plate on mould Deckring m
top platform Gichtbühne f

top pour fallend [ver]gießen; gießen
top pouring Fallendgießen n; fallender Guß m
top-pouring pig iron ladle Roheisenpfanne f mit Obenentleerung
top rake Neigungswinkel m (Spanen)
top roll Oberwalze f
top roll pressure Oberdruck m
top side of the strip Bandoberseite f
top tool carrier Obersatteltraverse f
top up auffrischen; nachschärfen (Beizbad)
top water Leitungswasser n
torch Brenner m
torch cutting Brennschneiden n
torch deseaming Brennputzen n
torch for lighting fuse Stichflamme f
torch welding Gasschweißen n
torpedo ladle Torpedopfanne f
torque Drehmoment n; Walzarbeit f
torsion Drehung f; Verdrillen n; Verwinden n; verwinden
torsional buckling Drillknicken n
torsional fatigue endurance limit Verdrehdauerfestigkeit f; Verdrehungswechselfestigkeit f; Verdrehwechselfestigkeit f
torsional fatigue strength Verdrehdauerfestigkeit f; Verdrehwechselfestigkeit f
torsional-flexural buckling Biegedrillknicken n
torsional strength Verdrehfestigkeit f
torsional stress Verdrehbeanspruchung f
torsional vibration test[ing] stand Drehschwingprüfstand m
torsion failure Verdrehungsbruch m
torsion fatigue test Dauerverdrehversuch m
torsion impact test Schlagdrehversuch m
torsion resistance Torsionssteifigkeit f
torsion test Verdrehversuch m
tortuosity factor Labyrinthfaktor m
total carbon Gesamtkohlenstoff m
total decarburization Auskohlung f

total immersion test Dauertauchversuch *m*
total plastic strain bleibende Gesamtverformung *f*
total radiation pyrometer Gesamtstrahlungspyrometer *n*
total reliability Gesamtverfügbarkeit *f* (EDV)
total specimen Gesamtprobe *f*
total weight Gesamtgewicht *n*
touch tasten
touching lever Fühlhebel *m*; Tasthebel *m*
touch rod Kontaktelektrode *f*
touch-up Retuschieren *n*
tough at subzero temperature kaltzäh
toughness Zähigkeit *f*
tower washer Naßreiniger *m*
town gas Leuchtgas *n*; Stadtgas *n*
town water Leitungswasser *n*
TP monitor Dialogmonitor *m*
trace Gleis *n*; Spur *f*; anreißen; nachspüren; pausen; verfolgen
trace element Stahlbegleitelement *n*
trace of curve Kurvenverlauf *m*
trace press Strangpresse *f*
tracer Taster *m* (Fühlersteuerung)
tracer-controlled fühlergesteuert
tracer gas Indikatorgas *n*
tracers Spurenelemente *npl*
tracing Stoffflußverfolgung *f*
track Bahn *f*; Gleis *n*
trackbound gleisgebunden
track cable Tragseil *n*
tracker ball Rollkugel *f*
tracking Verfolgung *f*
track laying machine Gleisbaumaschine *f*
track material Eisenbahnzeug *n*; Oberbaumaterial *n*
track time Reisezeit *f* (eines Blockes); Transportdauer *f* (bei Blöcken); Übergabezeit *f* (von Blöcken)
traction Ziehen *n*
tractoloader Schürflader *m*
tractor Schlepper *m*
trade balance Handelsbilanz *f*
trade mark Schutzmarke *f*; Warenzeichen *n*; Werksmarke *f*; gesetzlich geschützter Name *m*
trade scrap Sammelschrott *m*
trade union Gewerkschaft *f*
traditional melting herkömmliche Erschmelzung *f*
traffic Verkehr *m*
trail edge Nebenschneide *f*
trailer Anhänger *m* (Wagen)
trailing end hinteres Ende *n*
trailing pointer Schleppzeiger *m*
trailing thermocouple Schleppthermoelement *n*
train Straße *f*; Strecke *f*; Zug *m*
trainee Anlernling *m*
training Einarbeitung *f*
train of stands nebeneinander angeordnete Walzgerüste *npl*
tram Lore *f*
tramlines parallele Längsfehler *mpl* durch Überwalzen
tramp element Begleitelement *n*; Spurenelement *n*; Stahlbegleitelement *n*
tram[way] rail Rillenschiene *f*
transcrystalline corrosion transkristalline Korrosion *f*
transcrystalline fracture transkristalliner Bruch *m*
transducer Meßumformer *m*; Signalumformer *m*
transfer übertragen; Übertragung *f*
transfer car Förderwagen *m*; Zubringerwagen *m*
transfer element Übertragungsglied *n*
transfer of heat Wärmeübergang *m*; Wärmeübertragung *f*
transfer printing Transferdruck *m*
transfer table [railway] Schiebebühne *f*
transform umformen
transformation Umwandlung *f*
transformation point Haltepunkt *m*
transformation range Umwandlungsbereich *m*
transformation substructure Umwandlungsuntergefüge *n*
transformation temperature Umwandlungstemperatur *f*

transformer Transformator *m*; Umformer *m*; Umspanner *m*
transformer sheet steel Transformatorenstahl *m*
transformer tap Transformatorstufe *f* (sekundär)
transgranular corrosion transkristalline Korrosion *f*
transient response Übergangsfunktion *f*
transition metal Übergangsmetall *n*
transition point Umwandlungspunkt *m*; Übergangspunkt *m*
transit time Laufzeit *f*
translating device Signalumformer (EDV) *m*
translational motion Schubbewegung *f*
translator Zuordner *m*
transmission Übersetzung *f*; Übertragung *f*
transmission gear Vorgelege *n*
transmission range Vorstrahlbereich *m* (Röntgen)
transmission shaft Übertragungswelle *f*
transmitter Geber *m*; Meßumformer *m*
transparent cut Dünnschliff *m*
transport and conveying plant Transportanlage *f*
transportation means Verkehrsmittel *n*
transport box Transportkasten *m*
transport guidance Transportführung *f*
transporting appliance Transportgerät *n*
transport number Überführungszahl *f*
transverse bending test Querbiegeversuch *m*
transverse corner crack Kantenquerriß *m*
transverse crack Querriß *m*
transverse extrusion of rods and tubes Quer-Strangpressen *n*
transverse facial crack Flächenquerriß *m*
transverse impact extrusion Quer-fließpressen *n*
transverse lap Querfalte *f*
transverse microsection Querschliff *m*
transverse rod [impact] extrusion Voll-Quer-Fließpressen *n*
transverse roller table Kreuzrollgang *m*
transverse rolling Querwalzen *n*
transverse sampling Querprobenahme *f*
transverse section Querschnitt *m*
transverse strain Querdehnung *f*
transverse test specimen Querprobe *f*
transverse tubular extrusion Hohl-Quer-Strangpressen *n*
transverse tubular impact extrusion Hohl-Quer-Fließpressen *n*
transverse wave Schubwelle *f* (Ultraschallprüfung)
trap Falle *f*; Klappe *f*; aufhalten; abschließen; auffangen (Gas); einschließen
trapezoids Trapezstahl *m*
travel Durchgang *m*; Lauf *m*; fahren
travelling fahrbar
travelling crane Laufkran *m*
travelling field pump Wanderfeldpumpe *f*
travelling [fire] grate Wanderrost *m*
travelling hopper Zubringerwagen *m*
travelling roller table fahrbarer Rollgang *m*
travel time Laufzeit *f*
traversing wheel Laufrad *n*
tray Kasten *m*; Kübel *m*; Schale *f*; Schüssel *f*
tread Lauffläche *f*
tread roll Laufflächenwalze *f*
treat bearbeiten; behandeln; verarbeiten
treated surface nachbehandelte Oberfläche *f*
treated water aufbereitetes Wasser *n*
treating Bearbeitung *f*
treatise Abhandlung *f*; Aufsatz *m*
treatment Behandlung *f*; Verfahren *n*
tree (surface defect) Rutschstelle *f*

trellis Gitter n
trench Graben m; Grube f; Rinne f; Schram m (Bergwerk)
trend Entwicklung f; Entwicklungsrichtung f; Grundrichtung f; Verlauf m
trepanned core Radialbohrkern m
trepanning Ausstechen n
trestle Bock m; Gerüst f; Gestell n
trial Probe f; Probefahrt f; Versuch m
trial plant Versuchsanlage f
trial run Probefahrt f
triangle head cap screw Dreikantschraube f
triangular dreieckig
triangular section Dreilagenblech n
triangular section steel Dreikantstahl m
tribology Tribologie f
tricalcium silicate Tricalciumsilicat n
trickle sickern; tropfen
trickling filter Tropfkörper m (Wasserreinigung)
trigger Auslöser m (EDV)
trim abgraten; abstechen; besäumen; putzen
trimming Abgraten n; Besäumen n
trimming lathe Abstechdrehbank f
trimming shear Besäumschere f
trip auslösen; schalten
triple cast bloom Vorblock-Drillingsguß m
triple casting Drillingsguß m
trolley Laufkatze f
trommel test Trommelprobe f
Tropenas converter seitlich blasender Konverter m
trouble Beschwerde f; Störung f; Verwerfung f
troubles due to an excess of lime Kalkelend n
troubles due to an excess of sulphur Schwefelelend n
trough Behälter m; Rinne f; Zwischenpfanne f
trough conveyor Trogförderer m
trough rubbish Rinnenschutt m
trough sections Rinneneisen n
trough shaped steel sleeper Trogschwelle f
truck Hubwagen m; Karre f; Lastkraftwagen m
true mean wahrer Mittelwert m
trueness to ga[u]ge Maßhaltigkeit f
true tensile stress Reißfestigkeit f
true to dimension maßgenau
true to shape formgerecht
true to size maßgenau
trumpet Eingußrohr n; Gießtrichter m; Trichter m
truncated abgestumpft; gestutzt (Statistik)
truncated frequency distribution Rumpfverteilung f
trunnion Ritzel n; Zapfen m (Konverter)
trunnion ring Tragring m
truss Fachwerk n; Strebe f; Stütze f
try prüfen; versuchen
TTT characteristics ZTU-Kennwerte mpl
tub Kübel m; Wanne f
tube Rohr n; Röhre f
tube bend Rohrbogen m
tube bending machine Rohrbiegemaschine f
tube billet Röhrenknüppel m
tube blank Rohling m; Rohrluppe f
tube cooler Rohrkühler m
tube cutting-off bench Rohrabstechbank f
tube drawing Rohrziehen n
tube drawing bench Rohrziehbank f
tube drawing with a plug Rohrstopfenzug m
tube furnace Rohrofen m
tube-piercing bench Rohrstoßbank f
tube plate Röhrenblech n
tube radiator Röhrenradiator m
tube [rolling] mill Rohrwalzwerk n; Röhren-Walzwerk n
tube round Rohrrohling m
tube rounds Halbzeug n; Halbzeug n für Röhren; Röhrenrundstahl m
tube sinking Rohrziehen n
tube sinking bench Rohrziehbank f
tube square Rohrrohling m

tube strip Röhrenstreifen *m*
tube strip rolling mill Röhrenstreifen-Walzwerk *n*
tube welding plant Rohrschweißanlage *f*
tub filling Kübelbegichtung *f*
tubing Rohrziehen *n*
tubular rohrförmig
tubular bifurcated rivet wire röhrenförmiger zweigeteilter Nietedraht *m*
tubular mould Rohrkokille *f*
tubular product Rohrerzeugnis *n*
tubular recuperator Röhrenrekuperator *m*
tubular steel scaffolding Stahlrohrgerüst *n*
tubular strander Rohrverseilmaschine *f*
tumbler Putztrommel *f*; Rommelfaß *n*; Scheuerfaß *n*
tumbler strength (am.) Trommelfestigkeit *f*
tumbling Rommeln *n*; Scheuern *n*
tumbling barrel Rommelfaß *n*; Scheuerfaß *n*
tundish Gießwanne *f*; Verteiler *m*; Zwischengefäß *n* (Stranggießen); Zwischenpfanne *f*
tundish car Verteilerwagen *m*
tuned abgestimmt (EDV)
tungsten Wolfram *n*
tungsten arc spot welding Wolfram-Lichtbogenpunktschweißen *n*
tungsten carbide alloy Hartmetall *n*; Hartmetall-Legierung *f*
tungsten inert gas arc welding Wolfram-Inertgas-Schweißen *n*
tungsten steel Wolframstahl *m*
tunnel Eingußrohr *n* (steigender Guß)
tunnel type furnace Kanalofen *m*
tup Bär *m*; Fallbirne *f*; Fallbär *m*
turbine blade sections Profile *npl* für Turbinenschaufeln
turboblower Kreiselgebläse *n*
turbulence reduction method Wirbelreduktionsverfahren *n*
turbulent wirbelig
turbulent burner Wirbelbrenner *m*

turn Drehung *f*; Umdrehung *f*; drehen; kanten
turn down umlegen (Sauerstoffkonverter)
turn-down of rolling stock Skibildung *f* am Walzgut
turned finish gedreht (Oberflächenzustand)
turner Dreher *m*
turning Dreharbeit *f*; drehbar
turning lathe Drehbank *f*
turning motion Drehbewegung *f*
turning over device Kantvorrichtung *f*
turning place Drehpunkt *m* des Wechselwagens
turnings Drehspäne *mpl*
turning techniques Drehverfahren *n*
turning tool Drehmeißel *m*; Drehmesser *n*; Drehstahl *m*
turn into line with beidrehen (Kristall vor der Erstarrungsfront)
turnkey (mini plants) schlüsselfertig
turn of a coil Windung *f*
turn off abdrehen
turn over kanten; umschlagen; umfallen (im Kaliber); umschlagen (im Kaliber); wenden
turn-over gear Wendevorrichtung *f*
turn-round (of goods) Güterumschlag *m*
turntable Drehscheibe *f*; Drehtisch *m*
turn-up of rolling stock Skibildung *f* am Walzgut
turret lathe Revolverdrehbank *f*
tuyre Blasform *f*; Düse *f*; Form *f*; Windform *f*
tuyre area Düsenquerschnitt *m*
tuyre bottom Düsenboden *m*
tuyre holder Düsenhalter *m*
tuyre level Blasformebene *f*
tuyre nozzle Formenrüssel *m*
tuyre snout Formenrüssel *m*; Rüssel *m*
tuyre stock Düsenstock *m*
twenty-roll stand Zwanzigwalzengerüst *n*
twin-bore Doppelbohrung *f*
twin draught compound coke oven

Zwillingszug-Verbundkoksofen *m*
twin drive Einzelwalzenantrieb *m* bei Duo-Umkehrstraßen (Zwillingsantrieb); Zwillingsantrieb *m*
twin journal box Zwillingsachsbüchse *f*
twinning Zwillingsbildung *f*
twin strand casting machine Zweistrang-Gießmaschine *f*
twist Drall *m*; Verdrehung *f*, verdrallen; Verwindung *f*, verdrehen
twist drill Schlangenbohrer *m*; Spiralbohrer *m*
twisted [reinforcement] bulb steel Drillwulststahl *m*
twisted strip verzogenes Band *n*
twist guide Drehführung *f*
twisting Tordieren *n*
twist[ing] guide Drallbüchse *f*, Drallführung *f*
twisting machine Verwindemaschine *f*
twisting moment Drillmoment *n*
twisting strength Drehfestigkeit *f*, Verdrehfestigkeit *f*
twisting stress Verdrehbeanspruchung *f*
twisting with rotary tool movement Verdrehen *n*
two-high cold reduction mill Duo-Kaltwalzwerk *n*
two-high mill Zweiwalzen-[Duo]-Walzwerk *n*
two-high [rolling] mill Duostraße *f*; Zweiwalzengerüst *n*
two-high [rolling] stand Duowalzwerk *n*; Zweiwalzengerüst *n*
two-high stand of rolls Zweiwalzengerüst *n*
two-phase region Mischungslücke *f*
two-position controller Zweipunktregler *m*
two-roll straightening machine Zwei-Walzen-Richtmaschine *f*
two shifts operation Zweischichtbetrieb *m*
two sided clad steel Dreilagenstahl *m*
two-slag practice Zweischlackenverfahren *n*

two-stage zweistufig
two-step action Zweipunktregler *m*
two step ag[e]ing Zweistufenauslagern *n*
two-stroke cycle gas engine Zweitakt-Gasmaschine *f*
two way soaking pit Zweiweg-Tiefofen *m*
tying wire Bindedraht *m*
type Bauart *f*
type of corrosion Korrosionsart *f*
type sample Ausfallmuster *n*
tyre Bandage *f*, Radreifen *m*
tyre cord wire Reifencorddraht *m*

U

U-fired soaking pit umkehrflammenbeheizter Tiefofen *m*
UHP furnace Hochleistungslichtbogenofen *m*
U-leather Ledermanschette *f*
ultimate bending strength Biegebruchfestigkeit *f*
ultimate strength Zugfestigkeit *f*
ultimate stress Bruchspannung *f*
ultimate tensile strength Bruchfestigkeit *f*
ultrahigh power [arc] furnace Hochleistungs-[Lichtbogen]ofen *m*
ultrasonic examination method Ultraschallprüfverfahren *n*
ultrasonic image Schallbild *n*
ultrasonic shear wave Ultraschall-Scherwelle *f*
ultrasonic testing Ultraschallprüfung *f*
ultrasonic testing apparatus Ultraschallimpuls[prüf]gerät *n*
ultrasonic wave Überschallwelle *f*
ultrasonic welding Ultraschallschweißen *n*
unalloyed steel unlegierter Stahl *m*
unbiased frei von systematischen Fehlern; unbeeinflußt; unbelastet; unparteiisch; unverfälscht; unverzerrt

unbonded strain ga[u]ge Setzdehnungsmesser *m*
unburnt gas Frischgas *n*
uncoil abwickeln
uncoiler Ablaufhaspel *f*; Abrollhaspel *f*
uncoiling device Kronengestell *n*
uncoiling reel Abrollhaspel *f*
uncontrolled cooling Luftabkühlung *f*; ungesteuerte Kühlung *f*
uncouple auskuppeln; entkuppeln
undeformed chip thickness Spanungsdicke *f*
underburdening Untermöllerung *f*
undercoiling wickeln von unten
under construction in Bau *m*
undercut Hinterschneidung *f*
undercutting Unterhöhung *f* (Fräslöcher)
underdraft Unterzug *m*
underfeed furnace Unterschubfeuerung *f*
underfeed stocker Unterschubfeuerung *f*
underfeed stoker Rostbeschicker *m*
underfilling (ingot defect) Stoffmangel *m*
underfloor duct Unterflurleitung *f*
undergrate air firing Unterwindfeuerung *f*
undergrate firing Unterfeuerung *f*
underground unter Tage
underground gasification (of coal) Untertagevergasung *f* (von Kohle)
underground level Grube *f*; Grube *f* (Untertagebau)
underground winning Gewinnung *f* unter Tage; Grubenbau *m*
underhearth cooling Bodenkühlung *f* (Hochofen)
undersintered untersintert
undersize Mindermaß *n*; Siebdurchgang *m*; Unterkorn *n*; Untermaß *n*
undertaking Unternehmen *n*
underwinding wickeln von unten
undesirable element unerwünschtes Begleitelement *n*
undesulphurised nicht entschwefelt

unemployed [man] Arbeitsloser *m*
unemployment benefit Arbeitslosenunterstützung *f*
unequal angle ungleichschenkliges Winkeleisen *n*
unequal [leg] angle Winkelstahl *m* mit ungleichen Schenkeln
uniaxial elongation ebener Dehnungszustand *m*
uniaxial stress ebener Spannungszustand *m*
unidirected gleichgerichtet
uniflow furnace Einwegofen *m*
uniform einheitlich
uniform attack (corrosion) gleichmäßiger Angriff *m*
uniform elongation Gleichmaßdehnung *f*
uniformity Gleichmäßigkeit *f*
unimodal eingipflig
uninflammable coal magere Steinkohle *f*
union Gewerkschaft *f*; Verbindung *f*
unit Einheit *f*; Los *n*
unitary einheitlich
unit cell Elementarwürfel *m*; Elementarzelle *f*
unit construction principle Baukastenprinzip *n*
unit form Einheitsformat *n*
unit load Flächeneinheitslast *f*
unit of heat Kalorie *f*; Wärmeeinheit *f*
unit shape Einheitsformat *n*
universal bending off machine Universalabkantmaschine *f*
universal coiling machine Universalwickler *m*
universal computer universaler Rechner *m*
universal cutting machine Universalbrennschneidemaschine *f*
universal mill Universalstahlwalzwerk *n*
universal [mill] plate Breitflachstahl *m*; Universalstahl *m*
universe Kollektiv *n* (Großzahlforschung)
unkilled steel unberuhigter Stahl *m*

unload entladen; löschen
unloading facilities Entladeanlage f
unnotched specimen Vollstab m
U notch U-Kerb m
unpickled ungebeizt
unscrew abschrauben
unsintered body Preßling m
unskilled workman Hilfsarbeiter m; ungelernter Arbeiter m
unsuitable unpassend
unwind abwickeln; abziehen
unwinding box Ablaufkasten m
unworkable bed Flöz n nichtabbauwürdiges
upbending test Stauchversuch m
upcut milling Gegenlauffräsen n
upend hochkant stellen
up-ender Kippstuhl m
upending by the electric heating method Elektroanstauchen n
upending Flachrecken n mit Breitung
uphill casting steigendes Gießen n
upkeep Instandhaltung f; Unterhaltung f; Wartung f
upmilling Gegenlauffräsen n
upper bainite structures obere Zwischenstufe f
upper caloric value oberer Heizwert m
upper die block oberer Schmiedesattel m (das Obergesenk)
upper frame [cope] Oberkasten m
upper punch Oberstempel m
upper ram Oberbär m; Oberkolben m
upper roll Oberwalze f
upper shelf Hochlage f
upper yield point obere Streckgrenze f
upright Ständer m
up-running steigendes Gießen n
upset anstauchen; stauchen (schmieden); umfallen (im Kaliber); umschlagen (im Kaliber)
upset forging compression Stauchen n
upset pass Stauchstich m
upsetting Stauchen n
upsetting machine Stauchmaschine f

upsetting test Stauchversuch m
upsetting wire Stauchdraht m
upsetting with electric resistance heating Elektrostauchverfahren n
upsetting Flachrecken n mit Breitung
upshot Endergebnis n; Fazit n
uptake Fuchs m; Kanal m; Luftkanal m; Zug m
use Benutzung f; Verarbeitung f; Verwendung f; Verwertung f; benutzen; verarbeiten; verwenden; vorgeschmiedetes Stück n; vorschmieden
use hot blast heißblasen
user facility Leistungsmerkmal n
user program procedure Kommandoprogramm n
U-shaped frequency distribution U-förmige Häufigkeitsverteilung f
utilisation Verwertung f
utility patent Gebrauchsmuster n

V

vacancy Leerstelle f
vacant site in lattice Gitterfehlstelle f
vacation Ferien pl
vacuum Leere f; Unterdruck m
vacuum arc melting Vakuumlichtbogenschmelzen n
vacuum casting Vakuumgießen n
vacuum channel-type furnace Vakuumrinnenofen m
vacuum circulation process Vakuumumlaufverfahren n
vacuum cleaner Staubsauger m
vacuum deposition Vakuumbedampfen n
vacuum electron beam welding Grobvakuum-Elektronenstrahlschweißen n
vacuum hot extraction Heißextraktion f; Vakuumheißextraktion f
vacuum hot wall furnace Vakuumheißwandofen m
vacuum induction melting Vakuuminduktionsschmelzen n

vacuum ingot casting Vakuumblockguß *m*
vacuum ladle degassing Vakuum-Pfannendurchlaufentgasung *f*
vacuum levitation melting Vakuumschwebeschmelzen *n*
vacuum lift process (DH-process) Vakuumheberverfahren *n* (DH-Verfahren)
vacuum melting plant Vakuumschmelzanlage *f*
vacuum plasma melting Vakuumplasmaschmelzen *n*
vacuum refining Vakuumfrischen *n*; Vakuumraffination *f*
vacuum remelting Umschmelzen *n* unter Vakuum
vacuum sintering bell Vakuumsinterglocke *f*
vacuum stream degassing Vakuumgießstrahlentgasung *f*
vacuum treatment Vakuumbehandlung *f*
vacuum tube lamp Leuchtstofflampe *f*; Leuchtstoffröhre *f*
vagabond current corrosion Streustrom-Korrosion *f*
valency Wertigkeit *f*
valency electron Valenzelektron *n*
valid gültig
valley location Tallage *f* (Atomreihe)
valuation Beurteilung *f*; Bewertung *f*; Schätzung *f*
value Wert *m*
valve Schieber *m*; Ventil *n*
valve seal-type top-charging Gichtverschluß *m* durch Tellerventile
valve seat Ventilsitz *m*
valve spring wire Ventilfederdraht *m*
valve steel Ventilstahl *m*
valve tongue Schieberzunge *f*
vanadium Vanadium *n*
vanadium steel Vanadinstahl *m*
vane Flügel *m*; Schaufel *f*
vapor deposition Aufdampfen *n* (Metallüberzug)
vaporization Verdampfen *n*
vaporise verdampfen

vaporize abrauchen; verdampfen
vapour Dampf *m*
vapour pressure Dampfdruck *m*
variability Veränderlichkeit *f*
variable Größe *f*; Veränderliche *f*; veränderlich
variable costs veränderliche Kosten *pl*
variable prime costs bewegliche Herstellungskosten *pl*
variance analysis Streuungszerlegung *f*
variance comparison Soll-Ist-Vergleich *m*
variate Wert *m* der Veränderlichen; verändern; zufällige Veränderliche *f*
variation Schwankung *f*; Streuung *f*
variation in dimension Abmaß *n*; Maßabweichung *f*
variation in hardness Härteverlauf *m*
varnish Lack *m*; lackieren
varnished lackiert
varnishing Firnissen *n*
vary verändern
varying unterschiedlich
vat Bottich *m*; Kübel *m*
V-belt Keilriemen *m*
V-die bending Knickbiegen *n*
vehicle Fahrzeug *n*
vehicle spring Fahrzeugfeder *f*
vein Ader *f*; Flöz *n*; Gang *m* (des Hochofens); Gangspalte *f*
vein fissure Gangspalte *f*
velocity Geschwindigkeit *f*
velocity of descent Sinkgeschwindigkeit *f*
velocity of exit Austrittsgeschwindigkeit *f*
velocity potential Geschwindigkeitspotential *n*
vent Luftzug *m*; Wind *m*; lüften
ventilating device Belüfter *m*
ventilating flap Belüftungsklappe *f*
ventilating system Entlüftungsanlage *f*
ventilation Belüftung *f*; Entlüften *n*
ventilation plant Lüftungsanlage *f*

ventilator Gebläse *n*; Lüfter *m*; Ventilator *m*
ventilator cowl Lüftungsaufsatz *m*
venting Entlüftung *f*
verification Nachprüfung *f*; Prüfen *n* auf Richtigkeit
verifier Prüfer *m* (Maschine)
verify nachprüfen; prüfen; überprüfen
verifying machine operator Prüfer *m* (Arbeiter)
versatile vielseitig
vertex Scheitelpunkt *m* (eines Winkels)
vertex angle Spitzwinkel *m*
vertical boring and turning mill Karusselldrehbank *f*
vertical continuous casting installation Senkrecht-Stranggießanlage *f*
vertical cutting Vertikalschneiden *n*
vertical down senkrecht nach unten
vertical flue oven Horizontalkammerofen *m*
vertical furnace charging hoist senkrechter Gichtaufzug *m*
vertically adjustable heb- und senkbar; senkrecht verstellbar
vertical turret boring machine Karusselldrehbank *f*; Senkrecht-Bohrmaschine *f*
vertical type continuous casting plant with bending of the strand Stranggießanlage *f* vertikaler Bauart mit Strangabbiegung
vertical up senkrecht nach oben
vertical welding Senkrechtschweißung *f*
vessel Bottich *m*; Gefäß *n*; Konverter *m*
V-form bending Keilbiegen *n*
vibrating apparatus Rüttelgerät *n*
vibrating conveyor Schwingförderer *m*
vibrating frame Windungstransportgerüst *n*
vibrating lay conveyor Windungstransportgerüst *n*
vibrating screen Rüttelsieb *n*; Schüttelsieb *n*

vibrating sieve Rüttelsieb *n*; Schüttelsieb *n*
vibrational corrosion Schwingungsrißkorrosion *f*
vibration damper Schwingungsdämpfer *m*
vibration testing machine Schwingungsprüfmaschine *f*
vibrator Rüttler *m*; Schwinger *m* (Ultraschall)
vibratory mill Schwingmühle *f*; Vibrationsmühle *f*
vice Schraubstock *m*
Vickers hardness Vickershärte *f*
video-signal Fernsehsignal *n*
vignol rail Vignolschiene *f*
virtual input virtueller Eingang *m*
viscosity Viskosität *f*; Zähigkeit *f*
viscous dickflüssig; zähflüssig
visioplasticity Visioplastizität *f*
vitreous slag Schlackenglas *n*; glasige Schlacke *f*
vitrify dichtbrennen (ff. Steine); glasig werden; sintern; verschlacken
V-notch Spitzkerb *m*
V-notch specimen Spitzkerbprobe *f*
void Fehlstelle *f*; Höhlung *f*; Pore *f*
voidage Lückengrad *m*
voids fraction Lückengrad *m*
volatile flüchtig
volatile components flüchtige Bestandteile *mpl*
volatile matter flüchtige Bestandteile *mpl*
volatilise verdampfen; verflüchtigen
voltage Spannung *f* (elektr.)
voltage regulator Spannungsregler *m*
voltage tap Spannungsstufe *f*; Transformatorstufe *f* (sekundär)
volume Rauminhalt *m*; Volumen *n*
volume change Volumenänderung *f*
volume concentration Volumenkonzentration *f*
volume expansion Raumausdehnung *f*
volume fraction Volumenbruch *m*
volume of blast Windmenge *f*
volume of cases Zahl *f* der Fälle

volume ratio Raumerfüllung f
volume regulator Mengenregler m
volume stability Raumbeständigkeit f
volumeter Mengenmesser m
volumetric liquid counter volumetrischer Flüssigkeitszähler m
vortex Wirbel m
voucher copy Belegexemplar n

W

wad vorgeformte dünne Metallschicht f
wage Lohn m
wage conforming to the tarif Tariflohn m
wage costs Lohnkosten pl
wage earner Lohnempfänger m
wage incentive Lohnanreiz m
wagon Wagen m; Waggon m
wagon hoist Wagenaufzug m
wagon weighbridge Gleiswaage f; Wiegebrücke f
walking-beam annealing furnace Balkenherd-Glühofen m
walking beam conveyer Hubbalkenförderer m
walking beam furnace Hubbalkenofen m
walking beam system Hubsystem n
walking beam [type] heating furnace Balkenherdofen m
wall Mauer f; Wand f
wall arch nose Gewölbenase f; Gewölbezwickel m
walling up Ausmauerung f
wall loss Wandverlust m
wall thickness Wanddicke f
wall thickness tester Wanddickenmesser m
wall up aufmauern; vermauern
wap Windung f
warehouse Lager n; Lagerhalle f
warehouse control Lagerwesen n
warehouse equipment Betriebslagereinrichtung f; Magazineinrichtung f

warehouse locations master file Lagerplatzstamm m
warehouse master file Lagerortstamm m
warehouse on-hand quantity Lagerbestand m
warm erwärmen
warm up anwärmen
warm work hardening Warm-Kalt-Verfestigen n
warm working Halbwarmverformung f
warp verziehen; werfen
warping Verwerfung f; Verzug m
washer Unterlegscheibe f; Wäscher m
washery slag Waschberge mpl
wash heating furnace Abschweißofen m
washing attack Auswaschung f
wash[ing] heat Schweißhitze f (zum Abschweißen und Entzundern von Blöcken)
washing tower sludge Gichtschlamm m
wash tower Berieselungsturm m
waste Abfall m; Ausschuß m; Schrott m
waste air Abluft f
waste casting Fehlguß m
waste coal Abfallkohle f
waste disposal Abfallbeseitigung f; Müllbeseitigung f
waste gas Abgas n; verbrauchtes Gas n
waste gas control Abgasüberwachung f
waste gas main Abgasabführung f
waste gas probe Abgas-Entnahmesonde f
waste gas recirculation Abgasumwälzung f
waste gas recirculation heating Abgas-Umwälzbeheizung f
waste heat boiler Abhitzekessel m; Abwärmekessel m
waste heat flue Abgaskanal m
waste heat recuperation Abwärmeverwertung f
waste heat steam recovery Abhitze-

dampfgewinnung f
waste heat utilization Abhitzeverwertung f; Abwärmeverwertung f
waste heat utilization plant Abwärme-Verwertungsanlage f
waste incineration plant Abfallverbrennungsanlage f
waste materials Abfallstoffe mpl
waste pickle liquor Beizablauge f; Beizabwasser n
waste product Abfallerzeugnis n
waster Ausschußblech n; Fehlguß m
waste sheet Ausschußblech n
waste water Abwasser n
waste water clarifying plant Abwasser-Kläranlage f
waste water cleaning Abwasserreinigung f
waste water pump Abwasserpumpe f
waste water recovering plant Abwasser-Rückgewinnungsanlage f
waste-wax process Wachsausschmelz-Verfahren n
water Wasser n
water atomising Wasserzerstäubung f
water based wasserlöslich
water bath Wasserbad n
water bearing stratum wasserführende Schicht f
water boiler tube Siederohr n
water borne wasserlöslich
water circulation Wasserkreislauf m
water clearing Wasserklärung f
water cooled cable wassergekühltes Kabel n
water cooling Wasserkühlung f
water-cooling system Wasserkühlung f
water [cooling] wheel Wasserkühlrad n
water equivalent Wasserwert m
water feeding Wasserversorgung f
water fit for industrial use Brauchwasser n
water fittings Wasserarmaturen fpl
water gas Wassergas n
water ga[u]ge Wasserstandsanzeiger m; Wassersäule f

waterglass Wasserglas n
water harden Wasserhärten n
water-hardened spring steel wassergehärteter Federstahl m
water-hardened wire rod Wasserdraht m; wassergehärteter Walzdraht m
water hardening Wasserhärten n
water hardening steel Wasserhärter m
water level regulator Wasserstandsregler m
water mill Kühlstraße f
water pollution Wasserverschmutzung f
water power Wasserkraft f
water pressure pump Preßwasserpumpe f
water purifying Wasserreinigung f
water quenching followed by tempering Wasservergüten n
water sampling device Wasserprobe-Entnahmegerät n
water separator Wasserabscheider m
watersoluble binding wasserlösliche Bindung f
water spray collector Naßabscheider m
water-spray granulated slag sand wassergranulierter Schlackensand m
water supply Wasserversorgung f
water tank Wasserkasten m
water-tight wasserdicht
water-tight partition wall Schott n
water tower Wasserturm m
water trough Löschtrog m
water turbine Wasserturbine f
water vapour Wasserdampf m
water wheel Wasserfangkasten m
wattless current Blindstrom m
wattless power (arc furnace) Blindlaststoß m
wave attenuation Schallschwächung f
wave length Wellenlänge f
wave number Wellenzahl f
waviness Welligkeit f
wavy edges Randwellen fpl (Bandfehler)

way Lauf *m*; Weg *m*
weak current Schwachstrom *m*
weak gas Schwachgas *n*
weak gas firing Schwachgasheizung *f*
weakly caking coal Magerkohle *f*
weak spheroidising schwachkörnige Einformung *f*
wear Abnutzung *f*; verschleißen
wearability Abnutzungsbeständigkeit *f*
wear [and tear] Abnutzung *f*; Verschleiß *m*
wear by rubbing abreiben
wear hardening Kalthärtung *f*; Kaltverfestigung *f*
wear index Verschleißzahl *f*
wear off abnutzen
wear of the lining Verschleiß *m* der Ausmauerung
wear of top face Flächenverschleiß *m*; Freiflächenverschleiß *m*
wear resistance Abnutzungsbeständigkeit *f*; Verschleißfestigkeit *f*
wear resistant verschleißfest
wear resisting collar Verschleißring *m*
wear [resisting] life Verschleißstandzeit *f*
wear resisting part Verschleißteil *n*
wear resisting steel verschleißfester Stahl *m*
wear test Verschleißprüfung *f*
weather verwittern
weathering steel wetterfester Stahl *m*
weathering test Bewitterungsversuch *m*
weave with electrode (welding) pendeln mit Schweißelektrode
web Steg *m* (Träger)
web girder Vollwandträger *m*
wedge Keil *m*; Keilstein *m*; Wölbstein *m*
wedge adjusting equipment Keilanstellung *f*
wedge brick Ganzwölber *m* (ff. Stein)
wedge draw cupping test Keilzug-Tiefungsverfahren *n*
wedge-draw specimen Keilzugprobe *f*
wedge-draw test Zipfelzugprobe *f*

wedge section keilförmiger Querschnitt *m* (Band)
wedge shape keilförmiger Querschnitt *m* (Band)
weekend commuter Wochenendpendler *m*
week-end iron Sonntagseisen *n*
wege-action cutting Keilschneiden *n*
weighbridge Brückenwaage *f*; Plattformwaage *f*
weighed sample Einwaage *f*
weighing hopper Wiegebunker *m*
weighman Wiegemeister *m*
weight Gewicht *n*
weight deviation Gewichtsabweichung *f*
weighted average gewogenes Mittel *n*
weighted mean gewogenes Mittel *n*
weighting Gewichtung *f*
weighting curve Bewertungskurve *f*
weight per meter Metergewicht *n*
weight saving construction Leichtbauweise *f*
weir across ladle mouth (to retain slag) Sperrbrücke *f*
weld Naht *f*; Schweißnaht *f*; Schweißung *f*
weldability Schweißbarkeit *f*
weldable steel schweißbarer Stahl *m*
weld bead bend test Aufschweißbiegeversuch *m*
welded body Schweißkörper *m*
welded butt joint geschweißte Stumpfnaht *f*
welded container geschweißter Behälter *m*
welded joint Schweißverbindung *f*; geschweißter Stoß *m*
welded pipe geschweißtes Rohr *n*
welded wire fabric Baustahlmatte *f*
welded wire mesh Baustahlmatte *f*
welded wire reinforcing fabric Betonstahlmatte *f*
welder Schweißer *m*
welding Schweißen *n*; Schweißung *f*; Verschweißen *n*
welding apparatus and tool Schweißwerkzeug *n*

welding appliance Schweißvorrichtung f
welding bead Schweißraupe f
welding blow-pipe Schweißbrenner m
welding burr Schweißgrat m
welding department Schweißwerk n
welding electrode Schweißelektrode f
welding joint Schweißfuge f; Schweißstoß m
welding machine Schweißmaschine f
welding material Schweißwerkstoff m
welding plant Schweißwerk n
welding rectifier Schweißgleichrichter m
welding rod Drahtelektrode f; Schweißdraht m; Stabelektrode f
welding seam Schweißnaht f
welding shop Schweißwerk n
welding stud Anschweißschraube f
welding torch Schweißbrenner m
welding transformer Schweißumformer m
welding wire Schweißdraht m
weld nugget Schweißkern m
weld on anschweißen; aufschweißen
weld position Schweißlage f
weld toe Einbrandkerbe f
weld up zuschweißen
well Bohrloch n; Brunnen m; Gestell n; Schacht m
well planned planmäßig
well wagon Tiefladewagen m
wet and dry bulb thermometer Thermometer n zur Feuchtigkeitsmessung
wet bottom gas producer Schlackenabstich-Gaserzeuger m
wet cooler Wasserkühlrad n
wet cooling tower Naßkühlturm m
wet drawing Naßzug m
wet drawn wire naß gezogener Draht m (mit heller Oberfläche)
wet dust removing Naßentstaubung f
wet electro filter Naßelektrofilter m
wet galvanising Naßverzinkung f
wet [gas] cleaning Naß[gas]reinigung f
wet grinding Naßmahlung f

wet magnetic dressing naßmagnetische Aufbereitung f
wet-puddling Puddeln n im flüssigen Zustand
wet quenching Naßlöschen n
wet scrubber Hordenwäscher m; Naßreiniger m
wet separator Naßabscheider m
wet sizing Naßklassieren n
wet spraying mass Schlämmspritzmasse f
wet storage stain Weißrost m
wettability Benetzbarkeit f
wetting agent Benetzungsmittel n
wetting angle of contact Benetzungswinkel m
wetting power Benetzungsfähigkeit f
wharf Rampe f
wheel base Radstand m
wheel body Radkörper m
wheel disc Radscheibe f
wheel hub Radnabe f
wheel rim Radkranz m
wheel set Radsatz m
wheel strip width Rollenbandbreite f
wheels with spring action by rubber gummigefederte Räder npl
wheel tire Radreifen m
wheting Dengeln n
whetstone Schleifstein m
whetting material Schleifmittel n
whim Haspel f; Winde f
whip wippen
whipping of the work rolls Durchbiegen n der Arbeitswalzen
whirl Wirbel m
whirler Wirbler m
whirl gate Wirbeleinguß m
whisker Fadenkristall m; Haarkristall m
whiskers Bart m (Nägel)
white annealing Weißglühen n
white arsenic Arsenik n
white cast iron weißes Gußeisen n
white heart malleable [cast] iron Weißguß m; weißer Temperguß m
white heat Weißglut f
white hot weißglühend

white lime Weißkalk *m*
white noise weißes Rauschen *n*
white pickler Weißbeize *f*
white pig [iron] weißes Roheisen *n*
white rust Weißrost *m*
wide end up (W.E.U.) mould Kokille *f* mit dem weiten Ende oben
wide-flanged beam Breitflanschträger *m*
wide-flanged joist Breitflanschträger *m*
wide flat steel Breitflachstahl *m*
widen breiten; erweitern; weiten
wide plate Blech *n* breites
wide-plate test Großzugversuch *m*
wide sheet Blech *n* breites
wide strip mill Bandwalzwerk *n*; Breitband-Walzwerk *n*
width Breite *f*
width of a bite Bißweite *f*
width of cratering Kolkbreite *f*
width of the hearth Herdbreite *f*
width of wear band Verschleißmarkenbreite *f*
wild phase scharfe Phase *f*
wild steel kochender Stahl *m*
win gewinnen
winch Göpel *m*; Haspel *f*; Winde *f*
winch house Windenhaus *n*
wind Wind *m*; aufwickeln; fördern; haspeln
wind box Düsenboden *m*; Saugkasten *m* (Sinter); Windkasten *m*
winding Winden *n*
winding drum Auflaufhaspel *f*
winding engine house Maschinenhaus *n*
winding gear Fördermaschine *f*
winding in coils Aufwickeln *n* in Rollen
winding machine Spulmaschine *f*
winding reel Wickelhaspel *f*
winding rope Förderseil *n*
winding tower Förderturm *m*
windlass Haspel *f*; Winde *f*
window drip section Wasserschenkelstahl *m*
window framing steel Fensterstahl *m*
wind up aufspulen

wing screw Flügelschraube *f*
winning of coal Kohlengewinnung *f*
wiper Abstreifer *m*; Abwischer *m*
wire Draht *m*; Draht *m* (gezogener); Leitung *f* (elektr.)
wire annealing Drahtglühen *n*
wire brush Drahtbürste *f*
wire cable Drahtseil *n*
wire coil Drahtring *m*
wire cutter Drahtschere *f*; Drahtzange *f*
wire die Ziehstein *m*
wire drawer Drahtzieher *m*
wire drawing Drahtziehen *n*
wire drawing block Drahtzug *m*
wire drawing grease Drahtziehfett *n*
wire drawing machine Drahtziehmaschine *f*
wire drawing plant Drahtzieherei *f*
wire electrode Drahtelektrode *f*
wire fabric Betonstahlmatte *f*
wire-fence Drahtzaun *m*
wire ga[u]ge Drahtdicke *f*; Drahtlehre *f*
wire gauze Drahtgaze *f*
wire glass Drahtglas *n*
wire laying Leitungsverlegen *n*
wire nail Drahtstift *m*
wire netting Drahtgeflecht *n*
wire patenting furnace Drahtpatentierofen *m*
wire peeling machine Drahtschälmaschine *f*
wire product Drahterzeugnis *n*
wire rod Draht *m* (Walzdraht); Runddraht *m*; Walzdraht *m*
wire rod for screws Schrauben[walz]draht *m*
wire rod mill Drahtwalzwerk *n*
wire [rod] reel Drahthaspel *f*
wire [rolling] mill Drahtwalzwerk *n*
wire rope Drahtseil *n*
wire shot Drahtkorn *n*
wire strand Drahtader *f*; Drahtlitze *f*
wire twisting machine Drahtverwindeanlage *f*
wire welding machine Drahtschweißmaschine *f*

wireworking machine Drahtbearbeitungsmaschine f
wiring diagram Wirkschaltbild n
withdraw absenken
withdrawal roll Abziehwalze f; Strangförderwalze f (Strangguß); Abziehrolle f
withdrawal speed Absenkgeschwindigkeit f (Stranggießen)
withdraw (die/powder met.) abziehen
withdrawing machine (furnace) Auszugmaschine f (Ofen)
wobbler Kleeblattzapfen m; Kuppelzapfen m
wobbling device Wobbeleinrichtung f
Woehler diagram Wöhlerlinie f
Wood's metal Wood-Metall n
woodruff key Scheibenfeder f
work Arbeit f; abbauen (gewinnen); bearbeiten
workability Verarbeitbarkeit f (spanlos)
workable abbauwürdig
work annealing Zwischenglühen n
work-bench Werkbank f
work clamp (earthing clamp) Polzwinge f
work done in twisting Drallarbeit f
worker Arbeiter m
work expended Arbeitsaufwand m
work harden verfestigen
work hardened structure verfestigtes Gefüge n
work hardening Kalthärtung f; Kaltverfestigung f; Verfestigung f; Verfestigung f durch Kaltverformung
work holding attachment Aufspannvorrichtung f
working Führung f; Gang m (des Hochofens)
working angle Wirkwinkel m (Spanen)
working capacity Leistung f
working conditions Arbeitsbedingungen fpl
working face Arbeitsfläche f
working group Arbeitsgruppe f
working heat Warmformgebungshitze f

working hour Arbeitsstunde f
working lining Verschleißfutter n
working mean vorläufiges Mittel n
working of the melt Führung f der Schmelze
working of trenches Schrämarbeit f
work[ing] part Werkstück n
working party Arbeitsgemeinschaft f
working peak torque höchstes Betriebsmoment n
working platform Arbeitsbühne f
working pressure Betriebsdruck m
working program Arbeitsplan m
working radius Ausladung f (Drehkran)
work[ing] roll Arbeitswalze f
working stage Arbeitsbühne f
working stress Belastbarkeit f; Gebrauchsspannung f
working stroke Arbeitshub m
working the heat Führung f der Schmelze
working time Arbeitszeit f
working up the wall Randgängigkeit f (Hochofen)
working voltage Betriebsspannung f
working with a basic slag basische Schlackenführung f
working with an acid slag saure Schlackenführung f
work in progress Erzeugnisse npl in der Fertigung
work lead (am.) Erdungskabel n
workman Arbeiter m
workmen's quarter Arbeitersiedlung f
work output Arbeitsleistung f
work physiology Arbeitsphysiologie f
workpiece Walzgut n (Walzstück); Werkstück n
work proceeding Arbeitsablauf m
work psychology Arbeitspsychologie f
works Hütte f; Werk n
works' certificate Werkszeugnis n
works' test certificate Werksprüfzeugnis n
works' transport Werktransport m
works accident Betriebsunfall m
works annealed sheet Feinblech n

works cost accounting betriebliches Rechnungswesen *n*
works engineering specifications Betriebsblatt *n* (z.B. SEB)
workshop Werkstatt *f*; Werkstätte *f*
workshop installation Werkstätteneinrichtung *f*
workshop lighting Werkstattbeleuchtung *f*
works manager Betriebschef *m*; Betriebsleiter *m*
work sociology Arbeitssoziologie *f*
works practice Arbeitsweise *f*
works railway Werksbahn *f*
works scheduling Arbeitsvorbereitung *f*
works scrap Rücklaufschrott *m*
work study Arbeitsstudium *n*
work task Arbeitsaufgabe *f*
worm Schnecke *f*
worm extruder Schneckenpresse *f*
worm gear Schneckengetriebe *n*
worm rim Schneckenkranz *m*
worm wheel Schneckenrad *n*
worn die ausgeschlissener Ziehstein *m*
wortle Zieheisen *n*
wortle plate Ziehlochplatte *f*
wrap umwickeln; wickeln
wrapping test Wickelversuch *m*
wreck abwracken
wrench Drehung *f*; Drehung *f* (Schraubenschlüssel); verdrehen
wringer roll Abquetschrolle *f* (Beizen)
wrist pin Kurbelzapfen *m*
wrought iron Schmiedeeisen *n*; Schweißeisen *n*
wrought steel Schmiedestahl *m*; Schweißstahl *m*
wustite Wüstit *n*

X

xeroradiography Xeroradiographie *f*
X-ray analysis Röntgenanalyse *f*
X-ray diffraction pattern Röntgenbeugungsdiagramm *n*
X-ray fluorescence analysis Röntgenfluoreszenzanalyse *f*
X-ray interference Röntgeninterferenz *f*
X-ray investigation röntgenographische Untersuchung *f*
X-ray radiometer Röntgenstrahlenmeßgerät *n*
X-ray scan picture Röntgenrasterbild *n*
X-ray testing apparatus Röntgenprüfeinrichtung *f*

Y

yard Lagerplatz *m*
yellow brass Messing *n*
yield Austrag *m* (Erz); Ergebnis *n*; Ertrag *m*; Gehalt *m*; ausbringen; fließen; nachgeben; strecken
yield criterion Fließbedingung *f*
yielding Fließvorgang *m*
yielding phenomenon Fließvorgang *m*
yield point Streckgrenze *f*
yield point at elevated temperature Warmstreckgrenze *f*
yield pressure Fließdruck *m*
yield strength Streckgrenze *f*
yield stress Fließspannung *f*; Formänderungsfestigkeit *f*; Streckspannung *f*
yield stress in shear Schubfließspannung *f*
yield stress under tensile load Zugfließspannung *f*
Young's modulus Elastizitätsmodul *m*
Y-roller table Hosenrollgang *m*

Z

zeds Z-Stahl *m*
zees (am.) Z-Stahl *m*
zero dead stop Nullanschlag *m*
zero setting Nulleinstellung *f*

zinc Zink *n*
zinc coated sheet verzinktes Blech *n*
zinc coating Verzinken *n*; Verzinkung *f*
zinc coating furnace Verzinkungsofen *m*
zinc coating kettle Verzinkungspfanne *f*
zinc coating plant Verzinkungsanlage *f*
zinc coating shop Verzinkerei *f*
zinc destillation plant Feinzink-Destillationsanlage *f*

zinc for [zinc] coating Verzinkereizink *m*
zinc plate Zinkblech *n*
zinc sheet Zinkblech *n*
zinc stearate Zinkstearat *n*
zircon[ium] Zirkon[ium] *n*
zirconium silicate Zirkonsilicat *n*
zone melting Zonenschmelzen *n*
zone of contact Eingriffsbereich *m*
zone of fusion Schmelzzone *f*
zoning Zonenbildung *f*
Z-sections Z-Stahl *m*